EXPLORING THE LIMITS OF PERSONNEL SELECTION AND CLASSIFICATION

EXPLORING THE LIMITS OF PERSONNEL SELECTION AND CLASSIFICATION

Edited by

John P. Campbell
Deirdre J. Knapp

LEA LAWRENCE ERLBAUM ASSOCIATES, PUBLISHERS
2001 Mahwah, New Jersey   London

All views expressed in this book are those of the authors and do not necessarily reflect the official opinions or policies of the U.S. Army Research Institute (ARI) or the Department of the Army. Most of the work described was conducted under contract to ARI: MDA903-82-C-0531 (Project A), MDA903-89-C-0202 (Career Force), and MDA903-87-C-0525 (Synthetic Validity). Editing of this book was funded in part by ARI contract MDA903-92-C-0091.

Lawrence Erlbaum Associates, Inc., Publishers
10 Industrial Avenue
Mahwah, NJ 07430

Cover design by Kathryn Houghtaling Lacey

Library of Congress Cataloging-in-Publication Data

Exploring the limits of personnel selection and classification / John P. Campbell and Deirdre J. Knapp, editors.
    p.   cm.
    Includes bibliographical references and index.
    ISBN 0-8058-2553-3 (cloth : alk. paper)
    1. Employee selection.   2. Personnel management.   3. Performance standards.
I. Campbell, John Paul, 1937–   II. Knapp, Deirdre J.   III. Title.

    HF5549.5.S38 E97   2001
    658.3'112—dc21

                                                               00-061691

Books published by Lawrence Erlbaum Associates are printed on
acid-free paper, and their bindings are chosen for strength and
durability.

Printed in the United States of America
10 9 8 7 6 5 4 3 2 1

Contents

V

List of Figures

List of Tables

Preface

Beginning in the early 1980s and continuing through the middle 1990s, the U.S. Army Research Institute for the Behavioral and Social Sciences (ARI) sponsored a comprehensive research and development program to evaluate and enhance the Army's personnel selection and classification procedures. It was actually a set of interrelated efforts, collectively known as "Project A," that were carried out by the sponsor (ARI) and a contractor consortium of three organizations (the American Institutes for Research—AIR, the Human Resources Research Organization—HumRRO, and the Personnel Decisions Research Institute—PDRI).

As will be described in Chapter One, Project A engaged a number of basic and applied research objectives pertaining to selection and classification decision making. It focused on the entire selection and classification system for enlisted personnel and attempted to address research questions and generalize findings within this system context. It involved the development and evaluation of a comprehensive array of predictor and criterion measures using samples of tens of thousands of individuals in a broad range of jobs sampled representatively from a population of jobs. Every attempt was made to fully represent the latent structure of the determinants (i.e., predictors) of performance, and the latent structure of performance itself, for entry level skilled occupations and for supervisory positions. It was a rare opportunity that produced a great deal of knowledge and experience that we think should be shared and preserved. It is our belief that the Army's occupational structure and performance requirements have many more similarities than differences when compared to the nonmilitary sectors, and that the findings of Project A have considerable generalizability. The number of jobs and sample sizes involved are larger than many meta-analyses.

Over the 12 plus years that Project A was conducted, a technical research report was produced each year to document the research and development activities of the preceding year. In addition, there were comprehensive "final reports" for each major phase. These reports and other more specific technical reports pertaining to particular topics have been published by ARI and are available through the Defense Technical Information Center (DTIC). Although these reports contain comprehensive and detailed information about the research program, it would take one a very long time to cognitively process them all. A summary of the very first phase of Project A (the concurrent validation effort) was reported in a special issue of *Personnel Psychology* (Summer 1990). Many other specific questions and issues addressed by the research program have been reported in the published literature and in a large number of conference presentations. However, none of these sources provides a relatively accessible self contained report of the entire R&D research program and the issues it raised, including the extensive longitudinal validation effort, which focused on the prediction of both entry-level performance and supervisory/leadership performance.

The purpose of this book, therefore, is to provide a concise and readable description of the entire Project A research program between two covers. We would like to share the problems, strategies, experiences, findings, lessons learned, and some of the excitement that resulted from conducting the type of project that comes along once in a lifetime for an industrial/organizational psychologist.

We hope that this book will be of interest to I/O psychologists and graduate students, and those in related fields, who are interested in personnel selection and classification research. The text could serve as a supplemental reading for courses in selection, classification, human resource management, and performance assessment; and could also serve as resource material for other areas in which I/O psychology students often have limited exposure (e.g., large-scale data collection and database management procedures). We believe that experienced researchers and consultants can also learn from the methods and results produced by this R&D program, even as the methodology and procedures that were used may lead them to challenge the "Project A approach."

We assume that most readers will be technically knowledgeable, with a background in research methods and statistics. Those readers interested in more technical details than can be provided in a book of this length have the option of turning to the annual reports and other documents published by ARI, which are available to the public through DTIC. Readers with less of a technical background may well find information of interest in many of the chapters, particularly the summary chapters at the beginning and end of the volume.

ORGANIZATION OF THE BOOK

The book has 20 chapters, organized into seven parts. Part I, *Introduction and Major Issues*, introduces readers to the Project A research program, including the rationale for why it was conducted and the overall research plan. Chapter 3 is particularly important for giving the reader a framework from which to understand how the various pieces of the project fit together and describing the vernacular for referring to the various data collection activities and measures.

Part II, *Specification and Measurement of Individual Differences for Predicting Performance*, describes the design and development of the Project A predictor measures. Chapter 4 discusses how predictor constructs were selected for measurement. Chapter 5 discusses development of measures of cognitive, perceptual, and psychomotor abilities, and then Chapter 6 discusses the development of measures of personality, temperament, vocational interests, and work outcome preferences.

Part III, *Specification and Measurement of Individual Differences in Job Performance*, turns to the issue of criterion measurement, with Chapter 7 detailing the job analyses on which the measures were based and Chapter 8 describing those measures and the procedures that were used to develop them.

Part IV, *Developing the Database and Modeling Predictor and Criterion Scores*, discusses how Project A went about collecting validity data using the predictor and criterion measures described in Sections II and III and developing higher-level factor scores using these data. Data collection activities are described in Chapter 9. The development of factor scores for predictors (Chapter 10) and criteria (Chapter 11) were relatively complex endeavors, given the nature and number of measures included in the research, and required extensive discussion beyond the simple "basic" scores for each measure described in Parts II and III. Part IV closes with evidence of the criterion factor score reliability and examines the relationship between criterion measures collected at different points in time (i.e., predicting future performance from past performance).

Part V, *Selection Validation, Differential Prediction, Validity Generalization, and Classification Efficiency*, presents the longitudinal sample based estimates of selection validity for entry-level personnel (Chapter 13) and for individuals with more advanced tenure in the organization after promotion and reenlistment (Chapter 14). The use of Project A data as the basis for synthetic validation and validity generalization efforts is discussed in Chapter 15. Chapter 16 describes attempts to first model and then estimate the incremental gains obtained from "true" classifications, as compared to single stage selection. Part V closes with a discussion (Chapter 17) of how differences in the organizational context could affect performance itself, as well as the prediction of performance.

The application of Project A research findings is the subject of Part VI, *Application of Findings: The Organizational Context of Implementation*. Chapters 18 and 19 include extensive discussions of how follow-on research conducted by ARI examined ways to implement the Project A findings and facilitate their operational use. They illustrate how complex the operational system can be, in both expected and unexpected ways.

Section VII, *Epilogue*, closes the book by commenting upon the major implications of Project A for industrial/organizational psychology in particular and the study of individual differences in general.

The individuals involved in Project A all shared a very high level of mutual respect for each other and for the research program itself. In retrospect, the levels of collaboration, cooperation, and intensity of effort that were maintained over such a long period of time were beyond any reasonable expectation. Although we cannot expect those who did not share in this experience to feel as strongly about it as we do, we do want to provide a single archival record of this research and permit readers to take from it what is useful to them. And yes, we also hope that we can convey some sense of the excitement everyone felt over the entire period, and which is still ongoing.

Literally hundreds of psychologists, graduate students, and other individuals were involved in the design and implementation of Project A. Many of the individuals who were heavily involved have contributed chapters to this volume. However, it is important to understand that there were many more who made significant and sustained contributions. We cannot list them all, but they know who they are, and we thank them many times over. We would also like to thank profusely our Scientific Advisory Group (SAG)—Phil Bobko, Tom Cook, Milt Hakel, Lloyd Humphreys, Larry Johnson, Mary Tenopyr, and Jay Ulhaner—all of whom were with us for the entire life of the project and provided invaluable oversight, advice, and counsel. The editors also want to acknowledge the word-processing efforts of Dolores Miller, LaVonda Murray, and Barbara Hamilton in creating this volume. Resources toward the development of the book were contributed by the project sponsor (ARI) as well as the contractor organizations involved in the research (HumRRO, AIR, and PDRI). Finally, we wish to thank the Army Research Institute for having the courage to envision such an ambitious project in the first place, obtaining the resources to fund it, supporting it steadfastly, and contributing many talented researchers to the research team.

John Campbell
Deirdre Knapp

Foreword

First there was a concept. "... no two persons are born exactly alike, but each differs from each in natural endowments, one being suited for one occupation and another for another." Thus Plato introduced his discussion of selection and placement in the ideal state he depicted in *The Republic*. He proposed a series of "actions to perform" as tests of military aptitude, and gave the first systematic description of aptitude testing that we have on record. *The Republic* was written about 380 BCE. I've seen no evidence that Plato's testing program was actually implemented, but the concept is clear.

Next came practice. In the second century BCE, the Chinese implemented a selection testing program (see J. Gernet, *A History of Chinese Civilization*, Cambridge University Press, 1982; D. Bodde, *Essays on Chinese Civilization*, Princeton University Press, 1981). They began using performance on written tests as a means of selecting government administrators. Tests were used in this way for the next 20 centuries, and have endured because they apparently favored the selection of successful candidates. The Chinese story is fascinating, showing instances of problems that are instantly recognizable as contemporary issues in test score use and interpretation: group differences in scores, implementation of quotas (followed eventually by their rejection), differential access to educational and economic opportunity, and narrow coverage of the predictor domain.

Then the dawn of research. In April of 1917, the United States entered World War I. In just four months, a group of psychologists led by Robert M. Yerkes created the Army Alpha, the first large-scale, group-administered examination of general mental ability. Pilot studies were carried out to gather evidence of both convergent and discriminant validity, decades before these concepts were clearly enunciated.

Between implementation in September of 1917 and the end of the war in November of 1918, 1,700,000 examinees took the Alpha. Some 8,000 recruits with raw scores of 0 to 14 were discharged immediately for "mental inferiority," and 10,000 with raw scores of 15 to 24 were assigned to heavy labor battalions. On the other end of the score distribution, those with raw scores of 135 or higher were sent to officer candidate school. Robert M. Yerkes's monumental account of the development and use of the Alpha is well worth close study (*Psychological Examining in the United States Army*, Government Printing Office, 1921).

After the war there was a major boom in selection testing, and the research enterprise also picked up steam. However, practice and theory did not turn out to be highly congruent, and questions about appropriate uses of tests were readily raised and debated (including the "contemporary issues" enumerated above).

Research for understanding. In 1982, Project A was launched as a comprehensive and systematic investigation of the measurement and meaning of human differences. At long last, the inevitable shortcomings of narrowly focused, short-range, small sample, single investigator, single predictor, single criterion validation research could be overcome. The researchers would not be obliged to compromise research quality by limiting the scope of predictor constructs, using cross-sectional and concurrent designs, and having to make do with an available criterion measure. Indeed, in my judgment the greatest contribution from Project A is its elucidation and specification of the criterion space, something that we too cavalierly talk about as "performance." From the beginning we have dwelt on inventing and refining better predictors without paying proper conceptual and operational attention to what it is that we attempt to predict.

Quite simply, Project A is startling. If it is new to you, discover it in these pages. If it is already familiar, look again to see its original design, complete execution, and full complexity. It deserves to be emulated in many occupations and fields, such as teacher selection and licensure, and managerial and executive advancement, especially for multinational and global assignments. Project A epitomizes practical science and scientific practice.

Milton D. Hakel
Chair Project A Scientific Advisory Group
August 2000

About the Editors
and Contributors

Editors

Dr. John P. Campbell is professor of psychology and industrial relations at the University of Minnesota where he received his Ph.D. (1964) in psychology. From 1964 to 1966 he was assistant professor of psychology, University of California, Berkeley, and has been at Minnesota from 1967 to the present. Dr. Campbell has also been affiliated with the Human Resources Research Organization as a principal staff scientist since 1982. He was elected president of the Division of I/O Psychology of APA in 1977–78 and from 1974 to 1982 served as associate editor and then editor of the *Journal of Applied Psychology.* He is the author of *Managerial Behavior, Performance, and Effectiveness* (with M. Dunnette, E. Lawler, and K. Weick, 1970), *Measurement Theory for the Behavioral Sciences* (with E. Ghiselli and S. Zedeck, 1978), *What to Study: Generating and Developing Research Questions* (with R. Daft and C. Hulin, 1984), and *Productivity in Organizations* (with R. Campbell, 1988). He was awarded the Society of I/O Psychology Distinguished Scientific Contribution Award in 1991. From 1982 to 1994 he served as principal scientist for the Army's Project A research program. Current research interests indude performance measurement, personnel selection and classification, and modeling the person/job match.

Dr. Deirdre J. Knapp is manager of the Assessment Research and Analysis Program at the Human Resources Research Organization (HumRRO). She earned Ph.D. in industrial and organizational psychology from Bowling Green State University in 1984. Dr. Knapp was involved in Project A for a short time as a researcher with the U.S. Army Research Institute, then joined HumRRO in 1987 to co-manage the criterion measurement portion of Project A. She was the overall project director for the last several years of the research program. Her primary area of expertise is designing and developing performance assessments. This experience has covered many different contexts (e.g., to support validation research and occupational certification programs), many different types of jobs and organizations, and a variety of assessment methods (e.g., multiple choice tests, live simulations, and computerized adaptive testing). Dr. Knapp also has considerable experience conducting job/work analyses and developing strategies for collecting future-oriented job analysis information.

Contributors

Dr. Jane M. Arabian is assistant director, Enlistment Standards for the Accession Policy Directorate, Office of the Assistant Secretary of Defense, Force Management Policy, Pentagon, Washington, D.C. Prior to joining the Accession Policy Directorate in 1992, she conducted personnel research at the U.S. Army Research Institute where she was the contract monitor for the Synthetic Validity Project. As the Army's technical representative for two DoD initiatives, the DoD Job Performance Measurement Project and the Joint-Service Linkage Project, she coordinated application of Project A data. Both projects were conducted under the guidance of the National Academy of Sciences; the former established the relationship between enlistment aptitude scores and job performance while the latter led to the development of the model currently used to set accession quality benchmarks. Dr. Arabian earned her Ph.D. at the University of Toronto in 1982.

Dr. Bruce Barge is a director in the Organizational Effectiveness consulting practice within PricewaterhouseCoopers, responsible for the Western region. Bruce worked on Project A while employed at Personnel Decisions Research Institute in the early- to mid-1980s, focusing on noncognitive predictors such as biodata, vocational interests, and personality. He earned his Ph.D. from the University of Minnesota in 1987 and has spent the years since working in a variety of internal and external consulting leadership positions.

Dr. J. Anthony Bayless is a personnel research psychologist with the U.S. Immigration & Naturalization Service. He was involved in Project A as a researcher while working at the Human Resources Research Organization during his tenure there from 1990 to 1995. Dr. Bayless assisted with a component of the criterion measurement portion of the project. Dr. Bayless earned his Ph.D. from the University of Georgia in 1989.

Dr. Walter C. Borman is the chief executive officer of Personnel Decisions Research Institutes (PDRI). He was co-director of Project A's Task 4, the "Army-wide" criterion development effort and worked extensively on Task 1 (the analysis task) and Task 5 (the job-specific criterion development task). Dr. Borman earned his Ph.D. in I/O psychology from the University of California (Berkeley) in 1972.

Charlotte H. Campbell is manager of the Advanced Distributed Training Program of the Human Resources Research Organization (HumRRO). She was heavily involved throughout Project A, taking lead roles in the development of job-specific criterion measures and the concurrent and longitudinal validation data collection efforts. Ms. Campbell earned her M.S. from Iowa State University in 1974.

Dr. Mary Ann Hanson is currently working as an independent consultant. Until late 1999 she was a senior research scientist at Personnel Decisions Research Institutes (PDRI) and the general manager of their Tampa Office. While with PDRI, she was involved in many aspects of Project A including the development of predictor and criterion measures, collection and analyses of field test and validation data, and analyses to model job performance. Dr. Hanson earned her Ph.D. from the University of Minnesota in 1994.

Jim Harris is a principal with Caliber Associates. He was involved in Project A from its inception in 1982 until 1995. From 1985 forward he served as the project manager.

Dr. Jody Toquam Hatten is manager of People Research at the Boeing Company. She was involved in Project A from its inception until 1986 while working at Personnel Decisions Research Institute. As a Project A staff member, she participated in developing cognitive ability tests, both paper and computer-administered, for entry-level recruits and helped to construct performance appraisal measures for several military occupational specialties (MOS). Dr. Hatten earned her Ph.D. from University of Minnesota in 1994.

Dr. Lawrence M. Hanser is a senior scientist at RAND. He was one of the designers of Project A and one of the authors of its statement of work. He originally managed the development of a portion of Project A's criterion measurement research. He was the senior Army scientist responsible for overseeing Project A from approximately 1985 through 1988. Faced with the prospect of being a manager for the rest of his career, he escaped to RAND to remain a researcher, concerned with addressing public policy issues. Dr. Hanser earned his Ph.D. from Iowa State University in 1977.

Dr. R. Gene Hoffman, who has been with HumRRO for 19 years, is currently the manager of HumRRO's Center of Learning, Assessment, and Evaluation Research. He worked on a variety of criterion issues for Project A, including the identification of additional MOS to increase coverage of the MOS task performance domain. He was also involved with the Synthetic Validity effort for which he continued his work on structuring the task performance domain. Dr. Hoffman received his Ph.D. from the University of Maryland in 1976.

Dr. Leaetta Hough is president of the Dunnette Group, Ltd. She headed the team that conducted the literature review and predictor development of the noncognitive measures for Project A. She is co-editor of the four-volume *Handbook of Industrial & Organizational Psychology* and senior author of the personnel selection chapter in the 2000 edition of *Annual Review of Psychology.*

Ms. Janis S. Houston is a principal research scientist at Personnel Decisions Research Institutes (PDRI). She was involved in Project A from the beginning, primarily working on the predictor measures. She directed several of the predictor development teams and was the initial coordinator for the computer administration of predictors to the longitudinal sample of over 55,000 entry-level soldiers.

Dr. John Kamp was involved in the predictor development portion of Project A while a graduate student at the University of Minnesota and research associate at PDRI. He received his Ph.D. in 1984 and has since spent his career specializing in individual and organizational assessment and organization development. Dr. Kamp is currently director of product development for Reid Psychological Systems.

Dr. Rodney A. McCloy is a principal staff scientist at the Human Resources Research Organization (HumRRO). He worked on Project A both as a graduate student (under the tutelage of Dr. John P. Campbell) and as a HumRRO research scientist. His dissertation, based on Project A data, won the Society of Industrial and Organizational Psychology's S. Rains Wallace award for best dissertation. Dr. McCloy earned his Ph.D. from the University of Minnesota in 1990.

Dr. Jeffrey J. McHenry is HR director for U.S. Sales, Services and Support at Microsoft Corporation. He worked on both predictor and criterion development when he was employed at the Personnel Decisions Research Institute (1983–1985). He then joined the staff of the American Institutes for Research (1986–1988), where he continued to work on Project A as a member of the team responsible for modeling job performance and concurrent validation. Dr. McHenry earned his Ph.D. from the University of Minnesota in 1988.

Dr. Darlene M. Olson is manager of the Human Resource Management (HRM) Evaluation Staff at the Federal Aviation Administration (FAA). She was involved in Project A, as a research psychologist at the Army Research Institute, from the initiation of the research program in 1981 until 1989. She worked on the concurrent validation data collections, criterion development, examined gender-related differences on spatial predictor measures, and investigated the relationship between dimensions of the Army Work Environment and job performance. From 1988 to 1989 she served as the contract monitor. Dr. Olson earned her Ph.D. from the University of Maryland in 1985.

Dr. Scott H. Oppler is a managing research scientist for the American Institutes for Research (AIR), working in their Washington Research Center in Georgetown. He began working on Project A as a graduate student at the University of Minnesota in 1986 and as an intern at AIR in the summers of 1986 and 1987. After completing his dissertation in 1990, Dr. Oppler became deputy director of the data analysis task for the longitudinal validation portion of the project and participated in the design and execution of analyses associated with both the modeling and prediction of training and job performance.

Dr. Norman G. Peterson is a senior research fellow at the American Institutes for Research. He led the team that developed the experimental predictor battery for Project A and later was involved in research on synthetic validation methods using Project A data. Dr. Peterson earned his Ph.D. at the University of Minnesota and held prior positions at the State of Minnesota, Personnel Decisions Research Institute (where he was when he participated in Project A), and Pathmark Corporation.

Dr. Elaine Pulakos is vice president and director of Personnel Decisions Research Institute's Inc. (PDRI's) Washington D.C. office. She worked on Project A during a previous tenure at PDRI and as a researcher at the American Institutes of Research. She played a number of roles on the project, including leading the development of the performance rating scales and the supervisory role play exercises. Dr. Pulakos received M.A. (1983) and Ph.D. (1984) degrees from Michigan State University.

Dr. Douglas H. Reynolds is manager of assessment technology for Development Dimensions International (DDI). He currently leads an R & D department focused on the development and implementation of new behavioral and psychological assessments. Prior to joining DDI, Dr. Reynolds was with the Human Resources Research Organization (HumRRO), where he was involved in several aspects of the Project A effort. His activities spanned role playing and administering performance measures to evaluating the reliability of the criterion set. Dr. Reynolds earned his Ph.D. from Colorado State University in 1989.

Dr. Rodney L. Rosse is currently president of Alternatives for People with Autism, Inc., in Minnesota. He is also associated with American Institutes for Research as a senior research fellow. He was the primary architect of the custom hardware and software system used for the computer-administered part of the Project A experimental battery. He was also a major contributor to the statistical and psychometric approaches taken throughout Project A and the synthetic validation research that followed the project that built upon his prior work for the insurance industry. Dr. Rosse earned a Ph.D.

(1972) at the University of Minnesota and held prior positions at Personnel Decisions Research Institute (where he participated in Project A) and Pathmark Corporation.

Dr. Michael G. Rumsey is chief of the Selection and Assignment Research Unit at the U.S. Army Research Institute for the Behavioral and Social Sciences. He was involved in Project A from beginning to end, first as a task monitor and chief of the government research team in the performance measurement domain, and ultimately as contract monitor. Dr. Rumsey earned his Ph.D. from Purdue University in 1975.

Dr. Teresa L. Russell is a principal research scientist at the American Institutes for Research. She was a part of the Project A team at the Personnel Decisions Research Institute, Inc., from 1984 to 1990. She played a key role in the development of the predictor measures and was in charge of predictor data analyses for the longitudinal validation sample. In the early 1990s, she conducted fairness and other Project A data analyses while working for HumRRO. She received her Ph.D. in 1988 from Oklahoma State University.

Dr. Joyce Shields serves as a senior leader of the Hay Group. Prior to joining the Hay Group in 1985, Dr. Shields was a member of the Senior Executive Service and Director of the Manpower and Personnel Research Laboratory of the Army Research Institute (ARI). At ARI she was responsible for initiating and selling Project A and its companion Project B (which resulted in the Enlisted Personnel Allocation System—EPAS). Dr. Shields holds a Ph.D. in measurement and statistics from the University of Maryland, an M.A. in experimental psychology from the University of Delaware, and a B.A. in psychology from the College of William and Mary.

Dr. Clinton B. Walker, as a senior research psychologist at ARI, led the efforts to get the cognitive predictors from Project A implemented in various Army and joint-Service settings. Since his retirement from ARI in 1997, he has been an independent consultant on Army human resource issues. Dr. Walker has a Ph.D. in psychology from the University of Illinois.

Dr. Leonard A. White is a personnel research psychologist at the U.S. Army Research Institute for the Behavioral and Social Sciences. He became involved in Project A in 1983, initially on the criterion measurement portion and in the last few years of the research program on implementation issues relating to the Assessment of Background and Life Experiences (ABLE). Dr. White earned his Ph.D. from Purdue University in 1977.

Dr. Hilda Wing recently retired from the Federal Aviation Administration. While there, she initiated a selection project for air traffic control specialists that was modeled on Project A. She was the task monitor for Project A predictor development when she worked for the Army Research Institute from 1981 to 1985. She received her Ph.D. in experimental psychology from the Johns Hopkins University in 1969.

Dr. Lauress L. Wise earned his Ph.D. in psychological measurement from the University of California, Berkeley in 1975. He was a research scientist with the American Institutes for Research at the beginning of Project A. He served initially as the database director and then assumed responsibility for the database and analysis task from 1985 through 1990. In 1990, Dr. Wise took a position with the Defense Department, directing research and development for the Armed Services Vocational Aptitude Battery (ASVAB). Since 1994, Dr. Wise has served as the president of the Human Resources Research Organization (HumRRO), the prime contractor for Project A.

Dr. Mark C. Young is a research psychologist with the U.S. Army Research Institute for the Behavioral and Social Sciences (ARI). His work at ARI over the past ten years has focused on the development and validation of new personnel assessment measures that can be used to reduce Army attrition, while increasing job performance. Dr. Young's achievements at ARI have contributed to the Army's use of new personnel selection measures for improving the quality of enlisted accessions. Dr. Young earned his Ph.D. from Georgia State University in 1987, where he specialized in personnel psychology and measurement.

Ms. Winnie Y. Young is a private consultant specialized in database management and statistical analysis. She was involved in Project A from 1983 to 1990, while working for the American Institutes for Research, primarily as the database manager for the concurrent and longitudinal validation data collections. From 1995 to 1998, Ms. Young returned to work as an independent consultant for both the American Institutes for Research and the U.S. Army Research Institute. She was responsible for archiving the final Project A and Building the Career Force databases.

I

Introduction and Major Issues

1

Matching People and Jobs: An Introduction to Twelve Years of R&D

John P. Campbell

This book is about large-scale personnel research; or more specifically, about personnel selection and classification research on a scale never attempted before in terms of (a) the types and variety of information collected, (b) the number of jobs that were considered simultaneously, (c) the size of the samples, and (d) the length of time that individuals were followed as they progressed through the organization.

It is primarily an account of a research program, sponsored by the U.S. Army Research Institute for the Behavioral and Social Sciences (ARI), designed to address a broad set of selection and classification issues using a very large, but very integrated, database. The central focus of the research program, which incorporated two sequential projects, was the enlisted personnel selection and classification system in the United States Army.

Project A (1982–1989) and **Career Force** (1990–1994) worked from a common overall design. Project A covered all initial instrument development work and all data collections, which involved the assessment of training performance and job performance during the first tour of duty for enlisted personnel in the U.S. Army. The Career Force project involved the assessment and prediction of job performance during the second tour of duty, that is, after the individual reenlists and begins to take on supervisory responsibilities as a junior noncommissioned officer (NCO). In this book we will also describe the **Synthetic Validation Project** (1987–1990), which used the database generated by Project A/Career Force (generally referred to simply as "Project A") to evaluate alternative procedures for making selection and classification decisions when the decision rules cannot be developed using empirical validation data for each job.

Collectively, these projects attempted to evaluate the selection validity and classification efficiency of different kinds of prediction information for different selection and classification goals (e.g., maximize future performance, minimize turnover/attrition) using a variety of alternative decision rules (i.e., "models"). Tackling such an ambitious objective required the development of a comprehensive battery of new tests and inventories, the development of a wide variety of training and job performance measures for each job in the sample, four major worldwide data collections involving thousands of job incumbents for one to two days each, and the design and maintenance of the resulting database.

The truly difficult part was the neverending need to develop a consensus among all the project participants (of which there were many) regarding literally hundreds of choices among measurement procedures, analysis methods, and data collection design strategies. Although many such decisions were made in the original design stage, many more occurred continuously as the projects moved forward, driven by the target dates for the major data collections, which absolutely could *not* be missed. The project participants had to use the entire textbook (Campbell, 1986) and then to go considerably beyond it. The fact that all major parts of the projects were completed within the prescribed time frames and according to the specified research design remains a source of wonder for all who participated.

This book then is an account of 12 years (1982–1994) of personnel selection and classification research design, measure development, data collection, database management, and interpretation and implementation of research findings. We will take the remainder of this chapter to set the context within which these projects were designed, carried out, and interpreted. Subsequent chapters will discuss the basic design and organization of the projects, the measurement development work, the projects' attempts to "model" the latent structure of both prediction information and performance, and the major domains of research findings.

Although, as an example of a large complex organization, the U.S. Army has a number of specialized features, the argument here is that there is more than sufficient communality with complex organizations in the public and private sectors to make a great deal of generalization possible. It is also true that, as an employer, the Army has certain features that can make both research questions and research findings much clearer than in private sector organizations.

PERSONNEL SELECTION AND CLASSIFICATION IN MODERN SOCIETY

Everyone should recognize that current personnel research and human resource management in the developed, market-oriented economies carry along certain principles and operating assumptions. Some of these are old, and some are fairly recent.

Certainly, the development of large, privately owned organizations created to produce specific goods and services goes back less than 200 years and is largely a product of the industrial revolution. Within this context, it is legitimized by law and current custom that the employer has the right (and the obligation) to hire people who will do the "best job" or make the greatest contribution to the organization is goals and to reject those who will not.

The dominant value is that of the meritocracy, which dictates that individuals should receive rewards commensurate with their individual merit; and judgments of (i.e., measurement of) current merit, or forecasts of future merit, should be as fair and as accurate as possible. Distributing rewards according to family or class membership, or distributing them equally according to a strict equalitarian value system is not legitimized in our current political-economic system.

Further, there must be significant agreement across the economic system as to what "merit" means, such that it is at least potentially possible to measure an individual's level of merit in some meaningful way. If significant disagreement exists among the major parties as to what constitutes high merit, conflict will result. However, such conflict aside, there seems to be very high agreement that merit cannot be defined from the individual point of view. That is, for example, individuals cannot each decide for themselves what will constitute high merit, or high performance, and thereby give themselves promotions or pay raises. Self-employed people may do that if they wish, provided they do not violate civil or criminal statutes, and then take their chances; but an individual who works for someone else cannot. Obviously, the definition and assessment of merit in ways that best serve common goals is a critical and fundamental issue in human resource management.

A relevant question pertaining to the research reported in this book is whether the military services in general, and the Army in particular, share these same values with the private sector. That is, are the human resource management practices of the two kinds of organizations (i.e., military vs. civilian) based on the same goals and assumptions? If they are not, then research findings from one sector might be difficult to generalize to another.

This book is based on the conclusion that the assumptions that underlie human resource management in the military and nonmilitary sectors are very much the same. This makes the basic goals of recruitment, selection, training, career management, performance appraisal, and promotion also the same. Although the military services do not "sell" products or services, and they have somewhat different compensation practices, employment constraints, and management practices, they are not qualitatively unique. Human resource management "truths" that are discovered in military organizations should have broad applicability across many other sectors.

PERSONNEL SELECTION AND DIFFERENTIAL CLASSIFICATION: SOME BASIC ISSUES

Personnel selection is the decision process by which applicants are assigned to one of two possible outcomes (e.g., "hire" vs. "do not hire"). The decision could be with regard to hiring for a particular job or a particular class of jobs. Personnel classification, at least for the purpose of this book, refers to a decision process that requires each individual to be either not hired or hired and then assigned to one of two or more job alternatives. That is, if individuals are hired, there are alternative job assignments for which they could be considered. If there exist some set of assignment decision rules that will yield more benefit to the organization than random assignment, then there exists a potential classification gain. Consequently, the benefits from improving selection and classification procedures can accrue from two major sources. Better selection would bring in people whose predicted benefit would be higher, no matter what the job assignment (i.e., averaged across all the different jobs they could take). Better classification would, for all those people hired, achieve a better "fit" of individuals with different characteristics to jobs with different requirements.

The more any organization can learn about the benefits and costs of alternative methods for selecting and classifying the individuals who apply, the more effective its personnel management systems can be. Ideally, personnel management would benefit most from a complete simulation of the entire system that would permit a full range of "what if" questions focused on the effects of changes in (a) labor supply, (b) recruiting procedures, (c) selection and classification measures, (d) decision-making algorithms, (e) applicant preferences, (f) various organizational constraints, and (g) organizational goals (e.g., maximizing aggregate performance, achieving a certain distribution of individual performance in each job, minimizing attrition, minimizing discipline problems, or maximizing morale). Further, it would be desirable to have a good estimate of the specific costs involved when each parameter is changed.

However, describing, or "modeling," effective selection and classification in a large organization is a complex business. When considering all the variations in all the relevant components, there may be dozens, or even hundreds, of alternative models. Also, there is always at least one constraint on personnel decision-making specific to the organization, which complicates the decision model even further. The overall complexity of any real-world personnel management situation is such that it probably cannot be fully modeled by currently available analytic methods (Campbell, 1990).

It may not be possible even to *describe* all the potential parameters that influence the outcomes of a real-world selection/classification procedure. However, for purposes of setting the context for this series of projects, we start by simply listing some of the major parameters of selection and classification decision-making that we do know about, and the principal implications of each.

The Goal(s) of Selection/Classification

By definition, selection and classification decision procedures are implemented to achieve a particular objective, or set of objectives. Identifying the objective(s) for the selection/classification system is the most critical ingredient in the design of the system because it directly determines the appropriate input information and procedures to be used in decision-making.

Some possible alternative objectives are to (a) maximize the mean individual performance across jobs, (b) maximize the number of people above a certain performance level in each job, (c) maximize the correspondence of the actual distribution of performance in each job to a desired distribution, (d) minimize turnover across all jobs, (e) minimize the number of "problem" employees across all jobs, (f) fill all jobs with people who meet minimal qualifications, (g) maximize the utility, or value, of performance across jobs, or (h) minimize the cost of achieving a specific level of performance across jobs.

There are many important implications relative to these alternative decision-making objectives. For example, the procedure for maximizing average expected performance would not be the same as for maximizing average expected utility, if the utility of performance differs across jobs and/or the relationship of performance to performance utility within jobs is not linear.

If improving future performance is a goal, the way in which performance is to be defined and measured is also critical. For example, if major components of performance can be identified, then which component is to be maximized? If the objective is to maximize some joint function of multiple goals (e.g., maximize average performance and minimize attrition), then deciding on the combination rules is a major issue in itself. For example, should multiple goals be addressed sequentially or as a weighted composite of some kind?

Selection Versus Classification

A personnel decision-making system could give varying degrees of emphasis to selection versus classification. At one extreme, individuals could be selected into the organization and then assigned at random to k different jobs, or separate applicant pools could be used for each job. At the other extreme, no overall selection would occur and all available information would be used to make optimal job assignments until all available openings were filled.

In between, a variety of multiple step models could emphasize different objectives for selection and classification. For example, selection could emphasize minimizing turnover while classification could emphasize those aspects of individual performance that are the most job specific. For classification to offer an advantage over selection, jobs must, in fact, differ in terms of their requirements, predictability, difficulty level, or relative value (utility). Table 1.1 lists several other factors that also affect the decision process in varying degrees. Each of these factors is briefly discussed below.

The first two factors relate to the characteristics of the set of jobs to be filled. With regard to *job differences*, gains from classification (over selection plus random assignment) can be greater to the extent that (a) jobs differ in the knowledges, skills, and abilities (KSAs) required, and consequently a greater degree of differential prediction is possible; (b) jobs differ in terms the accuracy with which performance can be predicted

TABLE 1.1
Factors Influencing Effectiveness of
Selection and Classification Systems

Job differences
Number of jobs
Selection ratio
Applicant qualifications
Individual preferences
Predictor battery
Job fill requirements
Real time versus batch decision-making
Organizational constraints
Gains versus costs

and higher ability people are assigned to the more predictable jobs; (c) jobs differ in terms of the mean value or mean utility of performance; or (d) jobs differ in terms of the within job variance of performance or performance utility (i.e., SDy) and, other things being equal, higher ability people are assigned to jobs with higher SDy's. The *number of jobs* is also relevant. Other things being equal, the gains from classification are greater to the extent that the number of distinct jobs, or job families, is greater.

The next three factors, *selection ratio*, *applicant qualifications*, and *individual preferences*, relate to characteristics of the applicant pool. The gains from both selection and classification are greater to the extent that (a) the number of applicants exceeds the number of openings, (b) the mean qualification level of the applicant pool is high, and (c) applicant preferences correlate positively with the profile of jobs in which they are predicted to be most successful.

Obviously, the effectiveness of selection and classification decisions are also dependent upon characteristics of the *predictor battery*. Gains from selection are directly proportional to increases in the validity coefficient (R). Gains from classification are a joint function of the average R across jobs and the level of differential prediction across jobs that can be obtained by using a different predictor battery for each job or each job family. The nature of this joint function is perhaps a bit more complex than the conventional wisdom implies (e.g., Brogden, 1954).

Another set of factors that help determine the success of a selection and classification system relate to characteristics of the decision-making process, that is, *job fill requirements*, *real time versus batch decision-making*, and *organizational constraints*. Other things being equal (e.g., the total number of people to be assigned), the gains from classification are less to the extent that each job has a specified number (quota) of openings that must be filled. Similarly, to the extent that job assignments must be made in real time and the characteristics of future applicants during specified time periods must be estimated, the gains from classification will be reduced. The decrement will be greater to the extent that the characteristics of future applicants cannot be accurately estimated. And finally, in all organizations, the selection and classification decision-making process must operate under one or more constraints (e.g., budget limitations, training "seat" availability, hiring goals for specific subgroups, management priorities). In general, the existence of constraints reduces the gains from selection and classification. These effects must be taken into account.

The final factor listed in Table 1.1 is *gains versus costs*. The gains from selection and classification obtained by recruiting more applicants, recruiting higher quality applicants, improving the assessment of qualifications (e.g., a better predictor battery), enabling more informed individual preferences, and improving the assignment algorithm, are partially offset by increases in related costs. The primary cost factors are recruiting, assessment, applicant processing, training, separation, and system development (R&D). It is possible that a particular gain from improvements in classification could be entirely offset by increased costs.

Any attempt to fully model the selection and classification decision process in a real-world organization must take at least the above issues into account, and dealing with them systematically is anything but simple.

Some General Research Issues

In addition to the system parameters outlined above, any large-scale research and development effort directed at selection and classification must deal with a number of other issues that are viewed as critical by researchers and practitioners in the field. They were very much in the forefront as the Army research projects began.

The criterion problem.   Perhaps the oldest issue is still the most critical. In fact, as is noted in the next chapter, it was probably the single most important reason for the start of Project A/Career Force. Much of the development of human resource management policies and practices hinges on being able to evaluate alternative decision-making procedures in terms of their effects on the dependent variable of major interest—the criterion. Criterion measurement was/is a "problem" because it has been plagued by low reliability, low relevance, and too much contamination (e.g., Campbell, McCloy, Oppler, & Sager, 1993; Dunnette, 1963; Wallace, 1965). Effective personnel research must deal with this issue.

Types of validity evidence.   The issue of what constitutes validity evidence for the use of particular selection and classification procedures has been argued for some time (American Education Research Association, American Psychological Association, & National Council on Measurement in Education, 1985, 1999; Linn, 1988; Messick, 1988) and a number of positions are possible. For example, Messick's basic position is that validity is a unitarian concept and virtually any use of a psychological measure to make decisions about people must be supported by evidence that (a) supports the measure as a sample of a relevant content domain (content validation), (b) provides empirical evidence that scores on the measures are related to decision outcomes in the appropriate way (criterion-related validation), and (c) substantiates that the conceptual foundation for the measures is a reasonable one (construct validation). The classic historical view is that criterion-related validity, estimated from a longitudinal/predictive design is the fundamental validation evidence of greatest interest. Both the Society for Industrial and Organizational Psychology's *Principles for the Validation and Use of Personnel Selection Procedures* (1987) and the *Standards for the Development and Use of Psychological Tests* (1985, 1999), published jointly by the American Educational Research Association, the American Psychological Association, and the National Council on Measurement in Education, take a position between these two extremes, and argue that the kind of evidence required depends on the specific measurement objectives. From this perspective, each kind of evidence can be sufficient for certain prediction problems. It depends. The issue of the evidence requirement is a critical one if the measurement goal is to build a prediction system that can be used as the basis for making selection and classification decisions on an organization-wide basis. For a dynamic system of any size, it is simply not possible to generate comparable criterion-related validity estimates for each "job" in the system.

Validity generalization.   Related to the broad issue of evidence requirements is the question of how much variability exists in the predictive validity coefficient, when measures of the same construct are used to predict performance in different jobs within an organization or to predict performance in the same type of job across organizations. Hunter and Schmidt (1990) have shown convincingly that, after the masking effects of sampling error, differences in criterion reliabilities across studies, and differences in range restriction across studies are controlled, there is much less variation in validity estimates across studies and the remaining residual variance sometimes approaches zero. When the same predictor construct and the same performance construct are being measured, there is apparently very little situational specificity in the level of predictive validity when the true score on the criterion is being estimated. It can only be produced by genuine differences in the range of true scores across settings.

Differential prediction.   If the goal of a selection/classification system is to maximize the average level of predicted performance across job assignments, then the major gains from classification over selection result from differential prediction across jobs. That is, in the true score sense, the same person would not have the highest predicted performance score in each job. Because there is very little situational specificity for univariate prediction, classification gain can only be produced if the latent structure of performance, and by implication the job requirements, are different across jobs and the predictor battery is multidimensional. The extent to which this kind of differential prediction exists for a particular population of jobs is an empirical question. Among other issues, the battle lines between the general cognitive factor (g) and the multidimensional predictor battery have become readily apparent (e.g., Ree & Earles, 1991a).

BASIC FEATURES OF THE ARMY
ENLISTED PERSONNEL SYSTEM

In terms of the number of people it employs, the U.S. Army is considered a large organization. Between 1983 and 1989, it included approximately 760,000 active duty personnel (enlisted and officer) and approximately 1,190,000 uniformed personnel if you add in reserve component officers and enlisted personnel. In the late stages of Project A (1990–1993), the Army began a period of downsizing that has since stabilized. As of 1997, there were approximately 476,000 active duty personnel in the Army, up to about 838,000 if the reserve component is included. A large drop in size, but still a large organization by any standards.

In the beginning years of Project A, there were approximately 300,000 to 400,000 applicants per year for entry level Army positions. The number of new accessions (i.e., number of applicants who were hired) varied between roughly 106,000 and 132,000 per year between 1983 and 1989. Again as a result of downsizing initiatives, these numbers have declined considerably, from a low of about 57,000 in 1995 to a high of 76,000 in 1997. The first tour for these new accessions is an employment contract typically for a 2-, 3-, or 4-year period.

For enlisted personnel, during the 1983–1995 period, the number of different entry level jobs to which an individual could be assigned varied between 260 and 280. Although this number has decreased to about 200 as the Army has adjusted to its downsized state, there are still many different jobs for which a separate job description exists. In Army vernacular, a job is a Military Occupational Specialty (MOS) and for each MOS a *Soldier's Manual* specifies the major job tasks that are the responsibility of someone in that MOS. The distribution of first-term enlisted personnel over the 200+ MOS is very uneven. Some positions contain tens of thousands of people and some contain only a few dozen. A large N is not necessarily assured. Also, although a subset of MOS is designated as the category Combat Specialties, a very large proportion of the entry level jobs are skilled positions similar to that found in the civilian labor force. In fact, each MOS in the Army has been linked to its most similar civilian counterpart for vocational counseling and other purposes.

In the private sector, at this writing, there is considerable discussion of whether the term "job" is becoming an anachronism because of what is perceived as a marked increase in the dynamic nature of organizations. Because of global competition, products and services must be developed, produced, marketed, and updated or changed at a much faster pace than before. As a consequence, the content of jobs and interrelationships among jobs are seen as also entering a state of more or less constant change such that job descriptions don't stand still for long and individuals can't expect to "do the same thing" for long periods of time (Pearlman, 1995). Although it may be difficult to make cross-sector comparisons, the overall situation in the Army is probably not radically different. Considerable ongoing changes continue in missions, strategies, and equipment. It is not the case that the military services are static and the private sector is dynamic; both are living in very turbulent times.

It must also be said that the Army's human resource management situation has some unique features. We list the following as further background for the Project A/Career Force research.

- Every year a detailed budgeting process take place, which results in very specific goals for recruitment, hiring, and training. These goals are system-wide and tied directly to the fiscal year. If Congress cuts the budget, goals are changed. However, once goals are set, then it is best if the organization meets them exactly. For example, the planning and budgeting process determines the number of available training "seats" in each MOS at different times of the year and the ideal state is that each seat be filled (no empty seats and no standees) on the day each class starts. It is a delicate management task.

- Given that applicants are young and generally inexperienced, job histories are not required. Assessment of previous work experience plays no role in the selection and job assignment process (with certain exceptions, such as musicians).
- For each individual, the selection decision and the first tour job assignment is usually made in a relatively short space of time (about 2 days). After that, very little opportunity exists for changing training programs or changing MOS during the first tour of duty.
- In the private sector, almost all job applications are submitted for specific job openings, and personnel systems operate largely in a selection mode. In the Army, after an applicant has passed the basic selection screen, he or she is usually placed in a specific training program that leads to a specific job. Classification is a much bigger part of the personnel management system in the military than in the private sector.

OPERATIONAL SELECTION AND CLASSIFICATION DECISION-MAKING PROCEDURES

The major stages of the current operational selection, classification, and assignment procedure for persons entering enlisted service in the Army are described below. Although it is difficult to discuss recruitment, selection, and classification separately because of their interdependence, they are presented in chronological order.

Recruitment

The Army has succeeded in meeting or approximating its numerical recruitment quotas in most of the years following the change to an All Volunteer Force. Of course, the numbers that the Army has had to recruit in order to be successful have dropped somewhat with the downsizing of the force in the 1990s. The continued healthy state of the economy during this same period, however, has resulted in continued challenges to meeting recruiting goals.

TABLE 1.2
AFQT Mental Aptitude Categories

AFQT Category	Percentile Scores
I	93–100
II	65–92
IIIA	50–64
IIIB	31–49
IVA	21–30
IVB	16–20
IVC	10–15
V	1–9

Applicant quality is generally defined in terms of high school graduation status and scores on the Armed Forces Qualification Test (AFQT). The AFQT is a composite of four subtests (comprising verbal and math content) from the selection and classification instrument, the Armed Services Vocational Aptitude Battery (ASVAB), which is used by all the U.S. Armed Forces. AFQT scores are reported in percentiles relative to the national youth population and are grouped for convenience as shown in Table 1.2.

Because of their observed likelihood of success in training, the Army attempts to maximize the recruitment of those scoring within Categories I through IIIA. In addition, because traditional high school graduates are more likely to complete their contracted enlistment terms than are nongraduates and alternative credential holders, high school graduates are actively recruited as well.

To compete with the other Services and with the private sector for the prime applicant target group, the Army offers a variety of special inducements including "critical skill" bonuses and educational incentives. One of the most popular inducements has been the "training of choice" enlistment to a specific school training program, provided that applicants meet the minimum aptitude and educational standards and other prerequisites, and that training "slots" are available at the time of their scheduled entry into the program. Additional options, offered separately or in combination with "training of choice," include guaranteed initial assignment to particular commands, units, or bases, primarily in the combat arms or in units requiring highly technical skills. In recent years, a large proportion of all Army recruits, particularly in the preferred aptitude and educational categories, has been enlisted under one or more of these options.

The importance of aptitude measurement in recruiting decisions is exemplified in the prescreening of applicants at the recruiter level. For applicants who have not previously taken the ASVAB through the Department of Defense (DoD) high school student testing program, the recruiter administers a short Computerized Adaptive Screening Test (CAST) or the paper-and-pencil Enlistment Screening Test (EST) to assess the applicant's prospects of passing the ASVAB.

Applicants who appear upon initial recruiter screening to have a reasonable chance of qualifying for service are referred either to one of approximately 750 Mobile Examining Test Sites (METS) for administration of the ASVAB or directly to a Military Entrance Processing Station (MEPS) where all aspects of enlistment testing (e.g., physical examination) are conducted.

Selection and Classification at the Military Entrance Processing Station (MEPS)

ASVAB is administered as a computerized adaptive test (CAT-ASVAB) at the MEPS and as a paper-and-pencil test at the METS and in the student testing program (Sands, Waters, & McBride, 1997). ASVAB consists of the 10 subtests listed in Table 1.3. In addition to AFQT scores, subtest scores are combined to form 10 aptitude composite scores, based on those combinations of subtests that have been found to be most valid as predictors of successful completion of the various Army school training programs.

TABLE 1.3
ASVAB Subtests

Arithmetic Reasoning
Numerical Operations
Paragraph Comprehension
Word Knowledge
Coding Speed
General Science
Mathematics Knowledge
Electronics Information
Mechanical Comprehension
Automotive-shop Information

For example, the composite score for administrative specialties is based on the numerical operations, paragraph comprehension, word knowledge, and coding speed subtests. The composite score for electronics specialties is based on a combination of the scores for arithmetic reasoning, general science, mathematics knowledge, and electronics information. CAT-ASVAB includes an additional subtest that is not yet being used for operational decision-making purposes. Assembling Objects, a test developed as part of Project A, was added to CAT-ASVAB in 1993 to allow the battery to more clearly cover spatial abilities.

As stated above, eligibility for enlistment is based upon a combination of criteria: AFQT score, aptitude area composite scores, and whether or not the applicant is a high school graduate. The minimum standards are as follows:[1]

- *High school graduates* are eligible if they achieve an AFQT percentile score of 16 or higher and a standard score of 85 (mean of 100, standard deviation 20) in at least *one* aptitude area.
- *GED high school equivalency holders* are eligible if they achieve an AFQT percentile score of 31 or higher and a standard score of 85 in at least one aptitude area.
- *Nonhigh school graduates* are eligible only if they achieve an AFQT percentile score of 31 or higher and standard scores of 85 in at least *two* aptitude areas.

In addition to these formal minimum requirements, the Army may set higher operational cut scores for one or all of these groups. Physical standards are captured in the PULHES profile, which uses a general physical examination and interview to rate the applicant on General Physical (P), Upper torso (U), Lower torso (L), and Hearing, Eyes, and Psychiatric (HES). Scores of 1 or 2 (on a 5-point scale) are required on all six indicators to be accepted for military duty (though waivers may be extended to applicants with a score of 3 on one or two indicators). In addition to the PULHES, the Army also sets general height and weight standards for enlistment.

Qualified applicants do not typically enter active duty immediately but enter the Delayed Entry Program (DEP) where they await a training slot. The majority of enlistees enter the Army under a specific enlistment option that guarantees choice of initial school training, career field assignment, unit assignment, or geographical area. For these applicants, the initial

---

[1] Army Regulation 601-201, 1 October 1980, revised, Table 2-2.

classification and training assignment decision must be made prior to entry into service. This is accomplished at the MEPS by referring applicants who have passed the basic screening criteria (aptitude, physical, moral) to an Army guidance counselor, whose responsibility is to match the applicant's qualifications and preferences to Army requirements, and to make "reservations" for training assignments, consistent with the applicant's enlistment option.

For the applicant, this decision will determine the nature of his or her initial training and occupational assignment and future job assignment. For the Army, the relative success of the assignment process will significantly determine the aggregate level of performance and attrition for the entire force.

The classification and training "reservation" procedure is accomplished by the Recruit Quota System (REQUEST). REQUEST is a computer-based system to coordinate the information needed to reserve training slots for applicants. REQUEST uses minimum qualifications for controlling entry. Thus, to the extent that an applicant may minimally qualify for a wide range of courses or specialties, based on aptitude test scores, the initial classification decision is governed by (a) his or her own stated preference (often based upon limited knowledge about the actual job content and working conditions of the various military occupations), (b) the availability of training slots, and (c) the current priority assigned to filling each MOS.

The Army system currently incorporates a type of marginal utility constraint by specifying the desired distribution of AFQT scores in each MOS, which are termed quality goals.

Training

After the initial processing, all nonprior service Army recruits are assigned to a basic training program of 9 weeks, which is followed, with few exceptions, by a period of Advanced Individual Training (AIT), designed to provide basic entry-level job skills. Entrants into the combat arms and the military police receive both their basic training and their AIT at the same Army base (One Station Unit Training) in courses of about 3 to 4 months total duration. Those assigned to other specialties are sent to separate Army technical schools whose course lengths vary considerably, depending upon the technical complexity of the MOS.

In contrast to earlier practice, most enlisted trainees do not currently receive school grades upon completion of their courses, but are evaluated using pass/fail criteria. Those initially failing certain portions of a course are recycled. The premise is that slower learners, given sufficient time and effort under self-paced programs, can normally be trained to a satisfactory level of competence, and that this additional training investment is cost-effective. Those who continue to fail the course may be reassigned to other, often less demanding, specialties or discharged from service. One consequence of these practices is to limit the usefulness of the operational measures of training performance as criteria for selection/classification research.

Performance Assessment in Army Units

After the initial job assignment, most of the personnel actions affecting the career of the first-term enlistee are initiated by his or her immediate supervisor and/or the unit commander. These include the nature of the duty assignment, the provision of on-the-job or unit training, and assessments of performance, both on and off the job. These assessments influence such decisions as promotion, future assignment, and eligibility for reenlistment, as well as possible disciplinary action (including early discharges from service).

During an initial 3-year enlistment term, the typical enlistee can expect to progress to pay grade E-4, although advancement to higher pay grades for specially qualified personnel is not precluded. Promotion to E-2 is almost automatic after 6 months of service. Promotions to grades E-3 and E-4 normally require completion of certain minimum periods of service (12 and 24 months, respectively), but are subject to certain numerical strength limitations and specific commander approval. Unit commanders also have the authority to reduce assigned soldiers in pay grade, based on misconduct or inefficiency.

The Enlisted Evaluation System provides for an evaluation of both the soldier's proficiency in his or her MOS and of overall duty performance. The process includes a subjective evaluation based on supervisory performance appraisal and ratings that are conducted at the unit level under prescribed procedures. In addition, objective evaluations of physical fitness and job proficiency generally have been included in the system, particularly in the areas of promotion and retention.

In 1978, the Army replaced the MOS Proficiency Tests with the Skill Qualification Test (SQT). The SQT was a criterion-referenced performance-knowledge test that evaluated an individual's requisite knowledge and skill for performing critical job tasks satisfactorily. Scores from a soldier's last SQT were used in making promotion decisions for non-commissioned officer (NCO) positions. The SQT program was canceled in 1991 as a cost-saving measure. It was replaced with Self-Development Tests (SDT) that were given on an annual basis. These tests, however, have also been eliminated, thus further reducing archival information available for selection and classification research.

Reenlistment Screening

The final stage of personnel processing of first-term enlisted personnel is screening for reenlistment eligibility. This review considers such criteria as disciplinary records, aptitude area scores (based on ASVAB), performance appraisals, weight standards, and the rate of progression through the first tour salary grades.

By the time they start their first reenlistment, the cumulative losses resulting from attrition, reenlistment screening, and non-reenlistment of eligible personnel results in the reduction of the initial entering cohort to about 10 to 20 percent of the original number. In addition, not all of the individuals who reenlist are retained, or wish to be retained, in their original specialties, because an offer of retraining is often an inducement for reenlistment.

SUMMARY

It is against this background that the Army research projects were conducted. Despite the fact that it is smaller than it was when Project A began, the U.S. Army remains a large and complex organization with over 200 jobs at the entry level. Each year approximately 75,000 individuals must be recruited, selected, and "matched" with jobs such that all budgeted training slots are filled at the appropriate time, costs are contained, and the benefits from the person/job match are maximized. The system requires that each individual take only a short time to make critical decisions that are difficult to reverse. Applicants are not required to have any previous job experience, advanced education, or previous training. The available predictor information is limited to primarily to the ASVAB (but also includes high school diploma status and moral and physical standards) which, as of 1982, had not been "validated" against criterion measures of job performance.

The Army may indeed have the most difficult and complex personnel management task of any employer in the labor force.

2

A Paradigm Shift

Joyce Shields, Lawrence M. Hanser, and John P. Campbell

The overall design of the Project A/Career Force program was intended to be fundamentally different from the conventional paradigm that dominated personnel research from 1906 to 1982. In 1906, Hugo Münsterberg was credited with conducting the first personnel selection research study when he attempted to evaluate the validity of a new procedure for selecting streetcar operators for the Boston transit authority. For a sample of streetcar operators, a new test of psychomotor ability was correlated with criterion measures of performance and yielded a significant relationship (Münsterberg, 1913). With this study, the classic prediction model was born and it has dominated personnel research ever since (Campbell, 1990). The modus operandi became the estimation of the Pearson correlation coefficient when a single predictor score, or a single predictor composite score, and a single criterion measure of performance were obtained for a sample of job incumbents and the bivariate normal model was imposed on the distribution. Literally thousands of such estimates have been generated during this century (e.g., Ghiselli, 1973; Hunter & Hunter, 1984; Nathan & Alexander, 1988; Schmidt, 1988; Schmidt, Ones, & Hunter, 1992; Schmitt, Gooding, Noe, & Kirsch, 1984).

It is also characteristic of personnel research that through most of its history the enterprise has been carried out by individual investigators or co-investigators working on a specific problem with regard to a specific job or specific organization. Whether at a university, government agency, or private employer, the individual researcher has developed proposals, secured the necessary support, collected the data, and analyzed the results one study at a time. In a sense, personnel research has been a cottage industry composed of a number of single independent operators who defined their own research agenda and did not seek any kind of formal coordination among themselves.

There are probably many legitimate reasons why single investigators working to generate one bivariate distribution at a time has served as the dominant paradigm through most of our history. For one thing, the recurring problem of how best to select individuals for a particular job in a particular organization is a very real one, and a rational management will devote resources to solving such problems. It is not in the organization's best interest to spend money to solve similar or related problems in other organizations. Similarly, in the publish or perish world of the academic, the reinforcement contingencies that operate on faculty members tend to promote short-term efforts that have a high probability of payoff and that are firmly under the control of the individual whose career is on the line.

Certain structural and technological factors also might be identified as having worked against the establishment of long-term coordinated research projects that dealt with large parts of the personnel system at one time. First, the field of industrial and organizational psychology is not very large and the supply of research labor is limited. When the basic outline of Project A/Career Force was proposed, there was no single organization or university group that had the resources necessary to carry it out. Coalitions of organizations had to form. Also, until fairly recently, there were no means available for coordinating the efforts of researchers who are geographically scattered. Neither was there a technology for building a central database that could be accessed efficiently from remote locations.

In general, the dominant paradigm came to be so because of the constraints imposed by technology, because of the structural characteristics of the research enterprise itself, and because of the contingencies built into the reward structures for individual investigators.

There are of course exceptions to the above depiction of this dominant paradigm. Two of the more prominent ones are the AT&T Management Progress Study (Bray, Campbell, & Grant, 1974) and the Sears executive selection studies (Bentz, 1968). Both were programmatic in nature, were coordinated efforts over relatively long periods of time, and dealt with the prediction of success in a broad class of "management" jobs that varied by function and by level in the organization. The AT&T study is particularly noteworthy because it was a "blind" longitudinal study (over 20 years) that did not use the predictor information (scores from an assessment center) to make selection or promotion decisions. However, even with regard to these major exceptions, the number of different jobs was relatively circumscribed and the total sample sizes were still relatively small. For example, the AT&T management progress study began with a total sample size of 550 new college hires. In contrast, the longitudinal validation component of Project A/Career Force began with a sample of almost 50,000 new recruits.

PERSONNEL RESEARCH
IN THE MILITARY

Military personnel research, and research sponsored by the military, is an important segment of the total personnel research record during the 20th century. Actually, government sponsored personnel selection and classification using standardized measures of individual differences began in 1115 B.C. with the system of competitive examinations that led to appointment to the bureaucracy of Imperial China (DuBois, 1964). It soon included the selection/classification of individuals for particular military specialties, as in the selection of spear throwers with standardized measures of long-distance visual acuity (e.g., identification of stars in the night sky).

Systematic attempts to deal with selection/classification issues have been a part of military personnel management ever since (Zook, 1995). Military organizations have a critical need to make large numbers of complex personnel decisions in a short space of time. It was such a need that led to the Army sponsored effort to develop the first group intelligence tests during World War I. However, the centrality of criterion-related validation to a technology of selection and classification was not fully incorporated into military research until World War II, and research and development sponsored by the military has been the mainstay of growth in that technology from that time to the present.

The work of military psychologists during World War II is reasonably well-known and well-documented. The early work of the Personnel Research Branch of The Adjutant General's Office was summarized in a series of articles in the *Psychological Bulletin* (Staff, AGO, Personnel Research Branch, 1943 a, b, c). Later work was published in Technical Bulletins and in such journals as *Psychometrika, Personnel Psychology*, and *Journal of Applied Psychology*. The Aviation Psychology Program of the Army Air Forces issued 19 volumes, with a summary of the overall program presented in Volume I (Flanagan, 1948). In the Navy, personnel research played a smaller and less centralized role, but here too, useful work was done by the Bureau of Naval Personnel (Stuit, 1947).

Much new ground was broken. There were important advances in the development and analysis of criterion measures. Thorndike's textbook based on his Air Force experience presented a state-of-the-art classification and analysis of potential criteria (Thorndike, 1949). Improvements were made in rating scales. Checklists based on critical incidents were first used in the Army Air Force (AAF) program. Also, the sequential aspect of prediction was articulated and examined. Tests "validated" against training measures (usually pass/fail) were checked against measures of success in combat (usually ratings or awards). At least one "pure" validity study was accomplished, when the Air Force sent 1,000 cadets into pilot training without regard to their predictor scores derived from the classification battery. This remains one of the few studies that could report validity estimates without correcting for restriction of range. Historically, 1940 to 1946 was a period of concentrated development of selection and classification procedures, and further work during the next several decades flowed directly from it.

In part, this continuity is attributable to the well-known fact that many of the psychologists who had worked in the military research establishments during the war became leaders in the civilian research community after the war. It is also attributable to the less widely recognized fact that the bulk of the work continued to be funded by military agencies. The Office of Naval Research, the Army's Personnel Research Branch (and its successors), and the Air Force Human Resources Research installations were the principal sponsors.

The post war bibliography is very long. Of special relevance to Project A and Career Force is the work on differential prediction and classification models by Brogden (1946a, 1951) and Horst (1954, 1955); on utility conceptions of validity by Brogden (1946b) and Brogden and Taylor (1950a); on the "structure of intellect" by Guilford (1957); on the establishment of critical job requirements by Flanagan and associates (Flanagan, 1954); and on the decision-theoretic formulations of selection and classification developed by Cronbach and Gleser (1965) for the Office of Naval Research. The last of these (*Psychological Tests and Personnel Decisions*) was hailed quite appropriately as a breakthrough—a "new look" in selection and classification. However, the authors were the first to acknowledge the relevance of the initial work of Brogden and Horst. It was the culmination of a lengthy sequence of development.

As impressive and as important as the military sponsored research has been, it does not represent a major departure from the classic paradigm described above. Much of it has been directed at the development of new analytic technologies and has been conducted by the single principal investigator focusing on a specific problem or issue. Much of the substantive investigation has focused on a series of specific issues, such as selection for officer candidate school, pilot selection, attrition reduction, or making periodic improvements in the ASVAB and its predecessors. It was against this background that Project A/Career Force were formulated.

THE ORIGINS OF PROJECT A

The events that helped shape Army personnel policy and eventually resulted in Project A began in the 1970s. At the close of the Vietnam War in 1973, the draft came to an end and the All Volunteer Force was instituted. By 1975, first-term attrition had reached 26.6% among high school graduate enlistees and 51.4% among nonhigh school graduate enlistees, both record highs. Also in that year, only 58% of Army enlistees earned a high school diploma, compared with 90% in 1987. Although the size of the Army had been reduced drastically from the Vietnam War era, these high attrition rates placed an enormous burden on recruiting. These times were best summarized in a now famous Department of the Army white paper on the "Hollow Army" (Meyer, 1980).

In addition to changes in the personnel system, the Army was beginning the largest force modernization program since World War II. On-board computer systems were becoming commonplace; field units would use satellite communications for determining their location and shoulder-fired missiles would include state-of-the-art electronics for aircraft identification. Further complicating the ability to deal with the increasing technical demands of modern equipment was the prediction of a significant decline in the number of eligible youth, which was projected to begin about 1982 and continue through 1996. Obviously, the personnel needs of the Army were facing substantial change in a climate of declining labor supply.

The climate was also unfavorable to testing. The nation as a whole was questioning the fairness of tests. In 1978, the "Uniform Guidelines" (Equal Employment Opportunity Commission, 1978) were published. In 1981, the Congress had issued a directive that the Services must "develop a better

database on the relationship between factors such as high school graduation and entrance test scores, and effective performance." During the 1970s,
interest in, and support for, testing research in the Army had declined substantially. At that time, the Army Research Institute, the traditional home
for selection and classification research in the Army, was organized into
two laboratories: the Training Research Laboratory and the Organization
and Systems Research Laboratory. The latter included only a small team
devoted to selection and classification research. It was symptomatic of a
significant decline in military sponsored personnel research during the late
1960s and 1970s.

In 1980, ASVAB Forms 6/7, which were used operationally from 1976
to 1980, were discovered to have been misnormed. In 1980, as a result
of the misnorming, 50% of non-prior-service Army recruits were drawn
from the bottom 30% of the eligible youth population. More recently, more
than 60% of recruits have come from the top 50% of the youth population.
With this large influx of low-scoring recruits in the late 1970s, the U.S.
Congress began to question what difference entry test scores made in terms
of eventual performance in military occupations. That is, did it really matter
whether the Services recruited individuals from a higher percentile in the
youth population?

Previously, the Services had used measures of training performance to
assess the predictive validity of ASVAB. But Congress, mindful of the extra costs associated with recruiting high aptitude personnel in the military,
mandated that the Services answer the questions above thoroughly and convincingly. This meant that validating the ASVAB against carefully designed
measures of job performance was vital, and that each of the Services was responsible for conducting research to accomplish this. The research growing
out of this 1980 Congressional mandate became known as the Joint-Service
Job Performance Measurement/Enlistment Standards (JPM) Project.

The JPM research projects were coordinated through a Joint-Service
working group. Ongoing independent evaluation of the research program
was the responsibility of the Committee on the Performance of Military
Personnel within the National Research Council (Wigdor & Green, 1991).

Project A was the Army's contribution to the JPM project. It was a
contribution, and much more. The Army viewed the Congressional mandate as an opportunity to address a much larger set of personnel research
questions. Could other selection and classification measures be developed
to supplement the predictive power of the ASVAB? Could selection tests
be used to identify individuals more likely to complete their tour of service? Given the declining manpower pool, could tests be designed to

more efficiently use the available resources via better classification and allocation?

These questions cut across a number of Army commands and organizations, such that resolving them was important to a wide variety of policymakers, and there was great outside pressure to do so. As far as the Army was concerned, Project A did not spring from a desire to examine the issues related to validity generalization, or to rater accuracy, or to computerized testing, or from any basic desire to support industrial/organizational research. Rather, it grew from the need to address some very real policy issues and to improve the design and functioning of the Army's selection/classification decision procedures.

Upon examining the list of issues facing the Army in the late 1970s (including the Congressional mandate cited above), it was clear that a number of discrete policy research projects could have been designed to address them individually, and there were strong pressures to proceed in that direction. However, rather than simply pursuing piecemeal solutions to a laundry list of problems, a single comprehensive program of personnel research was established. Project A/Career Force was designed in such a way as to provide the basic data with which to resolve specific personnel management problems as well as to address longer term scientific issues.

Concurrently, ARI organized the Manpower and Personnel Research Laboratory to be responsible for this program of research. In the spring of 1981, a team of individuals from this technical area began to prepare the design specifications that were to become Project A. After several months of writing and rewriting, the Request for Proposals was released in the fall of 1981. In September 1982, a contract for Project A was signed with the Human Resources Research Organization (HumRRO) and its subcontractors, the American Institutes for Research (AIR) and Personnel Decisions Research Institute, Inc. (PDRI).

As discussed previously, the problems addressed by these projects are of great importance to the Army, and are of interest to many constituencies, including personnel and training proponents. Much of the line management responsibility in the Army is focused on attracting high-ability people, training them to a high degree of readiness, and maintaining a high degree of motivation and commitment. Effective personnel management is not characterized by add-on programs; it is a core line activity. If personnel researchers can demonstrate that they possess the necessary expertise and that they understand the Army, they are provided access.

Army management practices also require that researchers continue to provide information back to management in terms of options, alternatives, and evaluations—not just research reports. If the key policymakers have confidence and trust in the technical ability of the researchers and their understanding of the problems, they will continue to invest in the research effort and to provide time, access to sensitive data, and necessary support as well as trust and confidence. Not only has the Army management been open to results—whether or not prior beliefs are confirmed—but they have been willing to use the results to change and set policy.

SOME NECESSARY, BUT NOT SUFFICIENT, CONDITIONS

In addition to the developments within the Army that made a system-wide and long-term R&D effort the most attractive option, there were developments in the structure and technology of the personnel research enterprise that would also help make such a project possible. For example, advances in computerized database management and electronic communication made it possible to design, create, edit, update, and maintain a very large database in a very efficient manner. In addition, the database could be accessed for analysis and reporting purposes from anywhere in the world. What is routine now was new and liberating in 1982.

Advances in computerization also permitted the development of new testing technologies, as will be described in subsequent chapters. Computerization and the development of affordable, and powerful, linear programming algorithms made the estimation of classification efficiency and the comparison of alternative selection/classification strategies using the entire Army database a very manageable analytic problem. Certainly, the development of confirmatory techniques within the general domain of multivariate analysis models opened up a number of powerful strategies for generalizing research findings from a sample of jobs to the entire population of jobs in the organization's personnel system.

Finally, the realization in industrial and organizational psychology during the 1970s that one of our fundamental tasks is to learn things about an appropriately defined population, and not to learn more and more specific things about specific samples, changed the field's approach to the estimation of selection validity and classification efficiency. Meta-analysis and corrections for attenuation and restriction of range were no longer "risky" games to play. They were a conservative and necessary part of correct statistical estimation. They constituted giant steps forward, and these projects would make very little sense without them.

MANAGEMENT AND COLLABORATION

Because of what they tried to accomplish, the Army selection and classification projects probably constitute the largest, single research effort in the history of personnel research, by some orders of magnitude. As is outlined in the next chapter, there were a number of very large substantive pieces to the overall design, each of which was the concern of several investigators under the direction of a "task leader." The separate pieces were interdependent and had to come together on a specific date (perhaps several years in the future), such that a particular phase of the data collection could begin. The data collection dates were set far in advance and were driven by the requirement to assess a specific cohort of new recruits as it was inducted, finished training, moved on to the job, and then either left the Army or reenlisted. That is, once the overall project started, it could not stop or deviate to any significant degree from the agreed upon data collection schedule, which spanned an 8-year period. There was zero tolerance for failure, and the projects had to be managed with this reality in mind.

The successful management of the projects depended on successful and continual collaboration among all the participants. In this regard, the three contractor research organizations (HumRRO, AIR, and PDRI) and ARI were all equal and truly collaborative partners throughout the entire effort. The projects could not have been completed with even one weak link. It is to our own internal satisfaction that we finished with even more respect for each other than when we started.

GREAT EXPECTATIONS

In summary, in 1982 we hoped we had designed a research program that would bear directly on the major policy and design parameters of the selection/classification decision process such that the research results would be directly useful for meeting the system's needs, both as they existed initially and as changes took place. Simultaneously, we hoped that by considering an entire system and population of jobs at once, and by developing measures from a theoretical/taxonomic base, the science of industrial and organizational psychology would also be served. While this might not constitute a paradigm shift in the purest sense in which Kuhn (1970) discussed the phenomenon, we believe it represented a type of scientific revolution worthy of the term.

3

The Army Selection and Classification Research Program: Goals, Overall Design, and Organization

John P. Campbell, James H. Harris, and Deirdre J. Knapp

The Project A/Career Force research program involved two major validation samples, one concurrent and the other longitudinal. The concurrent sample, from which data were collected in 1985, allowed an early examination of the validity of the ASVAB, as well as a comprehensive battery of project developed experimental tests, to predict job performance for a representative sample of jobs. The longitudinal sample, from which data were collected from 1986 through 1992, allowed examination of the longitudinal relationship between ASVAB and the new predictors and performance at three stages in an individual's career. It also allowed determination of how accurately current performance predicts subsequent performance, both by itself and when combined with predictors administered at the time of selection.

This chapter describes the overall research design and organization of Project A/Career Force. It thus provides the framework within which the substantive work of the research was carried out. We begin by describing the research objectives in some detail, then provide an overview of the research design. For the most part, specific details regarding the various elements of the research will be provided in subsequent chapters. The sampling of jobs

(MOS) to include the research, however, is described more fully because this process is not presented elsewhere in this book. The chapter concludes with a description of the way in which the project was organized. This section is included to give the reader a picture of the required infrastructure to successfully manage a project of this magnitude and complexity.

SPECIFIC RESEARCH OBJECTIVES

The specific objectives of the research program incorporated the elements of a comprehensive and very broad criterion-related validation study. Moreover, the objectives span a continuum from operational/applied concerns to more theoretical interests. The major objectives may be summarized as follows:

Predictor Measurement

- Identify the constructs that constitute the universe of information available for selection/classification into entry-level skilled jobs given no prior job experience on the part of the applicant.

Criterion Measurement

- Develop measures of entry-level job performance that can be used as criteria against which to validate selection/classification measures.
- Develop a general model of performance for entry-level skilled jobs.
- Develop a complete array of valid and reliable measures of second-tour performance as an Army NCO, including its leadership/supervision aspects.
- Develop a model of NCO performance that identifies the major components of second-tour job performance.

Validation

- Validate existing selection measures (i.e., ASVAB) against training and job performance criterion measures.
- Based on the "best bet" constructs for enhancing selection and classification in this population of jobs, develop and validate a battery of new selection and classification measures.
- Carry out a complete incremental predictive validation of (a) the ASVAB and an experimental battery of predictors, (b) measures of

training success, and (c) the full array of first-tour performance criteria using the second-tour job performance measures as criteria.

- Estimate the degree of differential prediction across (a) major domains of predictor information (e.g., abilities, personality, interests), (b) major factors of job performance, and (c) different types of jobs.
- Determine the extent of differential prediction across racial and gender groups for a systematic sample of individual differences, performance factors, and jobs.
- Develop the analytic framework needed to evaluate the optimal prediction equations for predicting (a) training performance, (b) first-tour performance, (c) first-tour attrition and the reenlistment decision, and (d) second-tour performance, under conditions in which testing time is limited to a specified amount and when there must be a tradeoff among alternative selection/ classification goals (e.g., maximizing aggregate performance vs. minimizing discipline and low-motivation problems vs. minimizing attrition).

Other Research Objectives

- Develop a utility scale for different performance levels across jobs.
- Design and develop a fully functional and user-friendly research database that includes all relevant personnel data on the three cohorts of new Army accessions included in the research program.

OVERALL RESEARCH DESIGN

The first 6 months of the project were spent in planning, documenting, reviewing, modifying, and redrafting research plans, requests for participants/subjects, administrative support requests, and budgetary plans, as well as beginning the comprehensive literature reviews and job analyses. The final detailed version of the operative research plan was published as ARI Research Report No. 1332, *Improving the Selection, Classification, and Utilization of Army Enlisted Personnel: Project A Research Plan.*

Selection of the Sample of MOS (Jobs)

A goal of the project was to deal with the entire Army entry level selection and classification system at once, which at the time included approximately 275 different jobs. Obviously, data could not be collected from all of them so jobs (MOS) had to be sampled representatively. This meant there would be a trade-off in the allocation of research resources between the number of jobs researched and the number of incumbents sampled from each job: the more jobs that were included, the fewer the incumbents per MOS that could be assessed, and vice versa. Cost considerations dictated that 18 to 20 MOS could be studied if the initial goal was 500 job incumbents per job. This assumed that a full array of job-specific performance measures would be developed for only a subset of those MOS.

The sampling plan itself incorporated two principal considerations. First, a sample of MOS was selected from the total population of entry level MOS. Next, the required sample sizes of enlisted personnel within each MOS were specified. Because Project A was developing a system for a population of MOS, the MOS were the primary sampling units.

The selection of the sample of MOS proceeded through a series of stages. An initial sample was drawn on the basis of the following considerations:

1. High-density jobs that would provide sufficient sample sizes for statistically reliable estimates of new predictor validity and differential validity across racial and gender groups.
2. Representation of the Army's designated Career Management Fields (CMF), which are clusters of related jobs.
3. Representation of the jobs most crucial to the Army's mission.

The composition of the sample was examined from the perspective of mission criticality by comparing it with a list of 42 MOS identified by the Army as having high priority for mobilization training. The initial set of 19 MOS represented 19 of the Army's 30 Career Management Fields. Of the 11 CMF not represented, two were classified and nine had very small numbers of incumbents. The initial set of 19 MOS included only 5% of Army jobs, but represented 44% of the soldiers recruited in FY81. Similarly, of the total number of women in the Army, 44% were represented in the sample.

A cluster analysis of MOS similarity was carried out to evaluate and refine the sample. To obtain data for empirically clustering MOS, brief job descriptions were generated for about 40% of the MOS. This sample of 111 MOS included the 84 largest (300 or more new job incumbents yearly) plus an additional 27 selected randomly but proportionately by CMF. Each job description was limited to two sides of a 5 × 7 index card.

Members of the contractor research staff and Army officers ($N = 25$), serving as expert judges, sorted the sample of 111 job descriptions into homogeneous categories based on perceived similarities and differences in the described job activities. The similarity data were clustered and used to check the representativeness of the initial sample of 19 MOS. (That is, did the 19 MOS include representatives from all the major clusters of MOS derived from the similarity scaling?) On the basis of these results and additional guidance received from the project's Army Advisory Group (described later in this chapter), two MOS that had been selected initially were replaced. During the course of the project, several MOS subsequently changed names or identifiers and a few were added or deleted because requirements changed.

Table 3.1 shows the MOS ($N = 21$) that were studied over the course of the Project A/Career Force research program. "Batch A" MOS received the most attention in that soldiers in these jobs were administered a full array of first- and second-tour job performance measures, including hands-on work sample tests, written job knowledge tests, and Army-wide and

TABLE 3.1

Project A/Career Force Military Occupational Specialties (MOS)

Batch A		Batch Z	
MOS		*MOS*	
11B	Infantryman	12B	Combat engineer
13B	Cannon crewmember	16S	MANPADS Crewman
19E	M60 Armor crewman	27E	Tow/dragon repairer
19K	M1 Armor crewman[a]	29E	Comm-electronics radio repairer[b]
31C	Single channel radio operator	51B	Carpentry/masonry specialist
63B	Light-wheel vehicle mechanic	54B	NBC specialist[c]
71L	Administrative specialist	55B	Ammunition specialist
88M	Motor transport operator[d]	67N	Utility helicopter repairer
91A/B	Medical specialist/medical NCO[e]	76Y	Unit supply specialist
95B	Military police	94B	Food service specialist
		96B	Intelligence analyst[b]

[a]Except for the type of tank used, this MOS is equivalent to the 19E MOS originally selected for Project A testing.

[b]This MOS was added after the Concurrent Validation (CVI).

[c]This MOS was formerly designated as 54E.

[d]This MOS was formerly designated as 64C.

[e]Although 91A was the MOS originally selected for Project A testing, second-tour medical specialists are usually reclassified as 91B.

MOS-specific ratings. Soldiers in "Batch Z" MOS were not measured as extensively with regard to the job performance criterion measures.

Data Collection Design

The research plan incorporated three criterion-related research components: (a) validation using archival predictor and criterion data, (b) concurrent validation using experimental predictors and criteria, and (c) longitudinal validation using experimental predictors and criteria. The basic framework and major samples are depicted in Fig. 3.1.

Analyses of the available archival file data for soldiers who entered the Army in FY81/82 are represented in the leftmost box in Fig. 3.1. These analyses validated ASVAB scores against measures routinely administered to first-tour soldiers at that time. Results of these analyses were used to make modifications to the ASVAB aptitude area composite scores used by the Army to determine whether applicants are qualified for particular MOS.

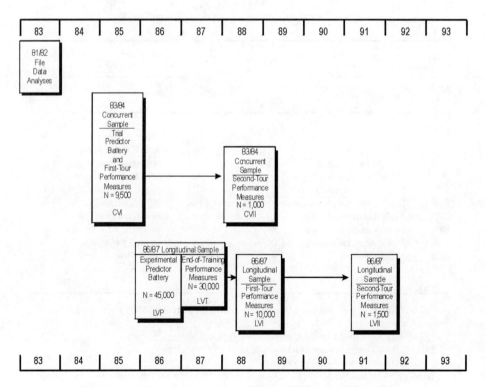

FIG. 3.1.   Project A/Career Force research flow and samples.

This early phase of the research program is not discussed in detail in this book, but details are provided in Eaton, Goer, Harris, and Zook (1984).

The primary focus of the research design encompassed two major cohorts, each of which was followed into their second tour of duty and which collectively produced six major research samples. The Concurrent Validation (CV) cohort, which entered the Army in FY83/84, was administered a battery of predictor measures and an array of training and first-tour performance measures concurrently in 1985/86 (CVI sample). In 1988 and early 1989, after they had reenlisted, many of these same soldiers were administered measures of second-tour performance (CVII sample). The Longitudinal Validation (LV) cohort of soldiers, who entered the Army in FY86/87, were followed through training and through their first two enlistment terms. The experimental predictors were administered during their first two days in the Army (LVP sample) and project-developed measures of training performance were administered at the completion of the job-specific technical training program (LVT sample). They were then followed into the field and administered first-tour performance measures in 1988–1989 (LVI sample) and second-tour performance measures in 1991–92 (LVII sample), if they had reenlisted.

Preliminary Data Collections

Development of the predictor and criterion measures administered during the major phases of this research involved dozens of smaller data collection efforts. For example, a "preliminary battery" of predominantly off-the-shelf predictor tests was administered to approximately 2,200 soldiers in four MOS. These data helped in the effort to construct a more tailored set of predictors. Development of the criterion measures involved a relatively large number of job analysis-related data collection activities (e.g., critical incident workshops, SME panels to review and rate job tasks).

The development of both predictor and criterion measures involved several pilot tests (generally involving fewer than 100 soldiers for the predictors and fewer than a dozen soldiers for the criteria) and field tests. There was a single predictor measure field test, which incorporated the full "Pilot Trial Battery" ($N = 303$). The first-tour performance measures were field tested several MOS at a time, for a total of six field tests ($N = 90$ to 596). Refinements following field testing produced the measures that were used in CVI.

In addition to supporting the development and refinement of the research instruments, the preliminary data collections (i.e., those occurring before

CVI) offered project staff considerable experience that proved invaluable for ensuring the success of the much more critical, larger-scale data collections described next.

Major Data Collections

As discussed previously, the major validation samples were drawn from two cohorts of soldiers, those who entered the Army in 1983–1984 and those who entered in 1986–1987. Each data collection involved on-site administration by a trained data collection team. The amount of pre-coordination required for these data collections was considerable. Each Army site supporting a data collection had to supply examinees, classrooms, and office space. For the predictor data collections (CVI and LVP), provision had to be made for the computers used to administer some of the experimental tests. The data collections involving administration of job performance measures required provision and scheduling of first- and second-line supervisors of tested soldiers to provide ratings, and terrain and equipment to support hands-on testing (e.g., tanks, trucks, rifles, medical supplies).

Each of the six major data collections is briefly characterized below in terms of the sample, timing, location, and duration (per soldier) of the data collection.

Concurrent validation (CVI) sample. The sample was drawn from soldiers who had entered the Army between July 1983 and June 1984, thus they had been in the Army for 18 to 24 months. Data were collected from these soldiers and their supervisors at 13 posts in the continental United States and at multiple locations in Germany. Batch A soldiers (see Table 3.1) were assessed for 1½ day on end-of-training and first-tour job performance measures and for ½ day on the new predictor measures (the Trial Battery). Batch Z soldiers were tested for ½ day on a subset of the performance measures and ½ day on the Trial Battery.

Longitudinal validation predictor (LVP) sample. Virtually all new recruits who entered the Army into one of the sampled MOS from August 1986 through November 1987 were tested. They were assessed on the 4-hour Experimental Battery (a revised version of the Trial Battery) within 2 days of first arriving at their assigned reception battalion where they did basic, and in some cases advanced, training. Data were collected over a 14-month period at eight reception battalions by permanent (for the duration of testing), on-site data collection teams.

Longitudinal validation end-of-training (LVT) sample. End-of-training performance measures were administered to those individuals in the LV sample who completed advanced individual training (AIT), which could take from 2 months to 6 months, depending on the MOS. The training performance measures required about ½ day to administer. Data collection took place during the last 3 days of AIT at 14 different sites.

Longitudinal validation first-tour (LVI) sample. The individuals in the 86/87 cohort who were measured with the Experimental Battery, completed training, and remained in the Army were assessed with the first-tour job performance measures when they had roughly between 18 and 24 months of service. Data collections were conducted at 13 posts in the United States and multiple locations in Europe (primarily in Germany). The administration of the criterion measures required 1 day for Batch A soldiers and ½ day for Batch Z soldiers.

Concurrent validation second-tour (CVII) sample. The same teams that administered the first-tour performance measures to the LVI sample administered second-tour performance measures at the same location and during the same time periods to a sample of junior NCOs from the 83/84 cohort in their second tour of duty (4 to 5 years of service). Every attempt was made to include second-tour personnel from the Batch A MOS who had been part of CVI. The CVII data collection required 1 day per soldier.

Longitudinal validation second-tour (LVII) sample. This samle includes members of the 86/87 cohort from the Batch A MOS who were part of the LVP (predictors), LVT (training performance measures), and LVI (first-tour job performance measures) samples and who reenlisted for a second tour. The revised second-tour performance measures were administered at 15 U.S. posts, multiple locations in Germany, and two locations in Korea. The LVII performance assessment required 1 day per examinee.

RESEARCH INSTRUMENT DEVELOPMENT

Predictor Development

A major research objective was to develop an experimental battery of new tests that had maximum potential for enhancing selection and classification decisions for the entire enlisted personnel system. So rather than the traditional approach of basing the selection of predictor constructs on a job analysis, the general strategy was to identify a universe of potential predictor constructs appropriate for the population of enlisted MOS and sample appropriately from it. The next steps were to construct tests for each construct sampled, and refine and improve the measures through a series of pilot and field tests. The intent was to develop a predictor battery that was maximally useful for selection and classification into an entire population of jobs, and that provided maximal incremental information beyond that provided by the ASVAB.

Predictor development began with an in-depth search of the personnel selection literature. Literature review teams were created for cognitive abilities, perceptual and psychomotor abilities, and noncognitive characteristics such as personality, interests, and biographical history. After several iterations of consolidation and review, the research team identified a list of 53 potentially useful predictor variables. A sample of 35 personnel selection experts was then asked to estimate the expected correlations between each predictor construct and an array of potential performance factors. The estimates were analyzed and compared to meta-analytic information from the empirical literature.

All the available information was then used to arrive at a final set of variables for which new measures would be constructed. As indicated previously, instrument construction efforts involved several waves of pilot tests and a major field test. Included in these efforts were the development of a computerized battery of perceptual/psychomotor tests, the creation of the software, the design and construction of a special response pedestal permitting a variety of responses (e.g., one-hand tracking, two-hand coordination), and the acquisition of portable computerized testing stations. Also developed were several paper-and-pencil cognitive tests and two inventories. One inventory assessed relevant vocational interests and the second focused on major dimensions of personality and biographical history.

Job Analyses

In contrast to the predictors, virtually all criterion development in Project A/Career Force was based on extensive job analyses, most of which focused on the Batch A MOS. Task descriptions, critical incident analysis, and interviews with SMEs were used extensively. Relevant job manuals and available Army Occupational Survey results were used to enumerate the complete population of major tasks ($n = 100-150$) for each MOS. The total array of tasks for each MOS was then grouped into clusters and rated for criticality and difficulty by panels of SMEs.

Additional panels of SMEs were used in a workshop format to generate approximately 700 to 800 critical incidents of effective and ineffective performance per MOS that were specific to each MOS, and approximately 1,100 critical incidents that could apply to any MOS. For both the MOS-specific and Army-wide critical incidents, a retranslation procedure was carried out to establish dimensions of performance.

Together, the task descriptions and critical incident analysis of MOS-specific and Army-wide performance were intended to produce a detailed content description of the major components of performance in each MOS. These are the job analyses results that were used to begin development of the performance criterion measures.

The job analysis goals for the second tour included the description of the major differences in technical task content between first and second tour and the description of the leadership/supervision component of the junior NCO position. The task analysis and critical incident steps used for first tour were also used for second tour. In addition, a special 46-item job analysis instrument, the Supervisory Description Questionnaire, was constructed and used to collect criticality judgments from SMEs. Consequently, the supervisory/leadership tasks judged to be critical for an MOS became part of the population of tasks for that MOS.

Performance Criteria

The goals of training performance and job performance measurement in Project A/Career Force were to define, or model, the total domain of performance in some reasonable way and then develop reliable and valid measures of each major factor. The general procedure for criterion development followed a basic cycle of a comprehensive literature review, extensive job analyses using several methods, initial instrument construction, pilot testing, instrument revision, field testing, and proponent (management) review. The specific measurement goals were to:

1. Develop standardized measures of training achievement for the purpose of determining the relationship between training performance and job performance.
2. Make a state-of-the-art attempt to develop job sample or "hands-on" measures of job task proficiency.
3. Develop written measures of job task proficiency to allow for a broad representation of job task proficiency.

4. Develop rating scale measures of performance factors that are common to all first-tour enlisted MOS (Army-wide measures), as well as for factors that are specific to each MOS.
5. Compare hands-on measurement to paper-and-pencil tests and rating measures of proficiency on the same tasks (i.e., a multitrait, multimethod approach).
6. Evaluate existing archival and administrative records as possible indicators of job performance.

The Initial Theory

Criterion development efforts were guided by a model that viewed performance as truly multidimensional. For the population of Army entry-level enlisted positions, two major types of job performance components were postulated. The first is composed of components that are specific to a particular job and that would reflect specific technical competence or specific job behaviors that are not required for other jobs. It was anticipated that there would be a relatively small number of distinguishable factors of technical performance that would be a function of different abilities or skills and would be reflected by different task content.

The second type includes components that are defined and measured in the same way for every job. These are referred to as Army-wide performance components and incorporate the basic notion that total performance is much more than task or technical proficiency. It might include such things as contributions to teamwork, continual self-development, support for the norms and customs of the organization, and perseverance in the face of adversity. Components of performance now known as "contextual performance" were included in this category.

In summary, the working model of total performance, with which Project A began, viewed performance as multidimensional within these two broad categories of factors or constructs. The job analysis and criterion construction methods were designed to explicate the content of these factors via an exhaustive description of the total performance domain, several iterations of data collection, and the use of multiple methods for identifying basic performance factors.

Training Performance Measures

Because a major program objective was to determine the relationships between training performance and job performance and their differential predictability, if any, a comprehensive training achievement test was constructed for each MOS. The content of the program of instruction was matched with the content of the population of job tasks, and items were written to represent each segment of the match. After pilot testing, revision, field testing, and Army proponent review, the result was a 150 to 200 item "school knowledge" test for each MOS included in the research. Rating scales were also developed for completion by peers and drill instructors.

First-Tour (Entry Level) Measures

Job performance criterion development proceeded from the two basic types of job analysis information. The task-based information was used to develop standardized hands-on job samples, paper-and-pencil job knowledge tests, and rating scales for each Batch A MOS. These measures were intended to assess knowledge and proficiency on critical tasks associated with each MOS. Roughly 30 tasks per MOS were covered by the written job knowledge tests and rating scales, and about one-half of those tasks were also tested using a hands-on format. Each measure went through multiple rounds of pilot testing and revision before being used for validation purposes.

The second major procedure used to describe job content was the critical incident method. Specifically, a modified behaviorally anchored rating scale procedure was used to construct rating scales for performance factors specific to a particular job and performance factors that were defined in the same way and relevant for all jobs. The critical incident procedure was also used with workshops of combat veterans to develop rating scales of expected combat effectiveness. Ratings were gathered from both peers and supervisors of first-tour soldiers and from supervisors only for second-tour soldiers. Rating scale development activities included the development of procedures for identifying qualified raters and a comprehensive training program.

The final category of job performance criterion measure was produced by a search of the Army's archival records for potential performance indicators. First, all possibilities were enumerated from the major sources of such records maintained by the Army. Considerable exploration of these sources identified the most promising indexes, which were then investigated further to determine their usefulness as criterion measures.

Second-Tour Measures

For performance assessment of second-tour positions, which is when individuals begin to take on supervisory/leadership responsibilities, the measurement methods used for first-tour were retained. The tasks selected for measurement overlapped with the first-tour tests, but new higher skill-level tasks were added. The administrative indices used for first-tour soldiers were slightly modified for use in the second tour. On the basis of second-tour critical incident analyses, the Army-wide and MOS-specific behavior-based scales were revised to reflect higher-level technical requirements and to add dimensions having to do with leadership and supervision. Further, based on job analysis survey data, supplemental scales pertaining to supervision and leadership responsibilities were added.

The increased importance of supervision responsibilities for enlisted personnel in the second tour of duty led to the inclusion of two measurement methods that had not been used for first-tour performance measurement. A paper-and-pencil Situational Judgment Test (SJT) was developed by describing prototypical judgment situations and by asking the respondent to select the most appropriate and the least appropriate courses of action. Three Supervisory Role-Play Exercises were developed to assess NCO performance in job areas that were judged to be best assessed through the use of interactive exercises. The simulations were designed to evaluate performance in counseling and training subordinates. A trained evaluator (role player) played the part of a subordinate to be counseled or trained and the examinee assumed the role of a first-line supervisor who was to conduct the counseling or training. Evaluators also scored the examinee's performance, using a standard set of rating scales. There were three simulations of 15 to 20 minutes each.

DATA ANALYSIS

Model Development: Analyses of the Latent Structure of Predictors and Criteria

Both predictor measurement and performance measurement produced a large number of individual scores for each individual. There were far too many to deal with, either as predictors in a battery to be evaluated or as criterion measures to be predicted. Consequently, considerable analysis effort was directed at reducing the total number of initial scores to a more manageable number. For the predictor side, this was accomplished primarily via factor analysis and expert judgments concerning optimal composite scores. The end result was a set of 28 basic predictor scores for the new Experimental Battery and 4 factor scores for the ASVAB.

The score reduction demands were much more severe for the performance criterion side. There were three distinct performance domains—training performance, first-tour job performance, and second-tour job performance. The content of several of the criterion measures differed across jobs, and there were many more individual scores for each person than there were on the predictor side.

The performance modeling procedure began with an analysis of the relationships among the 150+ first-tour performance criterion scores. Depending on the instrument, either expert judgment or exploratory factor analysis/cluster analysis was used to identify "basic" composite scores that reduced the number of specific individual scores but did not throw any information away. These analyses were carried out within MOS and resulted in 24 to 28 basic criterion scores for each job, which was still too many for validation purposes.

The next step was to use all available expert judgment to postulate a set of alternative factor models of the latent structure underlying the covariances among the basic scores. These alternative models were then subjected to a confirmatory analysis using LISREL. The first confirmatory test used the covariance matrix estimated on the CVI sample. The latent structure model that best fit the concurrent sample data was evaluated again using the LVI sample data. This was a true confirmatory test. The best fitting model in the concurrent sample was also pitted against a new set of alternatives at the time of the analysis of the longitudinal sample data. A similar procedure was followed to test the fit of alternative factor models to the basic criterion score covariance estimated from both the concurrent and longitudinal second tour samples (CVII and LVII).

Because there were far fewer criterion measures, a similar confirmatory procedure was not used to model training performance. Instead, expert judgment was used to group the training performance criteria into composites that paralleled the latent factors in the first-tour and second-tour performance models. The expert judgment based factors were then checked against the criterion intercorrelation matrix estimated from the training validation (LVT) sample.

In summary, the modeling analyses produced a specification of the factor scores (i.e., latent variables) that defined the latent structure of performance at each of three organizational levels, or career stages: end of training performance, first-tour job performance, and second-tour job performance. It is the performance factor scores at each of these three points that constitute the criterion scores for all subsequent validation analyses.

Validation Analyses

As stipulated by the original objectives, the next major step was to assess the validities of the ASVAB and the experimental predictor tests for predicting performance during training, during the first tour, and during the second tour after reenlistment. Four types of validation analyses were carried out. First, "basic validation" analyses were used to describe the correlations of each predictor domain (e.g., ASVAB, spatial, personality, interests) with each performance criterion factor. Second, incremental validity was examined by comparing the multiple correlations of the four ASVAB factors with a particular criterion with the multiple correlation for ASVAB plus each of the experimental predictor domains in turn. Third, three kinds of "optimal" prediction equations were compared in terms of the maximum level of predictive validity that could be achieved in the longitudinal prediction of first tour performance (LVI). Finally, for the prediction of performance in the second tour (LVII), the validity of alternative prediction equations using different combinations of test data and previous performance data were compared.

Scaling the Utility of Individual Performance

If it is true that personnel assignments will differ in value depending on the specific MOS to which an assignment is made and on the level at which an individual will perform in that MOS, then the payoff of a classification strategy that has a validity significantly greater than zero will increase to the extent that the differential values (utilities) of each assignment can be estimated and made a part of the assignment system. Therefore, there was a concerted effort to evaluate the relationship of performance to performance utility using a ratio estimation procedure to assign utility values to MOS by performance level combinations.

Estimation of Classification Gain

The last major step in the selection/classification analysis was to develop a procedure for estimating potential classification gain under varying conditions (e.g., variation in quotas, selection ratio, number of possible job assignments). A number of alternative methods were formulated, and evaluated using the data from the longitudinal first tour samples (LVI). One principal comparison was between the Brogden (1959) estimate of gains in mean predicted performance and a newly developed statistic referred to as gain in Estimated Mean Actual Performance.

PROJECT ORGANIZATION AND MANAGEMENT STRUCTURE

Management Structure

A strong need existed for a relatively substantial management structure for this research program. The magnitude and breadth of the work requirements meant that a dozen or more investigators might be working on a given task at any one time. An even greater build-up of personnel was required to support each of the major large-scale data collections included in the research plan. Multiply that by four or five major tasks and add the geographic dispersion of the researchers (across the U.S.) and data collection locations (worldwide), and the need for coordination and management control becomes clear.

Project A personnel were organized into five substantive task teams and one management team. It was also true that the project's organization had matrix-like properties in that one individual could participate in more than one team, as the occasion warranted. The task teams can be briefly characterized as follows:

Task 1. Database Management and Validation Analyses
Task 2. Development of New Predictors of Job Performance
Task 3. Measurement of Training Performance
Task 4. Measurement of Army-Wide Performance
Task 5. Measurement of MOS-Specific Performance
Task 6. Project Management

Activities related to general coordination and management requirements were subsumed under Task 6. The size and scope of the project were such that these requirements were not trivial in nature and needed to be recognized explicitly.

The management structure for Project A is illustrated in Fig. 3.2. Contractor efforts were directed and managed jointly by a Project Director and a Principal Scientist. These individuals reported directly to an ARI scientist who served as both Contracting Officer's Representative and ARI Principal Scientist. The work in each major project task area was directed

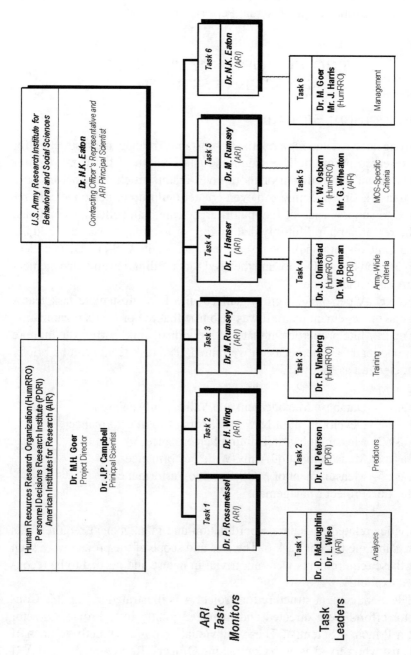

FIG. 3.2. Initial Project A organization.

48

by a Task Leader (depicted in the lower row of boxes in Fig. 3.2) and ARI appointed Task Monitors (depicted in the upper row) to assist in overseeing and supporting contractor activities. Contractor consortium and ARI investigators carried out research activities both independently and jointly.

We include Fig. 3.2 only to show the matching of contractor and ARI staff and to illustrate the form of the project management and contract review structure. There were of course a number of personnel changes over the life of the project. The work in the Career Force phase of the research program was organized in a similar fashion.

Oversight, Evaluation, and Feedback

A project of this scale had to maintain coordination with the other military departments and DoD, as well as remain consistent with other ongoing research programs being conducted by the other Services. The project also needed a mechanism for ensuring that the research program met high standards for scientific quality. Finally, a method was needed to receive feedback from the Army's management on priorities and objectives, as well as to identify problems. The mechanism for meeting these needs was advisory groups.

Figure 3.3 shows the structure and membership of the overall Governance Advisory Group, which was made up of the Scientific Advisory

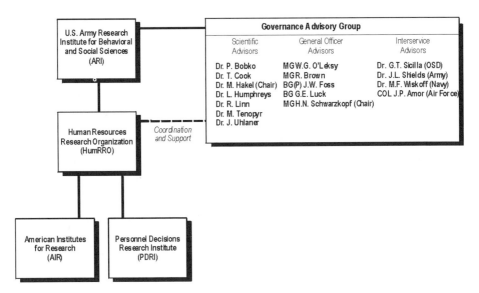

FIG. 3.3. Project A/Career Force Governance Advisory Group.

Group, Inter-Service Advisory Group, and the Army Advisory Group components.

The Scientific Advisory Group comprised recognized authorities in psychometrics, experimental design, sampling theory, utility analysis, applied research in selection and classification, and the conduct of psychological research in the Army environment. All members of the Scientific Advisory Group remained with the research effort from its beginning in 1982 to the end in 1994.

The Inter-Service Group comprised the Laboratory Directors for applied psychological research in the Army, Air Force, and Navy, and the Director of Accession Policy from the Office of Assistant Secretary of Defense for Manpower and Reserve Affairs. The Army Advisory Group included representatives from the Office of Deputy Chief of Staff for Personnel, Office of Deputy Chief of Staff for Operations, Training and Doctrine Command, Forces Command, and U.S. Army Europe.

ON TO THE REST OF THE STORY

Chapters 1 and 2 presented the context within which these projects were carried out and described the events and conditions that led to their being designed, funded, and started. Chapter 3 outlined the research goals and basic research design, and described the way the researchers' activities were organized and managed. The remaining chapters describe individual parts of the overall research program in more detail. Not every substantive activity of the research consortium is included. This chapter selection represents our collective judgment as to what would be most beneficial to have between two covers for a general audience of people interested in personnel research.

Chapter 3 is also intended to be a basic roadmap to help readers regain the big picture should they get so immersed in any given topic that the overall design departs from working memory. It was a critical management task for the project to make sure that everyone working on it had fully mastered this basic roadmap and could retrieve it whenever needed.

II

Specification and Measurement of Individual Differences for Predicting Performance

4

The Search for New Measures: Sampling From a Population of Selection/Classification Predictor Variables

Norman G. Peterson and Hilda Wing

Predictor variable selection and subsequent test development for a new predictor battery were a major part of Project A. This chapter presents an overview of the procedures used to determine what types of measures would be developed. The actual development of the measures is described in Chapter 5 for the cognitive, perceptual, and psychomotor tests and in Chapter 6 for the personality/temperament, vocational interest, and work outcome preference inventories.

At the start of Project A, as now, the ASVAB was the operational selection and classification battery used by all Services. The ASVAB previously had been validated against grades in entry level training courses but it had never been systematically validated against on-the-job performance. Given this context, the overall goal of predictor development in Project A was to construct an experimental test battery that would, when combined with ASVAB and bounded by reasonable time constraints, yield the maximum increment in selection and classification validity for predicting performance for Army entry-level jobs, both present and future. The research plan was also intended to provide for the evaluation and revision of the new predictor battery at several critical points over the life of the project. However, it was not part of the project's initial mission to recommend changes to the ASVAB subtests.

There was one additional pragmatic consideration. The Armed Services had been developing computer-adaptive testing technology prior to the beginning of Project A (cf., Sands, Waters, & McBride, 1997). It was widely anticipated that computerized testing technology would be routinely available for testing Armed Forces applicants well before the end of Project A. Therefore, to the extent that theoretical and empirical justification for this methodology could be found, the use of computer-administered testing technology was greatly encouraged.

OVERVIEW OF RESEARCH STRATEGY

The above considerations led to the adoption of a construct sampling strategy of predictor development. This is in contrast to the more common approach of basing predictor selection primarily on job analysis findings. An initial model of the predictor space, or potential population of relevant predictor variables, was developed by (a) identifying the major domains of individual differences that were relevant, (b) identifying variables within each domain that met a number of measurement and feasibility criteria, and (c) further selecting those constructs that appeared to be the "best bets" for incrementing validity (over current selection and classification procedures).

Ideally, this strategy would lead to the selection of a finite set of relatively independent predictor constructs that were also relatively independent of current predictor variables and maximally related to the criteria of interest. If these conditions were met, then the resulting set of measures should predict all or most of the criteria, yet possess enough heterogeneity to yield efficient classification of persons into different jobs. Obviously, previous research strongly suggested that such an ideal state could not be achieved. However, the goal was to move as far in that direction as possible.

If the latent structure of the relevant predictor variables and the latent structure of the relevant criterion domains (e.g., training performance, job performance, and turnover) could be modeled and confirmed with data, then the basic network of relationships between the two could be systematically investigated and modeled. Such a model would make it possible to predict whether the addition of a particular variable would be likely to improve selection or classification validity for a particular purpose.

Research Objectives

This general strategy led to the delineation of six specific research objectives for predictor development.

1. Define the population of measures of human abilities, attributes, or characteristics which are most likely to be effective in predicting future soldier performance and for classifying persons into MOS in which they will be most successful, with special emphasis on attributes not tapped by current measures.
2. Design and develop new measures or modify existing measures of these "best bet" predictor variables.
3. Develop materials and procedures for efficiently administering experimental predictor measures in the field.
4. Estimate and evaluate the reliability of the new selection/classification measures and their vulnerability to motivational set differences, faking, variances in administrative settings, and practice effects.
5. Determine the degree to which the validity of new selection and classification measures generalizes across jobs (MOS); and, conversely, the degree to which the measures are useful for classification, or the differential prediction of performance across jobs.
6. Determine the extent to which new selection/classification measures increase the accuracy of prediction over and above the levels of accuracy of current measures.

To achieve these objectives, the design depicted in Fig. 4.1 was followed. Several things are noteworthy about the research design. First, a large-scale literature review and a quantified coding procedure were conducted early in the project to take maximum advantage of accumulated research knowledge. A large-scale expert judgment study, which relied heavily on the information gained from the literature review, was then used to develop an initial model of both the predictor space and the criterion space. The Project A Scientific Advisory Group and researchers used this information, as well as results from the Preliminary Battery (described below), to determine what predictor constructs would be measured with project-developed instruments.

Second, Fig. 4.1 depicts several test batteries in ovals: Preliminary Battery, Demo Computer Battery, Pilot Trial Battery, Trial Battery, and Experimental Battery. These appear successively in time and allowed the modification and improvement of the new predictors as data were gathered and analyzed on each successive battery or set of measures.

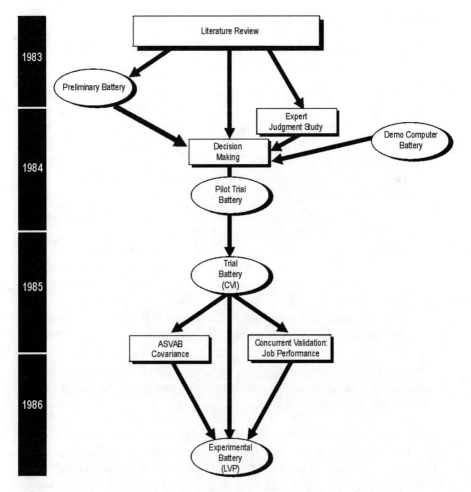

FIG. 4.1.   Flow chart of predictor measure development.

Third, the research plan included both concurrent (for the Trial Battery) and predictive (for the Experimental Battery) validation. Using both types of designs provided the opportunity to compare empirical results from concurrent and predictive validation on the same populations of jobs and applicants, using predictor and criterion measures that were identical or highly similar. Hypotheses generated by the concurrent analysis could be confirmed using the longitudinal analysis.

To implement this predictor identification and development plan, the research staff was organized into three "domain teams." One team concerned itself with temperament, biographical, and vocational interest variables and came to be called the "noncognitive" team. Another team concerned itself with cognitive and perceptual variables and was called the "cognitive" team. The third team concerned itself with psychomotor and perceptual variables and was labeled the "psychomotor" or sometimes the "computerized" team, because all the measures developed by that team were computer-administered.

To summarize, the development of new predictor measures used a comprehensive approach that tried to (a) define the population of potentially useful variables; (b) describe the latent structure of this population; (c) sample constructs from the population that had the highest probability of meeting the goals of the project; (d) develop operational measures of these variables; (e) pilot test, field test, and revise the new measures; (f) analyze their empirical covariance structure; (g) determine their predictive validities; and (h) specify the optimal decision rules for using the new tests to maximize predicted performance and/or minimize attrition.

The remainder of this chapter describes the major steps in predictor development up to the point where actual test construction for the designated variables was set to begin. Specifically, these steps were:

- Literature Search and Review
- Expert Forecasts of Predictor Construct Validity
- Evaluation of a Preliminary Battery of Off-the-Shelf Measures
- Evaluation of a Demonstration Computer Battery
- Final Identification of Variables Designated for Measurement

This chapter focuses on the overall procedure. Specifics regarding the literature review findings are presented in Chapters 5 and 6. Evaluation of the Demonstration Computer Battery is also described in more detail in Chapter 5.

LITERATURE SEARCH AND REVIEW

The principal purpose of the literature review was to obtain the maximum benefit from earlier selection/classification research that was in any way relevant for the jobs in the Project A job population. The search was conducted over a 6-month period by the three teams mentioned previously.

Method

Several computerized searches of all relevant databases resulted in identification of more than 10,000 sources. In addition, reference lists were solicited from recognized experts, annotated bibliographies were obtained from military research laboratories, and the last several years' editions of relevant research journals were examined, as were more general sources such as textbooks, handbooks, and relevant chapters in the *Annual Review of Psychology*.

The references identified as relevant were reviewed and summarized using two standardized report protocols: an article review form and a predictor review form (several of the latter could be completed for each source). These forms were designed to capture, in a standard format, the essential information from the various sources, which varied considerably in their organization and reporting styles. Each predictor was tentatively classified into an initial working taxonomy of predictor constructs (based on the taxonomy described in Peterson & Bownas, 1982).

Results

Three technical reports were written, one for each of three areas: cognitive abilities (Toquam, Corpe, & Dunnette, 1991); psychomotor/perceptual abilities (McHenry & Rose, 1988); and noncognitive predictors including temperament or personality, vocational interest, and biographical data variables (Barge & Hough, 1988). These documents summarized the literature with regard to critical issues, suggested the most appropriate organization or taxonomy of the constructs in each area, and summarized the validity estimates of the various measures for different types of job performance criteria. Findings from these reports are summarized in Chapters 5 and 6.

Based on the literature review, an initial list of all predictor *measures* of the constructs that seemed appropriate for Army selection and classification was compiled. This list was further screened by eliminating measures according to several "knockout" factors: (a) measures developed for a single research project only, (b) measures designed for a narrowly specified population or occupational group (e.g., pharmacy students), (c) measures targeted toward younger age groups, (d) measures requiring unusually long testing times, (e) measures requiring difficult or subjective scoring, and (f) measures requiring individual administration.

Application of the knockout factors resulted in a second list of candidate measures. Each of these measures was independently evaluated on the 12 factors shown in Table 4.1 by at least two researchers. A 5-point rating scale was applied to each of the 12 factors. Discrepancies in ratings were resolved by discussion. It should be noted that there was not always sufficient information for a measure to allow an evaluation on all factors. This second list of measures, each with a set of evaluations, was input to (a) the

TABLE 4.1

Factors Used to Evaluate Predictor Measures

1. Discriminability—extent to which the measure has sufficient score range and variance, (i.e., does not suffer from ceiling and floor effects with respect to the applicant population).
2. Reliability—degree of reliability as measured by traditional psychometric methods such as test-retest, internal consistency, or parallel forms reliability.
3. Group Score Differences (Differential Impact)—extent to which there are mean and variance differences in scores across groups defined by age, sex, race, or ethnic groups.
4. Consistency/Robustness of Administration and Scoring—extent to which administration and scoring is standardized, ease of administration and scoring, consistency of administration and scoring across administrators and locations.
5. Generality—extent to which predictor measures a fairly general or broad ability or construct.
6. Criterion-Related Validity—the level of correlation of the predictor with measures of job performance, training performance, and turnover.
7. Construct Validity—the amount of evidence existing to support the predictor as a measure of a distinct construct (correlational studies, experimental studies, etc.).
8. Face Validity/Applicant Acceptance—extent to which the appearance and administration methods of the predictor enhance or detract from its plausibility or acceptability to laypersons as an appropriate test for the Army.
9. Differential Validity—existence of significantly different criterion-related validity coefficients between groups of legal or societal concern (race, sex, age).
10. Test Fairness—degree to which slopes, intercepts, and standard errors of estimate differ across groups of legal or societal concern (race, sex, age) when predictor scores are regressed on important criteria (job performance, turnover, training).
11. Usefulness for Classification—extent to which the measure or predictor is likely to be useful in classifying persons into different specialties.
12. Overall Usefulness for Predicting Army Criteria—extent to which predictor is likely to contribute to the overall or individual prediction of criteria important to the Army (e.g., AWOL, drug use, attrition, job performance, training).

final selection of measures for the Preliminary Battery and (b) the final selection of constructs to be included in the expert judgment evaluation.

EXPERT FORECASTS OF PREDICTOR CONSTRUCT VALIDITY

Schmidt, Hunter, Croll, and McKenzie (1983) have shown that pooled expert judgments, obtained from experienced personnel psychologists, have considerable accuracy for estimating the validity that tests will exhibit in empirical, criterion-related validity research. Peterson and Bownas (1982) described a procedure that had been used successfully by Bownas and Heckman (1976); Peterson, Houston, Bosshardt, and Dunnette, Peterson

(1977); and Houston (1980); and Peterson, Houston, and Rosse (1984) to identify predictors for the jobs of firefighter, correctional officer, and entry-level occupations (clerical and technical), respectively. In this method, descriptive information about a set of predictors and the job performance criterion variables is given to "experts" in personnel selection and classification. These experts estimate the relationships between predictor and criterion variables by rating the relative magnitude of the expected validity or by directly estimating the value of the correlation coefficients.

The result of the procedure is a matrix with predictor and criterion variables as the rows and columns, respectively. Cell entries are experts' estimates of the degree of relationship between specific predictor variables and specific criterion variables. The interrater reliability of the experts' estimates is checked first. If the estimate is sufficiently reliable (previous research shows values in the .80 to .90 range for about 10 to 12 experts), the matrix of predictor-criterion relationships can be analyzed and used in a variety of ways. For example, by correlating the mean cell values in pairs of rows of the matrix (rows correspond to predictors) the intercorrelations of the predictors can be estimated, and by correlating the values in any two columns correlations between criteria can be estimated. The two sets of estimated intercorrelations can then be clustered or factor analyzed to identify either clusters of predictors within which the measures are expected to exhibit similar patterns of correlations with criterion components or clusters of criteria that are all predicted by a similar set of predictors.

For Project A, the clusters of predictors and criteria were important products for a number of reasons. First, they provided an efficient and organized means of summarizing the data generated by the experts. Second, the summary form permitted easier comparison with the results of meta-analyses of empirical estimates of criterion-related validity coefficients. Third, these clusters provided an initial model, or theory, of the predictor-criterion performance space. Consequently, we conducted our own expert judgment study of potential predictor validities. The procedure and results are summarized below. Complete details are reported in Wing, Peterson, and Hoffman (1984).

Method

Judges.   The experts who served as judges were 35 psychologists with experience and knowledge in personnel selection research and/or applications. Each expert was an employee of, or consultant to, one of the four organizations conducting Project A.

Predictor variables. As described previously, the literature reviews were used to identify the most promising predictor constructs. Fifty-three constructs were identified and materials describing each were prepared for use by the judges. These descriptive materials included names, definitions, typical measurement methods, summaries of reliability and validity findings, and similar information for at least one specific measure of the construct.

Criterion variables. The procedure used to identify job task categories was based on the job descriptions of a sample of 111 MOS that had been previously placed into 23 clusters by job experts as part of the process of selecting the sample of MOS to include in Project A (see Chapter 3). Criterion categories were developed by reviewing the descriptions of jobs within these clusters to determine common job activities. The categories were written to include a set of actions that typically occur together (e.g., transcribe, annotate, file) and lead to some common objective (e.g., record and file information). Fifty-three categories of task content were identified. Most of these applied to several jobs, and most of the jobs were characterized by activities from several categories. An example of one of these criterion categories is as follows:

> Detect and identify targets: using primarily sight, with or without optical systems, locate potential targets, and identify type (e.g., tanks, troops, artillery) and threat (friend or foe); report information.

The second type of criterion variable was a set of variables that described performance in initial Army training. On-site inspection of archival records and interviews with trainers for eight diverse MOS guided the definition of these variables. It was not practical to include MOS-specific training criteria, because there are so many entry level MOS in the Army's occupational structure. Instead, four general training criteria were defined: training success/progress; effort/motivation in training; performance in "theoretical" or classroom parts of training; and performance in practical, "hands-on" parts of training.

The final set of criterion variables consisted of nine general performance behavior categories and six broad outcome variables (e.g., attrition and reenlistment) obtained from the theoretical and empirical research described by Borman, Motowidlo, Rose, and Hanser (1987). Examples of the behavioral dimensions are "Following Regulations," "Commitment to Army Norms," and "Emergent Leadership."

In all, 72 possible criterion variables were identified and used in the expert judgment task. The reader should note that these are not the criterion variables that were subsequently produced by the extensive job analyses and criterion measurement efforts described in Chapters 7 and 8. The array of 72 constituted the best initial set that the available information could produce.

Procedure. Using the materials describing the criterion and predictor variables, each judge estimated the *true* validity of each predictor for each criterion (i.e., criterion-related validity corrected for range restriction and criterion measurement error). All judges completed the task very early in the project's second year.

Results

When averaged across raters, the mean reliability of the estimated cell validities was .96. The estimated correlations between the predictor and criterion variables were represented by these cell means, and factor analyses were based on these correlations. The most pertinent analysis for this chapter concerns the interrelationships of the predictor variables.

Table 4.2 shows the interpretation of the results of the factor analysis of the intercorrelations of the estimated validity profiles of the 53 predictor constructs. Factor solutions of from 2 to 24 factors were examined and eight interpretable factors were named. These are shown in the right-most column of Table 4.2. Based on an examination of their patterns of factor loadings, these eight factors appeared to be composed of 21 clusters of related predictor constructs. The lowest level in the hypothesized hierarchical structure shows the original 53 predictor constructs. The first five factors are composed of abilities in the cognitive, perceptual, and psychomotor areas while the last three factors are made up of traits or predispositions from the personality, biodata, and vocational interests areas. The only exceptions are the loading of Realistic and Artistic interests with Mechanical Comprehension on the Mechanical factor and Investigative interests on the Cognitive Ability factor.

The depiction of the predictor space provided by these analyses served to organize decision-making concerning the identification of predictor constructs for which Project A would develop specific measures. It portrayed the latent structure of potential predictor constructs as judged by knowledgeable experts.

TABLE 4.2
A Hierarchical Map of Predictor Domains

Constructs	Clusters	Factors
Verbal comprehension Reading comprehension Ideational fluency Analogical reasoning Omnibus intelligence/aptitude Word fluency	Verbal ability/ general intelligence	
Word problems Inductive reasoning/concept formation Deductive logic	Reasoning	
Numerical computation Use of formula/number problems	Number ability	Cognitive abilities
Perceptual speed and accuracy	Perceptual speed and accuracy	
Investigative interests	Investigative interests	
Rote memory Follow directions	Memory	
Figural reasoning Verbal and figural closure	Closure	
Two-dimensional mental rotation Three-dimensional mental rotation Spatial visualization Field dependence (negative) Place memory (visual memory) Spatial scanning	Visualization/spatial	Visualization/ spatial
Processing efficiency Selective attention Time sharing	Mental information processing	Information processing
Mechanical comprehension	Mechanical comprehension	Mechanical
Realistic interests Artistic interests (negative)	Realistic vs. artistic interests	
Control precision Rate control Arm-hand steadiness Aiming	Steadiness/precision	
Multilimb coordination Speed of arm movement	Coordination	Psychomotor

(Continued)

TABLE 4.2
(Continued)

Constructs	Clusters	Factors
Manual dexterity Finger dexterity Wrist-finger speed	Dexterity	
Sociability Social interests	Sociability	Social skills
Enterprising interests	Enterprising interests	
Involvement in athletics and physical conditioning Energy level	Athletic abilities/energy	Vigor
	Dominance/self-esteem	
Dominance Self-esteem		
Traditional values Conscientiousness Nondelinquency Conventional interests	Traditional values/conventionality/ nondelinquency	Motivation/ stability
Locus of control Work orientation	Work orientation/locus of control	
Cooperativeness Emotional stability	Cooperation/emotional stability	

PRELIMINARY BATTERY

The Preliminary Battery was intended to be a set of well developed "off-the-shelf" measures of variables that overlapped very little with the Army's existing preenlistment predictors. It would allow an early determination of the extent to which such predictors contributed unique variance not measured by operational predictors (i.e., the ASVAB).

Selection of Preliminary Battery Measures

As described earlier, the literature review identified a large set of predictor measures, each with ratings by researchers on 12 psychometric and substantive evaluation factors (see Table 4.1). These ratings were used to select a smaller set of measures as serious candidates for inclusion in the Preliminary Battery. There were two major practical constraints: (a) no apparatus or individualized testing methods could be used because of the relatively short time available to prepare for battery administration, and (b) only 4 hours were available for testing.

The predictor development team made an initial selection of "off-the-shelf" measures. This tentative list of measures, along with associated information from the literature review and evaluation, was reviewed by the ARI research staff, senior Project A staff members, and by several consultants external to Project A who had been retained for their expertise in various predictor domains. After incorporating the recommendations from this review process, the Preliminary Battery included the following measures:

• Eight perceptual-cognitive measures including five from the Educational Testing Service (ETS) French Kit (Ekstrom, French, & Harman, 1976), two from the Employee Aptitude Survey (EAS; Ruch & Ruch, 1980), and one from the Flanagan Industrial Tests (FIT; Flanagan, 1965). The names of the tests were: ETS Figure Classification, ETS Map Planning, ETS Choosing a Path, ETS Following Directions, ETS Hidden Figures, EAS Space Visualization, EAS Numerical Reasoning, and Flanagan Assembly.

• Eighteen scales from the Air Force Vocational Interest Career Examination (VOICE; Alley & Matthews, 1982).

• Five temperament scales adapted from published scales including Social Potency and Stress Reaction from the Differential Personality Questionnaire (DPQ; Tellegen, 1982), Socialization from the California Psychological Inventory (CPI; Gough, 1975), the Rotter I/E Scale (Rotter, 1966), and validity scales from both the DPQ and the Personality Research Form (PRF; Jackson, 1967).

• Owen's Biographical Questionnaire (BQ; Owens & Schoenfeldt, 1979). The BQ could be scored in one of two ways: (a) based on Owen's research, 11 scales could be scored for males and 14 for females, or (b) using 18 rationally developed, combined-sex scales developed specifically for Project A research. The rational scales had no item scored on more than one scale; some of Owen's scales included items that were scored on more than one scale. Items tapping religious or socioeconomic status were deleted from Owens' instrument for Project A use, and items tapping physical fitness and vocational-technical course work were added.

In addition to the Preliminary Battery, scores were available for the ASVAB, which all soldiers take prior to entry into service.

Evaluation of the Preliminary Battery

To test the instructions, timing, and other administration procedures, the Preliminary Battery was initially administered to a sample of 40 soldiers at Fort Leonard Wood, Missouri. The results of this tryout were used to adjust the procedures, prepare a test administrator's manual, and identify topics to be emphasized during administrator training.

Sample.   The battery was then administered by civilian or military staff employed on site at five Army training installations to soldiers entering Advanced Technical Training in four MOS: Radio Teletype Operator, Armor Crewman, Vehicle and Generator Mechanic, and Administrative Specialist. The experience gained in training administrators and monitoring the test administration provided useful information for later, larger data collection efforts. Analyses were conducted on the subsample ($n = 1850$) who completed the battery during the first 2 months of data collection.

Analyses.   Three types of analyses are summarized below. A full report is provided in Hough, Dunnette, Wing, Houston, and Peterson (1984).

Analyses of the psychometric properties of each measure indicated problems with some of the cognitive ability tests. The time limits appeared too stringent for several tests, and one test, Hidden Figures, was much too difficult for the population being tested. In retrospect, this was to be expected because many of the cognitive tests used in the Preliminary Battery had been developed on college samples. The lesson learned was that the Pilot Trial Battery measures needed to be accurately targeted (in difficulty of items and time limits) toward the population of persons seeking entry into the Army. No serious problems were indicated for the temperament, biodata, and interest scales. Item-total correlations were acceptably high and in accordance with prior findings, and score distributions were not excessively skewed or different from expectation. About 8% of subjects failed the scale that screened for inattentive or random responding on the temperament inventory, a figure that was in accord with findings in other selection research.

Covariance analyses showed that vocational interest scales were relatively distinct from the biographical and personality scales, but the latter two types of scales exhibited considerable covariance. Five factors were identified from the 40 noncognitive scales, two that were primarily vocational interests and three that were combinations of biographical data and personality scales. These findings led us to consider, for the Pilot Trial

Battery, combining biographical and personality item types to measure the constructs in these two areas. The five noncognitive factors had relatively low correlations with the Preliminary Battery cognitive tests. The median absolute correlations of the scales within each of the five noncognitive factors with each of the eight Preliminary Battery cognitive tests (i.e., a 5 x 8 matrix) ranged from .01 to .21.

Analysis of the ten ASVAB subtests and the eight Preliminary Battery cognitive tests confirmed the prior four factor solution for the ASVAB (Kass, Mitchell, Grafton, & Wing, 1983) and showed the relative independence of the ASVAB and the Preliminary Battery tests. Although some of the ASVAB-Preliminary Battery test correlations were fairly high (the highest was .57), most were less than .30 (49 of the 80 correlations were .30 or less, 65 were .40 or less). The factor analysis (principal factors extraction, varimax rotation) of the 18 tests showed all eight Preliminary Battery cognitive tests loading highest on a single factor, with none of the ASVAB subtests loading highest on that factor. The noncognitive scales overlapped very little with the four ASVAB factors identified in the factor analysis of the ASVAB subtests and Preliminary Battery cognitive tests. Median correlations of noncognitive scales with the ASVAB factors, computed within the five noncognitive factors, ranged from .03 to .32, but 14 of the 20 median correlations were .10 or less.

In summary, these analyses showed that the off-the-shelf cognitive and noncognitive measures were sufficiently independent from the ASVAB to warrant further development of measures of the constructs, but that these measures should be targeted more specifically to the Army applicant population. Biodata and temperament measures showed enough empirical overlap to justify the development of a single inventory to measure these two domains, but vocational interests appeared to require a separate inventory.

DEMONSTRATION COMPUTER BATTERY

As shown in Fig. 4.1, information from the development of a demonstration, computer-administered battery also informed the choice and development of measures for the Pilot Trial Battery. The development of this battery served to determine the degree of difficulty of programming such a battery and to determine the likely quality of results to be obtained using then-available portable microprocessors. The "demo" development, along with information gained during site visits at facilities that conducted computerized testing (e.g., the Air Force Human Resource

Research Laboratory), convinced the research team that the programming and technical problems to be faced in developing a portable, computer-administered battery were challenging, but surmountable. Valuable lessons were learned (see Chapter 5) in the context of the development of the computer-administered tests that were part of the Project A predictor batteries.

SELECTION OF VARIABLES
FOR MEASUREMENT

In March 1984, a critical decision meeting was held to decide on the new predictor measures to be developed for Project A. It was the first of a long series of decision meetings that occurred over the course of these two projects. Such meetings were for the purpose of making a project-wide decision about a particular course of action, given all the information available. These meetings were characteristically tense, lengthy, informative, candid, highly participative, and very interesting. Attendees at this meeting included all the principal investigators responsible for the work described in this chapter (the predictor development team), the principal scientist, a sub-committee of the Scientific Advisory Group, and research staff from ARI. Information reviewed and discussed came from all the sources described in this chapter, including the literature review, the expert judgment evaluation, initial analyses of the Preliminary Battery, and the demonstration computer battery. In addition, the predictor development team obtained and reported on information from visits to almost all major military personnel research laboratories and on-site observations of individuals during field exercises in the Army combat specialties. The predictor development group made initial recommendations for the inclusion of measures and these were extensively discussed, evaluated, and then modified.

Table 4.3 shows the results of the deliberation process. This set of recommendations constituted the initial array of predictor variables for which measures would be constructed and then submitted to a series of pilot tests and field tests, with revisions being made after each phase. The predictor categories or constructs are shown along with the priorities established at the decision meeting. In addition to developing measures of these predictors, a small number of additional predictors were introduced as the development research progressed. The primary addition was a questionnaire measure of preferences among work outcomes (described in Chapter 6).

TABLE 4.3
"Best Bet" Predictor Variables Rank Ordered, Within Domain, by Priority
for Measure Development

Cognitive Ability Variables

1. Spatial visualization/rotation
2. Spatial visualization/field independence
3. Spatial organization
5. Reaction time
4. Induction (reasoning)
5. Perceptual speed & Accuracy
6. Numerical ability
7. Memory

Psychomotor Abilities

1. Multilimb coordination
2. Control precision
3. Manual dexterity (later replaced by Movement judgment)

Biodata/Temperament Variables

1. Adjustment
2. Dependability
3. Achievement
4. Physical condition
5. Potency
6. Locus of control
7. Agreeableness/likeability
8. Validity Scales (not viewed as a predictor, per se, but a necessary component of this type of measure)

Interest Variables

1. Realistic
2. Investigative
3. Conventional
4. Social
5. Artistic
6. Enterprising

THE NEXT STEPS

This chapter describes the general procedure that was followed to identify the highest priority variables for measurement. Chapters 5 and 6 describe the research process that used the information accumulated to this point to develop the specific measures for the new test battery. These next two chapters represent approximately two years of development work.

5

The Measurement of Cognitive, Perceptual, and Psychomotor Abilities

Teresa L. Russell, Norman G. Peterson,
Rodney L. Rosse, Jody Toquam Hatten,
Jeffrey J. McHenry, and Janis S. Houston

The purpose of this chapter is to describe the development of the new predictor measures intended to assess cognitive, perceptual, and psychomotor abilities for the Project A Trial Battery. The development of the predictor measures related to temperament and interests is described in Chapter 6. The *Trial Battery* was the battery of new selection/classification tests used in the Concurrent Validation phase of Project A (CVI). The *Experimental Battery*, a revised version of the Trial Battery, was the test battery used in the Longitudinal Validation (LVP). The Experimental Battery is discussed in Chapter 10.

Chapter 4 described the procedure that was used to identify a relevant "population" of potential predictor constructs and to identify the highest priorities for measurement. The next step was to translate these general priorities into specific measurement objectives, develop the specific tests, and evaluate their psychometric properties. The literature review, extensive pilot testing, and evaluations using the CVI data were all part of this process.

This chapter is divided into two parts. The first part relies heavily on two of the Project A literature reviews (i.e., McHenry & Rose, 1988; Toquam, Corpe, & Dunnette, 1991), but incorporates a somewhat broader perspective and more recent research. The objectives of part one for both the cognitive/perceptual and psychomotor domains will be to (a) summarize the taxonomic theory, (b) briefly review the relevant validation research findings, and (c) identify existing measures of the most relevant constructs. An integration of this information with the identification of the "best bet" constructs described in Chapter 4 produced the initial specifications for the new tests to be developed. The second part of the chapter is a synopsis of a long series of test development steps that involved a number of pilot field test samples and numerous revisions that led to the versions of the tests that were used in the Concurrent Validation (CVI). A more detailed account of the development process can be found in J.P. Campbell (1987).

IDENTIFYING COGNITIVE AND PSYCHOMOTOR ABILITY CONSTRUCTS

The 20th century produced many efforts to identify human abilities and model their latent structure (e.g., Ackerman, 1996; Anastasi, 1982; Carroll, 1993; Lubinski & Dawis, 1992). Relative to personnel selection and classification, Thurstone's classic work (Thurstone, 1938; Thurstone & Thurstone, 1941) provided the cornerstone for much of abilities measurement. He administered 56 tests designed to tap a wide range of abilities to 218 subjects, and extracted 13 factors but could label only 9. In a separate study of eighth grade children, Thurstone and Thurstone identified seven primary mental abilities that were replicable in factor analyses: (a) verbal comprehension, (b) number, (c) word fluency, (d) space, (e) associative memory, (f) inductive reasoning, and (g) perceptual speed. However, different methods of factor analysis yield different results, and Spearman (1939) and Eysenk (1939) reanalyzed Thurstone's (1938) data to find a general factor (g) and more specific subfactors.

Several major alternative models of intellect have since been proposed. Two major frameworks are Vernon's (1950) hierarchical structure and Cattell's (1971) and Horn's (1989) distinction of fluid and crystallized intelligence. Vernon proposed that two major group factors emerge in factor analyses, after the extraction of g: (a) verbal-numerical (v:ed) and (b) practical-mechanical-spatial (k:m). Minor group factors, analogous to Thurstone's (1938) primary mental abilities, are subsumed by the two major group factors. More recent research continues to support Vernon's hierarchical structure of cognitive abilities (e.g., Ackerman, 1987).

The model described by Horn and Cattell (1966) integrates information processing research with traditional factor-analytic results and evidence from physiological studies of brain injury and other impairments to identify broad and narrow cognitive factors. Narrow (or primary) factors are ones for which the intercorrelations among subfactors are large; broad factors (second-order) are defined by tests that are not as highly intercorrelated. The model includes six broad cognitive abilities; the broadest of which are G_c and G_f. Acquired knowledge or *Crystallized Intelligence*, (G_c) underlies performance on knowledge or information tests. Broad Reasoning or *Fluid Intelligence* (G_f) subsumes virtually all forms of reasoning—inductive, conjunctive, and deductive. This distinction between cognitive ability as a reflection of acquired knowledge and cognitive ability as "relatively" domain free learning potential, reasoning capability, or general information processing efficiency/capability is virtually a universal component of discussions of human cognitive ability. The distinction has also been used to explain patterns of growth and decline in cognitive abilities over the life span. That is, it is domain free reasoning, or processing efficiency, that appears to decline after midlife while crystallized or knowledge-based intelligence can continue to rise. It also leads to the prediction that the factor structure of crystallized or knowledge based ability will become more differentiated as life progresses.

Although different theorists organize the lower order ability factors in somewhat different ways to form particular models of the latent structure, there is a great deal of consistency in the ability factors that constitute them. Summaries of the literature can be found in Carroll (1993); Ekstrom, French, and Harman (1979); Fleishman and Mumford (1988); Lubinski and Dawis (1992); McHenry and Rose (1988); Russell, Reynolds, and Campbell (1994); and Toquam et al. (1991).

Cognitive and Perceptual Abilities

Latent Structure

At the time predictor development in Project A began, a reasonable consensus from the literature was that nine major distinguishable cognitive abilities had been consistently measured, and replicated: (a) Verbal Ability, (b) Numerical Ability, (c) Reasoning, (d) Spatial Ability, (e) Perceptual Speed and Accuracy, (f) Memory, (g) Fluency, (h) Perception, and (i) Mechanical Aptitude (Horn, 1989; Toquam et al., 1991). Many of these abilities subsume one or more constructs that have factor-analytic support as distinguishable subfactors. Table 5.1 provides a brief definition of each ability as well as the names of the more specific constructs that they subsume.

TABLE 5.1
Cognitive and Perceptual Abilities

Verbal Ability—The ability to understand the English language. Includes constructs: verbal comprehension and reading comprehension.

Number/Mathematical Facility—The ability to solve simple or complex mathematical problems. Includes constructs: numerical computation, use of formulations, and number problems.

Spatial Ability—The ability to visualize or manipulate objects and figures in space. Includes constructs: space visualization, spatial orientation, two- and three-dimensional rotation, and spatial scanning.

Reasoning—The ability to discover a rule or principle and apply it in solving a problem. Includes constructs: inductive, deductive, analogical, and figural reasoning as well as word problems.

Memory—The ability to recall previously learned information or concepts. Includes constructs: associative or rote memory, memory span, and visual memory.

Fluency—The ability to rapidly generate words or ideas related to target stimuli. Includes constructs: associational, expressional, ideational, and word fluency.

Perception—The ability to perceive a figure or form that is only partially presented or that is embedded in another form. Includes constructs: flexibility of closure and speed of closure.

Perceptual Speed and Accuracy—The ability to perceive visual information quickly and accurately and to perform simple processing tasks with it (e.g., comparison).

Mechanical Aptitude—The ability to perceive and understand the relationship of physical forces and mechanical elements in prescribed situation.

Note. From Toquam, J.L., Corpe, V.A., & Dunnette, M.D. (1991). *Cognitive abilities: A review of theory, history, and validity* (ARI Research Note 91-28). Alexandria, VA: U.S. Army Research Institute for the Behavioral and Social Sciences.

Of course, cognitive abilities are intercorrelated, and a wealth of evidence supports the existence of a strong general factor (*g*) underlying cognitive test scores (e.g., Jensen, 1986). The concept of *g* has been characterized as "mental energy" (Spearman, 1927), the ability to learn or adapt (Hunter, 1986), the relative availability of attentional resources (Ackerman, 1988), working memory capacity (Kyllonen & Christal, 1990), and as the sum of acquired knowledge across a broad domain learned early in life (Lubinski & Dawis, 1992). A special task force appointed by the American Psychological Association to address the issue (Neisser, 1996) acknowledged the robust existence of *g*, but acknowledged that a definitive definition could not be given. In any case, it is a general factor that can be constituted several different ways and still produce much the same pattern of relationships (Ree & Earles, 1991a). The factor *g* may be assessed by elemental mental processes such as decision time on a letter recognition task (Kranzler & Jensen, 1991a, 1991b), by scores on information processing tasks (Carroll, 1991a, 1991b), or by scores on a variety of verbal reasoning tasks. However, g computed from one battery of tests is not identical to g from another battery of tests (Linn, 1986); that is, the true score correlation is not 1.0.

General factor g has a high degree of heritability (Humphreys, 1979), but is also influenced by the environment (Jensen, 1992). It is related to educational achievement and socio-economic status in complex ways (Humphreys, 1986, 1992). Factor g predicts job performance (Hunter, 1986; Ree, Earles, & Teachout, 1992; Thorndike, 1986) and training success (Ree & Earles, 1991b) and yields small positive correlations with a host of other variables (e.g., Vernon, 1990).

Moreover, existence of g does not preclude the existence of specific abilities and vice versa. Almost all researchers who study cognitive abilities acknowledge that specific abilities have been identified and replicated. The debate surrounds the magnitude and significance of the contribution of specific abilities in predictive validity settings over that afforded by g. Experts disagree over the amount of increment that is worthwhile (Humphreys, 1986; Linn, 1986).

Validation Evidence for Cognitive and Perceptual Abilities

Cognitive measures are valid predictors of performance for virtually all jobs (Ghiselli, 1973; Hunter, 1986). For the Project A cognitive ability literature review, we conducted a meta-analysis of validity estimates for cognitive predictors to identify measures likely to supplement the ASVAB (Toquam et al., 1991). Virtually all available studies published by 1983 that did not involve young children or college students were reviewed.

Estimated validities were arranged according to the type of criterion as well as the type of predictor and type of job. Jobs were organized into a taxonomy derived from the *Dictionary of Occupational Titles*. The major categories were (a) professional, technical, and managerial jobs, including military officers and aircrew as well as civilian managers and professionals; (b) clerical, including military and civilian office clerk and administrative jobs; (c) protective services, subsuming jobs like military police, infantryman, corrections officer; (d) service, comprising food and medical service jobs; (e) mechanical/structural maintenance, covering all mechanical and maintenance jobs; (f) electronics, including electricians, radio operators, radar and sonar technicians; and (g) industrial, including jobs such as machine operator and coal miner.

Criteria were organized into four categories: (a) education, including course grades and instructor evaluations; (b) training, composed of exam scores, course grades, instructor ratings, work sample and hands-on measures; (c) job proficiency, including supervisor ratings, job knowledge measures, and archival measures; and (d) adjustment, referring to measures of delinquency such as disciplinary actions and discharge conditions.

Validity estimates for verbal, reasoning, and number facility measures were relatively uniform across all job types. Reasoning was one of the better predictors of training and job performance outcomes for professional, technical, managerial, protective services, and electronics occupations. Spatial measures were effective predictors of training criteria in virtually all jobs, but particularly for electronics jobs. Perception and mechanical ability measures best predicted training outcomes for industrial, service, and electronics occupations. Perceptual speed and accuracy tests predicted education and training criteria in clerical, industrial, professional, technical, and managerial occupations. Memory and fluency measures were notable in that they have been used less frequently than other measures in validity studies. The available validity data suggested that fluency measures might be better predictors for professional, technical, and managerial jobs than for other jobs. Memory tests, on the other hand, have been useful predictors for service jobs.

Existing Measures of Cognitive and Perceptual Abilities

The ASVAB, the General Aptitude Test Battery (GATB), and other widely used batteries such as the Differential Aptitude Test (DAT) are differential aptitude batteries, philosophical descendants of Thurstone's (1938) attempt to define primary mental abilities. They are designed to reliably measure several specific abilities that differentiate people and/or jobs, usually for the purpose of career counseling or selection and classification decisions.

The Armed Services Vocational Aptitude Battery (ASVAB).
The ASVAB is a highly useful general purpose cognitive predictor (Welsh, Kucinkas, & Curran, 1990). ASVAB scores predict training success in a variety of jobs, and in all the Services. However, at the onset of Project A, the ASVAB had not been systematically validated against measures of job performance. For that reason, it was always the intent to include the then current ASVAB with the new project developed tests as part of the total battery to be validated with both the concurrent and longitudinal samples. Future changes to the ASVAB would be a function of all subsequent research data.

The content of the ASVAB stems from modifications of the Army General Classification Test (AGCT) and the Navy General Classification Test (NGCT) that were used during World War II (Schratz & Ree, 1989). These tests were designed to aid in assigning new recruits to military jobs (Eitelberg, Laurence, Waters, & Perelman, 1984). The tests resembled each other in content and covered such cognitive domains as vocabulary, mathematics, and spatial relationships. Separate batteries were used until the late 1970s when the military services developed a joint testing program. The resulting multiple-aptitude, group-administered ASVAB is now the primary selection and classification test used by the U.S. military for selecting and classifying entry level enlisted personnel.

The ASVAB that has been administered since 1980 includes 10 subtests, 8 of which are power tests and two of which are speeded. Table 5.2 shows the number of items that are included in each subtest, the amount of time it takes to administer each, and the internal consistency and alternate forms reliabilities of each. As noted, the average internal consistency reliability for the subtests is .86. The average alternate forms reliability is .79.

The factor structure of the ASVAB has been examined by a number of researchers over the years. The three most important findings are: (a) the

TABLE 5.2
Content and Reliability of ASVAB Subtests

| Subtest | Number of Items | Test Time (Minutes) | Reliability | |
			Internal Consistency	Alternate Forms
General Science (GS)	25	11	.86	.83
Arithmetic Reasoning (AR)	30	36	.91	.87
Word Knowledge (WK)	35	11	.92	.88
Paragraph Comprehension (PC)	15	13	.81	.72
Numerical Operations (NO)	50	03	*	.70
Coding Speed (CS)	84	07	*	.73
Auto & Shop Information (AS)	25	11	.87	.83
Mathematics Knowledge (MK)	25	24	.87	.84
Mechanical Comprehension (MC)	25	19	.85	.78
Electronics Information (EI)	20	09	.81	.72
Total/Average	334	144	.86	.79

*Internal consistency reliability not computed for speeded tests (Waters, Barnes, Foley, Steinhaus, & Brown, 1988).

general factor accounts for approximately 60% of the total variance (Kass, Mitchell, Grafton, & Wing, 1983; Welsh, Watson, & Ree, 1990), (b) in a number of factor analytic studies four factors have been identified and replicated (Kass et al., 1983; Welsh, Kucinkas, & Curran 1990), and (c) the four factors have been replicated for male, female, Black, White, and Hispanic subgroups separately (Kass et al., 1983). The four factors and ASVAB subtests that define them are as follows:

1. Verbal (WK and PC)
2. Speed (CS and NO)
3. Quantitative (AR and MK)
4. Technical (AS, MC, and EL)

General Science has loaded on the Verbal factor (Ree, Mullins, Mathews, & Massey, 1982) and has yielded split-loadings on the Verbal and Technical factors (Kass et al., 1983). Otherwise this factor solution is relatively straightforward and is highly replicable. Even so, over half of the variance in ASVAB scores is accounted for by the general factor (Welsh, Watson et al., 1990).

Although the ASVAB does cover an array of abilities, it is not a comprehensive basic ability measure. Project A researchers mapped the ASVAB against the nine abilities that emerged from the Project A literature review as shown in Table 5.3 (Toquam et al., 1991).

When Project A began, the ASVAB contained no measures of spatial ability, memory, fluency, or perception. After weighing the validity evidence for each of the ability constructs, it was concluded that it is probably

TABLE 5.3
Ability Factors Measured by ASVAB

Ability Factor	ASVAB Subtest(s)
Verbal ability	Word Knowledge, Paragraph Comprehension
Number ability	Mathematics Knowledge, Arithmetic Reasoning
Spatial ability	—
Reasoning	Arithmetic Reasoning
Memory	—
Fluency	—
Perception	—
Perceptual speed & accuracy	Coding Speed, Number Operations
Mechanical aptitude	Mechanical Comprehension

not critically important to measure fluency in the ASVAB because it appears to be more relevant for professional jobs. However, spatial ability was of high priority because it predicted training and job performance outcomes for six of the eight job types included in their review and served as one of the best predictors for Service and Industrial occupations. Similarly, measures of perception yielded moderate validities for six of the eight types of occupations and would seemingly be useful for military occupations. Although measures of memory had not been included in validity studies very often, Project researchers concluded that memory was very likely a relevant predictor for a number of military jobs (Toquam et al., 1991).

The General Aptitude Test Battery (GATB).   The U.S. Employment Service (USES) Test Research Program developed the GATB in 1947 to measure abilities that were generalizable to a large variety of occupations (HRStrategies, 1994). Prior to that time, the USES had developed literally hundreds of occupation-specific tests for use during the Depression and World War II. Factor analyses of combinations of 59 occupation-specific tests identified 10 aptitudes along with marker tests for each; two aptitudes were later merged. At the beginning of Project A, the GATB had 12 tests that measured eight aptitudes as shown in Table 5.4. GATB was recently renamed the Ability Profiler, but we will use the original name for purposes of this discussion.

TABLE 5.4
Content of the General Aptitude Test Battery

Aptitude		Test
V	Verbal aptitude	Vocabulary
N	Numerical aptitude	Computation
		arithmetic reasoning
S	Spatial aptitude	Three-dimensional space
P	Form perception	Tool matching
		Form matching
Q	Clerical perception	Name comparison
K	Motor coordination	Mark making
F	Finger dexterity	Assemble
		Disassemble
M	Manual dexterity	Turn
		Place

The GATB tests measure constructs very similar to those measured by the ASVAB (Peterson, 1993; Wise & McDaniel, 1991). In addition, it includes measures of form perception, spatial relations, and psychomotor abilities that were not included in the ASVAB.

Other major cognitive test batteries. The Project A literature review organized tests from four other major test batteries—Primary Mental Abilities (PMA), Flanagan Industrial Tests (FIT), Differential Aptitude Test (DAT), and Employee Aptitude Survey (EAS)—according to the nine abilities derived from the literature review. The result appears in Table 5.5. The tests can be thought of as "markers" or reliable measures for each of the abilities.

Selection of Constructs for Measurement

As detailed in Chapter 4, the predictor development strategy specified that the results of the literature review(s) should be combined with the results of the expert judgment study and presented to the Scientific Advisory Group for a decision as to what cognitive ability variables should have the highest priority for measurement development. Again, the priority rankings were a function of (a) the previous record of predictive validity for measures of the construct, (b) feasibility of measurement under the resource constraints of Project A, and (c) the potential that measures of the construct would provide incremental validity, relative to ASVAB, for relevant criterion variables.

Given the priorities that were subsequently set, the cognitive ability constructs in Table 5.5 that were subjected to measurement development were numerical ability, reasoning, spatial ability, perceptual speed and accuracy, and memory. Note that the highest priorities (from Fig. 4.3) were the subfactors of spatial ability. The verbal, fluency, perception, and mechanical aptitude constructs are not in the priority list, primarily because they were covered by the current ASVAB. The marker tests listed in Table 5.4 and Table 5.5 were used as a starting point for item development.

Psychomotor Abilities

Latent Structure

After examining the literature in the psychomotor domain, it was concluded that Fleishman's taxonomic work (e.g., 1967) had produced substantial research support for 11 psychomotor abilities. Table 5.6 provides definitions of these psychomotor abilities.

TABLE 5.5

Cognitive and Perceptual Ability Constructs Measured by Four Test Batteries

Cognitive Ability Construct	Battery and Test
Verbal ability	PMA Verbal meaning FIT Vocabulary EAS Verbal comprehension
Numerical ability	PMA Numerical facility DAT Numerical ability FIT Arithmetic EAS Numerical ability
Reasoning	PMA Reasoning FIT Judgment and comprehension FIT Mathematics and reasoning EAS Numerical reasoning EAS Verbal reasoning EAS Symbolic reasoning DAT Abstract reasoning FIT Planning DAT Verbal reasoning
Spatial ability	PMA Spatial relations DAT Spatial reasoning FIT Assembly EAS Visual pursuit EAS Space visualization
Perceptual speed and accuracy	PMA Perceptual speed DAT Clerical speed and accuracy FIT Inspection FIT Scales FIT Tables EAS Visual speed and accuracy
Memory	FIT Memory
Fluency	FIT Ingenuity EAS Word fluency
Perception	FIT Components FIT Patterns
Mechanical aptitude	DAT Mechanical reasoning FIT Mechanics

TABLE 5.6
Psychomotor Abilities (from Fleishman, 1967)

Multilimb Coordination—The ability to coordinate the movements of a number of limbs simultaneously, and is best measured by devices involving multiple controls (e.g., two-hand coordination tests).

Rate Control—This ability involves the timing of continuous anticipatory motor adjustments relative to changes in speed and direction of a continuously moving target or object.

Control Precision—The ability to make rapid, precise, highly controlled, but not overcontrolled, movements necessary to adjust or position a machine control mechanism (e.g., rudder controls). Control precision involves the use of larger muscle groups, including arm-hand and leg movements.

Speed of Arm Movement—The ability to make gross, discreet arm movements quickly in tasks that do not require accuracy.

Manual Dexterity—This ability involves skillful, well-directed arm-hand movements in manipulating fairly large objects under speeded conditions.

Finger Dexterity—The ability to make skillful, controlled manipulations of tiny objects involving, primarily, the fingers.

Arm-Hand Steadiness—The ability to make precise arm-hand positioning movements where strength and speed are minimized; the critical feature is the steadiness with which movements must be made.

Wrist, Finger Speed (also called tapping)—This ability is very narrow. It involves making rapid discrete movements of the fingers, hands, and wrists, such as in tapping a pencil on paper.

Aiming (also called eye-hand coordination)—This ability is very narrow. It involves making precise movements under highly speeded conditions, such as in placing a dot in the middle of a circle, repeatedly, for a page of circles.

Response Orientation—The ability to select the correct movement in relation to the correct stimulus, especially under highly speeded conditions (e.g., Choice Reaction Time tests).

Reaction Time—The ability to respond to a stimulus rapidly.

Predictive Validity Evidence

To construct a systematic picture of the existing predictive validity evidence for psychomotor abilities, previous study results were aggregated by type of test, type of job, and type of criterion (McHenry & Rose, 1988). The validity estimates for tests were organized according to Fleishman's classification scheme. The criterion and type of job definitions in the cognitive and perceptual abilities review literature were used in the psychomotor literature review as well. The bulk of the validation studies were conducted using GATB subtests; and a large number of validity estimates were reported for the GATB aptitudes Finger Dexterity, Manual Dexterity, and Wrist-Finger Speed. Conversely, measures of Control Precision, Rate Control, Aiming, Arm-Hand Steadiness, and Speed of Arm Movement have rarely been used.

As might be expected, measures of Multilimb Coordination have been effective predictors for a number of professional and technical jobs (which include pilots and aircrew) and protective service jobs (which include infantry and military police jobs). In contrast, Finger Dexterity, Manual Dexterity, and Wrist-Finger Speed predictors were most relevant to performance in industrial production jobs (e.g., assembler, bench worker, machine operator).

The results of the literature review were taken as evidence that certain psychomotor ability constructs were worth evaluating as potential supplements to the ASVAB. In particular, they offered the possibility of increasing differential prediction across MOS.

Existing Measures

Other than the GATB, there are very few widely used measures of psychomotor abilities. Most available tests were designed by the Services for use in aviator selection.

The Basic Attributes Test (BAT).   The Air Force developed the Basic Attributes Test (BAT) to supplement the cognitive-based Air Force Officer Qualification Test for pilot selection (Carretta, 1987a, 1987b, 1987c). The BAT is a battery of tests designed to measure cognitive, perceptual, and psychomotor aptitudes as well as personality and attitudinal characteristics (Carretta, 1987a, 1987b, 1987c, 1991, 1992). Several of the BAT subtests are descendants of the classic Army Air Force work and later work by Fleishman and his colleagues (e.g., Fleishman & Hempel, 1956). Other tests are based on more recent information-processing research. Descriptions of BAT subtests appear in Table 5.7.

Some BAT subtests have proven to be effective predictors (Bordelon & Kantor, 1986; Carretta 1987a, 1987b, 1987c, 1990, 1991, 1992; Stoker, Hunter, Kantor, Quebe, & Siem, 1987). The psychomotor abilities tests on the BAT have demonstrated strong relationships with success in Undergraduate Pilot Training, advanced training assignment, and in-flight performance scores. The cognitive/perceptual tests have not predicted training outcomes, although they have shown a relationship to in-flight performance measures.

Multi-Track Test Battery.   In 1988, the Army implemented the Multi-Track Test Battery for assigning flight students into four helicopter tracks (Intano & Howse, 1991; Intano, Howse, & Lofaro, 1991a, 1991b). The Multi-Track is actually an assembly of test batteries developed by the Army, Navy, Air Force, and National Aeronautics and Space Administration

TABLE 5.7

Basic Attributes Test (BAT) Battery Summary

Test Name	Length (mins)	Attribute Measured	Types of Scores	Cronbach Alpha	Guttman Split-Half
Two-hand coordination (rotary pursuit)	10	Tracking and time-sharing ability in pursuit	Tracking error x axis Tracking error y axis	.94 .95	.58 .65
Complex coordination (stick and rudder)	10	Compensatory tracking involving multiple axes	Tracking error x axis Tracking error y axis Tracking error z axis	.95 .99 .94	.62 .56 .41
Encoding speed	20	Verbal classification	Response time Response accuracy	.96 .71	.65 .40
Mental rotation	25	Spatial transformation and classification	Response time Response accuracy	.97 .90	.79 .71
Item recognition	20	Short-term memory, storage, search and comparison	Response time Response accuracy	.95 .54	.79 .55
Time-sharing	30	Higher-order tracking ability, learning rate and time-sharing	Tracking difficulty Response time Dual-task performance	.96	.80
Self-crediting word knowledge	10	Self-assessment ability, self-confidence	Response time Response accuracy	.89 .65	.72 .86
Activities interest inventory	10	Survival attitudes	Response time Number of high-risk choices	.95 .86	.70 .86

Source: Carretta (1991, 1992).

(NASA). It includes (a) five subtests from the Complex Cognitive Assessment Battery, which was developed by ARI; (b) two tests from the Air Force's BAT; (c) a questionnaire designed for NASA to assess attitudes and leadership potential (i.e., the Cockpit Management Attitude Questionnaire); and (d) the Complex Coordination/Multi-Tasking Battery (CCMB), which was developed by the Naval Aeromedical Research Laboratory. The CCMB contains seven computer-assisted subtests, in increasing difficulty. It begins with a relatively simple psychomotor task, then a dichotic listening task. Subsequent tasks require various combinations of psychomotor tasks, along with dichotic listening.

Selection of Constructs for Measurement

Based on similar considerations as for the cognitive ability tests, the Project A Scientific Advisory Group also established a priority ranking for the development of psychomotor ability measures. The original set of constructs included multilimb coordination, control precision, and manual dexterity. Subsequent development work resulted in manual dexterity being dropped from consideration and movement judgment (rate control) being added. All of these variables would be assessed using the project-developed computerized testing equipment. Again, the marker subtests from the GATB, BAT, and Multi-Track Test Battery served as a starting point for item development.

Summary

Although the ASVAB is a highly effective general purpose cognitive ability test battery, there are several parts of the aptitude domain that it did not measure. Most notably, it contained no measures of spatial, perceptual, and psychomotor abilities, all of which were likely to be valid predictors of performance in military jobs. These observations, coupled with the results of the predictor construct identification and evaluation process described in Chapter 4, led to the designation of the spatial, perceptual, and psychomotor constructs as critical variables for which Project A should develop predictor measures.

Test development for this part of the new predictor battery was the responsibility of two test development teams, one for the spatial constructs and one for the perceptual/psychomotor variables. The general process called for the team to begin with the variables that had been prioritized for test development and to assemble the most representative marker tests for each construct. Initial test specifications and item formats were based on the marker tests, and each experimental test was designed with the project's time, resource, and logistic constraints in mind. The measurement procedures, item content, and general sequence of pilot and field testing are described in the next section.

DEVELOPMENT OF THE SPATIAL, PERCEPTUAL, AND PSYCHOMOTOR MEASURES

Early in the test development process, it was decided that the spatial measures would be administered in paper-and-pencil form. Little information existed at that time about the comparability of different methods of measurement; it was not known whether administering a spatial test on the computer would change the nature of the construct being measured. Computerization of the psychomotor, perceptual speed and accuracy, and memory tests, however, was more straightforward and highly desirable. It would allow for precise measurement of responses to psychomotor items, manipulation of stimulus display intervals for the memory measures, and measurement of response times on the perceptual speed and accuracy tests.

Measurement of Spatial Abilities

Five spatial constructs were initially designated as critical for measurement. Brief descriptions of the 10 individual spatial tests, as initially designed, are given below, along with an explanation of the constructs the tests are intended to represent. Sample items for the six tests subsequently included in the Trial Battery are provided in Fig. 5.1. Note that all of these tests are paper-and-pencil.

Spatial Visualization—Rotation

Spatial visualization involves the ability to mentally manipulate components of two- or three-dimensional figures into other arrangements. The process involves restructuring the components of an object and accurately discerning their appropriate appearance in new configurations. This construct includes several subcomponents, two of which are rotation and scanning. The two tests developed to measure visual rotation ability are

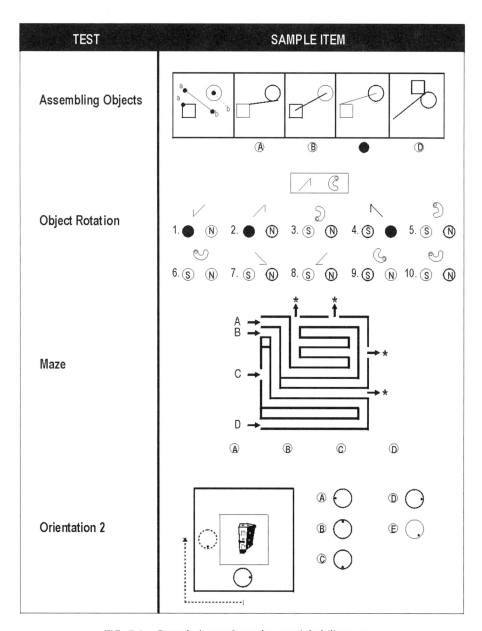

FIG. 5.1.   Sample items from the spatial ability tests.

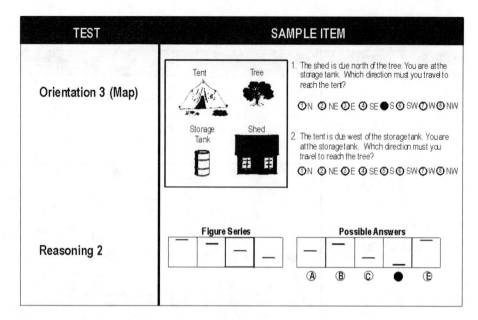

FIG. 5.1.   (Continued)

Assembling Objects and Object Rotation, involving three-dimensional and two-dimensional objects, respectively.

Assembling objects test.   This test was designed to assess the ability to visualize how an object will look when its parts are put together correctly (see Fig. 5.1). This measure was intended to combine power and speed components, with speed receiving greater emphasis. Each item presents components or parts of an object. The task is to select, from among four alternatives, the one object that depicts the components or parts put together correctly. Published tests identified as markers for Assembling Objects include the EAS Space Visualization (EAS-5) and the FIT Assembly.

Object rotation test.   The initial version (see Fig. 5.1) contained 60 items with a 7-minute time limit. The task involves examining a test object and determining whether the figure represented in each item is the same as the test object, only rotated, or is not the same as the test object (e.g., flipped over). Published tests serving as markers for the Object Rotation measure include Educational Testing Service (ETS) Card Rotations, Thurstone's Flags Test, and Shephard-Metzler Mental Rotations.

Spatial Visualization—Scanning

The second component of spatial visualization ability is spatial scanning, which requires the test taken to visually survey a complex field and find a pathway through it, utilizing a particular configuration. The Path Test and the Maze Test were developed to measure this component.

Path test.   The Path Test requires individuals to determine the best path between two points. A map of airline routes or flight paths is presented, and the task is to find the "best" path or the path between two points that requires the fewest stops. Published tests serving as markers for construction of the Path Test include ETS Map Planning and ETS Choosing a Path.

Maze test.   The first pilot test version of the Maze Test contained 24 rectangular mazes, with four entrance points and three exit points (see Fig. 5.1). The task is to determine which of the four entrances leads to a pathway through the maze and to one of the exit points. A 9-minute limit was established.

Field Independence

This construct involves the ability to find a simple form when it is hidden in a complex pattern. Given a visual percept or configuration, field independence refers to the ability to hold the percept or configuration in mind so as to distinguish it from other well-defined perceptual material.

Shapes test.   The marker test was ETS Hidden Figures. The strategy for constructing the Shapes Test was to use a task similar to that in the Hidden Figures Test while ensuring that the difficulty level of test items was geared more toward the Project A target population. The test was to be speeded, but not nearly so much so as the Hidden Figures. At the top of each test page are five simple shapes; below these shapes are six complex figures. Test takers are instructed to examine the simple shapes and then to find the one simple shape located in each complex figure.

Spatial Orientation

This construct involves the ability to maintain one's bearings with respect to points on a compass and to maintain location relative to landmarks. It was not included in the list of predictor constructs evaluated by the expert panel, but it had proved useful during World War II, when the AAF Aviation Psychology Program explored a variety of measures for selecting air crew personnel. Also, during the second year of Project A, a number of job observations suggested that some MOS involve critical job requirements of maintaining directional orientation and establishing location, using features or landmarks in the environment. Consequently, three different measures of this construct were formulated.

Orientation Test 1.   Direction Orientation Form B developed by researchers in the AAF Aviation Psychology Program served as the marker for Orientation Test 1. Each test item presents examinees with six circles. In the test's original form, the first, or Given, circle indicated the compass direction for North. For most items, North was rotated out of its conventional position. Compass directions also appeared on the remaining five circles. The examinee's task was to determine, for each circle, whether or not the direction indicated was correctly positioned by comparing it to the direction of North in the Given circle.

Orientation Test 2.   Each item contains a picture within a circular or rectangular frame (see Fig. 5.1). The bottom of the frame has a circle with a dot inside it. The picture or scene is not in an upright position. The task is to mentally rotate the frame so that the bottom of the frame is positioned at the bottom of the picture. After doing so, one must then determine where the dot will appear in the circle. The original form of the test contained 24 items, and a 10-minute time limit was established.

Orientation Test 3 (MapTest).   This test was modeled after another spatial orientation test, Compass Directions, developed in the AAF Aviation Psychology Program. Orientation Test 3 presents a map that includes various landmarks such as a barracks, a campsite, a forest, a lake (see Fig. 5.1). Within each item, respondents are provided with compass directions by indicating the direction from one landmark to another, such as "the forest is North of the campsite." They are also informed of their present location relative to another landmark. Given this information, the individual must determine which direction to go to reach yet another structure or landmark. For each item, new or different compass directions are given. This measure subsequently became known as the "Map test."

Induction/Figural Reasoning

This construct involves the ability to generate hypotheses about principles governing relationships among several objects. Example measures of induction include the EAS Numerical Reasoning (EAS-6), ETS Figure Classification, DAT Abstract Reasoning, Science Research Associates (SRA) Word Grouping, and Raven's Progressive Matrices. These paper-and-pencil measures present the test takers with a series of objects such as figures, numbers, or words. To complete the task, respondents must first determine the rule governing the relationship among the objects and then apply the rule to identify the next object in the series. Two different measures of the construct were developed for Project A.

Reasoning Test 1.   The plan was to construct a test that was similar to the task appearing in EAS-6, Numerical Reasoning, but with one major difference: Items would be composed of figures rather than numbers. Reasoning Test 1 items present a series of four figures; the task is to identify from among five possible answers the one figure that should appear next in the series.

Reasoning Test 2.   The ETS Figure Classification test, which served as the marker, requires respondents to identify similarities and differences among groups of figures and then to classify test figures into those groups. Items in Reasoning Test 2 are designed to involve only the first task. The test items present five figures, and test takers are asked to determine which four figures are similar in some way, thereby identifying the one figure that differs from the others (see Fig. 5.1).

Measurement of Perceptual and Psychomotor Abilities

A General Approach to Computerization

Compared to the paper-and-pencil measurement of cognitive abilities and the major noncognitive variables (personality, biographical data, and vocational interests), the computerized measurement of psychomotor and perceptual abilities was in a relatively primitive state at the time Project A began. Much work had been done in World War II using electro-mechanical apparatus, but relatively little development had occurred since then.

Microprocessor technology held out considerable promise and work was already under way to implement the ASVAB via computer-assisted testing methods in the Military Entrance Processing Stations. It was against this backdrop of relatively little research-based knowledge, but considerable excitement at the prospect of developing microprocessor-driven measurement procedures and the looming implementation of computerized testing in the military environment, that work began.

There were four phases of activities: (a) information gathering about past and current research in perceptual/psychomotor measurement and computerized methods of testing such abilities; (b) construction of a demonstration computer battery; (c) selection of commercially available microprocessors and peripheral devices, and writing of prototypic software; and (d) continued development of software and the design and construction of a custom-made response pedestal.

Information gathering.   In the spring of 1983, four military research laboratories were doing advanced work in computerized testing: (a) the Air Force Human Resources Laboratory (AFHRL) at Brooks Air Force Base, Texas, (b) the ARI Field Unit at Fort Rucker, Alabama, (c) the Naval Aerospace Medical Research Laboratory, Pensacola, Florida, and (d) the ARI Field Unit at Fort Knox, Kentucky. Experimental testing projects using computers at these sites had already produced significant developments.

Several valuable lessons emerged from interviews with researchers from each of the laboratories. First, large-scale testing could be carried out on microprocessor equipment available in the early 1980s (AFHRL was doing so). Second, to minimize logistic problems, the testing devices should be as compact and simple in design as possible. Third, it would be highly desirable for software and hardware devices to be as self-administering (i.e., little or no input required from test monitors) as possible and as resistant as possible to prior experience with typewriting or video games.

The demonstration battery.   The production of a demonstration battery served as a vehicle for (a) determining potential programming problems and (b) assessing the quality of results to be expected from a common portable microprocessor and a general purpose programming language. It was a short, self-administering battery of five tests programmed in BASIC on the Osborne 1.

Using the demonstration battery, the basic methods for controlling stimulus presentation and response acquisition through a keyboard were explored and techniques for developing a self-administering battery of tests were tried out. However, experience in developing and using the battery revealed that the BASIC language did not allow enough power and control for the optimal timing of events.

Selection of microprocessors and development of software. For purposes of this project, the desirable hardware/software configuration would need to be very reliable, highly portable, efficient, and capable of running the necessary graphics and peripherals.

Of the available commercial microprocessors at that point in time, the Compaq portable best met the criteria. It had a 256K random access memory, two 320 K-byte disk drives, a "game board" for accepting input from peripheral devices, and software for FORTRAN, PASCAL, BASIC, and assembly language programming. Initially six machines and commercially available joysticks were purchased. Some processes, mostly those that are specific to the hardware configuration, had to be written in IBM-PC assembly language. Examples include interpretation of the peripheral device inputs, reading of the real-time clock registers, calibrated timing loops, and specialized graphics and screen manipulation routines. For each of these identified functions, a PASCAL-callable "primitive" routine with a unitary purpose was written in assembly language. Although the machine-specific code would be useless on a different type of machine, the functions were sufficiently simple and unitary in purpose so they could be reproduced with relative ease.

It quickly became clear that the direct programming of every item in every test by one person (a programmer) was not going to be very successful in terms of either time constraints or quality of product. To make it possible for each researcher to contribute his/her judgment and effort to the project, it was necessary to take the "programmer" out of the step between test design and test production and enable researchers to create and enter items without having to know special programming.

The testing software modules were designed as "command processors," which interpreted relatively simple and problem-oriented commands. These were organized in ordinary text written by the various researchers using word processors. Many of the commands were common across all tests. For instance, there were commands that permitted writing of specified text to "windows" on the screen and controlling the screen attributes (brightness, background shade); a command could hold a display on the screen for a period measured to 1/100th-second accuracy. There were commands that caused the program to wait for the respondent to push a particular button.

Other commands caused the cursor to disappear or the screen to go blank during the construction of a complex display.

The design and construction of the response pedestal.

The standard keyboard and the available "off-the-shelf" joysticks were hopelessly inadequate for obtaining reliable data. Computer keyboards leave much to be desired as response acquisition devices—particularly when response latency is a variable of interest. Preliminary trials using, say, the "D" and "L" keys of the keyboard for "true" and "false" responses to items were troublesome with naive subjects. Intricate training was required to avoid individual differences arising from differential experience with keyboards. Moreover, the software had to be contrived so as to flash a warning when a respondent accidentally pressed any other key. The "off-the-shelf" joysticks were so lacking in precision of construction that the scores of a respondent depended heavily upon which joystick he or she was using.

A custom "response pedestal" was designed using readily available electronic parts and a prototype of the device was obtained from a local engineer (see Fig. 5.2) The first design could probably have been constructed in a home workshop. It had two joysticks, a horizontal and a vertical sliding adjuster, and a dial. The two joysticks allowed the respondent to use either the

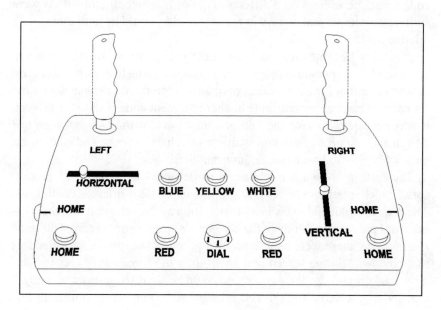

FIG. 5.2. The response pedestal.

left or right hand. The sliding adjusters permitted two-handed coordination tasks.

The response pedestal had nine button-switches, each of which was to be used for particular purposes. Three buttons (BLUE, YELLOW, and WHITE) were located near the center of the pedestal and were used for registering up to 3-choice alternatives. Also, near the center were two buttons (RED) mostly used to allow the respondent to step through frames of instructions and, for some tests, to "fire" a "weapon" represented in graphics on the screen.

Of special interest was the placement of the button-switches, which were called the "HOME" position with respect to the positions of other buttons used to register a response. The "HOME" buttons required the respondent's hands to be in the position of depressing all four of the "HOME" buttons prior to presentation of an item to which he or she would respond. Requiring the HOME button to be depressed before the test could proceed aided the control of the respondent's attention and hand position so as to further standardize the measurement of response latency. Using appropriately developed software, we were able to measure total response time but also to break it down into two parts: (a) "decision time," which is the interval between the appearance of the stimulus and the beginning of a response, and (b) "movement time," which is the time interval between the release of the HOME button and the completion of the response.

Perhaps the greatest difficulty regarding the response pedestal design arose from the initial choice of joystick mechanisms. Joystick design is a complicated and, in this case, a somewhat controversial issue. Variations in tension or movement can cause unacceptable differences in responding, which defeat the goal of standardized testing. "High-fidelity" joystick devices are available, but they can cost many thousands of dollars, which was prohibitively expensive in the quantities that were to be required for this project. The first joystick mechanism that was used in the response pedestals was an improvement over the initial "off-the-shelf" toys that predated the pedestals. It had no springs whatsoever so that spring tension would not be an issue. It had a small, lightweight handle so that enthusiastic respondents could not gain sufficient leverage to break the mechanism. It was inexpensive. Unfortunately, because this joystick had a "wimpy" feeling, it was greatly lacking in "face-validity" (or, sometimes called "fist-validity") from the Army's point of view. It was thought that the joystick was so much like a toy that it would not command respect of the respondents. Joysticks of every conceivable variety and type of use were considered. Ultimately, a joystick device was fashioned with a light spring for centering and a sturdy handle with a bicycle handle-grip. It had sufficient "fist-validity" to be accepted by all (or almost all), and it was sufficiently precise in design that we were unable to detect any appreciable "machine" effects over a series of fairly extensive comparisons.

Development of software for testing and calibrating the hardware was an important next step. The calibration software was designed such that test administrators could conduct a complete hardware test and calibration process. The software checked the timing devices and screen distortion, and calibrated the analog devices (joysticks, sliding adjusters, dial) so that measurement of movement would be the same across machines. It also permitted the software adjustment of the height-to-width ratio of the screen display so that circles would not become ovals or, more importantly, the relative speed of moving displays would remain under control regardless of vertical or horizontal travel.

Development of the Computerized Perceptual and Psychomotor Tests

The construct identification process summarized in Chapter 4 identified the general constructs with the highest priority for measurement. A careful consideration of the results of the literature reviews and expert judgment study together with the feasible capabilities of existing computerization technology translated the initial priorities into an array of seven constructs to be measured by the computer battery:

- Reaction Time and Response Orientation
- Short Term Memory
- Perceptual Speed and Accuracy
- Number Operations
- Psychomotor Precision
- Multilimb Coordination
- Movement Judgment

Field test versions of the tests designed to measure each of the constructs are described below.

Reaction Time and Response Orientation

These constructs involve the speed with which a person perceives the stimulus independent of any time taken by the motor response component of the classic reaction time measures. It is intended to be an indicator of processing efficiency and includes both simple and choice reaction time.

Simple reaction time: RT test 1.   The basic paradigm for this task stems from Jensen's research involving the relationship between reaction time and mental ability (Jensen, 1982). On the computer screen, a small box appears. After a delay period (ranging from 1.5 to 3.0 seconds) the word YELLOW appears in the box. The respondent must remove the preferred hand from the HOME buttons to strike the yellow key. The respondent must then return both hands to the ready position to receive the next item. Three scores are recorded for each item: (1) decision time (DT), or the amount of time lapsing from the presentation of the item to the release of the HOME buttons, (2) movement time (MT), the time from release of the HOME buttons to the depressing of another button, and (3) correct/incorrect to indicate whether the individual depressed the correct button.

Choice reaction time: RT test 2.   Reaction time for two response alternatives is obtained by presenting the word BLUE or WHITE on the screen. The test takers are instructed that, when one of these appears, they are to move the preferred hand from the HOME keys to strike the key that corresponds with the word appearing on the screen (BLUE or WHITE). Decision time, movement time, and correct/incorrect scores are recorded for each item.

Short-Term Memory

This construct is defined as the rate at which one observes, searches, and recalls information contained in short-term memory.

Short term memory test.   The marker was a short-term memory search task introduced by Sternberg (1966, 1969). The first stimulus set appears and contains one, two, three, four, or five objects (letters). Following a display period of 0.5 or 1.0 second, the stimulus set disappears and, after a delay, the probe item appears. Presentation of the probe item is delayed by either 2.5 or 3.0 seconds and the individual must then decide whether or not it appeared in the stimulus set. If the item was present in the stimulus set, the subject strikes the white key. If the probe item was not present, the subject strikes the blue key.

Parameters of interest include the number of letters in the stimulus set, length of observation period, probe delay period, and probe status (i.e., the probe is either *in* the stimulus or *not in* the stimulus set). Individuals receive scores on the following measures:

- Proportion correct.
- The grand mean decision time obtained by calculating the mean of the mean decision time (correct responses only) for each level of stimulus set length (i.e., one to five).
- Movement time.

Perceptual Speed and Accuracy

Perceptual speed and accuracy involves the ability to perceive visual information quickly and accurately and to perform simple processing tasks with the stimulus (e.g., make comparisons). This requires the ability to make rapid scanning movements without being distracted by irrelevant visual stimuli, and measures memory, working speed, and sometimes eye-hand coordination.

Perceptual speed and accuracy test.   Measures used as markers for the development of the computerized Perceptual Speed and Accuracy (PSA) Test included the EAS Visual Speed and Accuracy (EAS-4) and the ASVAB Coding Speed. The computer-administered PSA Test requires the ability to make a rapid comparison of two visual stimuli presented simultaneously and determine whether they are the same or different. Five different types of stimuli are presented: alpha, numeric, symbolic, mixed, and word. Within the alpha, numeric, symbolic, and mixed stimuli, the character length of the stimulus is varied. Four levels of character stimulus length are present: two, five, seven, and nine. Three scores are produced: proportion correct, grand mean decision time, and movement time.

Target identification test.   In this test, each item shows a target object near the top of the screen and three color-labeled stimuli in a row near the bottom of the screen. The task is to identify which of the three stimuli represents the same object as the target and to press, as quickly as possible, the button (BLUE, YELLOW, OR WHITE) that corresponds to that object. The objects shown are based on military vehicles and aircraft as shown on the standard set of flashcards used to train soldiers to recognize equipment being used by various nations (see Fig. 5.3). Several parameters were varied in the stimulus presentation. In addition to type of object, the position of the correct response (left or right side of the screen), the orientation of the

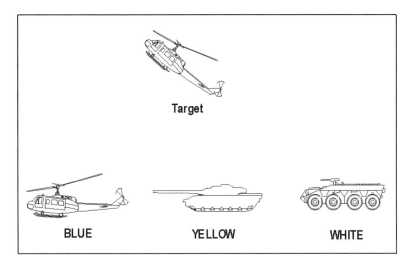

FIG. 5.3.   Sample target identification test item.

target object (facing in the same direction as the stimuli or in the opposite direction), variation in the angle of rotation (from horizontal) of the target object, and the size of the target object were incorporated into the test. Three scores are produced: proportion correct, grand mean decision time, and movement time.

Number Operations

This construct involves the ability to perform, quickly and accurately, simple arithmetic operations such as addition, subtraction, multiplication, and division.

Number memory test.   This test was modeled after a number memory test developed by Raymond Christal at AFHRL. Respondents are presented with a single number on the computer screen. After studying the number, the individual is instructed to push a button to receive the next part of the problem. When the button is pressed, the first part of the problem disappears and another number, along with an operation term such as "Add 9" or "Subtract 6" then appears. Once the test taker has combined the first number with the second, he or she must press another button to receive the third part of the problem. This procedure continues until a solution to the problem is presented. The individual must then indicate whether the solution presented is right or wrong. Test items vary with respect to number of

parts—four, six, or eight—contained in the single item, and the interstim-
ulus delay period. This test is not a "pure" measure of number operations,
because it also is designed to bring short-term memory into play. Three
scores are produced: proportion correct, grand mean decision time, and
movement time.

Kyllonen and Christal (1990) used a number memory test like this one
as a marker for Working Memory Capacity (WMC), the central construct
involved in information- processing. Kyllonen and Christal (1988) defined
working memory as the part of memory that is highly active or accessible
at a given moment. WMC is the ability to process and store information
simultaneously on complex tasks, regardless of content. That is, WMC is
general over types of processing, such as numerical and linguistic. Kyllonen
and Christal (1990) found that the General Reasoning factor correlated .80
to .88 with WMC in four large studies that used a variety of reasoning and
WMC measures.

Psychomotor Precision

This construct reflects the ability to make the muscular movements
necessary to adjust or position a machine control mechanism. The ability applies both to anticipatory movements where the stimulus condition
is continuously changing in an unpredictable manner and to controlled
movements where stimulus conditions change in a predictable fashion.
Psychomotor precision thus encompasses two of the ability constructs identified by Fleishman and his associates: control precision and rate control
(Fleishman, 1967).

Target tracking test 1.   This test was designed to measure control
precision, and the AAF Rotary Pursuit Test served as a model. For each
trial, the respondent is shown a path consisting entirely of vertical and
horizontal line segments. At the beginning of the path is a target box, and
centered in the box are crosshairs. As the trial begins, the target starts to
move along the path at a constant rate of speed. The respondent's task is to
keep the crosshairs centered within the target at all times. The respondent
uses a joystick, controlled with one hand, to control movement of the
crosshairs.

Item parameters include the speed of the crosshairs, the maximum speed
of the target, the difference between crosshairs and target speeds, the total
length of the path, the number of line segments comprising the path, and
the average amount of time the target spends traveling along each segment.

Two kinds of scores were investigated: tracking accuracy and improvement in tracking performance. Two accuracy measures were investigated: time on target and distance from the center of crosshairs to the center of the target. The test program computes the distance from the crosshairs to the center of the target several times each second, and then averages these distances to derive an overall accuracy score for that trial. Subsequently, to remove positive skew, each trial score was transformed by taking the square root of the average distance. These trial scores were then averaged to determine an overall tracking accuracy score.

Target shoot test.   This test was modeled after several compensatory and pursuit tracking tests used by the AAF in the Aviation Psychology Program (e.g., the Rate Control Test). For the Target Shoot Test, a target box and crosshairs appear in different locations on the computer screen. The target moves about the screen in an unpredictable manner, frequently changing speed and direction. The test taker controls movement of the crosshairs via a joystick and the task is to move the crosshairs into the center of the target, and to "fire" at the target. The score is the distance from the center of the crosshairs to the center of the target.

Several item parameters were varied from trial to trial, including the maximum speed of the crosshairs, the average speed of the target, the difference between crosshairs and target speeds, the number of changes in target speed (if any), the number of line segments comprising the path of each target, and the average amount of time required for the target to travel each segment.

Three scores were obtained for each trial. Two were measures of accuracy: (a) the distance from the center of the crosshairs to the center of the target at the time of firing, and (b) whether the subject "hit" or "missed" the target. The third score reflected speed and was measured by the time from trial onset until the subject fired at the target.

Multilimb Coordination

This ability does *not* apply to tasks in which trunk movement must be integrated with limb movements. It refers to tasks where the body is at rest (e.g., seated or standing) while two or more limbs are in motion.

Target tracking test 2.   This test is very similar to the Two-Hand Coordination Test developed by the AAF. For each trial, the respondent is shown a path consisting entirely of vertical and horizontal lines. At the beginning of the path is a target box, and centered in the box are crosshairs. As the trial begins, the target starts to move along the path at a constant rate of speed. The respondent manipulates two sliding resistors to control movement of the crosshairs. One resistor controls movement in the horizontal plane, the other in the vertical plane. The examinees's task is to keep the crosshairs centered within the target at all times. This test and Target Tracking Test 1 are virtually identical except for the nature of the required control manipulation.

Movement Judgment

Movement judgment is the ability to judge the relative speed and direction of one or more moving objects to determine where those objects will be at a given point in time and/or when those objects might intersect.

Cannon shoot test.   The Cannon Shoot Test measures the ability to fire at a moving target in such a way that the shell hits the target when the target crosses the cannon's line of fire. At the beginning of each trial, a stationary cannon appears on the video screen; the starting position varies from trial to trial. The cannon is "capable" of firing a shell, which travels at a constant speed on each trial. Shortly after the cannon appears, a circular target moves onto the screen. This target moves in a constant direction at a constant rate of speed throughout the trial, though the speed and direction vary from trial to trial. The respondent's task is to push a response button to fire the shell so that the shell intersects the target when the target crosses the shell's line of fire.

Three parameters determine the nature of each test trial: the angle of the target movement relative to the position of the cannon, the distance from the cannon to the impact point, and the distance from impact point to fire point.

Pilot and Field Testing the New Measures

Pilot and field testing allowed the opportunity to (a) improve and shorten the battery based on psychometric information, (b) investigate practice effects on the computer test measures, and (c) learn more about the relationship between video game experience and computer test performance. During pilot testing each instrument was administered one or more times to various small samples from Fort Campbell, Kentucky; Fort Carson, Colorado; and Fort Lewis, Washington. Based on feedback from the respondents, refinements were made in directions, format, and item wording. A few items were dropped because of extreme item statistics. However, the basic structure of each instrument remained the same until more data from the larger scale field tests became available.

The final step before the full Concurrent Validation (CVI) was a more systematic series of field tests of all the predictor measures, using larger samples. The outcome of the field test/revision process was the final form of the predictor battery (i.e., the Trial Battery) to be used in CVI. The full Pilot Trial Battery was administered at Fort Knox ($N = 300$) to evaluate the psychometric characteristics of all the measures and to analyze the covariance of the measures with each other and with the ASVAB. In addition, the measures were readministered to part of the sample to provide data for estimating the test-retest reliability of the measures. Finally, part of the sample received practice on some of the computer measures and were then retested to obtain an estimate of the effects of practice on scores on computer measures.

Psychometric and Factor-Analytic Data

In the field tests, the entire Pilot Trial Battery (not just the ability tests) required approximately 6.5 hours of administration time. However, the Trial Battery had to fit in a 4-hour time slot. Using all the accumulated information, particularly psychometric and factor-analytic data from the field test, revisions to shorten the ability test components of battery were made during a series of decision meetings attended by project staff and the Scientific Advisory Group.

Paper-and-pencil tests.   The Spatial Visualization construct was measured by three tests: Assembling Objects, Object Rotation, and Shapes. The Shapes Test was dropped because the previous evidence of validity for predicting job performance was judged to be less impressive than for the other two tests. Eight items were dropped from the Assembling Objects Test by eliminating items that were very difficult or very easy, or had low item-total correlations. The time limit was not changed, which made it more a power test than before. For the Spatial Scanning construct, the Path Test was dropped and the Mazes Test was retained with no changes. Mazes was a shorter test, showed higher test-retest reliabilities (.71 vs. .64), and gain scores, in a test retest comparison, were lower (.24 vs. .62 SD units). Reasoning Test 1 was evaluated as the better of the two tests for Figural Reasoning because it had higher reliabilities as well as a higher uniqueness estimate when compared to ASVAB. It was retained with no item or time limit changes, and Reasoning Test 2 was dropped. Of the three tests that measured the Spatial Orientation construct, Orientation Test 1 was dropped because it showed lower test-retest reliabilities (.67 vs. .80 and .84) and higher gain scores (.63 SD vs. .11 and .08 SD).

Computer-administered tests.   Besides the changes made to specific tests, several general changes designed to save time were made to the computer battery. Most instructions were shortened considerably. Whenever the practice items had a correct response, the participant was given feedback. Because virtually every test was shortened, rest periods were eliminated. Finally, the total time allowed for subjects to respond to a test item (i.e., response time limit) was set at 9 seconds for all reaction time tests.

None of the computer-administered tests were dropped, but a number of changes were made to specific tests. In some cases, items were added to increase reliability (e.g., Choice Reaction Time). Whenever it appeared that a test could be shortened without jeopardizing reliability, it was shortened (e.g., Perceptual Speed and Accuracy, Short Term Memory, Target Identification).

Practice Effects on Selected Computer Test Scores

Practice effects were analyzed via a 2×2 design with the two factors referred to as Group (practice vs. no practice) and Time (first administration vs. second administration). The results of the analyses of variance for the five tests included in the practice effects research showed only one statistically significant practice effect, the Mean Log Distance score on Target Tracking Test 2. There were three statistically significant findings for time, indicating that scores did change with a second testing, whether or not practice trials intervened between the two tests. Finally, the Omega squared value indicated that relatively small amounts of test score variance are accounted for by the Group, Time, or Time by Group factors. These data suggest that the practice intervention was not a particularly strong one. The average gain score for the two groups across the five dependent measures was only .09 standard deviations.

Correlations with Video Game-Playing Experience

Field test subjects were asked the question, "In the last couple years, how much have you played video games?" The five possible alternatives ranged from "You have never played video games" to "You have played video games almost every day" and were given scores of 1 to 5, respectively. The mean was 2.99, SD was 1.03 ($N = 256$), and the test-retest reliability was .71 ($N = 113$).

The 19 correlations of this item with the computer test scores ranged from $-.01$ to $+.27$, with a mean of .10. A correlation of .12 is significant at alpha $= .05$. These findings were interpreted as showing a small, but significant, relationship of video game-playing experience to the more "game-like" tests in the battery.

The Trial Battery

The final array of experimental cognitive, perceptual, and psychomotor tests for the Trial Battery is shown in Table 5.8. The Trial Battery was designed to be administered in a period of 4 hours during the Concurrent Validation phase of Project A, approximately 2 hours and 10 minutes of which was allocated to the spatial and perceptual/psychomotor ability tests. The remainder of this chapter briefly describes the basic predictor scores

TABLE 5.8
Spatial, Perceptual, and Psychomotor Measures in the Trial Battery

Tests	Number of Items	Time Required (minutes)
Spatial paper-and-pencil tests		
Reasoning test	30	12
Object rotation test	90	7.5
Orientation test	24	10
Maze test	24	5.5
Map test	20	12
Assembling objects test	32	16
Computer-administered tests		
Demographics	2	4
Reaction time 1	15	2
Reaction time 2	30	3
Memory test	36	7
Target tracking test 1	18	8
Perceptual speed and accuracy test	36	6
Target tracking test 2	18	7
Number memory test	28	10
Cannon shoot test	36	7
Target identification test	36	4
Target shoot test	30	5

that were derived from the Trial Battery based on analyses of CVI data. In Chapter 10, they will be compared to the basic predictor scores that were derived on the basis of the longitudinal validation data.

Psychometric Properties of the Trial Battery

The reliability estimates and uniqueness (from ASVAB) coefficients for scores on the cognitive, perceptual, and psychomotor tests appear in Table 5.9. In general, the battery exhibited quite good psychometric properties, with the exception of low reliabilities on some computer-administered test scores. As expected, the low reliabilities tended to be characteristic of the proportion correct scores on computer-administered perceptual tests. That is, the items can almost always be answered correctly if the examinee takes enough time, which restricts the range on the proportion correct scores. However, it increases the variance (and reliability) for the decision time scores.

Factor Structure

Factor-analysis of spatial test scores.   When factored alone, the six spatial tests form two factors (Peterson, Russell et al., 1992). Object Rotation and the Maze Test (speeded tests) load on the second factor and all other tests load on the first. Moreover, the distinction between the two factors appears to be power versus speed. When factored with other cognitive measures, the spatial tests consistently form a single factor of their own. Indeed, the four ASVAB factors identified in previous research (Kass et al., 1983; Welsh, Watson et al., 1990)—Verbal, Technical, Number, and Speed—emerged along with one spatial factor.

Factor-analysis of computer test scores.   Several findings emerged consistently across factor analyses of Pilot Trial Battery and Trial Battery data (Peterson, Russell et al., 1992). First, Target Tracking 1, Target Tracking 2, Target Shoot, and Cannon Shoot consistently form one factor: Psychomotor. Second, the pooled movement time variable usually has loadings split across three or four factors, although its largest loading is on the Psychomotor factor. Third, in factor analyses that include ASVAB subtests, one cross-method factor emerges, combining computer test scores on Number Memory with ASVAB Math Knowledge and Arithmetic Reasoning scores. In factor analyses without the ASVAB, Number Memory

TABLE 5.9

Psychometric Properties of Spatial, Perceptual, and Psychomotor Tests in the Trial Battery ($N = 9100$–9325)

Test	N	Mean	SD	Split-Half Reliability[a]	Test-Retest Reliability[b]	Uniqueness Estimate
Paper-and-Pencil Tests						
Assembling objects	9,343	23.3	6.71	.91	.70	.65
Object rotation	9,345	62.4	19.06	.99	.72	.81
Maze	9,344	16.4	4.77	.96	.70	.74
Orientation	9,341	11.0	6.18	.89	.70	.60
Map	9,343	7.7	5.51	.90	.78	.46
Reasoning	9,332	19.1	5.67	.87	.65	.54
Computer-Administered Tests[c]						
Target tracking 1						
Mean log(distance + 1)	9,251	2.98	.49	.98	.74	.82
Target tracking 2						
Mean log(distance + 1)	9,239	3.70	.51	.98	.85	.79
Target Shoot						
Mean log(distance + 1)	8,892	2.17	.24	.74	.37	.70
Mean time to fire	8,892	235.39	47.78	.85	.58	.78
Cannon shoot						
Mean absolute time	9,234	43.94	9.57	.65	.52	.56
Simple reaction time (SRT)						
Decision time mean	9,255	31.84	14.82	.88	.23	.87
Proportion correct	9,255	.98	.04	.46	.02	.44
Choice reaction time (CRT)						
Decision time mean	9,269	40.93	9.77	.97	.69	.93
Proportion correct	9,269	.98	.03	.57	.23	.55
Short-term memory (STM)						
Decision time mean	9,149	87.72	24.03	.96	.66	.93
Proportion correct	9,149	.89	.08	.60	.41	.55
Perceptual speed & accuracy (PSA)	9,244	236.91	63.38	.94	.63	.92
Decision time mean	9,244	.87	.08	.65	.51	.61
Proportion correct						
Target identification (TID)	9,105	193.65	63.13	.97	.78	.83
Decision time mean	9,105	.91	.07	.62	.40	.59
Proportion correct						
Number memory	9,099	160.70	42.63	.88	.62	.67
Final response time mean	9,099	142.84	55.24	.95	.47	.85
Input response time mean	9,099	233.10	79.72	.93	.73	.66
Operations time mean[d]	9,099	.90	.09	.59	.53	.39
Proportion correct						
SRT-CRT-STM-PSA-TID						
Pooled movement timed[d]	8,962	33.61	8.03	.74	.66	.71

[a] Split-half reliability estimates were calculated using the odd-even procedure with the Spearman-Brown correction for test length.

[b] Test-retest reliability estimates are based on a sample of 468 to 487 subjects. The test-retest interval was 2 weeks.

[c] Time scores are in hundredths of seconds. Logs are natural logs.

[d] Coefficient Alpha reliability estimates, not split-half.

scores form their own factor after four or five factors are extracted. Fourth, the Simple Reaction Time and Choice Reaction Time time scores form a factor—Basic Speed, and the proportion correct scores on those same tests form a factor—Basic Accuracy. Fifth, the Perceptual Speed and Accuracy (PSA) time score, PSA proportion correct, the Target Identification (TID) time score, and TID proportion correct often load together. Finally, the Short-Term Memory time score loads on the Basic Speed factor, and Short-Term Memory proportion correct loads with the more complex perceptual tests scores. When larger numbers of factors are extracted, Short-Term Memory scores form a factor.

Concurrent Validation Results

The CVI validation results were presented in McHenry, Hough, Toquam, Hanson, and Ashworth (1990) and will not be repeated here. However, Chapter 13 will present a comparison of the concurrent versus longitudinal validation results.

SUMMARY

This chapter described the development of the spatial ability, perceptual ability, and psychomotor ability tests that were constructed as part of Project A. The constructs selected for measurement within each domain were identified on the basis of (a) previous research on the latent structure of individual differences in that domain, (b) previous validation research relevant for the Army selection and classification setting, and (c) the judged probability that a well developed measure of the construct would add incremental selection/classification validity to the existing ASVAB. Six paper-and-pencil spatial tests and 10 computer administered psychomotor tests, yielding 26 separate scores (see Table 5.4), resulted from the development process. For purposes of the Concurrent Validation (CVI), the formation of the basic predictor composite scores for the ASVAB, the spatial tests, and the computerized tests relied principally on the factor analyses within each domain, as interpreted by the project staff and the Scientific Advisory Group. They were as follows.

- The nine ASVAB subtests were combined into four composite scores: Technical, Quantitative, Verbal, and Speed. In computing the Technical composite score, the Electronics Information subtest received a weight of one-half unit while the Mechanical Comprehension and Auto-Shop subtests received unit weights. This was done because a factor analysis indicated that the loading of the Electronics Information subtest on the Technical factor of the ASVAB was only about one-half as large as the loading of the Mechanical Comprehension and Auto-Shop subtests.

- The six spatial tests were all highly intercorrelated and were combined into a single composite score.
- Seven weighted composite scores were computed from the 20 perceptual-psychomotor test scores from the computerized battery as follows:
  — Psychmotor: all scores on Target Tracking 1, Target Tracking 2, Cannon Shoot, and Target Shoot.
  — Number Speed and Accuracy: all scores on the Number Memory Test.
  — Basic Speed: Simple and Choice Reaction Time decision time scores.
  — Basic Accuracy: Simple and Choice Reaction Time proportion correct scores.
  — Perceptual Speed: Decision time scores on Perceptual Speed and Accuracy and Target Identification.
  — Perceptual Accuracy: Proportion correct scores on Perceptual Speed and Accuracy and Target Identification.
- Movement Time: Movement time pooled across the five perceptual tests.

All subsequent CVI predictor validation analyses were based on these seven basic scores obtained from the new tests (i.e., one score from the spatial tests and six scores from the computerized measures). The CVI results are reported in McHenry et al. (1990). Changes to the predictor measures and to the predictor composite scores, for purposes of the Longitudinal Validation, are described in Chapter 10.

6

Assessment of Personality, Temperament, Vocational Interests, and Work Outcome Preferences

Leaetta Hough, Bruce Barge, and John Kamp

Project A invested much effort in the development of selection and classification predictor measures that were "different" than cognitive ability tests. They were collectively referred to as "noncognitive" measures, although this was something of a misnomer because *all* the predictor measures developed by the project require some kind of cognitive activity on the part of the respondent. As discussed in Chapter 4, the search for potentially useful noncognitive constructs led to an array of personality, biographical, interest, and motivational variables that were deemed worthy of predictor development. This chapter describes the development of the three paper-and-pencil inventories (personality/biographical, vocational interest, and work outcome preference) that were subsequently used to supplement the cognitive, perceptual, and psychomotor ability measures in the Project A predictor batteries.

PERSONALITY AND BIOGRAPHICAL
DATA: THE ABLE

A Brief History of Personality Measurement

This section describes the development of a personality/biographical inventory, the "Assessment of Background and Life Experiences" (ABLE). When Project A started, much of the scientific community believed that personality variables had little theoretical merit and were of little practical use for personnel decision making (Hough, 1989). In his 1965 book, Guion (1965) stated, "One cannot survey the literature on the use of personality tests without becoming thoroughly disenchanted" (p. 353), and concluded, "In view of the problems, both technical and moral, one must question the wisdom and morality of using personality tests as instruments of decision in employment procedures" (p. 379). In that same year, Guion and Gottier (1965), after a thorough review of the literature concluded that, though personality variables have criterion-related validity more often than can be expected by chance, no generalized principles could be discerned from the results. Just a few years earlier, Dunnette (1962) had urged a moratorium on construction of new personality tests until those already available were better utilized. However, Guion and Gottier (1965) noted that many studies they reviewed had used inadequate research designs and that much of the research had been badly conceived. This part of the review was widely ignored in favor of the much more critical comments in the Guion and Gottier article and Guion book (Dunnette & Hough, 1993).

A second wave of negative judgments about personality variables occurred when Walter Mischel (1968) published his influential book that started an intense debate about the nature of traits. Mischel asserted that evidence for the apparent cross-situational consistency of behavior was a function of the use of self-report as the measurement approach. Traits were an illusion. He proposed "situationism" as an alternative, stating that behavior is explained more by differences in situations than differences in people.

In addition to the theoretical challenges and the perceived lack of empirical evidence to support the use of personality variables, both academics and practitioners also worried about the intentional distortion of self descriptions particularly with regard to using self-report measures in an applicant setting. Equally important was the lay community's general negative perception of personality inventories. People resented being asked to respond to items they considered to be offensive. Such was the situation in the early 1980s when Project A began.

Identification of Relevant Personality Constructs as Predictors of Performance

Although Guion's review of criterion-related validities of personality scales had found little evidence for the usefulness of personality scales for predicting job performance, the underlying predictor-criterion relationships may have been obscured because those reviews had summarized validity coefficients across both predictor (personality) and criterion constructs. More specifically, we hypothesized that (a) if an adequate taxonomy of existing personality scales were developed and (b) existing validity coefficients were summarized within both predictor and criterion constructs, then meaningful and useful criterion-related validities would emerge.

Development of an Initial Taxonomy of Personality Scales

At the time the project began, no single well-accepted taxonomy of personality variables existed. Among researchers who had used factor analysis to explore the personality domain, Cattell, Eber, and Tatsuoka (1970) claimed that their list of 24 primary factors was exhaustive, whereas Guilford (1975) suggested 58. Research in the early 1960s by Tupes and Christal (1961) suggested that a smaller number of more general or higher order sources of variation accounted for the diverse concepts tapped by personality scales. They found that five basic dimensions, which they labeled Surgency, Agreeableness, Dependability, Emotional Stability, and Culture, emerged from factor analyses of peer ratings and nominations. Norman (1963) confirmed these same five dimensions, and some years later, Goldberg (1981) endorsed the primacy of these five higher order dimensions in the self-report domain.

We started with this five-category taxonomy, now known as the Big Five, but soon moved to Hogan's (1982) six-category taxonomy. Four of these, Agreeableness, Dependability, Emotional Stability, and Intellectance, are aligned with the Tupes and Christal (1961) factors. The other two dimensions, Ascendancy and Sociability, are components of Tupes' and Christal's Surgency factor. The project staff's previous experience using personality variables to predict job performance suggested that Ascendancy and Sociability correlated with job performance criteria differently.

This six-category taxonomy was then used to classify existing personality scales. The scales included in the taxonomic analysis were the 146 content scales of the 12 multiscale temperament inventories, which were, at the time, the most widely used in basic and applied research: the California Psychological Inventory (CPI; Gough, 1975), the Comrey Personality Scales (CPS; Comrey, 1970), the Multidimensional Personality Questionnaire (MPQ; Tellegen, 1982), the Edwards Personal Preference Schedule (EPPS; Edwards, 1959), the Eysenck Personality Questionnaire (EPQ; Eysenck & Eysenck, 1975), the Gordon Personal Profile-Inventory (GPPI; Gordon, 1978), the Guilford-Zimmerman Temperament Survey (GZTS; Guilford, Zimmerman, & Guilford, 1976), the Jackson Personality Inventory (JPI; Jackson, 1976), the Minnesota Multiphasic Personality Inventory (MMPI; W. Dahlstrom, Welsh, & L. Dahlstrom, 1972, 1975), the Omnibus Personality Inventory (OPI; Heist & Yonge, 1968), the Personality Research Form (PRF; Jackson, 1967), and the Sixteen Personality Factor Questionnaire (16 PF; Cattell et al., 1970).

The subsequent literature search attempted to locate entries for as many of the 146 x 146 between-scale correlation matrix cells as possible. Primary sources were test manuals, handbooks, and research reports. Just over 50% (5,313) of the 10,585 possible entries in the 146 x 146 matrix were obtained (Kamp & Hough, 1988).

Each scale was tentatively assigned to one of the six construct categories on the basis of item content, available factor-analytic results, and an evaluation of its correlations with other scales. Inspection of the resulting within-category correlation matrices allowed identification of scales whose relationships fit prior expectations poorly. For each of these scales, calculation of mean correlations with the scales constituting the other construct categories allowed classification into a more appropriate category.

A total of 117 of the 146 scales (80%) were classified into the six construct categories. The remaining 29 were classified as miscellaneous. The means and standard deviations of the within-category and between-category correlations, as well as the number of correlations on which these values are based, are given in Table 6.1. The mean correlations display an appropriate convergent-discriminant structure.

A Criterion Taxonomy

As mentioned above, it was hypothesized that if validities were summarized within both predictor and criterion constructs rather than across constructs, meaningful relationships would emerge. The initial taxonomy of criteria that was used consisted of the following:[1]

---

[1] This was done before Project A's criterion development work was completed.

TABLE 6.1

Mean Within-Category and Between-Category Correlations
of Temperament Scales

		Potency	Adjustment	Agreeableness	Dependability	Intellectance	Affiliation	Misc.
Potency	Mean	.46						
	SD	.16						
	N	146						
Adjustment	Mean	.20	.43					
	SD	.18	.19					
	N	321	165					
Agreeableness	Mean	.04	.24	.37				
	SD	.17	.16	.14				
	N	173	162	44				
Dependability	Mean	−.08	.13	.06	.34			
	SD	.16	.20	.17	.18			
	N	286	276	166	121			
Intellectance	Mean	.12	.02	.04	−.12	.40		
	SD	.15	.14	.16	.18	.19		
	N	175	193	94	162	52		
Affiliation	Mean	.09	.00	.10	.08	−.14	.33	
	SD	.21	.16	.17	.14	.15	.16	
	N	157	150	98	160	84	45	
Miscellaneous	Mean	.09	.12	.02	.02	.04	−.04	.05
	SD	.17	.18	.18	.18	.17	.15	.20
	N	392	419	215	361	242	208	246

Note: From "Criterion-Related Validities of Personality Constructs and the Effect of Response Distortion on those Validities" [Monograph] by Hough, Eaton, Dunnette, Kamp, and McCloy, 1990, *Journal of Applied Psychology*, 75, p. 584. Copyright 1990 by American Psychological Association. Reprinted by permission.

1. Job Proficiency: overall job performance, technical proficiency, advancement, job knowledge.
2. Training Success: instructor ratings, grades, field test scores, completion of training.
3. Educational Success: high school or college grades or grade point average, college attendance.
4. Commendable Behavior: employee records of commendations, disciplinary actions, reprimands, demotions, involuntary discharge, ratings of effort, hard work.
5. Law Abiding Behavior: theft, delinquent offenses, criminal offenses, imprisonment.

Review of Criterion-Related Validity Studies: Emergence of a Nine-Factor Personality Taxonomy

The literature search located 237 usable studies involving a total of 339 independent sample estimates of validity, which were categorized into the above predictor and criterion categories. The validity estimates within each predictor-criterion construct combination were summarized in terms of their mean and variability. One of the most important conclusions was that the highest criterion-related validities occurred for scales that had been classified into the Miscellaneous category.

An examination of the scales in the Miscellaneous category suggested that three additional constructs might be useful for summarizing the validities: Achievement, Locus of Control, and Masculinity (Rugged Individualism). They were added to the personality taxonomy, thereby increasing the number of personality constructs to nine. The definitions of the constructs in this nine-factor taxonomy are as follows:

1. **Affiliation:** The degree of sociability one exhibits. Being outgoing, participative, and friendly versus shy and reserved.
2. **Potency:** The degree of impact, influence, and energy that one displays. Being forceful, persuasive, optimistic and vital versus lethargic and pessimistic.
3. **Achievement:** The tendency to strive for competence in one's work.
4. **Dependability:** The person's characteristic degree of conscientiousness. Being disciplined, well-organized, planful, and respectful of laws and regulations, versus unreliable, rebellious, and contemptuous of laws and regulations.
5. **Adjustment:** The amount of emotional stability and stress tolerance that one possesses.
6. **Agreeableness:** The degree of pleasantness versus unpleasantness exhibited in interpersonal relations. Being tactful, helpful, and not defensive, versus touchy, defensive, alienated, and generally contrary.
7. **Intellectance:** The degree of culture that one possesses and displays. Being imaginative, quick-witted, curious, socially polished, and independent minded versus artistically insensitive, unreflective, and narrow.
8. **Rugged Individualism:** Refers to what is often regarded as masculine rather than feminine characteristics and values. Being decisive, action-oriented, independent, and rather unsentimental versus

empathetic, helpful, sensitive to criticism and personal rather than impersonal.

9. **Locus of Control:** One's characteristic belief in the amount of control he/she has or people have over rewards and punishments.

Criterion-related validities of these nine personality constructs for the five criteria, as well as the validities for all personality scales combined across constructs, are shown in Table 6.2. The validities are not corrected for unreliability or restriction in range. The best overall predictor appears to be Achievement, a construct that is not one of the Big Five. Potency, Achievement, and Locus of Control correlate .10 (uncorrected) or higher with Job Proficiency. However, of the five criteria examined, Job Proficiency is predicted least well. Achievement and Dependability correlate .33 and .23 with the Commendable Behavior factor. Dependability and Achievement correlate .58 and .42, respectively, with Law-Abiding Behavior, which is the best predicted of all the criterion factors. The only personality construct that appears to have little or no validity for any of the criteria in Table 6.2 is Affiliation. Table 6.2 summarizes criterion-related validities of personality variables from both concurrent and predictive validity studies. An important additional finding (not shown in the table) was that when the data are examined separately for predictive and concurrent validity studies, the pattern of results and the conclusions are the same.

In summary, these data provided considerable evidence that personality scales should be developed for Project A. The personality constructs targeted as potentially important predictors of performance in the Army were Potency, Adjustment, Agreeableness, Dependability, Achievement, and Locus of Control. The expert rating study described in Chapter 4 also indicated that these personality constructs warranted measurement. In addition, the construct Rugged Individualism was targeted for measurement because of evidence of its usefulness in predicting combat effectiveness (Egbert, Meeland, Cline, Forgy, Spickler, & Brown, 1958). However, the items written to measure this construct were ultimately included in the interest inventory (described later in this chapter).

ABLE Scale Development

The overall scale development effort was construct oriented, and a combination of rational and internal consistency scale construction strategies was used to write and revise the items forming each scale. Each item has

TABLE 6.2
Summary of Criterion-Related Validities

Personality Construct	Job Proficiency			Training Success			Educational Success			Commendable Behavior			Law-Abiding Behavior		
	No. r	Sum of Sample	Mean r	No. r	Sum of Sample	Mean r	No. r	Sum of Sample	Mean r	No. r	Sum of Sample	Mean r	No. r	Sum of Sample	Mean r
Affiliation	23	3,390	.00	—	—	—	9	2,953	.01	—	—	—	10	29,590	.29
Potency	274	65,876	.10	70	8,389	.07	128	63,057	.12	13	53,045	.08	2	5,918	.42
Achievement	28	2,811	.15	9	1,160	.21	31	12,639	.29	2	4,144	.33	22	25,867	.58
Dependability	141	46,116	.08	34	4,710	.11	42	18,661	.12	44	87,560	.23	15	36,210	.41
Adjustment	182	35,148	.09	69	8,685	.12	162	70,588	.20	6	20,555	.15	—	—	—
Agreeableness	87	22,060	.05	7	988	.08	15	7,330	.01	4	24,259	.08	—	—	—
Intellectance	46	11,297	.01	35	8,744	.02	8	3,628	.13	1	747	.24	3	6,152	-.02
Rugged individualism	28	3,007	.08	11	1,614	.03	27	12,358	-.02	1	7,923	.00	—	—	—
Locus of control	15	12,580	.11	2	225	.28	1	50	.32	1	7,666	.13	—	—	—
All personality constructs	824	202,285	.08	237	34,515	.08	423	191,264	.15	72	205,899	.16	52	103,737	.39

Note: Correlations are not corrected for unreliability or restriction in range. From "Development of personality measures to supplement selection decisions" (p. 367) by L. M. Hough, 1989, in B. J. Fallon, H. P. Pfister, & J. Brebner (Eds.), *Advances in Industrial Organizational Psychology,* Elsevier Science Publishers B.V. (North-Holland). Copyright 1989 by Elsevier Science Publishers B.V. Adapted by permission.

118

three response options that reflect the continuum defined by the construct. To prevent acquiescence response bias, however, the direction of scoring differs from item to item.

Personality/temperament and biodata items tend to differ from each other along the sign/sample continuum described by Wernimont and J.P. Campbell (1968). Biodata items are often suggested to be samples of past behavior. Temperament items are more often a sign, or an indicator, of a predisposition to behave in certain ways. Biodata measures have repeatedly demonstrated criterion-related validities that are among the highest of any of the types of predictors of job performance (see Schmitt, Gooding, Noe, & Kirsch, 1984; and Barge & Hough 1988). The intent was to capitalize on the biodata track record, but the lack of a construct orientation in most biodata research was a significant constraint.

While Owens (1976) and his colleagues had developed biodata scales factor analytically, their scales had not been validated as predictors of on-the-job work behavior. Moreover, the names of their factors, such as Sibling Rivalry, Parental Control versus Freedom, and Warmth of Parental Relationship did not appear to have counterparts in personality taxonomies. However, if biodata and personality scales tapped the same underlying constructs, biodata items could be written to measure personality constructs and thus merge the strengths of the biodata research with the construct orientation of personality theorists.

Early in Project A, the previously mentioned Preliminary Battery of off-the-shelf measures was administered to approximately 1800 enlisted soldiers. Eleven biodata scales from Owens' (1975) Biographical Questionnaire (BQ) and 18 scales from the U.S. Air Force (Alley, Berberich, & Wilbourn, 1977; Alley & Matthews, 1982) Vocational Interest Career Examination (VOICE) were administered as well as four scales from three personality inventories. The personality scales included the Social Potency and Stress Reaction scales of the MPQ (Tellegen, 1982), the Socialization scale of CPI (Gough, 1975), and Locus of Control (Rotter, 1966). The full array of scale scores was factor analyzed and the results suggested that the biodata and personality scales seemed to be measuring the same constructs (see Hough, 1993 for more detail). That is, biodata items/scales appeared to be samples of behavior that are the manifestation of individual difference variables that are also measured by personality items/scales. Consequently, it was concluded that both biodata and personality type items could be used to measure the targeted personality constructs.

An intensive period of item writing ensued and a large pool of candidate items was written. These were reviewed by a panel of project staff and a sample of items was selected for initial inclusion in the ABLE inventory. The principal criteria for item selection were: (a) the item was relevant for measuring a targeted construct, (b) it was clearly written, and (c) the content was "nonobjectionable."

ABLE Construct and Content Scale Definitions

The original design of the ABLE consisted of 10 content scales collectively intended to measure six personality constructs: Potency, Adjustment, Agreeableness, Dependability, Achievement, and Locus of Control. In addition, because it was beyond the purview of Project A to assess Physical Condition with physical ability tests, a self-report measure of physical condition was added to the list of constructs to be measured by ABLE, for a total of 11 content scales. Also, four response validity scales were developed to detect inaccurate self-description: Unlikely Virtues, Poor Impression, Self-Knowledge, and Nonrandom Response. The six constructs and their associated content scales are described below.

Potency. The Potency construct was measured with the *Dominance* and *Energy Level* scales. Dominance was defined as the tendency to seek and enjoy positions of leadership and influence over others. The highly dominant person is forceful and persuasive when adopting such behavior is appropriate. The relatively nondominant person is less inclined to seek leadership positions and is timid about offering opinions, advice, or direction. The Energy Level scale assesses the amount of energy and enthusiasm a person possesses. The person high in energy is enthusiastic, active, vital, optimistic, cheerful, and zesty, and gets things done. The person low in energy is lethargic, pessimistic, and tired.

Achievement. The Achievement construct was measured with the *Self-Esteem* and *Work Orientation* scales. Self-esteem was defined as the degree of confidence a person has in his or her abilities. A person with high self-esteem feels largely successful in past undertakings and expects to succeed in future undertakings. A person with low self-esteem feels incapable and is self-doubting. The Work Orientation scale assesses the tendency to strive for competence in one's work. The work-oriented person works hard, sets high standards, tries to do a good job, endorses the work ethic, and concentrates on and persists in the completion of the task at hand. The less work-oriented person has little ego involvement in his or her work, does not expend much effort, and does not feel that hard work is desirable.

Adjustment. The Adjustment construct was measured with the *Emotional Stability* scale, which assesses the amount of emotional stability and tolerance for stress a person possesses. The well-adjusted person is generally calm, displays an even mood, and is not overly distraught by stressful situations. He or she thinks clearly and maintains composure and rationality in situations of actual or perceived stress. The poorly adjusted person is nervous, moody, and easily irritated, tends to worry a lot, and "goes to pieces" in time of stress.

Agreeableness. The Agreeableness construct was measured with the *Cooperativeness* scale, which assesses the degree of pleasantness versus unpleasantness a person exhibits in interpersonal relations. The agreeable and likable person is pleasant, tolerant, tactful, helpful, not defensive, and is generally easy to get along with. His or her participation in a group adds cohesiveness rather than friction. A disagreeable and unlikable person is critical, fault-finding, touchy, defensive, alienated, and generally contrary.

Dependability. The Dependability construct was measured with three scales: *Traditional Values*, *Nondelinquency*, and *Conscientiousness*. The Traditional Values scale assesses a person's acceptance of societal values. The person who scores high on this scale accepts and respects authority and the value of discipline. The person who scores low on this scale is unconventional or radical and questions authority and other established norms, beliefs, and values. The Nondelinquency scale assesses a person's acceptance of laws and regulations. The person who scores high on this scale is rule abiding, avoids trouble, and is trustworthy and wholesome. The person who scores low on this scale is rebellious, contemptuous of laws and regulations, and neglectful of duty or obligation. The Conscientiousness scale assesses a person's tendency to be reliable. The person who scores high on the Conscientiousness scale is well organized, planful, prefers order, thinks before acting, and holds him- or herself accountable. The person who scores low tends to be careless and disorganized and to act on the spur of the moment.

Locus of Control. The Locus of Control construct was measured with the *Internal Control* scale, which assesses a person's belief in the amount of control people have over rewards and punishments. The person with an internal locus of control believes that there are consequences associated with behavior and that people control what happens to them by what they do. The person with an external locus of control believes that what happens to people is beyond their personal control.

Physical Condition.   The scale designed to tap this construct is called *Physical Condition*. The construct refers to one's frequency and degree of participation in sports, exercise, and physical activity. Individuals high on this dimension actively participate in individual and team sports and/or exercise vigorously several times per week. Those low on this scale participate only minimally in athletics, exercise infrequently, and prefer inactivity or passive activities to physical activities.

ABLE Response Validity Scales

Four response validity scales were developed to detect inaccurate self-descriptions. The rationale for each of them is described below.

Nonrandom Response scale.   The rationale for developing the Nonrandom Response scale was a concern that some respondents, when providing information for "research purposes only," would complete the inventory carelessly or in a random fashion. The items ask (a) about information that all persons are virtually certain to know or (b) about experiences that all persons are virtually certain to have had. The correct options are so obvious that a person responding incorrectly is either inattentive to item content or unable to read or understand the items.

Self-Knowledge scale.   The Self-Knowledge scale consists of items designed to elicit information about how self-aware and introspective the individual is. It was developed because research by Gibbons (1983) and Markus (1983) has shown that people who "know themselves" are able to provide more accurate self-descriptions than people who do not and that this greater accuracy moderates the relationship between self-descriptions and descriptions given by others. Believing that these results might generalize to the relationship between self-reports of personality and job-performance ratings provided by others, we developed a scale of self awareness to allow investigation of its affect on criterion-related validity.

Unlikely Virtues.   The Unlikely Virtues scale is intended to detect intentional distortion in a favorable direction in the volunteer applicant setting. The scale was patterned after the Unlikely Virtues scale of the

MPQ (Tellegen, 1982), the Good Impression scale of the CPI (Gough, 1975), and the L scale of the MMPI (Dahlstrom et al., 1972, 1975).

Poor Impression. The Poor Impression scale was developed to detect intentional distortion in an unfavorable direction in a military draft setting. It consists of items that measure a variety of negative personality constructs. A person who scores high on this scale has thus endorsed a variety of negative characteristics.

Revising the Initial Scales: Pilot and Field Tests

The subsequent development and refinement of the ABLE involved several steps. The first was editorial revision prior to pilot testing. The second was based on feedback and data from a pilot test at Fort Campbell, Kentucky. The third was based on feedback and data from a pilot test at Fort Lewis, Washington. The fourth was based on feedback and data from a field test at Fort Knox, Kentucky.

The editorial changes prior to pilot testing were made by project staff based on reviews of the instrument. This phase resulted in the deletion of 17 items and the revision of 158 items. The revisions were relatively minor. Many of the changes resulted in more consistency across items in format, phrasing, and response options, and made the inventory easier to read and faster to administer.

Fort Campbell pilot test. The initial 285-item inventory was administered to 56 soldiers and both their oral feedback and item responses were used to revise the ABLE. Two statistics were computed for each item: item-total scale correlation and endorsement frequency for each response option.

Thirteen items failed to correlate at least .15 in the appropriate direction with their respective scales. For the substantive scales, there were 63 items for which one or more of the response options were endorsed by fewer than two respondents. Seven items had both low item/total correlations and skewed response option distributions. Items were deleted if they did not "fit well" either conceptually or statistically, or both, with the other items in the scale and with the construct in question. If the item appeared to have a "good fit" but was not clear or did not elicit sufficient variance, it was revised rather than deleted.

The internal consistencies of the ABLE content scales were quite high and the item/scale statistics were reasonable. The participants had very few criticisms or concerns about the ABLE. Several soldiers did note the redundancy of the items on the Physical Condition scale and the 14-item scale was shortened to 9 items.

In addition to the ABLE, four well-established measures of personality were administered to 46 Fort Campbell soldiers to serve as marker variables: the Socialization scale of the CPI (Gough, 1975), the Stress Reaction scale and the Social Potency scale of the MPQ (Tellegen, 1982), and the Locus of Control scale (Rotter, 1966). Each ABLE scale correlated most highly with its appropriate marker variable, and by a wide margin. For example, the ABLE Dominance scale correlates much higher with MPQ Social Potency (.67) than with the other three marker scales, which are not part of the Dominance construct (−.24, .18, .22). Although these results were based on a small sample, they did indicate that the ABLE scales appeared to be measuring the constructs they were intended to measure.

Fort Lewis pilot test.   The revised ABLE was administered to 118 soldiers at Fort Lewis. Data screening reduced the sample to 106.

There were only three items where two of the three response choices were endorsed by fewer than 10% of the respondents (not including response validity scale items). After examining the content of these three items, it was decided to delete one and leave the other two intact. Also, 20 items were revised because one of the three response choices was endorsed by fewer than 10% of the respondents. The means, standard deviations, mean item-total scale correlations, and Hoyt (1941) reliability estimates were calculated for the screened group and the range of values for each statistic was judged to be reasonable and appropriate.

Fort Knox field test.   The revised ABLE, now a 199-item inventory, was administered to 290 soldiers at Fort Knox. Two weeks later, 128 of these soldiers completed the ABLE again. The data were examined for quality of responding (i.e., too much missing data or random responding) and 14 individuals were deleted at Time 1 and 19 at Time 2.

All the ABLE content scales showed substantial variance and high alpha coefficients (median .84, range .70 to .87). The test-retest reliability coefficients were also relatively high (median .79, range .68 to .83), and in most cases are close to the internal consistency estimates, indicating considerable stability.

The response validity scales exhibited the expected distributions. Unlikely Virtues and Self-Knowledge scores were nearly normally distributed with somewhat less variance than the content scales. The Nonrandom Response and Poor Impression scales showed markedly skewed distributions as would be expected for participants who responded attentively and honestly.

There were virtually no changes in mean scores for content scales between the two administrations for content scales. The response validity scales were somewhat more sensitive. However, the mean changes were not large except for the Nonrandom Response score, which went from 7.7 to 7.2 ($SD = .71$). The change in this mean score indicates that more subjects responded less attentively the second time around. Overall, these results were reassuring with respect to the way the content and response validity scales were designed to function.

Psychometric Characteristics of ABLE

The ABLE was part of the larger battery of newly developed Project A instruments (Trial Battery) that was administered during the Concurrent Validation (CVI). Participants were informed that the information would be used for research purposes only and that their responses would not affect their careers in the Army. The data were screened for quality, and the remaining inventories analyzed to determine response option endorsement, item and scale characteristics, structure of the ABLE scales, and correlations with other individual difference measures. Mean scale scores, standard deviations, and factor analyses were also computed separately for protected classes to evaluate the ABLE.

Results of Data Quality Screening

A total of 9,327 ABLE inventories were administered, and 139 were deleted because of excessive missing data, leaving 9,188, which were then screened for random responding. The decision rule was, if the person responded correctly to fewer than six of the eight Nonrandom Response scale items, his or her inventory was deleted. These deletions totaled 684, which represented 7.4% of the sample that survived the overall missing data screen. Slightly more males and minorities were screened out compared to females and whites. There were also slight variations across MOS, but no major differential effects on MOS sample sizes.

Some people conscientiously completed almost all the items, but neglected to answer a few. Consequently, data quality screens/rules were applied at the scale level as well. Inventories that survived the overall missing data and random responding screens were treated as follows:

1. If more than 10% of the items in a scale was missing, the scale score was not computed. Instead, the scale score was treated as missing.
2. If there were missing item responses for a scale, but the percent missing was equal to or less than 10%, then the person's average item response score for that scale was computed and used for the missing response(s).

Descriptive Statistics for ABLE Scales

Table 6.3 shows the number of items, sample size, means, standard deviations, median item-total scale correlations, internal consistency reliability estimates (alpha), and test-retest reliabilities for ABLE scales. The median

TABLE 6.3
ABLE Scale Statistics for Total Group[a]

	No. Items	Mean	SD	Median Item-Total Correlations	Internal Consistency Reliability (Alpha)	Test-Retest Reliability[b]
Able Content Scales						
Emotional stability	17	39.0	5.45	.39	.81	.74
Self-esteem	12	28.4	3.70	.39	.74	.78
Cooperativeness	18	41.9	5.28	.39	.81	.76
Conscientiousness	15	35.1	4.31	.34	.72	.74
Nondelinquency	20	44.2	5.91	.36	.81	.80
Traditional values	11	26.6	3.72	.36	.69	.74
Work orientation	19	42.9	6.06	.41	.84	.78
Internal control	16	38.0	5.11	.39	.78	.69
Energy level	21	48.4	5.97	.38	.82	.78
Dominance	12	27.0	4.28	.44	.80	.79
Physical conditions	6	14.0	3.04	.60	.84	.85
ABLE Response Validity Scales						
Unlikely virtues	11	15.5	3.04	.34	.63	.63
Self-knowledge	11	25.4	3.33	.36	.65	.64
Nonrandom response	8	7.7	0.59	.30	.—	.—
Poor impression	23	1.5	1.85	.20	.63	.61

[a] Total group after screening for missing data and random responding ($N = 8{,}461 - 8{,}559$).
[b] $N = 408$–412 for test retest correlation ($N = 414$ for Non-Random Response test-retest correlation).

item-total scale correlation for the content scales is .39 with a range of .34 to .60. The median internal consistency estimate for the content scales is .81 with a range of .69 to .84. The median test-retest reliability for the content scales is .78 with a range of .69 to .85. The median effect size (ignoring direction of change) for the differences in mean scale scores between Time 1 and Time 2 for the 11 content scales is .03. The ABLE content scales appeared to be psychometrically sound and to measure characteristics that are stable over time.

Internal Structure of ABLE

The intercorrelations among the ABLE content scales for the total group ranged from .05 to .73 with a median intercorrelation of .42. The internal structure of the ABLE was examined via principal component analysis of the scale intercorrelations with varimax rotation. The results for the total group appear in Table 6.4. Seven factors emerged. Similar factors emerged when analyses were performed separately according to ethnic group and gender (see Hough 1993 for more details). The scales loading on the Ascendancy factor are Dominance and Energy Level, which are the two scales intended to measure the Potency construct, as well as Self-Esteem and Work Orientation, the two scales intended to measure the Achievement construct. The four scales that load on the Dependability factor are Traditional Values, Nondelinquency, and Conscientiousness, which are the three scales intended to measure the construct Dependability, as well as Internal Control, the scale intended to measure the construct Locus of Control. The third factor, Adjustment, is made up of Emotional Stability and Cooperativeness, which were each intended to measure separate constructs. Poor Impression, a response validity scale, loads $-.81$ on the Adjustment factor, which is its highest loading. The other three response validity scales, Unlikely Virtues, Self-Knowledge, and Nonrandom Response, each form separate factors, as does the Physical Condition scale.

Examination of Response Distortion

Concern about intentional distortion is especially salient when self-report measures such as the ABLE are included in a selection or placement system. The possibility of response distortion is often cited as one of the main arguments against the use of personality measures in selection and placement. Considerable research has addressed this issue and the evidence is clear. People can, when instructed to do so, distort their responses in the desired direction (Dunnett, Koun, & Barber, 1981; Furnham & Craig, 1987; Hinrichsen, Gryll, Bradley, & Katahn, 1975; Schwab, 1971;

TABLE 6.4

ABLE Scales, Factor Analysis,[a] Total Group

	Factor I Ascendancy	Factor II Dependability	Factor III Social Adjustment	Factor IV Social Desirability	Factor V Self-Knowledge	Factor VI Physical Condition	Factor VII Nonrandom Response	h^2
Dominance	.81	.03	.13	.04	.15	.09	.03	.71
Self-esteem	.80	.12	.28	.05	.14	.07	.03	.76
Work orientation	.70	.50	.05	.16	.06	.13	.01	.79
Energy level	.68	.36	.36	.06	-.01	.19	.00	.77
Traditional values	.08	.82	.16	.13	.09	.02	.04	.73
Conscientiousness	.42	.67	.11	.23	.16	.05	.09	.72
Nondelinquency	.01	.67	.37	.40	.14	-.03	.09	.77
Internal control	.36	.66	.26	-.35	-.06	-.02	-.03	.77
Emotional stability	.48	.04	.74	.00	-.14	.06	.02	.80
Cooperativeness	.25	.33	.63	.26	.22	.02	.09	.70
Poor impression	-.12	-.28	-.81	.08	.07	-.09	-.04	.76
Unlikely virtues	.16	.21	.02	.83	-.09	.02	-.21	.81
Self-Knowledge	.21	.16	-.06	-.07	.92	.05	.01	.93
Physical Condition	.23	.02	-.10	.02	.05	.96	.00	.99
Non-Random Response	.04	.09	.08	-.16	.01	.00	.97	.98
								11.99

[a]Principal component, varimax rotation.

$N = 8,348$

Thornton & Gierasch, 1980; Walker, 1985). This appears to be true regardless of the type of item or scale construction methodology. For example, Waters (1965) reviewed a large number of studies showing that respondents can successfully distort their self descriptions on forced-choice inventories when they are instructed to do so; and Hough, Eaton, Dunnette, Kamp, and McCloy (1990) reviewed several studies that compared the validity of subtle and obvious items and concluded that subtle items are often less valid than obvious items, which may reduce overall scale validity.

The Project A design incorporated experiments on intentional distortion (faking) of noncognitive test responses. The purposes of the ABLE faking studies were to determine (a) the extent to which participants could distort their responses to temperament items when instructed to do so, (b) the extent to which the ABLE response validity scales detect such intentional distortion, and (c) the extent to which distortion might be a problem in an applicant setting.

The evaluation analyses were based on a variety of data collections. One data set was a faking experiment. The ABLE was administered to 245 enlisted soldiers who were tested under different instructional sets (i.e., honest, fake good, fake bad). Another data set consisted of the responses of applicant/soldiers who had been administered the ABLE under applicant-like conditions. These data could be compared to the responses of the soldiers who had completed the ABLE as part of CVI and had no reason to distort their responses.

Faking Experiment

Two hundred forty-five male soldiers were administered the ABLE under one honest and two faking conditions (fake good and fake bad). The significant parts of the instructions were as follows:

> **Fake Good:** Imagine you are at the Military Entrance Processing Station (MEPS) and you want to join the Army. Describe yourself in a way that you think will ensure that the Army selects you.

> **Fake Bad:** Imagine you are at the MEPS and you do not want to join the Army. Describe yourself in a way that you think will ensure that the Army does not select you.

> **Honest:** You are to describe yourself as you really are.

The design was repeated measures with faking and honest conditions counter-balanced. Approximately half the experimental group ($N = 124$)

received the honest instructions and completed the ABLE inventory in the morning. They then received the fake-good or fake-bad instructions and completed ABLE again in the afternoon. The other half ($n = 121$) completed ABLE in the morning with either fake-good or fake-bad instructions, and then completed ABLE again in the afternoon under the honest instructions. The within-subjects factor consisted of two levels: honest responses and faked responses. The first between-subjects factor (set) also consisted of two levels: fake good and fake bad. The second between-subjects factor (order) consisted of two levels, faked responses before honest responses and honest responses before faked responses. This was a 2 x 2 x 2 fixed-factor, completely crossed design and the analysis began with a multivariate analysis of variance (MANOVA). The findings for the interactions are central and the overall Fake x Set interaction for the 11 content scales was statistically significant at $p = .001$ indicating that, when instructed to do so, soldiers did distort their responses. The overall Fake x Set interaction for the response validity scales also was significant, indicating that the response validity scales detected the distortion. In addition, the overall test of significance for the Fake x Set x Order interaction effect was significant for both the content scales and the response validity scales, indicating that the order of conditions in which the participants completed the ABLE inventory affected the results.

Scale means, standard deviations, and relevant effect sizes for the first administration of the ABLE scales for each particular condition are shown in Table 6.5. First-administration results are presented because they reflect more accurately what the usual administrative situation would be in an applicant setting.

The effects of intentional distortion on content scales are clear. The median effect size of differences in ABLE content-scale scores between honest and fake-good conditions was .63. The median effect size of differences in ABLE content scale scores between honest and fake-bad conditions was 2.16. It is clear that individuals distorted their self-descriptions when instructed to do so. The effect was especially dramatic in the fake-bad condition.

Table 6.5 also shows the effect of distortion on the response validity scales. The standard score difference in mean scores on the Unlikely Virtues scale between the honest and fake-good conditions was .87. For the Poor Impression scale, the difference between the honest and fake-bad conditions was 2.78. In the fake-bad condition, the Nonrandom Response and Self-Knowledge scale means were also dramatically different from those in the honest condition.

TABLE 6.5

Effects of Faking on Mean Scores of ABLE Scales

ABLE Scale	Honest[a] (N = 111–119)		Fake Good[a] (N = 46–48)		Fake Bad (N = 40–41)		Effect Size[b]	
							Honest vs. Fake Good	Honest vs. Fake Bad
	Mean	S.D.	Mean	S.D.	Mean	S.D.		
Content scales								
Emotional stability	39.7	5.30	43.2	5.94	16.4	7.40	−.63 (−.14)	2.09 (−.14)
Self esteem	28.4	3.74	31.2	4.58	16.6	4.80	−.66 (−.64)	2.76 (.77)
Cooperativeness	41.3	5.51	43.8	6.62	25.6	8.09	−.41 (.06)	2.30 (.38)
Conscientious	33.0	4.59	35.9	5.77	20.6	6.91	−.56 (−.17)	2.16 (.31)
Nondelinquency	44.0	5.03	47.1	7.93	28.9	8.35	−.47 (.13)	2.25 (.63)
Traditional values	26.3	3.61	28.0	4.35	15.3	4.84	−.44 (−.24)	2.59 (1.00)
Work orientation	41.8	6.30	46.7	7.85	26.2	8.56	−.69 (−.33)	2.10 (.32)
Internal control	38.0	5.32	39.8	6.2	24.7	8.44	−.31 (.03)	1.94 (.22)
Energy level	49.1	6.13	53.9	7.11	29.9	8.75	−.73 (−.12)	2.58 (.45)
Dominance	27.2	4.53	30.4	4.56	16.9	5.71	−.70 (−.63)	2.02 (.32)
Physical condition	14.4	2.84	15.5	2.98	8.5	3.33	−.71 (−.07)	1.93 (.35)
Response validity scales								
Unlikely virtues	14.5	2.85	18.2	5.58	14.7	3.80	−.87	−.07
Self-knowledge	25.3	3.33	25.1	3.68	17.9	4.94	.05	1.78
Nonrandom response	7.6	.63	7.7	.57	2.9	2.48	−.17	3.04
Poor impression	1.4	2.03	1.1	1.65	15.4	8.02	.19	−2.78

[a] Scores are based on persons who responded to the condition of interest first.

[b] Effect size is the standardized difference between the mean scores in the two conditions (i.e., $\bar{x}_1 - \bar{x}_2 \div S.D._{pooled}$).

Note: From "Criterion-Related Validities of Personality Constructs and the Effect of Response Distortion on those validities" [Monograph] by Hough, Eaton, Dunnette, Kamp, and McCloy, 1990, *Journal of Applied Psychology*, 75, p. 588. Copyright 1990 by American Psychological Association. Adapted by permission.

Note: Values in parentheses are the effect sizes when unlikely Virtues or Poor Impression scale scores are regressed out of content scale scores in faking condition.

The Unlikely Virtues and Poor Impression scales were also used, via linear regression, to adjust ABLE content scale scores for faking good and faking bad. Table 6.5 also shows the adjusted mean differences in content scales (in parens) after regressing Unlikely Virtues from the Fake Good scores and Poor Impression from the Fake Bad scores. Table 6.5 shows that these response validity scales can be used to adjust content scales. However, two important unknowns remained: (a) Do the adjustment formulas developed on these data cross validate? and (b) Do they affect criterion-related validity?

Extent of Faking in an Applicant-Like Setting

Although the evidence is clear that people can distort their responses, whether they do in fact distort their responses when applying for a job is a different question. To obtain information about effect of setting on mean scores, ABLE was administered to 126 enlistees at the Minneapolis MEPS just after they were sworn in. Although they were not true "applicants," they were informed that their responses to the inventory would be used to make decisions about their careers in the Army. After completing ABLE, respondents were debriefed, and all questions were answered. After taking the ABLE, each respondent filled out a single-item form prior to debriefing and was asked, "Do you think your answers to these questionnaires will have an effect on decisions that the Army makes regarding your future?" Of the 126 recruits in this sample, 57 responded "yes," 61 said "no," and 8 wrote in that they did not know.

Table 6.6 compares these mean ABLE scale scores with the mean scores of two additional groups: (a) persons who completed the ABLE in the honest condition during the faking experiment and (b) the soldiers who completed ABLE as part of the Trial Battery administration during CVI. Only the people who completed the ABLE at the MEPS had any incentive to distort their self descriptions. These data suggest that intentional distortion may not be a significant problem in this applicant setting.

Summary of ABLE Development

The prevailing wisdom in the early- and mid-1980s was that personality variables had little or no validity for predicting job performance. Our competing hypothesis was that if an adequate taxonomy of personality scales were developed and validity coefficients were summarized within both predictor and criterion constructs, then meaningful criterion-related validities would emerge. A literature review resulted in a nine-factor personality taxonomy, and when criterion-related validities were summarized according to constructs, meaningful and useful validities emerged.

An inventory entitled "Assessment of Background and Life Experiences" (ABLE) was developed and included both personality and biodata items. The ABLE consists of 11 content scales and 4 response validity scales. The median internal consistency (alpha coefficients) of ABLE content scales was .81, with a range of .69 to .84. The median test-retest reliability

TABLE 6.6

Comparison of Mean ABLE Scale Scores of Applicants and Incumbents

	Applicants	Incumbents		
		Honest	Trial Battery	
		Experimental	Sample	Total
ABLE Scale	MEPS[a]	Condition[b]	(CVI)[c]	SD
Content scales				
Emotional stability	39.4	39.7	39.0	5.44
Self esteem	27.5	28.4	28.4	3.70
Cooperativeness	42.1	41.3	41.9	5.28
Conscientiousness	32.8	33.0	35.1	4.31
Nondelinquency	45.3	44.0	44.2	5.90
Traditional values	26.7	26.3	26.6	3.71
Work orientation	41.1	41.8	42.9	6.06
Internal control	39.9	38.0	38.0	5.11
Energy level	46.3	49.1	48.4	5.95
Dominance	25.1	27.2	27.0	4.29
Physical condition	12.9	14.4	14.0	3.04
Response validity scales				
Unlikely virtues	15.5	14.5	15.5	3.03
Self knowledge	23.8	25.3	25.4	3.33
Nonrandom response	7.8	7.6	7.4	1.18
Poor impression	1.0	1.4	1.5	1.85

[a]Sample size ranges from 119 to 125; MEPS = Military Entrance Processing Station.

[b]Sample size ranges from 111 to 119; Scores are based on persons who responded to the honest condition first.

[c]Sample size ranges from 8,461 to 9,188.

Note: From "Criterion-Related Validities of Personality Constructs and the Effect of Response Distortion on those Validities" [Monograph] by Hough, Eaton, Dunnette, Kamp, and McCloy, 1990, *Journal of Applied Psychology, 75*, p. 592. Copyright 1990 by American Psychological Association. Adapted by permission.

coefficient of ABLE content scales was .78, with a range of .69 to .85. Factor analysis of ABLE scales suggested seven underlying factors.

A series of studies on intentional distortion (faking) of ABLE responses indicated that (a) when instructed to do so, people can distort their responses in the desired direction; (b) ABLE response validity scales detect self descriptions that are intentionally distorted; (c) Unlikely Virtues scale scores can be used to adjust content scale scores to reduce variance associated with faking good, and the Poor Impression scale scores can be used to adjust content scale scores to reduce variance associated with faking bad; and (d) intentional distortion did not appear to be a significant problem in an applicant-like setting.

VOCATIONAL INTERESTS: THE AVOICE

Vocational interests are a second major domain of noncognitive variables that were judged to have significant potential for predicting job success. The subsequent development of an interest inventory, the AVOICE, is described below.

A Brief History of Interest Measurement

The first real attempt to assess interests systematically was probably that of E. L. Thorndike, who in 1912 asked 100 college students to rank order their interests as they remembered them in elementary school, high school, and currently. Another significant step occurred during a seminar conducted by C. S. Yoakum at Carnegie Institute of Technology in Pittsburgh in 1919. Graduate students in the seminar wrote approximately 1,000 interest items that formed the basis of many future interest inventories, including the *Strong Vocational Interest Blank* (SVIB, now called the "Strong"; Harmon, Hansen, Borgan, & Hammer, 1994), which was developed by E. K. Strong over a period of several decades beginning in the 1920s. Since 1960, the "Strong" has undergone three major revisions, the most recent in 1994 (see Harmon et al., 1994).

The basic premise of interest measurement is that people who select themselves into a specific occupation have a characteristic pattern of likes and dislikes that is different from people in other occupations and this information can be used to predict future occupational choices. By using comparisons with a general reference sample (e.g., "men-in-general") as the basis for empirically weighting items to differentiate between occupational groups, Strong successfully developed numerous occupational scales with impressive reliability and validity for predicting later occupational membership. However, although the empirical approach is a powerful one, it provides no consensus on the conceptual meaning of an interest score and thus no way of integrating interests into a broader theoretical framework of individual indifferences. Three historical developments have attempted to address this need: factor analysis of scale intercorrelations, construction of basic interest scales, and formulation of theories of interest.

Holland's Hexagonal Model

Whereas Strong and L. L. Thurstone, in the early 1930s, were the first to use factor analyses to investigate the latent structure of interests, Holland's (1973) six-factor hexagonal model is perhaps the best known and most widely researched. Holland's model can be summarized in terms of its four working assumptions:

1. In U.S. culture, most persons can be categorized as one of six types: realistic (R), investigative (I), artistic (A), social (S), enterprising (E), or conventional (C).
2. There are six corresponding kinds of job environments.
3. People search for environments that will let them exercise their skills and abilities, express their attitudes and values, and take on agreeable problems and roles.
4. One's behavior is determined by an interaction between one's personality and the characteristics of his or her environment.

Other constructs incorporated in the theory are differentiation, which is the degree to which a person or environment resembles many types or only a single type; congruence, the degree to which a type is matched with its environment; and calculus, the degree to which the internal relationships among the factors fit a hexagon.

Holland, Magoon, and Spokane (1981), in their *Annual Review of Psychology* chapter, reported that approximately 300 empirical studies regarding Holland's theory were conducted during the period 1964 to 1979. They concluded that, although evidence for the secondary constructs is mixed, the basic person-environment typology has been strongly supported, which is the same conclusion drawn by Walsh (1979) in his review of essentially the same literature.

The theory has had a major influence on vocational interest measurement in at least four respects (Hansen, 1983). First, the theory has prompted development of inventories and sets of scales to measure the six types. Second, it has stimulated extensive research on many aspects of vocational interests. Third, it has integrated and organized the relevant information under one system. Fourth, it has provided a simple structure of the world of work that is amenable to career planning and guidance.

Prediger (1982) attempted to uncover an even more basic set of dimensions that underlie the Holland hexagon and thus explain the link between interests and occupations. He reported two studies that provide support for the assertion that interest inventories work because they tap activity preferences that parallel work tasks. Results showed that two dimensions, things/people and data/ideas, accounted for 60% of the variance among a very large data set of interest scores. These dimensions were found to be essentially independent ($r = -.13$). In another study, both interest data from job incumbents and task analysis data from job analyses were scored on the two dimensions for a sample of 78 jobs. The correlations between interest versus task scores on the same factor ranged from the upper .60s to lower .80s. In understanding the link between interests and occupations, the emphasis is on activities and whether an individual's desired activities match an occupation's required activities.

Theory of Work Adjustment

Like Holland's theory, the Theory of Work Adjustment (TWA; Dawis & Lofquist, 1984) is based on the concept of correspondence between individual and environment. There are, however, some important differences.

The TWA model posits that there are two major parts of work personality, or suitability, for a job: the individual's aptitudes and his or her needs for various job rewards (or reinforcers) such as those assessed by the *Minnesota Importance Questionnaire* (MIQ), which is a measure of relative preferences for work outcomes. The work environment is also measured in two parts: (a) the aptitudes judged necessary to do the work and (b) the rewards offered by the job. The degree of correspondence can then be assessed between the individual's aptitudes and needs and the job's requirements and rewards. High correspondence between individual aptitudes and job requirements is associated with satisfactoriness of job performance, and high correspondence between the individual's needs and job reinforcers is associated with job satisfaction. Also, the degree of satisfactoriness moderates the relationship with job satisfaction and vice versa, ultimately resulting in a prediction of job tenure.

The TWA differs from Holland's model in the way in which it assesses both the work environment and the individual. Unlike the hexagonal approach, the TWA model includes measures of aptitude, and assesses vocational/motivational needs rather than interests. Some researchers have hypothesized that the individual's job relevant needs are determinants of vocational interests (Bordin, Nachman, & Segal, 1963; Darley & Hagenah, 1955; Roe & Siegelman, 1964; Schaeffer, 1953), whereas others believe that needs and interests reflect the operation of similar underlying variables (Strong, 1943; Thorndike, Weiss, & Dawis, 1968). However, Rounds (1981) has shown that needs and interests measure different aspects of vocational behavior.

The TWA specifies a set of 20 reinforcing conditions that can be used to assess both vocational needs and occupational rewards, and thus predict job satisfaction and satisfactoriness of performance. These 20 reinforcers were identified through extensive literature reviews and a programmatic series of subsequent research studies. The 20 dimensions are Ability Utilization, Achievement, Activity, Advancement, Authority, Company Policies, Compensation, Coworkers, Creativity, Independence, Moral Values, Recognition, Responsibility, Security, Social Service, Social Status, Supervision-Human Relations, Supervision-Technical, Variety, and Working Conditions.

Project A attempted to develop useful measures of both preferences for activities (i.e., interests) and preferences for rewards. The development of the preference for rewards inventory is described in a subsequent section.

Prior Criterion-Related Validity Research

The criterion-related validity of interest scales has been examined for a variety of criterion variables. The most common are occupational membership, job involvement and satisfaction, job proficiency, and training performance. Validities were summarized according to these variables as well as type of validation strategy, (i.e., concurrent or predictive).

Occupational Membership

The most popular criterion variable in previous research has been occupational membership. D. P. Campbell and Hansen (1981) reported the concurrent validity of the Strong-Campbell Interest Inventory (SCII) in terms of the percent overlap (Tilton, 1937) between the interest score distributions of occupational members and people-in-general. If a scale discriminates perfectly between the two groups, there is zero overlap, and if it does not discriminate at all, there is 100% overlap. Values for the occupational scales of the SCII range from 16–54% with a median of 34% overlap. The scales separated the two groups by about two standard deviations, on average.

A second method of assessing concurrent validity is to determine how well the scales separate occupations from each other rather than from people-in-general. D. P. Campbell (1971) reported the SVIB scores of more than 50 occupations on each of the other SVIB scales for both men and women. The median score for members of one occupation on the scales of other occupations was 25, as compared with a median score of 50 for members of an occupation on their own scale (standardized scores with mean of 50 and SD of 10).

Concurrent validity has also been demonstrated for the more homogeneous, basic interest scales. D. P. Campbell and Hansen (1981) reported that the SCII basic interests scales spread occupations' scores over 2 to 2.5 standard deviations, and that the patterns of high- and low-scoring occupations are substantially related to the occupations that people pursue. For example, astronauts were among the highest scorers on the "Adventure" scale and bankers were among the lowest.

The predictive validity of measured interests in forecasting later occupational membership has also been extensively investigated. Perhaps the classic study of this type is an 18-year follow-up of 663 Stanford University students who had completed the SVIB while still in college (Strong, 1955). D. P. Campbell and Hansen (1981) reviewed eight additional predictive validity studies and concluded that the "good" hit rate (McArthur, 1954) of the Strong inventories is approximately 50%.

For the *Kuder Preference Record*, hit rates were 53% in a 25-year follow-up (Zytowski, 1974), 63% in a 7- to 10-year follow-up (McRae, 1959), and 51% in a 12- to 19-year follow-up (Zytowski, 1976). Lau and Abrahams (1971) reported 68% in a 6-year follow-up with the *Navy Vocational Interest Inventory* whereas Gottfredson and Holland (1975) found an average 50% hit rate in a 3-year follow-up with the *Self-Directed Search*. The SVIB hit rates were 39% (corrected for base rate) in an 18-year follow-up (Worthington & Dolliver, 1977) and 50% in a 10-year follow-up (D. P. Campbell, 1971). Gade and Soliah (1975) reported 74% for graduation of college majors in a 4-year follow-up with the *Vocational Preference Inventory*.

Consistent throughout these studies is a demonstrated relationship between an individual's interests and the tendency to stay in a related job or occupation. This consistency is even more remarkable in light of the lengthy follow-up periods and the fact that interests are the only predictor information being considered.

Predicting Job Involvement/Satisfaction

Strong (1943) wrote that he could "think of no better criterion for a vocational interest test than that of satisfaction enduring over a period of time" (p. 385). Table 6.7 summarizes 21 correlational studies that used vocational

TABLE 6.7
Criterion-Related Validities: Job Involvement

	Job Satisfaction	Turnover
Number of studies	18	3
Mean correlation		
Overall	.31	.29
Predictive	.23	.29
Concurrent	.33	—
Correlation range	.01–.62	.19–.29
N Range	25–18,207	125–789
Median N	501	520

interests to predict job involvement and job satisfaction. It can be seen that the studies generally reported correlations of around .30, with concurrent investigations obtaining somewhat higher validities. Six of the studies were conducted with military personnel and obtained almost exactly the same results as with civilians. Overall, the investigations reported remarkably similar results, as evidenced by almost half of the median validities falling in the range of .25 to .35. The median sample size of these studies exceeds 500; considerable confidence can be placed in the replicability of these results.

Using mean differences, Kuder (1977) examined the differences in interests between satisfied members of occupations and their dissatisfied counterparts. He concluded that members of the dissatisfied group are much more likely to receive higher scores in other occupations than are the members of the satisfied group. A large number of additional studies have shown that group differences in interests are related to differences in job satisfaction: McRae (1959), Brayfield (1942, 1953), DiMichael and Dabelstein (1947), Hahn and Williams (1945), Herzberg and Russell (1953), North (1958), and Trimble (1965), among others. Lastly, Arvey and Dewhirst (1979) found that general diversity of interests was related to job satisfaction.

However, a number of other studies have found no significant relationship between interests and job satisfaction. These include Butler, Crinnion, and Martin (1972), Dolliver, Irvin, and Bigley (1972), Schletzer (1966), Trimble (1965), and Zytowski (1976).

D. P. Campbell (1971) observed that the generally modest relationships reported between interests and job satisfaction may be due to restriction in range. Job satisfaction studies have generally reported a high percentage of satisfied workers (around 80%), thus resulting in very little criterion variance. Another viewpoint, expressed by Strong (1955), is that job satisfaction is such a complex and variable concept that measuring it appropriately is difficult. With these factors in mind, the level of correspondence between interests, job satisfaction, and sustained occupational membership appears reasonable.

Predicting Job Proficiency

Strong's own investigation with life insurance agents showed that successful agents did receive higher interest scores on relevant interest scales than unsuccessful agents and that the correlation between sales production and interest scores was approximately .40. He added that many of those with low scores did not stay in the occupation, thus restricting the range in the predictor.

A number of other studies have shown that measured interests can differentiate between those rated as successful and unsuccessful within an occupation. For example, Abrahams, Neumann, and Rimland (1973) found that the highest interest quartile contained three times as many Navy recruiters rated effective as the lowest quartile. Similarly, Azen, Snibbe, and Montgomery (1973) showed that interest scores correctly classified 67% of a sample of deputy sheriffs in terms of job performance ratings.

Arvey and Dewhirst (1979) demonstrated that general diversity of interests was positively related to salary level. Along a similar line, D. P. Campbell (1965, 1971) reported that past presidents of the American Psychological Association, who have enjoyed outstanding professional success, have higher diversity of interest scores than psychologists-at-large.

In addition to the above, 14 studies were located that estimated the correlation between interest level and performance level (summarized in Table 6.8). The majority utilized ratings as the measure of job performance, although three studies examined the correlation of interests with archival production records.

Median validities are .20 for studies employing ratings as criteria and .33 for the studies using archival records. These values suggest a range of .20 to .30 for the overall correlation between measured interests and job performance, uncorrected for criterion unreliability or restriction of range.

TABLE 6.8
Criterion-Related Validities: Job Proficiency

	Ratings	Job Knowledge Tests	Archival Production
Number of studies	11	0	3
Median correlation			
Overall	.20	—	.33
Predictive	.20	—	.33
Concurrent	.25	—	
Correlation range	.01–.40	—	.24–.53
N Range	50–2,400	—	37–195
Median N	464	—	116

TABLE 6.9
Criterion-Related Validities: Training

	Objective Measures	Subjective Measures	Course Completion	Hands-On Measures
Number of studies	8	2	3	0
Median correlation				
Overall	.17	.35	.28	—
Predictive	.17	.35	.28	—
Concurrent	—	—	—	—
Correlation range	.02–.43	.28–.41	.23–.42	—
N Range	53–3,505	27–373	355–4,502	—
Median N	751	—	593	—

Predicting Training Performance

Table 6.9 summarizes 13 longitudinal correlational studies relevant to predicting training criteria. Ratings of training performance were predicted best, .35, and objective measures were predicted least well, .17, while a median of .28 was found for studies of course completion/noncompletion. Eight investigations used military samples and generally obtained higher validities than those obtained in civilian studies. In addition, the military studies included the use of much larger samples and have a training rather than academic emphasis.

Thus, it seems reasonable to expect the uncorrected correlation between interest and later training performance to generally fall around .25, and perhaps higher with instruments specifically constructed for a given set of training programs or jobs (as was often the case in the military research).

Summary of Criterion-Related Validity Studies

As part of the overall Project A literature review used to guide predictor development, more than 100 studies of different aspects of the criterion-related validity of measured interests were examined. Among the most thoroughly replicated findings is the substantial relationship between individuals' interests and sustained membership in an occupation. This relationship has been demonstrated for a wide variety of occupations and over lengthy periods of time. In addition, research has shown these preferences to have validity for predicting various aspects of job involvement, job proficiency, and training performance. The general magnitude of the estimates ranges from .20 to .30, in correlational terms, uncorrected for attenuation or range restriction. Much research has been conducted with military personnel, and the validities appear to be as high, or often higher, for these individuals and settings. In summary, the literature review suggested that an interest inventory would be potentially useful for placing and assigning individuals to jobs.

Development of the Army Vocational Interest Career Examination (AVOICE)

The seminal work of John Holland (1966) has resulted in widespread acceptance of a six-construct, hexagonal model of interests. The principal problem in developing an interest measure for Project A was not which constructs to measure, but rather how much emphasis should be devoted to the assessment of each.

Previous research had produced an interest inventory with excellent psychometric characteristics that had been developed for the U.S. Air Force. Alley and his colleagues (Alley et al., 1977; Alley & Matthews, 1982; Alley, Wilbourn, & Berberich, 1976) had used both rational and statistical scale construction procedures to develop the VOICE. It was the off-the-shelf (existing) measure included in the Preliminary Battery that was administered to approximately 1,800 enlisted soldiers before the concurrent validation began.

The AVOICE is a modified version of the VOICE. In general, items were modified to be more appropriate to Army occupations, and items were added to measure interests that were not included on the VOICE. The goal was to measure all of Holland's constructs, as well as provide sufficient coverage of the vocational areas most important to the Army.

The definitions of the factors assessed by AVOICE are as follows:

Realistic interests.   The realistic construct is defined as a preference for concrete and tangible activities, characteristics, and tasks. Persons with realistic interests enjoy the manipulation of tools, machines, and animals, but find social and educational activities and situations aversive. Realistic interests are associated with occupations such as mechanic, engineer, and wildlife conservation officer, and negatively associated with such occupations as social work and artist. The Realistic construct is by far the most thoroughly assessed of the six constructs tapped by the AVOICE, reflecting the preponderance of work in the Army of a realistic nature.

Conventional interests.   This construct refers to one's degree of preference for well-ordered, systematic and practical activities and tasks. Persons with Conventional interests may be characterized as conforming, efficient, and calm. Conventional interests are associated with occupations such as accountant, clerk, and statistician, and negatively associated with occupations such as artist or author.

Social interests. Social interests are defined as the amount of liking one has for social, helping, and teaching activities and tasks. Persons with social interests may be characterized as responsible, idealistic, and humanistic. Social interests are associated with occupations such as social worker, high school teacher, and speech therapist, and negatively associated with occupations such as mechanic or carpenter.

Investigative interests.   This construct refers to one's preference for scholarly, intellectual, and scientific activities and tasks. Persons with Investigative interests enjoy analytical, ambiguous, and independent tasks, but dislike leadership and persuasive activities. Investigative interests are associated with such occupations as astronomer, biologist, and mathematician, and negatively associated with occupations such as salesperson or politician.

Enterprising interests.   Enterprising interests refers to one's preference for persuasive, assertive, and leadership activities and tasks. Persons
with Enterprising interests may be characterized as ambitious, dominant,
sociable, and self-confident. Enterprising interests are associated with such
occupations as sales person and business executive, and negatively associated with occupations such as biologist or chemist.

Artistic interests.   This final Holland construct is defined as a person's
degree of liking for unstructured, expressive, and ambiguous activities and
tasks. Persons with Artistic interests may be characterized as intuitive, impulsive, creative, and nonconforming. Artistic interests are associated with
such occupations as writer, artists, and composer, and negatively associated
with occupations such as accountant or secretary.

Expressed interest scale.   Although not a psychological construct,
expressed interests were included in the AVOICE because of the extensive
research showing their validity in criterion-related studies (Dolliver, 1969).
These studies had measured expressed interests simply by asking respondents what occupation or occupational area was of most interest to them.
In the AVOICE, such an open-ended question was not feasible; instead,
respondents were asked how confident they were that their chosen job in
the Army was the right one for them.

The first draft of the AVOICE included 24 occupational scales, an 8-
item expressed interest scale, and 6 basic interest items. The items were
presented in five sections. The first section, "Jobs," listed job titles. The
second section, "Work Tasks," listed work activities and climate or work
environment conditions. The third section, "Spare Time Activities," listed
activities one might engage in during discretionary or leisure time. The
fourth section, "Desired Learning Experiences," listed subjects a person
might want to study or learn more about. The final section consisted of
the items from the expressed interest scale as well as the six basic interest
items. The response format for sections one through four was a five-point
preference format with "Like Very Much," "Like," "Indifferent," "Dislike,"
and "Dislike Very Much." The response format for items in section five
depended upon the particular question.

Pretesting and Field Testing the AVOICE

Two pretests ($N = 55$ and 114) were conducted and a review of the
results by project staff, together with verbal feedback from soldiers during
the pretests, resulted in minor word changes to 15 items. An additional

five items were modified because of low item correlations with total scale scores.

In a larger field test at Fort Knox, the AVOICE was administered to 287 first-tour enlisted personnel. Two weeks later, 130 of them completed the AVOICE again. Data quality screening procedures deleted approximately 6% of the 287.

In general, the AVOICE occupational scales showed good distributional properties and excellent internal consistency and stability. Coefficient alpha for the occupational scales ranged from .68 to .95 with a median of .86. The test-retest reliabilities ranged from .56 to .86 with a median of .76.

A principal factor analysis (with varimax rotation) of the occupational scale scores resulted in two factors, which were named Combat Support and Combat Related. The former is defined largely by scales that have to do with jobs or services that support the actual combat specialties. However, several scales showed substantial loadings on both factors. Most of these occur for scales loading highest on the first factor, and include Science/Chemical Operations, Electronic Communication, Leadership, and Drafting. Only one scale loading highest on the second factor has a substantial loading on the first factor, Electronics. This two-factor solution makes good intuitive sense and has practical appeal. It would seem helpful to characterize applicants as having interests primarily in combat MOS or in MOS supporting combat specialities.

The "Faking" Experiment

The same sample used to evaluate response distortion on the ABLE, 245 soldiers at Fort Bragg, were also administered the AVOICE under one honest and two faking conditions (fake combat and fake noncombat). Again, the design was a 2x2x2 completely crossed design with counterbalanced repeated measures for fake versus honest. Approximately half the experimental group received the honest instructions and completed the AVOICE inventory in the morning. In the afternoon they then received the fake-combat or fake-noncombat instructions and completed AVOICE again. The other half completed AVOICE in the morning with either fake-combat or fake-noncombat instructions and completed AVOICE again in the afternoon under the honest instructions.

After dividing the interest scales into two groups, combat related and combat support, a MANOVA showed that the overall Fake x Set interactions for both combat-related and combat-support scales were statistically significant indicating that, when instructed to do so, soldiers apparently did distort their responses. More specifically, 9 of the 11 combat-related

AVOICE scales appeared sensitive to intentional distortion, as well as 9 of 13 combat-support AVOICE scales. When told to distort their responses so that they would be more likely to be placed in combat-related occupational specialties (the fake combat condition), soldiers in general increased their scores on scales that were combat MOS related and decreased their scores on noncombat related scales. The opposite tended to be true in the fake noncombat condition.

However, because the Army is an all volunteer force, intentional distortion of interest responses may not be an operational problem. As part of the same study described for the ABLE, mean AVOICE scale scores were obtained under different conditions: an applicant-like setting (the Minneapolis MEPS sample described earlier) and two honest conditions (Fort Bragg and Fort Knox). There appeared to be no particular pattern to the mean score differences.

Psychometric Characteristics of AVOICE

The AVOICE was also part of the Trial Battery of new tests that were administered during CVI. After data screening, the remaining inventories were analyzed to determine response option endorsement, item and scale characteristics, and the covariance structure of the AVOICE scales.

A total of 10.3% of the scanned inventories were deleted for problems related to missing data and random responding. A slightly higher percent of males and minorities were deleted compared to females and whites.

Descriptive Statistics for AVOICE Scales

The AVOICE scales resulting from the field test were revised again using the data from the 8,399 CVI inventories that survived the data quality screens. The revisions were based on item-total scale correlations, factor analysis at the item level, clarity of interpretation, and practical considerations. The descriptive statistics of the revised scales are presented below.

Total group.   Table 6.10 shows the number of items, the sample size, means, standard deviations, median item-total scale correlations, internal consistency reliability estimates (alpha coefficients), and test-retest reliabilities for the revised AVOICE scales. The median item-total scale correlation for the scales is .66 with a range of .44 to .80. The median internal consistency estimate for the scales is .89 with a range of .61 to .94. The median test-retest reliability for the scales is .75 with a range of .54 to .84.

TABLE 6.10
AVOICE Scale Statistics for Total Group[a]

AVOICE Scale	No. Items	Mean	SD	Median Item-Scale Correlation	Internal Consistency Reliability (Alpha)	Test-Retest Reliability[b]
Clerical/administrative	14	39.6	10.81	.67	.92	.78
Mechanics	10	32.1	9.42	.80	.94	.82
Heavy construction	13	39.3	10.54	.68	.92	.84
Electronics	12	38.4	10.22	.70	.94	.81
Combat	10	26.5	8.35	.65	.90	.73
Medical services	12	36.9	9.54	.68	.92	.78
Rugged individualism	15	53.3	11.44	.58	.90	.81
Leadership/guidance	12	40.1	8.63	.62	.89	.72
Law enforcement	8	24.7	7.37	.65	.89	.84
Food service—professional	8	20.2	6.50	.67	.89	.75
Firearms enthusiast	7	23.0	6.36	.66	.89	.80
Science/chemical	6	16.9	5.33	.70	.85	.74
Drafting	6	19.4	4.97	.66	.84	.74
Audiographics	5	17.6	4.09	.69	.83	.75
Aesthetics	5	14.2	4.13	.59	.79	.73
Computers	4	14.0	3.99	.78	.90	.77
Food Service—employee	3	5.1	2.08	.54	.73	.56
Mathematics	3	9.6	3.09	.78	.88	.75
Electronic communication	6	18.4	4.66	.60	.83	.68
Warehousing/shipping	2	5.8	1.75	.44	.61	.54
Fire protection	2	6.1	1.96	.62	.76	.67
Vehicle operator	3	8.8	2.65	.51	.70	.68

[a]Total group after screening for missing data and random responding ($N = 8,224$–$8,488$).
[b]$N = 389$–409 for test-retest correlation.

Gender groups. Because male/female differences in interest patterns are a consistent empirical finding, scale means and standard deviations were calculated separately for men and women. The results appear in Table 6.11. The most noteworthy and expected differences between AVOICE interest scale scores for men and women are the higher or greater male interest in realistic occupations (Mechanics, Heavy Construction, Electronics, Combat, Rugged Individualism, Firearms Enthusiast, Fire Protection, and Vehicle Operator scales) and the higher or greater female interest in Clerical/Administrative, Aesthetics, and Medical Services activities.

TABLE 6.11
AVOICE Scale Means and Standard Deviations for Males and Females

	Male (N = 7,387 − 7,625)		Female (N = 832 − 864)	
	Mean	SD	Mean	SD
Clerical/administrative	38.9	10.54	45.8	11.11
Mechanics	33.0	8.97	24.0	9.35
Heavy construction	40.5	9.99	28.8	9.37
Electronics	39.4	9.71	29.1	9.92
Combat	27.0	8.24	21.5	7.71
Medical services	36.4	9.28	41.3	10.59
Rugged individualism	54.2	11.02	45.0	11.79
Leadership/guidance	39.9	8.58	41.8	8.89
Law enforcement	24.9	7.34	23.3	7.50
Food service/professional	20.0	6.41	22.3	6.96
Firearms enthusiast	23.7	5.99	6.5	5.85
Science/chemical	17.1	5.29	14.8	5.31
Drafting	19.6	4.91	17.6	5.18
Audiographics	17.6	4.09	17.7	4.11
Aesthetics	13.9	4.05	16.6	4.04
Computers	14.0	4.01	14.1	3.85
Food service/employees	5.1	2.08	5.2	2.10
Mathematics	9.6	3.07	9.8	3.28
Electronic communication	18.4	4.63	18.0	4.87
Warehousing/shipping	5.9	1.73	5.4	1.80
Fire protection	6.2	1.93	5.1	1.94
Vehicle operator	9.0	2.59	7.2	2.59

Note: A box indicates a difference in means of approximately one-half standard deviation or more.

MOS. Scale means and standard deviations were calculated separately for each MOS. The pattern of mean scale scores across MOS indicated considerable construct validity for the AVOICE scales. For example, Administrative Specialists score higher than all other MOS on the Clerical/Administrative scale; Light Wheel Vehicle Mechanics score higher than other MOS on the Mechanics scale and Carpentry/Masonry Specialists score higher than other MOS on the Heavy Construction scale. These results support a conclusion that AVOICE scales differentiate soldiers in different jobs in a meaningful way. Means and standard deviations were also calculated separately for men and women within MOS as well as for separate ethnic groups within MOS. Those data are available in Hough et al. (1987), Appendices D and E.

Internal Structure of AVOICE

The internal structure of the AVOICE scales was examined by factor analyzing the correlations among AVOICE scales for the total group as well as for ethnic and gender subgroups (principal component with varimax rotation). Although there was still evidence for the two higher order factors found using field test data, the subsequent revisions to the scales produced sets of more specific factors. When the correlations based on the full sample were factored, a 5-factor solution appeared to be most appropriate. However, the factor structure was more differentiated for specific subgroups.

The factor structure for Blacks was virtually the same as for Whites. The only difference between the 9-factor solution chosen for Whites and the 8-factor solution identified for Blacks is that two factors in the White solution, Structural Trades and Combat Related, merge for the Black sample (see Hough et al., 1987 for more detail).

The factor structures for men and women, as might be expected, exhibited more differences. The factors that are exactly the same are Food Service and Protective Services. The Graphic Arts factor of the female solution and the Technician-Artistic factor of the male solution are the same except the Aesthetics scale is included in the Technician-Artistic factor of the male solution, whereas it is not included in the Graphic Arts factor of the female solution. Two male factors, Structural/Machine Trades and Combat Related, merge in the female solution to form one factor (as they do for Blacks). The remaining scales, however, form very different factors for men and women. In total, a 7-factor solution for men and a 9-factor solution for women seem most appropriate (further details are given in Hough et al., 1987).

Summary

In summary, the AVOICE scales exhibited appropriate distributional properties and high reliabilities. They also seemed to have considerable construct validity as demonstrated by the pattern of scale score means within and across MOS. Not unexpectedly, men and women in the Army differ in their interests as reflected in their mean scale score differences. Those differences appear to map the differences in the general population.

WORK OUTCOME PREFERENCES: THE JOB ORIENTATION BLANK (JOB)

Development

As discussed previously, the Theory of Work Adjustment (TWA) specifies a set of 20 reinforcing outcomes (representing six factors) and measures relative preferences for those outcomes via an inventory called the *Minnesota Importance Questionnaire*. Project A sought to measure these six factors with the *Job Orientation Blank* (JOB). Table 6.12 shows the six factors, their associated scales, as well as one item written to measure each construct. The response format was the same as the AVOICE inventory, "Like Very Much," "Like," "Indifferent," "Dislike," and "Dislike Very Much."

The initial version of the JOB was included with the ABLE and AVOICE in the two pilot test samples ($N = 55$ and 114) and field test sample ($N = 287$) described previously. Based on pilot and field test results, only minor revisions were made to JOB items. The Trial Battery version of the JOB used in CVI consisted of 38 items and six scales.

Psychometric Characteristics of the JOB

The JOB was also part of the Project A Trial Battery that was administered to the CVI sample. The data were screened for quality using the same procedures applied to ABLE and AVOICE. From the total number of JOB inventories that were collected, 11.9% were deleted for problems related to missing data and random responding. The remaining sample of 8,239 was used to analyze the psychometric characteristics of the JOB.

Descriptive Statistics for JOB Scales

Factor analyses (principal factor with varimax rotation) of the JOB scales resulted in two factors. The 38 JOB items also were factored analyzed (principal factor with varimax rotation) and three factors were obtained. The first factor consisted of positive work environment characteristics, the second factor consisted of negative work environment characteristics, and the third factor consisted of items describing preferences for autonomous work

TABLE 6.12
JOB-Organizational Reward Outcomes

Scale	Sample Item
Achievement	
Achievement	Do work that gives a feeling of accomplishment
Authority	Tell others what to do on the job.
Ability utilization	Make full use of your abilities.
Safety	
Organizational policy	A job in which the rules are not equal for everyone.
Supervision—technical	Learn the job on your own.
Supervision—human resources	Have a boss that supports the workers.
Comfort	
Activity	Work on a job that keeps a person busy.
Variety	Do something different most days at work.
Compensation	Earn less than others do.
Security	A job with steady employment.
Working conditions	Have a pleasant place to work.
Status	
Advancement	Be able to be promoted quickly.
Recognition	Receive awards or compliments on the job.
Social status	A job that does not stand out from others.
Altruism	
Coworkers	A job in which other employees were hard to get to know.
Moral values	Have a job that would not bother a person's conscience.
Social services	Serve others through your work.
Autonomy	
Responsibility	Have work decisions made by others.
Creativity	Try out your own ideas on the job.
Independence	Work alone.

settings. The JOB appeared not to be measuring the intended work outcome constructs; only the autonomy scale appeared reasonable.

However, considerable prior research (Dawis & Lofquist, 1984) indicates that the six-factor structure has considerable validity. One hypothesis was that the reading level of the negatively worded items was too high for the present sample. A factor analysis of only the more simply stated items might result in a more meaningful structure. Nine of the 38 items were dropped and the items refactored. Six meaningful factors emerged: *Job Pride, Job Security, Serving Others, Job Autonomy, Job Routine*, and

Ambition. The JOB scales were reconstituted according to these six factors. The scales/constructs are described below.

Job pride.   Preferences for work environments characterized by positive outcomes such as friendly coworkers, fair treatment, and comparable pay.

Job security/comfort.   Preferences for work environments that provide secure and steady employment; environments where persons receive good training and may utilize their abilities.

Serving others.   Preferences for work environments where persons are reinforced for doing things for other people and for serving others through the work performed.

Job autonomy.   Preferences for work environments that reinforce independence and responsibility. Persons who score high on this construct prefer to work alone, try out their own ideas, and decide for themselves how to get the work done.

Job routine.   Preferences for work environments that lack variety, where people do the same or similar things every day, have about the same level of responsibility for quite a while, and follow others' directions.

Ambition.   Preferences for work environments that have prestige and status. Persons who score high on this scale prefer work environments that have opportunities for promotion and for supervising or directing others' activities.

Table 6.13 shows the number of items, the sample size, means, standard deviations, median item-total scale correlations, and internal consistency reliability estimates (alpha coefficients) for the revised JOB scales calculated on the CVI sample. The median item-total scale correlation for the scales is .39 with a range of .25 to .54. The median internal consistency estimate for the JOB is .58 with a range of .46 to .84. The revised JOB scales have reasonably good psychometric characteristics.

Scale means and standard deviations were also calculated separately for each MOS. A comparison of the different MOS scale score means indicated there is not a lot of variation in JOB scale score means across MOS. The

TABLE 6.13
JOB Scale Statistics for Total Group[a]

JOB Scales	No. Items	Mean	SD	Median Item-Total Correlation	Internal Consistency Reliability (Alpha)
Job pride	10	43.6	4.51	.54	.84
Job security/comfort	5	21.6	2.33	.43	.67
Serving others	3	12.1	1.83	.52	.66
Job autonomy	4	15.1	2.29	.31	.50
Job routine	4	9.6	2.30	.25	.46
Ambition	3	12.4	1.63	.35	.49

[a]Total group after screening for missing data and random responding ($N = 7{,}707\text{--}7{,}817$).

difference in highest and lowest mean scores were all less than one standard deviation for each JOB scale. The intercorrelations between JOB scales, computed for the total group, ranged from .07 to .61 (ignoring signs) with a median of intercorrelation of .23.

SUMMARY

This chapter described the theoretical and empirical foundations for developing a personality/biographical inventory, an interest inventory, and a work environment/outcome preference inventory. The objectives were to (a) identify a set of personality, vocational interest, and work needs variables likely to be useful in predicting soldier performance and for placing individuals in work situations that are likely to be satisfying; (b) develop a set of scales to measure those constructs; (c) revise and evaluate the scales until they had adequate psychometric properties; and (d) investigate the effects of motivational set on the scales. The approach to reviewing the literature, developing the scales, and evaluating the scales was construct-oriented, and a combination of rational and internal scale construction strategies was used to write and revise items forming each scale.

On the basis of considerable empirical evaluation, the ABLE, AVOICE, and JOB scales were judged to be psychometrically sound and appear to be relatively independent from each other. As part of a predictor set, the scales could potentially contribute reliable and unique information.

Chapter 10 describes the development of the basic predictor scores for each of these three inventories on the basis of analyses of the longitudinal validation data and compares the LV basic scores to the basic scores for the same three instruments that were used in CVI.

III

Specification and Measurement of Individual Differences in Job Performance

7

Analyzing Jobs for Performance Measurement

Walter C. Borman, Charlotte H. Campbell, and Elaine D. Pulakos

Job analysis is the cornerstone for all personnel practices. It provides the building blocks for criterion development and personnel selection, training needs analysis, job design or re-design, job evaluation, and many other human resources management activities. For Project A, it was the foundation for the development of multiple measures of performance for a representative sample of jobs at two different organizational levels.

Job analysis has been with us for a long time. Primoff and Fine (1988) argued that Socrates' concerns in the fifth century about work in society and how it might best be accomplished considered the problem in job analysis terms. In modern times, job analysis was an important part of the scientific management movement early in this century (Gael, 1988) and became an established part of personnel management procedures during and immediately after World War II. The criticality of job analysis was escalated by the Civil Rights Act of 1964 and its emphasis on fair employment practices was operationalized by the Uniform Guidelines on Personnel Selection (EEOC, 1978). Job analysis was identified as an important first step in ensuring such practices. At about the same time, the U.S. military services became very active in job analysis research and development, which led to the widespread use of the CODAP system (Mitchell, 1988). The Job Analysis Handbook (Gael, 1988) and the I/O Handbook chapter by Harvey (1991) provide exhaustive coverage of conceptual and practical issues in job analysis. Knapp, Russell, and J.P. Campbell (1993) discuss job analysis, with particular emphasis on how the military services approach this activity. Their report describes the various services' routine occupational analysis activities.

THE PROJECT A JOB ANALYSES: AN OVERVIEW

In any job analysis effort investigators must deal with a number of critical issues and assumptions. They vary from specific methodological concerns to broader issues about the changing nature of work itself (Howard, 1995).

Measurement Issues

One fundamental issue concerns whether the nature of work should be studied in the context of specific jobs or whether the boundaries that separate one job from another have become so dynamic that the term "job" is obsolete, and the elements that are used to analyze or describe work should make no reference to specific jobs. There is no better illustration of this issue than the effort to convert the Department of Labor's *Dictionary of Occupational Titles (DOT)*, which contains over 12,000 specific job descriptions, into an electronic occupational information network database (O*NET), which contains a much wider array of information referenced to approximately 1,100 "occupational units" (Peterson, Mumford, Borman, Jeanneret, & Fleishman, 1995). An occupational unit is described by a cluster of jobs that involve similar work content, but it is not described by a specific job or specific set of jobs. The O*NET organizes occupational information into domains such as ability requirements, knowledge and skill requirements, general work activities, and the context and conditions of work. Within each domain a basic taxonomy of descriptive variables has been developed that are not job specific and that can be used to provide a descriptive analysis of any job, occupation, or family of occupations. As will be apparent in subsequent sections, Project A took both views of "jobs."

Historically, another major issue has been the choice of the unit(s) of description for job analysis (Harvey, 1991). The choices range from specific job tasks, to general job behaviors, to the identification of job family or occupational membership, to the conditions under which the work is done, to inferences about the properties of individuals that are required to perform the work content in question. The terms "job-oriented" (e.g., job tasks, work behaviors) versus "person-oriented" (e.g., knowledges, skills, abilities) are often used to distinguish two major types of descriptors. The major alternatives might be referred to more accurately as descriptors for (a) the *content* of work, (b) the *outcomes* that result, (c) the *conditions* under which the work must be performed, and (d) the *determinants* of performance on the content in question under a given set of conditions. The determinants of performance (KSAOs in common parlance) can further be thought of as direct (e.g., current level of specific work relevant skill) or indirect (e.g., general cognitive ability). Yet another type of descriptor is implied by the advocates of cognitive job analysis (Glaser, Lesgold, & Gott, 1991). The critical descriptive units for a cognitive job analysis are the mental *processes* by which an expert (i.e., high performer) performs the work. The overall goals of Project A and the specific goals for its job analysis component suggested that the primary units of description should describe the *content* of the work people are asked to perform.

Finally, a critical measurement issue concerns the level of specificity/generality at which the content of work is described. At one extreme, the analysis could generate very general task descriptions that do not go much beyond the job title itself. At the other extreme, several hundred task elements, specific to a particular job, could be incorporated into a survey that is individualized for each job or position under study. Project A's attempt to stake out the middle ground is outlined below.

Goals

The central purpose of the job analysis work in Project A was to support job performance criterion development efforts. Consequently, the two major goals of the project's job analyses were to describe the dimensions of performance content in jobs as comprehensively and clearly as possible and to provide the basis for the development of multiple measures of each relevant performance factor. The intent was to push the state-of-the-art as far as possible. Multiple job analytic methods were used to generate a comprehensive description of the content of performance for each of the nine MOS (jobs) in "Batch A." The analyses were carried out both for entry level first-tour performance and for performance during the second tour (after reenlistment) during which the individual soldier begins to assume supervisory responsibilities.

Underlying Assumptions

A fundamental assumption was that job performance is multidimensional. Consequently, for any particular job, one specific objective is to describe the basic factors that comprise performance. That is, how many such factors are there and what is the basic nature of each?

For the population of entry-level enlisted positions in the Army, two major types of job performance content were postulated. The first is composed of performance components that are specific to a particular job. That is, measures of such components should reflect specific technical competence or specific job behaviors that are not required for other jobs within the organization. For example, typing correspondence would be a performance component for an administrative clerk (MOS 71L) but not for a tank crewmember (MOS 19E). Such components were labeled as "MOS-specific" performance factors.

The second type includes components that are defined in the same way for every job. These are referred to as "Army-wide" performance factors. The Army-wide concept incorporates the basic notion that total performance is much more than task or technical proficiency. It might include such things as contribution to teamwork, continual self-development, support for the norms and customs of the organization, and perseverance in the face of adversity. A much more detailed description of the initial framework for the Army-wide segment of performance can be found in Borman, Motowidlo, Rose, and Hanser (1987).

In summary, the working model of performance for Project A viewed performance as multidimensional within these two broad categories of factors. The job analysis was designed to identify the content of these factors via an exhaustive description of the total performance domain, using multiple methods.

The Overall Strategy

There are several different major approaches to conducting job analyses (Harvey, 1991), and different approaches are more (or less) appropriate for different purposes. A particular job analysis strategy may be ideal for one application (e.g., criterion development) but less useful for another application (e.g., training needs analysis).

Because the primary goal of job analysis in Project A was to support criterion development, methods that provided a description of job content were the central focus. Using a fairly traditional approach to job analysis, extensive questionnaire survey data, job incumbent and supervisor interviews, and existing job manuals were all used to generate exhaustive lists of tasks for each job. Most of the survey data were drawn from existing repositories of data routinely collected by the Army. Project researchers focused on the compilation of a large amount of existing task information. This information was then reviewed by SMEs and a sample of critical tasks were selected for performance measurement. The effort did not include a delineation of requisite knowledges, skills, and abilities, as is often included in this type of task-based job analysis.

Critical incident methodology (Flanagan, 1954), however, was used to generate a comprehensive sample of several hundred examples of effective and ineffective performance for each job. This involved a series of workshops with SMEs in which (a) critical incidents were collected and sorted into draft performance dimensions, (b) the incidents were resorted (i.e., retranslated) by the SMEs to ensure that the draft performance dimensions were adequate, and (c) the SMEs rated the performance level reflected by each of the critical incidents.

Both the task analyses and critical incident procedures incorporated the distinction between performance content that is common across all jobs, and performance content that is job specific. Both methods were used for the purpose of identifying the major components of performance in each job.

The remainder of this chapter describes the procedures and results for these two major methods for both entry level (first-tour) and supervisory (second-tour) positions. Transforming the job analysis results into fully functional performance measures is the topic for Chapter 8.

TASK ANALYSES FOR FIRST-TOUR
(ENTRY LEVEL) POSITIONS

As noted earlier, because of cost considerations, the comprehensive task analysis was carried out only for the nine jobs (MOS) in Batch A. The nine jobs were divided into two groups. Group I included 13B Cannon Crewman, 88M Motor Transport Operator, 71L Administrative Specialist, and 95B Military Police; and Group II included 11B Infantryman, 19E Armor Crewman, 31C Radio Operator, 63B Light Wheel Vehicle Mechanic, and 91A Medical Specialist. The initial task analysis procedures were used with Group I and then modified slightly to increase efficiency before proceeding with the analysis of Group II jobs. The task analysis procedure is described in detail in C. H. Campbell, R. C. Campbell, Rumsey, and Edwards (1986) and summarized below.

Specifying the Task Domain

The initial specification of the entry level tasks for each of the nine MOS was generated by synthesizing the existing job descriptions provided by the MOS-specific and common task Soldier's Manuals and the Army Occupational Survey Program (AOSP) results.

- *MOS-Specific Soldier's Manuals.* Each job's "proponent," the agency responsible for prescribing MOS policy and doctrine, publishes a manual that describes tasks that soldiers in the MOS are responsible for knowing and performing after a specified length of time. The number of entry-level (known as Skill Level 1) tasks varied widely across the nine MOS included in the study, from a low of 17 to more than 130.
- *Soldier's Manual of Common Tasks (SMCT).* The SMCT describes tasks that every soldier in the Army, regardless of MOS, must be able to perform (e.g., tasks related to first aid).
- *Army Occupational Survey Program (AOSP).* The Army periodically conducts a task analysis questionnaire survey for each MOS. The surveys are administered to incumbents at various career stages (i.e., Skill Levels) and provide information on the percent of individuals at each skill level who report that they perform each task. The number of tasks/activities in the surveys for the nine MOS in Batch A ranged from approximately 450 to well over 800.

Tasks compiled from all sources yielded a very large initial pool that incorporated considerable redundancy and variation in descriptive specificity. A multistep process was used to produce a synthesized list. First, the Skill Level 1 tasks from the Soldier's Manuals formed the initial core. Relevant AOSP questionnaire items were then subsumed under equivalent tasks from the Soldier's Manuals to eliminate redundancy of information from the two sources. Because the survey items were stated in much more elemental terms, task content that appeared only on the AOSP questionnaires was aggregated to a more molar level of description that was consistent with the task statements from the Soldier's Manuals. Tasks for which the survey data indicated very low frequency-of-performance were deleted. The synthesized list was then submitted to the proponent Army agency for review by a minimum of three senior NCOs or officers.

The result of the above activities generated the initial entry level task population for each MOS. The task lists for the nine MOS contained from 90 to 180 tasks. Several illustrative tasks (including common tasks and MOS-specific tasks for vehicle mechanics) are listed below:

- Determine a magnetic azimuth
- Administer first aid to a nerve agent casualty
- Perform operator maintenance on an M16A1 rifle
- Troubleshoot service brake malfunctions
- Replace wheel bearings

Subject Matter Expert (SME) Judgments

Based on projected cost considerations, it was the collective judgment of the research team that approximately 30 representative tasks should be selected as the basis for developing performance measures. The 30 tasks were to be selected for each MOS on the basis of SME judgments such that they would (a) represent all major factors of job content, (b) include the tasks judged to be the most critical for the MOS, and (c) have sufficient range of performance difficulty to permit measurement discrimination.

The SMEs were required to be either second or third tour NCOs, or officers who were Captains or above and who supervised, or had recently supervised, personnel in the MOS being reviewed. For the Group I MOS, 15 SMEs in each MOS served as judges. For the Group II MOS, some modifications in the review process were made (described below) and 30 SMEs in each of these MOS were used. Collection of SME data required approximately one day for each MOS, and three types of judgments were obtained: task similarity, task importance, and expected task performance variability/difficulty.

Forming task clusters.   A brief description of each task was printed on an index card, and SMEs were asked to sort the tasks into categories, based on their content, such that the tasks in each category were as similar as possible, and each group of tasks was as distinct as possible from the other groups. A matrix of intertask similarities was obtained by calculating the relative frequency with which a pair of tasks was clustered together. Following a procedure used by Borman and Brush (subsequently published in 1993), the similarities were converted to a correlation metric and then factored. The resulting factors for each MOS were named and defined and referred to thereafter as task clusters.

Task importance ratings.   Because the prevailing military situation (i.e., the conditions of work) could affect the rated importance of different tasks, an attempt was made to standardize the SMEs' frame of reference by providing a scenario that described the prevailing conditions. For the Group I MOS, all SMEs were given a scenario that described a looming European conflict, and specified a high state of training and strategic readiness, but did not involve an actual conflict.

Following collection of the Group I data, questions were raised about the nature of the scenario effect on SME judgments. As a consequence, three scenarios were used for the analysis of Group II. The neutral scenario (referred to as Increasing Tension) used for the Group I was retained. A less tense training scenario specifying a stateside environment, and a Combat European (nonnuclear) scenario in which a military engagement was actually in progress were also used. SMEs were divided into three groups, each of which was provided with a different scenario. Results showed that there were no significant scenario effects for task importance.

Performance distribution ratings.   To obtain judgments of the expected performance distribution for each task, SMEs were asked to sort 10 hypothetical job incumbents into five performance levels based on how they would expect a representative group of 10 soldiers to be able to perform the task. The mean and standard deviation of the distribution for the 10 soldiers were then calculated.

Summaries of the task data listed tasks ranked by importance within clusters. For each task, the summaries also included expected mean difficulty, expected performance variability, and frequency of performance (if available). Frequencies were taken from the AOSP survey data and supplemented with performance frequency estimates obtained during the SME review. For the Group II MOS, which obtained SME ratings under three scenarios, the rank ordering within clusters was determined by the Combat Scenario ranks. Table 7.1 shows the task clusters for two illustrative MOS.

Selecting Tasks for Measurement

The final step of the task analysis was to select subsets of tasks for the development of performance criterion measures.

Group I task selection.   A panel of five to nine experienced project personnel was provided with the task data summaries described above and

TABLE 7.1
Task Clusters for Two First Tour MOS

19E Armor Crewman	*63B Light Wheel Vehicle Mechanic*
First aid	First aid
Land navigation and map reading	Land navigation and map reading
Nuclear/biological/chemical weapons	Nuclear/biological/chemical weapons
Movement/survival in field	Movement/survival in field
Communications	Detect and identify threats
Mines and demolitions	Preventive/general maintenance
Prepare tank, tank systems, and	Brakes/steering/suspension systems
associated equipment for operations	Electrical systems
(except weapon systems)	Vehicle recovery systems
Operate tanks (except weapon systems)	Power train/clutch/engine systems
Prepare tank weapons systems for operations	Fuel/cooling/lubrication/exhaust systems
Operate tank weapon system	

asked to select 35 of the most critical tasks for each MOS. Five additional tasks were included because further internal and external reviews were to be conducted and the expectation was that some tasks might be eliminated in that process. No strict rules were imposed on panelists in making their selections, although they were told that high importance, relatively high frequency, and substantial expected performance variability were desirable and that each cluster should be sampled.

Results were analyzed with the objective of capturing each individual judge's decision policy. For each panelist, task selections were regressed on the task characteristics data (e.g., difficulty, performance variability) to identify individual selection policies. The equations were then applied to the task characteristics data to provide a prediction of the tasks each panelist would have selected if the panelist's selections were completely consistent with his or her general decision rules, as represented by the linear model.

In the second phase, panelists were provided their original task selections and the selection predicted by their regression captured policies. They were asked to review and justify discrepancies between the observed and predicted selections. Panelists independently either modified their selections or justified their original selections. Rationales for intentional discrepancies were identified and the regression equations adjusted.

The last phase of the panelists' selection procedure was a Delphi-type negotiation among panelists to merge their respective choices into 35 tasks for each MOS. The choices and rationales provided by panelists in the previous phase were distributed to all members, and each decided whether to retain or adjust prior selections. Decisions and revisions were collected, collated, and redistributed as needed until consensus was reached. For all MOS, three iterations were sufficient to obtain 30 tasks regarded as high priorities for measurement and five tasks as alternate selections. The resulting task selections were provided to each proponent agency for review. After some recommended adjustments, the final 30 tasks were selected.

Group II test task selection.   Based on experience with Group I, two modifications were made in the task selection process for Group II MOS. First, proponent agency representatives were introduced earlier in the process. Second, the regression analysis exercise was not used. Experience with Group I indicated that the use of regression based policy-capturing was prohibitively complex and time consuming when nonproject participants were introduced into the process. More important, the Group I results showed panelists' selections to be nonlinear. They interpreted the task data differently on the basis of specific knowledge of the MOS or the individual tasks. The linear model provided a relatively poor description of the task selection rules used by the SMEs.

The panel for the Group II task selections consisted of five to nine members of the project staff, combined with six military officers and NCOs from each MOS. These six were selected to provide minority and gender representation where possible (note that there are no women in the combat MOS). Panel members were provided a target number of tasks to be selected from each cluster, calculated in proportion to the number of tasks in each, with a total of 35 tasks to be selected. A second constraint prescribed a minimum of two tasks per cluster.

The initial task selection was performed independently by each SME. Next, each SME was provided a composite record of the choices made by the panel members and asked to independently select again, this time writing a brief justification for his or her selections. Members were again provided with a summary of the other panelists' selections along with the reasons for the selection and asked to independently make their selections a third time. Members were provided with a summary of these third round selections in a face-to-face meeting and asked to reach a consensus on the final list of 30 tasks. The end result of the task analysis was, for each of the nine MOS, a list of 30 critical tasks, which would become the focus of performance measurement.

CRITICAL INCIDENTS ANALYSIS
FOR FIRST-TOUR POSITIONS

The objective of the critical incidents job analyses (Flanagan, 1954) was to use a very distinct alternative method to identify the critical dimensions of performance for each of the nine MOS. These dimensions would subsequently form the basis for behavior-based performance rating scales (Borman, 1979a; Smith & Kendall, 1963); however, they would be the basis for other methods of measurement as well (e.g., the supervisory role plays described in the next chapter). Following the initial model (nonspecific and specific components), there was also a need to identify critical Army-wide performance dimensions that would be relevant for all 10 Batch Z MOS, as well as for other MOS beyond those studied in Project A.

Identification of MOS-Specific Performance Dimensions

The procedural steps for identifying specific critical dimensions within each of the nine MOS were: (a) conducting workshops to collect critical incidents of performance specific to the MOS, (b) analyzing the examples to identify an initial set of performance dimensions, and (c) conducting the retranslation exercise. (For a detailed description see Toquam, McHenry et al., 1988.)

Critical incident workshops. Almost all participants in the workshops were NCOs who themselves had spent two to four years as entry-level soldiers in these MOS and who were directly responsible for supervising first-tour enlistees in the MOS. Workshops for each MOS were conducted at six U.S. Army posts. Participants were asked to generate descriptions of performance incidents specific to their particular MOS, using examples provided as guides, and to avoid describing activities or behaviors that could be observed in any MOS (e.g., following rules and regulations, military appearance), because these requirements were being identified and described in other workshops. After four to five hours, the participants were asked to identify potential job performance categories, which were recorded on a blackboard or flip chart. Following discussion of the categories, the performance incidents written to that point were reviewed and assigned to one of the categories that had been identified. The remaining time was spent generating performance incidents for those categories that

TABLE 7.2
Performance Incident Workshops: Number of Participants
and Incidents Generated by MOS

	Number of Participants	Number of Incidents	Means Per Participant
11B	83	993	12.0
13B	88	1159	13.2
19E	65	838	12.0
31C	60	779	13.0
63B	75	866	11.6
71L	63	989	15.7
88M	81	1147	14.2
91A	71	761	10.7
95B	86	1183	13.8

contained few incidents. Results of the performance example workshops are reported in Table 7.2.

Sample critical incidents for two MOS appear below:

- This medical specialist was taking an inventory of equipment stored in a chest. He was careful to follow the inventory sheet to ensure that the chest was properly loaded.
- This medical specialist came upon a patient who was not breathing. Although she was supposed to know artificial respiration techniques, she did not. Therefore, she could not treat the patient and someone else had to do so.
- When the turn signals would not work on a truck, this 63B (vehicle mechanic) used the technical manual to trace and fix the problem.
- When told to replace the tail pipe on a 1/4 ton vehicle, this 63B did so, but failed to replace the gasket. The exhaust pipe leaked as a result.

Editing the performance examples and identifying dimensions. Project staff edited the 8,715 performance examples gathered across all nine MOS into a common format. For the editing and subsequent scale development work, small teams of researchers specialized in two or three of the individual MOS. After editing, and given the categories identified in the original workshops, the teams defined a revised set of categories or dimensions that as a set, seemed, to best summarize the content of the examples. That is, examples were sorted into categories according to their content to produce what were judged to be the most homogeneous dimensions.

Across all nine MOS, a total of 93 performance dimensions were identified. For individual MOS, the number varied from 7 to 13. These dimension labels and their definitions were used for the retranslation step.

Conducting the retranslation exercise and refining the dimension set. Confirmation that the dimension system provided a comprehensive and valid representation of job content required: (a) high agreement among judges that a specific incident represented the particular dimension of performance in which it was originally classified, (b) that all hypothesized dimensions could be represented by incidents, and (c) that all incidents in the pool could be assigned to a dimension (if not, dimensions could be missing). The retranslation task required SMEs to assign each incident to a dimension and to rate the level of performance reflected in the example on a 9-point scale. Retranslation data were collected by mail and in workshops for Group I MOS and in workshops only for Group II MOS. Because of the large number of incidents, each SME retranslated a subsample of approximately 200 incidents. Approximately 10 to 20 SMEs retranslated each incident. Retranslation data were analyzed separately for each MOS and included computing the (a) percentage agreement between raters in assigning incidents to performance dimensions, (b) mean effectiveness ratings, and (c) standard deviation of the effectiveness ratings.

For each MOS, performance incidents were identified for which at least 50% of the raters agreed that the incident depicted performance on a single performance dimension, and the standard deviation of the mean effectiveness rating did not exceed 2.0. These incidents were then placed in their assigned performance dimensions.

As mentioned above, the categorization of the original critical incident pool produced a total of 93 initial performance dimensions for the nine MOS, with a range of 7 to 13 dimensions per MOS. Based on the retranslation results, a number of the original dimensions were redefined, omitted, or combined. In particular, six were omitted, and in four cases, two dimensions were combined. One of the omissions was because too few critical incidents were retranslated into it by the judges. The other five were omitted because the factors represented tasks that were well beyond Skill Level 1 or were from a very specialized low-density "track" within the MOS (e.g., MOS 71L F5-Postal Clerk) that had very few people in it. Accordingly, the

TABLE 7.3
MOS-Specific Critical Incident Dimensions for Two First Tour MOS

19E Armor Crewman	*91A Medical Specialist*
Maintaining tank, hull/suspension system, and associated equipment	Maintaining and operating Army vehicles
Maintaining tank turret system/fire control system	Maintaining accountability of medical supplies and equipment
Driving/recovering tanks	Keeping medical records
Stowing and handling ammunition	Attending to patients' concerns
Loading/unloading guns	Providing accurate diagnoses in a clinic, hospital, or field setting
Maintaining guns	Arranging for transportation and/or transporting injured personnel
Engaging targets with tank guns	Dispensing medications
Operating and maintaining communication equipment	Preparing and inspecting field site or clinic facilities in the field
Establishing security in the field	Providing routine and ongoing patient care
Navigating	Responding to emergency situations
Preparing/securing tank	Providing instruction to Army personnel

retranslation results produced a final array of 83 performance dimensions with a range of 6 to 12 dimensions across MOS. The specific dimensions for two of the nine MOS are presented in Table 7.3. These dimensions, along with their scaled performance examples, provided the basis for the behavior-based rating scales to be described in Chapter 8.

Identification of Army-Wide Performance Dimensions

The analysis steps for identifying the Army-wide dimensions were the same as for the MOS-specific job analysis.

Critical incident workshops. Seventy-seven officers and NCOs participated in six one-day workshops intended to elicit critical incidents that were not job-specific but relevant for any MOS. A total of 1,315 behavioral examples were generated in the six workshops. Duplicate incidents and incidents that did not meet the specified criteria (e.g., the incident described the behavior of an NCO rather than a first-term soldier) were dropped from further consideration. This left a total of 1,111 performance examples. Two sample critical incidents are shown below:

- After being counseled on his financial responsibilities, this soldier continued to write bad checks and borrow money from other soldiers.
- While clearing a range, this soldier found and secured a military telephone that had been left at an old guard post.

Identifying dimensions.   After editing to a common format, project staff examined the performance examples and again identified performance dimensions by sorting critical incidents into homogeneous categories according to their content. After several iterations of the sorting task and discussions among the researchers, as well as with a small group of officers and NCOs, consensus was reached on a set of 13 dimensions. The dimension labels and short definitions were then placed in a protocol for the retranslation task.

Retranslation and revision.   The procedure for conducting this step was the same as that for the MOS-specific retranslation and utilized 61 SMEs (officers and NCOs). The criteria for retaining incidents were also the same and 870 of the 1,111 examples (78%) met these criteria. Two pairs of dimensions were combined because of confusion in sorting several of the examples into one or the other dimension. These revisions resulted in 11 Army-wide dimensions (Table 7.4).

TABLE 7.4
First Tour Army-Wide Critical Incident Dimensions

    A. Controlling own behavior related to personal finances, drugs/alcohol, and aggressive acts
    B. Adhering to regulations and SOP and displaying respect for authority
    C. Displaying honesty and integrity
    D. Maintaining proper military appearance
    E. Maintaining proper physical fitness
    F. Maintaining assigned equipment
    G. Maintaining living and work areas to Army-unit standards[a]
    H. Exhibiting technical knowledge and skill
    I. Showing initiative and extra effort on job/mission/assignment
    J. Developing own job and soldiering skills
    K. Leadership

---

[a]This dimension was subsequently eliminated on the basis of field test data and SME review.

As with the MOS-specific critical incident analysis, the definition of these Army-wide dimensions and the 870 successfully retranslated performance examples provided the foundation for the nonjob-specific behavior-based rating scales to be described in the next chapter.

Summary of First Tour Job Analyses

At the conclusion of the job analysis activities for first-tour soldiers, project researchers had identified for each of the nine Batch A MOS: (a) a representative sample of 30 critical Army-wide and MOS-specific tasks that would be the basis for the development of hands-on performance and written job knowledge tests, and (b) a set of 6 to 12 critical incident-based performance dimensions and associated scaled critical incidents that would be the basis for MOS-specific rating scales. In addition, a set of 11 critical incident-based performance dimensions and associated scaled critical incidents applicable to all first-tour soldiers, regardless of MOS, were identified. These would be the foundation for a set of Army-wide rating scales that could serve as criterion measures for all MOS included in the research, both Batch A and Batch Z.

SECOND-TOUR NCO JOB ANALYSES

There were three major goals for conducting the second-tour job analyses. The first was to describe the major differences between entry-level and second-tour performance content. A second goal was to describe the major differences across jobs at this higher level. The third goal was to describe the specific nature of the supervisory/leadership components of the second-tour jobs.

Army policy dictates that individuals at higher skill levels are responsible for performing all tasks at the lower skill levels as well. Consequently, the first-tour job analyses were used as a starting point. Perhaps the most substantial difference between the first-tour and second tour-jobs is that individuals are promoted to a junior NCO rank and begin to take on supervisory and leadership responsibilities. Identifying the components of leadership and supervisory performance became a special concern.

As in the first-tour analyses, task-based analyses and critical incident analyses were used to provide a comprehensive description of the major components of second-tour job content. In addition, interviews were conducted with small groups of NCOs to assess the relative importance of the supervisory versus technical components. Finally, additional standardized questionnaire measures were used to further describe specific supervisor and leadership responsibilities.

Task Analysis

First, technical tasks for each second-tour job were enumerated in the same manner as for the first-tour jobs. Specifically, information was combined from the Soldier's Manual (SMCT) for each MOS and from AOSP survey results. After being edited for redundancies and aggregated to a comparable level of generality, AOSP items that could not be matched with Soldier's Manual tasks were added to the task list for that MOS. The proponent Army agency for each MOS then reviewed the list for completeness and accuracy.

The initial task domains for the nine jobs contained between 153 and 409 tasks each, with a mean of 260. As for the first-tour analysis, additional task information was obtained from SMEs to aid in the selection of a representative sample of critical tasks. Specifically, judgments of task criticality and performance difficulty were obtained for the tasks in each MOS from panels of 15 officer SMEs who had recent field experience supervising second-tour NCOs in a specific MOS. Then, the first-tour task clusters were used as a starting point for categorizing the second-tour tasks. The sorting procedures were performed by members of the project staff. When second-tour tasks represented content that was not reflected in the first-tour task clusters, new clusters were formed.

Supervisory tasks. Supervisory/leadership activities were expected to be an important component of second-tour performance. The sources of task information used in the first-tour job analysis (AOSP and the SMCT), however, did not thoroughly address supervisory responsibilities. Therefore, project researchers sought out additional sources of this information for the second-tour job analysis. They identified two instruments previously developed by ARI: the *Supervisory Responsibility Questionnaire,* a 34-item instrument based on critical incidents describing work relationships between first-term soldiers and their NCO supervisors; and a comprehensive questionnaire checklist, the *Leader Requirements Survey,* which contained 450 items designed to describe supervisory/leadership activities at all NCO and officer ranks. Both instruments were based on extensive development work and took advantage of the large literature on military leader/supervisor behavior (Gast, C. H. Campbell, Steinberg, & McGarvey, 1987).

Project staff administered both surveys to samples of NCOs in each of the nine MOS. Approximately 50 NCOs received the *Leader Requirements Survey,* and 125 NCOs received the *Supervisory Responsibility Questionnaire.* All SMEs were asked to indicate the importance of each task for performance as a second-tour NCO for their MOS. Analysis of the *Supervisory Responsibility Questionnaire* data indicated that all the tasks were sufficiently important to be retained. The *Leader Requirements Survey* item ratings were used to select tasks that over half of the respondents indicated were essential to a second-tour soldier's job, and 53 leadership-related tasks were retained. Content analysis of the two task lists resulted in a single list of 46 tasks that incorporated all activities on both lists. These tasks, in eight rationally derived clusters, were added to the second-tour job task list for each of the nine jobs prior to the task selection process.

Task selection.   For each MOS, the SMEs then selected a sample of 45 tasks, 30 technical and 15 supervisory, that would be used as the basis for developing the second-tour performance measures. Task selection was based on the ratings of each task's criticality, expected difficulty, expected performance variability, and on the frequency of task performance. Cluster membership was taken into account by selecting tasks to be representative of the array of clusters that were identified for each job. As a final step, SMEs assigned an overall priority ranking from 1 to 45 for each task. Thus, the result of these procedures was a representative sample of the 45 most critical tasks for each MOS, rank ordered by their importance. There was considerable overlap between the first-tour and second-tour descriptions of job content. However, the second tour tasks tended to be more difficult and more complex.

Critical Incidents Analysis

The critical incident method was also used to identify dimensions of second-tour job content, but with some modification to the procedure used for first-tour jobs. In general, the existing first-tour dimensions were modified to make them appropriate for describing second-tour performance thus allowing the critical incidents analysis process to be conducted in a more abbreviated manner (e.g., with no retranslation step).

MOS-specific analysis.   As a first step, a critical incident analysis workshop was conducted with approximately 25 officers and NCOs in each of the nine target jobs to generate examples of effective, average, and

TABLE 7.5

Second-Tour MOS-Specific Critical Incident Workshops:
Numbers of Incidents Generated (by MOS)[a]

MOS	Number of Participants	Number of Incidents
11B	15	161
13B	14	58
19E	45	236
31C	21	212
63B	14	180
88M	31	184
71L	22	149
91A	20	206
95B	38	234

[a]Many of these participants also generated Army-Wide critical incidents as well.

ineffective second-tour MOS-specific job performance. Table 7.5 shows the number of incidents generated for each MOS, ranging from 58 to 236 with an average of 180. The incidents were then categorized by project staff, using the first-tour MOS-specific category system as a starting framework. If a second-tour incident did not fit into an already existing first-tour category, a new category was introduced. This procedure identified the category additions or deletions that were necessary to describe comprehensively critical second-tour performance.

Almost all of the first-tour MOS-specific performance categories were judged to be appropriate for second-tour MOS. However, for some dimensions, comparisons of the first- and second-tour critical incidents indicated that more was expected of second-tour soldiers than of their first-tour counterparts or that second-tour soldiers were responsible for knowing how to operate and maintain additional pieces of equipment. These distinctions were reflected by the differences in the examples that were used to represent performance levels on the second-tour dimensions.

For several MOS, the second-tour incidents suggested that MOS-specific supervisory performance categories should be incorporated into the job description. However, in developing such categories, care was taken not to duplicate the Army-wide leadership/supervision dimensions (described below) and to reflect aspects of supervision that were relevant only to

TABLE 7.6
MOS-Specific Critical Incident Dimensions for Two Second-Tour MOS

19E Armor Crewman	*91A/B Medical Specialist*
Maintaining tank, tank system, and associated equipment	Maintaining and operating army medical vehicles and equipment
Driving and recovering tanks	Maintaining accountability of medical supplies and equipment
Stowing ammunition aboard tanks	Keeping medical records
Loading/unloading weapons	Arranging for transportation and/or transporting injured personnel
Maintaining weapons	Dispensing medications
Engaging targets with tank weapon systems	Preparing and maintaining field site or clinic facilities in the field
Operating communications equipment	Provide routine and ongoing patient care
Preparing tanks for field problems	Responding to emergency situations
Assuming supervisory responsibilities in absence of tank commander	Providing health care and health maintenance instruction to Army personnel

the particular job in question. A total of six MOS-specific supervisory dimensions distributed over five MOS were generated.

Two examples of the MOS specific second-tour dimensions are shown in Table 7.6. For all nine jobs, approximately half of the dimensions were unchanged from the entry-level versions. For the remainder, revisions were made to reflect increased complexity and/or supervisory responsibilities that characterize the second-tour job. Only two of the original first-tour dimensions were dropped and three first-tour dimensions were each split into two second-tour dimensions, again reflecting increased complexity in job content.

Army-wide analyses.   Three workshops were conducted in which participants were asked to generate examples of second-tour performance episodes that would be relevant for second-tour performance in any MOS. Slightly over 1,000 critical incidents were generated by 172 officers and NCOs. As before, the incidents resulting from the workshops were edited to a common format and three project researchers independently sorted the incidents into categories based on content similarity, using the first-tour categories as a starting point. After resolving discrepancies in the three independent sortings, 12 preliminary dimensions of second-tour Army-wide performance were defined and named by the project staff. The nine

TABLE 7.7
Second-Tour Army-Wide Critical Incident Dimensions

A. Displaying technical knowledge/skill
B. Displaying effort, conscientiousness, and responsibility
C.[a] Organizing, supervising, monitoring, and correcting subordinates
D.[a] Training and developing
E.[a] Showing consideration and concern for subordinates
F. Following regulations/orders and displaying proper respect for authority
G. Maintaining own equipment
H. Displaying honesty and integrity
I. Maintaining proper physical fitness
J. Developing own job/soldiering skills
K. Maintaining proper military appearance
L. Controlling own behavior related to personal finances, drugs/alcohol, and aggressive acts

[a] New leadership/supervisory dimensions for second tour.

nonsupervisory performance dimensions resulting from the first-tour job analysis were retained for the second-tour descriptions. In addition, three additional generic supervisory dimensions emerged. The second-tour Army-wide performance dimensions are shown in Table 7.7.

Job Analysis Interviews

The job analysis interviews were 1-hour structured interviews conducted with small groups of five to eight NCOs in each of the nine jobs. These individuals were asked about the percentage of second-tour soldiers who would typically be in different duty positions, and about the usual activities of those individuals. Participants were also asked to indicate how many hours per week those individuals would likely spend on each of nine supervisory activities (identified in previous ARI research on NCOs) and each of two general areas of task performance (Army-wide vs. MOS-specific), and how important each of those 11 aspects of the job is for the second-tour soldier.

Further Defining the Leadership and Supervisory Components of NCO Performance

Both the task analysis and critical incident analysis identified supervisory/leadership components in the second-tour jobs. In seven of the MOS, a new task cluster was formed to represent MOS-specific tasks involving either tactical operations leadership or administrative supervision. Analysis of the MOS-specific critical incidents suggested additional MOS-specific supervisory dimensions for five of the nine MOS.

As mentioned previously, analysis of the Army-wide critical incidents led to the addition of three dimensions reflecting increased supervisory/leadership responsibilities across all MOS. These three dimensions in effect replaced a single first-tour leadership dimension. The nine other Army-wide dimensions produced by the first-tour critical incident analysis also appeared in the second-tour data.

These findings, as well as the results of the job analysis interviews, indicated that leadership and supervision represent a sizable proportion of the junior NCO position. For example, as judged by the previously described job analysis interview panels, from 35 to 80% of the NCO's time is spent on supervisory activities. Because of the sizable nature of the supervision/leadership component, the final step of the second-tour job analysis was to attempt a more detailed description of that content in terms of specific dimensions that might supplement the three Army-wide supervisory dimensions. To accomplish this, an item pool was created by first using project staff judgments to identify the tasks in each MOS task domain that represented leadership or supervision content. This total list, summed over the nine Batch A MOS, was edited for redundancy and then combined with the 46 items from the *Supervisory Responsibilities Questionnaire.* This produced a total pool of 341 tasks.

The pool of 341 individual task items was clustered into content categories by each of 12 Project A staff members, and each judge developed definitions of his or her categories. Next, the individual solutions were pooled using the method described in Borman and Brush (1993). Essentially, for each pair of task items, the proportion of the judges sorting these two items into the same cluster is computed, generating a matrix of similarities that is transformed to a correlation matrix by considering the patterns of these proportions across all other tasks for each task pair. The resulting 341×341 correlation matrix was factor analyzed, rotated to the varimax criterion, and the solution was compared to the individual judges' cluster sorts. A synthesized description of the dimensions was then written by the project staff (shown in Table 7.8).

The synthesized solution suggests nine interpretable supervisor dimensions. The dimensions represent a wide array of supervisory duties. The typical leader roles of directing, monitoring, motivating, counseling, informing, training subordinates, and completing administrative tasks are all included in the dimension set. Also included is a dimension that involves the leader setting a positive example and acting as a role model for subordinates.

TABLE 7.8

Supervision/Leadership Task Categories Obtained by Synthesizing Expert
Solutions and Empirical Cluster Analysis Solution

1. Planning Operations
   Activities that are performed in advance of major operations of a tactical or technical nature.
   It is the activity that comes *before* actual execution out in the field or workplace.

2. Directing/Leading Teams
   The tasks in this category are concentrated in the combat and military police MOS. They
   involve the actual direction and execution of combat and security team activities.

3. Monitoring/Inspecting
   This cluster includes interactions with subordinates that involve keeping an operation going
   once it has been initiated, such as checking to make sure that everyone is carrying out their
   duties properly, making sure everyone has the right equipment, and monitoring or evaluating
   the status of equipment readiness.

4. Individual Leadership
   Tasks in this cluster reflect attempts to influence the motivation and goal direction of
   subordinates by means of goal setting, interpersonal communication, sharing hardships,
   building trust, etc.

5. Acting as a Model
   This dimension is not tied to specific task content but refers to the NCO modeling the correct
   performance behavior, whether it be technical task performance under adverse conditions or
   exhibiting appropriate military bearing.

6. Counseling
   A one-on-one interaction with a subordinate during which the NCO provides support,
   guidance, assistance, and feedback on specific performance or personal problems.

7. Communication with Subordinates, Peers, and Supervisors
   The tasks in this category deal with composing specific types of orders, briefing subordinates
   and peers on things that are happening, and communicating information up the line to
   superiors.

8. Training Subordinates
   A *very* distinct cluster of tasks that describe the day-to-day role of the NCO as a trainer for
   individual subordinates. When such tasks are being executed, they are clearly identified as
   instructional (as distinct from evaluations or disciplinary actions).

9. Personnel Administration
   This category is made up of "paperwork" or administrative tasks that involve actually doing
   performance appraisals, making or recommending various personnel actions, keeping and
   maintaining adequate records, and following standard operating procedures.

Summary of Second-Tour Job Analyses

At the conclusion of the second-tour job analyses, project researchers had
identified for each Batch A MOS: (a) a sample of 45 technical and supervisory tasks that would form the basis for hands-on performance tests, (b)
a set of 7 to 13 critical incident dimensions to form the basis for MOS-
specific rating scales, and (c) a set of 12 critical incident-based dimensions

and an additional 9 supervisory dimensions to form the basis for Army-wide rating scales. This information, along with the critical incidents and additional information collected during the criterion measure development phase, was also used as the basis for developing a series of supervisory role-play exercises and a written, multiple-choice, supervisory situational judgment test.

SUMMARY

Again, the overall goal of criterion development in Project A/Career Force was to identify the critical components of performance in each job (MOS) and to use feasible state of the art methods to assess individual performance on each component. The job analyses described in this chapter identified those components. They consist of the task clusters produced by the task analyses (for both entry level and advanced positions within the same occupational specialty), the MOS-specific and Army-wide dimensions sets generated by the extensive critical incident analysis, and the components of leadership/supervision produced by the aggregation of task analysis, critical incident, questionnaire, and interview data. At this point, project researchers and the project advisory groups felt that they had been reasonably successful in identifying and portraying a comprehensive and valid picture of the relevant performance components in each job.

At the conclusion of the job analysis phase, the project was poised to begin an intense period of performance criterion development. Multiple methods of performance assessment were to be used, and their development is described in the next chapter.

8

Performance Assessment for a Population of Jobs

Deirdre J. Knapp, Charlotte H. Campbell,
Walter C. Borman, Elaine D. Pulakos,
and Mary Ann Hanson

The purpose of this chapter is to describe the criterion measures that were developed based on the job analysis work described in Chapter 7. All of the criterion measures can be found here, including those developed to assess performance at the end-of-training, during a soldier's first tour of duty (within the first three years), and during the second tour of duty (roughly between the next three to five years of enlistment).

Criterion development and the measurement of individual performance are critical for the evaluation of the validity of a personnel selection and classification system. If estimates of selection validity and classification efficiency are to be meaningful, performance criterion scores must depict individual differences in performance reliably and with high construct validity. From the organization's point of view, the value of any particular level of prediction accuracy (which must be estimated from empirical data using specific criteria) is a direct function of the relevance of the criterion. If the substantive meaning of the criterion and the degree to which it is under the control of the individual are unknown, then it is not possible to judge its importance to the organization's goals.

From the broader perspective of selection and classification research, the degree to which research data can be accumulated, meta-analyzed, and interpreted meaningfully is also a function of the degree to which predictor relationships are linked to major components of performance that have a generally agreed upon substantive meaning. For example, contrast two kinds of conclusions (i.e., things we know) based on the accumulated research data. First, the mean validity estimate for using general cognitive ability to predict performance, when the term "performance" represents a wide variety of unknown variables and when the unknown variables are measured by a variety of methods, is .40. Second, the mean validity estimates for using well developed measures of general cognitive ability and the conscientiousness factor (from personality assessment) to predict performance in the role of team member, when this component of performance has a broad consensus definition, are .30 and .45, respectively. Rather than be content with a single, overall, and not terribly meaningful representation of the research record (as in the first conclusion), it would be much more informative to have a number of substantive representations of what we know (as in the second conclusion).

Unfortunately, we simply know a lot more about predictor constructs than we do about job performance constructs. This was even more true at the beginning of Project A than it is today. There are volumes of research on the former, and almost none on the latter. For personnel psychologists, it is almost second nature to talk about predictor constructs. However, at the start of the project, the investigation of job performance constructs seemed limited to those few studies dealing with synthetic validity and those using the critical incidents format to develop performance factors. The situation has improved somewhat, and there is a slowly growing research record dealing with the substantive nature of individual job performance (e.g., Borman & Motowidlo, 1997; J.P. Campbell, Gasser, & Oswald, 1996; Organ, 1997). We would like to think, rightly or wrongly, that Project A was the major stimulus for finally getting job performance out of the black box and started down the path to construct validation. The remainder of this chapter and Chapter 11 attempt to describe how this came about.

CRITERION MEASUREMENT OBJECTIVES

This chapter describes the project's efforts to develop a comprehensive set of multiple performance criterion measures for each job (MOS) in the Project A sample. These criterion development activities resulted in the array of performance measures intended to meet the major criterion assessment objectives of the project; that is, a set of measures that would allow us to examine the multidimensional nature of performance and that would provide reliable and valid criterion "scores" for each performance dimension.

The job analyses described in Chapter 7 provided the building blocks for development of the performance measures. In Astin's (1964) terms, the job analyses yielded the conceptual criteria; that is, they specified the content of the important performance dimensions for the target jobs. The task analysis identified dimensions in terms of categories of critical job tasks; the critical incident analysis identified the important dimensions in terms of homogeneous categories of critical performance behaviors. The next major step was to develop the actual measurement procedures needed to assess individual performance on each performance dimension identified by the job analysis. The overall goal was to assess performance on all major performance components in each job using multiple measures.

As discussed in Chapter 7, criterion development efforts were guided by a theory of performance that views job performance as multidimensional. In Army enlisted jobs, this translates into an hypothesis of two general factors: job/MOS-specific performance and "Army-wide" performance. Within each of the two general factors, the expectation was that a small number of more specific factors could be identified. Moreover, it was assumed that the best measurement of performance would be achieved through multiple strategies to assess each performance dimension. With this theoretical backdrop, the intent was to proceed through an almost continual process of data collection, expert review, and model/theory revision.

We should point out that the Project A performance measures were intended to assess individual performance and not team/unit performance. This was because the project focused on the development of a selection/classification system that must make forecasts of individual performance without being able to anticipate the setting or unit to which the individual would eventually be assigned.

The next part of this chapter is organized into sections that describe the development of (a) training performance measures, (b) first-tour performance measures, and (c) second-tour performance measures. Scoring procedures and associated psychometric properties of the measures are presented next. The chapter ends with a discussion of selected measurement issues. Chapter 11 examines the underlying structure of performance using these measures.

At the outset, we must acknowledge that even with considerable time and resources to devote to performance measurement, the number of potential measurement methods that the state-of-the-art provides is relatively small. There are of course many different variations of the ubiquitous *performance rating*, which is the most frequently used, and most criticized, criterion measure in personnel research. In contrast, so-called "objective" indicators of performance or productivity maintained by the organization were traditionally highly valued as criterion measures (e.g., Cascio, 1991). In Project A, such measures are referred to as *administrative indices* of performance. *Job samples* or simulations (e.g., assessment centers, aircraft cockpit simulators) are less frequently used but potentially valuable as a method of performance assessment. Finally, in certain settings, such as the armed services, we will argue that written tests of *proceduralized job knowledge* can be appropriate as criterion measures. Our intent was to exploit multiple variations of each measurement method as fully as possible, and to use each one of them in the most construct valid way as possible.

DEVELOPMENT OF CRITERION MEASURES

Measures of Training Performance

Two measurement methods, ratings and written multiple-choice tests, were used to assess performance at the end of the individual's MOS-specific technical training course, which entailed 2 to 6 months of additional technical training beyond the basic training period. The training performance rating scales were a modified form of the first tour Army-wide behavior-based rating scales (to be described later in this chapter). Specifically, 3 of the 10 first-tour Army-wide dimensions were dropped because they were not suitable for trainees. The definitions and anchors for the remaining dimensions were simplified. Ratings were to be collected from four peers and the student's drill instructor.

Written training achievement tests were developed for each of the 19 MOS included in the research plan (Davis, Davis, Joyner, & deVera, 1987). A blueprint was developed for each test, which specified the content areas to be covered and the approximate number of items for each area. Final tests were expected to include approximately 150 items.

The test blueprints were derived through a synthesis of training curriculum documents and applicable Army Occupational Survey Program (AOSP) data. The AOSP job analysis data were used to help confirm the job relevance of the training curricula and to identify relevant content areas not explicitly covered in training. The rationale for including such content on the so-called "school knowledge" tests was to ensure that we would capture the incidental learning that trainees, particularly exceptional trainees, might be expected to gain during training. This might include learning that comes from outside study or extracurricular interactions with experienced Army personnel and other students.

Test items were drafted by project staff and consultants using information provided by Programs of Instruction, Soldier's Manuals, and other pertinent reference documents. Items had four to five response alternatives. The draft items were reviewed by job incumbents and school trainers and revised accordingly. In addition to suggesting modifications to test items, reviewers rated each item for importance and relevance. The items were then pilot-tested on a sample of approximately 50 trainees per MOS. The Batch A items were later field tested on samples of job incumbents in the first-tour field tests described later in this chapter. Field test data were used to compute classical test theory item statistics (item difficulties, percent examinees selecting each response option, and point-biserial correlations between item performance and performance on the whole test) and to estimate test reliability. Items were retained, revised, or dropped based on these analyses. Draft tests were reviewed by the Army proponent agency for each MOS, and then finalized for administration to job incumbents in the CVI (Concurrent Validation-First Tour) sample. The Batch Z tests were field tested concurrently with the CVI administration (i.e., over- length tests were administered and poor items were dropped before final CVI test scores were generated). Before administration at the end of training in the longitudinal validation (LVT), the tests were reviewed and revised once more to ensure that they reflected current equipment and procedural requirements. An additional review was required of the Batch Z tests, which were used as a surrogate job performance measure in the longitudinal validation, first-tour data collection (LVI). In the end, the so-called "school knowledge" tests used in these data collections contained from 97 to 180 (average 130) scored multiple choice items.

Performance Measures for First-Tour Job Incumbents

The development of several measures for multiple performance dimensions for the nine Batch A and 10 Batch Z MOS was a very large undertaking. A team approach was used in which a group of researchers took responsibility for each major category of measures and, within each category, measures for specific MOS became the responsibility of individual staff members.

The common goal of the different criterion measurement teams was to prepare the initial prototypes that could be pretested at one or more of six field test sites. The field tests involved MOS-specific sample sizes ranging from 114 to 178. Of the 1,369 job incumbents involved in the field tests, 87% were male and 65% were white.

All criterion measures were revised based on the field test results, readying them for administration to the CVI sample. The CVI data collection occurred three years before the measures would be administered again to first-tour soldiers in the LVI sample. Particularly for the hands-on and written job knowledge tests, considerable effort was required in this interim period to revise measures so that they would be consistent with new equipment and procedures. Other changes were made in an effort to improve the psychometric quality and/or administration procedures associated with several of the measures.

In the remainder of this section, the development of each major criterion measure is described.

Hands-On Job Sample Measures

Job sample measures are often viewed as the most desirable means of measuring performance because they require the application of job knowledge and procedural skills to performance on actual job tasks under standardized conditions (e.g., Asher & Sciarrino, 1974). Such measures also benefit from wide acceptance by laypersons because of their inherent credibility.

In Project A, job samples, or "hands-on" measures were used to assess both job-specific and common task performance. However, the high cost of developing and administering comprehensive job-specific measures, coupled with the large number of MOS sampled, made it infeasible to use this measurement method for all the MOS included in the full sample. Therefore, job samples were developed and administered only in the nine Batch A MOS.

Given the time frame for the project, the resources available, and the sample sizes specified by the research design, the job sample for each MOS needed to be administered one-on-one to 15 soldiers within a 4-hour timeframe. The tests were to be administered by eight senior NCOs (assigned to the post where data were being collected) under the direction of project staff. The NCOs were to both administer and score the hands-on measures.

Selecting job tasks for measurement. Job samples are relatively time-consuming to administer, and the number of critical job tasks that could be assessed was limited by the one-half day that the research design could make available. Project staff familiar with job sample assessment estimated that performance on roughly 15 tasks per MOS could be assessed in this amount of time. As described in Chapter 7, the task selection process resulted in the identification of approximately 30 tasks per MOS. The plan was to develop written job knowledge test questions for all 30 tasks, and to develop hands-on job sample measures for approximately 15 of those same tasks, which, again, were intended to be representative of the critical job tasks.

Development and field testing. Each job sample test protocol consisted of four major components: (a) specification of test conditions, including the required equipment and environment; (b) specification of the performance steps on which examinees would be scored; (c) instructions for examinees; and (d) instructions for the administrators/scorers.

Development of the hands-on measures was greatly facilitated by the availability of training manuals specifying the steps required to perform various tasks as well as standards of performance associated with those tasks. These training manuals and related materials were used to draft the initial versions of the job samples. Initial development efforts also benefited from the fact that many of the project staff had related military experience. That is, many of our criterion development researchers had considerable job knowledge as well as measurement expertise.

The specification of test conditions was designed to maximize standardization within and across test sites. For example, equipment requirements were limited to those that could be reasonably satisfied at all test sites. Construction specifications, if required, were very detailed. These specifications included such things as how to construct a simulated loading dock and how to select objects (e.g., buildings and trees) used to collect azimuth measurements. In some cases, equipment requirements included materials used in training (e.g., mannequins and moulage kits for medical tasks) to simulate task performance.

To maximize reliability and validity, the performance steps on which examinees were to be evaluated adhered to the following principles:

- Describe observable behavior only.
- Describe a single pass/fail behavior.
- Contain only necessary action.

- Contain a standard, if applicable (e.g., how much, how well, or how quickly).
- Include an error tolerance limit if variation is permissible.
- Include a sequence requirement only if a particular sequencing of steps is required by doctrine.

In most cases, the hands-on criterion scores were procedure-based. That is, they reflected what the soldier did (correctly or incorrectly) to perform the task. In some cases, however, product-based performance measures were included as well. For example, the task "Determine azimuth with a compass" was scored by determining whether the soldier correctly carried out each action step required to perform the task (process) and also by determining the accuracy of the obtained azimuth reading (product).

"Tracked" versions of the hands-on measures were prepared as necessary to accommodate using different types of equipment on the same task. For example, there were three types of field artillery equipment to which cannon crewmembers (13B) could be assigned. The tracked versions were intended to be parallel measures.

Following initial construction of the hands-on tests for each MOS, the lead test developer for the MOS met with four senior NCOs (administrators/scorers) and five incumbents (examinees) to conduct a pilot test. The sequential nature of the pilot test activities (i.e., review by senior NCOs, one-by-one administration to the five incumbents) allowed the measures to be revised in an iterative fashion. The revised measures were then evaluated in the larger scale field tests described previously.

Evaluating the reliability of the first-tour hands-on measures was problematic. Test-retest data were collected, but the retesting time frame was only a few days and some participants tended to resent having to take the test twice (thus performing at a substandard level on the second test). Other individuals received intense coaching between the two administrations. It was infeasible to develop alternate forms of the hands-on tests and no "shadow scoring" data were available on which to base inter-scorer reliability estimates. Within a task, internal consistency estimates would tend to be spuriously high because steps within the task would usually not be independent. Estimates of coefficient alpha computed using the total scores for each task (e.g., $k = 15$) as the components tended to be low, but the hands-on measures were not intended to be unidimensional. The only feasible reliability estimate is the corrected split half estimate based on an a priori division of the 15 task test scores into two parts that were judged to be as parallel as possible.

The unique nature of the hands-on tests also made difficult item evaluation and test revision based on statistical evidence. This was largely because steps within a task test were interdependent and sequential. Thus, for example, the elimination of very easy steps from the performance checklist served to interrupt the logical flow of the list and would likely confuse scorers. Therefore, most revisions to the hands-on tests made as a result of the field tests were based on observations of the test administration process. The major criterion used to select entire task tests for elimination was the extent to which the tests adequately simulated real-world task performance.

The final step in the development of the hands-on tests, as well as the other criterion measures, was proponent agency review. That is, the training command responsible for each MOS in the sample was asked to review the final set of measures. This step was consistent with the philosophy of obtaining input from SMEs at each major developmental stage and also was considered important for the credibility of the measures in the eyes of the organization. In general, considerable deference was given to the proponent judgments particularly when they were based on an understanding of planned changes in task requirements for the MOS. For example, in the year before CVI began, the military police (MOS 95B) were starting to shift toward a more combat-ready security role and away from a domestic police role. This was addressed by making several changes in the tasks to be assessed for that MOS.

Format.   The hands-on test forms had two major sections: (a) instructions to scorers and (b) the score sheet. The score sheet listed the performance steps with spaces alongside in which the scorer could check the examinee as go or no-go on each step. The score sheet also included spaces for identifying information (e.g., scorer and examinee identification codes), the text to be read aloud to examinees, and miscellaneous notes to the scorers. For LVI, a 7-point overall proficiency rating was added at the end of each task test. A copy of the measurement protocol for one task (Putting on a pressure dressing) is shown in Fig. 8.1. This example uses the format adopted for LVI and LVII.

Written Job Knowledge Measures

The Army may be one of the few organizations for which a measure of "current job knowledge" can be legitimized as a performance criterion. A major goal of the U.S. Army, as an organization, is to be "ready" to respond to conflict situations and threats to national security. For an individual, one component of being ready is to be knowledgeable about one's job. Consequently, people who maintain a high state of job knowledge are performing at a higher level than people who maintain a lower level of knowledge. In most other contexts, job knowledge is regarded as a determinant of performance but not performance itself.

A multiple-choice format was selected for the knowledge measures primarily because of cost and feasibility considerations. Development of high quality multiple-choice tests is still relatively difficult, however, because of inherent cueing, particularly between items, and the need to develop likely and plausible, but clearly incorrect, distractors. Because the number of plausible alternatives was somewhat dependent upon each test item, the number of response alternatives across items was allowed to vary, and ranged from two to five.

Put on field or pressure dressing

Equipment/Material Required

    2   Field dressings
          Padding or folded swath
          Red felt tip marker
          Medical mannequin or scorer's assistant
          Ground Cloth

Procedures to Set Up Test Site

1. Spread the ground cloth.

2. Mark the forearm of mannequin or the scorer's assistant with the felt tip marker to identify the wound.

3. Remove the field dressing from its protective package.

Procedures to be Performed Before Testing Each Soldier

1. Refold the field dressings along their original folds.

2. Lay the mannequin on the ground cloth or have the scorer's assistant lie on his/her back on the cloth.

Procedures to Conduct and Score Test

1. For PM 5 and PM 13, "Tied in a non-slip knot," consider any non-slip knot acceptable.

2. Check the tightness of the field pressure (PM 8) by inserting two fingers after the soldier applies the field dressing, before you give the instructions for manual pressure.

3. For the manual pressure phase, the scorer's assistant, if used, should keep the wounded arm below chest level until the tested soldier elevates it.

4. Check the tightness of the pressure dressing (PM 15) by trying to insert one finger after the test is over.

FIG. 8.1.   Sample hands-on test.

Check: <u>Yes</u> <u>No</u>

Scorer: _____   Soldier: _____   Know Soldier: ___ ___
Date: _____   ID#: _____   Soldier in CO: ___ ___
                                                            Supervise Soldier: ___ ___

This test covers your ability to use a field and pressure dressing. This soldier has a bleeding wound as indicated. He has no other injuries. You must stop the bleeding and protect the wound. Assume that you have just opened the dressing packet and the dressing is sterile.

PERFORMANCE MEASURES   GO   NO-GO

Field Dressing

1. Placed white side of dressing directly over wound.   ———   ———
2. Held dressing in place with one hand and used other hand
   to wrap one of the tails around the dressing.   ———   ———
3. Wrapped the other tail in the opposite direction.   ———   ———
4. Maintained sterility of dressing (must not touch side going toward wound. ———   ———
5. Tied the tails in a non-slip knot.   ———   ———
6. Tied knot so it was not directly over the wound.   ———   ———
7. Sealed edges of dressing with the tails (at least ½" overlap).   ———   ———
8. Tied dressing tight enough that it does not move, but loose enough that two
   fingers can be inserted between knot and dressing ties.   ———   ———

Manual Pressure

The wound continues to bleed.

9. Applied manual pressure to the wound (by hand) or at the elbow or armpit (by
   finger) until scorer gave further instructions.   ———   ———
10. Elevated the wound two to four inches above heart level while applying pressure. ———   ———

Pressure Dressing

You have applied pressure for ten minutes and the wound continues to bleed.

11. Placed padding on top of field dressing directly over wound.   ———   ———
12. Wrapped second dressing over padding and around limb.   ———   ———
13. Tied dressing in a non-slip knot.   ———   ———
14. Tied knot directly over wound.   ———   ———
15. Tied pressure dressing tight enough so only the tip of one finger can be
    inserted between the knot and pressure dressing ties.   ———   ———

FIG. 8.1. (Continued)

Although labeled as measures of job knowledge, the Project A tests were designed to be assessments of proceduralized knowledge (C.H. Campbell, R.C. Campbell, Rumsey, & Edwards, 1986). That is, the tests were characterized by three distinct properties intended to reflect realistic performance requirements. First, they either asked the examinee to perform a task (e.g., determine distance on a map) or to indicate how something should be done (e.g., how to determine if medical anti-shock trousers have been put on a patient properly). As with the hands-on measures, the objective of the knowledge tests was to measure the examinee's capability to perform a task, not to determine his or her underlying understanding of why it is performed in one way or another. Because of this requirement, job-relevant stimuli (e.g., illustrations, abstracts of technical manuals, protractors) were used liberally.

A second characteristic was that the test items were based on an analysis of common performance errors. This required considerable input from SMEs to understand if job incumbents tended to have problems knowing how to perform the task, where to perform it, when to perform it, and/or what the outcome of the task should be.

The third primary characteristic was that the distractors were, in fact, likely alternatives. They were based on an identification of what individuals tend to do wrong when they are unable to perform the task or task step correctly.

Development of the job knowledge measures.   Recall that a representative sample of 30 critical tasks was selected for job knowledge measurement in each Batch A MOS, and approximately half of these were assessed in the hands-on mode as well. Development of the written tests closely paralleled that of the hands-on measures, with the same developers generally working on each method for a particular MOS.

Project staff drafted test items, for each task, as described above. These items were pilot tested by having four senior NCOs in the MOS carefully review each item with the test developers. Five incumbents took the test as examinees and were debriefed to determine what types of problems, if any, they had understanding each item. The items were revised based on the pilot test findings and administered to a larger sample of incumbents in the first-tour criterion measure field tests.

Standard classical test theory item analysis procedures were used to evaluate the written test items. Item evaluation was conducted in the context of each task rather than across tasks. The first step was to check for keying errors and evidence of otherwise faulty items. The field test versions were longer than desired for administration to the validation samples. Items were selected for elimination based on their item statistics and using an iterative process within each of the 30 tasks to yield a set of items that produced the highest coefficient alpha (within task).

The reduced knowledge tests were reviewed by proponent agencies along with the hands-on measures. As with the hands-on measures, some changes were made based on the proponent's understanding of recent and anticipated changes in MOS-related procedures and requirements. The final tests covered approximately 30 tasks per MOS and contained 150 to 200 items each.

Rating Measures

Several different types of ratings were used. All scales were to be completed by both peer and supervisor raters who were given extensive rater orientation and training instruction.

Task rating scales.   Development of hands-on job samples and written job knowledge tests provided two methods of measurement for the MOS-specific and common tasks. As a third method of measuring task performance for soldiers in the Batch A MOS, numerical 7-point rating scales were used for assessing current performance on each of the tasks also measured by both the hands-on and job knowledge methods. Each rating was defined by the task name or label, and the rating instrument required raters to evaluate how effectively the individual performs the task (on a 7-point scale) and to indicate how often the rater had observed the soldier perform the task. A comparable task rating scale was developed for Batch Z soldiers. It required raters to evaluate soldier performance on 11 tasks common across MOS (e.g., first aid).

Although the other rating scales worked well in CVI, the task rating scales did not. Preliminary analyses indicated that they were generally not rated reliably, presumably because raters did not have the opportunity to witness performance on all of these very specific tasks. Many scales were left blank for this reason. Because of these problems, the task rating scales were not used in the CVI validation analyses and were not administered to the LV sample.

Army (organization)-wide and MOS (job)-specific behavior-based rating scales.   As described in Chapter 7, Project A's job analyses included both task analysis and critical incident analysis. We have described three measurement methods used to assess performance on a representative set of important job tasks. This section describes the two rating booklets designed to provide assessments of ratee performance on major dimensions of performance defined by categories of critical incidents of job behavior. The Army-wide and MOS-specific rating scales were each developed using essentially the same methodology (Pulakos & Borman, 1986; Toquam et al., 1988).

The critical incident workshops and retranslation activities described in Chapter 7 were conducted to support development of the Army-wide rating scales and the nine sets of MOS-specific behavior-based rating scales. During the course of these workshops, SMEs wrote thousands of critical incidents, which were retranslated into performance dimensions and became the dimensions included on each set of rating scales. There were 11 Army-wide dimensions (one of which was dropped after field testing) and 7 to 13 dimensions for each of the nine MOS identified through this process.

The effectiveness level ratings for each incident made by SMEs during the retranslation exercises were used to develop rating scale anchors with behavioral definitions at three different effectiveness levels. Behavioral definitions were written by summarizing the content of the performance examples reliably retranslated into that dimension and effectiveness level. Specifically, for each dimension, all behavior examples having mean effectiveness values of 6.5 or higher (on the 9-point scale) were reviewed, and a behavioral summary statement was generated that became the anchor for the high end of that rating scale. Similarly, all examples with mean effectiveness values of 3.5 to 6.4 were summarized to form the mid-level anchor, and examples with values of 1.0 to 3.4 were summarized to provide the anchor for low effectiveness. The same procedure was followed for each Army-wide and MOS-specific performance dimension.

A rater orientation and training program was designed to help ensure that ratings data collected in Project A would be as informative as possible. The program included a description of common rater errors (e.g., halo, recency). Enlarged sample rating booklets were used to depict what these errors look like (e.g., ratings across dimensions all the same or all high). Raters were also reminded that their ratings would be used for research purposes only. The rater training program is described in more detail in Pulakos and Borman (1986).

Revisions were made to the rating scales and the rater orientation and training program based on analyses of the field test data and observations of the project staff. Scale dimensions that tended to show low agreement among supervisor and/or peer raters were examined and revised in an effort to increase inter-rater agreement. Also, a few dimensions were collapsed when ratings on them were very highly correlated. Finally, field test observations suggested that some raters experienced difficulty with the amount of reading required by the scales. Therefore, all scale anchors were reviewed and edited to decrease reading requirements while trying not to incur any significant loss of information.

Examples of Army-wide and MOS-specific dimension rating scales are presented in Fig. 8.2. In addition to the 10 dimension ratings, the Army-wide rating booklet included two other scales—an overall effectiveness rating and a rating of potential for successful performance in the future as an NCO. These are shown in Fig. 8.3. The MOS-specific rating booklets also included two other scales—an overall MOS performance rating and a confidence rating. The latter scale gave the rater the opportunity to indicate how confident he or she was about the evaluations being made. Raters were also asked to indicate their position relative to the soldier (peer, first-line supervisor, or second-line supervisor). All rating scale booklets used a format that allowed raters to rate up to five individuals in a single booklet.

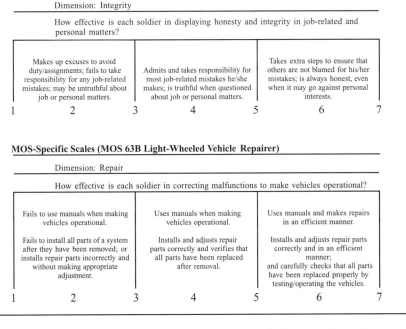

FIG. 8.2. Sample Army-wide and MOS-specific behavior-based rating scales.

OVERALL EFFECTIVENESS

The scales you have just made ratings on represent 10 different areas important for effective soldiering. This scale asks you to rate the <u>overall effectiveness</u> of each soldier, taking into account performance on all 10 of the soldiering categories.

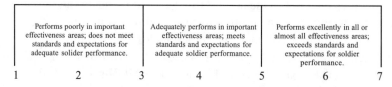

NCO POTENTIAL

On this rating scale, evaluate each soldier on his or her <u>potential effectiveness as an NCO</u>. At this point you are <u>not</u> to rate on the basis of present performance and effectiveness, but instead indicate how well each soldier is likely to perform as an NCO in his or her MOS (assume each will have <u>an opportunity</u> to be an NCO).

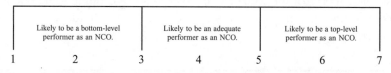

FIG. 8.3.   First tour overall and NCO potential ratings.

Expected Combat Performance

Army personnel spend a significant amount of their time training for combat. Fortunately, most job incumbents in the Project A samples had not experienced combat. The fact remained, however, that a soldier's ability to perform under degraded and dangerous conditions is central to the concept of performance in the military, and the complete absence of this aspect of performance from the assessment package was unacceptable to the sponsors of this research. Because realistic simulation of combat conditions was infeasible, it was necessary to try some other way to capture this aspect of performance.

The Combat Performance Prediction Scale (CPPS) was developed to measure *expected* performance under combat conditions. The rationale was that peers and supervisors knowledgeable about a soldier's day-to-day performance would be able to make reasonable predictions about how the soldier would perform under combat conditions (J. P. Campbell, 1987). Two difficulties associated with this approach were recognized from the outset. First, raters' opportunities to observe performance under any kind of adverse conditions (combat or otherwise) may often be limited. Second, most raters will not have had combat experience themselves, making it even more difficult for them to make the required predictions.

The CPPS was envisioned as a summated scale in which items represented specific performance examples (e.g., this soldier prepared defensive positions without being told to do so). Raters would be asked to estimate the likelihood that the soldier being rated would act in the manner depicted by the performance example. This format was adopted largely to reduce common method variance between the CPPS and the Army-wide behavior-based scales, both of which were designed to measure aspects of general soldiering performance.

Scale development.   Behavioral examples were generated in a series of critical incident workshops involving officers and NCOs who had combat experience (J. P. Campbell, 1987; C. H. Campbell et al., 1990). Additional examples were drawn from the Army-wide rating scale critical incident workshops described earlier. A sorting and retranslation exercise yielded five combat behavior dimensions: (a) cohesion/commitment, (b) mission orientation, (c) self-discipline/responsibility, (d) technical/tactical knowledge, and (e) initiative.

A draft version of the CPPS containing 77 items was field tested. Using a 15-point rating scale ranging from "very unlikely" to "very likely," raters indicated the likelihood that each soldier they were rating would perform as the soldier in the behavioral example performed. Ratings were obtained from 136 peer raters and 113 supervisor raters in five different jobs. Means and standard deviations for individual item ratings were within acceptable ranges, but the intraclass reliability for the total summated score (in which error was attributed to item heterogeneity and rater differences) was only .21. This estimate was increased to .56 when only the best 40 items were used to compute the total score. This set of 40 items was selected on the basis of content representation, psychometric properties (i.e., reliability, item-dimension correlation, and item-total correlation), and rater feedback regarding item rateability. Coefficient alpha for the shortened scale was .94.

The CPPS administered in CVI included the 40 items, rated on a 15-point scale, and a single 7-point rater confidence rating. This latter rating gave raters the opportunity to indicate how confident they were about the predictions they were being asked to make. A principal components analysis of the 40 substantive items yielded two factors. These were labeled "Performing Under Adverse Conditions" and "Avoiding Mistakes." The empirical evidence did not lend support to the five rational dimensions derived during scale development.

Before the CPPS was administered to soldiers in LVI, it was substantially revised. The revisions were intended to (a) reduce administration time requirements, (b) increase inter-rater reliability, and (c) ensure that the scale would be applicable for second-tour soldiers. With regard to this last point, it was initially believed that a completely different scale might be needed for second-tour personnel. After consulting with a group of combat-experienced SMEs, however, it became evident that one instrument would suffice. These SMEs identified three items on the CVI version of the instrument that they believed should be dropped and pronounced the remaining items suitable for both first- and second-tour incumbents.

A new version of the CPPS, containing the 37 remaining behavioral example items and using a 7-point (instead of a 15-point) rating format was field tested on a sample of more than 300 second-tour soldiers during the second-tour criterion measure field tests (described in the next section). Principal components analysis of the data failed to reveal a clear, meaningful factor structure. Therefore, items having the highest inter-rater reliabilities and item-total correlations, without regard to content representation, were selected for inclusion on the revised CPPS. The resulting instrument had 14 substantive items and the single rater confidence rating. This version of the CPPS was administered to soldiers in the LVI, LVII, and CVII samples.

Administrative Indices of Performance

In addition to the for-research-only measures constructed for purposes of the project, it was hoped that the Army's archival performance records might also be useful, in spite of the well-known problems associated with the use of operational indices of performance (e.g., productivity records, supervisor appraisals, promotion rate). Common problems include criterion contamination and deficiency (Borman, 1991; Guion, 1965; Smith, 1976).

The strategy for identifying promising administrative criterion measures involved (a) reviewing various sources of personnel records to identify potentially useful variables, (b) examining them for evidence of opportunity bias, and (c) evaluating their distributional properties. There was also some effort to improve the psychometric properties of these indices by combining individual variables into meaningful composites (Riegelhaupt, Harris, & Sadacca, 1987).

Several sources of administrative performance indices were examined. The Military Personnel Records Jacket (MPRJ) is a paper file of personnel records maintained for every active duty soldier. This file is continually updated and follows the soldier from one assignment to the next. The Enlisted Master File (EMF) is a centrally maintained computerized file containing a wide range of information about every enlisted soldier serving in the Army at any given time. It is a working file that is periodically overwritten with updated information taken from MPRJs. The Official Military Personnel File (OMPF) is a permanent historical record of an individual's military service, and is maintained on microfiche records. A systematic review of these data sources indicated that the MPRJ was by far the richest and most up-to-date archival source of performance information. Unfortunately, it was also the least accessible.

Variables available from one or more of the three sources were reviewed to identify criteria of interest. These potential criteria were studied further to examine their distributional properties and their relationships with other variables. For example, were indices theoretically related to cognitive ability significantly correlated with AFQT scores? Opportunity bias was examined by testing for score differences between various groups of soldiers (e.g., race and gender subgroups, soldiers in different job types or located at different posts).

This exercise resulted in the identification of seven variables with the highest potential for being useful criteria. These were:

1. Eligibility to reenlist,
2. Number of memoranda and certificates of appreciation and commendation,
3. Number of awards (e.g., Good Conduct Medal, Ranger Tab),
4. Number of military training courses completed,
5. Number of Articles 15 and Flag Actions (disciplinary actions),
6. Marksmanship qualification rating, and
7. Promotion rate (actual paygrade compared to average for soldiers with a given time in service).

The field test samples were used to collect comparative data on these indices and to evaluate the use of a self-report approach to measurement. A comparison of the three archival data sources showed that the MPRJ was the best source for most of these indices, but again, very difficult to retrieve. It was much more desirable to ask individuals to self report if it could be assumed that their answers would be accurate.

A brief questionnaire called the Personnel File Form was developed to collect self-report data on the variables listed above. In the field test, this measure was administered to 505 soldiers. In the same time frame, project staff collected data on the identical variables from the MPRJ for these same soldiers. Comparison of the two data sources indicated that self-report indices were actually better than the archival records (C. H. Campbell et al., 1990). When the two sources were not in exact agreement, the self reports appeared to be providing more up-to-date information. Soldiers were likely to report more negative as well as positive outcomes. Moreover, correlations with the Army-wide performance ratings collected during the field test were higher for the self-report indices than for the MPRJ indices.

Based on the field test findings, the self-report approach to the collection of administrative indices of performance was adopted. An exception to this was promotion rate, which was easily and accurately calculated using data from the computerized EMF. Also, as a result of the field test, the number of military courses taken was dropped as a measure because it had insufficient variability, and reenlistment eligibility was dropped as well. Two items were added. One was the individual's most recent Physical Readiness test score. This test is given to each soldier annually and includes sit-ups, push-ups, and a two-mile run. Also, for many years, enlisted personnel took an annual certification test to evaluate their job knowledge, so people in the sample were asked to report their most recent Skill Qualification Test (SQT) score. Identical versions of the self-report Personnel File Form were administered to first-tour soldiers in CVI and LVI.

Summary of the First-Tour (Entry Level) Job Performance Measures

For the concurrent validation (CVI), incumbents in Batch A MOS were scheduled for 12 hours of criterion measurement activities and soldiers in Batch Z MOS were scheduled for 4 hours. Table 8.1 summarizes the instruments that were administered at this time. Although the training achievement (school knowledge) tests were not designed to be measures of first-tour performance, they are listed here because they were administered to soldiers in Batch Z MOS during CVI.

As noted in Table 8.1, three auxiliary measures were administered in CVI along with the primary performance measurement instruments. A "Job History Questionnaire" was developed for each Batch A MOS. It listed the tasks tested on the written and/or job sample tests and asked soldiers to indicate how often they had performed each task over the previous 6 months and the last time they had performed each task. The Measurement Method Rating Form asked Batch A soldiers to indicate the fairness of each measurement method used to evaluate their performance. Finally, the Army

TABLE 8.1
Summary of First-Tour Criterion Measures

Performance Measures for Batch A MOS Only

Hands-on job sample tests covering 15 job tasks.
Written, multiple-choice job knowledge tests covering 30 job tasks.
MOS-Specific Rating Scales—6–10 behavior-based rating scales covering major aspects of job-specific performance; single rating of overall MOS performance; ratings on 15 MOS-specific tasks. (*Dropped MOS-specific task ratings in LVI*)
Job History Questionnaire—Auxiliary measure to assess frequency and recency of performance for 30 job tasks.
Measurement Method Rating—Auxiliary measure asking soldiers to rate the fairness of the assessment methods.

Performance Measures Common to Batch A and Batch Z MOS

Personnel File Form—Self-report administrative data such as awards, disciplinary actions, physical training scores, etc.
School Knowledge Test—Written, multiple-choice tests covering material taught in MOS-specific classroom training. (*Administered to Batch Z incumbents only in LVI*)
Army-Wide Rating Scales—10 behavior-based rating scales covering non-job-specific performance; single rating of overall effectiveness; single rating of NCO potential; ratings on 13 tasks common to all MOS. (*Dropped common task ratings in LVI*)
Combat Performance Prediction Scale—40-item summated rating scale assessing expected performance in combat. (*Reduced to 14 items in LVI*)
Army Work Environment Questionnaire—Auxiliary measure assessing situational/environment characteristics. (*Administered in CVI only*)
Army Job Satisfaction Questionnaire—Auxiliary measure to assess satisfaction with work, co-worker, supervision, pay, promotions, and the Army. (*Administered in LVI only*)

Note: Ratings were collected from both peers and supervisors. Number of tasks covered by hands-on and job knowledge tests is approximate.

Work Environment Questionnaire was a 141-item instrument assessing situational characteristics, such as availability of equipment, amount of supervisor support, skills utilization, perceived job importance, and unit cohesion (see Chapter 17 for further discussion of this measure).

Table 8.1 also summarizes the measures that were administered to soldiers in the LVI sample. Once again, both Batch A and Batch Z soldiers were assessed. School knowledge tests were not administered to the Batch A soldiers because they were administered during the LVT (end-of-training) data collection. These tests were re-administered to the Batch Z soldiers, however, because there were no other MOS-specific criterion measures available for soldiers in these occupations. The MOS-specific task ratings were also dropped.

With regard to the LVI auxiliary measures, a job satisfaction measure (Knapp, Carter, McCloy, & DiFazio, 1996) was added, and the Army Work Environment Questionnaire was dropped. Otherwise, the criterion measures administered during this data collection were essentially the same as those administered during CVI.

Development of the Second-Tour Criterion Measures

The goal of criterion measurement for second-tour job incumbents was to provide a comprehensive assessment of junior NCO performance. The job analyses of the second-tour soldier job indicated that there is considerable overlap between first- and second-tour performance requirements. Almost all of the overlap occurs in the technical content of the position, although NCOs are expected to perform at somewhat higher levels on the technical tasks. The differences occur because it is after their first reenlistment that Army personnel begin to take on leadership responsibilities. The job analysis results showed that supervisory and leadership responsibilities are substantial and critical, although, as always, there is variability across MOS.

In general, the job analysis findings also suggested that, with relatively few modifications, the first-tour technical performance criterion measures could be used to measure second-tour soldier performance. This simplified development of the second-tour technical hands-on and job knowledge tests. Further, the critical incidents job analysis for second tour also showed that almost all technical performance dimensions identified in the first-tour analysis were relevant to second-tour performance. This meant that almost all criterion development efforts could be concentrated in the supervisory/leadership domain.

The measures were prepared with the support of several relatively small data collections. Pilot tests for each MOS included four senior NCOs and five incumbents. Field test data were collected at three locations (Ft. Bragg, Ft. Hood, and Germany), resulting in data from 40 to 60 soldiers per MOS. In addition, development of the Situational Judgment Test required collecting information from 90 senior NCOs from a variety of MOS at the U.S. Army Sergeants Major Academy (USASMA). The administration of criterion measures to soldiers who had previously participated in CVI as first-tour soldiers (i.e., CVII) constituted a large-scale field test of the second-tour measures. Based on the CVII data, the criterion measures were revised, and then administered again to second-tour soldiers in the

Longitudinal Validation sample (LVII). As with the first-tour measures, the second-tour instruments were reviewed by Army proponent agencies prior to both the CVII and LVII data collections.

Modification of First-Tour Measurement Methods

Technical hands-on and written job knowledge measures. The second-tour job sample and job knowledge measures were developed using a similar procedure as for first-tour entry level positions. This similarity extends to the number and way in which the sample of critical tasks was selected. Because of the considerable overlap in the job content of first- and second-tour soldiers, it was even possible to use some of the same tests. When this happened, it was only necessary to ensure that the tests were current and, in the case of the written tests, to reduce the number of test items to fit into a shorter, 1-hour administration time. The item task content of the measures did change slightly, and the overall effect was to make second-tour measures somewhat more difficult.

Rating measures. The second-tour job analysis results identified six additional MOS-specific leadership dimensions and three Army-wide leadership dimensions. These findings led to the development of several additional rating scales for measuring supervisory performance. The second-tour rating scale measures of the non-leadership/supervisory performance factors were very similar to the rating scales for first tour. At this more advanced point in the soldiers' careers, however, it became increasingly difficult to identify several peers who were in a position to provide performance ratings. Indeed, collecting peer ratings in CVII met with only limited success. As a result, only supervisor ratings were collected in LVII.

Army-Wide and MOS-Specific Behavior-Based Rating Scales. Nine nonsupervisory Army-wide dimensions relevant for first-tour performance were confirmed by the second-tour critical incidents job analysis. Some of the summary statement anchors were revised slightly to reflect somewhat higher expectations for second-tour soldiers. In addition, three general leadership/supervisory dimensions were identified from critical incidents generated by participants in the "Army-wide" or non-job-specific critical incident workshops. For each of the three new dimensions, the critical incidents reliably retranslated into each dimension were used to write behavioral summary statements.

Supervisory Task Dimension Rating Scales.   As described in Chapter 7, the second-tour task analysis that was specifically devoted to the description of leadership/supervisory performance components identified nine task-based dimensions. Accordingly, these dimensions (see Table 7.8, Chapter 7) were reviewed for possible inclusion as additional rating scales. Two of the nine dimensions overlapped considerably with the Army-wide supervisory dimensions, but the remaining seven appeared to reflect additional performance dimensions. Consequently, a set of supervisory performance rating scales was created to measure the following dimensions: acting as a role model, communication, personal counseling, monitoring subordinate performance, organizing missions/operations, personnel administration, and performance counseling/correcting. As shown in Fig. 8.4, three evaluative statements were developed to anchor, respectively, the low, mid-range, and high levels of effectiveness for each dimension.

Expected Combat Performance.   As described previously, the version of the CPPS administered to first-tour soldiers in the LV sample was administered to second-tour soldiers as well.

Administrative measures.   A self-report Personnel File Form suitable for second-tour soldiers was developed by reviewing the contents of the first-tour form with officers and NCOs from the Army's Military Personnel Center. Information regarding the promotion process was obtained from

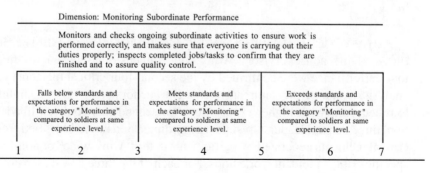

FIG. 8.4. Sample supplemental supervisory rating scale.

these SMEs as well as from current policy and procedure manuals. In addition to the information gathered on the first-tour soldiers, the second-tour form elicited information related to the soldier's promotion background and education. To distinguish between performance as a second-tour soldier versus as a first-tour soldier, respondents were asked to indicate how many commendations and disciplinary actions they received at different grade levels (i.e., E1–E3, E4–E5).

A draft version of the second-tour Personnel File Form was administered during the second-tour field test. Only minor changes were made to the form as a result of the field test data analysis.

New Measurement Methods for Second Tour

Based on a review of the literature and a careful consideration of the feasibility of additional measurement methods, two new methods were developed for assessing second-tour NCO job performance. The first was a set of assessment center-like role-play exercises, and the second was a written situational judgment test. The role-play exercises were intended to assess the one-on-one leadership components required for counseling and training subordinates, whereas the Situational Judgment Test (SJT) was intended to assess critical components of supervisory judgment across a broad range of situations, within the constraints of a paper-and-pencil format.

Supervisory role-play exercises. Role-play exercises were developed to simulate three of the most critical and distinct supervisory tasks for which junior NCOs are generally responsible. These tasks were:

- Counseling a subordinate with personal problems that affect performance.
- Counseling a subordinate with a disciplinary problem.
- Conducting one-on-one remedial training with a subordinate.

Information and data for the development of the supervisory simulations were drawn from a number of sources, including Army NCO training materials, the second-tour pilot tests, and the second-tour field tests. Ideas for a number of exercises were generated during the first two pilot tests, and the more promising scenarios were selected for further development in subsequent pilot tests. Selection of the task to be trained was accomplished by asking SMEs to nominate tasks that reflected a number of characteristics (e.g., limited time requirements, not already included in job samples or knowledge tests, standardized equipment and procedures across locations). Examination of these nominations indicated that no technical tasks reasonably met all the criteria. As a result, the "task" to be trained was the hand salute and about face—two drill and ceremony steps that often require remedial training.

The general format for the simulations was for the examinee to play the role of a supervisor. The examinee was prepared for the role with a brief (half page) description of the situation that he or she was to handle. The subordinate was played by a trained confederate who also scored the performance of the examinee.

The supervisory role-plays included (a) a description of the supervisor's (examinee's) role, (b) a summary of the subordinate's role, (c) a set of detailed specifications for playing the subordinate's role, and (d) a performance rating instrument. The scenarios are summarized in Table 8.2. The rating format modeled the hands-on test format in that it was in the form of a behavioral checklist. The checklist was based on Army NCO instructional materials. Initial pilot testing activities made liberal use of additional observer/scorers as a means of evaluating the reliability of the rating checklist.

The draft role-play exercises received their first complete tryout during the second-tour field tests. Practical constraints required that senior NCOs play the subordinate roles after less than half a day of training. No changes were made to the rating scales or administration protocol based on the field test experience. In the CVII data collection, however, the subordinates were played by civilians with prior military experience, hired and trained specifically for the data collection. These people were given a full day of training, which included a large number of practice runs with shadow scoring and feedback from trainers. Although all role-players learned all three roles, they were generally held responsible for mastering a single role.

The CVII experience suggested that, for the role of problem subordinate/scorer, an appreciation for standardization and other data collection goals was more useful than military experience for achieving reliable and valid measurement. As a result, the role-players who participated in the LVII data collection were professionals with research experience. The training they received was similar to that provided to the CVII role-players.

TABLE 8.2
Supervisory Role-Play Scenarios

Personal Counseling Role-Play Scenario

Supervisory Problem: PFC Brown is exhibiting declining job performance and personal appearance. Recently, Brown's wall locker was left unsecured. The supervisor has decided to counsel the soldier about these matters.

Subordinate Role: The soldier is having difficulty adjusting to life in Korea and is experiencing financial problems. The role-player is trained to initially react defensively to the counseling but to calm down if the supervisor handles the situation in a nonthreatening manner. The subordinate will not discuss personal problems unless prodded.

Disciplinary Counseling Role-Play Scenario

Supervisory Problem: There is convincing evidence that PFC Smith lied to get out of coming to work today. Smith has arrived late to work on several occasions and has been counseled for lying in the past. The soldier has been instructed to report to the supervisor's office immediately.

Subordinate Role: The soldier's work is generally up to standards, which leads the soldier to believe that he or she is justified in occasionally "slacking off." The subordinate had slept in to nurse a hangover and then lied to cover it up. The role-player is trained to initially react to the counseling in a very polite manner but to deny that he or she is lying. If the supervisor conducts the counseling effectively, the subordinate eventually admits guilt and begs for leniency.

Training Role-Play Scenario

Supervisory Problem: The commander will be observing the unit practice formation in 30 minutes. PVT Martin, although highly motivated, is experiencing problems with the hand salute and about face.

Subordinate Role: The role-player is trained to demonstrate feelings of embarrassment that contribute to the soldier's clumsiness. Training also includes making very specific mistakes when conducting the hand salute and about face.

Before the LVII administration, the rating procedure was also refined, both in terms of the items included on the checklists and the anchors on the scales used to rate each behavior. These changes were designed to make it easier for role-players to provide accurate and reliable ratings. A sample scale from the LVII rating protocol is shown in Fig. 8.5.

Prior to administration to the CVII sample, the role-play exercise materials were submitted to the U.S. Army Sergeants Major Academy (USASMA) for a proponent review. USASMA reviewers found the exercises to be an appropriate and fair assessment of supervisory skills, and did not request any revisions.

Asks open-ended, fact-finding questions that uncover important and relevant information.

5   =   Asks pertinent questions, picks up on cues, uncovers all relevant information, follows-up
          based on what the subordinate says.

3   =   Asks good questions but may not pick up on cues; uncovers most relevant information but
          may not follow-up based on the subordinate's response.

1   =   Fails to ask pertinent questions or ask questions at all; fails to uncover important information.

FIG. 8.5.   An example of a role-play exercise performance rating.

Situational Judgment Test (SJT)

The purpose of the SJT was to evaluate the effectiveness of judgments about how to most effectively react in typical supervisory problem situations. A modified critical incident methodology was used to generate situations for inclusion in the SJT, and the SMEs who generated situations were pilot test participants. SMEs were provided with the taxonomy of supervisory/leadership behaviors generated using the second-tour job descriptions and were given a set of criteria for identifying a "good" situation. Specifically, situations had to be challenging, realistic, and applicable to soldiers in all MOS. They must provide sufficient detail to help the supervisor make a choice between possible actions, and those actions must be adequately communicated in a few sentences.

Response options were developed through a combination of input from pilot test SMEs and examinees from the field tests. They wrote short answers (1 to 3 sentences) to the situations describing what they would do to respond effectively to each situation. Many of these SMEs also participated in small-group discussions to refine the situation, and additional alternatives often arose out of these group discussions. All of these possible responses were content analyzed by the research staff, redundancies removed, and a set of five to ten response options generated for each situation. Over the course of nine pilot test workshops, an initial set of almost 300 situations was generated.

Additional data were gathered on 180 of the best situations during the field tests. Field test examinees responded to experimental items by assessing the effectiveness of each listed response option on a 7-point scale, and by indicating which option they believed was most, and which was least, effective.

Following the field tests, a series of small group workshops were conducted at USASMA with 90 senior NCOs (Sergeants Major). At these workshops the SJT was revised and refined, and a scoring key was developed by asking the Sergeants Major panel to rate the effectiveness of each response alternative for a scenario. In the CVII version of the SJT, the examinee was asked to indicate what he or she believed to be the most effective and the least effective response to the problem in the scenario.

The final CVII version consisted of 35 test items (i.e., scenarios) selected on the basis of four criteria: (a) high agreement among SMEs from US-ASMA on "correct" responses and low agreement among junior NCOs, (b) item content that represented a broad range of the leadership/supervisory performance dimensions identified via job analyses, (c) plausible distractors (i.e., incorrect response options), and (d) positive USASMA proponent feedback. Three to five response options per item were selected. An example item is shown in Fig. 8.6. Examinees were asked to indicate the most and least effective response alternative for each situation. Because the SJT clearly required more extensive reading than the other Project A tests, there was concern that the Reading Grade Level (RGL) would be too high for this examinee population. However, the RGL of the test, as assessed using the FOG index, is fairly low (seventh grade).

Analysis of the CVII data indicated that the SJT yielded considerable variability across examinees and was relatively difficult (Hanson & Borman, 1992). Also, construct validity analyses showed that the SJT is a good measure of supervisory job knowledge (Hanson, 1994). To provide for a more comprehensive measure, 14 items were added to the LVII version of the test. These items were selected to be somewhat easier, on the whole, than the original item set.

You are a squad leader. Over the past several months you have noticed that one of the other squad leaders in your platoon hasn't been conducting his CTT training correctly. Although this hasn't seemed to affect the platoon yet, it looks like the platoon's marks for CTT will go down if he continues to conduct CTT training incorrectly. What should you do?

    a. Do nothing because performance hasn't yet been affected.

    b. Have a squad leader meeting and tell the squad leader who has been conducting training improperly that you have noticed some problems with the way he is training his troops.

    c. Tell your platoon sergeant about the problems.

    d. Privately pull the squad leader aside, inform him of the problem, and offer to work with him if he doesn't know the proper CTT training procedures.

FIG. 8.6. Example Situational Judgment Test item.

Summary of Second-Tour
Performance Measures

As noted in Chapter 3, only soldiers in Batch A MOS were included in the second-tour data collections. CVII and LVII examinees were scheduled for 8 hours of criterion measurement activities. Table 8.3 summarizes the instruments that were administered during CVII and LVII. Recall that peer ratings were collected in CVII but not in LVII.

As was true for the first-tour soldiers, several auxiliary measures were administered along with the primary performance measurement instruments. The Job History Questionnaire and the Army Job Satisfaction Questionnaire were administered to both the CVII and LVII samples. One supplemental measure used in CVII (the Measurement Method Rating Form) was dropped and another (the Supervisory Experience Questionnaire, an analog

TABLE 8.3
Summary of Second-Tour Criterion Measures

Hands-on job sample tests covering 15 job tasks.

Written, multiple-choice job knowledge tests covering 30 job tasks.

Role-plays covering three supervisory problems.

Situational Judgment Test—Multiple-choice items describing 35 common supervisory problems (LVII version included 49 items).

Personnel File Form—Self-report administrative data such as awards, disciplinary actions, physical training scores, etc.

Army-Wide Rating Scales—12 behavior-based rating scales covering non-job-specific performance; 7 scales covering supervisory aspects of performance; single rating of overall effectiveness; single rating of senior NCO potential.

MOS-Specific Rating Scales—7–13 behavior-based anchored rating scales covering major aspects of job- specific technical task proficiency. (*Single overall rating of MOS performance included in LVII version.*)

Combat Performance Prediction Scale—14-item summated rating scale assessing expected performance in combat.

Army Job Satisfaction Questionnaire—Auxiliary measure to assess satisfaction with work, co-workers, supervision, pay, promotions, and the Army.

Job History Questionnaire—Auxiliary measure to assess frequency and recency of performance for 30 job tasks.

Measurement Method Rating—Auxiliary measure asking soldiers to rate the fairness of the assessment methods. (*Not used in LVII.*)

Supervisory Experience Questionnaire—Auxiliary measure to assess experience with supervisory tasks. (*Not used in CVII.*)

Note: CVII ratings were collected from both peers and supervisors; LVII ratings were collected from supervisors only. Number of tasks covered by hands-on and job knowledge tests is approximate.

to the Job History Questionnaire) was added for LVII. Otherwise, the criterion measures administered during this data collection were essentially the same as those administered during CVII.

DEVELOPMENT OF BASIC SCORES

The criterion measures just described yielded literally hundreds of individual item-level scores. The first major analysis task, therefore, was to construct so-called "basic" scores for each measure and evaluate the psychometric properties of these scores. The derivation of these basic scores is described in this section. Chapter 11 discusses the factor analysis work that was used to further reduce the basic scores into an even smaller set of construct scores for the validation analyses.

Because the performance modeling work and most of the validation analyses were carried out using data from the Batch A MOS, results cited in this section are also based on the Batch A MOS. Although the discussion focuses on the longitudinal sample results, where possible, concurrent sample results are also provided for purposes of comparison.

Measures of Training Performance

Rating Scales

End-of-training ratings were collected from four peers and the soldiers' drill instructor. Following edits to remove suspicious data (i.e., data from raters with excessive missing data or who were extreme outliers), there were 191,964 rater/ratee pairs in the LVT (Longitudinal Validation-Training) data set. These ratings were distributed among 44,059 ratees. The average number of peer raters per ratee was 3.50 (SD = 1.21), and the average number of instructor raters per ratee was .86 (SD = .37).

Initial analyses were performed on a preliminary analysis sample of 100 ratees from each MOS with at least 600 ratees (McCloy & Oppler, 1990). For each ratee in this sample, only the instructor rater and two randomly-selected peer raters were included, for a total of 1,400 ratees and 4,200 rater/ratee pairs. The initial analyses included means, standard deviations, and interrater reliability estimates for each rating scale item. Exploratory factor analyses suggested that a single factor would be sufficient to account for the common variance associated with the ratings assigned by both the peer and instructor raters. In a series of confirmatory analyses, the single-factor model was compared to a four-factor model that had been previously derived using the first-tour Army-wide rating scales (described later in this chapter). Consistently across MOS and rater type (peer, instructor, or pooled), these analyses suggested an improved fit for the four-factor model.

Thus, the seven training rating scales were combined to yield four basic scores that corresponded to scores derived for the first-tour rating scales: (a) Effort and Technical Skill (ETS), (b) Maintaining Personal Discipline (MPD), (c) Physical Fitness and Military Bearing (PFB), and (d) Leadership Potential (LEAD). Further analyses indicated that the factor pattern of the ratings and the relationships between the ratings and the criteria was different for the instructor and peer ratings. Therefore, no pooled scores were calculated. Moreover, only the peer-based scores were used in validation analyses because these scores exhibited stronger relationships with the Experimental Predictor Battery scores than did the instructor-based scores.

Table 8.4 shows the means and standard deviations for the final training rating scale basic scores. To provide an indication of the reliability of these scores, Table 8.4 also provides single-rater and two-rater reliability estimates.

School Knowledge Tests

The school knowledge tests were administered to all Project A MOS in CVI and at the end of training in the longitudinal sample (LVT). The tests were administered again to Batch Z soldiers in LVI. Only the LVT scores were used in validation analyses, therefore, only those will be discussed here.

TABLE 8.4
Descriptive Statistics and Reliability Estimates for Training
Rating Scale Basic Scores

	Longitudinal Validation		Reliability	
Score	Mean	SD	1-rater	2-rater
ETS	4.44	0.89	.34	.51
MPD	4.64	1.01	.37	.54
PFB	4.75	0.85	.37	.54
LEAD	4.07	1.22	.32	.49

Note: Based on mean peer ratings of 4,343 LV Batch A soldiers.
Reliability estimates based on 34,442 individual peer ratings.

After deleting items with poor item statistics or that were otherwise problematic, three alternative sets of basic scores were investigated using confirmatory factor analysis techniques. Two of the scoring systems were based on work that had been done with the first-tour job knowledge tests, which will be discussed further in the next section. One system would combine the test items into six scores (e.g., safety/survival, communication, technical) and the other would have combined the items into two scores (basic and technical). A third possible scoring system would have resulted in a single percent-correct score across all items. The confirmatory analyses indicated that, across all MOS, the two factor score approach consistently demonstrated the best fit (see McCloy & Oppler, 1990 for further details).

Table 8.5 provides means and standard deviations for the two basic scores derived from the LVT school knowledge tests, both for the Batch A MOS and for all MOS combined. The CVI Batch A means are also shown for comparison.

Measures of First- and Second-Tour Performance

Generally-speaking, the exploratory analyses used to derive basic scores for the CVI first tour performance measures were applied in confirmatory analyses to derive basic scores for the LVI measures and for comparable second-tour measures. Therefore, the following discussion is organized by measurement method and encompasses both the first- and second-tour measures from both the concurrent and longitudinal validations.

TABLE 8.5

Descriptive Statistics for School Knowledge (Training Achievement) Basic Scores

Score	Longitudinal Validation			Concurrent Validation		
	N	Mean	SD	N	Mean	SD
Batch A MOS						
Basic knowledge	3,279	58.88	14.53	3,548	60.63	14.61
Technical knowledge	4,410	62.50	12.79	4,039	63.25	24.44
All MOS						
Basic knowledge	31,261	59.08	14.92			
Technical knowledge	43,620	63.11	12.63			

Hands-On and Written Job Knowledge Tests

To reduce the number of criterion scores derived from the hands-on and job knowledge tests, the task domains for each of the nine Batch A MOS were reviewed by project staff and tasks were clustered into a set of functional categories on the basis of task content. Ten of the categories (e.g., First Aid, Weapons, Navigate) applied to all MOS and consisted primarily of common tasks. In addition, seven of the nine MOS had two to five job-specific categories.

Three project staff independently classified all the 30 or so tasks tested in each MOS into one of the functional categories. The level of perfect agreement in the assignment of tasks to categories was over 90% in every MOS. Scores for each of the functional categories were then computed for the hands-on tests by calculating the mean of the percent "go" scores for the task tests within each category and for the job knowledge tests by calculating the percent correct across all items associated with tasks in the category. Scores were computed separately for the hands-on and job knowledge tests.

Prior to calculation of the functional scores, item statistics were computed for the multiple-choice job knowledge test items to correct any scoring problems and eliminate items that exhibited serious problems. Although there were explicit instructions on how to set up each of the hands-on tests, some differences in equipment and set-up across test sites were inevitable. Therefore, the task-level scores were standardized by test site. Finally, data imputation methods were applied to the task-level scores for both the hands-on and job knowledge tests before they were combined to yield functional category scores (see J.P. Campbell & Zook, 1994 for further details).

Separate principal components analyses were carried out for each MOS, using the functional category score intercorrelation matrix as the input. The results of these factor analyses suggested a similar set of category clusters, with minor differences, across all nine MOS. Thus, the ten common and the MOS-specific functional categories were reduced to six basic scores: (a) Communications, (b) Vehicles, (c) Basic Soldiering, (d) Identify Targets, (e) Safety/Survival, and (f) Technical.

These became known as the "CVBITS" basic scores and, although this set of clusters was not reproduced precisely for every MOS, it appeared to be a reasonable portrayal of the nine jobs when a common set of clusters was imposed on all.

The process of defining functional categories and deriving the CVBITS basic scores from these was replicated in LVI. In the longitudinal validation, however, confirmatory factor analysis techniques were used to assess the fit of the CVBITS model. These analyses were also used to test a two-factor model that combined the CVBITS scores into two scores: basic (CVBIS) and technical (T). The six-factor CVBITS model fit the data best and was therefore used in favor of the two-factor model. It is also true, however, that the two-factor model was used to compute higher-order so-called "construct" scores that were used for some analyses. Figure 8.7 depicts the hierarchical grouping scheme for the tasks that were tested with hands-on and written measures.

Given the very large number of individual scores, the means and standard deviations for the first-tour hands-on and job knowledge basic CVBITS scores are not provided here. The scores did, however, exhibit very reasonable distributional characteristics across MOS and measurement methods. Note that not every MOS had a score on each of the six possible basic scores. Note also that the hands-on tests did not measure one basic score (Identify Vehicles) for any of the MOS. The descriptive statistics calculated across MOS for both the Task Construct and Task Factor scores were very similar for the concurrent and longitudinal first-tour samples.

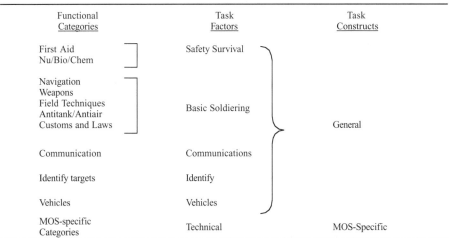

Functional Categories	Task Factors	Task Constructs
First Aid Nu/Bio/Chem	Safety Survival	
Navigation Weapons Field Techniques Antitank/Antiair Customs and Laws	Basic Soldiering	General
Communication	Communications	
Identify targets	Identify	
Vehicles	Vehicles	
MOS-specific Categories	Technical	MOS-Specific

Note: The Task Factors correspond to the six task groups known as CVBITS. The Task Constructs termed General and MOS-Specific refer to the same constructs that have previously been called Basic and Technical, or Common and Technical.

FIG. 8.7. Hierarchical relationships among Functional Categories, Task Factors, and Task Constructs.

To derive basic scores for the second tour hands-on and job knowledge tests, we tried to apply the same procedures as were used for the first-tour measures. Perhaps at least in part because of the much smaller sample sizes, the factor analysis results were largely uninterpretable. Moreover, the smaller sample sizes limited the use of sophisticated data imputation techniques making missing scores at the CVBITS level a fairly serious problem. Therefore, we elected to use only the higher-level two-factor score model (General and MOS-Specific) for the CVII and LVII hands-on and job knowledge tests.

Rating Measures

For each soldier in the two first-tour samples (CVI and LVI), the goal was to obtain ratings from two supervisors and four peers who had worked with the ratee for a least two months and/or were familiar with the ratee's job performance. For both CVI and LVI, there was an average of just less than three peer and about two supervisor ratings for each ratee. Analyses were conducted for these two rater groups separately and for the pooled supervisor and peer ratings. All final first-tour basic scores were based on the pooled ratings. The pooled ratings were computed by averaging the mean peer rating and mean supervisor rating for those soldiers who had at least one peer rating and one supervisor rating.

Obtaining peer ratings was problematic for second-tour soldiers. Although we knew that the greater autonomy of soldiers at this level and the limitations of our data collection process would make this task difficult, we tried to collect peer ratings in CVII. The result was that more than one-half of the second-tour soldiers did not receive *any* peer ratings, although we collected supervisor ratings in quantities comparable to first tour. We did not try to collect peer ratings at all during LVII, and basic scores for both CVII and LVII were based on mean supervisor ratings only.

Army-wide rating scales.   In CVI, the reduction of individual rating scales to a smaller set of aggregated scores was accomplished primarily through exploratory factor analysis. Principal factor analyses with a varimax rotation for the Army-wide scales were performed across MOS for peer raters, for supervisor raters, and for the combined peer and supervisor rater groups. Virtually identical results were obtained for all three rater groups, and a three-factor solution was chosen as most meaningful. The three factors were named (a) Effort and Technical Skill (ETS), (b) Maintaining Personal Discipline (MPD), and (c) Physical Fitness and Military

TABLE 8.6

Composition and Definition of LVI Army-Wide Rating Composite Scores

Factor Name and Definition	*Individual Rating Scales*
Effort and Technical Skill	
Exerting effort over the full range of job tasks; engaging in training or other development activities to increase proficiency; persevering under dangerous or adverse conditions; and demonstrating leadership and support toward peers.	Technical knowledge/skill Leadership Effort Self-development Maintaining equipment
Maintaining Personal Discipline	
Adhering to Army rules and regulations; exercising self-control; demonstrating integrity in day-to-day behavior; and not causing disciplinary problems.	Following regulations Self-control Integrity
Physical Fitness and Military Bearing	
Maintaining an appropriate military appearance and bearing, and staying in good physical condition.	Military bearing Physical fitness

Bearing (PFB). These three factors were replicated using the LVI data; definitions for each of the factors are provided in Table 8.6. Two ratings were not part of the factor analysis, "overall performance effectiveness" and "overall future potential for performance as an NCO." One of these (overall effectiveness) was retained as a single-item scale basic score.

Table 8.7 shows the mean scores and interrater reliability estimates for the four LVI Army-wide rating scale basic scores; the CVI results are provided as well. Overall, the rating distributions were as expected.

Several factor analyses were conducted on the second-tour soldier ratings from the CVII and LVII samples. Ratings on the nine nonsupervisory dimensions were factor analyzed so that the first- and second-tour factor structures could be directly compared. They were closely correspondent. Then the ratings on the 10 supervisory dimensions were factor analyzed, followed by a factor analysis of all 19 dimensions included together. Based on these results, a four-composite basic score model was adopted, which included the three factor scores used for first-tour soldiers and a fourth "Leading/Supervising" score. Table 8.8 shows basic information about the LVII basic Army-wide rating scale scores. The LVII means were generally

TABLE 8.7
Descriptive Statistics and Reliability Estimates for First Tour Army-Wide Ratings

Score	Concurrent Validation		Longitudinal Validation		Longitudinal Validation
	Mean	SD	Mean	SD	Reliability
ETS	4.42	0.78	4.36	0.92	.61
MPD	4.64	0.85	4.63	0.99	.60
PFB	4.87	0.88	4.77	1.00	.65
Overall	4.65	0.82	4.58	0.96	—

Note: Based on ratings on 4,039 CVI and 6,814 LVI Batch A soldiers; inter-rater reliability estimates based on pooled peer and supervisor ratings.

TABLE 8.8
Descriptive Statistics and Reliability Estimates for Second
Tour Army-Wide Ratings

Score	Concurrent Validation			Longitudinal Validation			Longitudinal Validation
	N	Mean	SD	N	Mean	SD	Reliability
ETS	918	5.04	1.03	1451	4.87	0.98	.63
MPD	920	5.16	1.09	1451	5.03	1.05	.60
PFB	925	5.18	1.17	1450	4.98	1.15	.70
LEAD	857	4.51	1.01	1388	4.40	0.94	.64

Note: Based on ratings on 857 CVII and 1,427 LVII soldiers.

lower than in CVII (because of the revised scale anchors) and the variability was similar. The interrater reliability for the LVII (and CVII) ratings was almost exactly the same as that found in the LVI and CVII analyses.

MOS-specific rating scales.   For the MOS-specific scales, exploratory analyses using principal factor analyses, with varimax rotation, were performed within MOS and separately for each rater type. The objective was to look for common themes that might be evident across MOS. This examination revealed a two-factor solution that could potentially be used across all nine Batch A MOS. The rating dimensions loading highest on

TABLE 8.9
Descriptive Statistics for MOS Rating Scales Overall Composite Score

MOS	First Tour (LVI)			Second Tour (LVII)		
	N	Mean	SD	N	Mean	SD
11B	907	4.67	0.71	315	5.10	0.84
13B	916	4.69	0.69	159	5.24	0.70
19E/K	825	4.75	0.73	147	5.23	0.91
31C	529	4.70	0.91	144	5.01	0.94
63B	752	4.53	0.90	190	4.70	0.79
71L	678	4.88	0.88	147	5.12	0.86
88M	682	4.78	0.77	85	5.15	0.80
91A	824	4.73	0.81	183	5.18	0.92
95B	452	4.66	0.70	150	4.93	0.68

one of the factors consisted mainly of core job requirements, while those loading highest on the second factor were more peripheral job duties. However, given the minimal conceptual distinction between the two factors, we decided to combine all the MOS scales into a single composite for each MOS. This single-composite scoring system was also adopted for LVI and for the second-tour (CVII and LVII) MOS-specific rating scales as well. Table 8.9 shows the means and standard deviations for the composite scores from LVI and LVII. The CVI and CVII descriptive statistics were highly similar. Table 8.10 shows the interrater reliability estimates for the LVI and LVII scores.

Combat performance prediction scale. The CVI version of the Combat Performance Prediction Scale was a summated scale based on 40 items. Exploratory factor analysis of the item ratings for different rater groups and across MOS consistently showed support for a two-factor solution. The second factor, however, was composed entirely of the instrument's negatively worded items. Therefore, a single summated composite score was adopted. In subsequent data collections (LVI, CVII, and LVII), the instrument was reduced to 14 items and again was scored by summing the items together to form a single composite score. Table 8.11 shows the CVI, LVI, and LVII expected combat performance scale scores and associated reliability estimates.

TABLE 8.10

MOS-Specific Ratings: Composite Interrater Reliability Results for LVI and LVII

	11B	13B	19K	31C	63B	71L	88M	91A/B	95B
LVI Composite									
$r_{kk}{}^a$	.51	.53	.51	.29	.57	.37	.50	.51	.61
LVII Composite									
r_{kk}	.63	.28	.59	.71	.46	.53	.39	.55	.36

Note: The total number of ratings used to compute reliabilities for each MOS ranges from 103 to 586. LVII analyses based on supervisor ratings only.

[a] k is the average number of ratings per ratee.

TABLE 8.11

Descriptive Statistics for Combat Performance Prediction Scale

	N	Mean	SD	Reliability
First-Tour				
LVI	5,640	62.41	10.84	.607
Second-Tour				
CVII	848	70.20	11.50	.575
LVII	1,395	70.69	12.37	.610

Note: CVI scores were based on a different version of the instrument, so the scores are not comparable to those described here.

Administrative Indices

Five scores were computed from the CVI self-report Personnel File Form: (a) number of awards and memoranda/certificates of achievement, (b) physical readiness test score, (c) M16 qualification, (d) number of Articles 15 and flag (i.e., disciplinary) actions, and (e) promotion rate. Promotion rate was a constructed score, which is the residual of pay grade regressed on time in service, adjusted by MOS. Only slight changes were made to the scoring system for LVI (e.g., the score distributions did not indicate the need to continue to standardize the number of Articles 15 and flag actions before summing them to yield a composite score).

TABLE 8.12

Descriptive Statistics for First-Tour Administrative Index Basic Scores

	Concurrent Validation		Longitudinal Validation	
	Mean	*SD*	*Mean*	*SD*
Awards and certificates	2.80	1.99	3.31	3.18
Physical readiness	255.39	32.90	238.66	33.43
Weapons qualification	2.21	0.77	2.28	0.76
Disciplinary actions	0.35	0.81	0.60	0.88
Promotion rate	0.02	0.54	0.00	0.60

Note: $N = 3,733–4,039$ CVI and $6,596–6,814$ LVI Batch A soldiers.

Table 8.12 shows descriptive statistics for the first-tour Personnel File Form.

The scoring system used for the second-tour Personnel File Form yielded the same five basic scores, but in the case of LVII, some of the computations were done a bit differently, and one score (Weapons Qualification) had to be dropped because of excessive missing data (this was true in CVII as well). The scoring of the awards and certificates composite was changed so that, instead of unit weighting each award, the awards were weighted by their relative importance, as indicated by the number of points they are given on the Army NCO promotion board worksheet. Also, the promotion rate score reflected the pay grade deviation score used for first-tour as well as the reported number of recommendations for accelerated promotion. Table 8.13 shows descriptive statistics for the second-tour Personnel File Form.

Situational Judgment Test

Procedures for scoring the LVII and CVII SJT were identical, involving consideration of five different basic scores. The most straightforward was a simple number correct score. For each item, the response alternative that was given the highest mean effectiveness rating by the experts (the senior NCOs at the Sergeants Major Academy) was designated the "correct" answer. Respondents were scored based on the number of items for which they indicated that the "correct" response alternative was the most effective.

TABLE 8.13
Descriptive Statistics for Second-Tour Administrative Index Basic Scores

Measure		N	Mean	SD
Awards and certificates[a]	CVII	928	10.53	5.63
	LVII	1,509	14.81	6.79
Disciplinary actions	CVII	930	.42	.87
	LVII	1,509	.36	.74
Physical readiness score	CVII	998	250.11	30.68
	LVII	1,457	249.16	30.76
Weapons qualification	CVII	1,036	2.52	.67
	LVII	1,498	2.59	.67
Promotion rate	LVII	1,463	100.07	7.84
Promotion rate	CVII	901	100.14	8.09
(CVII scoring)	LVII	1,513	99.98	7.48

[a]Differences in LVII and CVII results primarily reflect differences in response format.

The second scoring procedure involved weighting each response alternative by the mean effectiveness rating given to that response alternative by the expert group. This gave respondents more credit for choosing "wrong" answers that are still relatively effective than for choosing wrong answers that are very ineffective. These item-level effectiveness scores for the chosen alternative were then averaged to obtain an overall effectiveness score for each soldier. Averaging item-level scores instead of summing them placed respondents' scores on the same 7-point effectiveness scale as the experts' ratings and ensured that respondents were not penalized for missing data.

Scoring procedures based on respondents' choices for the least effective response to each situation were also examined. Being able to identify the least effective response alternatives might be seen as an indication of the respondent's knowledge and skill for avoiding these very ineffective responses, or in effect, to avoid "screwing up." As with the choices for the most effective response, a simple number correct score was computed—the number of times each respondent correctly identified the response alternative that the experts rated the least effective. To differentiate it from the number correct score based on choices for the most effective response, this score will be referred to as the L-Correct score, and the score based on choices for the most effective response (described previously) will be referred to as the M-Correct score.

Another score was computed by weighting respondents' choices for the least effective response alternative by the mean effectiveness rating for that response, and then averaging these item-level scores to obtain an overall effectiveness score based on choices for the least effective response alternative. This score will be referred to as L-Effectiveness, and the parallel score based on choices for the most effective responses (described previously) will be referred to as M-Effectiveness.

Finally, a scoring procedure that involved combining the choices for the most and the least effective response alternative into one overall score was also examined. For each item, the mean effectiveness of the response alternative each soldier chose as the least effective was *subtracted* from the mean effectiveness of the response alternative they chose as the most effective. These item-level scores were then averaged together for each soldier to generate the fifth total score. This score will be referred to as M-L Effectiveness.

Each of these scores was computed twice for the LVII soldiers, once using all 49 SJT items and once including only the 35 SJT items that had been administered to the CVII sample as well. The 35-item SJT scores were computed for two reasons. First, these scores can be more directly compared with the SJT scores for the CVII sample because they are based on the same set of items. Second, these scores can be used to determine whether adding 14 items did, as hoped, increase the internal consistency reliability of the SJT and decrease test difficulty.

The item-level responses from both the CVII and LVII samples were well-distributed across the response alternatives for each item. For example, the percentage of LVII respondents choosing the most popular response alternative for each item as the most effective ranged from 32 to 83, with a median of 53%. This suggests that the correct responses to SJT items were not at all obvious to the soldiers.

Table 8.14 presents descriptive statistics for the 35-item SJT for both the LVII and the CVII samples. This table includes the mean score for each of the five scoring procedures. The maximum possible for the M-Correct scoring procedure is 35 (i.e., all 35 items answered correctly). In the LVII sample, the mean M-Correct score for the 35-item SJT was only 17.51. The mean number of least effective response alternatives correctly identified by this group was only 15.64. The mean M-Correct score for the CVII sample was 16.52 and the mean L-Correct score was 14.86. Clearly the SJT was difficult for both the CVII and the LVII soldiers.

In addition, two-tailed t-tests revealed that the LVII sample had significantly higher M-Correct ($t = 5.93$, $p < .001$) and L-Correct ($t = 5.01$,

$p < .001$) scores than did the CVII sample. Likewise, the LVII sample also scored significantly higher than the CVII sample on the M-L Effectiveness score ($t = 6.75$, $p < .001$).

These differences between the LVII and CVII samples may be, in part, a function of the level of supervisory training the soldiers in each sample had received. Sixty-two percent of the LVII sample reported having received at least basic supervisory training, whereas only 53% of the CVII sample had received such training.

Table 8.14 also presents the standard deviation for each of the five scoring procedures. All of the scoring procedures resulted in a reasonable amount of variability in both the LVII and CVII samples. The internal consistency reliability estimates for all of these scoring procedures are also acceptably high. The most reliable score for both samples is M-L Effectiveness,

TABLE 8.14
Comparison of LVII and CVII SJT Scores: Means, Standard Deviations,
and Internal Reliability Estimates

Scoring Method	N	Mean	SD	Coefficient Alpha
LVII 49-Item SJT				
M-Correct[a]	1,577	25.84	5.83	.69
M-Effectiveness	1,577	4.97	.32	.74
L-Correct[a]	1,577	22.35	5.14	.60
L-Effectiveness[b]	1,577	3.35	.29	.76
M-L Effectiveness	1,576	1.62	.57	.81
LVII 35-Item SJT				
M-Correct[a]	1,580	17.51	4.11	.56
M-Effectiveness	1,580	4.99	.31	.64
L-Correct[a]	1,581	15.64	3.81	.48
L-Effectiveness[b]	1,581	3.47	.29	.65
M-L Effectiveness	1,580	1.53	.54	.72
CVII SJT (35 items)				
M-Correct[a]	1,025	16.52	4.29	.58
M-Effectiveness	1,025	4.91	.34	.68
L-Correct[a]	1,007	14.86	3.86	.49
L-Effectiveness[b]	1,007	3.54	.31	.68
M-L Effectiveness	1,007	1.36	.61	.75

[a]Maximum possible score is 35.
[b]Low scores are "better"; mean effectiveness scale values for L responses should be low.

probably because this score contains more information than the other scores (i.e., choices for *both* the most and the least effective responses).

Table 8.14 also presents descriptive statistics and reliability estimates for the 49-item version of the SJT in the LVII sample. All of the scoring methods for both versions of the SJT have moderate to high internal consistency reliabilities. The most reliable score for both versions is M-L Effectiveness. In addition, the longer 49-item SJT resulted in considerably higher reliability estimates for all of the scoring methods.

Comparing the various scoring strategies, the M-Correct and L-Correct scores appeared to have less desirable psychometric characteristics than the scores obtained using the other three scoring procedures. Further, the M-L Effectiveness score was the most reliable and was highly correlated ($r = .94$ and $-.92$) with both the M-Effectiveness and the L-Effectiveness scores. Therefore, the M-L Effectiveness score was used as the SJT Total Score.

A rational/empirical analysis of the item covariance resulted in six factor-based subscales that contained between six and nine items each. Definitions of these factor-based subscales are presented in Table 8.15. These subscales had potential for more clearly delineating the leadership/supervision aspects of the second-tour soldier job. They were included in one of the major alternative models of second-tour performance to be evaluated in subsequent confirmatory analyses (see Chapter 11).

Supervisory Role-Play Exercises

For the CVII sample, examinees were rated on their performance on each exercise independently. Using a 3-point scale, ratings were made on from 11 to 20 behaviors tapped by each exercise. The three rating points were anchored with a description of performance on the particular behavior being rated. Examinees were also rated on a 5-point overall effectiveness scale following each of the three exercises. Additionally, examinees were rated on a 5-point overall affect scale following the personal counseling exercise and on a 5-point overall fairness scale following the disciplinary counseling exercise.

The rating system used to evaluate LVII examinees was modified in several ways from CVII. First, the CVII analyses identified the scales that appeared to be (a) difficult to rate reliably, (b) conceptually redundant with other rated behaviors, and/or (c) not correlated with other rated behaviors in meaningful ways. These behavior ratings were dropped to allow raters to concentrate more fully on the remaining behaviors. Some of the behavioral

TABLE 8.15
Situational Judgment Test: Definitions of Factor-Based Subscales

---

1. *Discipline soldiers when necessary (Discipline).* This subscale is made up of items on which the most effective responses involve disciplining soldiers, sometimes severely, and the less effective responses involve either less severe discipline or no discipline at all. (6 items.)
2. *Focus on the positive (Positive).* This subscale is made up of items on which the more effective responses involve focusing on the positive aspects of a problem situation (e.g., a soldier's past good performance, appreciation for a soldier's extra effort, the benefits the Army has to offer). (6 items.)
3. *Search for underlying reasons (Search).* This subscale is made up of items on which the more effective responses involve searching for the underlying causes of soldiers' performance or personal problems rather than reacting to the problems themselves. (8 items.)
4. *Work within the chain of command and with supervisor appropriately (Chain/Command).* For a few items on this subscale the less effective responses involve promising soldiers rewards that are beyond a direct supervisor's control (e.g., "comp" time). The remaining items involve working through the chain of command appropriately. (6 items.)
5. *Show support/concern for subordinates and avoid inappropriate discipline (Support).* This subscale is made up of items where the more effective response alternatives involve helping the soldiers with work-related or personal problems and the less effective responses involve not providing needed support or using inappropriately harsh discipline. (8 items.)
6. *Take immediate/direct action (Action).* This subscale is composed of items where the more effective response alternatives involve taking immediate and direct action to solve problems and the less effective response alternatives involve not taking action (e.g., taking a "wait and see" approach) or taking actions that are not directly targeted at the problem at hand. (9 items.)

---

anchors were also changed to improve rating reliability, and the rating scale was expanded from 3 to 5 points. The overall effectiveness rating was retained, but the overall affect and fairness rating scales were eliminated. Thus, examinees were rated on each exercise on from 7 to 11 behavioral scales and on one overall effectiveness scale. By way of example, Fig. 8.8 shows the 7 behaviors soldiers were rated on in the Disciplinary Counseling exercise.

Another important difference between the CVII and LVII measures was the background of the evaluators. The smaller size of the LVII data collection allowed for the selection and training of role-players/evaluators who were formally educated as personnel researchers and who were employed full-time by organizations in the project consortium. In contrast, the scope of the LVI/CVII data collection required the hiring of a number of temporary employees to serve as role-players. Most of these individuals had no formal research training or related research experience. Informal observations of

1. Remains focused on the immediate problem.
2. Determines an appropriate corrective action.
3. States the exact provisions of the punishment.
4. Explains the ramifications of the soldier's actions.
5. Allows the subordinate to present his/her view of the situation.
6. Conducts the counseling session in a professional manner.
7. Defuses rather than escalates potential arguments.

FIG. 8.8. Behavioral scales from the disciplinary counseling role-play exercise.

the simulation training and testing across the two data collections suggest that, in comparison to the CVII exercises, the LVII exercises were played in a more standardized fashion and examinees were rated more consistently both within and across evaluators.

To develop a scoring system, descriptive analyses were conducted, followed by a series of factor analyses. Maximum likelihood factor analyses with oblique rotations were performed within each exercise. The factor analyses were within exercise because analyses of the CVII data indicated that, when the factor analyses included scales from multiple exercises, method factors associated with each exercise dominated the factor structure. Raw scale ratings and scale ratings standardized by MOS, evaluator, and test site were factor analyzed because there was some concern that non-performance-related variables associated with MOS, evaluator, and/or test site might affect the factor structure of the raw scale ratings. No orthogonal rotations were used because, based on the CVII analyses, the factors were expected to be at least moderately correlated.

The overall effectiveness ratings were not considered for inclusion in the basic scores because they are conceptually distinct from the behavior ratings. Interrater reliability estimates could not be computed because there were insufficient "shadow score" data to conduct the required analyses.

Scales were assigned to composite scores based primarily on the patterns of their relative factor loadings in the factor structure for each exercise. This procedure resulted in empirically derived basic scores for each exercise that seemed to have considerable substantive meaning.

Two basic scores were created to represent performance on the Personal Counseling exercise (see Table 8.16)—a Communication/Interpersonal Skills composite (6 scales) and a Diagnosis/Prescription composite (3 scales). One scale was not assigned to either composite score because the analyses of raw and standardized scale ratings disagreed about the factor on

TABLE 8.16
Descriptive Statistics for LVII Supervisory Role-Play Scores

	Mean	SD
Personal Counseling		
Communication/Interpersonal Skill	3.82	0.67
Diagnosis/Prescription	2.93	1.15
Disciplinary Counseling		
Structure	3.17	0.71
Interpersonal Skill	4.54	0.57
Communication	2.24	1.35
Training		
Structure	3.54	0.95
Motivation Maintenance	3.90	0.92

Note: $N = 1,456$–$1,482$. CVI scores not provided because the scoring systems were not comparable.

which the scale loaded highest and the scale's communality was relatively low. Two basic scores were generated for the Personal Counseling exercise in CVII as well; however, they were structured significantly differently than the LVII composites. Three basic scores were created to represent performance on the Disciplinary Counseling exercise—a Structure composite (3 scales), an Interpersonal Skill composite (2 scales), and a Communication composite (2 scales). Only two basic scores had been derived from the CVII Disciplinary Counseling exercise data. Finally, two basic scores were created to represent performance on the Training exercise. This included a Structure composite (5 scales) and a Motivation Maintenance composite (2 scales). Two scales were not assigned to either composite. Only one basic score was derived from the CVII Training exercise data.

Across all exercises, each basic composite score was generated by (a) standardizing the ratings on each scale within each evaluator, (b) scaling each standardized rating by its raw score mean and standard deviation, and (c) calculating the mean of the transformed (i.e., standardized and scaled) ratings that were assigned to that particular basic criterion composite. The ratings were standardized within evaluator because each evaluator rated examinees in only some MOS, and there was more variance in mean ratings across evaluators than there was in mean ratings across MOS. The standardized ratings were scaled with their original overall means and standard deviations so that each scale would retain its relative central tendency and variability.

Final Array of Basic Performance Scores

A summary list of the first-tour basic performance scores produced by the analyses summarized above is given in Table 8.17. The analyses of the second-tour performance measures resulted in the array of basic criterion scores shown in Table 8.18. These are the scores that were put through the final editing and score imputation procedures for the validation data files. The scores that formed the basis for the development of the first- and second-tour job performance models (described in Chapter 11) were also drawn from this array.

TABLE 8.17

Basic Criterion Scores Derived from First-Tour Performance Measures

---

Hands-On Job Sample Tests
    1. Safety-survival performance score
    2. General (common) task performance score
    3. Communication performance score
    4. Vehicles performance score
    5. MOS-specific task performance score

Job Knowledge Tests
    6. Safety/survival knowledge score
    7. General (common) task knowledge score
    8. Communication knowledge score
    9. Identify targets knowledge score
    10. Vehicles knowledge score
    11. MOS-specific task knowledge score

Army-Wide Rating Scales
    12. Overall effectiveness rating
    13. Technical skill and effort factor score
    14. Personal discipline factor score
    15. Physical fitness/military bearing factor score

MOS-Specific Rating Scales
    16. Overall MOS composite score

Combat Performance Prediction Scale
    17. Overall Combat Prediction scale composite score

Personnel File Form (Administrative)
    18. Awards and certificates score
    19. Disciplinary actions (Articles 15 and Flag Actions) score
    20. Physical readiness score
    21. M16 Qualification score
    22. Promotion rate score

TABLE 8.18
Basic Criterion Scores Derived from Second-Tour Performance Measures

Hands-On Job Sample Tests
    1. MOS-specific task performance score
    2. General (common) task performance score

Written Job Knowledge Tests
    3. MOS-specific task knowledge score
    4. General (common) task knowledge score

Army-Wide Rating Scales
    5. Effort and technical skill factor score
    6. Maintaining personal discipline factor score
    7. Physical fitness/military bearing factor score
    8. Leadership/supervision factor score
    9. Overall effectiveness rating score

MOS-Specific Rating Scales
    10. Overall MOS composite score

Combat Performance Prediction Scale
    11. Overall Combat Prediction scale composite score

Personnel File Form (Administrative)
    12. Awards and certificates score
    13. Disciplinary actions (Articles 15 and Flag actions) score
    14. Physical readiness score
    15. Promotion rate score

Situational Judgment Test
    16. Total test score *or, alternatively,* the following subscores
        a. Discipline soldiers when necessary
        b. Focus on the positive
        c. Search for underlying causes
        d. Work within chain of command
        e. Show support/concern for subordinates
        f. Take immediate/direct action

Supervisory Role-Play Exercises
    17. Personal counseling—Communication/Interpersonal skill
    18. Personal counseling—Diagnosis/Prescription
    19. Disciplinary counseling—Structure
    20. Disciplinary counseling—Interpersonal skill
    21. Disciplinary counseling—Communication
    22. Training—Structure
    23. Training—Motivation maintenance

SOME RELEVANT MEASUREMENT ISSUES

The measurement methods that were used for criterion assessment in Project A highlight a number of issues that perhaps need further discussion to document our rationale. Three issues are particularly relevant.

Hands-On Tests as the Ultimate Criteria

Hands-on job samples, assuming they are constructed and administered in an appropriate fashion, are very appealing. Because they require actual task performance, albeit under simulated conditions, they have an inherent credibility that is not shared with most other assessment methods. This credibility appears to explain why job samples were identified as the benchmark method by the National Academy of Science panel that evaluated the Joint-Service Job Performance Measurement (JPM) Project, of which Project A was a part (Wigdor & Green, 1991). The philosophy of the JPM National Academy of Sciences oversight committee was that job sample tests should be the standard by which other assessment methods are evaluated. That is, they come close to the elusive "ultimate criterion."

As is evident from this chapter, Project A did not share this view. Rather, the strategy was to use multiple measurement methods and recognize that all methods, including job sample tests, have advantages and disadvantages. Besides face validity and credibility, a major advantage of the standardized job sample is that individual differences in performance are a direct function of individual differences in current job skills. To the extent that (a) the tasks selected for the job sample are representative all the major critical job tasks and (b) the conditions of measurement approach the conditions of work in real settings, so much the better. To the extent that neither of these two things is true, construct validity suffers.

One disadvantage is that the Project A job samples had to be administered at many locations with different scorers and set-up conditions at each, and under different environmental conditions (heat, cold, rain, snow). Although test administrators standardized the measurement of conditions as much as possible, the reality was that there were many potential threats to the construct validity of the hands-on test scores and the data collection teams struggled with them continually.

Another major disadvantage of job samples when used as criterion measures is that, by design, the standardized assessment format attempts to control for individual differences in the motivation to perform. That is, the measurement method tries to induce all the participants to try as hard as they can and perform at their best. Their "typical" levels of commitment and effort should *not* be reflected in job sample scores. However, in an actual job setting performance, differences could occur because of motivational differences as well as because of differences in knowledge and skill. The distinction is nowhere better demonstrated than in the study of supermarket checkout personnel by Sackett, Zedeck, and Fogli (1988). Each person in the sample was scored for speed and accuracy on a standardized set of shopping carts. Presumably, everyone tried their best on the job sample. The nature of the organization's online computerized systems also made it possible to score samples of day-to-day job performance on exactly the same variables. Whereas both the standardized job sample scores and the actual day-to-day performance scores were highly reliable, the correlation between the two was relatively low. The explanation was that the actual day-to-day performance scores were influenced by individual differences in the motivation to perform whereas the standardized job sample scores were not because everyone was trying his or her best.

Because the standardized job sample does not allow motivational determinants of performance to operate, it cannot be regarded as the ultimate benchmark against which all other measurement methods are judged. It is simply one of several useful measurement methods and has certain advantages and disadvantages in the criterion measurement context.

In certain other contexts, such as the evaluation of skills training, the purpose of measurement may indeed be to control for motivational differences. In skills training, the goal of criterion measurement is to reflect the degree to which the knowledges and skills specified by the training goals were in fact mastered, and to control for the effects of motivation. Motivational differences are not the issue. This is not the case for the measurement of job performance. In the actual job setting, an individual performance level is very much influenced by effort level. If the selection system can predict individual differences in performance that are due to motivational causes, so much the better. Historically, in criterion-related validation research, it has not been well enough appreciated that the measurement method must correspond to the measurement goals in terms of the sources of variation that are allowed to influence individual differences on the criterion scores.

Finally, the most critical job context for military personnel is performance under extreme conditions. As discussed in the context of the rating scales measuring expected performance in combat, it does not appear possible to adequately simulate such conditions in a standardized scenario. The hands-on test method can do this no better than other methods used in this research. Indeed, it is arguable that other methods (e.g., ratings) are capable of providing more information related to performance in dangerous or otherwise stressful situations than the hands-on method.

Legitimacy of Job Knowledge Tests

Written tests of job knowledge have been disparaged for a lack of realism and because they only assess declarative knowledge (Knapp & J. P. Campbell, 1993). However, as we tried to demonstrate in Project A, such tests can be designed to maximize the performance-relatedness of both questions and response alternatives (i.e., more closely measure proceduralized knowledge). The clear advantages of this type of measure are its breadth of coverage and relatively low cost. A disadvantage is that to the extent that written tests reflect the knowledge determinant of performance, rather than performance itself, they are not measures of performance in most organizations. However, as noted previously, they might be taken as an indicator of "readiness" to perform. If readiness is a performance requirement, then demonstrating current proceduralized knowledge might well be considered performance behavior. The military services are one type of organization where this kind of performance requirement is legitimate. Personnel are selected and trained to a state of readiness for events that we hope will not occur.

The Case for Performance Ratings

Because they present such a complex and difficult perceptual, information processing, and judgment task, performance ratings are sometimes criticized for being little more than popularity contests and as containing such serious errors that they are rendered inaccurate as depictions of actual job performance (e.g., Landy & Farr, 1980). However, ratings also have two distinct advantages as performance measures. First, job performance dimensions can be aligned precisely with the actual performance requirements of jobs. That is, if a performance requirement can be stated in words, then it can directly form the basis for a rating dimension (e.g., Borman, 1991). Another way to say this is that rating dimensions that represent the important performance requirements for a job are, by their very nature, at least content valid (e.g., J. P. Campbell, McCloy, Oppler, & Sager, 1993). Thus, rating scales based on a job analysis *can*, at least theoretically, avoid being deficient. Second, ratings are a typical rather than maximal performance measure. For many purposes, it is desirable to have a measure that also reflects the motivational determinants of performance rather than just the knowledge and skill determinants. All of this is not to argue that the rating method is, by definition, free of contamination.

Beyond these conceptual advantages, there is evidence to suggest that ratings can have reasonable distributions, produce reliable data, measure separate dimensions of performance, possess little race or gender bias, and be comparatively independent from raters' liking of ratees. First, when ratings are gathered on a for-research-only (or developmental) basis and the raters are oriented toward attempting to provide accurate ratings, ratings have sufficient variability to differentiate well among ratees (e.g., Pulakos & Borman, 1986). Second, under similar favorable conditions, the reliability of a single rater's performance ratings is likely to be in the .50 to .60 range (e.g., Rothstein, 1990). Multiple raters can produce composite ratings with higher reliabilities.

Third, in Project A, using different samples of raters and ratees, we found a consistent three-factor solution (Effort/Leadership, Personal Discipline, and Military Bearing) in the peer and supervisor ratings of first-tour soldiers (Pulakos & Borman, 1986). Fourth, analyses of Project A data showed only very small mean differences for the effects of rater race or gender and ratee race or gender. Pulakos, White, Oppler, and Borman (1989), and Oppler, J. P. Campbell, Pulakos, and Borman (1992) found these small effect sizes when controlling for *actual* ratee performance by constraining the sample of raters and ratees such that each ratee was evaluated by both a male and female rater for the gender effect analysis and by both a black and white rater for the race effect analysis.

And finally, data from Project A suggest that friendship on the part of raters toward ratees does not have a substantial effect on ratings. In a path analysis, Borman, White, and Dorsey (1995) found that a liking/friendship rating factor had a nonsignificant path to both peer and supervisor overall job performance ratings.

In summary, well before the 360° assessment movement, Project A showed that, with appropriate attention paid to rating format development and rater orientation and training, ratings can provide highly useful and appropriate performance information. There is no doubt that ratings contain error. Nonetheless, the above evidence regarding the validity of performance ratings is encouraging, particularly in contrast to how ratings are usually characterized.

SUMMARY

At this point, the categories and dimensions of job content identified by multiple job analyses at two different organizational levels have been transformed into components of individual performance for which one or more measurement methods have been developed. A major goal regarding performance measurement was to push the state-of-the-art as far as the resource constraints of the project would allow. We wanted performance measurement to be as thorough and as construct valid as possible. The array of first-tour and second-tour measures portrayed in Tables 8.1 and 8.2 were the result. Subsequent chapters in this volume will examine the psychometric characteristics and construct validity of the alternative Project A measures, including ratings, in considerable detail. The longitudinal sample database (LVI and LVII) is described in Chapter 10. How this database was used to model the latent structure of first- and second-tour performance and to develop the final criterion scores for the major components of performance is described in Chapter 11.

IV

Developing the Database and Modeling Predictor and Criterion Scores

9

Data Collection and Research Database Management on a Large Scale

Deirdre J. Knapp, Lauress L. Wise,
Winnie Y. Young, Charlotte H. Campbell,
Janis S. Houston, and James H. Harris

The identification of critical variables, the development of instruments to measure these variables, specifications for sophisticated research designs, and the analysis and interpretation of data collected using those instruments and designs all constitute what we consider to be high science. Missing from the picture are the steps of lining up participants, getting the participants to complete the various instruments, translating their responses into machine-readable form, and creating an edited database with both item responses and summary scores for use in analyses. These latter steps constitute the less glamorous, but no less essential, components of conducting research. In many ways, these steps are the most difficult part because less attention is typically paid to data collection and database development, and therefore there is less literature to provide guidance.

Four general challenges were addressed in collecting Project A data and building the Longitudinal Research Data Base (LRDB). They were to:

- *Maximize sample sizes.* It proved amazingly easy to lose data points, again because of the size and complexity of the data collection efforts. The first goal was to test as many of the soldiers scheduled for testing as possible. The next was to minimize the chances that some participants would fail to complete some instruments. Finally, data editing procedures were used to check for and, where possible, recover missing pieces of information.

- *Standardize test administration as much as possible.* Measures were administered by a large number of test administrators at dozens of locations. For the hands-on tests and role-play exercises in particular, it was a significant challenge to standardize test conditions. It was essential, however, to take all possible steps to keep extraneous sources of variation from affecting the data as they were being collected.
- *Avoid mistakes in data handling.* Once collected, data can still be lost or damaged if not handled carefully. Ratings, score sheets, and answer sheets that cannot be linked to the right soldier are lost completely. Shipping data from one point to another is another step at which data might be lost or damaged. Moreover, errors can creep into a database because of problems with coding or entering data.
- *Make the resulting database maximally accessible.* Data must be carefully documented so that analysts and database managers can speak precisely about the data that are used in specific analyses. The data must also be stored in a form that will allow efficient access for both planned and special purpose analyses.

This chapter describes our struggles, successes, and failures in meeting these four challenges.

BACKGROUND

Most previous efforts to develop and validate selection tests have involved a much narrower range of measures and much smaller amounts of data than in Project A. Furthermore, the data collection procedures and the data that resulted from the procedures in these studies are not well-documented. For the most part, such validation data were collected by private companies for their own use, and there was little or no motivation for making them available for secondary analyses.

There were and are, however, some large projects that have involved careful documentation of data collection procedures and that also have made resulting data files available for secondary use. The validity database for the General Aptitude Test Battery (GATB) is one example of efforts to archive an extensive array of test and criterion information. Hunter (1980) demonstrated the power of secondary analyses of such data.

Several large scale research databases were well known and served as models, particularly in the development of the LRDB. Chief among these was the Project TALENT database (Wise, McLaughlin, & Steel, 1977). The TALENT database includes results from two days of cognitive, personality, interest, and background measures administered to over 400,000 high school youth in 1960. It also includes results from follow-up surveys conducted one, five, and eleven years after the high school graduation of the classes represented by these youth (the classes of 1960 through 1963) and from a retesting of a sample of the original 9th graders when they reached 12th grade. The original data collection involved the first large-scale use of scanning equipment. In fact, it was several years after the initial data collection before the scanners achieved sufficient capacity to record all of the item responses as well as the test scores. The follow-up surveys also pioneered the new versions of multipage scannable documents. Project TALENT also included a major effort to re-edit, reformat, and document the database in 1976 and 1977 after the final wave of follow-up data collection had been completed.

At the time Project A began, the National Assessment for Educational Progress (NAEP) provided what might be considered a negative example for our database. NAEP involved a complex matrix sampling approach in which each student completed a small sample of items. There were no attempts to create summary level scores and most analyses focused only on estimates of the proportion of students passing particular items. In the 1970s, the National Center for Education Statistics, the sponsor for this project, funded special studies to exploit the capabilities of the NAEP data. In part as an outgrowth of these studies, a major redesign of NAEP resulted. Today, the NAEP data and data collection procedures are much more extensively documented (Johnson & Zwick, 1990), although the research design is still so complicated that most researchers cannot analyze the data appropriately.

Better examples of data collection and documentation procedures were provided by longitudinal studies that followed in the footsteps of Project TALENT. The National Longitudinal Study of the Class of 1972 (NLS-72) and the High School and Beyond Study (beginning with high school sophomores in 1980) made extensive efforts to provide public use files with documentation that included base frequencies for most variables as well as a description of data collection procedures and efforts (albeit sometimes in vain) to describe appropriate uses of case weights in analyses. (See Sebring, B. Campbell, Glusberg, Spencer, & Singleton, 1987 for a good example of data documentation.)

One other example of a large data collection project that was nearly contemporaneous with the early stages of Project A was the Profile of American Youth Study. This study involved the collection of ASVAB test scores from a representative sample of 1980 youth, which provided the basis for current ASVAB norms. It was part of a larger series of studies, known as the National Longitudinal Surveys (NLS) of Labor Market Experience, sponsored by the Bureau of Labor Statistics and conducted by the Center for Human Resource Research at Ohio State University. These studies involved longitudinal follow-ups of several different worker cohorts, but the 1980 youth cohort, known as NLSY, is the only one with extensive test score information. The NLS pioneered some aspects of data documentation (Center for Human Resource Research, 1991) and was among the first to provide public use data on CD-ROM.

Most of the above projects did involve special studies of data collection procedures. Unfortunately, most of these efforts involved survey procedures that were not particularly relevant to the design of Project A. Procedures for collecting and recording "performance" tests, now of great interest to the educational community under the rubric of "authentic" tests, were largely unknown at that time. Work sample studies had been heard of, but were generally of such limited scope that issues in collecting and scoring the data were limited. Thus, although the above studies did provide some suggestions for data documentation, useful guidelines for relevant data collection procedures were largely nonexistent.

We obviously knew a lot more about data collection and database design and execution when we finished than when we started. In the sections that follow, we recount our approach to issues we faced in getting from new instruments to a database ready for analysis. It is hoped that this description will provide insights for researchers who are collecting data, no matter how small- or large-scale their efforts. We also hope that readers will share our sense of gratification that the data coming from data collections so fraught with potential problems turned out to be so useful and informative.

DATA COLLECTIONS

Research Flow

The Project A data collection design was described in Chapter 3 (see particularly Figures 3.3 and 3.5). In summary, there were six major data collections, two of which took place simultaneously (LVI and CVII).

- *Concurrent Validation (CVI)*—About 9,500 soldiers who entered the Army between July 1, 1983 and June 30, 1984 (FY 83/84) were tested for 1 to 2 days on predictors (the Trial Battery), training measures, and first-tour performance criterion measures. Ratings data were also collected from peers and supervisors of these soldiers. Data were collected at 13 locations in the United States and numerous locations throughout Germany.
- *Longitudinal Validation: Predictors (LVP)*—Approximately 45,000 new recruits were given the 4-hour Experimental Battery from August 20, 1986 through November 30, 1987 (FY 86/87). They were tested at all eight Army Reception Battalion locations.
- *Longitudinal Validation: Training (LVT)*—About 30,000 soldiers from the LVP cohort were assessed using the training criterion measures as they exited MOS-specific training from one of 14 different locations. Ratings from the soldiers' drill instructors were also collected.
- *Longitudinal Validation: First-Tour Performance (LVI)*—Roughly 10,000 soldiers from the LVP cohort were tested using first tour criterion measures. Testing occurred in 1987–1988 and lasted from 4 to 8 hours per soldier. Ratings data were also collected from peers and supervisors. Data were collected at 13 U.S. Army posts and multiple locations in Europe, primarily in Germany.
- *Concurrent Validation Followup: Second-Tour Performance (CVII)*—Second-tour job performance data were collected from about 1,000 soldiers in the FY 83/84 (CVI) cohort in a data collection effort that was conducted in conjunction with the LVI data collection. Testing lasted 1 day per soldier. Supervisor and peer ratings were also collected.
- *Longitudinal Validation: Second-Tour Performance (LVII)*—In 1991–1992, second-tour criterion measures were administered to about 1,500 soldiers in the LVP cohort. Testing lasted 1 day per soldier, and supervisor ratings were collected as well.

In addition to the major data collections, there were dozens of smaller-scale data collections required to conduct the job analyses and construct and field test the predictor and criterion measures. These supplementary data collections helped us to try out and refine data collection procedures and served as training grounds for preparing project staff, as well as the predictor and criterion instruments, for the larger data collections to come.

Data Collection Instruments

The data collection instruments administered to each cohort in the various data collections have been described in some detail in preceding chapters. A simplified summary of the measures used in the major data collections is provided in Table 9.1. Recall that the 21 MOS were divided into Batch A and Batch Z groups, with the Batch A MOS receiving a wider array of criterion measures than the Batch Z MOS. Note also that the summary lists include several auxiliary measures that, in the interest of space, have not been discussed at length in this book. The Army Work Environment Questionnaire assessed soldier attitudes toward characteristics of their environment. The MOS-specific Job History Questionnaire and the Supervisory Experience Questionnaire questioned soldiers about the recency and extent of experience with the tasks on which they were being tested. The Measurement Method Rating, which was administered at the end of the testing day, asked soldiers to indicate how fair and valid they felt each testing method was. Finally, a job satisfaction questionnaire was administered in several of the data collections.

Data Collection Methods

Testing Scenarios

The major data collections used one of two different scenarios depending upon the location of the examinees. The Longitudinal Validation predictor and end-of-training data collections represented one scenario in which soldiers were assessed on the predictor battery as they were processed into the Army or completed their initial technical training. Under this scenario, Project A test centers were in place for approximately 12 months at each in-processing and training location, and data were collected from *everyone* in the designated MOS. A civilian test site manager (TSM) was hired at each test location to manage the day-to-day data collection activities and was supported by from one to eight on-site test administrators (TAs), depending upon the volume of testing. All data collection staff were hired and trained by permanent project staff.

Both predictor and training data were collected at all eight Army reception battalions and end-of-training data were collected at an additional six sites where advanced training for some of the MOS was conducted. The 1985 CVI and subsequent job performance data collections (CVII, LVI, and LVII) required project staff to go out into the field to assess a sample of individuals from each MOS. Under this second scenario, data collection

TABLE 9.1
Measures Administered to 1983–1984 (CV) and 1986/1987 (LV)
Cohorts of Soldiers

Concurrent Validation	*Longitudinal Validation*

CVI: First-Tour Data Collection (1985)

Trial Battery
  Cognitive paper-and-pencil tests
  Noncognitive paper-and-pencil inventories
  Computer-administered tests

Written Criterion and Auxiliary Measures
  School Knowledge Test
  Job Knowledge Test (Batch A only)
  Personnel File Form
  Job History Questionnaire
  Army Work Environment Questionnaire
  Measurement Method Rating

Rating Scales (supervisor and peer raters)
  Army-Wide Rating Scales
  Army-Wide Rating Scale Supplement
    (Batch Z only)
  MOS-Specific Rating Scales (Batch A only)
  Task Rating Scales (Batch A only)
  Combat Performance Prediction Scale

Hands-On Job Sample Tests (Batch A only)

CVII: Second-Tour Data Collection (1988)—
  Batch A Only

Written Criterion and Auxiliary Measures
  Job Knowledge Test
  Situational Judgment Test
  Personnel File Form
  Job History Questionnaire
  Army Job Satisfaction Questionnaire
  Measurement Method Rating

Rating Scales (supervisor and peer raters)
  Army-Wide Rating Scales
  MOS-Specific Rating Scales
  Combat Performance Prediction Scale

Hands-On Job Sample Tests
Supervisory Role-Play Exercises

LVP: Predictor Data Collection (1986–1987)

Experimental Battery
  Cognitive paper-and-pencil tests
  Noncognitive paper-and-pencil inventories
  Computer-administered tests

LVT: End-of-Training Data Collection (1987)

Performance Ratings (Instructor and peer raters)
School Knowledge Test

LVI: First-Tour Data Collection (1988–1989)

Written Measures
  Job Knowledge Test (Batch A only)
  School Knowledge Test (Batch Z only)
  Personnel File Form
  Job History Questionnaire
  Army Job Satisfaction Questionnaire
  Measurement Method Rating

Rating Scales (supervisor and peer raters)
  Army-Wide Rating Scales
  MOS-Specific Rating Scales (Batch A only)
  Combat Performance Prediction Scale (males only)

Hands-On Job Sample Tests (Batch A only)

LVII: Second-Tour Data Collection (1991–1992)—
  Batch A Only

Written Measures
  Job Knowledge Test
  Personnel File Form
  Job History Questionnaire
  Situational Judgment Test
  Supervisory Experience Questionnaire
  Army Job Satisfaction Questionnaire

Rating Scales (supervisor raters only)
  Army-Wide Rating Scales
  MOS-Specific Rating Scales
  Combat Performance Prediction Scale

Hands-On Job Sample Tests
Supervisory Role-Play Exercises

sites were set up at Army installations throughout the United States, Germany, and in the case of the LVII data collection, South Korea. Data were collected by teams of test administrators comprising both permanent project staff and temporary hires who were supported by military personnel at each test site. Test administrator training took place in a central location and staff members were assigned to collect data at multiple locations. Data collection teams usually ranged in size from 5 to 10 persons and operated for varying periods, from a few days to several months.

Advance Preparations

Identifying test locations.   Deciding where to collect predictor and training data proved easy; there were only so many places that this could be done, and data collections were set up at all of them. However, once trained, American soldiers can end up in hundreds of different locations around the world. Not only that, most of them move every two to four years. Clearly, our data collectors could not go everywhere, and it was not feasible to bring soldiers to the data collectors at some central location.

The most critical considerations for deciding where data would be collected were the number of soldiers in the target MOS at each possible site and costs associated with traveling to the site. The Army's computerized Worldwide Locator System was used to identify the most promising test sites in the United States by looking for the highest concentrations of soldiers in the sample of 21 MOS selected for testing. Thirteen Army posts were selected in this manner. Specific data collection sites were designated in Europe through consultation with relevant Army personnel.

Research support.   The support required for this research was quite extensive. The process started with the submission of formal Troop Support Requests, which initiated procedures through the military chain of command. Briefings for commanders of installations asked to provide large-scale support were generally required to obtain their support for the data collections. Eventually, the requests reached the operational level of individual installations, at which time the installation appointed a Point-of-Contact (POC) to coordinate the delivery of required research support. For the predictor and end-of-training data collections (LVP and LVT), data collection activities had to be worked into demanding operational schedules. In addition, appropriate data collection facilities had to be made available. In some cases, this meant fairly significant adjustments to existing facilities (e.g., constructing or tearing down walls, installing electrical outlets).

For the criterion data collections, research support requirements were even more extensive—involving a larger variety of personnel and facilities, as well as hands-on testing equipment. Required personnel included examinees, their supervisors, senior NCOs to administer the hands-on tests, and additional NCOs to help coordinate the data collection activities. Indoor facilities were required to accommodate written testing, some hands-on job samples, supervisory role-play administration, supervisor rating sessions, and general office and storage needs. Large outdoor areas and motorpools were required for job sample performance assessment. Locally supplied equipment was necessary for each of the MOS that used job sample measurement. The necessary items included tanks, artillery equipment, trucks, rifles, grenade launchers, medical mannequins, and so forth. Supporting our research needs was no small order for our hosts.

The role of the installation POC was paramount. Installation POCs typically had to work nearly full time on scheduling personnel and arranging for equipment and facility requirements for several months prior to the data collection. A project staff member worked closely with the POC via phone contact, written correspondence, and one or two site visits. This process was facilitated in the last major data collection (LVII) with the development of a detailed POC manual, which walked the POC through all requirements and provided solutions to problems commonly encountered in orchestrating this type of data collection. Every examinee, supervisor, NCO hands-on test administrator, and piece of hands-on testing equipment that did not appear as scheduled was a threat to the success of the data collection. Even with the most thorough planning, scheduling, and follow-up, however, problems invariably arose and constant efforts by on-site project staff and military support personnel were required to maximize the amount of data collected.

Identifying/scheduling participants. In the CVI data collection and the LV predictor and end-of-training data collections, soldiers were identified for testing based on their MOS and accession date (i.e., the date they entered the Army). In CVI, a systematic sampling plan for determining the specific soldiers to be tested at each installation was developed. This involved giving installation POCs paper lists of eligible individuals. The lists were designed to oversample minority and female soldiers. POCs were instructed to go down the lists in order. The lists were oversized, so that if 20 soldiers in an MOS were to be assessed, 40 or more names would be provided on the list. This allowed for skipping people who had moved to another post or were otherwise unavailable. For the LVP and LVT data collections, all soldiers in the selected MOS who processed through the reception battalions and training schools during the testing timeframe were scheduled for testing.

In subsequent data collections, because of the longitudinal design, individuals had to be requested by name (actually by social security number [SSN]). For the Army, this was an unusual and difficult requirement. Soldiers change locations frequently and requests for troop support were often required a full year before data were scheduled to be collected. Moreover, installations were not accustomed to accommodating such requirements. Individual soldiers were very hard to schedule on any particular day for a variety of reasons, including unit training and leave requirements.

In preparation for the LVI/CVII data collection, the computerized Worldwide Locator System was used to determine the location of soldiers who previously took part in the CVI or Experimental Battery (LVP) data collections. Lists of soldiers identified as being at each installation were provided to installation POCs. The POCs used these lists to "task" (i.e., formally request and schedule) specific individuals. Before data collection even began, it became clear that insufficient numbers of CVI soldiers would be available. Accordingly, the decision was made to also include individuals in the desired MOS and time-in-service cohort who had not been included in the previous data collection. A similar strategy was used for LVI, though to a much lesser degree. Part of the rationale was that it increased the sample sizes for certain analyses without appreciably increasing the data collection effort.

To improve our ability to track the sample, a different strategy was adopted for the LVII data collection. In addition to negotiating for more flexibility (i.e., requesting more soldiers at more sites than we intended to test) with the troop support request process, each installation was provided with a set of diskettes containing the SSNs for every eligible soldier. Army personnel on site matched the SSNs on the diskettes with their own computerized personnel files to determine which soldiers were actually there. This provided the most accurate determination possible. The LVII sample was thus composed entirely of those who had taken the predictor battery and/or the first-tour performance measures. No supplemental sample was included.

Considerable precoordination effort in support of the LVII data collection had already taken place when there was a large-scale deployment of troops to Southwest Asia as part of Operations Desert Shield and Desert Storm. As a result, FORSCOM, which controls all field installations in the continental United States, invoked a moratorium on research support. The duration of the moratorium was uncertain and the data collection could not be indefinitely postponed because the criterion measures were not suitable for soldiers with more than 3 to 5 years of experience. This indeed was a crisis for the Project A research design. Fortunately, the flexibility of the new troop support request strategy saved the day. In the end, an unexpectedly large proportion of the data was collected in Germany and South Korea (where large numbers of troops relatively unaffected by the deployment were located). Also, the data collection window was expanded several months beyond that designated by the original research plan. Luckily, no more comparable trouble spots erupted.

Staffing.   As mentioned previously, the sites at which LV predictor and training data collections were conducted required a Test Site Manager (TSM) and supporting staffs of one to eight test administrators. Given the amount of organizational knowledge and negotiating skill required, retired NCOs or officers with previous training or assessment experience and considerable knowledge of the installation supporting the data collection were often selected to be TSMs.

With regard to the criterion-related data collections (including CVI), each test site required the following project personnel: one TSM, one to two Hands-On Managers, one to two Hands-On Assistants, and three to five Test Administrators (TAs). In addition to project staff, each installation provided personnel to support the data collection activities, including 8 to 12 senior NCOs for each MOS to administer and score the hands-on tests.

CVI, which involved administration of predictor, training, and first-tour performance criterion measures, required larger teams of data collectors. Most CVI teams also included a person whose primary task was to keep track of completed instruments and prepare the data for shipment.

Training.   Data collection procedures evolved through the course of the project and were documented in updated manuals provided to all data collection personnel. Data collection personnel, with the exception of the civilian on-site personnel hired for LVP and LVT, were trained in a central location for two to five days. Many staff members who were able to participate in multiple data collection efforts became very experienced with the requirements of the Project A data collections and with working in a military environment. This experience was essential to the success of the various data collections. Because of their relative complexity, particularly extensive training was provided for the rating scale administration procedures and the supervisory role-play simulations.

Ratings administration.   Determining who was to provide performance ratings was a formidable administrative task. Each day, participants indicated which of the other participants they could rate. Using this information, the TA assigned up to four peer raters for each ratee. The transitory nature of military assignments made it especially difficult to identify supervisory raters. The data collection team did as much as possible to ensure that raters had sufficient experience with the ratee to provide valid ratings, even if this turned out to be individuals not in the soldier's official chain of command.

The rater training program was developed specifically for Project A and is described fully in Pulakos and Borman (1986). The efforts of the rating scale administrators to train raters and convince them to be careful and thorough was key to obtaining performance rating data that turned out to be of exceptionally high quality.

Role-player training for the supervisory simulations lasted two to three days. There were three role-plays and each TA was assigned a primary role and a secondary role. Because we were not dealing with professional actors, role assignments were based to some degree on a match with the demeanor of the TA. There were many practice runs, and role-players were "shadow scored," meaning that others also rated the person playing the examinee. Scores were compared and discussed to ensure that the scoring scheme was being reliably applied. Role-players were also given considerable feedback on ways in which they could follow the role more closely.

It was also necessary to train the on-site NCOs to administer and score the hands-on job samples in a standardized fashion and to develop high agreement among the scorers as to the precise responses that would be scored as go or no-go on each performance step. This 1- to 2-day training session began with a thorough introduction to Project A, which generally went a long way toward increasing the NCOs' motivation. Over multiple practice trials of giving each other the tests, the NCOs were given feedback from project staff who shadow scored the practice administrations. One persistent problem was that NCOs were inclined to correct soldiers who performed tasks incorrectly, which is, after all, their job. Keeping them in an assessment rather than a training mode was a constant challenge.

Training procedures for hands-on scorers are described in more detail in R. C. Campbell (1985).

Data Collection Logistics

The daily data collection schedule and logistics varied considerably depending upon the data collection. Each is briefly described below.

Concurrent validation (CVI). For the CVI data collection, the predictor battery, end-of-training tests, and first-tour job performance criterion measures were administered. NCO hands-on test administrators were trained the day before their MOS was scheduled to begin. Data collections lasted from 4 to 6 weeks per installation.

Soldiers in the Batch A MOS were assessed for two consecutive days in groups of 30 to 45. They were subdivided into groups of 15 each and rotated through four half-day test administration sessions: (a) written and computerized predictor tests, (b) school knowledge test and peer ratings, (c) job knowledge test and other written measures, and (d) hands-on tests. (See Table 9.2 for an illustration of 45 soldiers divided into 3 groups of 15.) The rotational schedule allowed reducing the groups to manageable sizes for the hands-on tests and computerized predictor tests. Concurrent with the testing of examinees was the collection of performance ratings from their supervisors.

Batch Z soldiers, for whom no MOS-specific job performance measures were available, were divided into groups of 15 and rotated between two half-day test sessions: (a) the predictor battery and (b) end-of-training school knowledge test, peer ratings, and other Army-wide written criterion measures.

TABLE 9.2
Concurrent Validation Examinee Rotation Schedule

	Group A (n = 15)	Group B (n = 15)	Group C (n = 15)
Day 1: a.m.	Predictors	Job knowledge test/other	School knowledge test/ratings
Day 1: p.m.	Hands-on	Predictors	Job knowledge test/other
Day 2: a.m.	School knowledge test/ratings	Hands-on	Predictors
Day 2: p.m.	Job knowledge test/other	School knowledge test/ratings	Hands-on

LV predictor battery (LVP).   The 4 hours of testing required for the Experimental Battery were divided up in various ways depending upon the operational schedules of each of the eight reception battalions. In some cases, all testing was accomplished in one session, but in others, testing had to be divided into two or three blocks distributed across the 3-day in-processing timeframe.

For one MOS, infantrymen (11B), the number of new recruits was more than could be tested on the computerized battery with available equipment. All of the future infantrymen completed the paper-and-pencil predictor tests, but only about one-third were scheduled for the computerized pre-dictor test battery.

LV end-of-training (LVT).   As the new soldiers reached the end of their MOS-specific training programs, they were scheduled to take the writ-ten training achievement (school knowledge) test and to complete Project A performance ratings on their peers. Performance ratings were also collected from each trainee's primary drill instructor.

Longitudinal validation/first tour and concurrent validation/ second tour (LVI/CVII).   Although simpler than the CVI data collec-tion because no predictor data were collected, this data collection was much larger in terms of total sample size (15,000 vs. 9,000). Moreover, it was complicated by the need to maximize the number of name-requested indi-viduals and the requirement to assess both first- and second-tour personnel during the same site visit. Individuals in the Batch A MOS were tested for 1 day versus a half day for Batch Z.

Longitudinal validation/second tour (LVII).   Compared to the preceding criterion-related data collections, this one was relatively small and simple. Only second-tour personnel in the nine Batch A MOS were included, and only those previously tested in Project A were eligible.

Summary.   To get a picture of the complexity of the criterion-related data collections, keep in mind that there were separate performance mea-sures, with different equipment, administrator training, and scoring proce-dures for each Batch A MOS. There were also separate first- and second-tour measures within each Batch A MOS. Consequently, each criterion data collection was really 10 to 20 separate efforts. At the same time that person-nel in some MOS were being assessed, NCOs from other MOS were being trained to administer and score the hands-on job samples, and performance ratings were being collected from dozens of supervisors. Batch Z MOS data collections were also taking place concurrently with all of the Batch A testing activities.

On-Site Data Preparation

When testing thousands of people all over the world on numerous measures and collecting performance rating data from multiple raters for each, there is considerable room for error. Every effort was made at the outset to reduce data entry errors by establishing a comprehensive set of data verification and tracking procedures and thoroughly training data collectors to follow those procedures.

TAs were instructed to scan visually answer sheets and rating forms for problems before examinees and raters left the test site. Their training included the identification of errors commonly made on the various measures and errors that had particularly significant repercussions (e.g., a rater miscoding the identification of the soldiers he or she is rating). Log sheets were maintained by individual TAs to record circumstances that might explain missing or unusual data. This task was particularly challenging for the Hands-On Managers who encountered many difficulties in obtaining complete and accurate data. For example, equipment needed for a given hands-on test might have been unavailable during part of the test period leading to missing scores for a group of soldiers. In some cases, equipment was available, but it was somewhat different from the requested equipment and on-site changes to the scoring system had to be made accordingly. Such information was recorded on testing log sheets and/or examinee rosters. Additional logging requirements were also required for the ratings data to facilitate the matching of ratings to examinee records.

The TSM was responsible for conducting a final check of test forms being shipped from the test site. Data shipments were accompanied by detailed data transmittal forms, which included annotated personnel rosters, all relevant log sheets, and an accounting of all the data contained in the shipment (e.g., number of first-tour 95B examinee test packets; number of 88M supervisor rating packets).

Additional File Data

Except for the FY81/82 cohort in which all data were obtained from existing Army records, most research data for Project A were collected in the for-research-only data collections described here. Computerized Army personnel files, however, were accessed to obtain a variety of information regarding individuals in our research samples. Accession files were tapped to retrieve information such as ASVAB test scores, educational background, demographic indices, key dates in the enlistment process, and term of enlistment. To support future research efforts, active duty personnel files are still periodically monitored to get up-to-date information on promotions and turnover activity to support future research efforts.

DATABASE DESIGN AND MANAGEMENT

Designing the Longitudinal Research Database (LRDB)

This section describes the evolution of the LRDB plan prior to and during the first year of the project and then summarizes the subsequent adjustments and changes. That is, first there was the plan, and then there was how it really worked out.

At the start, ARI contemplated the mammoth amount of data that would be generated, worried about it, and required a detailed database plan as one of the first contract deliverables. Concerns about the database were both near-term and long-term. In the long run, the accuracy and completeness of the data and the comprehensiveness and comprehensibility of the documentation were the chief concerns. Near-term concerns included the speed with which new data were entered into the database and, especially, the efficiency of access to these data for a variety of analytic purposes.

The database plan that was developed at the beginning of the project covered (a) content specifications, (b) editing procedures, (c) storage and retrieval procedures, (d) documentation, and (e) security procedures. More detailed information may be found in Wise, Wang, and Rossmeissl (1983).

LRDB Contents

The question was what to include in the database, and the short answer was everything. All participant responses would be recorded in the database, including responses to individual items and all of the scores generated from those responses. Data from all pilot tests and field tests would be collected as well as data from the Concurrent and Longitudinal Validation studies.

What was more of an issue was the extent to which existing data from operational files would also be linked into the database. The proposed

LRDB included a listing of specific variables to be pulled from applicant and accession files, from the Army EMF, and from the Army Cohort Files maintained by the Defense Manpower Data Center. These same data were pulled quarterly from the EMF and annually from the Cohort Files to chart the progress of each soldier included in the database. In addition, SQT results were to be pulled from files maintained by the Training and Doctrine Command (TRADOC) for use as preliminary criterion measures. For the most part, this information was to be maintained for all 1981–82 accession and also for individuals in each of the two major research samples. More limited information, including at least operational ASVAB scores, was obtained for soldiers participating in pilot and field tests.

Although the original intent was to be all-encompassing, a number of additions were not anticipated. These additions had to do primarily with information used in sampling jobs and tasks and in developing the criterion instruments. For example, SME judgments about the similarity of different jobs were combined with operational information about accession rates, gender and racial group frequencies, and so forth, to inform the selection of the MOS sampling plan. Similar judgments about the importance, frequency, and similarity of specific job tasks were collected and used in sampling the tasks to be covered by the written and hands-on performance measures. Other additions included "retranslation ratings" of the critical incidents used in developing the performance rating scales and expert judgments of predictor-criterion relationships used to identify the most promising areas for predictor development.

The LRDB plan also included a beginning treatise on the naming of variables. At that time, the plan was to begin both variable and data file names with a two-character prefix. The first character would indicate the type of data. The second character would be a number indicating the data collection event from 1 for the FY81/82 cohort data through 9 for the LVII data. After the first two characters, the plan was to use relatively descriptive six-character labels. During the course of the project, additional conventions were adopted so that the third and fourth characters indicated instrument and score types and the last four characters indicated specific elements (e.g., tasks, steps, or items) within the instrument and score type. Although it was never possible for any one person to remember the names of all of the variables, the naming convention used made it relatively easy to find what you were looking for in an alphabetized list.

Editing Procedures

Analysts and research sponsors are, by nature, an impatient lot; therefore it was necessary to remind them of all of the important steps required between data entry and analysis to ensure accuracy. For example, when reading operational data, cases were encountered where ASVAB scores of record were shifted one or two bytes, leading to seriously out-of-range values or where the ASVAB form code was incorrect or missing, leading to an incorrect translation of raw, number correct scores to standardized subtest and composite scores. Invalid MOS codes and incorrect dates were also encountered. Sex and race codes were not always consistent from one file to the next. Even SSNs were sometimes erroneously coded.

The LRDB approach was to cross link as much information as possible to check each of the data elements on individual soldiers. Sequences of dates (testing, accession, training) were compiled and checked for consistency. MOS codes and demographic data from accession records, the EMF, the Cohort files, and training records were all checked for consistency. Also, the procedures used to identify and correct outliers became much more involved as the project went on.

Data Storage and Retrieval

At the beginning, we had a great plan. During the contract procurement process, the contractor team engaged a database consultant who helped identify a system that we believed would give us a clear advantage. The system, known as "RAPID," was developed and maintained by Statistics Canada, a branch of the Canadian government. Presumably, this system would be made available to the U.S. government at no charge. In fact, we found staff in the Bureau of Labor Statistics who also were interested in using this system and worked jointly with them on acquisition and installation. Apart from being cheap, RAPID had three attractive features. First, the data were stored in a transposed format (by variable rather than by subject). Most analyses use only a small subset of the variables in a file making it possible to read only the data for those variables without having to pass through all of the other data in the file. Second, RAPID employed a high degree of data compression. A categorical variable, such as an MOS code, might take on as many as 256 different values and still be stored in a single byte (rather than the three it otherwise took) and missing data indicators were stored as bits. Third, RAPID had convenient interfaces to SAS and SPSS and to a cross-tabulation program (later incorporated into SAS as PROC TABULATE) that was required by the research sponsor.

Reality is often different from expectation. After initial installation, tests were run and several unanticipated problems were discovered that made RAPID less attractive than originally believed. A major problem was that, because of the way RAPID files were indexed, they could only be stored on disk. The process of "loading" and "unloading" files from and to tape was cumbersome and costly. Tape copies were required for data security and unloading files after every update eliminated any access efficiencies. Reloading/rebuilding a RAPID file was more cumbersome than loading a file in other formats. Finally, the convenient interfaces to other software were not exactly as convenient as believed. RAPID was neither a real programming language (for generating composite variables) nor an analysis package. Analysts or database staff would have to maintain currency in two languages, RAPID and SAS (or SPSS) rather than one.

The decision was made to drop RAPID and use SAS as the system for maintaining all data files. SAS includes many features that facilitate file documentation including format libraries, the history option of PROC CONTENTS, and procedures and functions that are reasonably descriptive and well documented. In addition, SAS allowed the addition of user-defined procedures and several such procedures were developed for use in the project (e.g., procedures to compute coefficient alpha or inter-rater reliability estimates).

The primary mechanism for ensuring efficient access was to "chunk" the database into distinct files. This chunking included both a nesting of participants and a nesting of variables. Separate files were maintained for (a) all applicants in a given period, (b) all accessions during that period, and (c) participants in each of the major data collections, with distinct information on each file linkable through a scrambled identifier. We also maintained detailed item response files separately from files containing only summary score information. On the criterion side, separate item files were maintained for each MOS, because the content of the tests was different.

Documentation

The LRDB Plan called for a comprehensive infrastructure of data to describe the data in the data bank. This infrastructure would include information about data collection events (e.g., counts by sites, lists of instruments used, perhaps even staff assignments), instruments (copies of instruments and answer sheets with some indication of the names of the variables used in recording the responses), and data sets (names, locations, and flow charts showing the processes and predecessor files used in creating each data set). The design of the infrastructure was essentially a neural net model, where the user could begin at many different points (nodes) and find his or her way to the information that was required. Today, software engineers would use the term configuration management for the task of keeping the data and its documentation in harmony. Although we did not have a term for it, we did experience the constant struggle to keep the documentation consistent with the data.

At the heart of the documentation plan was a detailed codebook for each data set. This was not just a listing of variables, as you would get with a PROC CONTENTS. The intent was to show not only the codes used with each variable, but also the frequency with which those codes occurred in the data set. For continuous variables, complete summary statistics would be provided. Users could thus get some indication of the data available for analysis and have some constant counts against which to check results. Because there were a large number of files to be documented and a large number of variables in each of these files, some automation of the process of generating codebooks was essential. A SAS macro was developed that would take the output of a SAS PROC CONTENTS and an ancillary flag for each variable indicating whether frequencies or descriptive statistics was desired and generate the SAS code to produce most of the codebook. Although the process was never fully automated, the SAS program was used to good advantage. The codebooks just for the MOS specific CVI files were, in the aggregate, several feet thick (see Young, Austin, McHenry & Wise, 1986, 1987; Young & Wise, 1986a, 1986b).

Some aspects of the documentation scheme were not carried out as thoroughly as originally desired. Data collection events were thoroughly documented in technical reports, but not always online. Similarly, instrument files were maintained in file cabinets, but not necessarily online. System and program flow charts were not maintained in as much detail as proposed, because an easier and more comprehensive system of program documentation was identified. Output listings from all file creation runs were saved online and then allowed to migrate to backup tapes. It was thus always possible to retrieve any run and see, not only the SAS code used, but the record counts and other notes provided by SAS in the output log indicating the results of applying that code.

A plan for "online" assistance was developed to aid in the dissemination of file documentation and other useful information. Project staff from ARI and all three contractor organizations were assigned accounts on the mainframe computer system and a macro was placed in each user's log on profile that would execute a common profile of instructions. The database manager could thus insert news items that would be printed whenever any of the project staff logged on. Specially defined macros could also be inserted and thus made available for use by all project staff. The command "DIRECT" (for directory), for example, would pull up a list of the names, user IDs, and phone numbers of all project staff. Project staff became proficient at the use of e-mail for a variety of purposes including submitting workfile requests to the database manager. In point of fact, e-mail (a novelty at the time) became a very useful way of communicating, particularly among staff who worked diverse hours and/or in different time zones.

Security Procedures

There were two principal security concerns: privacy protection and ensuring the integrity of the database. The primary privacy issue was that information in the database not be used in operational evaluations of individual soldiers. A secondary concern was that outside individuals or organizations not get unauthorized access. The concern with integrity was that no one other than the database manager and his or her staff should have the capability of altering data values and that copies of all data should be stored off-site for recovery purposes. Both the privacy and integrity concerns were dealt with through a series of password protection systems that controlled file access. Another data security component was the encryption of soldier identifiers.

Data Coding, Entry, and Editing

Although sample sizes were too small to warrant the use of scannable forms for the second-tour samples (note that this was before the era of desktop publications capable of generating scannable forms), in the first-tour data collections, scannable answer sheets were used whenever possible to speed processing and minimize the possibility of data entry errors. Responses to all first-tour written tests and ratings were coded on scannable answer sheets. The primary exception, when key entry was required for both first- and second-tour soldiers, was with the hands-on job samples. Because the measures were different for each of the nine Batch A MOS, the volume of responses did not justify the expense of designing and programming scannable answer sheets. In addition, the instructions for coding responses to each task were changing up to the last minute, separate answer sheets were judged unwieldy for the scorers, and these tests were often administered under conditions where scannable answer sheets might not survive (e.g., the motor pool or in the rain). A great deal of effort was expended by the database staff in logging the hands-on score sheets, sorting them, checking names against rosters, and then shipping them to a data entry vendor where they were key-entered and verified.

For both the hands-on tests and the peer and supervisor ratings, soldiers were assigned a three-character identifier that was easier to enter than SSNs and also provided a degree of privacy protection. A great deal of effort was required, however, to make sure that the correct identifiers were used in all cases. This step involved printing rosters for each data collection site and then checking off instruments (manually for hands-on score sheets and then electronically for both ratings and score sheets after data entry). Duplicate or missing identifiers were resolved by retrieving the original documents where the soldier's name was written (but not scanned or entered) and comparing the name to the roster submitted by the data collectors and the roster generated from the background questionnaire. These steps were a major reason it took several months between the time data were received from the field and when "cleaned" files were available for analyses.

One editing procedure that emerged that was particularly noteworthy was the use of a "random response" index. In CVI, Batch A soldiers spent 2 full days taking tests. In the hands-on tests, because soldiers were watched individually by senior NCOs, it is likely that they generally did their best. On written tests, however, a much greater degree of anonymity was possible, and it was likely that some soldiers may have just filled in the bubbles without paying much attention to the questions. (The TAs would not let them leave until all of the bubbles were filled in, but it was not possible to be sure that every examinee actually read the questions.) Random responders were identified by plotting two relevant statistics and looking for outliers. The two statistics were the percent of items answered correctly (random responders would fall at the bottom end of this scale) and the correlation between the soldiers' item scores (right or wrong) and the overall "p-values" for each item. Individuals who were answering conscientiously would be more likely to get easier items correct than hard items. For participants responding randomly, the correlation between item scores and p-values would be near zero.

In analyzing random response results for written tests used in CVI, we noticed that some individuals appeared to answer conscientiously at first but then lapsed into random responding part way through the tests. To identify these "quitters," scores and random response indices were computed separately for the first and second half of each test. Outliers were identified where these measures were not consistent across both halves.

Further details of the editing procedures used with the CVI data may be found in Wise (1986). The procedures used with the LV data built upon the procedures developed for the CVI. Details on these procedures may be found in Steele and Park (1994).

Dealing with Incomplete Data

Notwithstanding the Project's best efforts to collect complete data on each individual in the CV and LV samples, the outcome was not perfect. The hands-on and ratings criteria experienced the most missing data. The hands-on data collection, for example, was heavily dependent on the availability and reliability of a wide variety of equipment. At times, equipment broke down and data were not available on the related task performance measures during the period before replacement equipment became available. However, other data collection activities had to proceed and the soldiers affected could not be called back. At other times, unexpected weather conditions precluded testing some tasks or mandated skipping other steps.

The rating data presented other issues. The most frequent problem was with participants who had recently transferred into a unit where there were no supervisors (or peers) on post who could provide ratings. There were also a few cases in which raters did not follow instructions and omitted sections.

Other reasons for incomplete data included soldiers who were not available for part of the scheduled time. Data were also missing in a few cases because soldiers were exceptionally slow in completing some of the tests and ran out of time.

By way of example, for the nine Batch A MOS in the CVI sample, fewer than 15% had absolutely complete data on every instrument. This is somewhat misleading, however, because greatest category of missing data was for the hands-on tasks and the majority of the time this was due to known variation in equipment that led to different "tracks" for different soldiers. Consequently, these "missing data" were actually scores on "parallel" forms.

Actual missing values were troublesome for two reasons. First, multivariate analyses were used in analyses of the criterion domain, and in such analyses, cases missing any values are typically deleted. This would mean throwing away a great deal of data on cases where only one or two variables were missing. Second, summary level criterion (and predictor) scores had to be generated for use in validity analyses. If scores could only be generated for cases with complete data, the number of cases remaining for the validity analyses would be unacceptably small. For these reasons, a great deal of attention was paid to the process of "filling in" the missing values using appropriate imputation procedures.

The general approach to missing data was to "fill in" data for instruments in which 90% or more of the data were present and generate the corresponding summary scores. When more than 10% of the data were missing, all summary scores from the instrument were set to missing. Traditional procedures for imputing missing data involve substituting variable or examinee means for the missing values. This strategy was used for the second-tour criterion samples because sample sizes were relatively small (see Wilson, Keil, Oppler, & Knapp, 1994 for more details). Even though the amount of data being imputed was very small and the impact of different procedures was likely to be minimal, efforts were made to implement a more sophisticated procedure for the other data collection samples.

The procedure of choice, PROC IMPUTE (Wise & McLaughlin, 1980), used the information that was available for an examinee to predict his or her score on the variables that were missing. For each variable with missing data, the distribution of that variable conditioned on the values of other variables was estimated using a modified regression. The algorithm used by PROC IMPUTE divided predicted values from a linear regression into discrete levels and then estimated (and smoothed) the conditional distribution of the target variable for each predictor level. This approach allowed for a better fit to situations where the relationship of the predicted values to the target measure was not strictly linear or where homoscedasticity of the conditional variances did not apply.

The value assigned by PROC IMPUTE to replace a missing value is a random draw from the conditional distribution of the target variable. The advantage of this particular approach over substituting the mean of the conditional distribution (i.e., predicted values in a regression equation) is that it leads to unbiased estimates of variances and covariances as well as means, although this advantage is paid for by slightly greater standard errors in the estimators of means. It should be noted that a very similar procedure has been adopted with NAEP to estimate score distributions from responses to a limited number of items, although in that case multiple random draws are taken from the estimated conditional distribution.

The "art" of applying PROC IMPUTE is in deciding which variables to use as predictors (conditioning variables). Several background variables and provisional scale scores for the instrument in question were used in imputing the missing values for each instrument. Details about the application of PROC IMPUTE may be found in Wise, McHenry, and Young (1986) and Young, Houston, Harris, Hoffman, and Wise (1990) for the CV data and in Steele and Park (1994) for the LV data.

FINAL SAMPLE SIZES

Tables 9.3 through 9.5 show the final post-imputation sample sizes from each of the major Project A data collections. Specifically, Table 9.5 shows the final post-imputation sample sizes for CVI and CVII. Note that the CVI figures reflect complete criterion and experimental predictor data. Table 9.4 shows the number of soldiers with either complete or partial data from the Longitudinal Validation predictor and end-of-training data collections (LVP and LVT). Note that many of the 11B soldiers are missing

TABLE 9.3
Concurrent Validation Sample Sizes (CVI and CVII)

	Numbers of CVI Soldiers Post-Imputation with Complete Predictor and Criterion Data		Numbers of CVII Soldiers Post-Imputation with Complete Criterion Data	
	Total N	Post-Imputation w/Complete data	Total N	Post-Imputation w/Complete data
Batch A MOS				
MOS				
11B	702	491	130	123
13B	667	464	162	154
19E	503	394	43	41
31C	366	289	103	97
63B	637	478	116	109
71L	514	427	112	111
88M	686	507	144	134
91A	501	392	106	98
95B	692	597	147	139
Total	5,268	4,039	1,063	1,006
Batch Z MOS				
MOS				
12B	704	544	n/a	n/a
16S	470	338		
27E	147	123		
51B	108	69		
54E	434	340		
55B	291	203		
67N	276	238		
76W	490	339		
76Y	630	444		
94B	612	368		
Total	4,162	3,006		

TABLE 9.4

Longitudinal Validation on Predictor and Training Sample Sizes (LVP and LVT)

	Numbers of LVP Soldiers Post-Imputation with Complete Computer and Paper-&-Pencil Battery Data		Numbers of LVT Soldiers Post-Imputation with Complete School Knowledge and Rating Data	
	Total N	Post-Imputation w/Complete data	Total N	Post-Imputation w/Complete data
Batch A MOS				
MOS				
11B	14,193	4,540	10,575	10,169
13B	5,087	4,910	5,288	5,128
19E	583	580	471	466
19K	1,849	1,822	1,659	1,645
31C	1,072	970	1,377	1,321
63B	2,241	2,121	1,451	1,389
71L	2,140	1,944	1,843	1,805
88M	1,593	1,540	1,913	1,867
91A	4,219	3,972	5,368	5,314
95B	4,206	4,125	3,776	3,704
Total	37,183	26,524	33,721	32,808
Batch Z MOS				
MOS				
12B	2,118	2,101	2,001	1,971
16S	800	783	694	675
27E	139	138	166	160
29E	257	216	306	296
51B	455	442	377	368
54E	967	888	808	787
55B	482	464	674	606
67N	334	329	408	379
76Y	2,756	2,513	2,289	2,195
94B	3,522	3,325	2,695	2,519
96B	320	304	253	235
Total	12,150	11,503	10,671	10,191

some predictor data because, as mentioned previously, the sheer volume of soldiers in-processing into this MOS exceeded the number that could be accommodated by the hardware required for the computerized predictor tests. Sample sizes for the LVI and LVII criterion data collections are provided in Table 9.5. Sample sizes for validation analyses were smaller than those shown here, because soldiers with complete criterion data did not necessarily have complete predictor data.

TABLE 9.5
Longitudinal Validation Criterion Sample Sizes (LVI and LVII)

	Numbers of LVI Soldiers Post-Imputation with Complete Criterion Data		Numbers of LVII Soldiers Post-Imputation with Complete Criterion Data	
	Total N	Post-Imputation w/Complete Data	Total N	Post-Imputation w/Complete Data
Batch A MOS				
MOS				
11B	907	896	347	281
13B	916	801	180	117
19E	249	241	168	105
19K	825	780	70	—[a]
31C	529	483	194	157
63B	752	721	157	129
71L	678	622	89	69
88M	682	662	222	156
91A	824	801	168	130
95B	452	451		
Total	6,814	6,458	1,595	1,144
Batch Z MOS				
MOS				
12B	840	719	n/a	n/a
16S	472	373		
27E	90	81		
29E	111	72		
51B	212	145		
54E	498	420		
55B	279	224		
67N	194	172		
76Y	789	593		
94B	831	605		
94B	128	110		
Total	4,444	3,514		

[a]No hands-on test or role-play data were collected from this MOS in LVII.

SUMMARY AND IMPLICATIONS

The planning and execution of the Project A data collections is a story (at least in our eyes) of truly epic proportions. Our purpose in recounting this story is to communicate the strategies that were used to maximize the completeness and accuracy of the data.

If there was a single lesson learned from our efforts, it is the need to plan carefully (and budget carefully) for data collection and data editing. These topics are not generally taught in graduate school, but are critical to the success of any significant research effort. A brief summary of more specific "lessons" illustrated by our efforts is presented here. First, the selection and training of data collectors is fundamental to the collection of data that are as clean and complete as possible. In addition, as many contingencies (e.g., equipment failures) as possible must be anticipated, and procedures for responding to these contingencies must be developed. The importance of pilot tests demonstrating the workability of data collection procedures cannot be overemphasized. We conducted multiple pilot tests in advance of each major data collection and made significant revisions to instruments and procedures as a result of each test. The early editing of data in the field greatly improved its quality and completeness, and it was often possible to resolve missing or inconsistent information at that time, whereas it would have been impossible later. Finally, for a variety of reasons, it is inevitable that some data will be missing. Hard decisions about when to delete and how and when to impute must be made.

Enhancements to the Research Database

After Project A concluded, some attention was given to enhancements of the LRDB.

Continued Improvements in Documentation

Originally, separate codebooks were generated for each MOS, resulting, for example, in a 10-volume codebook for the CVI data collection. Since 1994, extensive revisions were made to the contents and procedures for generating codebooks. Expanded content includes a general overview of the project plan, a description of the research sample, details on the data collection procedures, a listing of available documentation and codebooks, and a bibliography of available references and publications. Furthermore, a more detailed description of data processing procedures, the extent and treatment of missing data, and the final sample was provided for each data collection. The ordering of variables within each codebook was also changed: related variables were grouped together and the information common to all MOS was printed first, followed by information specific to the instruments used for the individual MOS. By using a condensed and more user-friendly approach, the codebook for each data collection could include more information, and still be reduced from ten volumes to one volume.

Addition of Data

On a regular basis, data from the EMF are abstracted and added to the latest data collection cohort. The data that are being added include paygrade information, promotion rate, re-enlistment, and attrition information. These data are part of ARI's ongoing research efforts.

Reformating of Data for Analyses on PCs

With most researchers using PCs to analyze data, it would be desirable to have the project A data available in PC format as well as in a mainframe format. Although currently there is no plan or funding available to reformat data for PC usage, it would be feasible to abstract a smaller set of data on diskette or even on CD-ROM for PC use. In addition to providing the data in either raw data format or in SAS system file format, additional information could also be developed to help users select variables and run simple statistics on subsets of the sample.

10

The Experimental Battery: Basic Attribute Scores for Predicting Performance in a Population of Jobs

Teresa L. Russell and Norman G. Peterson

As described in Chapters 4, 5, and 6, the development of the Experimental Battery was an iterative process using data from three successive phases: the Pilot Trial Battery administered in the Project A field tests, the Trial Battery administered in the Concurrent Validation (CVI), and the Experimental Battery administered as part of the Longitudinal Validation (LV) effort, and the subject of this chapter.

As it was configured at the start of the Longitudinal Validation, more than 70 individual test or scale scores could be obtained from the Experimental Battery. Entering such a large number of scores into a prediction equation presents obvious problems, especially for jobs with relatively small sample sizes, and it was necessary to reduce the number of scores. On the other hand, each measure had been included because it was deemed important for predicting job performance. Consequently, it was also important to preserve, as much as possible, the heterogeneity, or critical elements of specific variances of the original set of test scores. A major goal for the analysis of the Experimental Battery reported in this chapter was to identify the set of basic predictor composite scores that balanced these considerations as effectively as possible.

Data from the Trial Battery and the Experimental Battery differ in several ways. Some of the measures were revised significantly after the CVI analyses. Also, the Experimental Battery was administered to a much larger sample that was longitudinal, rather than concurrent, in nature. Both samples are large enough to produce stable results, but there are major differences in terms of the examinees' relative length of experience in the organization and its possible effects on the measures in the predictor battery.

Of the approximately 50,000 individuals who were tested during the longitudinal predictor data collection (LVP), about 38,000 had complete predictor data (i.e., both the computer-administered and paper-and-pencil measures). Because of cost considerations regarding computerized administration, over 11,000 new entrants in the high-volume combat MOS (11B) were given the paper-and-pencil measures only. To conserve computing resources, most intrabattery analyses were conducted on an initial sample of 7,000 soldiers with complete predictor data. This sample, called "Sample 1," is a random sample stratified on race, gender, and MOS. When appropriate, findings from Sample 1 were subjected to confirmatory analyses on a second stratified random sample ($N = 7,000$), called "Sample 2." Both subsamples were drawn from the sample of new accessions having complete predictor data. Although the basic N for each subsample was 7,000, the numbers vary slightly for the various analyses. For the most part, results reported in this chapter are based on Sample 1 analyses.

The Experimental Battery includes three major types of instruments: (a) paper-and-pencil tests designed to measure spatial constructs; (b) computer-administered tests of cognitive, perceptual, and psychomotor abilities; and (c) noncognitive paper-and-pencil measures of personality, interests, and job outcome preferences. Names of the instruments and the constructs they were designed to measure appear in Table 10.1. The Trial Battery versions of the instruments were described in detail in Chapters 5 and 6.

The remainder of this chapter discusses each type of test domain in turn and describes the analyses that produced the array of composite scores which then became the "predictors" to be validated. The discussion covers only the experimental project developed measures. The validation analyses also included the ASVAB, as it was then constituted. There are essentially four scoring options for the ASVAB: (a) the 10 individual test scores, (b) the four factor scores previously described, (c) a total score of the 10 individual tests, and (d) the Armed Forces Qualification Test (AFQT) composite of 4 of the 10 individual tests.

TABLE 10.1
Experimental Battery Tests and Relevant Constructs

Test/Measure	Construct
Paper-and Pencil Spatial Tests	
Assembling objects	Spatial Visualization-Rotation
Object Rotation	Spatial Visualization-Rotation
Maze	Spatial Visualization-Scanning
Orientation	Spatial Orientation
Map	Spatial Orientation
Reasoning	Induction
Computer-Administered Tests	
Simple Reaction Time	Reaction Time (Processing Efficiency)
Choice Reaction Time	Reaction Time (Processing Efficiency)
Short-Term Memory	Short-Term Memory
Perceptual Speed and Accuracy	Perceptual Speed and Accuracy
Target Identification	Perceptual Speed and Accuracy
Target Tracking 1	Psychomotor Precision
Target Shoot	Psychomotor Precision
Target Tracking 2	Multilimb Coordination
Number Memory	Number Operations
Cannon Shoot	Movement Judgment
Temperament, Interest, and Job Preference Measures	
Assessment of Background and Life Experiences (ABLE)	Adjustment
	Dependability
	Achievement
	Physical Condition
	Leadership (Potency)
	Locus of Control
	Agreeableness/Likability
Army Vocational Interest Career Examination (AVOICE)	Realistic Interest
	Conventional Interest
	Social Interest
	Investigative Interest
	Enterprising Interest
	Artistic Interest
Job Orientation Blank (JOB)	Job Security
	Serving Others
	Autonomy
	Routine Work
	Ambition/Achievement

PAPER-AND-PENCIL SPATIAL TESTS

The only spatial test that underwent changes between the concurrent and longitudinal validation was Assembling Objects, a measure of spatial visualization. Four items were added and three items were revised because of a ceiling effect. There were no large differences between the LV and CV samples in means and standard deviations of test scores for the five unchanged tests. On most tests, the LV sample performed slightly better and with slightly greater variability than did the CV sample. On the whole, performances of the two samples were very similar.

For the six spatial tests, several methods of screening data were investigated because it was difficult to differentiate "might-be-random responders" from low-ability examinees. However, so few examinees would have been screened out for four of the six tests, even if there had been no confusion with low-ability examinees, that no special screening was applied to any of the six tests. If an examinee had at least one response, he or she was included and all items were used to compute scores.

Psychometric Properties of Spatial Test Scores

Table 10.2 presents the means and standard deviations for the LV sample, with the CV sample distributional data provided for comparison purposes. The distributions are quite similar across the two samples. Table 10.3 summarizes coefficient alpha and test-retest reliabilities obtained in three data

TABLE 10.2
Spatial Test Means and Standard Deviations

Test	Mean		SD	
	LV	CV	LV	CV
Assembling Objects	23.5	23.3	7.15	6.71
Object Rotation	59.1	62.4	20.15	19.06
Maze	16.9	16.4	4.85	4.77
Orientation	12.2	11.0	6.21	6.18
Map	7.9	7.7	5.45	5.51
Reasoning	19.5	19.1	5.44	5.67

Note: LV Sample 1 $n = 6,754$–$6,950$; CV sample $n = 9,332$–$9,345$.

TABLE 10.3

Spatial Reliability Comparisons Between Pilot Trial Battery, Trial Battery,
and Experimental Battery Administrations

	Internal Consistency (Alpha)			Test-Retest	
Test	PTB (n = 290)	TB (n = 9332–9345)	EB[a] (n = 6754–6950)	PTB (n = 97–125)	TB (n = 499–502)
Assembling Objects[b]	.92	.90	.88	.74	.70
Object Rotation[c]	.97	.97	.98	.75	.72
Maze[c]	.89	.89	.90	.71	.70
Orientation	.88	.89	.89	.80	.70
Map	.90	.89	.88	.84	.78
Reasoning	.83	.86	.85	.64	.65

[a]LV Sample 1.

[b]Contained 40 items in the Fort Knox field test and 32 items in the CV administration. Time limits were 16 minutes for both the PTB and TB. The EB version contains 36 items and has an 18-minute time limit.

[c]Object Rotation and Maze tests are designed to be speeded tests. Alpha is not an appropriate reliability coefficient but is reported here for consistency. Correlations between separately timed halves for the Pilot Trial Battery were .75 for Object Rotation and .64 for Maze (unadjusted).

collections (CV, LV, and a test-retest sample conducted prior to CV). Similar levels of reliability were obtained across the different samples. As indicated by Table 10.4, the patterns of correlations among the tests are also similar across the CV sample and the two initial LV samples.

Subgroup Differences

Gender

A gender difference on tests of spatial ability is a prevalent finding (Anastasi, 1958; Maccoby & Jacklin, 1974; McGee, 1979; Tyler, 1965). For example, the precursor to the current ASVAB included a Space Perception test. Kettner (1977) reported test scores for 10th, 11th, and 12th grade males and females. In total, 656 males and 576 females were included in the sample. Male means consistently exceeded female means on Space Perception; effect sizes were .32 SD for 10th graders, .51 SD for 11th graders, and .34 SD for 12th graders.

An important historical finding is that the magnitude of the gender difference varies considerably with type of test (Linn & Petersen, 1985; Sevy,

TABLE 10.4

Spatial Measures: Comparison of Correlations of Number Correct Score in
Concurrent and Longitudinal Validations

| Test | CV (N = 9332–9345)/LV Sample 1 (N = 6941–6950) (CV/LV) | | | | |
	Object Rotation	Maze	Orientation	Map	Reasoning
Assembling Objects	.41/.46	.51/.51	.46/.50	.50/.52	.56/.56
Object Rotation		.50/.51	.37/.42	.39/.42	.38/.44
Maze			.40/.41	.44/.42	.45/.48
Orientation				.53/.54	.48/.49
Map					.52/.51

1983). Linn and Petersen performed a meta-analysis of standardized mean differences between males' and females' scores. They grouped spatial tests into three categories: (a) spatial perception and orientation tests, (b) mental rotation tests that included both two- and three-dimensional rotation tests, and (c) spatial visualization tests that resembled the Experimental Battery Reasoning and Assembling Objects tests. The spatial perception effect sizes were not sufficiently homogeneous for meta-analysis (see Hedges, 1982) and were, therefore, partitioned by age. Studies of subjects over 18 years of age produced an effect size of .64 SD favoring males, whereas the effect size for subjects under 18 years of age was .37 SD favoring males. The mental rotation effect sizes were also not homogeneous, but this time the effective partitioning variable was two- versus three-dimensional rotation tests. The effect size for two-dimensional tests was .26 SD favoring males, whereas the effect size for three-dimensional tasks was nearly a full standard deviation (.94 SD) favoring males. The effect sizes for spatial visualization (the largest category of studies) were homogeneous. The average effect size was .13 SD; no changes in gender differences in spatial visualization were detected across age groups. A separate meta-analysis by Sevy (1983) yielded essentially the same results; three-dimensional rotation tasks produced the largest effect size, and paper form board and paper folding tasks yielded the smallest effect.

As shown in Table 10.5, observed gender differences on the Project A spatial tests are consistent with the meta-analytic findings (i.e., gender differences vary with the type of test). Gender differences are small to nonexistent on the Reasoning and Assembling Objects tests—tests that

TABLE 10.5
Effect Sizes of Subgroup Differences on Spatial Tests[a]

Test	Male-Female Effect Size (d)[b]	White-Black Effect Size (d)[b]
Assembling Objects	.06	.84
Object Rotation	.21	.69
Maze	.35	.94
Orientation	.35	.91
Map	.30	1.08
Reasoning	−.01	.77

[a]LV Sample 1. $N \approx 6,900$.
[b]d is the standardized mean difference between group means. A positive value indicates a higher score for the majority group.

resemble Linn and Petersen's visualization tests. Differences of one-half to about one-third of an SD were observed on the other tests across samples.

Race Differences

Both verbal and non-verbal I.Q. test data frequently yield differences between White and Black means that approximate 1.0 SD (Jensen, 1980). As shown in Table 10.5, differences on the Project A spatial tests ranged from about two-thirds of an SD to one SD. The Map Test and the Maze Test produced the largest differences; the Object Rotation Test produced the smallest.

Forming Composites of the Spatial Test Scores

When the spatial tests were factor analyzed, either one or two factors typically emerged. Table 10.6 shows results from principal factor analyses (R^2 in the diagonal). Parallel analysis estimates of eigenvalues for random data (Allen & Hubbard, 1986; Humphreys & Montanelli, 1975) suggested that one or at most two factors should be retained. Solutions from CVI and the two LV analysis samples are highly similar. The Object Rotation Test and Maze Test (speeded tests) load on the second factor and all other tests load on the first. The second factor appears to be a method (speededness) factor that does not reflect a meaningful homogeneous construct.

TABLE 10.6

Comparison of Spatial Paper-and-Pencil Test Factor Loadings for Three Samples[a]

Test	Factor I Concurrent/Sample 1/Sample 2	Factor II Concurrent/Sample 1/Sample 2
Map	.60/.59/.58	.37/.38/.38
Orientation	.56/.57/.56	.34/.37/.35
Assembling Objects	.54/.55/.54	.47/.49/.50
Reasoning	.59/.54/.54	.40/.46/.42
Maze	.38/.38/.37	.57/.57/.55
Object Rotation	.32/.36/.34	.52/.54/.52
Eigenvalue	1.56/1.54/1.49	1.24/1.35/1.26

Note: Concurrent sample $N = 7939$; LV Sample 1 $N = 6929$, LV Sample 2 $N = 6436$.
[a]Principal factor analysis with varimax rotation.

When factored with other cognitive measures (i.e., the ASVAB subtests and/or computer measures), the spatial tests consistently form a single factor of their own (N.G. Peterson, Russell et al., 1990). That would suggest that the spatial tests should be pooled to form one composite. However, members of the project's Scientific Advisory Group (L. Humphreys, personal communication, March 1990) noted that there are little or no gender differences on the Reasoning Test and Assembling Objects Test whereas differences on the other tests are consistent with those found in previous research. This might suggest grouping the two gender-neutral tests to form a composite. If the two speeded tests were grouped together, that would leave the Maze Test and the Orientation Test as an orientation factor. Consequently, the most extremely differentiated view would posit three factors: speed, orientation, and "figural" (Reasoning and Assembling Objects). Additional confirmatory (using LISREL) and second-order analyses (the Schmid-Leiman transformation) were carried out to further evaluate these alternatives to a one factor solution.

The Schmid-Leiman analysis showed that all tests had large loadings on the second-order general factor. Loadings on the speed and orientation specific factors were small, and loadings on the figural factor are essentially zero, suggesting that virtually all reliable variance in the Assembling Objects and Reasoning tests is tapped by the general factor. Comparative confirmatory analyses also showed that a one-factor solution produced the best fit. However, the decision on the number of spatial test composites required consideration of practical concerns as well as research findings. Some reasons for using more than one composite were that (a) the Army may wish in the future to administer fewer than six of the paper-and-pencil tests, (b) it might be useful to have a gender-neutral spatial composite (Reasoning), and (c) the specific factors might predict different criteria.

There were also several reasons for using one composite for all tests. First, including more than one spatial composite in prediction equations would reduce degrees of freedom, a consideration that may be important for within-MOS analyses where Ns may be small. Second, all six tests had "strong" loadings on the general factor (ranging from .62 for Maze to .75 for Assembling Objects); moreover, the loadings on the specific factors were moderate to small. Third, the constructs defined by alternate solutions were not highly meaningful.

The final resolution reflected the fact that, for the situation for which these tests are intended (i.e., selection/classification of applicants into entry-level enlisted Army occupations), there was no reason to expect a spatial speed factor to be particularly useful. Moreover, the figural factor is better measured by a unit-weighted composite of all six tests than by a composite of two tests, and the orientation factor did not appear to explain much variance unique from the general spatial factor. Therefore, one unit-weighted composite of the six spatial test scores was used. For settings in which the Army may wish to use fewer than six tests to test spatial abilities, the Assembling Objects Test is a good measure of the general factor, and it consistently yields smaller gender and race differences than the other tests.

COMPUTER-ADMINISTERED MEASURES

None of the computer tests changed substantively between CV and LV, although some minor changes were made in the instructions and the test software. The full computer battery took about 1 hour to administer. The mean test times for each test for the CV and initial LV samples were highly similar; new recruits took about the same amount of time as the first-tour incumbents.

The 10 computer tests can be divided into two groups: (a) cognitive/perceptual tests and (b) psychomotor tests. The cognitive/perceptual tests include Simple Reaction Time, Choice Reaction Time, Perceptual Speed and Accuracy, Short-Term Memory, Target Identification, and Number

Memory. With the exception of Number Memory, three scores are recorded for each item on these tests: decision time, movement time, and correct/incorrect; Number Memory has three time scores and a proportion correct score. The item scores on the psychomotor tests (Target Tracking 1, Target Tracking 2, Target Shoot, and Cannon Shoot) are in either distance or time units. In either case, the measurement reflects the precision with which the examinee has tracked or shot at the target.

Special Considerations in Scoring Computer-Administered Tests

Computerization resulted in new scoring choices. When time scores are used, the parameters that define the test items become particularly important because those parameters influence expected reaction times. Also, the individual distributions on choice reaction time tests can be highly skewed, and it is important to consider alternative scoring possibilities (e.g., mean, median, log scores).

Test Parameters

The items on the computer tests can be described in terms of several parameters. For example, the Perceptual Speed and Accuracy (PSA) test has three defining parameters: (a) the number of characters in the stimulus (i.e., two, five, or nine characters), (b) the type of stimulus (letters, numbers, symbols, or a mix of these), and (c) the position of correct response.

The effect of such parameters on the scoring procedure could be considerable, especially when the possibility of missing item data is taken into account. Missing time score data could occur if the subject "timed-out" on the item (i.e., did not respond to an item before the time limit expired) or answered the item incorrectly. If the examinee has missing scores for only the more difficult items, a mean time score computed across all items will be weighted in favor of the easier items, and vice versa. For example, decision time on PSA increases with the number of characters in the item. If a test-taker misses or times-out on many of the difficult items, his or her reaction time pooled across all items without regard to the critical parameters might appear "fast." It is also important to note that examinees are less likely to get the "harder" items correct; that is, proportion correct decreases as the number of characters in the stimulus increases. This will result in more missing data for the harder items because incorrect items are not used to compute decision time.

A series of ANOVAs showed that examinees' scores on particular items are influenced, sometimes to a great degree, by the parameters of those items

(Peterson, Russell et al., 1990). We concluded that decision time scores should first be computed within levels of the major parameter affecting decision time. Taking the mean within each parameter level and computing the mean of means as a final score ensures equal weight to items at different parameter levels.

Alternative Scores

There has been little systematic research on alternate scoring methods for reaction time tests, and opinions are mixed. For example, Roznowski (1987) found that median reaction time scores had greater test-retest reliabilities than means on simple and choice reaction time tests. Philip Ackerman (personal communication, 1990) prefers to use mean reaction times and suggests that inclusion of aberrant responses may enhance the validity of the measure. Other researchers have used the median or have removed aberrant responses before computing the mean.

Three alternate methods of scoring decision time (DT) for each reaction time test were compared. The methods were:

- The median.
- The "clipped" mean (the mean DT after elimination of the examinee's highest and lowest DT).
- The 3SD rule: The mean DT computed after deleting DTs that are more than three standard deviations outside the examinee's untrimmed mean.

For tests having critical item parameters (i.e., PSA, Short-Term Memory, Target Identification, and Number Memory), alternate scores were computed within parameter levels and means were taken across parameter levels. For example, the PSA median score is the mean taken across the median DT for two-character items, the median DT for five-character items, and the median DT for the nine-character items. We also examined median, clipped, and 3SD rule alternate scores for movement time on these tests.

Comparison of the test-retest and split-half reliabilities achieved with the different scores led to three conclusions. First, the alternative scoring procedures had the greatest impact on Simple Reaction Time DT, where the median was the most reliable score. Second, for the other tests, the clipping procedure usually resulted in better reliability; there were, however, no large differences in reliability across methods. Third, with regard to movement time, the split-half reliability for the median was greater than that for clipped and 3SD rule means; the test-retest reliability of the mean of the median movement time was highest, .73. The pooled median was clearly the best movement time score.

Psychometric Properties of Basic Scores from Computer-Administered Tests

Twenty basic scores were selected for further analysis. Means and standard deviations are shown in Table 10.7. Reliability estimates for the cognitive/perceptual test scores appear in Table 10.8. The tables provide data

TABLE 10.7
Computer-Administered Cognitive/Perceptual Test Means
and Standard Deviations

Measure	Experimental Battery[a] (Longitudinal Validation) Sample 1 (N = 6436)		Trial Battery (Concurrent Validation) (N = 9099–9274)	
	Mean[b]	SD	Mean	SD
Simple Reaction Time: Decision Time Mean	28.43	7.68	31.84	14.82
Simple Reaction Time: Proportion Correct	.98	.05	.98	.04
Choice Reaction Time: Decision Time Mean	38.55	7.70	0.93	9.77
Choice Reaction Time: Proportion Correct	.98	.04	.98	.03
Perceptual Speed & Accuracy: Decision Time Mean	227.11	62.94	236.91	63.38
Perceptual Speed & Accuracy: Proportion Correct	.86	.08	.87	.08
Short Term Memory: Decision Time Mean	80.48	21.90	87.72	24.03
Short Term Memory: Proportion Correct	.89	.07	.89	.08
Target Identification: Decision Time Mean	179.42	59.60	193.65	63.13
Target Identification: Proportion Correct	.90	.08	.91	.07
Number: Memory: Input Response Time Mean	141.28	52.63	142.84	55.24
Number: Memory: Operations Time Pooled Mean	208.73	74.58	233.10	79.71
Number Memory: Final response Time Mean	152.83	41.90	160.70	42.63
Number Memory: Proportion Correct	.86	.10	.90	.09
Pooled Mean Movement Time[c]	28.19	6.06	33.61	8.03

[a]Experimental Battery data were screened for missing data before reliabilities were computed.

[b]Mean response time values are reported in hundredths of seconds.

[c]Movement Time is pooled across Simple Reaction time, Choice Reaction Time, Short-Term Memory, Perceptual Speed and Accuracy, and Target Identification.

TABLE 10.8

Reliability Estimates for Computer-Administered Cognitive/Perceptual
Test Scores

	Split-Half Estimates		Test-Retest Estimates
	TB (N = 9099–9274)	EB[a] (N = 6215–6096)	TB Rescored Measure With EB Scoring (N = 473–479)
Simple Reaction Time: Decision Time Mean	.88	.83	.40
Simple Reaction Time: Proportion Correct	.46	.50	.00
Choice Reaction Time: Decision Time Mean	.97	.58	.68
Choice Reaction Time: Proportion Correct	.57	.93	.23
Perceptual Speed & Accuracy: Decision Time Mean	.94	.96	.66
Perceptual Speed & Accuracy: Proportion Correct	.65	.62	.49
Short Term Memory: Decision Time Mean	.96	.97	.66
Short Term Memory: Proportion Correct	.60	.50	.36
Target Identification: Decision Time Mean	.97	.97	.76
Target Identification: Proportion Correct	.62	.66	.34
Number Memory: Input Response Time Mean	.95	.94	.47
Number Memory: Operations Time Pooled Mean	.93	.95	.72
Number Memory: Final Response Time Mean	.88	.90	.61
Number Memory: Proportion Correct	.59	.59	.57
Pooled Mean Movement Time[b]	.74	.97	.73

[a]Experimental Battery data were screened for missing data before reliabilities were computed. Values in the table are for Sample 1.

[b]Movement Time is pooled across Simple Reaction Time, Choice Reaction Time, Short-Term Memory, Perceptual Speed and Accuracy, and Target Identification.

281

from CVI and the LV Sample 1. The Decision Mean Time scores all show extremely high split-half (or within testing session) reliabilities, and adequate test-retest reliabilities, except for Simple Reaction Time, which has a low test-retest reliability. This was to be expected as the Simple Reaction Time test has few items and largely serves to acquaint the examinee with the testing apparatus.

The Proportion Correct scores yield moderate split-half reliabilities and low to moderate test-retest reliabilities. The lower reliabilities for Proportion Correct scores were expected because these tests were designed to produce the most variance for decision time, with relatively low variance for proportion correct. That is, ample time was allowed for examinees to make a response to each item (9 seconds).

Means and standard deviations for the psychomotor test scores are shown in Table 10.9. Reliability estimates are given in Table 10.10. The split-half reliabilities are uniformly high. The test-retest correlations are high for the two tracking test scores, but are low to moderate for Cannon Shoot and Target Shoot. Even so, there remains a large amount of reliable variance for predicting performance.

TABLE 10.9
Computer-Administered Psychomotor Tests Means and Standard Deviations

	Concurrent Validation (N = 8892–9251)		Longitudinal Validation Sample 1 (N = 6436)	
	Mean[a]	SD	Mean	SD
Target Tracking 1				
Mean Log (Distance + 1)	2.98	.49	2.89	.46
Target Tracking 2				
Mean Log (Distance + 1)	3.70	.51	3.55	.52
Target Tracking 1				
Mean Log (Distance + 1)	2.17	.24	2.20	.23
Mean Time-to-Fire	235.39	47.78	230.98	50.18
Cannon Shoot				
Mean Absolute Time Discrepancy	43.94	9.57	44.03	9.31

[a]Time-to-fire and time-discrepancy measures are in hundredths of seconds. Logs are natural logs.

TABLE 10.10

Reliability Estimates for Computer-Administered Psychomotor Test Scores

	Split-Half Estimates		Test-Retest Estimates	
	TB	*EB*	*TB*	*TB Rescored with EB Scoring*
	(N = 9099–9274)	*(N = 6215–6096)[a]*	*(N = 473–479)*	
Target Tracking 1				
Mean Log (Distance + 1)	.98	.98	.74	b
Target Tracking 2				
Mean Log (Distance + 1)	.98	.98	.85	b
Target Tracking 1				
Mean Log (Distance + 1)	.74	.73	.37	.42
Mean Time-to-Fire	.85	.84	.58	.58
Cannon Shoot				
Mean Absolute Time				
Discrepancy	.65	.64	.52	b

[a]Values are for LV Sample 1; EB data were screened for missing data before reliability estimates were computed.

[b]TB and EB scoring methods are the same for this test.

Subgroup Differences

Gender Differences

Subgroup differences on the perceptual tests are shown in Table 10.11. For the most part, the effect sizes for the decision time measures fluctuated between 0 to .20 SD, males being typically higher than females. For Target Identification decision time, we consistently found about a .5 SD difference in means, favoring men. On the proportion correct scores, almost all of the effect sizes favored women. The largest effect was on PSA proportion correct, where women consistently outperformed men by over one-third of an SD.

On the psychomotor test scores (shown in Table 10.12), male scores were considerably higher than female scores, as is typically true for psychomotor tests of coordination (McHenry & Rose, 1988). The Target Shoot time score had the smallest effect (about .5 SD), and the largest differences (over 1.25 SD) were observed for the two tracking tests. Similarly, men performed better on movement time than women, by about .5 SD.

TABLE 10.11

Computer-Administered Tests: Subgroup Effect Sizes on Perceptual Test Scores[a]

	Test Time		Proportion Correct	
Measures	Male-Female Effect Size(d)[b]	White-Black Effect Size(d)	Male-Female Effect Size(d)	White-Black Effect Size(d)
Simple Reaction Time	.09	−.02	−.02	.14
Choice Reaction Time	−.10	.00	−.18	.16
Short Term Memory	.11	.17	−.19	.11
Perceptual Speed and Accuracy	.19	.04	−.33	.13
Target Identification	.47	.66	−.01	.23
Number Memory Final Time	.11	.66	.06	.35
Number Memory Input Time	−.13	.41		
Number Memory Operations Time	.22	.42		

[a]LV Sample 1. Approximate samples sizes were: 6000 Males, 880 Females, 4700 White, and 1700 Black.
[b]d is the standardized mean difference between group means. A positive sign indicates higher scores for the majority group.

Race Differences

For the decision time measures, effect sizes ranged from zero to about two-thirds SD (see Table 10.11), with whites scoring higher than blacks where differences occurred. For the proportion correct scores, differences were about .1 SD. As shown in Table 10.12 on the psychomotor tests, differences were about .5 SD.

Forming Composites of Computer-Administered Test Scores

Over the course of Project A, we conducted numerous factor analyses of the computer-administered test scores (e.g., principal components, common factors, with and without spatial test scores and ASVAB subtest scores). In conjunction with the factor analyses, parallel analyses (Humphreys & Montanelli, 1975; Montanelli & Humphreys, 1976) were used to inform the decision about the number of factors to extract.

As noted in Chapter 5, using the CVI data, six basic predictor scores were derived from the 20 computerized test scores. Based on the LVP data,

TABLE 10.12

Computer-Administered Tests: Subgroup Effect Sizes on Psychomotor Test
Scores[a]

Measures	Male-Female Effect Size(d)[b]	White-Black Effect Size(d)
Target Tracking 1 Distance Score	1.26	.70
Target Tracking 2 Distance Score	1.26	.87
Target Shoot Distance Score	.88	.25
Target Shoot Time Score	.48	.50
Cannon Shoot Time Score	.99	.48
Pooled Movement Time	.51	.38

[a]LV Sample 1. Approximate samples sizes were: 6000 Males, 880 Females, 4700 White,
and 1700 Black;

[b]d is the standardized mean difference between group means. A positive sign indicates
higher scores for the majority group.

the 20 computer-administered test scores were grouped into eight basic composite scores. Four of these composites can be extracted readily from the factor-analytic findings; they had virtually identical counterparts in CVI:

1. *Psychomotor:* Sum of Target Tacking 1 Distance, Target Tracking 2 Distance, Target Shoot Distance, and Cannon Shoot Time Score. The Target Shoot Time Score was included in the CVI Psychomotor composite, but was dropped in LV because its reliability was relatively low and excluding this score would enhance the homogeneity and meaningfulness of the Psychomotor composite; all remaining constituent variables have high loadings on this factor.

2. *Number Speed and Accuracy:* Subtract Number Memory Time Score from Number Memory Proportion Correct, or reflect the time score and add them. Proportion Correct scores are scaled so that higher scores are "better," while Time scores are scaled so that lower scores are better. Two more Number Memory time scores, Input Time and Final Response Time, were included in the CVI composite. However, including all four scores appeared to be unnecessary to produce a reliable composite.

3. *Basic Speed:* Sum Time Scores for Simple Reaction Time and Choice Reaction Time.

4. *Basic Accuracy:* Sum Proportion Correct Scores for Simple Reaction Time and Choice Reaction Time.

Also, as in CVI, two composites for the PSA and Target Identification scores were identified:

5. *Perceptual Speed:* Sum of PSA Time Score and Target Identification Time Score.
6. *Perceptual Accuracy:* Sum of PSA Proportion Correct and Target Identification Proportion Correct.

When raw scores are used, the PSA Time Score, PSA Proportion Correct, Target Identification (TID) Time Score, and TID Proportion Correct often load together. More specifically, the time scores and proportion correct scores both load positively on the same factor. The correlations between the speed and proportion correct scores for these tests are positive. This suggests that individuals who respond quickly are less accurate and those who respond slowly are more accurate. In contrast, on Short-Term Memory and Number Memory, the speed and proportion correct scores are negatively correlated. The fact that Short-Term Memory speed and proportion correct scores correlate negatively, and PSA and TID speed and proportion correct scores correlate positively is one additional reason for forming a separate Short-Term Memory composite.

A review by the project's Scientific Advisory Group suggested that the correlations between different scores on the same test (e.g., PSA Decision Time and Proportion Correct) might be inflated because the multiple scores, initially recorded for a single item, are not independent. A way of removing this dependence is to compute each score on alternate split halves of the test and to use these scores in subsequent factor analyses. Consequently, one score was computed using one half of the items and the other score used the alternate set of items.

The alternate score correlations for PSA and Target Identification were somewhat lower than those for the total scores, suggesting that item interdependence does inflate the total score correlation to some degree for these two tests. Factor solutions based on alternate scores were also compared with those based on total scores. Based on these analyses, separate composites were computed for the speed and proportion correct scores as described above.

The above six scores had comparable counterparts in CVI. A review of all the accumulated information about the scores showed that two more composites had good support:

7. *Movement Time:* Sum Median Movement Time scores on Simple Reaction Time, Choice Reaction Time, PSA, Short-Term Memory, and Target Identification.

8. *Short-Term Memory:* Subtract Short-Term Memory Decision Time from Short-Term Memory Proportion Correct, or reflect the time score and add them.

The pooled movement time variable was not used during CVI. However, the LV analyses showed that its internal consistency and test-retest reliability improved substantially when medians were used. Also, it should not be placed in the psychomotor composite because the psychomotor scores involve movement judgment and spatial ability as well as coordination. Movement time is a more basic measure of movement speed.

For the CVI, Short-Term Memory scores were placed in composites with PSA scores and Target Identification scores. However, the Short-Term Memory scores simply do not fit well conceptually or theoretically with the other test scores, and they do form a separate empirical factor, when enough factors are extracted.

Summary of Cognitive Test Basic Scores

Analysis of the LV data, in conjunction with the CVI results, yielded 13 basic predictor scores. The ASVAB analyses confirmed the 4-factor solution, the spatial tests were scored as one factor, and eight basic scores were derived from the computerized tests.

ASSESSMENT OF BACKGROUND AND LIFE EXPERIENCES (ABLE)

Several changes were made to the Trial Battery version of the ABLE to form the Experimental Battery version. These changes were made in two phases. First, 10 items were deleted because they were either part of the AVOICE inventory (see following section), had low item-total correlations, were difficult to interpret, or appeared inappropriate for the age of the applicant population. The inventory that resulted is called the Revised Trial Battery version of the ABLE. Then 16 items were modified based on item statistics computed on the concurrent data and reviewers' comments, and the instructions were changed slightly to allow for the use of a separate answer sheet. This was the Experimental Battery version.

The Revised Trial Battery ABLE is simply a new way of scoring the CVI data, taking into account the first set of changes described above. The distinction between these versions of the inventory is important because the results obtained for the Experimental Battery (LVI sample) are compared to those obtained for the Revised Trial Battery (CVI sample).

Data Screening

The same procedures that were used to screen the CVI sample were used for the LV data. That is, records were removed from the data set if (a) respondents answered fewer than 90% of the questions or (b) they answered incorrectly three or more of the eight questions in the Nonrandom Response scale. This scale includes questions that should be answered correctly by all persons who carefully read and respond to the questions. (On average, 92% of the people answered each of the items correctly.)

The number and percentage of persons eliminated from the CV and LV samples by the missing data and Nonrandom Response scale screens are shown in Table 10.13. In comparison to the CV sample, more persons were screened from the LV sample by the Nonrandom Response scale screen and fewer were removed by the missing data screen. This resulted in a slightly smaller proportion of persons screened by the two procedures combined. In general, a high rate (over 90%) of the sample appeared to read and answer the questions carefully.

For inventories surviving these screens, missing data were treated in the following way. If more than 10% of the item responses in a scale were

TABLE 10.13
Comparison of CV and LV ABLE Data Screening Results

	Number		Percent	
	CV	LV	CV	LV
Number of Inventories Scanned	9359	7000	100.0	100.0
Deleted Using Overall Missing Data Screen	171	40	1.8	0.6
Deleted Using Nonrandom Response Screen	684	565	7.3	8.1
Respondents Passing Screening Criteria	8504	6395	90.9	91.3

missing, the scale score was not computed; instead the scale score was treated as missing. If there were missing item responses for a scale but the percent missing was equal to or less than 10%, then the person's average item response score for that scale was computed and used for the missing response.

Analyses to Verify Appropriateness of the Scoring Procedures

Scale scores were formed according to the scoring procedure developed during earlier phases of the project. Each item was then correlated with each ABLE scale, and these correlations were compared to within-scale, item-total correlations (with the item removed from the total). Few items correlated substantially higher with another scale than with their own scale. In total, 13 of the 199 items (7%) correlated higher with another scale than with their own scale by a margin of .05 or more.

Given this relatively small number, we decided to retain the previously established scoring procedure. The aim was to maintain the conceptual framework established previously while maximizing the external (i.e., predictive) validity of the scales.

Psychometric Properties of ABLE Scores

In CVI, the Revised Trial Battery was found to have adequate reliability and stability and to correlate with job performance in the Army (McHenry, Hough, Toquam, Hanson, & Ashworth, 1990). Therefore, the Revised Trial Battery descriptive statistics were used as a benchmark against which to compare the psychometric characteristics of the Experimental Battery version of the ABLE. The means, standard deviations, and internal consistency reliability estimates for each of 15 ABLE scale scores for the Revised Trial Battery and Experimental Battery are reported in Table 10.14. Test-retest reliabilities obtained for the Revised Trial Battery are also presented. Test-retest data were not collected in the longitudinal sample.

As shown in the table, LV respondents tended to score higher than CVI respondents. In particular, LV respondents scored more than half an SD higher than CVI respondents on the Cooperativeness, Nondelinquency, Traditional Values, and Internal Control scales. This may be due to differences in the LV and CVI testing conditions because LV respondents

TABLE 10.14
Comparison of ABLE Scale Scores and Reliabilities From the Trial
(CV) and Experimental (LV) Batteries

ABLE Scale	No. of Items CV/LV	Mean		SD		Internal Consistencey Reliability (Alpha)		Test-Retest Reliability[a]
		CV	LV	CV	LV	CV	LV	CV
Emotional Stability	17	39.0	40.0	5.5	5.6	.81	.84	.74
Self-Esteem	12	28.4	28.7	3.7	3.7	.74	.78	.78
Cooperativeness	18	41.9	44.4	5.3	4.9	.81	.80	.76
Conscientiousness	15	35.1	36.7	4.3	4.1	.72	.73	.74
Nondelinquency	20	44.2	47.8	5.9	5.5	.81	.78	.80
Traditional Values	11	26.6	29.0	3.7	2.9	.69	.64	.74
Work Orientation	19	42.9	45.2	6.1	6.1	.84	.86	.78
Internal Control	16	38.0	41.7	5.1	4.4	.78	.76	.69
Energy Level	21	48.4	50.4	6.0	6.0	.82	.84	.78
Dominance	12	27.0	27.2	4.3	4.6	.80	.84	.79
Physical Condition	6	14.0	13.3	3.0	3.0	.84	.81	.85
Unlikely Virtues	11	15.5	16.8	3.0	3.4	.63	.66	.63
Self-Knowledge	11	25.4	26.2	3.3	3.1	.65	.59	.64
Nonrandom Response	8	7.7	7.7	.6	.6	—	—	.30
Poor Impression	23	1.5	1.2	1.8	1.6	.63	.62	.61

[a]$N = 408–414$.
Note: $N_{CV} = 8450$, Sample 1 $N_{LV} = 6390$

completed the inventory during their first few days in the Army whereas CVI respondents had been in the Army for 18 to 30 months. LV respondents may have believed (in spite of being told the contrary by the test administrators) that their responses to the inventory would affect their Army career and thus responded in a more favorable direction. Indeed, LV respondents on average scored more than one third of an SD higher than CVI respondents on the Unlikely Virtues scale, a measure of the tendency to respond in a socially desirable manner. Internal consistency reliabilities remained acceptable for these scales, however, with reliability estimates for the 11 content scales ranging from .64 (Traditional Values) to .86 (Work Orientation).

TABLE 10.15

ABLE Subgroup Effect Sizes

ABLE Scale	Male-Female Effect Size[a] (d)	White-Black Effect Size (d)
Emotional Stability	.18	−.21
Self-Esteem	.09	−.23
Cooperativeness	−.11	−.27
Conscientiousness	−.18	−.25
Nondelinquency	−.33	−.22
Traditional Values	−.11	−.10
Work Orientation	−.14	−.27
Internal Control	−.25	.07
Energy Level	−.04	−.15
Dominance	.17	−.26
Physical Condition	.54	−.23
Unlikely Virtues	.00	−.21
Self-Knowledge	−.21	−.29
Non-Random Response	−.05	.17
Poor Impression	−.07	.06

Note: LVI Sample. N for males = 5519–5529; N for females = 865–866; N for Whites = 4429–4433; N for Blacks = 1510–1514.

[a] d is the standardized mean difference between group means. A positive value indicates higher scores for the majority group.

Analysis of Subgroup Differences

As shown in Table 10.15, women scored slightly higher than men on Nondelinquency, Internal Control, and Self-Knowledge. Men scored, on average, a half SD higher than women on the Physical Condition scale. In general, however, gender differences tended to be small.

Effect sizes for race differences are also presented in Table 10.15. Race differences also tended to be quite small, with blacks scoring slightly higher than whites on most of the 11 content scales.

Formation of ABLE Composites

The correlations between content scale scores were higher in the LV sample for 51 of the 54 intercorrelations. Also, all of the correlations between the Unlikely Virtues scale and the content scales were higher in the LV sample than in the CV sample, indicating perhaps more social desirability bias in LV responses. Greater social desirability bias could account for higher correlations among all of the scales. It also can make it more difficult to identify conceptually meaningful clusters of scale scores.

Both principal components and principal factor analyses were used to identify possible composites. Whereas principal factor analysis would produce a set of factors that are more likely to be stable over different samples, principal components analysis was also conducted to discover whether smaller, additional, interpretable factors might emerge.

Four possible sets of composites suggested by these factor and component analyses were compared using LISREL (Jöreskog & Sörbom, 1986). The differences among the sets reflected the choices about where to assign a few of the scales resulting from multiple factor loadings.

However, the differences in factor composition were not very great and the differences in "fit" across the four alternatives were also not very large. Based on all considerations, the final LV composite score model is shown in Table 10.16, along with the composite model used in the CV analyses (McHenry et al., 1990).

ARMY VOCATIONAL INTEREST CAREER EXAMINATION (AVOICE)

Several modifications were made to the Trial Battery version of the AVOICE to form the Experimental Battery version. These changes were made in two phases. First, to form the Revised Trial Battery version based on analyses of the CV data, numerous items were either dopped or moved from one scale to another based on rational considerations, item-total scale correlations, factor analysis at the item level, clarity of interpretation, and practical considerations. None of these changes entailed adding or modifying items. Thus, the Revised Trial Battery scores can be obtained for persons in both samples.

In the second phase, 16 items were added to increase the stability and reliability of the scales, one item was modified to better fit the AVOICE response format, and the instructions were modified slightly to allow for the use of separate answer sheets. The 182-item inventory that resulted from both sets of changes is the Experimental Battery version that was administered in the LVP data collection.

TABLE 10.16
ABLE Composites for the Longitudinal and Concurrent Validations

Longitudinal Validation Composites	*Concurrent Validation Composites*
Achievement Orientation	**Achievement Orientation**
Self-Esteem	Self-Esteem
Work Orientation	Work Orientation
Energy Level	Energy Level
Leadership Potential	**Dependability**
Dominance	Conscientiousness
	Nondelinquency
Dependability	
Traditional Values	**Adjustment**
Conscientiousness	Emotional Stability
Nondelinquency	
	Physical Condition
Adjustment	Physical Condition
Emotional Stability	
Cooperativeness	
Cooperativeness	
Internal Control	
Internal Control	
Physical Condition	
Physical Condition	

Note: Four ABLE scales were not used in computing CV composite scores. These were Dominance, Traditional Values, Cooperativeness, and Internal Control.

Data Screening

Cases were screened if more than 10% of their data were missing. Four methods to detect careless or low-literacy respondents were investigated: a chi-square index to detect patterned responding, a Runs index to detect repetitious responding, an Option Variance index to detect persons who tend to rely on very few of the (five) response options, and an empirically derived Unlikely Response scale. These indexes were developed by hypothesizing and measuring patterns of responses that would be produced only by careless or low-literacy respondents and were investigated because of the desire to screen the AVOICE respondents directly on AVOICE data, rather than relying on ABLE Nonrandom scale screens.

TABLE 10.17
CV and LV AVOICE Data Screening Results

	Number		Percent	
	CV	LV	CV	LV
Number of Inventories Scanned	9359	7000	100.0	100.0
Deleted Using Overall Missing Data Screen	200	141	2.1	2.0
Deleted by at least one of the four response validity screens (LV Battery only) or by the ABLE Nonrandom Response Scale (CV only)	760	527	8.1	7.5
Respondents Passing Screening Criteria	8399	6332	89.7	90.5

The detection scales were newly developed, and there was some concern about erroneously removing inventories that had, in fact, been conscientiously completed. Consequently, conservative cut scores were used, and respondents who scored beyond them were flagged. If flagged by one or more of the indexes, a case was removed from the sample. The results of this screen and the missing data screen are presented in Table 10.17, along with the screening results obtained in the CVI sample (in which the ABLE Nonrandom Response Scale and 10% missing data screens were applied). Overall, using the method of screening directly on AVOICE responses resulted in deleting a slightly smaller proportion of the sample.

For the inventories surviving these screens, if more than 10% of the item responses in a scale were missing, the scale score was treated as missing. If item responses were missing for a scale, but the percent missing was equal to or less than 10%, then the scale midpoint (3) was used in place of the missing response. The midpoint was chosen because the effect on the overall mean for the entire group would be less than if the average of the nonmissing items in the scale were used.

Psychometric Properties of AVOICE

Table 10.18 compares Revised Trial Battery (CV) and Experimental Battery (LV) AVOICE descriptive statistics, including means, standard deviations, median item-total correlations, and internal consistency (alpha) reliability estimates. Test-retest reliability estimates for the Revised Trial Battery are also presented (test-retest data were not collected in LV).

TABLE 10.18

AVOICE Scale Scores and Reliabilities for the Revised Trial (CV) and
Experimental (LV) Batteries

AVOICE Scale	No. of Items CV	LV	Mean CV	LV	SD CV	LV	Internal Consistency Reliability (Alpha) CV	LV	Test-Retest Reliability[a] CV
Clerical/Admin	14	14	39.6	40.0	10.8	10.2	.92	.92	.78
Mechanics	10	10	32.1	32.9	9.4	9.4	.94	.95	.82
Heavy Construction	13	13	39.3	38.7	10.5	9.7	.92	.91	.84
Electronics	12	12	38.4	37.8	10.2	9.6	.94	.93	.81
Combat	10	10	26.5	33.8	8.3	7.5	.90	.88	.73
Medical Services	12	12	36.9	37.4	9.5	9.4	.92	.91	.78
Rugged Individualism	15	16	53.3	59.2	11.4	10.4	.90	.88	.81
Leadership/Guidance	12	12	40.1	41.7	8.6	8.3	.89	.89	.72
Law Enforcement	8	8	24.7	26.8	7.4	6.7	.89	.87	.84
Food Service—Prof	8	8	20.2	20.9	6.5	6.4	.89	.87	.75
Firearms Enthusiast	7	7	23.0	25.1	6.4	5.9	.89	.88	.80
Science/Chemical	6	6	16.9	17.1	5.3	5.0	.85	.82	.74
Drafting	6	6	19.4	19.4	5.0	4.9	.84	.83	.74
Audiographics	5	5	17.6	17.3	4.1	3.8	.83	.79	.75
Aesthetics	5	5	14.2	14.4	4.1	4.1	.79	.78	.73
Computers	4	4	14.0	13.1	4.0	4.0	.90	.89	.77
Food Service—Empl	3	6	5.1	12.2	2.1	4.4	.73	.85	.73
Mathematics	3	3	9.6	9.3	3.1	3.0	.88	.85	.75
Electronic Comm	6	6	18.4	19.9	4.7	4.2	.83	.81	.68
Warehousing/Shipping	2	7	5.8	20.4	1.7	5.0	.61	.85	.54
Fire Protection	2	6	6.1	19.8	2.0	4.4	.76	.81	.67
Vehicle Operator	3	6	8.8	17.8	2.6	4.5	.70	.78	.68

[a] $N = 389$–409 for test-retest correlations.

Note: $N_{CV} = 8400$, LV Sample 1 $N_{LV} = 6300$.

Several findings are noteworthy. In general, the LV sample tended to score higher on most of the scales, especially Combat, Law Enforcement, Firearms Enthusiast, Food Service—Employee, and Fire Protection. Where mean scores increased, standard deviations tended to decline. Still, internal consistency reliabilities all remained quite high, ranging from .78 to .95. Adding items to some scales produced the expected increase in reliability.

TABLE 10.19
AVOICE Subgroup Effect Sizes

AVOICE Scale	Male-Female Effect Size[a] (d)	White-Black Effect Size (d)
Clerical/Administrative	−.77	−.95
Mechanics	.69	.10
Heavy Construction	.90	.09
Electronics	.72	−.37
Combat	.95	.35
Medical Services	−.48	.42
Rugged Individualism	.85	.98
Leadership/Guidance	−.20	−.34
Law Enforcement	.21	.25
Food Service—Professional	−.24	−.48
Firearms Enthusiast	1.17	.47
Science/Chemical	.24	.00
Drafting	.28	−.04
Audiographics	−.19	−.37
Aesthetics	−.67	−.39
Computers	−.07	−.73
Food Service—Employee	−.06	−.49
Mathematics	−.16	−.41
Electronic Communications	.01	−.44
Warehousing/Shipping	.03	−.53
Fire Protection	.42	.14
Vehicle Operator	.36	−.15

Note: $N = 5450$–5530 (males); $N = 788$–802 (females)
[a]d is the standardized mean difference between group means. A positive value indicates a higher score for the majority group.

Subgroup Differences

Means and standard deviations for the AVOICE scales by gender are shown in Table 10.19. Mean scores for men exceeded the means for women on 13 of the 22 scales. In particular, men tended to score higher on Mechanics, Heavy Construction, Electronics, Combat, Rugged Individualism, and Firearms Enthusiast. Women scored higher on Clerical/Administrative, Medical Services, and Aesthetics.

Effect sizes by race are also shown in Table 10.19. There are substantial score differences on these scales. Mean scores for blacks, for instance, were higher than those for whites on 15 of the 22 scales, and eight of these differences are greater than .40. Whites scored substantially higher on two scales, Rugged Individualism and Firearms Enthusiast.

Formation of AVOICE Composites

As expected, correlations among the AVOICE scales are generally low, with some moderate to high correlations (of the 231 correlations, about 20% [52] are .40 or greater). This indicates a relatively successful result in terms of measuring independent areas of vocational interest. Given the large number of predictors available in LV, however, we attempted to identify clusters of AVOICE scales that could be combined to form composite scores, thus reducing the number of predictors.

A principal components analysis was used to identify sets of AVOICE scales that cluster together empirically. The method of parallel analysis (Humphreys & Montanelli, 1975; Montanelli & Humphreys, 1976) indicated that as many as 22 components underlie the 22 scales, highlighting the difficulty of clustering scales intended to measure different constructs. Through a series of factor analyses, however, several clusters or pairs of scales appeared consistently. Similar to the procedure for the ABLE, 10 different models for combining the scales were hypothesized based on these analyses, and the relative fit of the 10 models were compared using LISREL (Jöreskog & Sörbom, 1986). An 8-factor model was selected because it fit the data best and was the most interpretable. However, none of the models provided a particularly close fit to the data.

The CVI and LV composite formation models for AVOICE are presented side-by-side in Table 10.20. As shown, there are eight LV composites and six CVI composites; the CVI Skilled Technical composite has been separated into three more homogeneous composites—Interpersonal, Administrative, and Skilled/Technical.

JOB ORIENTATION BLANK (JOB)

Two sets of changes were made to the Trial Battery version of the JOB to form the Experimental Battery version. The first phase resulted in a revised method for scoring the JOB on the CVI data, called the Revised Trial Battery. These changes were incorporated into the pretest of the Experimental Battery version of the JOB scales. Also, five negatively worded items that had been dropped from the original Trial Battery scales were changed to positive statements and added back. The other four items that had been removed from the original JOB Trial Battery scales were not revised to a

TABLE 10.20
AVOICE Composites for the Longitudinal and Concurrent Validations

Longitudinal Validation Composites	*Concurrent Validation Composites*
Rugged/Outdoors	***Combat-Related***
Combat	Combat
Rugged Individualism	Rugged Individualism
Firearms Enthusiast	Firearms Enthusiast
Audiovisual Arts	***Audiovisual Arts***
Drafting	Drafting
Audiographics	Audiographics
Aesthetics	Aesthetics
Interpersonal	***Skilled/Technical***
Medical Services	Clerical/Administrative
Leadership/Guidance	Medical Services
Skilled/Technical	Leadership/Guidance
Science/Chemical	Science/Chemical
Computers	Data Processing
Mathematics	Mathematics
Electronic Communications	Electronic Communications
Administrative	***Food Service***
Clerical/Administrative	Food Service—Professional
Warehousing/Shipping	Food Service—Employee
Food Service	***Protective Services***
Food Service—Professional	Law Enforcement
Food Service—Employee	Fire Protection
Protective Services	***Structural/Machines***
Fire Protection	Mechanics
Law Enforcement	Heavy Construction
Structural/Machines	Electronics
Mechanics	Vehicle/Equipment Operator
Heavy Construction	
Electronics	
Vehicle Operator	

Note: Warehousing/Shipping was not included in a CV composite.

lower reading level because in their simplified version they were extremely similar to items already in the JOB. Thus, the pretest version for the Experimental Battery inventory consisted of 34 items. The pretest version was administered to 57 Army enlisted trainees and the item-total scale correlations were examined. Five items were dropped.

The above-described changes were then incorporated into the final Experimental Battery version and two new items were added as well, one to the Job Routine scale and one to the Serving Others scale. Finally, the response option "Indifferent" was changed to "Doesn't Matter."

The Experimental Battery version of the JOB consisted, then, of 31 items and six scales: Job Pride, Job Security/Comfort, Serving Others, Job Autonomy, Job Routine, and Ambition.

Data Screening

The JOB, like the AVOICE, contained no scales designed to detect careless or low-literacy persons, so screening indexes similar to those developed for the AVOICE were used. They were developed by hypothesizing and quantitatively capturing patterns of responses that might be produced only by persons who either respond carelessly or do not understand the questions. A cut score was established for each index at the extreme of the distribution, resulting in relatively few persons being screened by each index.

As in the CVI sample, two screens were used: the 10% missing data rule and the ABLE Nonrandom Response scale screen. Overall, the screening indexes developed for the JOB removed a slightly smaller proportion of respondents from the LV sample, as compared to the CVI sample (9.7% vs. 11.9%). For the inventories surviving these screens, missing data were treated in the same way as for the AVOICE.

Psychometric Properties of JOB

Table 10.21 compares Revised Trial Battery (CVI) and Experimental Battery (LV) JOB scale score descriptive statistics, including means, standard deviations, and reliabilities. LV respondents scored substantially higher than CVI respondents on two of the scales—Job Security/Comfort and Job Routine—and lower on Job Autonomy. In general, internal consistency (alpha) reliabilities are higher in the LV sample, compared to the CVI sample, with estimates ranging from .59 to .80. These are fairly high reliabilities for scales as short as these.

Subgroup Differences

Subgroup differences for the JOB scales by gender and race are presented in Table 10.22. On the average, women score higher than men on four of the six scales. In particular, they tend to value serving others and job security

TABLE 10.21

Comparison of JOB Scale Scores and Reliabilities for Revised Trial (CV) and
Experimental (LV) Batteries

JOB Scale	No. of Items		Mean		SD		Internal Consistency Reliability (Alpha)	
	CV	LV	CV	LV	CV	LV	CV	LV
Job Pride	10	10	43.6	44.1	4.5	4.0	.84	.79
Job Security/Comfort	5	6	21.6	27.1	2.3	2.4	.67	.76
Serving Others	3	3	12.1	12.1	1.8	2.0	.66	.80
Job Autonomy	4	4	15.1	14.5	2.3	2.4	.46	.63
Job Routine	4	4	9.6	11.1	2.3	2.6	.46	.63
Ambition	3	4	12.4	16.4	1.6	2.2	.49	.67

Note: $N_{CV} = 7800$, LV Sample 1 $N = 6300$.

TABLE 10.22

JOB Subgroup Effect Sizes

JOB Scale	Male-Female Effect Size[a] (d)	White-Black Effect Size[a] (d)
Job Pride	−.22	−.15
Job Security/Comfort	−.39	−.34
Serving Others	−.54	−.20
Job Autonomy	.11	.00
Routine	−.07	−.42
Ambition	.13	−.23

Note: LV Sample 1. $N = 5450$–5530 (males); $N = 788$–802
(females), $N = 4423$–4480 (Whites); $N = 1480$–1514 (Blacks).
[a]d is the standardized mean difference between group means.
A positive value indicates a higher score for the majority group.

TABLE 10.23
Longitudinal Validation: Model
for Formation of JOB Composites

Scale	Composite
Pride	
Job Security	High Job Expectations
Serving Others	
Ambition	
Routine	Job Routine
Autonomy	Job Autonomy

more than men do. Race differences tend to be small, with blacks scoring higher than whites on five of the six scales.

Formation of JOB Composites

In an effort to identify composites of JOB scales that cluster empirically and rationally, a series of principal components and principal factor analyses of the scale scores was carried out. The CVI and LV factor structures are extremely similar. There appears to be one main factor composed of Job Pride, Job Security/Comfort, Serving Others, and Ambition. Two individual scales appear to measure their own unique constructs: Job Routine and Job Autonomy. Consistent with this finding, neither Job Routine nor Job Autonomy correlate highly with any of the other JOB scales. Given the similarity of the CVI and LV factor structure, the CV composite formation strategy was used for the LV data. These composites are shown in Table 10.23.

SUMMARY OF THE EXPERIMENTAL BATTERY

This summary is organized according to the four major phases in the analysis of the Experimental Battery: screening data, forming basic scores, describing their psychometric characteristics, and developing recommendations for composite scores.

Data Screening

All instruments had been administered to several sequential samples over the course of earlier phases of the project allowing successive refinement of both measurement and administration procedures. The intention of the LV data screening was to identify two types of undesirable data sets: excessive amounts of missing data and "suspect" data, or test responses that may have been made carelessly, inattentively, or in an otherwise uninformative manner. The predictor instruments differ in their susceptibility to these sources. The computer-administered measures have relatively small amounts of missing data because the presentation of items and recording of responses is under automated control, whereas with the paper-and-pencil instruments the examinee is free to skip items. The paper-and-pencil spatial tests all have time limits, whereas the temperament/biodata, interest, and job preference inventories do not, and a missing response means different things with regard to these instruments. Different screening strategies were used for the various instruments.

For computer-administered tests, very few examinee/test cases were eliminated with the initial screening criteria. Overall, 94% of the samples analyzed had complete data for all computer-administered tests. For the ABLE, AVOICE, and JOB, data screening techniques shared a common minimum data screen. That is, an examinee had to have responded to 90% of the items on an instrument or the examinee was not scored for that instrument. For the ABLE, the Nonrandom Response Scale was applied as an additional screen and about 9% of ABLE examinees were eliminated. Four new data-screening techniques were developed for the AVOICE and JOB and approximately 10% of the examinees were eliminated using these techniques.

Descriptive Statistics
and Psychometric Properties

With regard to the psychometric properties of the experimental predictors, a primary concern was to compare the longitudinal (LV) sample results to the concurrent (CVI) sample results. There were some score distribution differences (especially for ABLE scales, where most scale scores were elevated in the LV sample, and a few AVOICE scales that showed higher mean scores in the LV sample), but generally the differences were not large. For most test/scale scores, the variances were very similar. The effects of attrition over the course of the first term in the Army did not result in reduced variance of the CVI scores as compared to LV sample scores. The reliability coefficients and score intercorrelations were remarkably similar across the two data collections, and factor analyses showed highly similar solutions. Some test/scale scores increased in reliability because of instrument revisions and modifications in scoring methods. In summary, these data showed a very high degree of consistency and regularity across cohorts.

Formation of Composite Scores

The basic score analyses produced a set of 72 scores. This number was too large for general validation analyses involving techniques that take advantage of idiosyncratic sample characteristics, such as ordinary least squares multiple regression. Therefore, a series of analyses was conducted to determine an appropriate set of composite predictor scores that would preserve the heterogeneity of the full set of basic scores to the greatest extent possible. These analyses included exploratory factor analyses and confirmatory factor analyses guided by considerable prior theory and empirical evidence (McHenry et al., 1990; Peterson et al., 1990). A final set of 31 composites was identified and is shown in Table 10.24. The intercorrelation matrix of the 31 scores is shown in Table 10.25.

A FINAL WORD

The basic scale scores and composite scores described here are the results of the implementation of the predictor development design described in Chapters 3 and 4. The design was fully completed in almost every respect. Collectively, the Experimental Battery and the ASVAB were intended to be a comprehensive and representative sample of predictor measures from the population of individual differences that are relevant for personnel selection and classification. The parameters of the Experimental Battery were necessarily constrained by the available resources and administration time, which were considerable, but not unlimited. Within these constraints, the intent was to develop a battery of new measures that was as comprehensive and relevant as possible, while realizing that the tradeoff between bandwidth and fidelity is always with us.

TABLE 10.24

Experimental Battery: Composite Scores and Constituent Basic Scores

ASVAB Composites	Computer-Administered Test Composites[a]	ABLE Composites	AVOICE Composites
Quantitative	Psychomotor	Achievement Orientation	Rugged Outdoors
Math Knowledge	Target Tracking 1 Distance	Self-Esteem	Combat
Arithmetic Reasoning	Target Tracking 2 Distance	Work Orientation	Rugged Individualism
Technical	Cannon Shoot Time Score	Energy Level	Firearms Enthusiast
Auto/Shop	Target Shoot Distance	Leadership Potential	Audiovisual Arts
Mechanical Comprehension	Movement Time	Dominance	Drafting
Electronics Information	Pooled Movement Time	Dependability	Audiographics
Speed	Perceptual Speed	Traditional Values	Aesthetics
Coding Speed	Perceptual Speed & Accuracy (DT)	Conscientiousness	Interpersonal
Number Operations	Target Identification (DT)	Nondelinquency	Medical Services
Verbal	Basic Speed	Adjustment	Leadership Guidance
Word Knowledge	Simple Reaction Time (DT)	Emotional Stability	Skilled/Technical
Paragraph Comprehension	Choice Reaction Time (DT)	Cooperativeness	Science/Chemical
General Science	Perceptual Accuracy	Cooperativeness	Computers
Spatial Test Composite	Perceptual Speed & Accuracy (PC)	Internal Control	Mathematics
Assembling Objects Test	Target Identification (PC)	Internal Control	Electronic Communication
Object Rotation Test	Basic Accuracy	Physical Condition	Administrative
Maze Test	Simple Reaction Time (PC)	Physical Condition	Clerical/Administrative
Orientation Test	Choice Reaction Time (PC)	JOB Composites	Warehousing/Shipping
Map Test	Number Speed and Accuracy	High Job Expectations	Food Service
Reasoning Test	Number Speed (Operation DT)	Pride	Food Service - Professional
	Number Memory (PC)	Job Security	Food Service - Employee
	Short-Term Memory	Serving Others	Protective Services
	Short-Term Memory (PC)	Ambition	Fire Protection
	Short-Term Memory (DT)	Job Routine	Law Enforcement
		Routine	Structural/Machines
		Job Autonomy	Mechanics
		Autonomy	Heavy Construction
			Electronics
			Vehicle Operator

[a] DT = Decision Time and PC = Proportion Correct

TABLE 10.25

Correlations Between Experimental Battery Composite Scores for Longitudinal Validation Sample 1

	1	2	3	4	5	6	7	8	9	10	11	12	13	14	15
1. Spatial	—														
2. ASVAB Verbal	.44	—													
3. ASVAB Quantitative	.58	.55	—												
4. ASVAB Speed	.17	-.01	-.22	—											
5. ASVAB Technical	.55	.63	.50	-.10	—										
6. Psychomotor	.43	.22	.25	.05	.38	—									
7. Perceptual Speed	.34	.17	.19	.17	.15	.31	—								
8. Perceptual Accuracy	.17	.12	.12	.06	.10	.07	-.43	—							
9. Number Speed/Accuracy	.37	.30	.57	.32	.24	.22	.21	.10	—						
10. Basic Speed	.10	-.01	.07	.18	-.06	.17	.31	-.12	.15	—					
11. Basic Accuracy	.09	.06	.08	.04	.05	.03	.02	.09	.08	-.01	—				
12. Short-Term Memory	.27	.08	.17	.22	.05	.21	.34	.03	.25	.27	.09	—			
13. Movement Time	.20	.06	.08	.10	.14	.31	.24	-.09	.09	.10	-.09	.18	—		
14. High Job Expectations	-.09	-.02	-.05	.08	-.08	-.07	-.03	.00	-.04	.02	-.02	.00	.03	—	
15. Job Routine	-.20	-.33	-.24	-.01	-.25	-.13	-.08	-.03	-.13	-.02	-.01	-.05	-.06	.08	—
16. Job Autonomy	.02	.08	.05	-.02	.11	.01	.00	-.02	-.01	.04	-.02	-.04	.00	.30	.07
17. Achievement Orientation	.07	.06	.10	.10	.08	.07	.03	.00	.05	.05	-.01	.05	.10	.35	-.10
18. Leadership Potential	.05	.10	.09	.08	.08	.08	.05	-.01	.04	-.01	-.01	.04	.08	.35	-.16
19. Dependability	.01	.01	.03	.08	.01	-.01	-.01	.07	.00	.04	.02	.06	.04	.29	.08
20. Adjustment	.09	.09	.10	.05	.11	.10	.04	.00	.05	.02	-.02	.05	.08	.20	-.12
21. Cooperativeness	.03	.04	.04	.06	.03	.05	-.01	.05	.02	.02	.01	.05	.04	.28	.00
22. Internal Control	.11	.12	.10	.07	.07	.05	.02	.05	.07	.01	.03	.07	.07	.22	-.06
23. Physical Conditions	-.01	-.06	.01	.04	-.02	.14	.09	-.09	.04	.10	-.07	.03	.12	.14	-.03
24. Rugged/Outdoors	.20	.18	.08	-.11	.36	.32	.14	-.02	.02	-.01	.00	.01	.17	.10	-.03
25. Audiovisual Arts	.03	.07	.04	.03	.00	.00	.00	.04	-.05	-.01	.01	.02	.02	.28	.01
26. Interpersonal	-.06	.03	.03	.10	-.10	-.07	-.02	.01	.00	.03	.00	.04	.03	.48	-.01
27. Skilled/Technical	.02	-.07	.12	.11	-.03	.00	-.03	.04	.06	.02	.00	.06	.02	.26	.08
28. Administrative	-.16	-.22	-.10	.10	-.24	-.19	-.14	.03	-.06	-.02	.00	-.01	-.08	.23	.29
29. Food Service	-.11	-.13	-.06	.03	-.15	-.13	-.10	.01	-.06	-.04	.01	-.04	-.06	.07	.23
30. Protective Services	.04	.02	-.03	-.01	.08	.11	.08	-.04	-.01	.03	.06	.04	.08	.20	.05
31. Structural/Machines	.02	-.12	-.06	-.10	.18	.11	-.04	-.01	-.04	-.04	-.01	-.03	.06	.06	.17

TABLE 10.25
(Continued)

	16	17	18	19	20	21	22	23	24	25	26	27	28	29	30	31
16. Job Autonomy	—															
17. Achievement Orientation	.22	—														
18. Leadership Potential	.24	.66	—													
19. Dependability	.07	.61	.33	—												
20. Adjustment	.14	.70	.53	.40	—											
21. Cooperativeness	.07	.59	.39	.60	.53	—										
22. Internal Control	.07	.54	.33	.51	.44	.45	—									
23. Physical Conditions	.09	.49	.35	.22	.36	.22	.18	—								
24. Rugged/Outdoors	.18	.22	.18	.07	.20	.09	.13	.19	—							
25. Audiovisual Arts	.20	.23	.21	.19	.15	.21	.13	.07	.17	—						
26. Interpersonal	.18	.41	.47	.30	.29	.31	.25	.19	.15	.56	—					
27. Skilled/Technical	.19	.30	.25	.25	.21	.21	.18	.11	.21	.58	.55	—				
28. Administrative	.07	.14	.12	.21	.06	.13	.07	.01	.01	.45	.47	.58	—			
29. Food Service	.03	.03	.04	.06	.00	.04	-.01	-.02	.01	.30	.29	.26	.56	—		
30. Protective Services	.15	.22	.23	.15	.15	.16	.13	.14	.52	.19	.38	.24	.21	.14	—	
31. Structural/Machines	.15	.09	.04	.01	.06	.05	.01	.11	.52	.28	.14	.42	.37	.29	.37	—

Note: $N = 4623$.

11

Modeling Performance in a Population of Jobs

John P. Campbell, Mary Ann Hanson, and Scott H. Oppler

This chapter describes efforts to develop a coherent framework, or "model," with which to use and interpret the criterion data for training performance, entry level (first-tour) job performance, and supervisory (second-tour) performance. No previous research efforts had ever collected so much performance information on so many people on so many jobs. At the outset, we did not expect the level of consistent interpretability that was eventually achieved.

BACKGROUND

As detailed in Chapters 7 and 8, both the first-tour and second-tour jobs were subjected to extensive job analyses. Three principal measurement methods were used at both organizational levels to assess performance on the job tasks and performance dimensions identified via the job analyses: (a) job knowledge tests, (b) hands-on job samples, and (c) rating scales using a variety of types of scale anchors. A fourth type of performance index consisted of a select number of administrative indices of the type found in the individual's personnel records (e.g., number of disciplinary actions, combined number of awards and commendations). For the supervision and leadership components of performance that were identified in the job analyses of second-tour positions, two additional measurement methods were used: (a) the Situational Judgment Test and (b) three role-play exercises (as described in Chapter 8).

The overall goal of the research design was to measure *all* major components of performance in each job in each sample to the fullest extent possible, and with more than one method. Although this was a laudable goal, it also had its downside. As described in Chapter 8, it produced literally hundreds of individual "scores" for each job. One major issue then was how to get from this very large number to a more manageable number of performance scores that could be used as criterion measures for validation purposes.

Given the initial model of performance described in Chapters 3 and 7, which posited a finite but small number of distinguishable factors within the two broad components of organization-wide versus job-specific factors, there were two major steps that were taken to arrive at a model for the latent structure of performance for entry level jobs, for supervisory jobs, and for training performance as well. By *latent structure* is meant a specification of the factors or constructs that best explain the pattern of observed correlations among the measures, when each factor is represented by several measures, and the factor scores are interpreted as the individual's standing on a major distinguishable component of performance.

Development of Basic Scores

The first major step was to reduce the large number of individual task, item, scale, and index scores to a smaller number of *basic* scores that were composites of the single scores. These composites did not throw any specific scores away; they were formed with the objective of losing as little information about specific variance as possible. As described in Chapter 8, the methods for forming the basic scores were a combination of expert judgment, cluster analysis, and exploratory factor analysis. For both the first-tour and the second-tour MOS in the samples, the number of basic criterion scores that were finally agreed upon varied from 22 to 27 per job.

Confirmatory Factor Analysis

Having 22 to 27 criterion scores is still far too many with which to deal in selection and classification research. Consequently, the second major step was to specify via confirmatory techniques the basic constructs or latent factors that could be used to represent the 20+ scores. For both entry level and supervisory jobs this was carried out in a two-stage process, corresponding to a "quasi" confirmatory analysis using the concurrent (CVI, CVII) samples and a subsequent more stringent confirmatory test using the longitudinal (LVI, LVII) samples.

The basic procedure was to request the project staff to offer alternative models, or hypotheses, for the latent structure in the context of the concurrent sample data. The alternative hypothesized models were compared for relative goodness of fit using the concurrent sample data and LISREL software. This was done for both a First-Tour Performance Model and a Second-Tour Performance Model. The best fitting model was subsequently put through another confirmatory test when the longitudinal sample data became available.

The models that best survived this two-stage process, and which offered the best explanation for the pattern of correlations among the observed criterion scores, then became the set of specifications for how the criterion measures should be combined and scored to yield a meaningful set of criterion scores for validation purposes.

A CONFIRMATORY TEST OF THE FIRST-TOUR PERFORMANCE MODEL

Development of the Concurrent Validation Model

The derivation of the concurrent validation first-tour performance model was described in J.P. Campbell, McHenry, and Wise (1990). The initial concurrent validation model of first-tour performance specified the five performance factors shown in Table 11.1. Additionally, the CVI model included two measurement method factors, a "ratings factor" and a "paper-

TABLE 11.1
Definitions of the First-Tour Job Performance Constructs

1. *Core Technical Proficiency* (CTP)
   This performance construct represents the proficiency with which the soldier performs the tasks that are "central" to the MOS. The tasks represent the core of the job, and they are the primary definers of the MOS. This performance construct does not include the individual's willingness to perform the task or the degree to which the individual can coordinate efforts with others. It refers to how well the individual can execute the core technical tasks the job requires, given a willingness to do so.

2. *General Soldiering Proficiency* (GSP)
   In addition to the core technical content specific to an MOS, individuals in every MOS also are responsible for being able to perform a variety of general soldiering tasks—for example, determines a magnetic azimuth using a compass; recognizes and identifies friendly and threat vehicles. Performance on this construct represents overall proficiency on these general soldiering tasks. Again, it refers to how well the individual can execute general soldiering tasks, given a willingness to do so.

3. *Effort and Leadership* (ELS)
   This performance construct reflects the degree to which the individual exerts effort over the full range of job tasks, perseveres under adverse or dangerous conditions, and demonstrates leadership and support toward peers. That is, can the individual be counted on to carry out assigned tasks, even under adverse conditions, to exercise good judgment, and to be generally dependable and proficient? While appropriate knowledge and skills are necessary for successful performance, this construct is meant only to reflect the individual's willingness to do the job required and to be cooperative and supportive with other soldiers.

4. *Maintaining Personal Discipline* (MPD)
   This performance construct reflects the degree to which the individual adheres to Army regulations and traditions, exercises personal self-control, demonstrates integrity in day-to-day behavior, and does not create disciplinary problems. People who rank high on this construct show a commitment to high standards of personal conduct.

5. *Physical Fitness and Military Bearing* (PFB)
   This performance construct represents the degree to which the individual maintains an appropriate military appearance and bearing and stays in good physical condition.

and-pencil test," or written, factor. The two methods factors are defined as a specific kind of residual score. For example, for all scores based on ratings, the general factor was computed and all variance accounted for by other measures was partialed from it. The residual, or ratings method factor, is the common variance across all ratings measures that cannot be accounted for by specific factors or by any other available performance measures. A similar procedure was used to identify a paper-and-pencil test method factor. The two methods factors were used to enable the substantive components of performance to be more clearly modeled without being obscured by these two general factors. This does not imply that *all* the variance in the two method factors is necessarily criterion contamination or bias. The construct meaning for the two factors must be investigated independently. For example, for a given set of observable performance measures, the methods factor scores can in turn be partialed from the observed factor scores and results compared for the observed versus the residual versus the methods factor itself.

Because the model was developed using the concurrent sample data, it could not be confirmed using the same data. J.P. Campbell et al. (1990) described the LISREL analyses of the concurrent validation data as "quasi" confirmatory. The evaluation of the CVI first-tour performance model using data from an independent sample (LVI) can, however, be considered confirmatory.

Method of Confirming First-Tour Model Using the Longitudinal Validation Sample

Sample

The CVI model was based on data from the nine jobs, or "Batch A MOS," for which a full set of criterion measures had been developed (C.H. Campbell et al., 1990). In the LVI sample, there are 10 "Batch A" jobs, including the nine from the CVI sample plus MOS 19K. 19E and 19K both refer to tank crewmen. Only the equipment (i.e., the tank) is different. (Note also that the MOS designation of Motor Transport Operators was changed from 64C in the CVI sample to 88M in the LVI sample.) All individuals in the LVI sample with complete performance data (see Chapter 9) are included in the analyses reported here. The number of these soldiers within each MOS is shown in Table 11.2.

Measures/Observed Scores

The basic criterion scores described in Chapter 8 (Table 8.13) are the observed scores that were used to generate the intercorrelation matrices for the confirmatory analyses. Altogether, the LVI first-tour performance measures were reduced to 22 basic scores. However, because MOS differ in their task content, not all 22 variables were scored in each MOS, and there was some slight variation in the number of variables used in the subsequent analyses. Also, Combat Performance Prediction Scores were not available for female soldiers in LVI, so they were not used in the modeling effort. (This was also the case for the CVI data.) Means, standard deviations, and

TABLE 11.2
LVI Confirmatory Performance Model Factor Analysis Sample Sizes

11B	Infantryman	896
13B	Cannon Crewman	801
19E	M60 Armor (Tank) Crewman	241
19K	M1 Armor (Tank) Crewman	780
31C	Single Channel Radio Operator	483
63B	Light-Wheel Vehicle Mechanic	721
71L	Administrative Specialist	622
88M	Motor Transport Operator	662
91A	Medical Specialist	801
95B	Military Police	451

intercorrelations among the variables for each of the 10 jobs are given in J.P. Campbell and Zook (1991).

Analyses

Confirmatory factor-analytic techniques were applied to each MOS individually, using LISREL 7 (Jöreskog & Sörbom, 1989). In general, the covariances among the unobserved variables, or factors, are represented by the phi matrix. The diagonal elements of this matrix are fixed to one in these analyses, so that the off diagonal elements represent the correlations among the unobserved variables. In all cases, the model specified that the correlation among the two method factors and those between the method factors and the performance factors should be zero. This specification effectively defined a method factor as that portion of the common variance among measures from the same method that was not predictable from (i.e., correlated with) any of the other related factor or performance construct scores.

Parameters estimated for each MOS were the loadings of the observed variables on the specified common factors, the unique variances or errors for each observed variable, and the correlations among the unobserved variables. The fit of the model was assessed for each MOS using the chi-square statistic and the root mean-square residual (RMSR). The chi-square statistic indicates whether the matrix of correlations among the variables reproduced using the model is different from the original correlation matrix. The RMSR summarizes the magnitude of the differences between entries in the reproduced matrix and the original matrix.

The first model fit to the LVI data was a five-factor CVI model. As in the CVI analyses, out-of-range values were sometimes encountered in a number of MOS for the correlations among the factors, for the unique variances, and/or for the factor loadings. In the CVI analyses, this difficulty was resolved by setting the estimates of unique variance equal to one minus the squared multiple correlation of the corresponding variable with all other variables. When out-of range values persisted, the estimate of unique variance was reset to .05.

For the LVI analyses, only the second step was taken; that is, for those variables for which the initial estimate of the uniqueness coefficient was negative (2 out of 22), the estimates were set at .05, and the model was rerun. Thus, the uniqueness coefficient for the Physical Fitness and Military Bearing rating was set to .05 for each of the 10 MOS, as was the uniqueness coefficient for the Maintaining Personal Discipline rating for 11B, 19E, and 88M. This was necessary for Physical Fitness and Military Bearing in both the CVI and LVI analyses. This is most likely because an identification problem in the model caused by the fact that the Physical Fitness and Military Bearing performance factor is defined by only two variables, one of which (the Physical Readiness test score) is only marginally related to the other variables in the model. These actions had the desired effect of making the uniqueness matrix for each MOS positive definite and bringing the factor correlations and factor loadings back into range.

After the fit of the five-factor model was assessed in each MOS, four reduced models (all nested within the five-factor model) were examined. These models are described below. As with the five-factor model, the fit of the reduced models was assessed using the chi-square statistic and the RMSR. Also, to maintain the nested structure of the models, the uniqueness estimates that were set to .05 for the five-factor models were also set to .05 for each of the reduced models.

Finally, as had been done in the original CVI analyses, the five-factor model was applied to the Batch A MOS simultaneously (using LISREL's multigroups option). This model constrained the following to be invariant across jobs: (a) the correlations among performance factors, (b) the loadings of all the Army-wide measures on the performance factors and on the rating method factor, (c) the loadings of the MOS-specific scores on the rating method factor, and (d) the uniqueness coefficients of the Army-wide measures. As described above, the unique variance for the Physical Fitness and Military Bearing rating was fixed to .05 for all 10 MOS, as was the unique variance for the Maintaining Personal Discipline rating for 11B, 19E, and 88M.

Results: Confirmatory
Analyses Within Jobs

The specifications for the five-factor CVI model were fit to the LVI data for each MOS sample. However, for 11B all of the variables obtained from the hands-on and job knowledge tests were specified to load on the General Soldiering Proficiency factor (thus resulting in only a four-factor model for this MOS) because 11B is the basic infantry position for which these common tasks form the "technical" component.

For comparison purposes, the five-factor model described above was also applied back to the CVI data. To make the comparison as interpretable as possible, the results were computed using exactly the same procedures as for the LVI analyses. Thus, these results are different from those previously reported (J.P. Campbell et al., 1990) in that they include only those basic scores that were also available for the LVI analyses.

The fit of the five-factor model for each MOS in the LVI and CVI samples is reported in Table 11.3. Note that the RMSRs for the LVI data are very similar to those for the CVI data. In fact, for three of the MOS

TABLE 11.3
Comparison of Fit Statistics for CVI and LVI Five-Factor Solutions: Separate
Model for Each Job

	CVI				LVI			
	n	RMSR	Chi-Square	df	n	RMSR	Chi-Square	df
11B[a]	687	.063	198.1	88	896	.044	213.8	88
13B	654	.066	218.9	114	801	.059	244.1	114
19E	489	.043	143.0	114	241	.072	148.9	114
19K[b]					780	.049	236.8	114
31C	349	.060	205.5	148	483	.077	290.4	148
63B	603	.047	129.8	99	721	.065	219.6	99
64C/88M[c]	667	.053	140.0	84	662	.057	221.4	84
71L	495	.067	99.8	71	622	.045	108.3	71
91A	491	.050	162.2	98	801	.056	245.6	98
95B	686	.046	236.7	130	451	.061	199.4	130

[a] Fit statistics for MOS 11B are for four-factor model (all factors except Core Technical Proficiency).
[b] MOS 19K not included in Concurrent Validation sample.
[c] MOS 64C in CVI is designated as MOS 88M in LVI.

(11B, 13B, and 71L), the RMSRs for the LVI data are smaller than those for the CVI data. The model developed using the CVI data fit the LVI data quite well.

Reduced Models

To determine if information would be lost by trying to fit a more parsimonious model, four reduced models were also examined using the LVI data. Each of the reduced models retained the two method factors and the specification that these method factors be uncorrelated with each other and with the performance factors.

For the *four-factor model*, the Core Technical Proficiency and General Soldiering Proficiency performance factors were collapsed into a single "can do" performance factor. Specifications for the Effort and Leadership, Maintaining Personal Discipline, and Physical Fitness and Military Bearing performance factors were not altered. The *three-factor model* retained the "can do" performance factor model, but also collapsed the Effort and Leadership and Maintaining Personal Discipline performance factors into a "will do" performance factor. Once again, specifications for the Physical Fitness and Military Bearing performance factor were not changed. For the *two-factor model*, the "can do" performance factor was retained; however, the Physical Fitness and Military Bearing performance factor became part of the "will do" performance factor. Finally, for the *one-factor model*, the "can do" and "will do" performance factors (or, equivalently, the five original performance factors) were collapsed into a single performance factor. The RMSRs for the four reduced models, as well as for the five-factor model, are provided in Table 11.4. These results suggest that a model composed of only four performance factors (combining the CTP and GSP performance factors) and the two method factors fit the LVI data almost as well as the original model. However, further reductions resulted in poorer fits.

Results: Confirmatory Factor Analyses Across Jobs

The above results indicate that the parameter estimates for the five-factor model were generally similar across the 10 MOS. The final step was to determine whether the variation in some of these parameters could be attributed to sampling variation. To do this, we examined the fit of a model in which the following were invariant across jobs: (a) the correlations among

TABLE 11.4

LVI Root Mean-Square Residuals for Five-, Four-, Three-, Two-, and
One-Factor Performance Models

	Root Mean-Square Residuals				
MOS	Five Factors	Four Factors	Three Factors	Two Factors	One Factor
11B[a]	.044	.044	.064	.092	.134
13B	.059	.063	.071	.070	.114
19E	.072	.072	.098	.141	.212
19K	.049	.049	.069	.091	.134
31C	.077	.084	.119	.147	.163
63B	.065	.066	.074	.079	.104
71L	.045	.053	.054	.078	.150
88M	.057	.057	.072	.100	.150
91A	.056	.056	.058	.122	.159
95B	.061	.060	.071	.095	.123

[a]Five- and four-factor models are the same for MOS 11B.

performance factors, (b) the loadings of all the Army-wide measures on
the performance factors and on the rating method factor, (c) the loadings of
the MOS-specific score on the rating method factor, and (d) the uniqueness
coefficients for the Army-wide measures.

J.P. Campbell et al. (1990) indicated that this is a relatively stringent
test for a common latent structure across jobs. They stated that it is "quite
possible that selectivity differences in different jobs would lead to differences in the apparent measurement precision of the common instruments or
to differences in the correlations between the constructs. This would tend
to make it appear that the different jobs required different performance
models, when in fact they do not" (p. 324).

The LISREL 7 multigroups option required that the number of observed
variables be the same for each job. However, as was the case for the CV
data, for virtually every MOS at least one of the CVBITS variables had not
been included in the LVI job knowledge or hands-on tests. To handle this
problem, the uniqueness coefficients for these variables were set at 1.00,
and the observed correlations between these variables and all the other
variables were set to zero. It was thus necessary to adjust the degrees of
freedom for the chi-square statistic by subtracting the number of "observed"

correlations that we generated in this manner. (Likewise, it was necessary to adjust the RMSRs for this analyses.)

The chi-square statistic for this model, based on 1,332 degrees of freedom, was 2,714.27. This result can be compared to the sum of the chi-square values (2,128.24) and degrees of freedom (1,060) for the LVI within-job analyses. More specifically, the difference between the chi-square for one model fits all, and the chi-square associated with the 10 separately fit models (i.e., $2,714.27 - 2,128.24 = 586.03$) is itself distributed according to chi-square, with degrees of freedom equal to the difference between the degrees of freedom associated with the former and the sum of the degrees of freedom associated with the latter (i.e., $1,332 - 1,060 = 272$).

These results indicate that the fit of the five-factor model is significantly worse when the parameters listed above are constrained to be equal across the 10 jobs. Still, as shown in Table 11.5, the RMSRs associated with the across-MOS model are not substantially greater than those for the within-job analyses. (The average RMSR for the across-MOS model is .0676; the average for the within-MOS models is .0585.)

TABLE 11.5
Root Mean-Square Residuals for LVI Five-Factor Performance
Model: Same Model for Each Job

| | Root Mean-Square Residual | |
MOS	Same Model for Each Job	Separate Model for Each Job[a]
11B[b]	.073	.044
13B	.068	.059
19E	.080	.072
19K	.054	.049
31C	.073	.077
63B	.071	.065
71L	.062	.045
88M	.063	.057
91A	.069	.056
95B	.063	.061

[a]See Table 11.4.
[b]Root mean-square residual for MOS 11B is for four-factor model (all factors except Core Technical Proficiency).

Determining the Performance Factor Scores

Criterion construct scores for the validation analyses were based on the five-factor model. Although the four-factor model has the advantage of greater parsimony than the five-factor model, the five-factor model offers the advantage of corresponding to the criterion constructs generated in the CVI validation analyses. The five LVI scores are composed of the basic LVI performance scores as shown in Table 11.6, and were computed as described below.

The *Core Technical Proficiency* construct is composed of two components—the MOS-specific technical score from the hands-on (job sample) tests and the MOS-specific technical score from the job knowledge tests. For this and all other constructs, the components were unit weighted; that is, they were combined by first standardizing them within MOS and then adding them together.

The *General Soldiering Proficiency* construct is also composed of two major components. The first component is operationally defined as the sum of each of the CVBITS scores (except the technical score, which is a component of the Core Technical Proficiency construct) from the hands-on

TABLE 11.6
Five Factor Model of First Tour Performance (LVI)

Latent Variable	Scores Loading on Latent Variables
Core Technical Proficiency (CTP)	MOS-Specific Hands-on Job Sample
	MOS-Specific Job Knowledge
General Soldiering Proficiency (GSP)	General Hands-On Job Sample
	General Job Knowledge
Effort and Leadership (ELS)	Admin: Awards/Certificates
	Army-Wide Ratings: Technical
	Skill and Effort Factor
	Overall Effectiveness Rating
	MOS Ratings: Overall Composite
Personal Discipline (MPD)	Admin: Disciplinary Actions
	Admin: Promotion Rate
	Army-Wide Ratings: Personal Discipline Factor
Physical Fitness/Military Bearing (PFB)	Admin: Physical Readiness Score
	Army-Wide Ratings: Physical Fitness/Military Bearing Factor

test. The second component is defined as the sum of the CVBITS scores (again, excluding the technical score) from the job knowledge test. Refer to Chapter 8 for a description of the CVBITS factor scores.

The *Effort and Leadership* criterion construct is composed of three components, the first of which corresponds to the single rating for Overall Effectiveness. The second component is composed of two subcomponents, both of which are also standardized within MOS. The first is one of the three factor scores derived from the Army-wide rating scales (i.e., the Army-wide Effort and Leadership factor) and consists of the unit-weighted sum of five different scales (Technical Skill, Effort, Leadership, Maintain Equipment, Self-Development). The second subcomponent is the average of the MOS-specific rating scales. The third and final component is the administrative measure identified as Awards/Certificates.

The *Maintaining Personal Discipline* construct is composed of two major components. The first component is the Maintaining Personal Discipline score derived from the Army-wide ratings and consists of the unit-weighted sum of three different scales (Following Regulations, Integrity, Self-Control). The second component is the sum of two standardized administrative measures: Disciplinary Actions and the Promotion Rate score.

The fifth criterion construct, *Physical Fitness and Military Bearing*, is also composed of two major components. The first component is the Physical Fitness and Military Bearing score derived from the Army-wide ratings and consists of the unit-weighted sum of two different scales (Military Appearance, Physical Fitness). The second component corresponds to the administrative measure, identified as the Physical Readiness score.

Criterion Residual Scores

As in the CVI analyses, five residual scores, for the five criterion constructs, were created using the following procedure. First, a paper-and-pencil "methods" factor was created by partialing from the total score on the job knowledge test that variance shared with all of the non-paper-and-pencil criterion measures (i.e., hands-on scores, rating scores, and administrative records). This residual was defined as the paper-and-pencil method score. Next, this paper-and-pencil method score was partialed from each of the job knowledge test scores used to create the Core Technical Proficiency and General Soldiering Proficiency constructs (as described above). The resulting "residualized" job knowledge test scores were then added to the hands-on scores (which were not residualized) to form residual Core Technical Proficiency and General Soldiering Proficiency scores.

A similar procedure was used to create residual criterion scores for the Effort and Leadership, Maintaining Personal Discipline, and Physical Fitness and Military Bearing constructs. First, a "total" rating score was computed by standardizing and summing the overall effectiveness rating score, the three Army-wide rating factor scores, and the average MOS-specific rating score. Next, a ratings "method" score was created by partialing from the total rating score of all ratings that variance associated with all of the nonrating criterion measures. The resulting method score was then partialed from the rating components of the Effort and Leadership, Maintaining Personal Discipline, and Physical Fitness and Military Bearing constructs. Finally, these residualized rating scores were then combined with the appropriate administrative measures (which were not residualized in any way) to form residual scores for the last three criterion constructs.

Criterion Intercorrelations

The five "raw" criterion construct scores and the five residual criterion construct scores were used to generate a 10×10 matrix of criterion intercorrelations for each Batch A MOS. The averages of these correlations are reported in Table 11.7. These results are very similar to the correlations that were reported by J.P. Campbell et al. (1990) for the CVI sample, which are also shown. Note that the similarity in correlations occurs despite the

TABLE 11.7

Mean Intercorrelations Among 10 Summary Criterion Scores for the Batch A
MOS in the (CVI) and LVI Samples (Decimals omitted)

Summary Criterion Score	CTP Raw	GSP Raw	ELS Raw	MPD Raw	PFB Raw	CTP Res	GSP Res	ELS Res	MPD Res	PFB Res
CTP (raw)	1.00									
GSP (raw)	(53)57	1.00								
ELS (raw)	(28)25	(27)26	1.00							
MPD (raw)	(19)16	(16)18	(59)58	1.00						
PFB (raw)	(03)06	(04)06	(46)48	(33)36	1.00					
CTP (residual)	(88)88	(39)41	(35)30	(26)20	(03)07	1.00				
GSP (residual)	(38)40	(89)88	(33)32	(23)23	(04)06	(44)45	1.00			
ELS (residual)	(47)41	(45)42	(65)70	(44)43	(25)26	(45)40	(43)42	1.00		
MPD (residual)	(23)20	(19)22	(28)28	(89)88	(17)17	(25)20	21(23)	(48)46	1.00	
PFB (residual)	(04)07	(05)07	(19)20	(19)21	(92)90	(−01)04	(01)03	(28)29	(20)21	1.00

fact that the CVI results are based on criterion construct scores that were created using the full array of basic scores available for that sample, and not just those scores used to create the construct scores for the LVI sample.

Concluding Comments

These results indicate that the five-factor model of first-tour job performance developed using the concurrent validation sample fit the longitudinal validation data quite well and to approximately the same degree that it did in the concurrent sample. This conclusion holds for the relationships among the latent performance factors (as indicated by the results of the LISREL analyses) as well as for the correlations among the observed criterion construct scores. Cast against the atheoretical history of the "criterion problem" in personnel research, these results were remarkable, and seemed to hold considerable promise for the development of new and better performance theory.

The results also indicate that a four-factor model (in which the Core Technical Proficiency and General Soldiering Proficiency factors were combined into a single "can do" factor) fit the LVI data almost as well as the five-factor model.

However, despite the relatively large relationship between Core Technical Proficiency and General Soldiering Proficiency, validation results reported for the CVI sample did indicate that somewhat different equations were needed to predict the two performance constructs (Wise, McHenry, & J.P. Campbell, 1990). Furthermore, those results also indicated that the hypothesis of equal prediction equations across jobs could be rejected for the Core Technical construct but not for General Soldiering. Based on these previous results, and the results reported in this chapter, it seems justifiable to use the criterion construct scores associated with all five factors in the longitudinal validation analyses reported in Chapter 13.

MODELING SECOND-TOUR PERFORMANCE

As with first-tour performance, analyses of the performance data collected from the second-tour concurrent validation (CVII) and second-tour longitudinal validation (LVII) samples proceeded from the assumption that total performance comprises a small number of relatively distinct components such that aggregating them into one score covers up too much information about relative proficiency on the separate factors. The analysis objectives were again to develop a set of basic criterion scores and to determine which model of their latent structure best fits the observed intercorrelations.

A preliminary model of the latent structure of second-tour soldier performance was developed based on data from the CVII sample (J.P. Campbell & Oppler, 1990). After scores from each measurement instrument were defined, the development of the model began with an examination of the correlations among the CVII basic criterion scores. Exploratory factor analyses suggested five to six substantive factors, generally similar to those in the first-tour model, and also suggested method factors for at least the ratings and the written measures.

The exploratory results were reviewed by the project staff members and several alternative models were suggested for "confirmation." Because the sample sizes were limited, it was not feasible to conduct split-sample cross-validation within the concurrent sample. The initial results were thus primarily suggestive, and needed to be confirmed using the LVII sample performance data. Given these caveats, three major alternative models and several variations within each of these models were evaluated using the CVII data.

Development of the CVI Model

Procedure

Because the MOS second-tour sample sizes were relatively small, tests of the models were conducted using the entire CVII sample. The basic scores listed in Figure 8.14 were used, with the exception of the Combat Performance Prediction Scales, which had not been administered to female soldiers. Basic criterion scores were first standardized within each MOS, then the intercorrelations among these standardized basic scores were computed across all MOS. The total sample matrix was used as input for the analyses.

The correlation matrix was submitted to confirmatory factor analyses using LISREL 7 (Jöreskog & Sörbom, 1989). To determine whether the use of correlation matrices was appropriate in the present analyses, several analyses were conducted a second time using the variance-covariance matrices, as suggested by Cudeck (1989). Results indicated that correlation matrices were, in fact, appropriate for the models tested.

LISREL 7 was used to estimate the parameters and evaluate the fit of each of the alternative models. Goodness of fit was assessed using the same indices as for the first-tour modeling analyses. Again, as Browne and Cudeck (1993) pointed out, the null hypothesis of exact fit is invariably false in practical situations and is likely to be rejected when using large samples. However, comparison of these chi-square fit statistics for nested models allows for a test of the significance of the decrement in fit when parameters (e.g., underlying factors) are removed (Mulaik et al., 1989).

CVII Results

The model that best fit the CVII data will be referred to as the Training and Counseling model. This model is very similar to the model of first-tour soldier performance discussed earlier. The primary difference is that this second-tour model was expanded to incorporate the supervisory aspects of the second-tour NCO position. Some of these elements were represented by a sixth factor, called Training and Counseling Subordinates, which included all scores from the supervisory role-play exercises. The role-play scores defined a new factor in large part because they show a good deal of internal consistency, but have very low correlations with any of the other performance measures. Two other supervisory measures, the Situational Judgment Test and the Leading/Supervising rating composite, were constrained to load on the factor called Achievement and Leadership. Finally, whereas promotion rate was part of the Personal Discipline factor in the model of first-tour performance, the revised promotion rate variable fit more clearly with the Achievement and Leadership factor in the second-tour model. Apparently, for soldiers in their second tour of duty, a relatively high promotion rate is due to positive achievement rather than simply the avoidance of disciplinary problems.

The CVII Training and Counseling model has one undesirable characteristic: the Training and Counseling factor itself confounds method variance with substantive variance. One of the objectives in generating alternative hypotheses of the underlying structure of second-tour soldier performance to be tested using the LVII data was to avoid this problem.

Development of the LVII Model

The second-tour longitudinal sample data (LVII) provided an opportunity to confirm the fit of the CVII Training and Counseling model in an independent sample. An additional objective was to evaluate the fit of alternative *a priori* models. In general, the LVII data should provide a better understanding of second-tour performance because the sample is larger than the

CVII sample and because several of the individual performance measures were revised and improved based on the results of the CVII analyses. For the LVII sample, several alternative models of second-tour soldier performance were first hypothesized. The fit of these alternative models was then assessed using the LVII data and compared with the fit of the CVII Training and Counseling model. Once a best fitting model was identified, analyses were conducted to assess the fit of a hierarchical series of more parsimonious models. Finally, the fit of the new model identified using the LVII data was tested with the CVII data.

Expert Generated Alternatives

Definitions of LVII basic criterion scores were circulated to the project staff, and a variety of hypotheses concerning the nature of the underlying structure of second-tour soldier performance were obtained. These hypotheses were consolidated into one principal alternative model, several variations on this model, and a series of more parsimonious models that involved collapsing two or more of the substantive factors. The principal alternative, the Consideration/Initiating Structure model, differs from the CVII Training and Counseling model primarily in that it includes two leadership factors. The composition of these two factors—given their traditional labels of Consideration and Initiating Structure—is based on the general findings of the Ohio State Leadership Studies and virtually all subsequent leadership research (Fleishman, 1973; Fleishman, Zaccaro, & Mumford, 1991). Based on staff judgments, each of the Situational Judgment Test (SJT) subscores and the role-play scores was assigned rationally to one of these two factors. Because the majority of the scales contained in the Army-wide ratings Leading/Supervising composite appear to involve initiating structure, this score was assigned to the Initiating Structure factor.

However, some of the rating scales included in the Army-wide Leading/Supervising rating composite are clearly more related to consideration than to structure. Thus, one variation of this model that was tested involved rationally assigning the scales from this basic rating score to the appropriate leadership factor. Another variation on this model was to assign *both* of the scores from the Personal Counseling exercise to the Consideration factor, because this entire exercise could be seen as more related to consideration than to initiating structure.

The analysis plan was to first compare the fit of the Consideration/Initiating Structure model and the variations of this model with each other and with the fit of the CVII Training and Counseling model, and to identify the alternatives that best fit the LVII covariance structure. The next set of analyses involved comparing a series of nested models to determine the extent to which the observed correlations could be accounted for by fewer underlying factors.

LVII Model Fitting Procedures

Procedures used to conduct confirmatory factor analyses for the LVII data were essentially identical to those for CVII except for one additional fit index, the Root Mean Square Error of Approximation (RMSEA) that was not provided by LISREL 7. RMSEA can be interpreted as a measure of the residual error variance per degree of freedom when a specific model is fit to the data (Browne & Cudeck, 1993). Because additional parameters will not *necessarily* improve the fit of a model as assessed by the RMSEA, this fit index does not encourage the inclusion of unimportant or theoretically meaningless parameters just to improve model fit. Browne and Cudeck suggest that a value of .08 or less for the RMSEA can be interpreted as indicating a reasonable fit of the model to the data.

LVII Results

The fit of the Training and Counseling model is shown in Table 11.8. The fit of this model in the LVII sample is remarkably similar to the fit of this same model in the CVII sample, especially considering that the performance data were collected several years apart using somewhat different measures.

Tests of the Consideration/Initiating Structure model, and its variations, resulted in a relatively poor fit to the data (e.g., RMSR values greater than .09) and the program encountered a variety problems in estimating the parameters for these models. To determine whether there were reasonable alternative models of second-tour performance that had been overlooked, a series of additional exploratory analyses were conducted. The LVII total sample (including 11B) was randomly divided into two subsamples: 60% of the sample was used to develop alternative models and 40% was set aside for confirming any new models that were identified.

The matrix of intercorrelations among the basic criterion scores for the developmental subsample was examined by the project staff and a variety of alternative models were tested for fit in the developmental sample. A number of these alternatives tried different arrangements of the role-play exercise, Situational Judgment Test, and rating scale scores while still pre-serving two leadership factors. None of these alternatives resulted in a good

TABLE 11.8

LISREL Results: Comparisons of Overall Fit Indices for the Training and
Counseling Model and the Leadership Model in the LVII and CVII Samples[a,b]

Sample	N	Chi-Square	df	GFI	RMSR	RMSEA (CI)[c]
LVII Sample						
Training and	1,144	652.27	185	.95	.041	.048
Counseling Model						(.044–.052)
Leadership Model	1,144	649.27	178	.95	.043	.048
						(.044–.052)
CVII Sample						
Training and	1,006	376.76	129	.96	.043	.044
Counseling Model						(.039–.049)
Leadership Model	1,006	353.66	124	.96	.040	.043
						(.038–.048)

[a]The basic criterion scores used in modeling performance for these two samples differed somewhat.
[b]The T&C model was developed using the CVII sample; the Leadership model was developed using the LVII sample.
[c]The 90% confidence interval for each RMSEA estimate is shown in parentheses.

fit with the data. However, a model that collapsed the Consideration and
Initiating Structure factors into a single Leadership factor, that included a
single Role-Play Exercise method factor, and for which the promotion rate
variable was moved to the new Leadership factor *did* result in a considerably
better fit.

The Leadership Model

Table 11.9 shows the six factor "Leadership Factor" model that was developed based on these exploratory analyses.[1] This model was tested in the
holdout sample, and the parameter estimates were very similar to those obtained in the developmental sample. Table 11.8 shows the overall fit indices
for this model using the total LVII sample and compares these fit indices
with those obtained for the Training and Counseling model. The fit of the
new Leadership Factor model to the LVII data is, for all practical purposes,

---

[1]Note the model includes the overall Combat Performance Prediction Scale (CPPS) score. This
score was not used in the LVII modeling exercise because it was not used in the CVI modeling exercise.
The score was subsequently added in the hypothesized part of the model, and the model was retested
to ensure goodness-of-fit.

TABLE 11.9
Leadership Factor Model

Latent Variable	*Scores Loading on Latent Variables*
1. Core Technical Proficiency (CT)	MOS-Specific Hands-on Job Sample
	MOS-Specific Job Knowledge
2. General Soldiering Proficiency (GP)	General Hands-On Job Sample
	General Job Knowledge
3. Achievement and Effort (AE)	Admin: Awards and Certificates
	Army-Wide Ratings: Effort/Technical Skill Factor
	Overall Effectiveness Rating
	MOS Ratings: Overall Composite
	Combat Prediction: Overall Composite
4. Personal Discipline (PD)	Admin: Disciplinary Actions (reversed)
	Army-Wide Ratings: Personal Discipline Factor
5. Physical Fitness/Military Bearing (PF)	Admin: Physical Readiness Score
	Army-Wide Ratings: Physical Fitness/Military Bearing Factor
6. Leadership (LD)	Admin: Promotion Rate
	Army-Wide Ratings: Leading/Supervising Factor
	RP—Disciplinary Structure
	RP—Disciplinary Communication
	RP—Disciplinary Interpersonal Skill
	RP—Counseling Diagnosis/Prescription
	RP—Counseling Communication/Interpersonal Skills
	RP—Training Structure
	RP—Training Motivation Maintenance
	SJT—Total Score
Written Method	Job-Specific Knowledge
	General Job Knowledge
	SJT—Total Score
Ratings Method	Four Army-Wide Ratings Composites
	Overall Effectiveness Rating
	MOS Ratings: Total Composite
	Combat Prediction: Overall Composite
Role-Play Exercise Method	All Seven Role-Play (RP) Exercise Scores

identical to the fit of the Training and Counseling model to these same data. The 90% confidence intervals for the RMSEAs overlap almost completely. Because these models have an equally good fit and because the Leadership Factor model does not confound method variance with substantive variance, the Leadership Factor model was chosen as the best representation of the latent structure of second-tour performance for the LVII data.

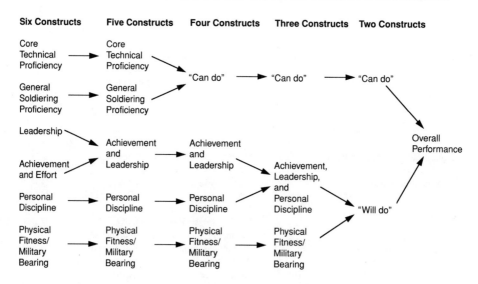

FIG. 11.1. Final LVII criterion and alternate criterion constructs based on increasingly parsimonious models.

For confirmatory purposes, the Leadership Factor model was also fit to the CVII data (Table 11.8). The results are virtually identical to the fit obtained in the LVII sample.

Next, the Leadership Factor model was used as the starting point to develop a nested series of more parsimonious models, similar to a series of nested models that were tested in the LVI sample. Figure 11.1 illustrates the order in which the six substantive factors in the Leadership Factor model were collapsed. The first of these nested models is identical to the full Leadership Factor model except that the Achievement and Effort factor has been collapsed with the Leadership factor. In other words, these two factors were replaced with a single factor on which included all the variables that had previously loaded on either Achievement and Effort or on Leadership. The final model collapses all of the substantive factors into a single overall performance factor. Because these more parsimonious models are nested within each other, the significance of the loss of fit can be tested by comparing the chi-square values for the various models.

Fit indices calculated by applying the models to the CVII data are shown in Table 11.10. In general, as the models become more parsimonious (i.e., contain fewer underlying factors) the chi-square values become larger and the fit to the data is not as good. However, the first nested model that involved collapsing the Leadership factor with the Achievement and Effort

TABLE 11.10
LISREL Results Using CVII Data: Overall Fit Indices for a Series of Nested
Models That Collapse the Substantive Factors in the Leadership Factor Model

Model	Chi-Square	df	GFI	RMSR	RMSEA (CI)[a]
Full Model (6 factors)	353.66	124	.96	.040	.043 (.038–.048)
Single Achievement Leadership Factor (5 factors)	370.83	129	.96	.040	.043 (.038–.048)
Single "Can Do" Factor (4 factors)	430.10	133	.96	.042	.047 (.042–.052)
Single Achievement/Leadership/ Personal Discipline Factor (3 factors)	464.80	136	.95	.043	.049 (.044–.054)
Single "Will Do" Factor (2 factors)	574.27	138	.94	.048	.056 (.051–.061)
Single Substantive Factor	722.83	139	.92	.054	.065 (.060–.069)

Note: N = 1,006.
[a]The 90% confidence interval for each RMSEA estimate is shown in parentheses.

factor resulted in a very small decrement, and the change in chi-square is very small. Similarly, collapsing the two "can do" factors resulted in a very small reduction in model fit. Based on these results, a model with only four substantive factors (and three method factors) can account for the data almost as well as the full Leadership Factor model. Collapsing additional factors beyond this level resulted in larger decrements in model fit. The model with a single substantive factor has an RMSR value of .065, indicating that even this model accounts for a fair amount of the covariation among the LVII basic criterion scores. It should be remembered that this model still includes the three method factors (Written, Ratings, and Role-Play Exercise), so this result is partly a reflection of the fact that a good deal of the covariation among these scores is due to shared measurement method.

A wide variety of additional nested analyses were also conducted to determine how the order in which the factors are collapsed affects the fit of the resulting models. These results, taken as a whole, indicate that the order in which the factors were originally collapsed results in the smallest decrement in model fit at each stage. Results of these nested analyses are, in general, very similar to those obtained using the first-tour performance data from the LVI sample.

Identifying the Leadership Component of Performance

Results of the performance modeling analyses for second-tour jobs show that both the Training and Counseling model and the Leadership Factor model fit the data well. Because the substantive factors do not confound method and substantive variance, the Leadership model was chosen as the best representation of the latent structure of second-tour soldier performance.

Efforts to identify more specific leadership components within the general leadership factor were not successful, even though the LVII contained a greater variety of basic criterion scores related to leadership than did the CVII. This could indicate that the current performance measures are not sensitive to the latent structure of leadership performance, that leadership responsibilities at the junior NCO level are not yet well differentiated, or that the latent structure is actually undimensional. Given the robust findings from the previous literature that argue for multidimensionality, the explanation is most likely some combination of reasons one and two.

The promotion rate variable was included on the Leadership construct primarily because it was expected to share a great deal of variance with leadership and supervisory performance. Individuals with more leadership potential are more likely to be promoted, and individuals who have been promoted more are likely to have obtained more experience in leading and supervising other soldiers. The fact that promotion rate fit very well on the Leadership factor confirmed this expectation. In the model of first-tour performance, promotion rate fit most clearly on the Personal Discipline factor.

In addition to the Leadership factor itself, the six-factor Leadership model of second-tour performance also includes performance constructs that are parallel to those identified for first-tour soldiers, and thus is quite correspondent with the CVI/LVI model of performance as well. This is consistent with the results of the second-tour job analysis, which indicated that second-tour soldiers perform many of the same tasks as the first-tour soldiers and, in addition, have supervisory responsibilities. In summary, even though its incremental goodness of fit compared to the five and four factors alternative is not large, the Leadership Factor model is the most consistent with the data in the confirmatory samples and is also the clearest portrayal of the differences between entry level and initial supervisory performance.

Creating LVII Criterion Construct Scores for Validation Analyses

The performance criterion scores for use in validation analyses are based on the full Leadership Factor model, with six substantive factors. A description of the computation of the six performance factor scores follows.

The *Core Technical Proficiency* factor comprises two basic scores: the job-specific score from the hands-on tests and the job-specific score from the job knowledge tests.

Similarly, the *General Soldiering Proficiency* factor comprises two basic scores: the general soldiering score from the hands-on tests and the general soldiering score from the job knowledge tests. Soldiers from MOS 11B do not have scores on this construct because no distinction is made between core technical and general soldiering tasks for this MOS.

The *Personal Discipline* factor comprises the Personal Discipline composite from the Army-wide ratings, which is the average of ratings on three different scales (Following Regulations/Orders, Integrity, and Self-Control), and the disciplinary actions score from the Personnel File Form.

The *Physical Fitness and Military Bearing* factor also comprises two basic scores: the Physical Fitness and Military Bearing composite from the Army-wide ratings, which is the average of ratings made on two scales (Military Appearance and Physical Fitness) and the physical readiness score, which was collected on the Personnel File Form.

The *Achievement and Effort* criterion factor comprises four composite scores and the single rating of overall effectiveness. The four composites are (a) the Technical Skill/Effort composite from the Army-wide ratings (the average of ratings on Technical Knowledge/Skill, Effort, and Maintain Assigned Equipment); (b) the overall MOS composite, which is the average across all of the behavior-based MOS-specific rating scales; (c) the composite score from the Combat Performance Prediction scales; and (d) the awards and certificates score from the Personnel File Form. Scores for the three rating composites (a, b, and c) were first combined, with each of the individual scores unit weighted. This score was then treated as a single subscore and combined with the two remaining subscores (i.e., the awards and certificates score, and the overall effectiveness rating).

The *Leadership* factor is made up of four major components. The first is the unit-weighted sum of all seven basic scores from the Personal Counseling, Training, and Disciplinary Role-Play Exercises. The second is the Leading/Supervising score from the Army-wide ratings, which is the average across nine rating scales related to leadership and supervision. The third is the total score from the Situational Judgment Test, and the fourth is the promotion rate score.

In computing scores for each of these factors, the major subscores were unit weighted. That is, they were combined by first standardizing each within MOS and then adding them together. These scoring procedures gave approximately equal weight to each measurement method, minimizing potential measurement bias for the resulting criterion construct scores.

Table 11.11 shows the intercorrelations among these six criterion construct scores. These intercorrelations reflect whatever method variance is present and varying degrees of covariation are reflected among the factors. However, one feature of the matrix is that the most uniform intercorrelations are displayed by the leadership factor. As will be seen in the next chapter, this is most likely not due to differential reliabilities across the composite scores. A more likely explanation (although probably not the only one) is that good leadership is partly a direct function of expertise on the other components of performance as well, even highly technical factors.

TABLE 11.11
Intercorrelations for LVII Performance Construct Scores

Criterion Factor Scores	CT Core Technical	GP General Proficiency	AE Achievement/ Effort	PD Personal Discipline	PF Physical Fitness	LD Leadership
CT Construct	1.00					
GP Construct	.51	1.00				
EA Construct	.29	.24	1.00			
PD Construct	.15	.13	.51	1.00		
PF Construct	.10	.06	.41	.36	1.00	
LD Construct	.44	.45	.55	.41	.30	1.00

Note: N = 1,144.

SUMMARY

This chapter has described the modeling of performance at two stages of an individual's career in the U.S. Army: (a) toward the end of the first tour of duty (entry level performance in skilled jobs) and (b) and toward the end of the second tour of duty (advanced technical performance plus initial supervisory and leadership responsibilities). Performance scores are also available from the conclusion of the prescribed technical training (training performance), as described in Chapter 8. The latent structure of performance showed considerable consistency across all three organizational levels and represented total performance in terms of a set of either five or six major factors.

The standardized simple sum composite scores for each factor constitute the criterion factor scores that have been used in all subsequent validation analyses. Because of its consistency across career stages, this basic structure permits very meaningful comparisons of performance at one stage with performance at another stage. The correlation of performance with performance and the prediction of each performance factor with the complete predictor battery will be examined in detail in the following chapters.

12

Criterion Reliability and the Prediction of Future Performance from Prior Performance

Douglas H. Reynolds, Anthony Bayless, and John P. Campbell

A major overall goal of personnel selection and classification research is to estimate population parameters, in the usual statistical sense of estimating a population value from sample data. For example, a population parameter of huge interest is the validity coefficient that would be obtained if the prediction equation developed on the sample was used to select all future applicants from the population of applicants. The next three chapters focus on this parameter in some detail. The sample value is of interest only in terms of its properties as an efficient and unbiased estimate of a population value.

In personnel research, there are at least two major potential sources of bias in sample estimates of the population validity. First, restriction of range in the research sample, as compared to the decision (applicant) sample, acts to bias the validity estimate downward. Second, if the sample data are used to develop differential weights for multiple predictors (e.g., multiple regression) and the population estimate (e.g., of the multiple correlation coefficient) is computed on the same data, then the sample estimate is biased upward because of fortuitous fitting of error as valid variance. For virtually all Project A analyses, the sample values have been corrected for these two sources of bias. That is, the bias in the sample estimator was reduced by using the multivariate correction for range restriction and the Rozeboom (1978) or Claudy (1978) correction for "shrinkage."

It also seems a reasonable goal to estimate the validity of the predictor battery for predicting true scores on performance. That is, the criterion of real interest is a performance measure that is not attenuated by unreliability. If different methods are used to measure the same performance factor, the estimate of validity would differ across methods simply because of differences in reliability. To account for these artifactual differences in validity estimates and to provide an estimate of a battery's validity for predicting true scores on a performance dimension, the sample-based estimates can be corrected for attenuation.

This chapter reports the results of two sets of analyses. The first deals with the estimation of the reliability coefficient for each performance factor score specified by the performance model for the end-of-training, for first-tour performance, and for second-tour performance. The second set of analyses provides estimates of the true score correlation of performance at one organizational level with performance at the next level.

ESTIMATING CRITERION RELIABILITIES

Corrections for attenuation are an accepted procedure for removing the downward bias in the population estimates that is caused by criterion un-reliability. Consequently, one of the project's analysis tasks was to develop reliability estimates for each of the performance factors used as criterion measures in each of the principal research samples. Once the reliability estimates were available, the final corrections to the major validity estimates could be made.

Reliability Computation

Reliability estimates were calculated for the CVI, LVT, LVI, and LVII performance factor scores. All performance factor scores in these samples have the same general form: Each is a linear composite of several standardized basic criterion scores that may themselves be a linear composite of specific criterion scores. Consequently, all reliability estimates were derived using a modification of a formula given in Nunnally (1967) for the reliability of a composite of weighted standardized variables.[1] This formulation of composite reliability requires the intercorrelations among the variables in a composite, the weight applied to each variable, and the reliability of each variable. All intercorrelatons among the variables that constitute each composite were computed within MOS, within each of the data collection samples. The computations are described in more detail below.

Weights for each variable are a function of the manner by which the variables in each composite were combined. When standardized variables are simply added together to form a composite score, all components receive equal weight. When components are combined into subcomposites before being added together to create a larger composite, components are differentially weighted. For example, if three standardized variables are added to form a composite, each would receive equal weight (e.g., .33). If two of the three variables were added together, restandardized, and added to the third variable, the sum of the weights of the first two variables would equal the weight of the third (e.g., .25, .25, .50). The weights for each criterion variable were applied in accordance with the manner by which the variables were combined in each composite under consideration.

Generally, reliability estimates were computed at the MOS level for MOS-specific measures and across MOS for Army-wide measures. The Army-wide rating scales were the only exception; rating-scale based reliabilities were adjusted to account for differences in the average number of raters in each MOS. The methods for estimating the reliability of the various project criterion measures are described in the following sections.

Training Achievement, Job Knowledge, and Hands-on Criterion Measures

The reliability analyses for the school knowledge, job knowledge, and hands-on measures were conducted separately for each criterion composite and each MOS. Split-half reliability estimates were obtained for the job knowledge and training achievement criterion measures using an odd-even

---

[1] Composite reliability was derived using the following equation:

$$r_{yy} = 1 - \frac{\sum w_j^2 - \sum w_j^2 r_{xx}}{\sum w_j^2 + 2\sum\sum w_j w_k r_{jk}}$$

where w_j = the weight for component j, w_k = the weight for component k, r_{xx} = the reliability estimates for each component, and r_{jk} = the intercorrelation between the total scores on the components.

split method. Estimates of the reliability of equivalent forms were derived for the hands-on criterion measure by having a subject matter expert (who was familiar with the various MOS and their tasks) separate "equivalent" tasks into two groups. Scores for each criterion measure were derived by summing the constituent items or tasks of each half or equivalent form and correlating them within criterion measure to produce split-half reliability estimates. These estimates were corrected using the Spearman-Brown prophecy formula.

For those MOS that required tracked tests (i.e., different forms of the tests were necessary for some MOS because different types of equipment were used within the MOS), corrected split-half reliability estimates were derived for each track. To obtain a single reliability estimate for the tracked MOS, the weighted average of the corrected reliability estimates across tracks was computed.

Rating Scales

Three types of rating scales were used across the four samples examined here: (a) Army-wide scales, (b) combat prediction scales, and (c) MOS-specific scales. K-rater reliability (interrater agreement) estimates for each MOS are available for all MOS-specific rating measures; those estimates were used here (J. P. Campbell, 1987; J. P. Campbell & Zook, 1991; J. P. Campbell & Zook, 1994).

Reliability estimates for the Army-wide ratings were computed differently depending on how the rating scale scores were constructed in each sample. In the LVT sample, only peer ratings were used in computing the composite scores. Similarly, in the LVII sample, only supervisor ratings were used. In these samples, the single-rater intraclass correlation reliability estimate computed across all cases and MOS in the sample was adjusted by the average number of peer (LVT) or supervisor (LVII) raters within each MOS.

In the CVI and LVI samples, an average of the peer and supervisor ratings was used to develop the criterion composites. For these samples, rating reliability was estimated by using an intraclass correlation analogous to Cronbach's alpha, where the reliability of the combined ratings is a function of the variance of the individual components (i.e., the peer or the supervisor ratings) and the variance of the combined ratings.

All of the required variances were computed for each rating scale basic score within MOS to produce an estimate of the reliability. The reliability estimates for the combat prediction scales used in the CVI sample were also developed using this procedure. Rating scale basic scores were used in composites involving effort, leadership, personal discipline, and physical fitness in each of the data collection samples.

Role-Plays

The LVII data collection included three role-plays (supervisor simulation exercises). The seven basic factor scores resulting from these measures were added together to form a role-play total score. The reliability of the role-play total score was estimated as an unweighted linear composite (Nunnally, 1967; equation 7–11). This formulation requires the variances of each of the seven basic role-play scores, the variance of the total score, and the reliability of each of the seven basic scores. The required variances were computed, across MOS, with LVII data. However, because of the very small number of soldiers who were shadow-scored in the LVII data collection (i.e., who were scored by two raters instead of one), the reliabilities for the individual role-plays could not be computed for LVII data. Instead, single-rater reliability estimates computed for the CVII supervisory role-plays were used; these reliabilities were reported in J.P. Campbell and Zook (1990). The resulting reliability estimate was .791 for the LVII role-play scores. These scores were used as one component of the LVII Leadership composite.

Administrative Measures

A number of administrative measures were used in the four data collections examined here. These included the Awards and Certificates score, the Disciplinary Actions score, the Promotion Rate score, and the Physical Readiness score. The reliability of each of these scores was conservatively estimated to be .90 across all MOS. This "arm-chair" estimate was based on the small but probable error that may result from soldiers incorrectly remembering, or purposefully distorting, their self-reported administrative data. Administrative measures were used in composites involving effort, leadership, personal discipline, and physical fitness in each of the data collection samples.

Situational Judgment Test

Prior project research has estimated the internal-consistency reliability of the SJT at .81 across all MOS (J.P. Campbell & Zook, 1994). This estimate was used as one component of the LVII Leadership composite.

TABLE 12.1

Median Reliabilities (Across Batch A MOS) for the LVT, LVI, and LVII
Performance Factor Scores

LVT		LVI		LVII	
Factor	r_{xx}	Factor	r_{xx}	Factor	r_{xx}
Tech	.895	CTP	.800	CTP	.706
Basic	.795	GSP	.774	GSP	.731
ETS	.661	ELS	.847	AE	.857
MPD	.685	MPD	.810	PD	.797
PFB	.670	PFB	.824	PFB	.829
LEAD	.641			LDR	.857

Note: Tech = Technical Knowledge Score   CTP = Core Technical Proficiency
Basic = Basic Knowledge Score   GSP = General Soldiering Proficiency
ETS = Effort and Technical Skill   ELS = Effort and Leadership
MPD = Maintaining Personal Discipline   AE = Achievement and Effort
PFB = Physical Fitness/Military Bearing   PD = Personal Discipline
LEAD = Leadership Potential   LDR = Leadership

Results

The individual performance factor reliabilities for each Batch A MOS in
each sample are reported in J.P. Campbell and Zook (1994). Median reliabilities across MOS are shown in Table 12.1. In general, the reliabilities
of the factors are quite high. There are several reasons for this result. First,
the individual components had gone through a lengthy development process that attempted to maximize their relevant variance. Second, the data
collections themselves had been carried out as carefully as possible. Third,
each criterion factor score is a composite of a number of components. Finally, when ratings served as component measures, multiple raters were
used. In fact, the reliabilities of the factors that are based largely on ratings measures are as high as, or higher than, the factor scores based on the
hands-on and/or knowledge tests. The reliabilities of the "will-do" factors
for the training performance factors tend to be somewhat lower than for the
"can-do" factors because the number of scales in each composite is smaller.

It is important to note that "halo" did not contribute to these reliability estimates for criterion composites that included rating scale scores.
Interrater agreements were first estimated for each single rating score. The

reliability of the composite was then estimated in a manner analogous to the Spearman-Brown.

TRUE SCORE CORRELATIONS OF PAST PERFORMANCE WITH FUTURE PERFORMANCE

The first application of the correction for attenuation was to the correlations of performance with performance. That is, the performance factor scores obtained at one point in time were correlated with performance factor scores obtained at a later point in time in a true longitudinal design. As described previously, the longitudinal component of the Project A design provided for collection of performance data at three points in time: (a) at the end of training (LVT); (b) during the first tour of duty (LVI); and (c) during the second tour of duty (LVII). It was virtually an unparalleled opportunity to examine the consistencies in performance over time from the vantage point of multiple jobs, multiple measures, and a substantive model of performance itself.

The general question of how accurately individual job performance at one level in the organization predicts job performance at another level is virtually a "classic problem" in personnel research. It has critical implications for personnel management as well. That is, to what extent should selection for a different job or promotion to a higher level position be based on an evaluation of an individual's performance in the previous job, as compared to alternative types of information that might be relevant? In the Army context, it is a question of the extent to which promotion or reenlistment decisions should be based on assessments of prior performance.

This general question encompasses at least two specific issues. First, the degree to which individual differences in future performance can be predicted from individual differences in past performance is a function of the relative stability of performance across time. Do the true scores for individuals change at different rates even when all individuals are operating under the same "treatment" conditions? The arguments over this question sometimes become a bit heated (Ackerman, 1989; Austin, Humphreys, & Hulin, 1989; Barrett & Alexander, 1989; Barrett, Caldwell, & Alexander, 1985; Henry & Hulin, 1987; Hulin, Henry, & Noon, 1990).

The second issue concerns whether the current and future jobs possess enough communality in their knowledge, skill, or other attribute requirements to produce valid predictions of future performance from past performance. Perhaps the new job is simply too different from the old one. For example, the degree to which "managers" should possess domain-specific expertise has long been argued. Just as an army should not be equipped and trained to fight only the last way, the promotion system should not try to maximize performance in the *previous* job. One implication of this issue depends on whether similar and dissimilar components of performance for the two jobs can be identified and measured. If they can, then the pattern of correlations across performance components can be predicted, and the predictions evaluated.

The data from Project A/Career Force permit some of the above issues to be addressed. Extensive job analyses, criterion development, and analyses of the latent structure of MOS performance for both first tour and second tour have attempted to produce a comprehensive specification of performance at each level. The models of performance for training performance, first-tour performance, and second-tour performance summarized in Chapter 11 provide some clear predictions about the pattern of convergent and divergent relationships. The results of the prior job analyses also suggest that while the new NCO (second tour) is beginning to acquire supervisory responsibilities, there is a great deal of communality across levels in terms of technical task responsibilities. Consequently, first- and second-tour performance should have a substantial proportion of common determinants.

The LVT × LVI, LVI × LVII, and LVT × LVII intercorrelations both corrected and uncorrected for attenuation are shown in Tables 12.2, 12.3, and 12.4. Three correlations are shown for each relationship. The top figure is the mean correlation across MOS corrected for restriction of range (using the training sample as the population) but not for attenuation. These values were first corrected for range restriction within MOS and then averaged (weighted across MOS). The first value in the parentheses is this same correlation after correction for unreliability in the measure of "future" performance, or the criterion variable when the context is the prediction of future performance from past performance. The second value within the parentheses is the value of the mean intercorrelation after correction for unreliability in both the measure of "current" performance and the measure of future performance. It is an estimate of the correlation between the two true scores.

The reliability estimates used to correct the upper value were the median values (shown in Table 12.1) of the individual MOS reliabilities. The mean values across MOS were slightly lower and thus less conservative than the median.

TABLE 12.2
Zero-Order Correlations of Training Performance (LVT) Variables With First-Tour
Job Performance (LVI) Variables: Weighted Average Across MOS

	LVT:TECH	LVT:BASC	LVT:ETS	LVT:MPD	LVT:PFB	LVT:LEAD
LVI: Core Technical Proficiency (CTP)	**.48** (.54/.57)	.38 (.42/.45)	.22 (.25/.26)	.15 (.17/.18)	.05 (.06/.06)	.18 (.20/.21)
LVI: General Soldiering Proficiency (GSP)	.49 (.56/.62)	**.45** (.51/.57)	.23 (.26/.29)	.17 (.19/.22)	.04 (.05/.05)	.16 (.18/.20)
LVI: Effort and Leadership (ELS)	.21 (.23/.28)	.17 (.18/.23)	**.35** (.38/.47)	.25 (.27/.33)	.28 (.30/.37)	.35 (.38/.47)
LVI: Maintain Personal Discipline (MPD)	.17 (.19/.23)	.14 (.16/.19)	.31 (.34/.42)	**.36** (.40/.48)	.21 (.23/.28)	.27 (.30/.36)
LVI: Physical Fitness and Bearing (PFB)	−.01 (−.01/−.01)	−.02 (−.02/−.03)	.26 (.29/.34)	.13 (.14/.17)	**.44** (.48/.58)	.31 (.34/.41)
LVI: NCO Potential (NCOP)	.18 (.23/.25)	.16 (.21/.23)	.35 (.45/.56)	.26 (.34/.41)	.29 (.37/.45)	.36 (.46/.58)

Note: Total pairwise Ns range from 3,633–3,908. Corrected for range restriction. Correlations between matching variables are in bold. Leftmost coefficients in parentheses are corrected for attenuation in the future criterion. Rightmost coefficients in parentheses are corrected for attenuation in both criteria.

Labels:
LVT: Technical Total Score (TECH) LVT: Maintain Personal Discipline (MPD)
LVT: Basic Total Score (BASC) LVT: Physical Fitness and Bearing (PFB)
LVT: Effort and Technical Skill (ETS) LVT: Leadership Potential (LEAD)

In general, training performance is a strong predictor of performance during the first tour of duty. For example, the single-scale peer rating of leadership potential obtained at the end of training has a correlation of .46 with the single-scale rating of NCO potential obtained during the first tour, when the NCO potential rating is corrected for attenuation. The correlation between the true scores is .58. Correlations of first-tour performance with second-tour performance are even higher, and provide strong evidence for

TABLE 12.3
Zero-Order Correlations of First-Tour Job Performance (LVI) Variables With
Second-Tour Job Performance (LVII) Variables: Weighted Average Across MOS

	LVI:CTP	LVI:GSP	LVI:ELS	LVI:MPD	LVI:PFB	LVI:NCOP
LVII: Core Technical Proficiency (CTP)	.44 (.52/.59)	.41 (.49/.55)	.25 (.30/.33)	.08 (.10/.11)	.02 (.02/.03)	.22 (.26/.29)
LVII: General Soldiering Proficiency (GSP)	.51 (.60/.68)	**.57** (.67/.76)	.22 (.26/.29)	.09 (.11/.12)	−.01 (−.01/−.01)	.19 (.22/.25)
LVII: Effort and Achievement (EA)	.10 (.11/.12)	.17 (.18/.20)	**.45** (.49/.53)	.28 (.30/.33)	.32 (.35/.38)	.43 (.46/.50)
LVII: Leadership (LEAD)	.36 (.39/.42)	.41 (.44/.47)	**.38** (.41/.45)	.27 (.29/.32)	.17 (.18/.20)	.41 (.44/.48)
LVII: Maintain Personal Discipline (MPD)	−.04 (−.04/−.05)	.04 (.04/.05)	.12 (.13/.15)	**.26** (.29/.32)	.17 (.19/.21)	.16 (.18/.20)
LVII: Physical Fitness and Bearing (PFB)	−.03 (−.03/−.04)	−.01 (−.01/−.01)	.22 (.24/.27)	.14 (.15/.17)	**.46** (.51/.56)	.30 (.33/.36)
LVII: Rating of Overall Effectiveness (EFFR)	.11 (.14/.16)	.15 (.19/.22)	.35 (.45/.49)	.25 (.32/.36)	.31 (.40/.44)	**.41** (.53/.68)

Note: Total pairwise Ns range from 333–413. Corrected for range restriction. Correlations between matching variables are in bold. Leftmost coefficients in parentheses are corrected for attenuation in the future criterion. Rightmost coefficients in parentheses are corrected for attenuation in both criteria.

Labels:
LVI: Core Technical Proficiency (CTP)   LVI: Maintain Personal Discipline (MPD)
LVI: General Soldiering Proficiency (GSP)   LVI: Physical Fitness and Bearing (PFB)
LVI: Effort and Leadership (ELS)   LVI: NCO Potential (NCOP)

using measures of first-tour performance as a basis for promotion, or for the reenlistment decision. The true score correlation between the first-tour single-scale rating of NCO potential and the second-tour single-scale rating of overall effectiveness is .68.

The pattern of correlations in Table 12.3 also exhibits considerable convergent and divergent properties. The most interesting exception concerns

TABLE 12.4

Zero-Order Correlations of Training Performance (LVT) Variables With
Second-Tour Job Performance (LVII) Variables: Weighted Average Across MOS

	LVT:TECH	LVT:BASC	LVT:ETS	LVT:MPD	LVT:PFB	LVT:LEAD
LVII: Core Technical Proficiency (CTP)	**.48** (.57/.60)	.41 (.49/.52)	.22 (.26/.28)	.15 (.18/.19)	.08 (.10/.10)	.17 (.20/.21)
LVII: General Soldiering Proficiency (GSP)	.49 (.57/.64)	**.43** (.50/.56)	.19 (.22/.25)	.11 (.13/.14)	.06 (.07/.08)	.11 (.13/.14)
LVII: Effort and Achievement (EA)	.10 (.11/.13)	.15 (.16/.20)	**.25** (.27/.33)	.17 (.18/.23)	.19 (.21/.25)	.24 (.26/.32)
LVII: Leadership (LEAD)	.32 (.35/.43)	.39 (.42/.53)	.29 (.31/.39)	.19 (.21/.26)	.15 (.16/.20)	**.25** (.27/.34)
LVII: Maintain Personal Discipline (MPD)	.08 (.09/.11)	.09 (.10/.12)	.21 (.24/.28)	**.26** (.29/.35)	.16 (.18/.22)	.21 (.24/.28)
LVII: Physical Fitness and Bearing (PFB)	−.05 (−.05/−.07)	−.01 (−.01/−.01)	.12 (.13/.16)	.07 (.08/.09)	**.32** (.35/.42)	.21 (.23/.28)
LVII: Rating of Overall Effectiveness (EFFR)	.11 (.14/.15)	.16 (.21/.23)	.24 (.31/.38)	.18 (.23/.28)	.17 (.22/.26)	.21 (.27/.35)

Note: Total pairwise Ns range from 333–413. Corrected for range restriction. Correlations between matching variables are in bold. Leftmost coefficients in parentheses are corrected for attenuation in the future criterion. Rightmost coefficients in parentheses are corrected for attenuation in both criteria.

Labels:
LVT: Technical Total Score (TECH)   LVT: Maintain Personal Discipline (MPD)
LVT: Basic Total Score (BASC)   LVT: Physical Fitness and Bearing (PFB)
LVT: Effort and Technical Skill (ETS)   LVT: Leadership Potential (LEAD)

the prediction of second-tour leadership performance. Virtually all components of previous performance (i.e., first tour) are predictive of future leadership performance, which has important implications for modeling the determinants of leadership. For example, based on the evidence in Table 12.3, one might infer that effective leadership is a function of being a high scorer on virtually all facets of performance. The least critical determinant is military bearing and physical fitness which some might call "looking like a leader."

In subsequent chapters, the criterion reliability estimates will be used to examine the "corrected" coefficients for additional relationships of special interest. For example, what happens when *all* available predictor information is used in an *optimal* fashion to predict subsequent performance and the sample estimate is fully corrected for both restriction of range and criterion unreliability?

V

Selection Validation, Differential Prediction, Validity Generalization, and Classification Efficiency

13

The Prediction of Multiple Components of Entry-Level Performance

Scott H. Oppler, Rodney A. McCloy,
Norman G. Peterson, Teresa L. Russell,
and John P. Campbell

This chapter reports results of validation analyses based on the first-tour longitudinal validation (LVI) sample described in Chapter 9. The questions addressed include the following: What are the most valid predictors of performance in the first term of enlistment? Do scores from the Experimental Battery produce incremental validity over that provided by the ASVAB? What is the pattern of predictor validity estimates across the major components of performance? How similar are validity estimates obtained using a predictive versus concurrent validation design? When all the predictor information is used in an optimal fashion to maximize predictive accuracy, what are the upper limits for the validity estimates? This chapter summarizes the results of analyses intended to answer these questions and others related to the prediction of entry-level performance.

THE "BASIC" VALIDATION

This chapter will first describe the validation analyses conducted within each predictor domain. We call these the basic analyses. The final section will focus on maximizing predictive accuracy using all information in one equation.

Procedures

Sample

The results reported in this chapter were based on two different sample editing strategies. The first mirrored the strategy used in evaluating the Project A predictors against first-tour performance in the concurrent validation phase of Project A (McHenry, Hough, Toquam, Hanson, & Ashworth, 1990). To be included in those analyses, soldiers in the CVI sample were required to have complete data for all of the Project A Trial Battery predictor composites, as well as for the ASVAB and each of the CVI first-tour performance factors. Corresponding to this strategy, a validation sample composed solely of individuals having complete data for all the LV Experimental Battery predictors, the ASVAB, and the LVI first-tour performance factors was created for longitudinal validation analyses. This sample is referred to as the "listwise deletion" sample.

Table 13.1 shows the number of soldiers across the Batch A MOS who were able to meet the listwise deletion requirements. LVI first-tour performance measures were administered to 6,815 soldiers. Following final editing of the data, a total of 6,458 soldiers had complete data for all of the first-tour performance factors. The validation sample was further reduced because of missing predictor data from the ASVAB and the LV Experimental Battery. Of the 6,319 soldiers who had complete criterion data *and*

TABLE 13.1

Missing Criterion and Predictor Data for Soldiers Administered LVI
First-Tour Performance Measures

Number of soldiers:
- in the LVI Sample 6,815
- who have *complete* LVI criterion data 6,458
- *and* who have ASVAB scores 6,319
- *and* who were administered LV Experimental Battery
  (either paper-and-pencil *or* computer tests) 4,528
- *and* for whom no predictor data were missing 3,163

---

whose ASVAB scores were accessible, 4,528 were administered at least a portion of the Experimental Battery (either the paper-and-pencil tests, the computer tests, or both). Of these, the total number of soldiers with complete predictor data was 3,163.

The number of soldiers with complete predictor and criterion data in each MOS is reported in Table 13.2 for both the CVI and LVI data sets. With the exception of the 73 soldiers in MOS 19E, the soldiers in the right-hand column of the table form the LVI listwise deletion validation sample. MOS 19E was excluded from the longitudinal validation analyses for three reasons. First, the sample size for this MOS was considerably smaller than that of the other Batch A MOS (the MOS with the next smallest sample had 172 soldiers). Second, at the time of the analyses the MOS was being phased out of operation. Third, the elimination of 19E created greater correspondence between the CVI and LVI samples with respect to the composition of MOS (e.g., the ratio of combat to noncombat MOS).

In the alternative sample editing strategy, a separate validation sample was identified for each set of predictors in the Experimental Battery (see below). More specifically, to be included in the validation sample for a given predictor set, soldiers were required to have complete data for each of the first-tour performance factors, the ASVAB, and the predictor composites in that predictor set only. For example, a soldier who had data for the complete

TABLE 13.2
Soldiers in CVI and LVI Data Sets With Complete Predictor
and Criterion Data by MOS

MOS		CVI	LVI (Listwise Deletion Sample)
11B	Infantryman	491	235
13B	Cannon Crewmember	464	553
19E[a]	M60 Armor Crewmember	394	73
19K	M1 Armor Crewmember	—	446
31C	Single Channel Radio Operator	289	172
63B	Light-Wheel Vehicle Mechanic	478	406
71L	Administrative Specialist	427	252
88M	Motor Transport Operator	507	221
91A	Medical Specialist	392	535
95B	Military Police	597	270
Total		4,039	3,163

[a]MOS 19E not included in validity analyses.

set of ABLE composites (as well as complete ASVAB and criterion data), but was missing data from the AVOICE composites, would have been included in the "setwise deletion" sample for estimating the validity of the former test, but not the latter.

There were two reasons for creating these setwise deletion samples. The first reason was to maximize the sample sizes used in estimating the validity of the Experimental Battery predictors. The number of soldiers in each MOS meeting the setwise deletion requirements for each predictor set is reported in Table 13.3. As can be seen, the setwise sample sizes are considerably larger than those associated with the listwise strategy.

The second reason for using the setwise strategy stemmed from the desire to create validation samples that might be more representative of the examinees for whom test scores would be available under operational testing conditions. Under the listwise deletion strategy, soldiers were deleted from the validation sample for missing data from any of the tests included in the Experimental Battery. In many instances, these missing data could be attributed to scores for a given test being set to missing because the examinee failed to pass the random response index for that test, but not for any of the other tests. The advantage of the setwise deletion strategy is that none of the examinees removed from the validation sample for a given test

TABLE 13.3

Soldiers in LVI Setwise Deletion Samples for Validation of Spatial, Computer, JOB, ABLE, and AVOICE Experimental Battery Composites by MOS

| | Setwise Deletion Samples | | | | |
MOS	Spatial	Computer	JOB	ABLE	AVOICE
11B	785	283	720	731	747
13B	713	670	657	753	673
19E[a]	88	86	83	80	87
19K	548	539	512	495	527
31C	221	204	208	200	208
63B	529	499	498	468	507
71L	328	302	300	291	287
88M	279	289	258	263	257
91A	643	619	613	597	625
95B	316	306	307	294	302
Total	4,450	3,797	4,156	4,072	4,220

[a]MOS 19E not included in validity analyses.

were excluded solely for failing the random response index on a different test in the Experimental Battery.

As a final note, there is no reason to expect systematic differences between the results obtained with the listwise and setwise deletion samples. However, because of the greater sample sizes of the setwise deletion samples, as well as the possibly greater similarity between the setwise deletion samples and the future examinee population, it is possible that the validity estimates associated with these samples may be more accurate than those associated with the listwise deletion sample.

Predictors

The predictor scores used in these analyses were derived from the operationally administered ASVAB and the paper-and-pencil and computerized tests administered in the Project A Experimental Battery. For the ASVAB, three types of scores were examined. These scores, listed in Table 13.4, include the nine ASVAB subtest scores (of which the Verbal score is a composite of the Word Knowledge and Paragraph Comprehension subtests), the four ASVAB factor composite scores, and the AFQT (Armed Forces Qualification Test), which is the most direct analog to general cognitive aptitude (i.e., g).

The scores derived from the Experimental Battery were described in Chapter 10 and are listed again in Table 13.5. Note that three different sets

TABLE 13.4
Three Sets of ASVAB Scores Used in Validity Analyses

ASVAB Subtests
 General Science
 Arithmetic Reasoning
 Verbal (Word Knowledge and Paragraph Comprehension)
 Numerical Operations
 Coding Speed
 Auto/Shop Information
 Mathematical Knowledge
 Mechanical Comprehension
 Electronics Information

ASVAB Factor Composites
 Technical (Auto/Shop Information, Mechanical Comprehension, Electronics Information)
 Quantitative (Mathematical Knowledge, Arithmetic Reasoning)
 Verbal (Word Knowledge, Paragraph Comprehension, General Science)
 Speed (Coding Speed, Numerical Operations)

AFQT (Word Knowledge, Arithmetic Reasoning, Paragraph Comprehension, Mathematical Knowledge)

TABLE 13.5

Sets of Experimental Battery Predictor Scores Used in Validity Analyses

Spatial Composite	**ABLE Rational Composites**
Spatial	Achievement Orientation
	Adjustment
Computer Composites	Physical Condition
Psychomotor	Internal Control
Perceptual Speed	Cooperativeness
Perceptual Accuracy	Dependability
Number Speed and Accuracy	Leadership
Basic Speed	
Basic Accuracy	**ABLE-168 Composites**
Short-Term Memory	Locus of Control
Movement Time	Cooperativeness
	Dominance
JOB Composites	Dependability
Autonomy	Physical Condition
High Expectations	Stress Tolerance
Routine	Work Orientation
AVOICE Composites	**ABLE-114 Composites**
Administrative	Locus of Control
Audiovisual Arts	Cooperativeness
Food Service	Dominance
Structural/Machines	Dependability
Protective Services	Physical Condition
Rugged/Outdoors	Stress Tolerance
Social	Work Orientation
Skilled Technical	

of ABLE scores are listed in Table 13.5. The development of the first set, labeled the ABLE Rational Composites, was described in Chapter 10. The other two sets, labeled ABLE-168 and ABLE-114, were based on results of factor analyses of the ABLE items. ABLE-168 was scored using 168 of the ABLE items, and ABLE-114 was scored using only 114 items. The development of these scores is described by White (1994), and summarized in Chapter 18.

Criteria

The first-tour performance measures collected from the LVI sample generated a set of 20 basic scores that were the basis for the LVI performance modeling analysis reported in Chapter 11. Those analyses indicated that the factor model originally developed with the CVI data also yielded the best fit when applied to the LVI data. Again, this model specified the existence of five substantive performance factors and two method factors ("written" and "ratings"). The two methods factors were defined to be orthogonal to the substantive factors, but the correlations among the substantive factors were not so constrained.

The five substantive factors and the variables that are scored on each are again listed in Table 13.6. As in the scoring of the CVI data, both a raw and a residual score were created for each substantive factor. The residual scores for the two "can do" performance factors (Core Technical Proficiency [CTP] and General Soldiering Proficiency [GSP]) were constructed by partialing out variance associated with the written method factor, and the residual scores for the three "will do" scores were constructed by removing variance associated with the ratings method factor.

Consistent with the procedures used for CVI, the GSP factor scores (raw and residual) created for soldiers in MOS 11B (Infantry) are treated as CTP scores in the validity analyses. (Tasks that are considered "general" to the Army for soldiers in most other MOS are considered central or "core" to soldiers in 11B.) In addition to the raw and residual performance factors and the two method factors, total scores from the Hands-On and Job Knowledge

TABLE 13.6
LVI Performance Factors and the Basic Criterion Scores That Define Them

---

Core Technical Proficiency (CTP)
    Hands-On Test—MOS-Specific Tasks
    Job Knowledge Test—MOS-Specific Tasks

General Soldiering Proficiency (GSP)
    Hands-On Test—Common Tasks
    Job Knowledge Test—Common Tasks

Effort and Leadership (ELS)
    Admin: Number of Awards and Certificates
    Army-Wide Rating Scales Overall Effectiveness Rating Scale
    Army-Wide Rating Scales Effort/Leadership Ratings Factor
    Average of MOS Ratings Scales

Maintaining Personal Discipline (MPD)
    Admin: Number of Disciplinary Actions
    Admin: Promotion Rate Score
    Army-Wide Rating Scales Personal Discipline Ratings Factor

Physical Fitness and Military Bearing (PFB)
    Admin. Index—Physical Readiness Score
    Army-Wide Rating Scales Physical Fitness/Bearing Ratings Factor

---

tests were also used in the validation analyses reported in this chapter as validation criteria for comparative purposes.

Analysis Steps

The basic validation analyses consisted of the following steps. First, the listwise deletion sample was used to compute multiple correlations between each set of predictor scores and the five raw substantive performance factor scores (listed in Table 13.6), the five residual performance factor scores, the two method factor scores, and the total scores from the Hands-On and Job Knowledge tests. All multiple correlations were computed separately by MOS and then averaged across MOS. Also, prior to averaging, all results reported here were corrected for multivariate range restriction (Lord & Novick, 1968) and adjusted for shrinkage using Rozeboom's Formula 8 (1978). Corrections for range restriction were made using the 9 × 9 intercorrelation matrix among the subtests in the 1980 Youth Population. Results that have not been corrected for range restriction are reported in Oppler, Peterson, and Russell (1994).

In the second step, the listwise deletion sample was used to compute incremental validity estimates for each set of Experimental Battery predictors (e.g., AVOICE composites or computer composites) over the four ASVAB factor composites. These validity estimates were computed against the same criteria used to compute the validities in the first set of analyses. Once again, the results were computed separately by MOS, corrected for range restriction and adjusted for shrinkage, and then averaged.

Next, the setwise deletion samples were used to compute multiple correlations and incremental validities (over the four ASVAB factor composites) between each set of Experimental Battery predictors and the criteria used in the first two steps. As with the results of the first two steps, these results were also computed separately by MOS, corrected for range restriction and adjusted for shrinkage, and averaged. These results were then compared with the results computed using the listwise deletion sample.

Finally, the listwise deletion sample was used once more to compute multiple correlations and incremental validity estimates (over the four ASVAB factors) for each set of predictors in the Experimental Battery, this time with the results adjusted for shrinkage using the Claudy (1978) instead of the Rozeboom formula. This step was conducted to allow comparisons between the first-tour validity results associated with the longitudinal sample and those that had been reported for the concurrent sample (for which only the Claudy formula was used; see McHenry et al., 1990).

Results

Multiple Correlations for ASVAB and Experimental Battery Predictors (Based on Listwise Deletion Sample)

Estimated multiple correlations for each predictor domain.

Multiple correlations for the four ASVAB factors, the single spatial composite, the eight computer-based predictor scores, the three JOB composite scores, the seven ABLE composite scores, and the eight AVOICE composite scores are shown in Table 13.7.

As indicated above, these results have been corrected for range restriction and adjusted for shrinkage using Rozeboom Formula 8. Based on

TABLE 13.7
Mean of Multiple Correlations Computed Within-Job for LVI Listwise Deletion
Sample for ASVAB Factors, Spatial, Computer, JOB, ABLE, and AVOICE

Criterion[a]	No. of MOS[b]	ASVAB Factors [4]	Spatial [1]	Computer [8]	JOB [3]	ABLE [7]	AVOICE [8]
CTP (raw)	9	62 (13)	57 (11)	47 (16)	29 (13)	21 (09)	38 (08)
GSP (raw)	8	66 (07)	64 (06)	55 (08)	29 (13)	23 (14)	37 (07)
ELS (raw)	9	37 (12)	32 (08)	29 (15)	18 (14)	13 (11)	17 (15)
MPD (raw)	9	17 (13)	14 (11)	10 (16)	06 (13)	14 (11)	05 (10)
PFB (raw)	9	16 (06)	10 (04)	07 (07)	06 (06)	27 (07)	05 (09)
CTP (res)	9	46 (17)	42 (15)	29 (22)	17 (12)	08 (11)	28 (12)
GSP (res)	8	51 (10)	51 (08)	41 (10)	18 (11)	12 (12)	26 (09)
ELS (res)	9	46 (18)	41 (13)	37 (20)	23 (15)	21 (15)	24 (16)
MPD (res)	9	18 (13)	14 (12)	08 (16)	07 (11)	13 (11)	06 (10)
PFB (res)	9	20 (10)	12 (08)	09 (11)	07 (06)	28 (10)	09 (11)
Written	9	54 (13)	49 (12)	43 (18)	29 (16)	23 (12)	29 (14)
Ratings	9	12 (09)	09 (07)	07 (09)	06 (09)	03 (05)	02 (07)
HO-Total	9	50 (14)	48 (11)	38 (15)	18 (13)	11 (11)	28 (09)
JK-Total	9	71 (08)	65 (07)	58 (10)	36 (14)	31 (08)	41 (08)

Note: Results corrected for range restriction and adjusted for shrinkage (Rozeboom Formula 8). Numbers in parentheses are standard deviations. Numbers in brackets are the numbers of predictor scores entering prediction equations. Decimals omitted.

[a] CTP = Core Technical Proficiency; GSP = General Soldiering Proficiency; ELS = Effort and Leadership; MPD = Maintaining Personal Discipline; PFB = Physical Fitness and Military Bearing; HO = Hands-On; JK = Job Knowledge.

[b] Number of MOS for which validity estimates were computed.

the listwise deletion sample, the results in this table indicate that the four ASVAB factors were the best set of predictors for the raw CTP, GSP, ELS, and MPD performance factors, the residual CTP, GSP, ELS, and MPD performance factors, the written and ratings method factors, and the Hands-On and Job Knowledge total scores. The spatial composite and the eight computer composites were next in line, except for MPD, where the ABLE composites and spatial composite were next. The seven ABLE composites had the highest level of validity for predicting the raw and residual PFB factor, with the ASVAB factor composites second.

Comparisons of alternative ASVAB scores.   The average multiple correlations for the three different sets of ASVAB scores are reported in Table 13.8. The results indicate that the four ASVAB factors consistently had higher estimated validities than the other two sets of scores, whereas the AFQT tended to have the lowest.

TABLE 13.8

Mean of Multiple Correlations Computed Within-Job for LVI Listwise Deletion
Sample for ASVAB Subtests, ASVAB Factors, and AFQT

Criterion	No. of MOS[a]	ASVAB Subtests [9]	ASVAB Factors [4]	AFQT [1]
CTP (raw)	9	61 (14)	62 (13)	57 (15)
GSP (raw)	8	66 (07)	66 (07)	62 (08)
ELS (raw)	9	34 (16)	37 (12)	34 (12)
MPD (raw)	9	14 (15)	17 (13)	14 (15)
PFB (raw)	9	10 (09)	16 (06)	12 (06)
CTP (res)	9	45 (18)	46 (17)	39 (19)
GSP (res)	8	50 (10)	51 (10)	45 (09)
ELS (res)	9	44 (22)	46 (18)	43 (20)
MPD (res)	9	13 (14)	18 (13)	15 (15)
PFB (res)	9	15 (11)	20 (10)	15 (11)
Written	9	54 (14)	54 (13)	55 (12)
Ratings	9	09 (10)	12 (09)	11 (10)
HO-Total	9	49 (14)	50 (14)	43 (16)
JK-Total	9	71 (09)	71 (08)	69 (09)

Note: Results corrected for range restriction and adjusted for shrinkage (Rozeboom Formula 8). Numbers in parentheses are standard deviations. Numbers in brackets are the numbers of predictor scores entering prediction equations. Decimals omitted.

[a]Number of MOS for which validity estimates were computed.

TABLE 13.9

Mean of Multiple Correlations Computed Within-Job for LVI Listwise Deletion
Sample for ABLE Rational Composites, ABLE-168, and ABLE-114

Criterion	No. of MOS[a]	ABLE Composites [7]	ABLE-168 [7]	ABLE-114 [7]
CTP (raw)	9	21 (09)	25 (07)	26 (10)
GSP (raw)	8	23 (14)	26 (11)	28 (13)
ELS (raw)	9	13 (11)	15 (12)	16 (12)
MPD (raw)	9	14 (11)	15 (11)	17 (12)
PFB (raw)	9	27 (07)	27 (07)	27 (07)
CTP (res)	9	08 (11)	12 (09)	16 (12)
GSP (res)	8	12 (12)	14 (14)	19 (14)
ELS (res)	9	21 (15)	21 (15)	22 (17)
MPD (res)	9	13 (11)	14 (12)	17 (11)
PFB (res)	9	28 (10)	29 (10)	28 (10)
Written	9	23 (12)	24 (11)	24 (09)
Ratings	9	03 (05)	03 (05)	03 (04)
HO-Total	9	11 (11)	13 (12)	18 (12)
JK-Total	9	31 (08)	32 (08)	33 (09)

Note: Results corrected for range restriction and adjusted for shrinkage (Rozeboom Formula 8). Numbers in parentheses are standard deviations. Numbers in brackets are the numbers of predictor scores entering prediction equations. Decimals are omitted.

[a] Number of MOS for which validity estimates were computed.

Comparisons of alternative ABLE scores.

The average multiple correlations for the three sets of ABLE scores are reported in Table 13.9. The multiple correlations for the second set of alternate ABLE factor scores (those based on the reduced set of items) were consistently higher than those for the other two. Note that the validity estimates for the ABLE Rational composites tended to be the lowest of the three sets of ABLE scores.

Incremental Validities for the Experimental Battery Predictors Over the ASVAB Factors (Based on Listwise Deletion Sample)

Incremental validities by predictor type.   Incremental validity results for the Experimental Battery predictors over the ASVAB factors are shown in Table 13.10. This table reports the average multiple correlations

TABLE 13.10
Mean of Incremental Correlations Over ASVAB Factors Computed Within-Job for
LVI Listwise Deletion Sample for Spatial, Computer, JOB, ABLE Composites,
and AVOICE

Criterion	No. of MOS[a]	ASVAB Factors (A4) [4]	A4+ Spatial [5]	A4+ Computer [12]	A4+ JOB [7]	A4+ ABLE Comp. [11]	A4+ AVOICE [12]
CTP (raw)	9	62 (13)	63 (13)	61 (14)	61 (13)	61 (13)	62 (13)
GSP (raw)	8	66 (07)	68 (07)	66 (07)	66 (07)	66 (07)	66 (07)
ELS (raw)	9	37 (12)	36 (13)	35 (13)	36 (13)	34 (17)	33 (16)
MPD (raw)	9	17 (13)	16 (14)	16 (15)	14 (15)	23 (14)	10 (15)
PFB (raw)	9	16 (06)	13 (08)	09 (08)	17 (08)	30 (06)	12 (10)
CTP (res)	9	46 (17)	47 (17)	44 (18)	45 (18)	43 (19)	46 (19)
GSP (res)	8	51 (10)	53 (09)	51 (10)	50 (10)	50 (10)	50 (10)
ELS (res)	9	46 (18)	47 (18)	44 (21)	45 (21)	45 (22)	44 (21)
MPD (res)	9	18 (13)	15 (14)	15 (14)	14 (14)	22 (14)	12 (13)
PFB (res)	9	20 (10)	18 (12)	13 (11)	20 (11)	34 (10)	18 (13)
Written	9	54 (13)	55 (13)	51 (18)	54 (13)	54 (12)	52 (17)
Ratings	9	12 (09)	11 (08)	09 (10)	09 (10)	09 (08)	05 (08)
HO-Total	9	50 (14)	52 (13)	49 (14)	49 (15)	48 (14)	49 (15)
JK-Total	9	71 (08)	72 (08)	71 (09)	71 (08)	71 (08)	71 (08)

Note: Results corrected for range restriction and adjusted for shrinkage (Rozeboom Formula 8). Numbers in parentheses are standard deviations. Numbers in brackets are the numbers of predictor scores entering prediction equations. Multiple Rs for ASVAB Factors alone are in italics. Underlined numbers denote multiple Rs greater than for ASVAB Factors alone. Decimals omitted.

[a]Number of MOS for which validity estimates were computed.

of each set of Experimental Battery predictors in combination with the four ASVAB factors. These results, based on the listwise deletion sample, were adjusted for shrinkage using the Rozeboom formula and corrected for range restriction. Numbers that are underlined indicate validity estimates higher than those obtained with the four ASVAB factors alone (which are reported in italics).

The results indicate that the spatial composite adds slightly to the prediction of the raw and residual Core Technical and General Soldiering performance factors, as well as to the written method factor and the Hands-on and Job Knowledge total scores. They also show that the seven ABLE composites contribute substantially to the prediction of the raw and residual Personal Discipline and Physical Fitness performance factors.

Multiple Correlations and Incremental Validities Over the ASVAB Factors for the Experimental Battery Predictors (Based on the Setwise Deletion Samples)

Multiple correlations by predictor domain. Multiple correlations for the spatial composite, the eight computer-based composite scores, the three JOB composite scores, the seven ABLE composite scores, and the eight AVOICE composite scores based on the setwise deletion samples described above are reported in Table 13.11. Like the validity results based on the listwise deletion sample reported in Table 13.7, these results have been adjusted for shrinkage using the Rozeboom formula and corrected for range restriction.

TABLE 13.11

Mean of Multiple Correlations Computed Within-Job for LVI Setwise Deletion
Samples for Spatial, Computer, JOB, ABLE Composites, and AVOICE

Criterion	No. of MOS[a]	Spatial [1]	Computer [8]	JOB [3]	ABLE Composites [7]	AVOICE [8]
CTP (raw)	9	58 (11)	49 (16)	31 (13)	21 (09)	39 (07)
GSP (raw)	8	65 (06)	55 (08)	32 (13)	24 (14)	38 (07)
ELS (raw)	9	33 (08)	30 (15)	19 (14)	12 (11)	20 (12)
MPD (raw)	9	14 (11)	10 (16)	06 (13)	15 (11)	05 (11)
PFB (raw)	9	08 (04)	13 (07)	07 (06)	28 (07)	09 (09)
CTP (res)	9	43 (15)	31 (22)	17 (12)	10 (11)	29 (09)
GSP (res)	8	51 (08)	40 (10)	21 (11)	14 (12)	28 (09)
ELS (res)	9	41 (13)	36 (20)	24 (15)	21 (15)	26 (06)
MPD (res)	9	13 (12)	10 (16)	06 (11)	15 (11)	07 (13)
PFB (res)	9	11 (08)	10 (11)	09 (06)	30 (10)	12 (10)
Written	9	51 (11)	46 (16)	31 (17)	25 (11)	32 (15)
Ratings	9	09 (08)	09 (09)	07 (08)	04 (06)	03 (07)
HO-Total	9	50 (11)	38 (15)	20 (13)	13 (11)	30 (07)
JK-Total	9	66 (07)	60 (10)	38 (14)	30 (08)	43 (08)

Note: Results corrected for range restriction and adjusted for shrinkage (Rozeboom Formula 8). Numbers in parentheses are standard deviations. Numbers in brackets are the numbers of predictor scores entering prediction equations. Decimals omitted.
[a] Number of MOS for which validity estimates were computed.

TABLE 13.12
Mean of Multiple Correlations Computed Within-Job for ASVAB Factors Within
Each of the Five LVI Setwise Deletion Samples

Criterion	No. of MOS[a]	ASVAB Factor (Spatial) [4]	ASVAB Factor (Computer) [4]	ASVAB Factor (JOB) [4]	ASVAB Factor (ABLE Comp.) [4]	ASVAB Factor (AVOICE) [4]
CTP (raw)	9	63 (10)	62 (11)	63 (11)	62 (12)	64 (11)
GSP (raw)	8	66 (07)	65 (07)	67 (07)	66 (07)	67 (07)
ELS (raw)	9	37 (10)	37 (12)	37 (11)	36 (11)	37 (11)
MPD (raw)	9	16 (13)	15 (13)	15 (12)	16 (13)	16 (12)
PFB (raw)	9	16 (08)	19 (05)	16 (07)	15 (09)	16 (09)
CTP (res)	9	47 (12)	46 (13)	47 (14)	47 (14)	48 (13)
GSP (res)	8	51 (06)	50 (08)	51 (08)	51 (08)	52 (07)
ELS (res)	9	47 (12)	46 (15)	47 (14)	46 (14)	47 (14)
MPD (res)	9	15 (13)	14 (12)	14 (13)	14 (14)	16 (13)
PFB (res)	9	21 (10)	21 (09)	20 (09)	20 (11)	21 (10)
Written	9	56 (13)	55 (12)	58 (11)	55 (14)	56 (14)
Ratings	9	10 (10)	11 (11)	11 (08)	11 (10)	10 (10)
HO-Total	9	51 (09)	50 (11)	50 (12)	50 (11)	51 (10)
JK-Total	9	71 (09)	71 (08)	72 (08)	71 (09)	72 (09)

Note: Results corrected for range restriction and adjusted for shrinkage (Rozeboom Formula 8). Numbers in parentheses are standard deviations. Numbers in brackets are the numbers of predictor scores entering prediction equations. Decimals omitted.
[a]Number of MOS for which validity estimates were computed.

The multiple correlations computed with the setwise samples are very similar to those computed with the listwise sample. However, the multiple correlations based on the setwise samples are consistently very slightly higher. As noted earlier, we did not expect the validity estimates to either increase or decrease systematically across the listwise and setwise deletion samples. Furthermore, we can offer no plausible theoretical or statistical explanation for these differences. Therefore, attempting to interpret these findings may not be appropriate.

Incremental validities by predictor domain.   Incremental validity results associated with the setwise deletion samples can be found in Tables 13.12 and 13.13. Table 13.12 reports the multiple correlations for the four ASVAB factors alone (as computed separately in each of the

TABLE 13.13

Mean of Incremental Correlations Over ASVAB Factors Computed Within-Job for
LVI Setwise Deletion Samples for Spatial, Computer, JOB, ABLE Composites,
and AVOICE

Criterion	No. of MOS[a]	ASVAB Factors (A4) + Spatial [5]	A4+ Computer [12]	A4+ JOB [7]	A4+ ABLE Composites [11]	A4+ AVOICE [12]
CTP (raw)	9	64 (10)	61 (11)	63 (11)	61 (12)	64 (11)
GSP (raw)	8	69 (06)	66 (07)	67 (07)	66 (08)	66 (07)
ELS (raw)	9	37 (10)	36 (14)	37 (11)	36 (13)	36 (11)
MPD (raw)	9	15 (13)	15 (15)	12 (13)	24 (13)	11 (14)
PFB (raw)	9	15 (08)	17 (05)	17 (07)	32 (04)	15 (10)
CTP (res)	9	48 (12)	45 (14)	46 (14)	45 (14)	47 (14)
GSP (res)	8	54 (06)	50 (08)	51 (08)	50 (07)	50 (07)
ELS (res)	9	47 (12)	43 (20)	46 (15)	46 (15)	46 (14)
MPD (res)	9	14 (13)	13 (15)	13 (13)	22 (12)	11 (14)
PFB (res)	9	20 (11)	18 (11)	20 (10)	36 (08)	21 (11)
Written	9	57 (13)	53 (17)	58 (12)	55 (13)	54 (18)
Ratings	9	10 (09)	11 (11)	11 (09)	11 (07)	06 (09)
HO-Total	9	53 (09)	49 (11)	50 (12)	49 (11)	50 (11)
JK-Total	9	73 (08)	71 (09)	72 (08)	71 (09)	71 (09)

Note: Results corrected for range restriction and adjusted for shrinkage (Rozeboom Formula 8).
Numbers in parentheses are standard deviations. Numbers in brackets are the numbers of predictor
scores entering prediction equations. Underlined numbers denote multiple Rs greater than for ASVAB
Factors alone (as reported in Table 13.12). Decimals omitted.
[a]Number of MOS for which validity estimates were computed.

setwise deletion samples), whereas Table 13.13 reports the multiple correlations for the four ASVAB factors along with each set of predictors in the
Experimental Battery. Numbers underlined in Table 13.13 indicate multiple correlations that are higher than those based on the ASVAB factors
alone. Once again, results are adjusted for shrinkage using the Rozeboom
formula and corrected for range restriction.

The incremental validity results based on the setwise samples are practically identical to those based on the listwise sample. Again, the primary
difference between the two sets of results is that the level of validity estimates are sometimes slightly lower for the listwise sample than for the
setwise samples.

Comparison Between Validity Results Obtained With Longitudinal and Concurrent Samples

Multiple correlations by predictor domain. The final set of results from the first-tour basic validity analyses concerns the comparison between the validity results associated with the longitudinal data (i.e., LVI) and those reported for the concurrent validation data (CVI). Table 13.14 reports the multiple correlations for the ASVAB factors and each set of experimental predictors as computed for the listwise sample in both data sets. Note that there are differences between the CVI and LVI data in the number of predictor composites included in some of the experimental predictor sets. In particular, for the CVI analyses, there were only six computer composites, four ABLE composites, and six AVOICE composites. The results in Table 13.14 have been adjusted for shrinkage and corrected for range restriction. As previously indicated, the adjustments for shrinkage in this step were all made using the Claudy formula, rather than the Rozeboom. This is because the CVI results were not analyzed using the Rozeboom formula. The primary difference between the two corrections is that the Claudy formula estimates the multiple correlation of the population regression equation when applied to the population, whereas the Rozeboom estimates the multiple correlation of the sample-based regression equation when applied to the population. Given the sample sizes in Project A, the difference between the two estimates should be relatively slight.

Also, because the relative sizes of the validity coefficients across the different predictor sets and criterion constructs should be unaffected by the particular adjustment formula used, the comparison between the LVI and CVI results based on the Claudy adjustment should be very much the same as for Rozeboom adjustment. Indeed, a comparison of the Claudy- and Rozeboom-adjusted results for the LVI sample shows that the pattern of results is almost identical (although, as would be expected, the level of estimated validities is slightly higher for the Claudy-adjusted results).

The results in Table 13.14 demonstrate that the patterns and levels of estimated validities are very similar across the two sets of analyses. Still, there are several differences worth pointing out. Specifically, in comparison to the results of the CVI analyses: (a) the LVI estimated validities of the "cognitive" predictors (i.e., ASVAB, spatial, computer) for predicting

TABLE 13.14

Comparison of Mean Multiple Correlations Computed Within-Job for LVI and
CVI Listwise Deletion Samples for ASVAB Factors, Spatial, Computer, JOB,
ABLE Composites, and AVOICE

Criterion	No. of MOS[a]	ASVAB Factors		Spatial		Computer		JOB		ABLE Comp.		AVOICE	
		LV [4]	CV [4]	LV [1]	CV [1]	LV [8]	CV [6]	LV [3]	CV [3]	LV [7]	CV [4]	LV [8]	CV [6]
CTP (raw)	9	63	63	57	56	50	53	31	29	27	26	41	35
GSP (raw)	8	67	65	64	63	57	57	32	30	29	25	40	34
ELS (raw)	9	39	31	32	25	34	26	22	19	20	33	25	24
MPD (raw)	9	22	16	14	12	15	12	11	11	22	32	11	13
PFB (raw)	9	21	20	10	10	17	11	12	11	31	37	15	12
CTP (res)	9	48	47	42	37	35	37	20	21	18	22	33	28
GSP (res)	8	53	49	51	48	44	41	22	22	19	21	31	26
ELS (res)	9	48	46	41	41	40	38	25	27	26	31	29	32
MPD (res)	9	23	19	14	15	14	13	12	10	21	28	13	15
PFB (res)	9	24	21	12	11	17	14	11	10	32	35	16	14

Note: Results corrected for range restriction and adjusted for shrinkage (Claudy Formula). Numbers
in brackets are the numbers of predictor scores entering prediction equations. Decimals omitted.

[a] Number of MOS for which validity estimated were computed.

the "will do" performance factors (ELS, MPD, and PFB) are higher, (b) the
LVI estimated validities of the ABLE composites for predicting the "will
do" performance factors are lower, and (c) the LVI estimated validities of
the AVOICE composites for predicting the "can do" performance factors
(CTP and GSP) are higher.

Further exploration of ELS and ABLE.   As shown in the data
reported above, the largest difference between the CVI and LVI validation
results was in the prediction of the Effort and Leadership (ELS) performance factor with the ABLE basic scores. Corrected for restriction of
range and for shrinkage, the validity of the four ABLE composite scores in
CVI was .33 for ELS and the validity of the seven ABLE composite scores
in LVI was .20. When cast against the variability in results across studies in the extant literature, such a difference may not seem all that large
or very unusual. However, because the obtained results from CVI, CVII,

and LVI have been so consistent, in terms of the expected convergent and divergent results, we initially subjected this particular difference to a series of additional analyses in an attempt to determine the source of the discrepancy.

First, the discrepancy does not seem to arise from any general deterioration in the measurement properties of either the ABLE or the ELS composite in the LVI sample. For example, while the correlation of the ABLE with ELS and MPD went down, the ABLE's correlations with CTP and GSP went up slightly. Similarly, a decrease in the validity with which ELS is predicted is characteristic only of the ABLE. The validity estimates associated with the cognitive measures, the JOB, and AVOICE for predicting ELS actually increased by varying amounts. Consequently, the decrease in validity seems to be specific to the ABLE/ELS correlation and, to a lesser extent, the ABLE/MPD correlation.

Other potential sources of the discrepancy that might exert more specific effects include the following:

- Differences in the way the ABLE was scored in CVI versus LVI. The CVI ABLE analyses included four rationally defined construct scores whereas the LVI analyses were based on seven ABLE composites.
- A possible response bias in the LVI ABLE that affects differentially the validity estimates for predicting different components of performance.
- Measurement contamination in the CVI ABLE that *differentially* inflated validity estimates across performance factors.
- Different content for Effort/Leadership in CVI versus LVI. For example, the rating scales for expected combat performance were a part of ELS for CVI but not for LVI.
- Possible differences in the construct being measured by ELS in CVI versus LVI. That is, because of the rater/ratee cohort differences, the ratings may actually have somewhat different determinants.

While obtaining a definitive answer would subsequently require additional research and analyses, the available database was used initially to rule out a number of explanations.

Results of follow-up analysis. The follow-up analyses were able to rule out two possible additional sources of the CVI/LVI validity differences. First, differences in the composition and number of ABLE basic scores from CVI to LVI do not account for the differences in patterns of validity. We recomputed ABLE composites for the LVI data using the

TABLE 13.15

Multiple Correlations, Averaged Over MOS, for Alternative Sets of ABLE Scores
With Selected Criterion Scores in the LVI Sample

Criterion	ABLE Rational Composites (7)	ABLE-168	ABLE-114	ABLE Composites (4)	
				LV	CV
CTP (raw)	.27	.30	.31	.24	.26
GSP (raw)	.29	.31	.33	.24	.25
ELS (raw)	.20	.22	.24	.20	.33
EL2[a] (raw)	.19	.21	.23	.20	—
MPD (raw)	.22	.22	.24	.21	.32
PFB (raw)	.31	.32	.31	.31	.37

Note: Corrected for restriction of range and adjusted for shrinkage.
[a]EL2 = LV recalculated on CV basis.

composite scoring rules from CVI to determine whether differences in CVI to LVI validity estimates were related to the composition and number of ABLE composites. As shown in Table 13.15, the principal differences between LVI validity estimates for the ABLE scored using CVI keys versus scored using LVI keys were: (a) validity estimates against CTP and GSP dropped somewhat when the CVI key was used, but (b) there were no differences between CVI and LVI keyed validity estimates for the "will do" criteria (i.e., validities did not go up when the CVI key was used with LVI data).

Second, differences in the composition of the Effort/Leadership factor score from CVI to LVI do not account for differences in estimated validity. The LVI-ELS criterion has fewer ratings than the CVI-ELS criterion did, making the weighting of Ratings to Awards smaller than it was in CVI. We reweighted the Rating and Awards components of ELS to make their relative contribution to the construct more similar to CVI. We then compared the validity estimates resulting from both ELS scores. As shown in Table 13.15, there was essentially no difference between them.

The available evidence did *not* rule out two other possible explanations for the different ABLE/ELS correlations. First, there may have been a change in the nature of the construct being measured by the ELS criterion components, which may account for the lower ABLE/ELS validity in the LVI sample. That is, the true score variance of the determinants of ELS might be different for CVI and LVI (e.g., the LVI sample shows greater variability in skill but more uniform levels of motivational determinants). To address this issue, we compared the CVI versus LVI intercorrelations among the variables constituting the ELS criterion. The zero-order correlations between the components of ELS and the Hands-On, Job Knowledge, and ASVAB composite scores were also compared. There was no discernible evidence that the meaning of the scores was different across the two samples.

Second, there is evidence for the possible effects of some degree of response bias in the ABLE during the LVI data collection. Recall that the Experimental Battery was administered just a day or two after induction. The new recruits may easily have ascribed operational importance to the scores even though they were informed otherwise.

As shown in Table 13.16, the Social Desirability scale scores were almost one-half standard deviation higher for the LVI sample than for the CVI sample. Also, mean scores on some of the individual ABLE content scales were higher for the LVI sample than for the CVI sample. Specifically, Internal Control, Traditional Values, Nondelinquency, Locus of Control, and Dependability yielded the greatest CVI to LVI differences. In contrast, there were no differences between the samples on Dominance, and the CVI sample outscored the LVI sample on the Physical Condition scale.

Note that the pattern of CVI to LVI differences in means on the content scales is quite different from those observed during the Trial Battery faking experiment (i.e., the comparison between Honest vs. Fake Good experimental instructions) conducted during the Trial Battery field tests (Peterson, 1987). In the Faking Good condition, the participants changed in the positive direction on all the scales at about the same magnitude, whereas CVI versus LVI differences vary by scale. Dominance, for example, was strongly faked good (effect size = .70) in the faking study, while there was no difference between CVI and LVI on this scale.

A "ceiling effect" occurs when most people obtain high scores on a test. For the CVI sample, the only scale with a ceiling effect was Physical Condition. For the LVI data, the largest ceiling effects occur for Traditional Values and Internal Control, and from the factor-based scores, for Locus of Control. In short, variance is attenuated on these scales.

Additionally, as reported in Table 13.17, the correlations between Social Desirability and the ABLE composite scores are also higher for the LVI sample by about .10. Consider, for example, the seven rational composites used in the LVI analyses. Correlations between Social Desirability and these composites for the CVI sample ranged from .08 to .34 with a mean of .19; for the LVI sample, these correlations ranged from .16 to .41 with a mean of .27.

Finally, we also compared CVI and LVI intercorrelations for a variety of sets of ABLE scores: (a) composites formed using CV rules, (b) composites formed using LV rules, and (c) composites formed using the two factor-based scoring keys. Regardless of the scoring method used, LVI correlations are about .06 to .10 higher than those from CVI data. These results are reported in detail in Oppler et al. (1994).

A limited conclusion.   In general, at this point the somewhat lower correlation of ABLE with Effort/Leadership in LVI seemed at least partially to result from the effects of two influences. First, the greater influence of the social desirability response tendency in LVI seems to produce more positive manifold (i.e., higher intercorrelations for the LVI ABLE basic scores), as contrasted with CVI. This could also lower the correlation of the regression-weighted ABLE composite with ELS, whereas it might not have the same effect with the Core Technical and General Soldiering factors.

Another component of the explanation is the negative correlation between the Social Desirability scale and AFQT. High Social Desirability responders tend to have lower AFQT scores. AFQT and Social Desirability correlated −.22 in the CV sample and −.20 in the LV sample. This would tend to lower the correlation between ABLE and ELS if the correlations between ABLE and ASVAB and between ASVAB and ELS are positive, which they are. Given the above potential explanations, a more definitive answer must await the additional research reported in Chapter 18.

Predicting the True Scores

So far in this chapter, none of the estimated validities have been corrected for criterion unreliability. Table 13.18 shows a comparison of the corrected versus uncorrected estimates for the basic predictor domain multiple correlations that were calculated using the setwise deletion samples.

In general, because of the uniformly high reliabilities for the criterion scores, which are composites of several "basic" scores, the correction

TABLE 13.16

Means, Effect Sizes, and Ceiling Effects for ABLE Scale and Factor-Based Scores, CVI and LVI[a]

Score	No. of Items[b]	CV (N = 8346) Mean	SD	Ceiling[c]	LV (N = 7007) Mean	SD	Ceiling[c]	Effect Size d[d]	Honest vs. Fake Good d[e]
Content Scales									
ABLE Scale 1: Emotional Stability	17	38.98	5.45	-.21	40.14	5.34	-.03	.22	.63
ABLE Scale 2: Self-Esteem	12	28.43	3.71	-.04	28.80	3.85	.13	.10	.66
ABLE Scale 3: Cooperativeness	18	41.89	5.28	-.29	44.41	4.92	.05	.49	.41
ABLE Scale 4: Conscientiousness	15	35.06	4.31	-.31	36.67	4.06	-.05	.38	.56
ABLE Scale 5: Nondelinquency	20	44.25	5.91	-.66	47.82	5.43	-.24	.63	.47
ABLE Scale 6: Traditional Values	11	26.60	3.72	.28	28.98	2.92	.62	.70	.44
ABLE Scale 7: Work Orientation	19	42.92	6.07	-.32	45.16	6.09	.05	.37	.69
ABLE Scale 8: Internal Control	16	38.02	5.11	.05	41.59	4.46	.56	.74	.31
ABLE Scale 9: Energy Level	21	48.44	5.97	-.44	50.41	5.94	-.12	.33	.73
ABLE Scale 10: Dominance	12	27.01	4.27	-.10	27.06	4.57	.04	.01	.70
ABLE Scale 11: Physical Condition	6	13.96	3.05	.67	13.42	2.96	.45	-.18	.71
Response Validity Scales									
ABLE Scale 12: Social Desirability	11	15.46	3.04		16.89	3.41		.45	.87
ABLE Scale 13: Self-Knowledge	11	25.45	3.33		26.21	3.13		.23	-.05
ABLE Scale 14: Non-Random Response	8	7.70	.57		7.68	.59		-.03	.17
ABLE Scale 15: Poor Impression	23	1.51	1.85		1.13	1.58		-.22	-.19

Factor-Based Scores

	N	MN	SD	d	MN	SD	d	d
Factor: Work Orientation (168 items)	45	104.68	12.29	−.47	109.82	12.31	−.05	.42
Factor: Stress Tolerance (168 items)	29	66.61	8.52	.39	68.59	8.68	−.12	.23
Factor: Dominance (168 items)	23	52.36	7.06	−.36	52.98	7.50	−.14	.09
Factor: Dependability (168 items)	33	74.04	9.57	−.61	79.64	8.49	−.28	.62
Factor: Locus Control (168 items)	17	41.41	5.44	.24	45.47	4.37	.74	.81
Factor: Cooperate (168 items)	16	37.36	4.82	−.21	39.58	4.48	.12	.48
Factor: Physical Condition (168 items)	8	18.90	3.55	.56	18.31	3.48	.36	−.17
Factor: Work Orientation (114 items)	28	64.53	8.73	−.23	67.73	8.60	.11	.37
Factor: Stress Tolerance (114 items)	15	34.80	5.13	.01	35.69	5.03	.15	.18
Factor: Dominance (114 items)	19	42.72	6.16	−.32	43.16	6.57	−.11	.07
Factor: Dependability (114 items)	21	48.19	7.06	−.10	52.24	6.15	.25	.61
Factor: Locus Control (114 items)	13	31.82	4.57	.43	35.33	3.51	.96	.85
Factor: Cooperate (114 items)	10	23.54	3.39	.10	25.09	3.01	.37	.48
Factor: Physical Condition (168 items)	8	18.90	3.55	.56	18.31	3.48	.36	−.17

[a]CV and LV samples have been edited for missing data and random responding. Only individuals with complete ABLE data are included.

[b]CV and LV data are scored on the same keys. The keys for CV and LV do not differ in number of items.

[c]The difference between the point two standard deviations above the mean and the maximum possible number of points in SD units. That is, ceiling effect = $MN + 2*SD - Maximum Possible)/SD$. Higher positive values suggest a ceiling effect.

[d]The standardized difference between CV and LV scores. Positive effect sizes occur when LV scores are higher than CV; $d = (MN_{LV} - MN_{CV})/SD_{pooled}$.

[e]From Hough et al. (1990). Honest condition $N = 111–119$; Fake good condition $N = 46–48$. Positive effect sizes indicate higher scores by the Fake Good condition.

371

TABLE 13.17
Correlations Between ABLE Rational Composite Scores and ABLE Social
Desirability Scale

		ABLE-CV Composites (4)	ABLE-LV Composites (7)
CV sample	Range of r	.08–.35	.08–.34
	Mean r	.22	.19
LV sample	Range of r	.16–.45	.16–.41
	Mean r	.31	.27

TABLE 13.18
Mean of Multiple Correlations Computed Within-Job for LVI Setwise Deletion
Sample for ASVAB Factors, Spatial, Computer, JOB, ABLE, and AVOICE.
Comparisons of Estimates Corrected vs. Uncorrected for Criterion Unreliability

Criterion[a]	No. of MOS[b]	ASVAB Factors [4]	Spatial [1]	Computer [8]	JOB [3]	ABLE [7]	AVOICE [8]
CTP (89)	9	63 (71)	58 (64)	49 (55)	31 (35)	21 (24)	39 (44)
GSP (88)	8	66 (75)	65 (74)	55 (61)	32 (36)	24 (27)	38 (43)
ELS (92)	9	37 (40)	33 (36)	30 (33)	19 (21)	12 (13)	20 (22)
MPD (90)	9	16 (18)	14 (16)	10 (11)	06 (07)	15 (17)	05 (06)
PFB (91)	9	16 (18)	08 (09)	13 (14)	07 (08)	28 (31)	09 (10)

Note: Results corrected for range restriction and adjusted for shrinkage (Rozeboom Formula 8).
Correlations in parentheses are corrected for criterion unreliability. Numbers in brackets are the numbers
of predictor scores entering prediction equations. Decimals omitted.
[a]CTP = Core Technical Proficiency; GSP = General Soldiering Proficiency; ELS = Effort and
Leadership; MPD = Maintaining Personal Discipline; PFB = Physical Fitness and Military Bearing.
[b]Number of MOS for which validity estimates were computed.

for attenuation does not change the overall pattern of validity estimates.
The increase in individual coefficients is of course proportional to the
uncorrected estimate. Perhaps the most notable features are the surpris-
ingly high estimates for predicting the first two factors from the interest
measures.

MAXIMIZING SELECTION VALIDITY FOR PREDICTING FIRST-TOUR PERFORMANCE

The basic analyses discussed so far did not use all the information from ASVAB and the Experimental Battery in one equation so as to maximize the degree of predictive accuracy that can be obtained from the full predictor battery. Consequently, we next considered the complete array of full prediction equations for each of the five performance criterion factors in each of the nine Batch A MOS ($5 \times 9 = 45$) and attempted to determine the minimum number of equations that could be used without loss of predictive accuracy. For example, for any particular criterion factor, does each MOS require a unique equation (i.e., nine equations) or will fewer unique equations, perhaps only one, yield the same level of validity in each MOS?

Once the minimum number of equations had been identified, the next step was to estimate the maximum validity (selection efficiency) that could be obtained from a "reduced" prediction equation when the purpose for reducing the length of the test battery was either to (a) maximize selection efficiency, or (b) maximize classification efficiency. With respect to the latter, if the goal was to reduce the number of predictors so as to increase the differences in the equations across MOS (or across criterion factors within MOS), how did that goal affect the selection efficiency of the battery?

The next chapter (Chapter 14) will discuss the analyses that attempted to estimate the maximum validity that could be obtained when prior information about job performance is combined with the available ASVAB and Experimental Battery scores to predict performance during the second tour after reenlistment. Here, we consider the estimation of maximum potential validities for predicting first-tour, or entry level, performance.

Differential Prediction Across Criterion Constructs and Across MOS

The specific purpose here was to consider the extent to which the number of equations developed to predict first-term performance could be reduced from 45 (9 jobs $\times$ 5 equations, one equation per job for each of the five LVI criterion constructs) while minimizing the loss of predictive accuracy. Two separate sets of analyses were conducted—one to evaluate the reduction of equations across criterion constructs, within-MOS, and the other to evaluate the reduction of equations across MOS, within criterion construct.

Sample

To be included in the analyses, soldiers were required to have complete LVI criterion data, complete ASVAB data, and complete data for all composites derived from the Experimental Battery. This resulted in a total sample of 3,086 soldiers (11B = 235; 13B = 551; 19K = 445; 31C = 172; 63B = 406; 71L = 251; 88M = 221; 91A = 535; and 95B = 270).

Predictors

For the present investigation, two sets of predictors were examined. The first set of predictors included the four ASVAB factor composites, plus the one unit-weighted spatial test composite and the eight composite scores obtained from the computerized test measures (for a total of 13 predictors). The second set of predictors included the four ASVAB factors, plus the seven ABLE and eight AVOICE subscale composite scores (for a total of 19 predictors).

Criteria

Up to eight criteria were used in these analyses. These criteria included the five criterion constructs corresponding to the five factors from the LVI performance model (Core Technical Proficiency [CTP], General Soldiering Proficiency [GSP], Effort and Leadership [ELS], Maintaining Personal Discipline [MPD], and Physical Fitness and Military Bearing [PFB], plus three higher-order composites of these five constructs. The three higher-order composites (labeled Can-Do, Will-Do, and Total) were formed by standardizing and adding together CTP and GSP (Can-Do), standardizing and adding together ELS, MPD, and PFB, (Will-Do), and standardizing and adding together Can-Do and Will-Do (Total).

Analysis Procedures

Reducing equations across criterion constructs. For the analyses examining the reduction in prediction equations across criterion constructs, the data were analyzed using a variant of the Mosier (1951) double cross-validation design as follows. Soldiers in each job were randomly split into two groups of equal size, and predictor equations developed for each of the five LVI performance factors (i.e., CTP, GSP, ELS, MPD, and PFB) in one group were used to predict each of the five performance factors in the other group (and vice-versa). More specifically, after the soldiers were divided into groups, covariance matrices (comprising the predictors and criterion measures described above) were computed in each group and corrected for multivariate range restriction. As before, these corrections were made using the covariances among the ASVAB subtests in the 1980 Youth Population (Mitchell & Hanser, 1984). Next, prediction equations were developed for each of the five criteria using the corrected covariance matrix in each group. The prediction equations developed in each group were then applied to the corrected covariance matrix of the other group to estimate the cross-validated correlation between each predictor composite and each of the five criterion constructs. Finally, the results were averaged across the two groups within each job, and then averaged across jobs (after weighting the results within each job by sample size).

In addition to analyzing the data separately by job, a set of analyses was also conducted using data that had been pooled across jobs. Specifically, the two covariance matrices per job described above were used to form two covariance matrices that had been pooled across jobs (i.e., each pooled covariance matrix was formed by pooling the data from one of the matrices computed for each job). These pooled matrices were then analyzed using the same procedures described in the preceding paragraph, except that at the end it was not necessary to average the results across job.

Reducing equations across jobs. For the analyses examining the reduction in prediction equations across jobs, two sets of procedures were used. For the first set, a general linear model analysis was used to determine whether the predictor weights varied significantly across jobs. For the second set, an index of discriminant validity was used to estimate the extent to which predictive accuracy was improved when each job was allowed to have its own equation when predicting performance for a given criterion construct.

The analyses were conducted using two different subsets of the criterion measures. For the first set of predictors (ASVAB, spatial, and computer composites), a subset of five criteria was predicted: CTP, GSP, ELS, Can-Do, and Total. For the second set of predictors (ASVAB, ABLE, and AVOICE composites), a second subset of criteria was created by including MPD, PFB, and Will-Do in place of CTP, GSP, and Can-Do. The criteria for each set were chosen because they were considered the most likely to be predicted by the predictors in those sets. Note that ELS was included in both sets because the LVI basic validation analyses indicated that it was predicted by predictors in both sets.

General Linear Model.   For the general linear model analyses, deviation scores were created within job for all predictors and criteria. This was done to eliminate intercept differences across jobs that may have been caused by differences in selection requirements across jobs. The data were then pooled across jobs and a series of full and reduced linear models were estimated (one set per criterion for each predictor set). For the full models, regression weights were allowed to vary across job in the prediction of a given criterion measure; for the reduced models, regression weights were constrained to be equal across MOS. Finally, the multiple correlations associated with the full and reduced models were compared.

Discriminant Validity.   For the discriminant validity analyses, raw data were used to compute a single covariance matrix for each job, which was then corrected for multivariate range restriction. For each predictor set-criterion combination (e.g., the predictor set with ASVAB, spatial, and computer composites and CTP), these matrices were then used to develop prediction equations separately for each job. The multiple correlations associated with these equations were adjusted for shrinkage and averaged across jobs. This average is referred to here as the mean absolute validity. Next, the prediction equation developed in each job was correlated with performance in all of the other jobs. These across-job correlations were also averaged (but were not adjusted for shrinkage, because they did not capitalize on chance). The mean of these correlations is referred to here as the mean generalizability validity. Finally, discriminant validity was computed as the difference between the mean absolute validity and the mean generalizability validity.

Results

The pooled results of using equations developed for each of the five criterion factors to estimate the validity of each equation for predicting scores on the other four criterion factors are shown in Tables 13.19 and 13.20. When reading down the columns, the cross-validated correlation of the weighted predictor composite with its own criterion factor should be higher than the correlations of composites using weights developed on different criterion factors. This was the general result although the differences

TABLE 13.19

Differential Prediction Across Performance Factors: Mosier Double
Cross-Validation Estimates (Predictor set: ASVAB, Spatial, Computerized Tests)

Prediction Equation	Criterion Construct Scores				
	CTP	GSP	ELS	MPD	PFB
CTP	61[a]	—	37[b]	14	−03
GSP	—	—	—	—	—
ELS	58	—	37	16	02
MPD	40	—	29	16	04
PFB	−05	—	06	05	14

Note: Using pooled covariance matrixes with MOS 11B included; no GSP scores are given because 11B does not have GSP scores.

[a] Diagonal values are mean (across MOS) double cross-validated estimates using prediction equation developed for that specific criterion.

[b] Off diagonal values are mean (across MOS) double cross-validated estimates when a prediction equation developed on one criterion factor is used to predict scores on another.

were not very large in some cases. Again, two different predictor sets were used in the analyses. Table 13.19 used the ASVAB + Spatial + Computerized measures, and Table 13.20 used the ASVAB + ABLE + AVOICE.

Based on the results of the within MOS analysis it was decided, for purposes of future analyses, to maintain a unique equation for each of the criterion factors.

For the comparisons of criterion prediction equations across jobs the interpretation of the general linear model results were ambiguous because of the considerable disparity in degrees of freedom between the analysis of the full equation and the analysis of the reduced equations (e.g., 117 vs. 13 for predicting CTP). The difference between the adjusted and unadjusted estimates of R were so large that it swamped all the effects. The estimate of discriminant validity was approximately .03 for CTP, which constitutes only weak evidence for retaining a unique CTP prediction equation for each MOS. A grouping of the Batch A MOS into "job families" may have produced higher discriminant validity and reduced the number of unique equations from 9 to 3 or 4. However, it was decided for purposes of the current analysis, not to cluster MOS at this point. Using a unique equation

TABLE 13.20
Differential Prediction Across Performance Factors: Mosier Double
Cross-Validation Estimates (Predictor set: ASVAB, ABLE, AVOICE)

Prediction Equation	*Criterion Construct Scores*				
	CTP	*GSP*	*ELS*	*MPD*	*PFB*
CTP	59[a]	—	37[b]	16	−02
GSP	—	—	—	—	—
ELS	54	—	39	19	08
MPD	33	—	28	26	10
PFB	−04	—	09	07	29

Note: Using pooled covariance matrixes with MOS 11B included; no GSP scores are given because 11B does not have GSP scores.

[a]Diagonal values are mean (across MOS) double cross-validated estimates using prediction equation developed for tha specific criterion.

[b]Off diagonal values are mean (across MOS) double cross-validated estimates when a prediction equation developed on one criterion factor is used to predict scores on another.

for CTP for each MOS would constitute a benchmark for later analysis. It was also decided to use the same equation across jobs for the ELS, MPD, and PFB performance factors. This was consistent with the previous results of the concurrent validation analyses. The equation for GSP was not considered further in the subsequent analyses.

In summary, a reduction of the 45 equations to a set of 12 (nine for CTP and one each for ELS, MPD, and PFB) was judged to be a conservative interpretation of the data and to be consistent with the conceptual interpretation of these variables. Consequently, all subsequent analyses in this chapter are focused on this subset of 12 unique prediction equations.

Validity Estimates for Full and Reduced Equations

The objectives for this final part of the analysis were to estimate the predictive validity, in the LVI sample, (a) of the full ASVAB + Experimental Battery predictor set minus JOB ($k = 28$) for the 12 unique equations identified in the previous analysis, and (b) of the same set of 12 unique equations after they were reduced in length with the goal of preserving either maximum selection efficiency or maximum classification efficiency.

Analysis Procedures

The full prediction equations. For each of the 12 unique prediction situations identified in the previous analysis (i.e., one equation for CTP in each MOS and one equation for all MOS for ELS, MPD, and PFB), the appropriate covariance matrices, corrected for range restriction, were used to compute full least squares estimates of the multiple correlation between the full predictor battery (ASVAB plus the Experimental Battery) and the relevant criterion score. This estimate was adjusted using Rozeboom's (1978) Formula 8. The correlations of the weighted composite of all predictors with the criterion were also computed for equal weights for all predictors and when the zero order validity estimates were used as weights. For unit weights and validity weights, no negative weights were used except for AVOICE. For the AVOICE subscores, if a particular composite had a negative correlation with the criterion, the score was weighted negatively.

The validity estimates for predicting CTP were averaged across MOS. All validity estimates were corrected for attenuation in the criterion measure using the reliability estimates reported in Chapter 12.

Obtaining the reduced equation. The reduced equations were obtained via expert judgment using a panel of three experts from the Project A staff. The task for the SMEs was to identify independently what they considered to be the optimal equations, in each of the 12 unique situations, for maximizing selection validities and the optimal equations for maximizing classification efficiency. The judgment task was constrained by stipulating in each case that the prediction equations (i.e., for selection and for classification) could contain no more than 10 predictors. The judges were free to use fewer variables if they thought that a smaller number would reduce error while preserving relevant variance, or would improve classification efficiency without significantly reducing the overall level of selection validity.

The information used by the SMEs for the judgment task consisted of all prior LVI and CVI validation analyses and a factor analysis of the predictor battery, using a pooled 26×26 correlation matrix, which stipulated that the full set of 26 factors (unrotated) should be extracted. The factor scores were then correlated with pooled ELS, MPD, and PFB scores and with the CTP score in each MOS.

Each judge then identified two sets of 12 reduced equations. After looking at the results from each of the other SMEs, the judges revised their specifications. Remaining differences were eliminated via a series of discussions that were intended to reach a consensus. The zero order correlations, regression weights, and predictor battery validity estimates were then recomputed for the two sets (selection vs. classification) of reduced equations.

Expert judgment was used instead of hierarchical regression, or an empirical evaluation of all possible combinations, because the latter was computationally prohibitive and the former runs the risk of too much sample idiosyncracy. In fact, there is no one optimal procedure for identifying such predictor batteries. For any procedure there is a trade-off between adjusting for the capitalization on sample specific chance factors and being able to maximize an unbiased estimate of the population validity.

Results

Tables 13.21 and 13.22 show the results for the SME reduced equations in comparison to the results for the full equations using multiple regression weights. The body of each table contains the recomputed standardized regression weights. Also shown are the foldback and adjusted (via the Rozeboom correction formula) multiple correlations for the reduced equations and the validity estimates using zero order validity weights and unit weights. For comparison purposes, the multiple correlations using the full regression weighted ASVAB plus Experimental Battery predictor set are shown at the bottom of Table 13.21. The results for the reduced equations for ELS, MPD, and PFB are shown in Table 13.23.

In terms of comparisons across MOS, the following points seem relevant. They are based on the overall pattern and relative magnitudes of the recomputed regression weights.

Relative to selection validity for CTP, it is the Quantitative and Technical Knowledge factors on the ASVAB that make the greatest contribution. Overall, among the ASVAB factor scores, they yield the largest and most frequent regression weights. However, Perceptual Speed and Verbal do seem to make a contribution to potential classification

TABLE 13.21

SME Reduced (Optimal) Equations for Maximizing Selection Efficiency for
Predicting Core Technical Proficiency (CTP) in LVI

	Regression Wts. by MOS								
	11B	13B	19K	31C	63B	71L	88M	91A	95B
ASVAB									
Quant	.079	.220	.128	.138	.098	.326	.198	.176	—
PercSp	.135	—	—	.073	.047	.101	—	.130	−.041
Tech Kn	.317	.115	.124	.222	.332	—	.193	.208	—
Verbal	.061	.049	.129	.016	.050	.294	—	.100	.408
SPATIAL									
Total score	.196	.275	.308	.242	.198	.155	.264	.186	.388
COMPUTERIZED									
Movem'ttime	.136	—	—	—	.044	.059	—	—	.059
Num sp&Acc	.094	—	—	—	—	—	—	—	—
Perc Acc	—	.040	—	—	—	.079	—	.059	—
Perc Spd	—	—	—	—	—	—	—	—	—
Psychmotor	—	.034	—	—	—	—	.065	−.021	—
ShorttermM	—	—	—	.029	.106	.010	.138	.092	.125
Basic Spd	—	—	—	.066	—	—	—	—	—
Basic Acc	—	—	—	—	—	—	—	—	.086
ABLE									
Ach Orient	.002	—	.017	—	.014	−.058	—	—	.002
Adjustment	.000	−.046	−.036	—	—	—	—	—	—
Phys.Cond	—	—	—	—	—	—	—	—	—
I/E Control	—	.046	—	—	—	—	—	—	.059
Coopt'ness	—	—	—	—	—	—	.069	—	—
Dependability	—	.106	.079	.133	.073	—	.070	.040	−.070
Leadership									
AVOICE									
Admin'tive	—	—	—	—	—	—	—	—	—
Audio/Vis'l	—	—	—	—	—	.102	—	—	—
Food Serv	—	—	—	−.156	—	—	−.179	—	—
Mechanical	—	—	—	—	.007	—	.262	—	—
ProtectSer	—	—	—	—	—	—	—	—	—
Rug'outdr	.010	−.008	.056	.044	—	—	−.081	.077	.041
Social	—	—	—	—	—	—	—	—	—
Technical	—	—	—	—	—	.031	—	—	—

TABLE 13.21

(Continued)

	Regression Wts. by MOS								
	11B	*13B*	*19K*	*31C*	*63B*	*71L*	*88M*	*91A*	*95B*
N	235	551	445	172	406	251	221	535	270
Reduced Eq.									
FoldBack R	.789	.642	.637	.712	.710	.845	.719	.763	.836
Adjusted R	.765	.624	.617	.663	.691	.829	.683	.751	.820
Validity wts	.773	.625	.626	.693	.691	.827	.687	.756	.798
Unit wts	.737	.580	.556	.691	.651	.757	.632	.741	.665
Full Eq.									
Foldback R	.810	.663	.659	.768	.722	.861	.745	.777	.853
Adjusted R	.747	.614	.596	.650	.670	.821	.649	.748	.813

Note: Dashes indicate that the particular predictor was not included in the reduced equation for that MOS.

efficiency, as judged by the SMEs. They were selected as predictors and had substantial regression coefficients for only a few MOS. The spatial composite from the Experimental Battery was a uniformly strong contributor to selection validity and provided relatively little potential classification efficiency, except for distinguishing 71L and 91A from all other MOS.

Among the computerized measures, Movement Time and Short-term Memory were judged to make the most consistent contribution to selection validity (they were selected for the greatest number of MOS in Table 13.21), whereas Perceptual Speed, Psychomotor Ability, and the accuracy scores seem to make the greatest contribution (although small) to classification efficiency, as indicated by the specificity with which they were assigned to MOS in Table 13.22.

For the ABLE, it is the Dependability scale that is judged to make the greatest contribution to selection validity. The ABLE was seen as contributing very little to potential classification efficiency.

For the AVOICE, the Rugged Outdoor scale was selected as making the most consistent contribution to selection validity, and the AVOICE seems to have considerable potential for making a contribution to classification

TABLE 13.22

SME Reduced (Optimal) Equations for Maximizing Classification Efficiency for
Predicting Core Technical Proficiency (CTP) in LVI

	Regression Wts. by MOS								
	11B	*13B*	*19K*	*31C*	*63B*	*71L*	*88M*	*91A*	*95B*
ASVAB									
Quant	—	.279	—	—	.136	.480	—	.395	—
PercSp	.154	.024	—	—	—	—	—	—	—
Tech Kn	.353	—	.228	.248	.354	—	.234	.274	.213
Verbal	—	—	—	—	—	.360	—	—	.298
SPATIAL									
Total score	.214	.327	.406	.285	.209	—	.331	—	.297
COMPUTERIZED									
Movem'ttime	.121	—	—	—	.046	.089	—	—	.049
Num sp&Acc	.123	—	—	.153	—	−.046	—	—	—
Perc Acc	—	.039	—	—	—	.104	—	—	—
Perc Spd	—	—	.032	—	—	—	.035	—	—
Psychmotor	—	.048	—	—	—	—	.024	—	—
ShorttermM	—	—	—	.029	.116	—	.147	.150	.129
Basic Spd	—	—	—	.067	—	—	—	—	.026
Basic Acc	—	—	—	—	—	—	—	—	.083
ABLE									
Ach Orient	—	—	.014	—	—	—	—	.031	−.033
Adjustment	—	—	—	—	—	—	—	—	—
Phys.Cond	—	—	—	—	—	—	—	—	—
I/E Control	.041	.039	—	—	—	—	—	—	.047
Coopt'ness	—	—	—	—	—	—	.110	—	—
Dependability	—	.086	.079	.143	.074	—	—	.050	—
Leadership	—	—	—	—	—	—	—	—	—
AVOICE									
Admin'tive	−.101	—	—	—	—	—	—	—	−.006
Audio/Vis'l	—	—	—	—	—	.127	—	—	—
Food Serv	.030	—	—	−.154	—	—	−.159	—	.005
Mechanical	—	.038	—	—	—	—	.185	—	—
ProtectSer	—	—	—	—	—	—	—	—	—
Rug'outdr	—	—	.021	.030	—	—	—	.094	—
Social	—	—	—	—	—	−.037	—	—	—
Technical	.098	—	—	—	.041	—	—	−.103	—

TABLE 13.22
(Continued)

	Regression Wts. by MOS								
	11B	*13B*	*19K*	*31C*	*63B*	*71L*	*88M*	*91A*	*95B*
N	235	551	445	172	400	251	221	535	270
Reduced Eq.									
FoldBack R	.792	.636	.622	.710	.710	.835	.707	.750	.842
Adjusted R	.770	.621	.606	.670	.695	.823	.672	.740	.826
Validity wts	.776	.614	.605	.696	.702	.811	.674	.737	.825
Unit wts	.744	.568	.521	.675	.652	.750	.613	.585	.749

Note: Dashes indicate that the particular predictor was not included in the reduced equation for that MOS.

efficiency. The pattern of weights in Table 13.22 is very distinctive and seems to be consistent with the task content of the respective MOS.

The reduced equations for ELS, MPD, and PFB in Table 13.23 (which were obtained only for the goal of maximizing selection validity) show what are perhaps the expected differences in the equations. ASVAB is much more important for predicting ELS than for predicting MPD and PFB. The pattern of ABLE weights is consistent with expectations, and the AVOICE is judged to contribute virtually nothing to the prediction of these three factors.

The mean results across MOS for predicting CTP are shown in Table 13.24. In general, differential predictor weights do provide some incremental validity over unit weights. However, zero-order validity coefficients as weights are virtually as good as regression weights, and the reduced equations yield about the same level of predictive accuracy as the full equations. In fact, the reduced equations do slightly better.

Perhaps the most striking feature in Table 13.24 is the overall level of the correlations. The estimated validities are very high. The best available estimate of the validity of the Project A/Career Force predictor battery for predicting Core Technical Proficiency is contained in the last column of the table, which is the adjusted multiple correlation corrected for unreliability in the criterion (i.e., CTP in LVI). The estimated validities (averaged

TABLE 13.23

SME Reduced (Optimal) Equations for Maximizing Selection Efficiency for
Predicting Will-Do Criterion Factors

| | *Regression Wts. by Criterion Factors* | | |
	ELS	*MPD*	*PFB*
ASVAB			
Quant	.059	.073	.010
PercSp	.075	—	—
Tech Kn	.189	.088	—
Verbal	—	—	—
SPATIAL			
Total score	—	—	—
COMPUTERIZED			
Movem'ttime	.050	—	.052
Num sp&Acc	—	—	—
Perc Acc	—	—	—
Perc Spd	—	—	—
Psychmotor	—	—	—
ShorttermM	.056	.040	—
Basic Spd	—	—	—
Basic Acc	—	—	—
ABLE			
Ach Orient	—	—	.064
Adjustment	—	—	—
Phys.Cond	—	—	.245
I/E Control	—	−.086	—
Coopt'ness	—	—	—
Dependability	.088	.207	.049
Leadership	.047	—	—
AVOICE			
Admin'tive	—	—	—
Audio/Vis'l	—	—	—
Food Serv	—	—	—
Mechanical	—	—	—
ProtectSer	—	—	—
Rug'outdr	—	—	—
Social	—	—	—
Technical	—	—	—

TABLE 13.23
(Continued)

| | *Regression Wts. by Criterion Factors* | | |
	ELS	*MPD*	*PFB*
N	3086	3086	3086
Reduced Eq.			
FoldBack R	.354	.232	.310
Adjusted R	.347	.224	.304
Validity wts	.346	.202	.297
Unit wts	.341	.187	.252
Full Eq.			
Foldback R	.372	.277	.346
Adjusted R	.349	.243	.321

Note: Dashes indicate that the particular predictor was not included in the reduced equation for that criterion.

TABLE 13.24
Estimates of Maximizing Selection Efficiency Aggregated over MOS
(Criterion is Core Technical Proficiency)

| | *Mean Selection Validity* | | | | |
	Unit Wts.	*Valid. Wts.*	*Fold Back-R*	*Adj. R*	*Corr. R^a*
Full equation (all predictors)	.570	.697	.762	.701	(.772)
Reduced equation (selection)	.668	.720	.739	.716	(.789)
Reduced equation (classification)	.651	.716	.734	.714	(.786)

[a]Corrected for criterion unreliability.

over MOS) in this column are $.78 \pm .01$. The reduced equations produce this level of accuracy, which does break the so-called validity ceiling, just as readily as the full equation, with perhaps more potential for producing classification efficiency. The analyses that attempt to estimate the actual gains in classification efficiency are reported in Chapter 16.

SUMMARY AND CONCLUSIONS

The preceding analyses of basic validation results and the "optimal battery" results for the LVI sample produced a number of noteworthy findings in relation to the objectives that guided this round of analyses. Generally speaking, the ASVAB was the best predictor of performance. However, the composite of spatial tests provided a small amount of incremental validity for the "can do" criteria and the ABLE provided larger increments for two of the three "will do" criteria (Maintaining Personal Discipline, and Physical Fitness and Bearing).

With regard to the alternative ASVAB scoring options for prediction purposes, results indicate highly similar results across three methods, with a very slight edge going to multiple regression equations using the four ASVAB factor scores in the equation. These factors are unit-weighted composites of the ASVAB subtests.

In the evaluation of several ABLE scoring options, the method using factor scores computed from a subset of all the ABLE items proved to have generally higher estimated validities, but the differences were not large. The issues surrounding the need for shorter forms are discussed in greater detail in Chapter 18.

One of the most interesting findings is the comparison between the longitudinal validation and the concurrent validation results. Such comparisons are rare, because it is extremely difficult to conduct a concurrent validation and longitudinal validation study in the same organization on the same set of varied jobs using essentially the same predictors and criteria. It is particularly noteworthy because the predictors and criteria are comprehensive and carefully developed *and* the sample sizes are large. Aside from the concurrent versus longitudinal design difference, only cohort differences (both examinees and raters/scorers) can explain any disparities in the validation results.

Generally, the pattern and level of the validity coefficients are highly similar across the two samples. The correlation between the CV and LV coefficients in Table 13.14 is .962 and the root mean squared difference between the two sets of coefficients is .046.

Note, however, that the correlation is not 1.00, nor is the RMS difference zero. As we described previously, the validity estimates are lower for predicting the "will do" criteria in the longitudinal sample than in the concurrent sample. Although several explanations for these findings were ruled out, the possibility that the differences may have been due to changes in the response patterns of examinees in the longitudinal sample could not be. This finding is particularly important in that the timing and conditions under which the ABLE was administered to the longitudinal sample is probably much closer to operational than that associated with the administration of the ABLE to the examinees in the concurrent sample. Again, these issues are revisited in Chapter 18 in the context of the implementation of research results.

Consistent with the results from CVI, the analysis of the LVI data for the Batch A MOS indicated differential prediction across performance factors within MOS and differential prediction across MOS for the CTP factor but not for the other performance factors. For this set of 12 unique equations, the best estimate of the population value for selection validity is the observed correlation corrected for restriction of range, unreliability in the criterion, and the fitting of error by the predictor weighting procedure. The resulting estimates of the population validity are very high, both for the equations using all predictors and the equations using a reduced set of predictors ($k < 10$). Predictor sets selected to maximize classification efficiency also yield high selection validity. To the extent that it exists, differential validity across MOS is judged to be a function of the ASVAB, the computerized perceptual and psychomotor measures, and the AVOICE. Estimates of actual classification gains for the various equations will be presented in a subsequent chapter (Chapter 15).

14

The Prediction of Supervisory and Leadership Performance

Scott H. Oppler, Rodney A. McCloy, and John P. Campbell

During their second tour of duty, Army enlisted personnel are expected to become considerably more expert in their positions and to begin taking on supervisory and leadership responsibilities. This is analogous to the first promotion to a supervisory position in the private sector. As in civilian human resource management, a number of critical questions arise with regard to selection and promotion decisions for supervisory and leadership positions. This chapter addresses the following: To what extent do pre-employment (i.e., pre-enlistment) measures predict performance beyond the entry level, or first term of enlistment? Does early performance predict later performance, when additional responsibilities such as supervision are required? What is the optimal combination of selection and classification test information and first-tour performance data for predicting second-tour job performance? This chapter summarizes the results of analyses intended to answer these and other questions. Recall, as described in Chapters 9 and 11, that both the concurrent and longitudinal samples were followed into their second tour of duty and their performance was assessed again.

We will first present the results of analyses designed to estimate the basic validities for ASVAB and Experimental Battery predictors against the second-tour performance factors as well as the incremental validities for the Experimental Battery predictors over the four ASVAB factor composites. Next, we will compare the estimated validities and incremental validities of the Experimental Battery predictors reported for LVI with those estimated for LVII. Thirdly, we will report the correlations between performance in the first tour and performance in the second tour. Finally, we evaluate the incremental validity of first-tour performance over the ASVAB and Experimental Battery for predicting second-tour performance.

THE BASIC VALIDATION ANALYSES

Procedure

Sample

These analyses are based on a different sample editing procedure than was used in Chapter 13. The previous longitudinal first-tour (LVI) analyses used both "listwise deletion" and "setwise deletion." The listwise deletion samples were composed of soldiers having complete data for all the Experimental Battery predictors, the ASVAB, and the LV first-tour performance factors. For the setwise procedure, soldiers were required to have complete data for each of the first-tour performance factors, the ASVAB, and the predictor scores in a particular set.

The number of soldiers with complete predictor and criterion data (the listwise deletion sample) in each MOS is shown in Table 14.1 for both the LVI and LVII samples. Note that in the LVII sample only two MOS (63B and 91A) have more than 100 soldiers with complete predictor and criterion data. Indeed, 88M had such a small sample size that these soldiers were excluded from the validation analyses. Also, recall from Chapter 9 that no MOS-specific criteria or supervisory simulation data were administered to soldiers in the 31C MOS, so those soldiers were also excluded from the LVII validation analyses. The number of soldiers in each MOS in the LVII sample who were able to meet the setwise deletion requirements is larger, but even this relaxed sample selection strategy resulted in three MOS (19K, 71L, and 88M) with sample sizes of fewer than 100 soldiers.

Consequently, a third sample editing strategy termed "predictor/criterion setwise deletion" was used. Specifically, to be included in the validation sample for a given criterion/predictor set pair, soldiers were required to have

TABLE 14.1

Soldiers in LVI and LVII Data Sets With Complete Predictor and Criterion Data by MOS

MOS		LVI	LVII
11B	Infantryman	235	83
13B	Cannon Crewmember	553	84
19K	M1 Armor Crewman	446	82
31C[a,b]	Single Channel Radio Operator	172	—
63B	Light-Wheel Vehicle Mechanic	406	105
71L	Administrative Specialist	252	77
88M[b]	Motor Transport Operator	221	37
91A/B	Medical Specialist	535	118
95B	Military Police	270	93
Total		3,163	679

[a]MOS-specific and supervisory simulation criterion data were not collected for MOS 31C in LVII.

[b]MOS 31C and 88M were not included in LVII validity analyses.

complete data for the ASVAB, the predictor scores in the predictor set being examined, and only the specific criterion score being predicted. Thus, in addition to not requiring complete predictor data for every analysis, the third strategy also did not require complete data for all of the criterion scores.

This further increased the available sample sizes, and Table 14.2 reports the number of soldiers in each MOS meeting the predictor/criterion setwise deletion sample criteria for the Core Technical Proficiency criterion. This table indicates that 88M was now the only MOS with fewer than 100 soldiers, regardless of the predictor set. Similar results and sample sizes were found for the other criterion constructs.

Based on these findings, all analyses reported in this chapter were conducted using samples selected with the predictor/criterion setwise deletion strategy. However, because of the small sample size, 88M (along with 31C) was not included.

Predictors

The predictor scores were the same as those used in the first-tour validation analyses reported in the preceding chapter.

TABLE 14.2
Soldiers in LVII Sample Meeting Predictor/Criterion Setwise Deletion Data
Requirements for Validation of ASVAB Scores and Spatial, Computer,
JOB, ABLE, and AVOICE Experimental Battery Composites Against
Core Technical Proficiency by MOS

| | *Predictor Sets* | | | | | |
MOS	ASVAB	Spatial	Computer	JOB	ABLE	AVOICE
11B	333	322	112	301	297	309
13B	170	165	152	159	148	156
19K	156	130	130	122	123	129
63B	169	147	139	136	132	140
71L	147	115	104	105	109	102
88M[a]	84	56	54	51	52	53
91A/B	205	191	174	185	165	183
95B	160	149	140	142	133	145
Total	1,424	1,275	1,005	1,201	1,159	1,217

[a]MOS 88M was not included in LVII validity analyses.

Criteria

The second-tour measures generated a set of over 20 basic scores that were the basis for the LVII performance modeling analysis reported in Chapter 11. The model of second-tour performance (labeled the Leadership Factor model) specified six substantive performance factors and three method factors ("paper-and-pencil," "ratings," and "simulation exercise"). The three methods factors were defined to be orthogonal to the substantive factors, but the correlations among the substantive factors were not so constrained.

The six substantive factors and the variables that are scored on each are listed again in Table 14.3. Three of the six correspond exactly to factors in the first-tour model developed using the Concurrent Validation (CVI) sample and confirmed using LVI (Oppler, Childs, & Peterson, 1994). These factors are Core Technical Proficiency (CTP), General Soldiering Proficiency (GSP), and Physical Fitness and Military Bearing (PFB). Consistent with the procedures used for LVI, the GSP factor scores created for soldiers in

TABLE 14.3
LVII Performance Factors and the Basic Criterion Scores That Define Them

Core Technical Proficiency (CTP)
    Hands-On Test—MOS-Specific Tasks
    Job Knowledge Test—MOS-Specific Tasks

General Soldiering Proficiency (GSP)
    Hands-On Test—Common Tasks
    Job Knowledge Test—Common Tasks

Achievement and Effort (AE)
    Admin: Number of Awards and Certificates
    Army-Wide Rating Scales Overall Effectiveness Rating Scale
    Army-Wide Rating Scales Technical Skill/Effort Ratings Factor
    Average of MOS Rating Scales
    Average of Combat Prediction Rating Scales

Personal Discipline (PD)
    Admin: Number of Disciplinary Actions
    Army-Wide Rating Scales Personal Discipline Ratings Factor

Physical Fitness and Military Bearing (PFB)
    Admin: Physical Readiness Score
    Army-Wide Rating Scales Physical Fitness/Bearing Ratings Factor

Leadership (LDR)
    Admin: Promotion Rate Score
    Army-Wide Rating Scales Leading/Supervising Ratings Factor
    Supervisory Role-Play – Disciplinary Structure
    Supervisory Role-Play – Disciplinary Communication
    Supervisory Role-Play – Disciplinary Interpersonal Skill
    Supervisory Role-Play – Counseling Diagnosis/Prescription
    Supervisory Role-Play – Counseling Communication/Interpersonal Skills
    Supervisory Role-Play – Training Structure
    Supervisory Role-Play – Training Motivation
    Situational Judgment Test—Total Score

MOS 11B are treated as CTP scores in the validity analyses. (Tasks that are considered "general" to the Army for soldiers in most other MOS are considered central or "core" to soldiers in 11B.)

Two of the second-tour performance factors—Achievement and Effort (AE) and Personal Discipline (PD)—have a somewhat different composition than their first-tour counterparts (Effort and Leadership [ELS] and Maintaining Personal Discipline [MPD], respectively). That is, the second-tour Achievement and Effort factor contains one score (the average of the Combat Performance Prediction Rating Scales) that was not included in the first-tour Effort and Leadership factor and does not include any rating scales reflective of leadership performance. Also, the second-tour Personal Discipline factor is missing one score (Promotion Rate) that was incorporated in the first-tour version of that factor. The sixth second-tour performance factor—Leadership (LDR)—has no counterpart in the first-tour performance model, although it does include the Promotion Rate score that had previously been included in the first-tour MPD factor and all rating scales reflective of leadership performance.

In addition to the six performance factors, four additional criteria were used in the analyses reported here. Two of these are variations of the Leadership factor. The first variation (LDR2) does not include the Situational Judgment Test (SJT) total score that was included in the original Leadership factor, and the second variation (LDR3) does not include either the SJT or the scores from the supervisory role-play exercises. The other two criteria included in the validation analyses are the total scores from the Hands-On job sample and the written Job Knowledge measures.

Analysis Steps

In the first set of analyses, multiple correlations between the set of scores in each predictor domain and the substantive performance factor scores, the two additional leadership performance factor scores, and the total scores from the Hands-On and Job Knowledge measures were computed separately by MOS and then averaged. Results were computed both with and without correcting for multivariate range restriction (Lord & Novick, 1968). Corrections for range restriction were made using the 9×9 intercorrelation matrix among the subtests in the 1980 Youth Population. All results were adjusted for shrinkage using Rozeboom's (1978) Formula 8.

In the second set of analyses, incremental validity estimates for each set of Experimental Battery predictors (e.g., AVOICE composites or computer composites) over the four ASVAB factor composites were computed against the same criteria used to compute the estimated validities in the first set of analyses. Once again, the results were computed separately by MOS and then averaged. Also, the results were computed both with and without correcting for range restriction, and were adjusted for shrinkage using the Rozeboom formula. All analyses used the predictor/criterion setwise deletion sample.

Basic Validation Results

Multiple Correlations for ASVAB and Experimental Battery Predictors

Multiple correlations for the four ASVAB factors, the single spatial composite, the eight computer-based predictor scores, the three JOB scores, the seven ABLE scores, and the eight AVOICE scores are reported in Table 14.4. Using the predictor/criterion deletion sample, these results were computed separately by MOS and then averaged. These results have also been adjusted for shrinkage using the Rozeboom formula and corrected for range restriction.

The results in Table 14.4 indicate that the four ASVAB factors were the best set of predictors for all of the criterion performance factors except

TABLE 14.4

Mean of Multiple Correlations Computed Within-Job for LVII Samples for
ASVAB Factors, Spatial, Computer, JOB, ABLE Composites, and AVOICE:
Corrected for Range Restriction

Criterion[a]	No. of MOS[b]	ASVAB Factors [4]	Spatial [1]	Computer [8]	JOB [3]	ABLE [7]	AVOICE [8]
CTP	7	64 (10)	57 (11)	53 (11)	33 (17)	24 (19)	41 (12)
GSP	6	63 (06)	58 (05)	48 (10)	28 (19)	19 (17)	29 (24)
AE	7	29 (14)	27 (13)	09 (11)	07 (12)	13 (17)	09 (15)
PD	7	15 (12)	15 (10)	12 (12)	03 (05)	06 (10)	06 (10)
PFB	7	16 (11)	13 (06)	03 (06)	07 (08)	17 (15)	09 (13)
LDR	7	63 (14)	55 (08)	49 (13)	34 (21)	34 (20)	35 (24)
LDR2	7	51 (16)	46 (12)	35 (19)	26 (21)	25 (22)	25 (24)
LDR3	7	47 (13)	39 (12)	31 (15)	19 (18)	23 (17)	20 (21)
HO-Total	7	46 (13)	41 (14)	33 (21)	24 (11)	12 (15)	21 (18)
JK-Total	7	74 (05)	67 (03)	58 (06)	37 (16)	29 (17)	44 (14)

Note: Predictor/criterion setwise deletion sample. Adjusted for shrinkage (Rozeboom Formula 8). Numbers in brackets are the numbers of predictor scores entering prediction equations. Numbers in parentheses are standard deviations. Decimals omitted.

[a]CTP = Core Technical Proficiency; GSP = General Soldiering Proficiency; AE = Achievement and Effort; PD = Personal Discipline; PFB = Physical Fitness/Military Bearing; LDR = Leadership; LDR2 = Leadership minus Situational Judgment Test; LDR3 = Leadership minus Situational Judgment Test and Supervisory Role-Play Exercises; HO = Hands-On; JK = Job Knowledge

[b]Number of MOS for which validity estimates were computed.

PFB. The highest multiple correlation was between the ASVAB factors and the Job Knowledge score (R = .74), whereas the lowest was with the PD and PFB scores (R = .15 and .16, respectively).

With the exception of the prediction of PFB with the ABLE composites, the spatial composite was the next best predictor. The pattern of multiple correlations for the spatial composite was highly similar to the ASVAB pattern.

The three JOB composites, the seven ABLE composites, and the eight AVOICE composites had different patterns of multiple correlations for the different criterion performance factors. The AVOICE was highest among the three for CTP, GSP, LDR, and the Job Knowledge score, while JOB was highest for the Hands-On criterion; ABLE was highest for AE, PFB, LDR2, and LDR3.

In general, with regard to the ABLE, the highest correlations are with the Leadership factor and the Core Technical Proficiency factor. Comparatively, the correlations of the ABLE with Achievement and Effort and with Personal Discipline are lower. In large part this reflects the emergence

TABLE 14.5

Mean of Multiple Correlations Computed Within-Job for LVII Samples for
ASVAB Subtests, ASVAB Factors, and AFQT: Corrected for Range Restriction

Criterion	No. of MOS[a]	ASVAB Subtests [9]	ASVAB Factors [4]	AFQT [1]
CTP	7	64 (10)	64 (10)	61 (08)
GSP	6	62 (07)	63 (06)	58 (09)
AE	7	28 (10)	29 (14)	28 (13)
PD	7	12 (11)	15 (12)	16 (11)
PFB	7	10 (08)	16 (11)	16 (06)
LDR	7	64 (10)	63 (14)	62 (15)
LDR2	7	51 (13)	51 (16)	50 (16)
LDR3	7	46 (13)	47 (13)	45 (14)
HO-Total	7	45 (12)	46 (13)	43 (13)
JK-Total	7	74 (05)	74 (05)	70 (06)

Note: Predictor/criterion setwise deletion samples. Adjusted for shrinkage (Rozeboom Formula 8). Numbers in brackets are the numbers of predictor scores entering prediction equations. Numbers in parentheses are standard deviations. Decimals omitted.

[a]Number of MOS for which validity estimates were computed.

of a separate leadership factor and the fact that the promotion rate index produced a better fit for the LVII model when it was scored as a Leadership component than as a component of the Personal Discipline factor. A faster promotion rate for second-tour personnel is more a function of good things that happen rather than an absence of negative events that act to slow an individual's progression, as it was for first-tour positions.

Comparisons of alternative ASVAB scores.   The average multiple correlations for the three different sets of ASVAB scores are reported in Table 14.5. The results indicate that, as before, the four ASVAB factors tended to have slightly higher estimated validities than the other sets of scores, whereas the AFQT tended to have slightly lower estimated validities. Each column of this table is based on exactly the same set of samples.

Comparisons of alternative ABLE scores.   The average multiple correlations for the three sets of ABLE scores are reported in Table 14.6. The results indicate that the pattern and levels of multiple correlations

TABLE 14.6
Mean of Multiple Correlations Computed Within-Job for LVII Samples for ABLE
Composites, ABLE-168, and ABLE-114: Corrected for Range Restriction

Criterion	No. of MOS[a]	ABLE Composites [7]	ABLE- 168 [7]	ABLE- 114 [7]
CTP	7	24 (19)	30 (10)	27 (15)
GSP	6	19 (17)	18 (16)	18 (17)
AE	7	13 (17)	12 (14)	11 (17)
PD	7	06 (10)	05 (09)	04 (07)
PFB	7	17 (15)	16 (16)	16 (14)
LDR	7	34 (20)	26 (25)	27 (25)
LDR2	7	25 (22)	24 (23)	25 (23)
LDR3	7	23 (17)	19 (18)	20 (19)
HO-Total	7	12 (15)	12 (13)	14 (14)
JK-Total	7	29 (17)	30 (13)	28 (15)

Note: Predictor/criterion setwise deletion samples. Adjusted for shrinkage (Rozeboom Formula 8). Numbers in brackets are the numbers of predictor scores entering prediction equations. Numbers in parentheses are standard deviations. Decimals omitted.
[a]Number of MOS for which validity estimates were computed.

were generally very similar across the three sets. However, the ABLE com-
posites were somewhat better predictors of LDR ($R = .34$) than were the
ABLE-168 and ABLE-114 factor scores ($R = .26$ and $.27$, respectively).
Again, the estimates in each column were computed on the same samples.

Incremental Validity Estimates for the Experimental Battery Over the ASVAB

Incremental validity results for the Experimental Battery predictors over
the ASVAB factor composites are reported in Table 14.7. The results
indicate that there were no increments to the prediction of any of the
performance components for the computer, JOB, or AVOICE composites.
The spatial composite added slightly to the prediction of GSP, AE, and
JK-Total, and the ABLE composites added an average of .05 to the prediction of PFB (from $R = .13$ for ASVAB alone to $R = .18$ for ASVAB

TABLE 14.7

Mean of Incremental Correlations Over ASVAB Factors Computed Within-Job for
LVII Samples for Spatial, Computer, JOB, ABLE Composites, and AVOICE:
Corrected for Range Restriction

Criterion	No. of MOS[a]	ASVAB Factors (A4) + Spatial [5]	A4 + Computer [12]	A4 + JOB [7]	A4 + ABLE Composites [11]	A4 + AVOICE [12]
CTP	7	65 (11)	63 (10)	65 (11)	65 (11)	64 (13)
GSP	6	<u>62</u> (08)	62 (10)	60 (11)	60 (10)	57 (12)
AE	7	<u>33</u> (10)	10 (14)	30 (15)	24 (20)	20 (18)
PD	7	16 (12)	16 (17)	14 (15)	13 (12)	06 (11)
PFB	7	12 (10)	08 (11)	13 (11)	<u>18</u> (15)	11 (16)
LDR	7	63 (12)	61 (15)	63 (13)	<u>65</u> (13)	62 (13)
LDR2	7	51 (17)	48 (20)	49 (20)	50 (24)	48 (19)
LDR3	7	45 (20)	41 (21)	42 (23)	45 (22)	40 (24)
HO-Total	7	46 (15)	43 (17)	44 (15)	43 (21)	39 (23)
JK-Total	7	<u>75</u> (05)	73 (06)	74 (06)	74 (06)	73 (06)

Note: Predictor/criterion setwise deletion samples. Adjusted for shrinkage (Rozeboom Formula
8). Numbers in brackets are the numbers of predictor scores entering prediction equations. Numbers in
parentheses are standard deviations. Underlined numbers denote multiple Rs greater than for ASVAB
Factors alone (as reported in Table 3.13 of Oppler, Peterson, & Rose [1994]). Decimals omitted.

[a] Number of MOS for which validity estimates were computed.

and ABLE together). The estimates of incremental validity for each of the three sets of ABLE scores over the ASVAB factors were very similar.

COMPARISON BETWEEN VALIDITY RESULTS OBTAINED WITH FIRST-TOUR AND SECOND-TOUR SAMPLES

The next set of results concerns the comparison between the validity estimates computed for the first-tour Longitudinal Validation (LVI) sample and those reported for the second-tour Longitudinal Validation (LVII) sample.

Levels of Validity

The multiple correlations for the ASVAB factors and each domain of experimental predictors for LVI and LVII are shown in Table 14.8. The estimates have been corrected for range restriction and adjusted for shrinkage.

Note that the first-tour results are based on the setwise deletion strategy described above and the LVII analyses did not include two MOS (31C and 88M). Also, as described earlier, there were differences between the components of the Achievement and Effort (AE) and Personal Discipline (PD) factors computed for soldiers in the LVII sample and their corresponding factors in the LVI sample (Effort and Leadership [ELS] and Maintaining Personal Discipline [MPD], respectively).

The results in Table 14.8 demonstrate that the patterns and levels of estimated validities are very similar across the two organizational levels, especially for the four ASVAB factor composites. The greatest discrepancies concern the multiple correlations between the ABLE composites and two of the three "will do" criterion factors: [Maintaining] Personal Discipline and Physical Fitness and Military Bearing. Specifically, the multiple correlation between ABLE and the discipline factor decreases from .15 in LVI to .06 in LVII, and the multiple correlation between ABLE and Physical Fitness and Military Bearing decreases from .28 to .17.

Some of the decrease in the ABLE's ability to predict the Personal Discipline factor may be due to the removal of the Promotion Rate score. The estimated validities of the other predictors were not similarly affected

TABLE 14.8

Comparison of Mean Multiple Correlations Computed Within-Job for ASVAB
Factors, Spatial, Computer, JOB, ABLE Composites, and AVOICE Within LVI
and LVII Samples: Corrected for Range Restriction

	No. of MOS[b]		ASVAB Factors [4]		Spatial [1]		Computer [8]		JOB [3]		ABLE [7]		AVOICE [8]	
Criterion[a]	LVI	LVII	LVI	LVII	LVI	LVII	LVI	LVII	LVI	LVII	LVI	LVII	LVI	LVII
CTP	9	7	63	64	58	57	49	53	31	33	21	24	39	41
GSP	8	6	66	63	65	58	55	48	32	28	24	19	38	29
ELS/AE	9	7	34	29	33	27	30	09	19	07	12	13	20	09
MPD/PD	9	7	16	15	14	15	10	12	06	03	15	06	05	06
PFB	9	7	12	16	08	13	13	03	07	07	28	17	09	09
HO-Total	9	7	50	46	50	41	38	33	20	24	13	12	30	21
JK-Total	9	7	73	74	66	67	60	58	38	37	30	29	43	44

Note: LVI setwise deletion samples; LVII predictor/criterion setwise deletion sample. Adjusted for shrinkage (Rozeboom Formula 8). Numbers in brackets are the numbers of predictor scores entering prediction equations. Decimals omitted.

[a]CTP = Core Technical Proficiency; GSP = General Soldiering Proficiency; ELS = Effort and Leadership (LVI); AE = Achievement and Effort (LVII); MPD = Maintaining Personal Discipline (LVI); PD = Personal Discipline (LVII); PFB = Physical Fitness/Military Bearing; HO = Hands-On; JK = Job Knowledge

[b]Number of MOS for which validity estimates were computed.

by this scoring change. Again, the highest correlation for the ABLE in LVII was with the Leadership factor ($R = .34$). The LVII Leadership factor includes the promotion rate index, all scores derived from the supervisory role-plays, *and* the Army-wide rating scale Leading and Supervising factor, which was part of the ELS factor in CVI and LVI. In effect, these differences were expected to decrease the ABLE correlations and increase the ASVAB correlations with the LVII Achievement and Effort factor, which is more reflective of technical achievement than was the ELS factor in LVI and CVI. The expected patterns are what were found, and they lend further support to the construct validity of the performance models.

Predicting True Scores

Finally, Table 14.9 shows the validity estimates corrected for unreliability in the second-tour performance measures and compares them to the uncorrected estimates previously shown in Table 14.4. Again, the criterion

TABLE 14.9
Mean of Multiple Correlations Computed Within-Job for LVII Samples for
ASVAB Factors, Spatial, Computer, JOB, ABLE Composites, and AVOICE:
Corrected for Range Restriction. Comparison of Estimates Corrected vs.
Uncorrected for Criterion Unreliability

Criterion[a]	No. of MOS[b]	ASVAB Factors [4]	Spatial [1]	Computer [8]	JOB [3]	ABLE [7]	AVOICE [8]
CTP	7	64 (76)	57 (68)	53 (63)	33 (39)	24 (29)	41 (49)
GSP	6	63 (74)	58 (67)	48 (56)	28 (33)	19 (22)	29 (34)
AE	7	29 (31)	27 (29)	09 (10)	07 (07)	13 (14)	09 (10)
PD	7	15 (17)	15 (17)	12 (13)	03 (03)	06 (07)	06 (07)
PFB	7	16 (17)	13 (14)	03 (03)	07 (08)	17 (18)	09 (10)
LDR	7	63 (68)	55 (59)	49 (53)	34 (37)	34 (37)	35 (38)

Note: Predictor/criterion setwise deletion sample. Adjusted for shrinkage (Rozeboom Formula 8). Numbers in brackets are the numbers of predictor scores entering prediction equations. Numbers in parentheses are corrected for criterion unreliability. Decimals omitted.
[a]CTP = Core Technical Proficiency; GSP = General Soldiering Proficiency; AE = Achievement and Effort; PD = Personal Discipline; PFB = Physical Fitness/Military Bearing; LDR = Leadership.

reliability estimates used to make the corrections are those presented in Chapter 12.

Summary of Basic Validation Analyses

The preceding analyses of basic validation results for the LVII second-tour sample produced results that were largely consistent with those obtained during the basic validation analyses for the entry level LVI sample.

Furthermore, not only were the LVII results similar in pattern to those of the LVI analyses, they were also similar in magnitude (with the notable exception of some of the ABLE validities, which were substantially lower in LVII). In particular, the multiple correlations between the ASVAB factor composites and second-tour criterion scores were rarely more than .02–.03 lower than the multiple correlations between the ASVAB factors and the corresponding first-tour criteria. Given the length of time between the collection of the first- and second-tour performance measures (approximately three years), this level of decrement in estimated validities is remarkably small.

With regard to the options for using ASVAB subtest scores to form prediction equations, the LVII results indicate highly similar results across the three methods examined with a slight advantage going to the equations using the four factors. Similar results were obtained for the LVI sample.

The method using factor scores computed from the subset of 114 ABLE items proved to have generally higher estimated validities in the LVI sample, although the differences were not large. In comparison, the LVII results indicate that the estimated validities of the three sets of scores were very similar.

Finally, the results of the present analyses indicate that the estimated validity of ASVAB as a predictor of the Leadership factor, even uncorrected for criterion attenuation, is quite high ($R = .63$ for the four ASVAB factor composites), as are the validities for the other cognitive predictors in the Experimental Battery. In fact, none of the predictor sets (including the JOB, ABLE, and AVOICE) had multiple correlations of less than .34 with this criterion. Furthermore, multiple correlations between ASVAB and the two modified versions of this score ($R = .51$ for LDR2, and $R = .47$ for LDR3) indicate that the relationships between the ASVAB and the Leadership factor cannot be explained purely as being due to shared "written verbal" method variance. The only "paper-and-pencil" component of the Leadership factor—the Situational Judgment Test—was not used in computing LDR2 or LDR3.

THE PREDICTION OF SECOND-TOUR PERFORMANCE FROM PRIOR PERFORMANCE

Besides determining the validity of the selection and classification test battery for predicting performance as an NCO during the second tour of duty, the study design also permits the prediction of future performance from current performance. In a civilian organization this is analogous to asking whether current job performance in a technical, but entry level, position predicts future performance as a supervisor.

As described in Chapter 12, to examine the prediction of second-tour performance from first-tour performance the five factors from the first-tour (LVI) performance model were correlated with the six factors identified by the second-tour performance model. Also included in the matrix was a single scale rating of NCO (i.e., leadership) potential based on first-tour performance and a single scale rating of overall performance obtained for second-tour incumbents. The resulting 6 × 7 matrix of cross correlations was generated by calculating each of the 42 correlations within each of the second-tour jobs. The individual correlations were then averaged across the nine jobs.

All correlations were corrected for restriction of range by using a multivariate correction that treated the six end-of-training performance factors (see Chapter 12) as the "implicit" selection variables on the grounds that, in comparison to other incidental selection variables, these factors would have the most to do with whether an individual advanced in the organization.

Making the corrections in this way means that the referent population consists of all the soldiers in the LV sample who had completed their training course. This is the population for which we would like to estimate the prediction of second-tour performance with first-tour performance, and it is the population for which the comparison of the estimated validities of the experimental predictor tests and training criteria as predictors of future performance is the most meaningful. As long as the implicit selection variables are the best available approximation to the explicit selection variables, the corrected coefficients will be a better estimate of the population values than the uncorrected coefficients, but they will still be an underestimate (Linn, 1968). Because the degree of range restriction from the end of training (EOT) to first-tour job incumbency (LVI) is not great, the effects of the corrections were not very large.

The 6 (LVI) by 7 (LVII) correlation matrix is shown as Table 14.10. The composition of the five first-tour performance factors and the six second-tour performance factors are as shown previously in Chapter 11. Two correlations are shown for each relationship. The left-hand figure is the mean correlation across MOS corrected for restriction of range (using the training sample as the population) but not for attenuation. These values were first corrected for range restriction within MOS and then averaged. The value in the parentheses is the same correlation after correction for unreliability in the measure of "future" performance, or the criterion variable when the context is the prediction of future performance from past performance. The reliability estimates used to correct the upper value were the median values of the individual MOS reliabilities described in Chapter 12. The mean values across MOS were slightly lower and thus less conservative than the median.

The correlations of first-tour performance with second-tour performance are quite high, and provide strong evidence for using measures of first-tour performance as a basis for promotion, or for the reenlistment decision. The correlation between the first-tour single-scale rating of NCO potential and

TABLE 14.10

Zero-Order Correlations of First-Tour Job Performance (LVI) Criteria With
Second-Tour Job Performance (LVII) Criteria: Weighted Average Across MOS

	LVI:CTP	LVI:GSP	LVI:ELS	LVI:MPD	LVI:PFB	LVI:NCOP
LVII: Core Technical Proficiency (CTP)	44 (52)	41(49)	25 (30)	08 (10)	02 (02)	22 (26)
LVII: General Soldiering Proficiency (GSP)	51(60)	*57 (67)*	22 (26)	09 (11)	−01 (−01)	19 (22)
LVII: Effort and Achievement (EA)	10 (11)	17 (18)	*45 (49)*	28 (30)	32 (35)	43 (46)
LVII: Leadership (LEAD)	36 (39)	41(44)	*38* (41)	27 (29)	17 (18)	41 (44)
LVII: Maintain Personal Discipline (MPD)	−04 (−04)	04 (04)	12 (13)	*26 (29)*	17 (19)	16 (18)
LVII: Physical Fitness and Bearing (PFB)	−03 (−03)	−01 (−01)	22 (24)	14 (15)	*46 (51)*	30 (33)
LVII: Rating of Overall Effectiveness (EFFR)	11 (14)	15 (19)	35 (45)	25 (32)	31 (40)	41 (53)

Note: Total pairwise Ns range from 333–413. Corrected for range restriction. Correlations between matching variables are underlined. Leftmost coefficients are not corrected for attenuation. Coefficients in parentheses are corrected for attenuation in the criterion (second-tour performance). Decimals omitted.

Labels:
LVI: Core Technical Proficiency (CTP)   LVI: Maintain Personal Discipline (MPD)
LVI: General Soldiering Proficiency (GSP)   LVI: Physical Fitness and Bearing (PFB)
LVI: Effort and Leadership (ELS)   LVI: NCO Potential (NCOP)

the second-tour single-scale rating of overall effectiveness, corrected for unreliability in the second tour rating, is .53.

There is also a reasonable pattern of convergent and divergent validity across performance factors, even without correcting these coefficients for attenuation and thereby controlling for the effects of differential reliability. The greatest departure from the expected pattern is found in the differential correlations of the two "can do" test-based factors (i.e., CTP and GSP). Current CTP does not always correlate higher with future CTP than current GSP correlates with future CTP. The correlation patterns for the "will do" factors, which are based largely on ratings, virtually never violate the expected pattern. The one possible exception to the consistent results for the "will do" factors is the predictability of the leadership performance factor for second-tour personnel. This component of NCO performance is predicted by almost all components of past performance. Such a finding is consistent with a model of leadership that views leadership performance as multiply determined by technical, interpersonal, and motivational factors.

"OPTIMAL" PREDICTION OF SECOND-TOUR PERFORMANCE

Having examined separately the validity of the test battery and the validity of entry level performance for predicting later supervisory performance, the next logical step was to combine them in the same equation. For a small sample of individuals for whom second-tour performance measures are available, the Project A database can also provide ASVAB scores, Experimental Battery scores, and first-tour performance measures. Consequently, for such a sample it was possible to estimate the validity with which the components of second-tour performance could be predicted by alternative combinations of ASVAB factor scores, Experimental Battery predictor composites, and LVI performance factor assessments.

Sample and Analysis Procedure

For these analyses, soldiers were required to have complete data on (a) the four ASVAB composites, (b) nine of the Experimental Battery basic scores, (c) the five LVI performance criteria, and (d) five of the six LVII performance scores. Listwise deletion was favored over pairwise deletion in this case because a number of different kinds of variables were combined in the

TABLE 14.11

Variables Included in Optimal Prediction of Second-Tour Performance Analyses

---

PREDICTORS

ASVAB: Quantitative   Experimental Battery: Spatial
        Speed   Rugged/Outdoors Interests (AVOICE)
        Technical   Achievement Orientation (ABLE)
        Verbal   Adjustment (ABLE)
                                                       Physical Condition (ABLE)
                                                       Cooperativeness (ABLE)
                                                       Internal Control (ABLE)
                                                       Dependability (ABLE)
                                                       Leadership (ABLE)

First-Tour Performance (LVI): Can-Do (CTP + GSP)
                               Will-Do (ELS + MPD + PFB)

LVII CRITERIA

        Core Technical Proficiency (CTP)
        Leadership (LDR)
        Effort/Achievement (EA)
        Will-Do (LDR + EA + MPD + PFB)

---

same equation raising the possibility of ill-conditioned covariance matrices (e.g., not positive definite). In light of the multivariate adjustment applied to the primary covariance matrix (i.e., correction for range restriction), the loss of sample size was considered less detrimental to the analyses than the possibility of a poor covariance structure. Only a subset of Experimental Battery predictors was included so that the predictor/sample size ratio remained reasonable for the LVII analyses. The variables are listed in Table 14.11.

Two MOS did not appear in the analyses—19E (too few soldiers) and 31C (no LVII criterion scores). Sample sizes for each of the MOS constituting the LVII analytic samples ranged from 10 to 31 and the total number of usable cases was 130.

The basic procedure was to calculate the multiple correlations for a selected set of hierarchical regression models. The correlations reflect (a) correction for range restriction using the procedure developed by Lawley and described by Lord and Novick (1968, p. 147), and (b) adjustment for shrinkage using Rozeboom's Formula 8 (1978).

For the prediction of second-tour performance, the procedure used to correct for range restriction is a function of the specific prediction, or personnel decision, being made, which in turn governs how the population parameter to be estimated is defined. There are two principal possibilities.

First, we could be interested in predicting second-tour or supervisory performance at the time the individual first applies to the Army. In this case, the referent population would be the applicant sample. Second, we could be interested in the reenlistment decision and in predicting second-tour performance from information available during an individual's first tour. In this case, the referent population is all first-tour job incumbents; it is the promotion decision that is being modeled.

For these analyses the relevant decision was taken to be the promotion decision and a covariance matrix containing the ASVAB composites, the selected Experimental Battery predictors, LVI Can-Do and Will-Do composites, and the five basic LVI criterion composites served as the target matrix. The end-of-training (EOT) measures were treated as incidental, rather than explicit, selection variables. The matrix was calculated using scores from all first-tour (LVI) soldiers having complete data on the specified measures ($N = 3,702$).

Results

A summary of the results is shown in Table 14.12. A hierarchical set of three equations for predicting four LVII performance factors are included. The four second-tour performance criterion scores were (a) the Core Technical Proficiency (CTP) factor, (b) the Leadership (LDR) factor, (c) the Achievement and Effort (EA) factor, and (d) the Will-Do composite of EA, LDR, MPD, and PFB. The three alternative predictor batteries follow:

1. ASVAB alone (4 scores).
2. ASVAB + the Experimental Battery (4 + 9 scores).
3. ASVAB + the Experimental Battery + LVI Performance (4 + 9 + 1 scores). The LVI performance score is either the Can-Do composite of (CTP + GSP) or the Will-Do composite of (ELS + MPD + PFB), depending on the criterion score to be predicted. The LVI Can-Do composite was used in the equation when CTP was being predicted, and the LVI Will-Do composite was used in the equation when the LVII LDR, EA, and Will-Do criterion scores were being predicted.

Three estimates of each validity are shown in Table 14.12: (a) the unadjusted, or foldback multiple correlation coefficient, (b) the multiple R corrected for shrinkage, and (c) the zero order correlation of the unit weighted

TABLE 14.12

Multiple Correlations for Predicting Second-Tour Job Performance (LVII) Criteria
from ASVAB and Various Combinations of ASVAB, Selected Experimental
Battery Predictors, and First-Tour (LVI) Performance Measures:
Corrected for Restriction of Range and Criterion Unreliability

| LVII Criterion | Type | *Predictor Composite* | | | |
		A	A + X	A + X + 1	1
CTP	Unadj	69	80	80	35
	Adj	64	69	68	35
	Unit	52	39	42	35
Can-Do	Unadj	72	83	86	54
	Adj	68	74	76	54
	Unit	60	50	54	54
LDR	Unadj	43	61	76	53
	Adj	36	43	65	53
	Unit	40	43	50	53
EA	Unadj	23	30	58	54
	Adj	00	00	38	54
	Unit	16	13	21	54
Will-Do	Unadj	18	33	62	57
	Adj	00	00	47	57
	Unit	14	15	23	57

Note: Unadj and Adj reflect raw and shrunken (by Rozeboom, 1978, Formula 8) multiple correlations, respectively. Decimals omitted.

    Key: A = ASVAB factors (Quant, Speed, Tech, Verbal).

       X = Experimental Battery (Spatial, Rugged/Outdoors Interests, Achievement Orientation, Adjustment, Physical Condition, Internal Control, Cooperativeness, Dependability, Leadership).

       1 = The LVI Can-Do or Will-Do composite.

predictor composite with the criterion. All three estimates have been corrected for unreliability in the criterion measures.

When predicting Core Technical Proficiency, the fully corrected estimate of the population validity using ASVAB alone is .64. Adding the Experimental Battery raises it to .69, but LVI performance does not add incrementally. The corresponding increments for the Can-Do composite criterion are .68 to .74 to .76. First-tour performance information adds considerably more to the prediction of LDR, EA, and the Will-Do composite.

For example, for LDR, the validities go from .36 (ASVAB alone) to .43 (ASVAB + EB) to .65 (ASVAB + EB + LVI).

The results for the EA and Will-Do criteria scores show the danger of developing differential weights for multiple predictors when the sample size is small and the true score relationships are not overly high. In such cases, regression weights can be less useful than unit weights and adding additional predictors with low zero validities can result in a lower overall accuracy for the prediction system.

SUMMARY AND CONCLUSIONS

The above results show again that cognitive ability measures are very predictive of the technical components of performance and the estimated level of predictive accuracy is not reduced very much as the job incumbents progress from being in the organization 2 to 3 years to having 6 to 7 years of experience and promotion to a higher level job. Over this time interval at least, the validity of cognitive tests does not decline.

Although the sample size available for estimation is small, the data show reasonably clearly that the incremental value of prior performance over cognitive ability for predicting future performance is with regard to the future leadership and effort components. Conversely, while prior performance has a strong correlation with all components of future performance, it does not provide incremental validity over cognitive ability measures when the criterion consists of measures of technical task performance that attempt to control for individual differences in motivation and commitment.

Overall, the estimated validities for predicting both technical performance and leadership/supervisory performance after reenlistment and promotion are quite high. This is true even when the observed correlations are corrected back to the first tour sample and not to the applicant population. If all information is used, promotion decisions can be made with considerable accuracy.

15

Synthetic Validation and Validity Generalization: When Empirical Validation is Not Possible

Norman G. Peterson, Lauress L. Wise, Jane Arabian, and R. Gene Hoffman

Using Project A results, optimal prediction equations could be developed for 9 or 21 Military Occupational Specialties, depending on the performance measures used, and classification efficiency could be examined across the same MOS. However, the Army must select and assign people to approximately 200 jobs. How are the decisions for the other 180 jobs to be informed?

There are three major ways to approach this issue:

- Empirical validation studies, like those conducted in Project A, could be carried out for all MOS.
- Because the 21 MOS in Project A/Career Force were selected to be representative of clusters of many more MOS judged to be similar in content within each cluster, validity generalization could be assumed for all MOS in the cluster.
- A synthetic validation procedure could be used to select a predictor battery for each MOS. The 21 MOS in the Project A sample provide a means for empirically validating any such synthetic procedures.

411

The last strategy was the focus of the Synthetic Validation Project. Although this research used Project A data, it was not part of the Project A /Career Force project, per se.

A GENERAL OVERVIEW

The "synthetic validity" approach was first introduced by Lawshe (1952) as an alternative to the situational validity approach, which requires separate validity analyses for each job in the organization. Balma (1959) defined synthetic validity as "discovering validity in a specific situation by analyzing jobs into their components, and combining these validities into a whole."

Guion (1976) provided a review of several approaches to conducting synthetic validation. The approach most relevant to the problem at hand involves:

- identifying a taxonomy of job components that can account for the content of performance across a range of jobs,
- using criterion-related validity information or expert judgment to estimate the validity of potential predictors of each component of job performance, and
- developing predictor composites for each job by combining the prediction equations for each of the job components that are relevant to the job.

The usefulness of this approach depends on three critical operations.

First, the taxonomy of relevant job components must be reasonably exhaustive of the job population under consideration, such that the critical parts of any particular job can be described completely by some subset of the taxonomy.

Second, it must be possible to establish equations for predicting performance on each component, such that the prediction equation for a given component is independent of the particular job and there are reliable differences between the prediction equations for different components. To the extent that the same measures predict all components of performance to the same degree, the prediction equations will necessarily be the same across jobs, and a validity generalization model would apply.

Third, synthetic validation models assume that overall job performance can be expressed as the weighted or unweighted sum of performance on the critical individual components. Composite prediction equations are typically expressed as the corresponding sum of the individual component prediction equations, assuming that errors in estimating different components of performance are uncorrelated.

PROJECT DESIGN

The general design of the Synthetic Validity Project was as follows. After a thorough literature search (Crafts, Szenas, Chia, & Pulakos, 1988) and review of alternative methods for describing job components, three approaches for describing job components were evaluated. These were based on our own and previous work in constructing taxonomies of human performance (e.g., J. P. Campbell, 1987; Fleishman & Quaintance, 1984; Peterson & Bownas, 1982).

The first was labeled *Job Activities*. The components were defined as general job behaviors that are not task specific, but that can underlie several job tasks. Examples might be "recalling verbal information" or "driving heavy equipment." Some concerns were that it may be difficult to develop a taxonomy of behavior in sufficient detail to be useful, that the judgments of job relevance might be difficult, and that general "behaviors" as descriptors may not be accepted by those making the judgments.

The descriptive units in the second approach were *Job Tasks*. An initial list of performance tasks was developed in Project A from available task descriptions of the 111 enlisted jobs with the largest number of incumbents. These descriptions provided a basis for defining job components that are clusters of tasks, called task categories, rather than individual tasks. The chief advantages of this model were a close match to previous empirical validity data and the familiarity of Army Subject Matter Experts (SMEs) with these kinds of descriptions. The primary concerns were that the task category taxonomy might not be complete enough to handle new jobs and that the relationships of individual predictors to performance on task categories might be difficult to determine reliably and accurately.

For these first two approaches, SMEs were asked to make various ratings, including (a) the frequency with which the activities/tasks categories were performed on the focal job, (b) their importance for successful performance, and (c) the difficulty of reaching and maintaining an acceptable level of proficiency on the task or activity.

The third descriptive unit was called the *Individual Attribute*. Individual attributes are job requirements described in terms of mental and physical abilities, interests, traits, and other individual difference dimensions. A variety of rating and ranking methods were tried out to obtain SME judgments of the expected validity of the attributes for predicting performance on specific jobs. The chief concerns were that there might not be any SMEs with enough knowledge about both the job and the human attribute dimensions to describe job requirements accurately, and that this approach might not be as acceptable to policy makers as a method based on more specific job descriptors.

The project then followed an iterative procedure. The previous literature and the predictor and criterion development efforts in Project A were used by the project staff to develop an initial taxonomy for the job activity, task category, and individual attribute descriptors. After considerable review and revision, a series of exploratory workshops was then conducted with Army SMEs to assess the completeness and clarity of each of the alternative job analysis descriptor taxonomies. These initial development efforts were followed by three phases of further development and evaluation. In Phase I, initial procedures were tested for three of the Project A MOS (Wise, Arabian, Chia, & Szenas, 1989). In Phase II, revised procedures were tested for seven more Project A MOS (Peterson, Owens-Kurtz, Hoffman, Arabian, & Whetzel, 1990). The final revisions of the procedures were tested in Phase III using all 20 Project A MOS and one MOS not sampled by Project A (Wise, Peterson, Hoffman, Campbell, & Arabian, 1991). Throughout, the emphasis was on the identification and evaluation of alternative approaches to the implementation of synthetic validation.

GENERAL PROCEDURE FOR THE DEVELOPMENT AND EVALUATION OF ALTERNATIVE SYNTHETIC PREDICTION EQUATIONS

In general, the development of the synthetic prediction equations involved using expert judgment to establish (a) the linkages between the individual attributes (predictors) and each of the substantive components of performance (defined either as Job Activities or Task Categories), and (b) the linkages between each of the activity or task components and each of the jobs (MOS) under consideration (see Figure 15.1). The performance component to MOS linkage was made for each of three criterion constructs. The three criteria were Core Technical Proficiency and General Soldiering Proficiency, as assessed in Project A and as defined in Chapter 11, and Overall Performance, which was a weighted sum of all five criterion components specified for first-tour soldiers by the Project A model. There was also a

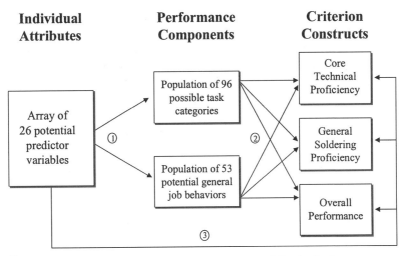

Individual Attributes   **Performance Components**   **Criterion Constructs**

① = Estimated (by psychologist SMEs) correlation between each predictor variable and each task category and each general job behavior.

② = Judgments (frequency/importance) by Army SMEs for the relevance of each task category and each general job behavior for each performance criterion for each specific MOS.

③ = Estimated (by psychologist SMEs) correlation between each predictor variable and each criterion variable for each specific MOS.

FIG. 15.1.   Model of alternative synthetic prediction equations.

judgment of the direct linkage of each attribute to performance on the three criterion variables for each job.

The weights for the attributes to component linkages and the attributes to specific MOS performance variables were provided by psychologist SMEs. The weights for the component to job linkage were provided by Army SMEs. The linkage weights were used in various ways (described in the following sections) to form predictor score composites composed of a weighted sum of relevant attributes.

The psychologists' judgments of the attribute/component and attribute/ job linkages were expressed in correlation terms. That is, for example, they estimated the expected correlation between a predictor and performance on a job component. The Army SME linkage judgments were made on three different response scales: frequency, importance, and difficulty. All three judgments used a 5-point Likert scale.

Evaluations of synthetic validity procedures focus on two indices— absolute validity and discriminant validity—which must be estimated from sample data. Absolute validity refers to the degree to which the synthetic equations are able to predict performance in the specific jobs for which they were developed. For example, how well would a particular synthetic equation derived for soldiers in 19K predict Core Technical Proficiency in that MOS if it could be applied to appropriate sample data? Data from Project A were used to obtain empirical estimates of these validities. The second criterion, discriminant validity, refers to the degree to which performance in each job is better predicted by the synthetic equation developed specifically for that job, than by the synthetic equations developed for the other MOS. For instance, how much better can the synthetic equation developed for 19K predict Core Technical Proficiency in that MOS than the synthetic equations developed to predict Core Technical Proficiency in each of the other MOS? Empirical estimates of correlations relevant to this criterion were also derived from data collected in Project A.

Within these basic steps, several different methods were used to form alternative predictor equations. The equations varied by the criterion being predicted, the method of forming the attribute-by-component weights, the method of forming the component-by-job weights, and the techniques used to directly "reduce" the number of predictor measures included in the final equation.

Variables

The Criterion Predicted

Scores for both Core Technical and Overall Performance criteria were available from the Project A database, so it was possible to evaluate the validity of synthetic equations for predicting both. For developing the synthetic equations, only the component-by-job weights are affected. When the object of prediction was Core Technical Proficiency, the task category judgments for Core Technical Proficiency were used, and when the object of prediction was Overall Performance, the task category judgments for Overall Performance were used.

Attribute-By-Component Weights

Three different methods were used to form the attribute-by-component weights. One method for developing prediction equations for each job component used attribute weights that were directly proportional to the attribute-by-component validities estimated by psychologists. This was called the validity method. A second alternative was to use zero or one weights (called the 0-1 attribute weight method). In this alternative, all attributes with mean validity ratings for a component less than 3.5 (corresponding to a validity coefficient of .30) were given a weight of 0 and all remaining attributes were given a weight of 1. A third alternative was identical to the 0-1 weight, except that when a mean validity rating was 3.5 or greater, the weight given was proportional to the estimated validity (as in the first method) rather than set to 1. This was called the 0-mean weighting method.

Attribute-By-Job-Weights

The direct linkage between the attributes and MOS specific performance was expressed either as a correlation or as a rank ordering of the criticality of attributes for each MOS.

Component-By-Job or "Criticality" Weights

With regard to these "criticality" weights, one issue was whether the use of cutoffs or thresholds (that is, setting lower weights to zero) produced higher discriminant validities without sacrificing much absolute validity. Another issue was whether the grouping of similar MOS into clusters might produce synthetic equations with higher absolute or discriminant validities than those produced by MOS-specific equations. Therefore, four types of criticality weights based on the mean task importance ratings could be computed for an MOS or for a cluster of MOS. The same four could be computed for frequency and difficulty, although not all were.

1. Mean importance ratings computed across all SMEs for an MOS, labeled "MOS Mean Component Weights."
2. Mean importance ratings computed across all SMEs for an MOS transformed such that means < 3.5 were set to zero, and means above 3.5 were left as is, labeled "MOS Threshold Component Weights."
3. Mean of "MOS mean" importance ratings for MOS that were similar in terms of their mean task importance profiles (determined by performing a Ward and Hook clustering of all MOS based on the appropriate profiles; see below), labeled "Cluster Mean Component Weights."
4. Transformed "Cluster Mean" ratings, using the same cutoff criteria (set to zero if < 3.5), labeled "Cluster Threshold Component Weights."

To obtain the criticality weights described in procedures 3 and 4 above, the MOS were clustered by correlating their profiles of mean task category importance scores, and then performing a Ward and Hook clustering on the

TABLE 15.1

MOS Clusters Based on Mean Task Importance for Core Technical Proficiency
and Overall Performance

CORE TECHNICAL PROFICIENCY

Cluster	MOS
1. Electronics	27E, <u>29E</u>, 31C, <u>31D</u>
2. Administration/Support	55B, 71L, 76Y, 91A, 94B, <u>96B</u>
3. Combat	11B, 12B, 13B, 16S, 19K, 54B, 95B
4. Mechanical/Construction	51B, 63B, 67N, 88M

OVERALL PERFORMANCE

Cluster	MOS
1. Electronics/Repair	27E, <u>29E</u>, 31C, <u>31D</u>, 63B, 67N
2. Administration/Support	55B, 71L, 76Y, 88M, 91A, 94B, <u>96B</u>
3. Combat	11B, 12B, 13B, 16S, 19K, 51B, 54B, 95B

Note: No attribute x job performance validity matrix is available for the underlined MOS (29E, 31D, 96B). These MOS were not included in the synthetic
equation analyses.

correlation matrices (Wilkinson, 1988). This was done for both the Core
Technical importance ratings and the Overall importance ratings. These
analyses were carried out for the 21 MOS included in all phases of the Synthetic Validity Project. Four clusters were selected as the most meaningful
solution for the Core Technical importance ratings, and labeled as Electronics, Administration/Support, Combat, and Mechanical/Construction. Three
clusters were selected as the most meaningful solution for the Overall importance ratings: Electronics/Repair, Administration/Support, and Combat.
The clusters are shown in Table 15.1. The MOS identifiers are shown in
Table 15.2.

Evaluation Sample Data

The empirical predictor measure and job performance data used to evaluate
the synthetic methods were taken from the Project A Concurrent Validation

TABLE 15.2

MOS Included in Each Phase of Project and Sample Size for Project A CV Data

MOS	Label	SV Phase	CV Sample Size
11B	Infantryman	1	491
12B	Combat Engineer	3	544
13B	Cannon Crewmember	3	464
16S	MANPADS Crewmember	2	338
19K	Armor Crewmember	2	394
27E	Tow/Dragon Repairer	3	123
29E[a]	Radio Repairer	3	—
31C	Single Channel Radio Operator	3	289
31D[a]	Mobile Subscriber Equipment Transmission System Operator	3	—
51B	Carpentry and Masonry Specialist	3	69
54B	Chemical Operations Specialist	3	340
55B	Ammunition Specialist	3	203
63B	Light Wheel Vehicle Mechanic	1	478
67N	Utility Helicopter Repairer	2	238
71L	Administrative Specialist	1	427
76Y	Unit Supply Specialist	2	444
88M	Motor Transport Operator	2	507
91A	Medical Specialist	2	392
94B	Food Service Specialist	2	368
95B	Military Police	3	597
96B[a]	Intelligence Analyst	3	—

[a] No Project A data available.

(CV) database. The overall data set included predictor and job performance measures collected on soldiers in 19 different jobs. Eighteen of these jobs (MOS) were included in either Phase I, II, or III of this project. All 18 MOS were used to evaluate the validity of the synthetic equations. Table 15.2 shows the designations and names of these MOS, as well as the phase in which they were included and their CV sample size.

The individual predictor measures included in the Project A Trial Battery were described in Chapters 5 and 6. Wise et al. (1989) described the identification of specific measures in the Project A data set corresponding to 26 of the 30 items in the Synthetic Validity Project's attribute taxonomy. These 26 measures were used in the analyses reported here. Thus, validity ratings were not used for four attributes not associated with Project A measures.

Chapter 11 described the identification and measurement of five factors of first-tour, entry level job performance. For the synthetic validation analyses, the job-specific factor (Core Technical Proficiency), and an overall performance measure that is a weighted combination of all five performance factors (Sadacca, Campbell, White, & DiFazio, 1989) were used as criteria. Project A validity analyses showed that significant differences across jobs were found in the predictors of job-specific proficiency but not for the other four factors. Discriminant validity could not legitimately be expected for any other performance components. However, it is both of scientific and practical interest to determine the validity of the synthetic methodology for predicting overall job performance as well.

The CV samples differed by MOS in terms of the heterogeneity and mean levels of the predictor scores. In addition, because of prior selection, all MOS had higher and less variable predictor scores than the overall pool from which applicants are drawn. A two-step procedure was used to adjust for range restriction. The 1980 Youth Population sample to which the ASVAB was administered was used as the target population. First, the covariances among the 26 predictor measures (corresponding to the attributes) were computed for each of the 18 MOS-specific samples and adjusted for differences between the samples and the Youth Population related to the covariances of the ASVAB subtests.[1] This provided estimates of the covariances among the attribute measures for the Youth Population, if all of the Project A predictor measures been administered to them. (Assumptions underlying these estimates are described in Lord & Novick, 1968.)

Second, covariances were computed for each of the 18 job-specific samples that included 26 predictors plus the Core Technical and Overall Performance criterion construct scores. These covariances were then adjusted for differences between the job specific sample and the estimated Youth Population covariances. These corrections provided estimates of the covariances among the 26 predictors and Core Technical and Overall Performance in each of the 18 MOS for the 1980 Youth Population.

Once the covariances of the predictor and criterion measures are estimated for each job, validities for any proposed synthetic composite of the predictors can be estimated through relatively direct matrix manipulations. For the synthetic equations reported here, there were two steps in forming a synthetic predictor score composite. First, scores on individual Project A measures of the attributes were standardized, weighted

---

[1]We initially used a different, less traditional method of estimating the population predictor intercorrelation matrix. However, follow-up simulation analyses convinced us that the more traditional method was best. See Rosse and Peterson (1991) for a full description of the investigation of this matter.

(by the psychologists' estimated validities), and summed to form a predicted score for each job component. These predicted job component scores were then weighted (according to the job component criticality ratings by the Army SMEs) and summed to form the predicted job performance score.

Reduction of Number of Predictors

As a practical matter, it is unlikely that any organization could ever use all 26 attribute measures to predict performance. One obvious method for reducing the number of predictors is to use only the ASVAB measures. Three Project A predictor score composites that matched the Synthetic Validity attributes consisted of ASVAB subtests. These three composites closely parallel measures of the ASVAB Verbal, Numerical, and Technical factors. Synthetic equations were constructed using only these three measures, with their associated attribute-by-component weights. This method was called the ASVAB reduction.

Two other methods employed stepwise regression to reduce the number of predictors. In the first, the full synthetic equation was first constructed using all attribute-by-component and component-by-job weights, and then the predictor contributing the least to predicting the full synthetic equation was dropped. This process continued until the reduced equation correlated less than .95 with the full equation. This method was called the .95 stepwise reduction. The second stepwise method used the same reduction technique except that it continued until only five predictors remained. Five was chosen arbitrarily, but it seemed to be a reasonable number from a practical viewpoint. Obviously, if a synthetic equation is being developed for a job for which there are no empirical data, it is not possible to evaluate the accuracy of the predictor reduction effects for that job. The current project tried to estimate only the general effects of such reductions.

Empirical Weights

In addition to the synthetically produced predictor composites, "empirical" prediction equations based on sample data were developed using least-squares regression of the 26 predictor measures against the Core Technical and Overall Performance criterion composites within each of the 18 MOS. Equations were also developed for each MOS using the three ASVAB predictors against the Core Technical criterion and against the Overall Performance criterion.

When the same empirical data that were used to develop the predictor composites were also used to estimate the validity of the empirical composites (e.g., when the equation developed on the 19K sample was applied to the 19K sample), the biased estimates were adjusted to yield unbiased estimates of cross-validated coefficients for these composites.[2] However, no adjustments were made when the validity of the empirical equation developed for one job for predicting performance in a different job was estimated. This is because the criterion data for the other jobs were not used in the development of the empirical weights, therefore removing the possibility of positive bias because of error-fitting.

THE PRELIMINARY PHASES OF EVALUATION

Phases I and II focused on (a) evaluating the alternative models for describing job components, (b) evaluating SME/rater differences, and (c) evaluating alternative response scales for assessing job component and individual attribute criticalities. After identifying the most useful component descriptions, SME/raters, and response scales, Phase III involved a full-scale evaluation of alternative methods for generating synthetic prediction equations and a comparison of synthetic estimates to sample based empirical estimates and to validity generalization estimates.

The results of the two preliminary phases will be noted only briefly. A full description can be found in Wise et al. (1989) and Peterson et al. (1990).

---

[2]We used three different adjustments to correct the bias. Two of these were from Claudy (1978). One provided an estimate of the population multiple correlation coefficient (i.e., the coefficient that would result if one could obtain the actual population weights for the least squares equation, Equation 12, p. 603) and one provided an estimate of the validity coefficient in the population for the sample-derived weights (unnumbered equation, p. 606). These two methods of adjustment were arrived at through empirical means based on some Monte Carlo work. The third adjustment is from Rozeboom (1978, Equation 8, p. 1350), which also provides an estimate of the population validity coefficient for the sample-derived weights. We had used Claudy's estimate of the population multiple correlation in the first two phases, but decided that an estimate of the validity coefficient in the population when using the sample-derived weights was the more appropriate estimate for the actual applied problem of predicting job performance for future Army applicants using weights derived from Project A samples. We wished to continue to provide the earlier estimate as well as to try out two different estimates of the validity coefficient, one (Claudy's) that was empirically based and one (Rozeboom's) that was derived analytically and fairly widely accepted as an accurate estimate of the validity of sample-derived weights (see Mitchell & Klimoski, 1986).

Phase I

The goal in Phase I was to obtain and evaluate relevant SME judgments for three MOS: 11B (Infantryman), 63B (Light-Wheel Vehicle Mechanic), and 71L (Administrative Specialist). First, three job analysis instruments for identifying tasks, activities, or attributes were used to obtain job descriptions and link the component to jobs. Second, predictor constructs were linked via expert judgment to the job components. Another major goal was to evaluate the degree to which job descriptions might vary by characteristics of SMEs, such as differences in rank and type of command (i.e., an operational unit versus a training installation). About 200 SMEs participated in the Phase I research. They provided various ratings for the three job component models on the three target MOS.

The results of the literature review and the job analysis results from Project A were synthesized to develop the Job Activity Questionnaire and the Army Task Questionnaire. After extensive pretesting, the final forms of these instruments contained 53 Activities and 96 Task Categories, respectively. The Project A predictor literature search and expert judgment study was used to generate a taxonomy of 30 predictor attributes.

Judgments were collected from 69 psychologists about the validity of the 30 psychological attributes (all but four of which had corresponding tests or scales in the Project A predictor battery) for predicting performance on each of 53 job activities and each of 96 job tasks, in the job activity and task category models, respectively. These judgments were the data from which were derived the various predictor-by-job component weights. The psychologists also used the attribute model to estimate the validity of the attributes for predicting performance in the three Army MOS included in Phase I.

Of the 69 psychologists, 46 were members of the research team's organizations and 23 were outside experts. The outside experts could be divided into five groups: members of the Project A Scientific Advisory Group ($n = 4$), past-presidents of the Society of I/O Psychology ($n = 5$), APA Fellows ($n = 6$), APA members ($n = 6$), and other ($n = 2$). One important research question for synthetic validation concerned the extent to which the characteristics or qualifications of these psychologists might affect the validity of synthetic equations formed using their judgments. The psychologists who made the validity judgments were asked about their familiarity with the military and their experiences in applied personnel research. They were also asked about their familiarity with the Army's Project A because of concerns about possible contamination of judgment data because of exposure to Project A information. This information was analyzed and

TABLE 15.3
Single Rater Reliability Estimates of Phase I Job Description and Validity Ratings

	MOS		
	11B	63B	71L
Task category importance for			
Core technical proficiency	.52	.36	.40
Overall job performance	.52	.43	.44
Job activity importance for			
Core technical proficiency	.36	.23	.43
Overall job performance	.36	.25	.34
Attribute			
Validity (Military SMEs)	.31	.34	.45
Validity (Psychologists)	.42	.55	.52

several subgroups of the judges were formed: military familiarity (low or high), psychological experience (low or high), the intersections of these two kinds of groups (e.g., high military familiarity and low psychological experience), and knowledge of Project A (low, moderate, high).

Phase I analyses showed that there were essentially no consistent differences across these psychologist subgroups in terms of inter-rater reliability. Results from Phase I also showed that Army SMEs were able to use the three job component models to reliably describe the content of these jobs. Table 15.3 shows, for the Task Category and Job Activity instruments, single-rater reliability estimates of importance ratings for Core Technical Proficiency and Overall Job Performance. Table 15.3 also shows reliability estimates for attribute validity ratings from military SMEs (those with the relevant job knowledge about Army jobs), and from psychologists, for predicting the Core Technical Proficiency performance criterion in each of the three MOS. The reliabilities of criticality ratings for Task Categories were generally higher than for the other descriptors. Also, the psychologist SMEs seemed to be the more reliable raters of potential attribute validity.

Phase II

One objective of Phase II was to replicate the results from Phase I on a larger set of jobs: 16S (MANPADS Missile Crewman), 19E/K (Armor/ Tank Crewman), 67N (Utility Helicopter Repairer), 76Y (Unit Supply

Specialist), 88M (Motor Transport Operator), 91A/B (Medical Specialist), 94B (Food Service Specialist). Over 400 NCOs and officers participated, about 55% from operational units and 45% from training units.

Another objective was to expand the types of job component descriptors and evaluate the alternatives on this broader range of jobs with the goal of identifying a preferred model. Consequently, a fourth type of job descriptor was developed, which combined the task and activity models. It was labeled the "hybrid" model and the intent was to achieve an even more comprehensive coverage of job components. The four job descriptor methods were compared on a number of distributional and psychometric properties. Further, the methodology for using the attribute model was expanded to include a rank ordering of the attributes in addition to attribute validity estimates. That is, for the Job Activity, Task Category, or Hybrid component descriptors, the judges either estimated the relative validity of each attribute (predictor) for predicting each component or rank ordered the estimated relative validities of the attributes for each component. For the attribute model, the judged validities of the 30 attribute variables for predicting performance in an MOS were either estimated or rank ordered for each MOS.

As shown in Table 15.4, acceptable single-rater reliability estimates of importance ratings for Core Technical Proficiency and Overall Job Performance were obtained via the Task Category, Job Activity, and Hybrid instruments. Table 15.4 also shows sufficient reliability estimates for attribute validity ratings and rankings for Core Technical Proficiency. However, it is apparent that the importance ratings for the Task Category descriptors consistently yielded the highest inter-rater reliabilities.

In identifying a preferred job descriptor model, emphasis was also placed on the model's ability to produce predictor equations that provided acceptable validity for each job as well as differential prediction among jobs. Several methods for forming job component weights for each MOS were evaluated in Phase II. They involved various combinations of frequency and importance ratings. Three variations, labeled "threshold" methods, assigned nonzero weights to components with mean frequency or core technical importance ratings that were above a specified cutoff (i.e., threshold). To take one example, all task categories with a mean SME importance rating of less than 3.5 (on a 5-point scale) for a particular job (MOS) were given a weight of zero for that job.

As will be described in more detail in the next section, once the relevant components were identified and weighted for each MOS, the mean SME estimated validities of each attribute variable for predicting performance on

TABLE 15.4
Reliability Estimates of Phase II Job Description and Validity Ratings

| | MOS | | | | | | |
	16S	19K	67N	76Y	88M	91A	94B
Task category importance for							
Core technical proficiency	.46	.55	.54	.73	.50	.43	.43
Overall job performance	.56	.55	.56	.47	.48	.48	.44
Job activity importance for							
Core technical proficiency	.44	.37	.38	.24	.39	.26	.27
Overall job performance	.47	.35	.34	.22	.36	.27	.25
Hybrid importance for							
Core technical proficiency	.41	.43	.38	.35	.44	.34	.33
Overall job performance	.46	.42	.39	.37	.42	.36	.34
Attribute ratings							
Core technical proficiency	.21	.22	.30	.22	.21	.16	.15
Attribute rankings							
Core technical proficiency	.38	.40	.53	.48	.38	.41	.37

a component were aggregated over the relevant components, and weighted by the relative importance of the component to the job. Also, a variety of predictor (attribute) weighting procedures were used for the synthetic prediction equations, ranging from mean estimate validities to 0-1 weights based on an estimated "validity threshold."

Table 15.5 is an example of a consistent set of evaluation results. Both mean estimated predictor validities and 0-1 weights were used to weight predictors and estimate validity for predicting Core Technical Performance in an MOS. Both the synthetic and the "empirical composites" were estimated from Project A sample data. Absolute validity refers to the estimates obtained when the equation (empirical or synthetic) for an MOS was used to make predictions (empirical or synthetic) in that MOS. Discriminant validity refers to the mean reduction in estimated validities when the equation developed for an MOS was used to make predictions for all other MOS. The more the decrement, the greater the discriminant validity.

The Task Category model emerged as the preferred job descriptor instrument primarily because it had higher absolute and discriminant validities than the other models, but also because it had adequate reliability levels and was acceptable to Army SMEs. However, the synthetic equations did

TABLE 15.5
Comparing Synthetic and Empirical Composites Obtained in Phase II

	Mean Absolute Validity			Mean Discriminant Validity		
Composites	V^a	R^b	U^c	V^a	R^b	U^c
Empirical composites		.69			.08	
Synthetic composites						
Task category	57		.61	.01		.02
Job activity	52		.53	.01		.01
Hybrid	53		.55	.01		.02
Attribute ratings	51		.31	.01		.01

Note: Mean validities were calculated by averaging across the seven Phase II MOS, across the threshold models, and across the criticality variations.
[a]V = Validity estimates as predictor weights.
[b]R = Regression derived predictor weights.
[c]U = 0/1 weights for predictors.

not take advantage of all the potential absolute and discriminant validity, as represented by the sample based least squares estimates, labeled "Empirical composites" in Table 15.5.

To test the differences in validities between the psychologist subgroups, we developed separate prediction equations using the mean validity judgments from each of the subgroups. Two types of job component models were employed—one that used mean officer/NCO ratings of the importance of 53 activities for Core Technical performance and one that used mean officer/NCO ratings of the importance of 96 task categories for Core Technical performance. The focal MOS were the seven used in Phase II.

Additional results (not shown) indicated very little advantage for any of the psychologist subgroups in terms of absolute validity or discriminant validity. Familiarity with the military and amount of applied psychological experience did not appear to appreciably influence the usefulness of the validity judgments made by the psychologists used in this research. Furthermore, experience with Project A had no pronounced effect. These were not necessarily unwelcome findings, because it meant that the descriptive and instructional materials used in the process of collecting the attribute-by-component validity judgments did not require special knowledge or experience on the part of the psychologists to produce reliable judgments that could lead to the construction of valid prediction equations.

The above are only a sampling of the evaluation data generated in Phase I and II. The total array of these results suggested that the "best bet" synthetic validation strategy was to concentrate on the Task Category component, use importance ratings as criticality ratings for the component-by-job linkage, and psychologist validity estimates as the weights for the attribute-by-component linkage. The direct attribute to job model was set aside. Phase III then evaluated a number of variations within this basic strategy.

PHASE III EVALUATION

Having identified the Task Category model as the preferred job descriptor instrument, the primary objectives of Phase III were to collect data on a broader array of MOS and to more fully evaluate and compare alternative methods for creating predictor equations, including the more traditional methods of validity generalization. To do this, all the MOS for which Project A data were available were used. This allowed the empirical comparison of validities resulting from the application of the synthetic and traditional validity generalization methods, because actual predictor and criterion data were available.

First, the psychometric characteristics of the Army Task Questionnaire will be discussed, followed by the analyses used to evaluate alternative synthetic equations and their comparison to empirical and validity generalization estimates.

Analysis of the Army Task Questionnaire

In Phases I and II, the Army Task Questionnaire emerged as the preferred job description instrument. This section describes the Army Task Questionnaire in more detail and reexamines the issues of reliability and discrimination among MOS in light of data from the larger, Phase III MOS sample.

The Army Task Questionnaire consists of 96 task categories that describe job content in terms of the tasks performed. It is designed to describe all entry-level positions in the Army. Seventeen task dimensions divide the 96 task categories at an intermediate level (see Figure 15.2 for illustration). Sixteen of these dimensions are further collapsed into four major divisions: (a) maintenance, (b) general operations, (c) administrative, and (d) combat. The 17th dimension, Supervision, is left separate. The development of the Army Task Questionnaire is described in detail in Chia, Hoffman, Campbell, Szenas, and Crafts (1989).

I. Maintenance
    A. Mechanical Systems Maintenance
        1. Perform operator maintenance checks and services
        2. Perform operator checks and services on weapons
        3. Troubleshoot mechanical systems
        4. Repair weapons
        5. Repair mechanical systems
        6. Troubleshoot weapons

> This level is not shown for remaining task categories

    B. Electrical and Electronic Systems Maintenance

II. General Operations
    C. Pack and Load
    D. Vehicle and Equipment Operations
    E. Construct/Assemble
    F. Technical Procedures
    G. Make Technical Drawings

III. Administrative
    H. Clerical
    I. Communication
    J. Analyze Information
    K. Applied Math and Data Processing
    L. Control Air Traffic

IV. Combat
    M. Individual Combat
    N. Crew-served Weapons
    O. Give First Aid
    P. Identify Targets

    Q. Supervision (not included in any of the four major divisions)

FIG. 15.2. Illustration of the task category taxonomy.

In using the Army Task Questionnaire, SMEs were asked to consider the entire range of duty assignments for soldiers with 24 months experience beyond Basic Training and Advanced Individual Training (AIT) in their particular MOS. SMEs first rated how frequently the tasks in each category are performed by such soldiers on a scale from 0 (Never; this task is not part of the job) to 5 (Most Often; this task is performed much more often than most other tasks). After providing Frequency ratings for all 96 task categories, participants rated the Importance and Difficulty of only those categories with nonzero Frequency ratings. Importance ratings were collected for each of three specifications of job performance: Core Technical, General Soldiering, and Overall Job.

SMEs then provided Difficulty ratings by answering the following question: "How difficult is it to reach and maintain an acceptable level of proficiency in this task?" using a scale from 1 (Very Easy; this task can be performed correctly after less than an hour of instruction and performed again correctly a year later with little or no practice in between) to 5 (Very Difficult; this task can be performed correctly after several weeks of instruction and performed again correctly only if it is practiced regularly).

Samples for Task Questionnaire Analysis

Eleven MOS were included in the Phase III analyses of the Task Questionnaire. SME sample sizes for each MOS ranged from 17 to 81. Two-hundred and seventy-four NCOs and 156 officers from operational units participated; 147 NCOs, 74 officers, and 35 civilians were from training units. Ten Army installations were visited to collect data from these SMEs.

Reliability

Reliability questions revolve around two overlapping issues: (a) Do raters within the same rater group agree with each other? and (b) Do raters from the different rater groups agree? An alternative way to phrase the second issue is: Do raters combined from all rater groups agree with each other? These questions were addressed separately for each MOS, and the results summarized across MOS.

Inter-rater reliability was calculated using an analysis of variance framework that treats task categories (the objects of measurement) as fixed, raters as random, and includes both rater variance and rater-by-task category variance as measurement error. Formulas may be found in Brennan (1983).

Single-rater reliability estimates. Single-rater estimates are useful for comparing differences among rater groups and MOS, and they provide the basic data, using the Spearman-Brown Prophecy Formula, for specifying the number of raters needed to achieve a particular level of reliability. Table 15.6 summarizes the single-rater reliability estimated by presenting mean estimates across the MOS for each rating scale and across all rating scales. Reliability estimates were computed only for rater groups with four or more raters. A series of orthogonal, planned comparisons were conducted to test statistical significance.

The Frequency and Importance reliability estimates are not detectably different, but estimated reliabilities for Difficulty are lower than those for Frequency and Importance. Comparisons of raters at different ranks showed

TABLE 15.6

Army Task Questionnaire Single Rater Mean Reliability Estimates by Rater Type
and Command

	Training Unit				Operational Unit			Combined			
	NCO	OFF	CIV	TOT	NCO	OFF	TOT	NCO	OFF	CIV	TOT
N[a]	11	7	4	11	10	9	10	11	9	4	11
Frequency	.55	.55	.49	.54	.57	.58	.56	.55	.57	.48	.55
N[a]	11	7	4	11	10	9	10	11	9	4	11
CTI	.52	.49	.44	.49	.52	.54	.52	.52	.52	.43	.50
GSI	.51	.53	.43	.49	.54	.56	.54	.52	.55	.42	.52
OJI	.53	.52	.43	.51	.56	.57	.56	.54	.55	.42	.53
N[a]	11	7	4	11	10	9	10	11	9	4	11
Difficulty	.39	.38	.38	.38	.43	.45	.43	.41	.43	.37	.41
N[a]	55	35	20	55	50	45	50	55	45	20	.55
All scales	.50	.50	.43	.48	.52	.54	.52	.51	.52	.42	.50
N[a]	44	28	16	44	40	36	40	44	36	16	44
Frequency & importance	.53	.52	.45	.51	.55	.56	.54	.53	.55	.44	.52

Note: CTI = Core Technical Importance, GSI = General Soldiering Importance, OJI = Overall Job Importance.

[a] Number of reliability coefficients included in the analyses.

no differences. Finally, raters from operational units agreed more among themselves than raters from training units ($F_{1,103} = 6.12$, $p < .02$).

The single-rater estimates are relatively high for all scales and for all rater groups. Because of the large number of raters in the sample, many of the reliabilities for the mean ratings approach .99. Making projections for multiple-rater reliabilities based on the single-rater reliability estimates, group reliabilities would exceed .90 for all of the Frequency and Importance ratings with as few as 10 raters.

Agreement among rater groups. If the different groups are providing different mean task category ratings, then reliabilities estimated across groups will be lower than the separate reliabilities estimated within each rater group. Table 15.6 shows that NCO and officer reliabilities average only slightly higher than total group reliabilities, usually no more than .02. Certainly, any across-group differences that do exist have no practical impact on the level of reliability of the ratings.

Three additional tests—overall level differences, differences in numbers of nonzero ratings, and profile correlations—were conducted separately for each of the five rating scales. Differences in profile means between the various rater groups were tested to determine whether some rater groups consistently give higher ratings than others. Differences in relative profile shape were examined by computing correlations between rater group profiles. This analysis indicates whether some rater groups give higher ratings to subsets of task categories.

The results in Table 15.7 indicate that NCOs, compared to Officers, consistently make higher average ratings on Frequency and Importance and lower (i.e., easier) average ratings on task Difficulty. Such results may occur because NCOs identify more task categories as relevant to their MOS and therefore give nonzero ratings to more task categories, or because they give higher ratings to the relevant tasks. If NCOs, compared to Officers, are identifying a larger set of task categories as relevant to their MOS, then there is a possibility that the NCO profiles will lead to the selection of a larger set of predictors for the MOS. Another difference is that civilians provide lower average ratings than either NCOs or Officers on all scales except Difficulty. Also, command differences occur for Frequency, Overall Job Importance, and Difficulty. In each case, training unit ratings average higher than operational unit ratings. However, the size of most of these differences is small. Differences for the Difficulty scale tend to be larger,

TABLE 15.7
Mean Level of Army Task Questionnaire Ratings for Five Rater Groups

| | Rater Group | | | | |
| | NCO | | Officer | | Civilian |
Scale	Training Unit	Operational Unit	Training Unit	Operational Unit	Training Unit
N of raters	672	672	672	672	288
Frequency	1.51	1.47	1.47	1.42	1.18
Core Tech Importance	1.68	1.65	1.57	1.54	1.30
Gen Soldier Importance	1.70	1.66	1.60	1.59	1.31
Overall Job Importance	1.81	1.74	1.72	1.70	1.45
Difficulty	1.62	1.48	1.76	1.61	1.48

TABLE 15.8

Proportion of Nonzero Rated Task Categories for Four Rater Groups

	Rater Group			
	NCO		Officer	
Scale	Training Unit	Operational Unit	Training Unit	Operational Unit
N of rater	672	672	672	672
Frequency	0.54	0.52	0.55	0.53
Core Technical Importance	0.58	0.55	0.57	0.56
General Soldier Importance	0.58	0.55	0.58	0.56
Overall Job Importance	0.59	0.56	0.61	0.59
Difficulty	0.64	0.58	0.68	0.63

about .11 to .14 between ranks and the same order of magnitude between commands. Civilian ratings were generally about .30 to .35 lower than soldier ratings, which reflects a somewhat different perspective.

Examination of proportions of nonzero ratings was conducted by converting rating group mean profiles to profiles of 1s and 0s. Group means of 0.0 for task categories occur only when all raters within a group rate the item as zero. Rather than requiring that all raters indicate a zero, task categories with mean ratings of less than 1.0 were recorded as zero. Table 15.8 presents the proportions of nonzero rated task categories. The data suggest that the NCOs and officers differ because of differences in importance level ratings for the relevant task categories and not because of differences in the proportion of task categories judged to be relevant.

Table 15.9 presents the mean intercorrelations among the four rater group profiles. While the correlations are high, they are not perfect. This suggests that every group profile may be considered highly similar to the other group profiles, but each also offers some unique variance in task category ratings. Recall that these group profiles are highly reliable so it is difficult to dismiss the unique information as unreliable noise.

While reliability and distributional difference alone cannot determine the most appropriate group of MOS raters, particularly when the differences are small, the data do suggest that careful consideration should be given before using civilians. Their perspective is the most divergent, and the constituency they represent may be the least certain.

TABLE 15.9
Mean Intercorrelations Among Task Questionnaire Profiles, for Rater Groups

	Training NCOs	Operational NCOs	Training Officers	Operational Officers	Matrix mean r w/civilians (w/o civilians)
Frequency Scale:					
Operational NCOs	0.93				
Training Officers	0.90	0.90			
Operational Officers	0.90	0.94	0.90		.89
Training Civilians	0.85	0.85	0.86	0.84	(.93)
Core Technical Importance Scale:					
Operational NCOs	0.93				
Training Officers	0.87	0.87			.87
Operational Officers	0.88	0.94	0.89		(.89)
Training Civilians	0.84	0.84	0.85	0.83	
General Soldiering Importance Scale:					
Operational NCOs	0.93				
Training Officers	0.89	0.92			.84
Operational Officers	0.90	0.95	0.92		(.92)
Training Civilians	0.87	0.87	0.84	0.84	
Overall Job Importance Scale:					
Operational NCOs	0.93				
Training Officers	0.90	0.92			.89
Operational Officers	0.90	0.95	0.91		(.92)
Training Civilians	0.87	0.85	0.83	0.84	
Difficulty Scale:					
Operational NCOs	0.90				
Training Officers	0.85	0.88			
Operational Officers	0.84	0.92	0.87		.85
Training Civilians	0.80	0.84	0.78	0.81	(.88)
N of raters:					
Training NCOs	1056				
Operational NCOs	960	960			
Training Officers	672	672	672		
Operational Officers	864	864	672	864	
Training Civilians	384	384	288	384	384

Scale Intercorrelations

Using a multitrait–multimethod matrix framework, data from both the
Phase I and II MOS (10) and the Phase III MOS (11) were analyzed to in-
vestigate relative discriminant and convergent validities. In these analyses,
MOS served as Traits and five possible response scales as Methods. Each

Mean Discriminant (Same Scale, Different MOS) Correlations

Scale	Phase III MOS		Phase I and II MOS	
	r	$1 - r^2$	r	$1 - r^2$
Frequency	.63	.60	.63	.60
Core Technical Importance	.58	.66	.58	.66
General Soldier Importance	.88	.23	.86	.26
Overall Job Importance	.75	.43	.75	.44
Difficulty	.68	.54	—	—

correlation was between two sets of mean ratings across the 96 Task Categories. That is, the Task Category profiles for each type of rating scale for each MOS were intercorrelated.

Discrimination Among MOS

Discriminant correlations are the task profile correlations computed between different MOS assessed by the same rating scale. Table 15.10 shows the average of these correlations for each rating scale. Phase I and II results are displayed for comparison.

The Phase III discriminant correlations are virtually identical to those based on the 10 Phase I and II MOS. As expected, the Core Technical Importance scale shows the greatest discrimination among the MOS, and the General Soldiering Importance scale shows the least. It is interesting that the two scales that address the relevance of the task categories to the whole job (i.e., the Frequency and Overall Job Importance scales) are somewhat different in the extent to which they discriminate among the MOS.

Although these correlations appear relatively high, the Core Technical average discriminant correlation of .58 may be interpreted to mean that any MOS shares, on the average, 34% of its variance in task category ratings with any other MOS. If there were no measurement error, 66% of the MOS variance in task category ratings would be unique. As shown in the prior sections on reliability, task category ratings with this many raters are highly reliable, suggesting that the 66% unique variation may not be too much of an overestimate. On the other hand, the discriminant correlations for General Soldiering Importance ratings suggest that no more than 23% of the variation in task category ratings is MOS-specific.

Convergence of Rating Scales

Convergent correlations are the correlations of mean task category profiles between different rating scales within each MOS. These are presented in Table 15.11 for Phase III MOS. The pattern of results from the Phase III MOS again parallel previous results. The Frequency, Core Technical Importance, and Overall Job Importance scales are essentially redundant. The General Soldiering Importance scale is the least redundant with the other scales, but only slightly.

A second source of information concerning the redundancy of the rating scales comes from the average off-diagonal (different scale, different MOS) correlations presented in Table 15.12. The usual expectation is that these correlations will not be high. However, they are in the same range as the

TABLE 15.11
Mean Off-Diagonal (Different Scale, Same MOS) Correlations

	Freq	Core Tech Importance	Gen Soldier Importance	Overall Job Importance
Core Technical Importance	.99			
General Soldier Importance	.91	.90		
Overall Job Importance	.97	.97	.97	
Difficulty	.93	.94	.92	.97

TABLE 15.12
Mean Off-Diagonal (Different Scale, Different MOS) Correlations

	Freq	Core Tech Importance	Gen Soldier Importance	Overall Job Importance
Core Technical Importance	.59			
General Soldier Importance	.73	.69		
Overall Job Importance	.67	.65	.81	
Difficulty	.61	.59	.74	.69

TABLE 15.13

Mean Convergent (Different Scale, Same MOS) Correlations Based on Relevant
(1) versus Nonrelevant (0) Indices and Original Mean Ratings

	Freq	Core Tech Importance	Gen Soldier Importance	Over Job Importance
Core Technical Importance				
1/0 Scoring	.96			
Task Means	.98			
General Soldier Importance				
1/0 Scoring	.90	.89		
Task Means	.89	.87		
Overall Job Importance				
1/0 Scoring	.89	.96	.94	
Task Means	.97	.96	.97	
Difficulty				
1/0 Scoring	.84	.88	.94	.93
Task Means	.93	.94	.91	.96

discriminant correlations presented in Table 15.10. This again suggests that the different scales are providing much the same information about the MOS.

An issue concerning the Army Task Questionnaire rating scales is that their correlations are inflated by the multiple zero ratings that MOS are expected to have in common. The convergent and discriminant correlations for the 11 Phase III MOS were recomputed using the previously described index of 1s and 0s presenting a dichotomy of relevant versus nonrelevant tasks. Tables 15.13 and 15.14 present these recalculated correlations along with the original correlations. With the exception of the discriminant correlations for the General Soldiering Importance scale, the convergent and discriminant correlations for the recoded task category profiles show little, if any, difference from those for the task category means. These findings strongly suggest that it may not matter how frequently performed or how important a task category is, but simply that it is relevant to the job.

Conclusions About the Task Questionnaire

Three conclusions may be reached regarding the Army Task Questionnaire. First, it provides highly reliable descriptions of Army MOS. In fact, using the worst case reliability (.40 single-rater reliability for 55B Core Technical

TABLE 15.14

Mean Discriminant (Same Scale, Different MOS) Correlations Based on Relevant
(1) versus Non-relevant (0) Indices and Original Mean Ratings

Scale	1/0 Scoring	Task Mean Ratings
Frequency	.59	.63
Core Technical Importance	.56	.58
General Soldier Importance	.69	.88
Overall Job Importance	.66	.75
Difficulty	.64	.68

Importance), only 14 raters would be needed to boost the reliability of mean ratings to .90. Second, the Core Technical Importance rating does differentiate among MOS. Third, within a job, ratings of Frequency, Core Technical Importance, and Overall Job Importance are highly redundant. They basically provide information about whether or not a task category is relevant to the MOS. General Soldiering Importance is the least redundant of the scales and, reflecting the structure of a common set of tasks for all Army MOS, shows the least discrimination among the MOS.

Analyses of Absolute and Discriminant Validity

Given the criterion predicted, the type of component-by-job weights, the type of attribute-by-component weights, and the method used to reduce the number of predictors in the equation, there were 40 different types of synthetic equations generated for each of the 18 MOS. Table 15.15 shows the absolute and discriminant validities for each of the 40 synthetic validation equations when they were evaluated with empirical data. Each of the 40 absolute validity estimates shown in this table is the mean validity computed across the 18 MOS. To provide an estimate of the statistical significance of the differences between these absolute validities, we computed the two-way analysis of variance with MOS (18 levels) and Method (40 levels) as main effects, and the MOS × Method interaction as the error term. The mean squares from the ANOVA were .021 for Method, .269 for MOS, and .002 for the interaction effect, which is the mean squared error. The value of the interaction effect is the standard error for comparing the absolute validities.

TABLE 15.15
Absolute and Discriminant Validity Estimates by Synthetic Validity Method

| | Attribute-by-Component Weights | | | Methods of Reducing Predictor Sets | | |
Job Component Weights (96 Task Categories)	Mean Validity Estimates	0-1 Weights	0-Mean Weights	.95 Stepwise Reduction	Top 5 Stepwise Reduction	ASVAB[a] Reduction
Core Technical Proficiency						
MOS						
Mean importance	.55[b]/.00[c]	.63/.01	.64/.01	.55/.00	.56/.00	.64/.00
Threshold importance	.56/.01	.62/.02	.62/.02	—	—	.65/.00
Cluster						
Mean importance	.55/.00	.63/.00	.64/.00	.56/.01	.57/.01	.64/.00
Threshold importance	.57/.01	.63/.01	.64/.01	—	—	.64/.00
Least squares[d] (corrected)	67/.06				.66/.03	
Overall Performance						
MOS						
Mean importance	.56/.00	.59/.00	.59/.00	.56/.00	.56/.00	.57/.00
Threshold importance	.56/.00	.57/.01	.57/.01	—	—	.57/.00
Cluster						
Mean importance	.56/−.01	.59/.00	.59/.00	.56/.00	.56/.00	.57/.00
Threshold importance	.56/.00	.56/.00	.56/.00	—	—	.57/.00
Least squares[4] (corrected)	61/.01				.57/.01	

[a] Project A Measures: A1AVERBL, A1AQUANT + B3CCNMSH, and A1ATECH.

[b] Absolute Validity = mean validity coefficient computed across 18 MOS.

[c] Discriminant Validity = mean absolute validity minus mean validity obtained by applying MOS equations developed for different MOS to a target MOS, computed across all 18 MOS.

[d] Absolute and discriminant validities for the least squares equations, using all 26 predictors (first set of figures) or using the 3 ASVAB predictors (second set of figures). The absolute validity was computed on adjusted coefficients, using Rozeboom's Formula #8.

Thus, the 95% confidence interval is plus or minus .004 around each coefficient. Basically, this means that a difference of .01 between absolute validity coefficients is statistically significant. This level of difference is probably not practically significant, but it should be kept in mind that even very small differences in validity can be meaningful for organizations with a huge volume of annual selection decisions (e.g., the U.S. Army).

Also shown in Table 15.15, for comparison, are the absolute and discriminant validities for the least squares equations, using the Rozeboom correction to compute the absolute validity estimates.

In general, the synthetic equations produced high levels of absolute validity and low levels of discriminant validity. The lowest absolute validity for a synthetic equation in Table 15.15 is .55, whereas the highest discriminant validity is .02. The values for the least squares equations in Table 15.15 show the maximum values that we might expect for these data. The least squares values show maximum discriminant validities for the full set of predictors of .06 for Core Technical and .01 for Overall, and discriminant validities for the ASVAB only of .03 for Core Technical and .01 for Overall Performance. Thus, in the best case (0-1 or 0-mean attribute weights with MOS threshold component weights for Core Technical), it appears that the synthetic equations obtain about 95% of the absolute validity and 33% of the discriminant validity of the least squares equations.

Influence of the Criterion

In general, the Core Technical Proficiency criterion appears to be better predicted than the Overall Performance criterion, although both are well predicted by the synthetic methods. This is especially so for synthetic equations using 0-1 or 0-mean validity weights for the attribute-by-component weights (r of .62 or .64 versus .56 to .59). Synthetic equations containing only ASVAB predictors also do not predict the Overall Performance criterion as well as the Core Technical Proficiency criterion (r of .64 or .65 versus .57). Given the generally low level of estimated discriminant validity obtained, it is not surprising that there is little difference between the estimated discriminant validities for the two criteria.

Influence of the Attribute-by-component Weights

The 0-1 weights and 0-mean weights produced nearly identical results and showed higher absolute validities than did the mean validity weights, especially for Core Technical Proficiency (r of .62 to .64 versus r of .55 to .57). The 0-1 and 0-mean weights produced slightly higher levels of discriminant validity, but these were still very low (no more than .02).

Influence of the Component-by-job Weights

Variations in methods of forming these weights appeared to have little impact on either absolute validity or discriminant validity, although there does appear to be a small reduction in absolute validity for predicting Overall Performance when using threshold weights.

Influence of Method of Reducing the Number of Predictors in the Synthetic Equation

The two stepwise reduction methods produced almost identical results, about .56 absolute validity and .00 or .01 discriminant validity. This is not too surprising when one considers that the .95 stepwise reduction method produced equations having seven or eight predictors and that the top five stepwise reduction method produced equations that correlated about .92 or .93, on average, with the full synthetic equation (mean validities and MOS mean component weights, no reduction method applied). Also, inspection of the attribute weights produced by the two methods (not shown here) shows considerable overlap in the weighted attributes. In general, the attributes most frequently weighted across reduction method and MOS were Verbal Ability, Reasoning, Spatial Ability, Memory, Eye-Limb Coordination, Work Orientation, Interest in Using Tools, Interest in Technical Activities, and Interests in Leadership. Thus, the two methods produced equations that stepped down from 26 predictors to 5 to 8 predictors and correlated about .92 to .95 with the full equation. A noteworthy feature of these results is the consistency of obtained validity for the reduced equations compared to the full equations (the first column contains the full equation validity corresponding to the reduced equation). The difference in the validities is never more than .02. This demonstrates that the stepwise method is preserving the level of validity in the original, nonreduced equation.

Use of only ASVAB predictors produces estimated validities for Core Technical Proficiency equal to the validities for the best nonreduced synthetic equations. This is not surprising because Project A results have already shown that the new predictors developed for Project A provide very little incremental validity for predicting this particular criterion. No discriminant validity was found for the ASVAB-only synthetic equations, also not surprising given that there was very little discriminant validity (.03) for the least squares equations.

With regard to predicting Overall Performance, the ASVAB-only equations do equally well or .02 lower when compared to the nonreduced, synthetic equations. The Overall Performance criterion is a weighted sum of all five Project A criterion constructs, so we might have expected a bit more improvement when all the predictors were included. No discriminant validity was obtained here either, but there was even less available because the discriminant validity for the least squares equations was just .01.

Comparison of Synthetic Validation to Validity Generalization

Synthetic validation is one method of developing prediction equations for jobs for which no empirical validity data are available. Another alternative is validity generalization (Schmidt & Hunter, 1981). Very briefly, for validity generalization, jobs for which appropriate empirical data do not exist are compared to existing jobs for which such data do exist. If a match is made between a new job and an existing job, or a sample of existing jobs, then the validity evidence for the existing job(s) is deemed relevant for the new job. This allows the selection methods for the existing job to be used for the new job. Of course, new jobs need not be matched to specific existing jobs. They could be matched to clusters of existing jobs, or, in the extreme, research could be carried out to demonstrate that one equation could serve to predict performance for all jobs in an organization (or however the population of relevant jobs is defined). For synthetic validation to receive serious consideration, it must provide validity results at least comparable to those provided by the validity generalization model.

There is not universal agreement on the appropriate index for the degree to which a new job matches an existing job. However, using the Army Task Questionnaire to match jobs on their task content profile would seem to be a reasonable approach. Computation of correlations between the mean task profiles should provide a useful index of the extent to which jobs are similar in task requirements performed on the job.

Method of Comparison of Synthetic and Validity Generalization Methods

For these analyses, 9 of the 18 MOS in the Project A database were considered to be the "existing" jobs and 9 of them to be the "new" jobs. The "existing" jobs were the Batch A MOS for which there were more comprehensive data and generally larger samples. The "new" jobs were the 9 Batch Z MOS.

First, correlations were computed between the Army Task Questionnaire profiles (on mean ratings of importance for Core Technical Proficiency) for the Batch A and Batch Z MOS to identify the "existing" job that was most similar to each "new" job. The Core Technical cluster to which each Batch A and Batch Z MOS belonged was also identified.

Second, the empirical least squares equation for the "existing" job that most closely matched each "new" job was applied to the sample data from the "new" jobs. This provided an estimate of the absolute generalized validity for each new job. As before, the difference between the mean absolute validity and the mean off-diagonal validity provided an estimate of the discriminant validity for the method.

Third, a least squares empirical equation for each of the four Core Technical clusters was developed by using the pooled predictor-Core Technical criterion correlations (pooled across all Batch A MOS in a cluster) together with the predictor intercorrelations computed across the entire Project A CV sample. These matrices had already been corrected for range restriction because of selection into the Army and the MOS. The appropriate cluster equation for each Batch Z MOS (i.e., the equation for the cluster to which the MOS belonged) was then used to compute a composite score, which was correlated with Core Technical Proficiency to provide an estimate of the absolute validity for this method for each Batch Z MOS. The estimate of discriminant validity was obtained in the same way as before.

Fourth, a least squares empirical equation was developed for all Batch A MOS by pooling across all nine jobs. This equation was applied to all nine Batch Z MOS to provide an estimate of the absolute validity for a "General" model of validity transportability. Of course, there is no discriminant validity possible for this method because only one equation is used.

Fifth, the validity coefficients (and the absolute and discriminant validities derived from them) obtained for the Batch Z MOS when these validity generalization models are used were compared with those obtained when each of the Batch Z MOS "own" empirical least squares equation is used, and with those obtained when the various forms of the synthetic method are used.

Results

Table 15.16 shows the correlations between Army Task Questionnaire profiles for the Batch A and Batch Z MOS. The highest correlation in each column represents the closest match to an existing job. Each of the Batch Z jobs appear to have an acceptably high correlation with a Batch A MOS (> .70), indicating a close match, except for 51B (.58). Also, most of the matches do not have close rivals. Note that 12B and 16S both match most closely with 11B, and that 51B, 55B, and 94B all match most closely with 88M.

Table 15.17 shows the validity coefficients produced when the empirical least squares equations for the Batch A MOS are applied to the Batch Z MOS. These are cross-validity coefficients and require no shrinkage

TABLE 15.16

Correlations Between Army Task Questionnaire Profiles (Mean Importance
Ratings for Core Technical Proficiency) for Project A Batch A and Batch
Z MOS Included in the Synthetic Validity Project: Highest Column
Correlations Underlined

Batch A MOS	Batch Z MOS ("New" Jobs)								
(Existing Job)	12B	16S	27E	51B	54B	55B	67N	76Y	94B
11B	.85	.92	.41	.44	.81	.66	.54	.48	.49
13B	.65	.76	.45	.52	.87	.67	.63	.53	.54
19K	.66	.80	.52	.33	.72	.49	.58	.40	.38
31C	.59	.75	.71	.44	.79	.53	.71	.57	.54
63B	.67	.78	.69	.53	.79	.69	.85	.60	.63
71L	.54	.62	.45	.35	.67	.68	.57	.82	.67
88M	.73	.84	.55	.58	.83	.79	.76	.68	.71
91A	.45	.55	.40	.30	.61	.55	.53	.59	.60
95B	.77	.85	.41	.42	.80	.66	.66	.57	.53

TABLE 15.17

Validity Coefficients of Least Squares Equations for Predicting Core Technical
Proficiency, When Developed on Batch A MOS and Applied to Batch Z MOS:
Highest Column Entries Underlined

Equation from	Applied to Batch Z MOS										
Batch A MOS	12B	16S	27E	51B	54B	55B	67N	76Y	94B	Mean	SD
11B	.64[a]	.50[a]	.70	.88	.71	.67	.77	.56	.65	.68	.10
13B	.62	.50	.65	.97	.70[a]	.70	.78	.43	.59	.66	.15
19K	.63	.50	.70	.83	.72	.58	.83	.56	.65	.67	.11
31C	.59	.46	.74[a]	.86	.72	.66	.74	.64	.66	.67	.11
63B	.55	.31	.61	.80	.62	.62	.76[a]	.38	.47	.57	.15
71L	.45	.50	.54	.76	.63	.47	.59	.59[a]	.70	.58	.10
88M	.64	.45	.65	.84[a]	.72	.62[a]	.80	.55	.63[a]	.66	.11
91A	.59	.48	.67	.89	.72	.64	.84	.54	.64	.67	.13
95B	.60	.53	.66	.82	.72	.57	.75	.61	.68	.66	.09
Mean	.59	.47	.66	.85	.70	.61	.76	.54	.63		
SD	.06	.06	.05	.06	.04	.06	.07	.08	.06		

[a]Validity coefficient for Batch Z MOS using the equation developed on Batch A MOS that is most
similar in terms of ATQ Profile correlation, Mean = .67, SD = .10.

adjustment. The highest column entries, or Batch Z validities, are underlined and the estimate for the "most similar" MOS is asterisked. In only one case does the highest validity for a Batch Z MOS occur for the "most similar" Batch A equation, 27E. Thus, using the "closest job match" method would not produce the highest generalized validities possible from the set of existing jobs. In general, however, the method does produce relatively high validities; the mean of the asterisked validity coefficients is .67 with a standard deviation of .10.

The means and standard deviations of the rows and columns also provide interesting information. The row means are an estimate of the validity generalization for a particular Batch A MOS (existing job) equation. An equation with a relatively high mean and low standard deviation provides generally high validity generalization estimates across all new jobs, while an equation with a relatively low mean and high standard deviation provides validity generalization estimates that vary across new jobs. Differences in means range from .57 to .68, and the standard deviations are from .09 to .15. The means and standard deviations of the column coefficients provide information about the relative predictability of the Batch Z MOS (new jobs). MOS 51B and 67N appear to be the most predictable, whereas 16S appears to be the least predictable.

Table 15.18 presents the validity generalization estimates when the "General" and cluster equations are applied to the Batch Z MOS. The "appropriate" cluster coefficients (i.e., those found for the cluster [e.g., combat, electronics] to which the Batch Z MOS belongs) are underlined. The appropriate coefficients are the highest of the cluster coefficients for five of the nine MOS (12B, 54B, 67N, 76Y, and 94B). The average appropriate validity coefficient was .68 with a standard deviation of .08, which are the same as the average and standard deviation for the "General" equation.

Table 15.19 presents the mean validity estimates for the nine "new" (Batch Z) jobs using the empirical equation (the validity coefficient obtained if the validity research could actually be carried out, as it was for these jobs), the "MOS Match" equation, the appropriate Cluster equation, the General equation, and the eight forms of the synthetic validity equations. Examination of the mean absolute validity estimates in this table shows that the General and Cluster equations provide the highest average validity (.68), other than the "own" equation, followed by the "MOS-Match" equation (.67). This is closely followed by the synthetic equations that combine 0-1 or 0-mean attribute weights with MOS mean component weights (.66) and the synthetic equations that combine 0-1 or 0-mean attribute weights with threshold component weights (.65). There is virtually no difference

TABLE 15.18

Validity Coefficients of General and Cluster Least Squares Equations for
Predicting Core Technical Proficiency, Developed on Batch A MOS and
Applied to Batch Z MOS

Batch Z MOS	General Equation	Mechanical Equation	Administrative Equation	Combat Equation	Electronics Equation
12B	.65	.64	.60	.64	.61
16S	.51	.41	.54	.52	.48
27E	.74	.66	.71	.73	.71
51B	.87	.79	.86	.88	.78
54B	.74	.68	.72	.73	.70
55B	.69	.67	.64	.69	.64
67N	.78	.77	.73	.77	.70
76Y	.61	.52	.63	.59	.62
94B	.68	.57	.72	.67	.65
Mean	.68	.63	.68	.69	.65
SD	.08	.11	.09	.10	.08

Mean of appropriate cluster coefficients (underlined) = .68
SD of appropriate cluster coefficients (underlined) = .08

Note: The correlations of the 26 attributes with Core Technical Proficiency for the four clusters
(M, A, C, E) were estimated by the pooled correlations of the Batch A MOS in each cluster and, for
the General group, by pooling all of the Batch A correlations.

in standard deviations of the validity coefficients; they range from .08 to
.10. Thus, all of the generalization methods provide high absolute validities as do several of the synthetic methods, but only the Batch A cluster
method provides absolute validity as high as the General method. The General method requires the collection of no additional data about new jobs,
albeit the additional data required of other methods is not overly costly
(completion of Army Task Questionnaires by 15 to 30 SMEs).

Table 15.19 also shows the discriminant validity coefficients for all the
methods. Note that the discriminant validity for the "own" equation is
.05, which we have regarded as the upper limit for this particular sample of
jobs. However, the Batch A "MOS-Match" or Batch A Cluster discriminant
validity probably more nearly provides the theoretical upper limit for the
applied situation for which the generalization and synthetic models are
intended, that is, applying information from existing jobs to new jobs for
which "own" equations are not available. These two discriminant validity

TABLE 15.19
Absolute and Discriminant Validity Coefficients for Predicting Core Technical
Proficiency (Computed Across Nine Batch Z MOS) for Equations Developed
from Various Methods

Equation	Absolute Validity	Discriminant Validity
"Own" Least Squares	.70[a]	.05
Batch A "MOS-Match" Least Squares	.67	.03
Batch A Cluster Least Squares	.68	.01
Batch A General Least Squares	.68	.00
Full Synthetic (Mean Attribute Validities and MOS Mean Component Weights)	.56	−.01
Top 5 Stepwise Reduction	.58	−.02
0-1 Attribute Weights	.66	.00
O-Mean Attribute Weights	.66	.00
Threshold Component Weights	.58	.00
0-1 Attribute Weights and Threshold Component Weights	.65	.01
0-Mean Attribute Weights and Threshold Component Weights	.65	.02

[a] The absolute validity estimate for "own" least squares equations were computed on coefficients adjusted with Rozeboom's Formula #8 (1978). Other absolute validity estimates were computed on coefficients that did not require adjustments.

values are .03 and .01. Discriminant validities for the other transportability and synthetic methods range from −.02 to .02.

Conclusions: Validity of Synthetic Validity Models

Most importantly, synthetic validity methods in almost any form provide acceptably high levels of absolute validity for Core Technical and Overall Performance. The highest estimated validities are achieved for predicting Core Technical Proficiency in which the attribute-by-component weights are formed by giving zero weight for cells with lower estimates of validity (.64). The lowest achieved estimated validities are .55. These values compare favorably to validities achieved by using least squares equations developed on the MOS themselves, which average about .67 for Core Technical Proficiency. Synthetic validity methods show very little discriminant validity. However, in this data set, there appears to be only a moderate amount of discriminant validity potentially available for the Core Technical criterion.

The most important comparison, in terms of the operational viability of the synthetic methods for the Army, is that of comparing generalization methods to synthetic methods. This is because one of these two types of methods must be used to develop an equation for a new MOS or an existing MOS for which empirical validation research cannot be completed. The analyses addressing this comparison (see Table 15.19) show that the generalization methods produce absolute and discriminant validities that are as high or higher than the synthetic methods. The Batch A Cluster and Batch A General least squares methods achieved the highest absolute validity (.68). The Batch A cluster method has discriminant validity of .01, while there is zero discriminant validity for the General method, which uses a single least squares equation developed across nine Army MOS. The Batch A "MOS-Match" method achieved absolute validity of .67, only slightly lower than the Cluster and General methods, and achieved the highest discriminant validity (.03) of any synthetic or generalization methods investigated. The choice between the Batch A Cluster and MOS-Match methods hinges on the trade-off between absolute validity and discriminant validity. Use of either method assumes the appropriate cluster or MOS match for a new MOS can be identified. The method used in this project (i.e., obtaining Army Task Questionnaire profiles for new MOS and correlating them with profiles for "existing" MOS) is an example of a method that can provide this information.

SUMMARY AND DISCUSSION

The Synthetic Validity Project developed and evaluated a series of alternative procedures for (a) analyzing jobs in terms of their critical components, (b) obtaining expert judgments of the validities of an array of individual attributes for predicting the critical components of performance, and (c) establishing prediction equations for specific jobs when criterion-related validation data are not available. The work of the project was firmly grounded in previous research and theory (Crafts et al., 1988). Relatively large samples of judges were used in each phase across a larger number of jobs than had been used in any previous study. The availability of the Project A data provided a rare opportunity to compare alternative synthetic methods to actual empirical results. As a result, the Synthetic Validity Project was able to investigate a number of issues never addressed before.

As a consequence of the results obtained in Phases I and II, the attribute model and job behaviors model were set aside and the Army Task Questionnaire became the component model of choice. Although all methods provided very reliable descriptions, the task questionnaire yielded somewhat greater discriminability across MOS and seemed to have higher acceptability among the judges. However, the other component models did not perform poorly. The job task method was the best of a set of reasonable options.

The several different types of item response scales were very highly intercorrelated. However, the task importance ratings for the Core Technical, General Soldiering, and Overall Performance aspects of the job do provide different information. In general, the importance scale seemed to be more useful than the ratings of frequency or difficulty.

Although there were some very slight differences between SME groups, differences in SME supervisory level, or organizational point of view (a training vs. operational unit orientation) appear to make virtually no difference in the usefulness of the job analysis data for synthetic validation. Similarly, expert judgments about the validity of individual attributes for predicting performance on job components proved to be particularly robust across psychologist judges who exhibited a fairly wide range of relevant psychological training and experience. In addition, attribute weighting methods that set low values of estimated validity to zero improve the discriminant validity of the resulting equations, with perhaps a slight loss in absolute validity.

The synthetic validation methods produced equations that have only slightly lower absolute validities, when evaluated with empirical data, than least squares equations developed directly on the jobs themselves, depending on the criterion and method of forming the synthetic equation. In general, the levels of absolute validity are about 95% of what is achieved with MOS specific least squares equations, while levels of discriminant validity are about 33% of those achieved by the least squares equations. Also, the synthetic equations produce results very similar to more traditional validity generalization methods when both methods are applied to the problem of identifying an appropriate prediction equation for a job for which no empirical validation can be undertaken. However, the MOS-match method may not always produce an acceptable equation. That is, a new MOS may not correlate highly enough (in terms of Army Task Questionnaire profile correlations) with an existing MOS to warrant confidence in the use of an associated equation. In such cases, the synthetic method will almost always be able to produce an acceptable equation because knowledgeable SMEs are easier to find than a matching job with empirical data.

What do these results mean for personnel research in general? First, it appears that the use of appropriately qualified judges to form prediction equations via synthetic models will lead to prediction equations that are nearly as valid as generalized equations. Second, for the data analyzed in this project, synthetically developed equations appeared to be nearly as valid as least squares equations developed via a full-blown, criterion-related validation study that uses work sample tests, job knowledge tests, and supervisory ratings as criteria and employs a sufficient sample size ($N > 250$). These results support work by Schmidt and colleagues (e.g., Schmidt, Hunter, Croll, & McKenzie, 1983) concerning the usefulness of expert judgments in validation research. Third, we did not find large amounts of discriminant validity across jobs. However, the relative pattern of discriminant validities was as it should be for the different criterion measures. That is, discriminant validity was greatest when estimated against the Core Technical Proficiency criterion and less when General Soldiering or Overall Performance was used. If differential validity is to be observed, it must come from genuine differences in the core task content, which in turn have different ability and skill requirements.

In retrospect, it may be reasonable to expect only a moderate amount of differential validity. First-tour MOS in the Army come from only one subpopulation of the occupational hierarchy, entry-level skilled positions, and do not encompass any supervisory, managerial, advanced technical, or formal communication (i.e., writing and speaking) components. However, a major consideration in all of this is that, although the potential for differential prediction appears to be only moderate, the gain in mean performance obtained by capturing this amount of differential prediction in an organization wide classification system may still be considerable. Evidence supporting this possibility is presented in Chapter 16.

Another issue that needs additional investigation is the difference between matching jobs on the basis of their task requirements and matching them on the basis of their prediction equations. Recall that the empirically based prediction equation transported from the MOS with the highest "task match" did *not* always yield validities that were higher, or as high, as prediction equations from other MOS. The fact that such is not the case implies that the job analytic methods so far developed do not capture everything that the empirical weights do. Why is that? It may be that the Task Questionnaire (and by implication, many other job analysis instruments) puts too much emphasis on the technical task content of a job and neglects other major components of performance, such as are represented in the Project A performance model. The investigation of the reasons for the lack of correspondence in matching task profiles versus matching prediction equations would offer additional clues about how job analytic methods might be made even more sensitive to differential job requirements.

In summary, for this subpopulation of jobs, the synthetic methods are reasonable ways to generate prediction procedures in situations where no empirical validation data are available. Absolute and discriminant prediction accuracy will suffer somewhat because the synthetic methods tend to weight the array of predictors more similarly across jobs than do the empirical estimation procedures. Finally, it seems clear from these results that personnel psychology has learned a great deal about the nature of jobs and the individual differences that forecast future performance on jobs. For many subpopulations of the occupational hierarchy, such as the one considered in this project, expert judges can take advantage of good job analysis information almost as well as empirical regression techniques.

16

Personnel Classification and Differential Job Assignments: Estimating Classification Gains

Rodney L. Rosse, John P. Campbell, and Norman G. Peterson

So far in this volume we have only considered the selection problem, or the accuracy with which performance in a specific job can be predicted. Classification considers the problem of estimating aggregate outcomes if there can be a choice of job assignments for individuals. The objectives of the first part of this chapter are to (a) summarize the major issues involved in modeling the classification problem, (b) review alternative methods for estimating classification efficiency, and (c) outline the major alternative strategies for making differential job assignments. In the second part of the chapter, we report on the use of a recently developed method to estimate the potential classification gains of using the Project A Experimental Battery to make job assignments.

PART 1: MODELING THE CLASSIFICATION PROBLEM

Major Issues

The classification problem has a number of critical facets. Consider just the following:

• What is the goal, or maximizing function, to be served by the selection/classification procedure? There are many options, ranging from minimizing attrition costs to maximizing aggregate utility across all personnel assignments for a given period. Obviously, before gains from classification can be estimated, the specific goal(s) to be maximized, minimized, or optimized must be chosen.

• What are the major constraints within which the classification system must operate? Such things as assignment quotas, assignment priorities, and cost constraints will have important effects on the gains that can be achieved.

• For a particular classification goal and a particular set of constraints, how should the predictor battery be constituted such that classification gain is maximized? Will maximizing selection validity within each job also produce the optimal battery for classification? Are there tradeoffs to make?

• Once the classification goal, assignment constraints, and the specifications for the prediction function are prescribed, the issue arises as to how best to estimate the potential classification gain. That is, given the specified constraints, what is the estimated gain from classification if the predictor information were used in the optimal fashion? Evaluating alternative estimates of this potential classification gain is a topic for this chapter.

• Given a particular level of potential classification gain, how much can be realized by a specific operational assignment system? This is analogous to asking how much of the estimated gain (e.g., in utility terms) from a new selection procedure will actually be operationally realized. For example, not everyone who is offered a job will take it, or it may not be possible to get people to accept their optimal job assignment.

Classification Objectives and Constraints

Applicant assignment procedures are controlled by the specified objectives and constraints for selection and classification. Objectives define the functions to be maximized by the classification process. Constraints define the minimum standards that must be met by any acceptable classification solution. When a problem has both objectives and constraints, the constraints are of primary importance, in the sense that maximization of the objectives considers only candidate solutions that meet all constraints. On the other hand, additional capability beyond the minimum standard can add value to an assignment system if the additional capability helps to satisfy a desirable, and specifiable, objective.

When an optimal procedure, such as linear programming, is used to solve a classification problem, the objectives are represented as continuous functions to be maximized, whereas constraints are represented by inequalities among variables that must be satisfied. However, it is in some sense arbitrary whether a particular factor is considered an objective or a constraint.

For example, we could easily frame a classification problem as one of minimizing the total cost required to meet specific performance standards. In this case, minimizing cost would be the objective, and the performance standards would be the constraints on the classification process. Alternatively, the problem could be formulated as one of maximizing performance, subject to cost constraints. This approach reverses the role of objective and constraint from the first formulation. A third approach would maximize a function that combines cost and performance, such as a weighted average (the weight assigned to cost would be negative). This approach has no constraints, because both of the relevant variables are considered part of the objective.

It is possible for all three methods to arrive at the same solution, if the constraints, objective functions, and weights are set appropriately. However, in general, optimal solutions will satisfy the constraints exactly, or very nearly so, and then attempt to maximize (or minimize) the objective function. In the previous example, additional performance generally requires additional cost. Thus, if performance is considered to be a constraint in a classification problem, then the optimal classification will barely meet the performance standards, while minimizing cost. However, if the constraints are set too low, then the optimization procedure may reach a solution that, in reality, is unacceptable. Alternatively, if the constraints are set too high, there will be little room for the optimization of the objectives to occur.

Wise (1994) identified a number of potential goals that could be addressed by selection and classification decisions, depending on the organization's priorities. The goals, as described below, pertain to the military, but are also generalizable to civilian organizations.

- **Maximize percentage of training seats filled with qualified applicants**. When the classification goal is stated in this way, the specifications for qualified applicants are a constraint. If the fill rate is 100%, the quality constraint could be raised.
- **Maximize training success**. Training success could be measured via course grades, peer ratings, and instructor ratings. Success could be represented with a continuous metric or a dichotomy (e.g., pass/fail).
- **Minimize attrition**. Any index of attrition must be defined very carefully and would ideally take into account the time period during which the individual attrited, as noted by McCloy and DiFazio (1996).
- **Maximize aggregate job performance across all assignments**. In terms of a multifactor model of performance, the maximizing function could be based on any one of the factors, or some weighted composite of multiple factors.
- **Maximize qualified months of service**. As used in previous research, this term refers to the joint function of attrition and performance when performance is scored dichotomously as qualified/not qualified.
- **Maximize aggregate total career performance**. This goal would be a joint function of individual performance over two or more tours of duty.
- **Maximize the aggregate utility of performance**. In this instance, the performance metric would be converted to a utility, or value of performance, metric that could change assignment priorities as compared to making job assignments to maximize aggregate performance.
- **Maximize percentage of job assignments that meet specific performance goals**. The current personnel assignment system "quality goals" fall in this category. The assignment rules could use one cut score as a minimum standard for each job or it could define maximum and minimum proportions of individuals at each of several performance levels.
- **Maximize the social benefit of job assignments**. Potential indicators of such a goal could be things such as the percentage of minority placements or the potential for civilian employment after the first tour.

This list illustrates the variety of goals that may be served by selection and classification processes. The individual goals are not mutually exclusive, but neither are they totally correspondent with each other, and no organization could be expected to try to optimize all of them at once. Some of these goals, such as maximizing training seat fill rates, are in close chronological proximity to the classification process, and can be easily measured. Others, such as total career performance, cover a period of time that may be many years removed from the classification process. Finally, some are "nested" within others, such as maximizing total performance utility, which is really maximizing total performance, where levels of performance have been evaluated on a utility metric.

One important feature is that most of the goals on the previous list could be stated as either objectives or constraints. In addition, there are other constraints under which the classification system must operate, the most obvious being cost. Other constraints are quotas for total accessions and for individual jobs, and minimum performance standards.

Different classification procedures focus on different objectives and constraints, and employ different methods to determine the optimal allocation of applicants to jobs. No existing method addresses all of the goals described above.

Classification via Multiple Regression versus Multiple Discriminant Analysis

At the most general level, there are two types of personnel classification models. One is the regression-based model, which begins by deriving least square estimates of performance separately for each job, using all predictors. The regression models have been labeled "maximization methods" to indicate that job performance is the criterion to be maximized by optimal assignment of applicants to different positions. The second is the discriminant-based model, which derives least square estimates to maximally predict membership (or perhaps performance above a certain level) in a job. Group membership itself is the criterion of interest.

Advocates of regression methodology do not view jobs as natural groupings in the same sense as classes or species in biology, the discipline within which the discriminant methodology was developed: "The model [discriminant analysis] is much less appropriate in personnel decisions where there is no theory of qualitatively different types of persons" (Cronbach & Gleser, 1965, p. 115).

Advocates of discriminant methods, however, take exception to fundamental assumptions of regression methodology. Specifically, they question whether it is appropriate to predict performance for an individual without knowing if the individual is a member of the same population on whom the regression equation was estimated. Rulon, Tiedeman, Tatsuoka, and Langmuir (1967) note, "We seldom bother to estimate an individual's similarity to those who are in the occupation before using the multiple regression relationship for the occupation" (p. 358). In the Army context, this raises the issue of whether the effects of self-selection for different MOS are strong enough to produce different subpopulations within the applicant pool.

The problem of predicting performance for individuals who may not come from the same population as the sample on which the equations were derived does not have an entirely adequate empirical solution. Horst (1954) noted that the misestimated regression weights, which are a symptom of this problem, can be largely corrected with corrections for restrictions in range using applicants for all jobs as the applicant population; and we have used this methodology in Project A. Consider the case, however, in which the incumbents in a job (e.g., mechanic) are uniformly high on an important predictor in the applicant population (e.g., mechanical interests and aptitude). Self-selection might be so extreme that the within-job regression equation developed to predict performance would not include this predictor because of its severely restricted range. When this equation is then applied to the general population of applicants, there would be the potential for high predicted performance scores for applicants who actually have low scores on important but range-restricted (and thus unweighted) predictors (e.g., mechanical interests and aptitude). Differential prediction would suffer.

Restriction in range of predictor variables also violates the assumption of equal within-group covariance matrices in discriminant analysis. The application of correction formulas is subject to the same concerns as in the case of extreme selection discussed above.

Using regression procedures in classification of personnel was first discussed in theoretical terms in work by Brogden (1946a, 1951, 1954, 1955, 1959) and by Horst (1954, 1956). Their framework consists of an established battery of tests optimally weighted to predict performance separately for each job. The key assumptions are that the relationships between predictors and performance are multidimensional and that the ability (and other personal characteristics), determinants of performance vary across jobs or job families.

Although Brogden and Horst shared a common framework, they focused on different aspects of the classification problem. Horst's concern was with establishing procedures to select tests to form a battery that maximizes differential prediction across jobs. Brogden assumed that the battery of tests is a given and concentrated on estimating the increase in assignment efficiency achieved by classification methods.

The majority of research on classification in the discriminant analysis tradition has used noncognitive predictors, such as vocational interests and personality constructs. Research on interests using the discriminant model dates back to Strong's (1931) publication of the Strong Vocational Interest Blank and the demonstration, through his research, that different occupational groups reliably differ on patterns of interests.

One classification methodology emerging from this tradition is Schoenfeldt's (1974) assessment classification method. This development can be seen as a union of efforts to develop taxonomies of jobs (e.g., McCormick, Jeanneret, & Mecham, 1972) and of persons (Owens, 1978; Owens & Schoenfeldt, 1979). Although the original conception was developmental in nature and the first empirical study involved college student interests and their subsequent choice of major fields of study (Schoenfeldt, 1974), later empirical investigations attempted to link interest-based clusters of persons with jobs or job clusters (Brush & Owens, 1979; Morrison, 1977).

The other major theoretical analysis of discriminant-based classification is the work of Rulon and colleagues (Rulon et al., 1967). This approach calculates probabilities of group membership based upon similarities of patterns of predictors between applicants and means of job incumbents. Rulon et al. (1967) assume multivariate normality in the distribution of predictor scores and derive a statistic (distributed as chi-square) to represent the distance in multivariate space between an individual's pattern of scores and the centroids for the various jobs. These distances can be converted into probabilities of group membership, and assignment can be made on this basis. In an attempt to link the discriminant and regression approaches, Rulon et al. (1967) include a derivation of the joint probability of membership and success in a group. The measure of success is limited to a dichotomous acceptable/not acceptable performance criterion.

A more recent application of discriminant-based methods used the large Project TALENT database of high school students to develop equations that predict occupational attainment from ability, interest, and demographic information (Austin & Hanisch, 1990). This research involved dividing occupations into 12 categories and then calculating discriminant functions to predict occupational membership 11 years after high school graduation. Prediction in this case was very impressive; the first five discriminant functions accounted for 97% of the variance between groups with the majority (85%) accounted for by the first two functions. The first function could be interpreted as a general ability composite whereas the second function weighted mathematics ability and gender heavily. The final three functions accounted for relatively little variance and had much less clear interpretations.

One critical issue in comparing the regression and discriminant approaches is the nature of the membership criterion. Humphreys, Lubinski, and Yao (1993) expressed enthusiasm for group membership as an "aggregate criterion" of both success in, and satisfaction with, an occupation. They noted that the composite nature of the membership criterion addresses method variance and temporal stability concerns that have been problematic for regression methodology. The quality of the group membership criterion, however, is critically dependent on the nature of the original classification system and subsequent opportunities to "gravitate" within the organization to reach the optimal job, as well as on the forces that produce attrition from the original sample of incumbents. The more gravitation that occurs and the more that the causes of attrition are related to performance, the more valuable the job membership criterion becomes. Discriminant-based classification is most useful when the employment situation involves free choices and/or free movement over a period of time and attrition occurs for the "right" reasons. When these conditions do not exist, discriminant procedures do not provide useful new information.

Wilk, Desmarais, and Sackett (1995) provided limited support for within-organization gravitation. Specifically, they noted the movement of high general ability employees into jobs of greater complexity. Additionally, they found that the standard deviation of ability scores tended to decrease with longer experience in a job providing further indirect evidence for gravitation. Discriminant analysis has been most effective in research that considers broader occupational criterion groups and longer periods that allow for crucial gravitation to create meaningful groupings (e.g., Austin & Hanisch, 1990). However, despite the popularity of discriminant methodology and its success in predicting occupational membership, without stronger evidence for substantial gravitation and/or appropriate attrition, it seems inappropriate for classification research within organizations.

In some very real sense, the regression model and the discriminant function do not have the same goals and cannot be compared directly. However, in any major evaluation of a selection/classification system, the design might best be thought of as having a repeated measures component that evaluates the classification gain for several kinds of objectives. Also, whereas results in terms of probability of correct classification may produce little or no information for the organization in terms of quantifying improvements in performance, this type of information could be very useful to applicants for advising and counseling purposes.

Predictor Selection for Classification

Brogden (1955) and others have argued that the maximum potential gain from classification will occur when the most valid predictor battery for each individual job is used to obtain predicted criterion scores for that job for each person, and these predicted criterion scores are what are used to make job assignments. However, this means that each individual must be measured on each predictor, no matter what subset of them is used for each job. Consequently, the total number of predictors aggregated across jobs could get very large. As a consequence, one major issue is how to choose a battery that will maximize potential classification efficiency for a battery of a given length, or more generally, for a given cost. The available methods for making such a battery selection are limited. We know of only two analytic methods, which are discussed below.

The Horst method. The value of the predictors used for classification depends upon their ability to make different predictions for individuals for different jobs. Differential validity in this context refers to the ability of a set of predictors to predict the differences between criterion scores on different jobs. Horst (1954) defined an index of differential validity (H_d) as the average variance in the difference scores between all pairs of criteria accounted for by a set of tests. It is not feasible to calculate H_d directly, because criterion scores are not available for more than one job for any individual. Consequently, Horst suggested substituting least squares estimates (LSEs), or the predicted criterion scores, for the actual criterion scores.

When H_d is calculated based on LSEs of criterion performance, then the index may be calculated from the matrix of covariances between the LSEs, denoted C, and the average off-diagonal element of C, as shown in the following equation:

$$H_d = tr\, C - l'Cl/m$$

where $tr\, C$ is the sum of the diagonal elements (or trace) of C, l is a vector with each element equal to one, and m is the number of jobs.

The Abrahams et al. method. An alternative to the Horst method would be to use a stepwise procedure to select predictors that maximize the mean selection validity across jobs. This is congruent with goals of the Brogden model but it provides a means to eliminate tests from the total pool such that all applicants do not take all tests.

For samples of Navy enlisted personnel, Abrahams, Pass, Kusulas, Cole, and Kieckhaefer (1993) used this approach to identify optimum combinations of 10 ASVAB subtests and 9 new experimental tests to maximize selection validities of batteries ranging in length from one to nine subtests. For each analysis, the steps were as follows: (a) the single test that had the highest weighted average validity across training schools (i.e., jobs) was selected, (b) multiple correlations were computed for all possible combinations of the first test with each of the remaining tests, and (c) the average multiple correlation (over jobs) was then computed for each test pair, and the combination with the highest weighted average was selected. This process was repeated until all remaining tests were included. The idea is that, at each step, the subtests currently in the prediction equation represent the test battery of that length that maximizes average absolute selection validity.

Three limitations are associated with this method. First, it does not allow subtests to be dropped at later stages (i.e., the procedure uses forward stepwise regression only), and the particular combination of subtests at the *n*th step may not be the battery of *n* tests that maximizes mean absolute validity. Second, this method seeks only to identify the optimal battery relative to the mean absolute validity across jobs; it does not account for potential classification efficiency or adverse impact. One implication of this difficulty is that, for a test battery of any length, the combination of subtests identified by this method may produce a relatively low level of differential validity compared to another combination of subtests with a similar level of mean absolute validity, but a higher level of differential validity. A final limitation of this method is that, whereas the number of subtests in a test battery is related to the cost of administering the battery, the actual test battery administration time might provide a more accurate assessment of cost.

Abrahams et al. (1994) addressed this latter concern in a subsequent analysis. They used an iterative procedure described by Horst (1956) and Horst and MacEwan (1957) to adjust test lengths, within a total time constraint, to maximize the differential validity of a battery for a specific time allotment. The tradeoff is between validity and reliability through successive iterations. Changes in predictor reliabilities as a function of estimates of changes in test length (via the Spearman-Brown) are used to recompute the necessary predictor intercorrelation and predictor validity matrices. These are then used, in turn, to recompute predictor weights that maximize differential validity.

Evaluating all possible combinations. It is not possible to choose a combination of predictors that simultaneously optimizes both selection validity and classification efficiency, or absolute validity and differential validity. It is possible, however, to calculate all the indices of test battery performance for every possible combination of subtests that fall within a given test administration time interval, to provide information about the consequences for various tradeoffs. These combinations of subtests can then be rank-ordered according to each index of test battery performance. For instance, the top 20 test batteries ranked on the basis of maximum absolute validity can be compared to the top 20 test batteries ranked on the basis of maximum differential validity. An advantage of this method is that it provides explicit information necessary to evaluate tradeoffs: If subtests are included to optimize test battery performance on one index, how will the battery perform on the other indices?

This approach was one of those followed in the Joint Services Enhanced Computer Administered Test (ECAT) validation study designed to evaluate different combinations of 19 ASVAB and ECAT subtests in predicting end-of-training performance (Sager, Peterson, Oppler, Rosse, & Walker, 1997). Data were collected from 9,037 Air Force, Army, and Navy enlistees representing 17 military jobs. The analysis procedures used three time intervals; included two ASVAB subtests (Arithmetic Reasoning and Word Knowledge) in every potential test battery; and evaluated absolute validity, differential validity, classification efficiency, and three types of adverse impact (White/Black, White/Hispanic, and Male/Female).

Results indicated that no single test battery (within each time interval) simultaneously optimized all the test battery indices examined. The researchers identified tradeoffs associated with maximizing absolute validity or classification efficiency versus minimizing all three types of adverse impact, and with minimizing M-F adverse impact versus minimizing either W-B or W-H adverse impact. The same approach was used on Project A data, focusing on each of three different Project A criterion measures (Sager et al., 1997).

Methods for Estimating Classification Gains

Given that a maximizing function, or classification goal, has been decided upon (e.g., mean predicted performance) and that a predictor battery has been identified, the next issue concerns how the level or magnitude of classification efficiency can actually be estimated. For example, under some set of conditions, if the full Project A Experimental Battery were used to make job assignments in an optimal fashion, what would be the gain in mean predicted performance (MPP) as compared to random assignment after selection, or as compared to the current system?

As is the case in other contexts, there are two general approaches to this issue. The first would be to use a statistical estimator that has been analytically derived, if any are available. The second is to use Monte Carlo methods to simulate a job assignment system and compute the gains in mean predicted performance that are produced in the simulation. Each of these approaches is discussed below.

Brogden's Analytic Solution

Early on, Brogden (1959) demonstrated that significant gains from classification are possible, even for predictors of moderate validity. He showed that, given certain assumptions, MPP will be equal to the mean actual performance for such a classification procedure, and that classification based on the full LSE composites produces a higher MPP than any other classification procedure. The assumptions that limit the generalizability of this result are the following:

1. The regression equations predicting job performance for each job are determined from a single population of individuals. In practice, this assumption is infeasible because each individual has only one job. Consequently, as Brogden stated (1955, p. 249), "Regression equations applying to the same universe can be estimated through a series of validation studies with a separate study being necessary for each job."
2. There is an infinite number of individuals to be classified. Simulation research by Abbe (1968) suggests that the result is robust with respect to this assumption. However, as discussed later in the chapter, if the samples of applicants to be assigned are not relatively large, cross-validation of MPP does become an issue.
3. The relationships between the test scores and criterion performance are linear.

Brogden (1951, 1959) provided a method of estimating the MPP of a full LSE classification procedure, based on the number of jobs, the intercorrelation between job performance estimates, and the validity of the performance estimates. The development of this measure is based on the following assumptions:

1. There is a constant correlation (r) between each pair of performance estimates.
2. The prediction equations for each job have equal validity (v).

3. The population of people being assigned is infinite. This assumption is used to avoid consideration of job quotas.

From these assumptions Brogden (1959) showed that the mean predicted performance, expressed as a standard score, is given by the following equation:

$$\text{MPP} = v\sqrt{1 - r}\, f(m)$$

where $f(m)$ is a function that transforms

$$v\sqrt{1 - r}$$

the Brogden Index of Classification Efficiency (BCE), into the mean predicted performance standard score as a function of the number of jobs (m) and the selection ratio. The greater the number of jobs, everything else being equal, and/or the lower the selection ratio, the greater the gain in MPP.

This result has several important implications regarding the determination of MPP. First, MPP is directly proportional to predictor validity. Second, because MPP depends on $(1 - r)^{1/2}$, substantial classification utility can be obtained even when predictors are positively correlated. For example, Brogden (1951; adapted by Cascio, 1991) illustrated that using two predictors to assign individuals to one of two jobs can increase MPP substantially over the use of a single predictor even when the intercorrelation between the predictors is 0.8. Third, the results indicate that MPP increases as the number of jobs (or job families) increases. The increase will be a negatively accelerated function of the number of jobs; for example, going from two to five jobs will double the increase in MPP, while going from 2 to 13 jobs will triple the increase in MPP (Hunter & Schmidt, 1982).

The assumptions of equal predictor validities and intercorrelations are simplifications that allow for an easy, analytical determination of MPP. For more realistic cases in which validities and intercorrelations vary, MPP may be estimated using simulations.

Estimates of Gains From Simulations

When Brogden's assumptions are relaxed, analytical estimation of MPP becomes more complicated. Following methods used by Sorenson (1965), Johnson and Zeidner (1990, 1991), along with several of their colleagues (e.g., Statman, 1992), have applied simulation methods that they call synthetic sampling to examine the gains in MPP for a variety of classification procedures. There have been several summaries of their work, most notably those of Johnson and Zeidner (1990, 1991); Johnson, Zeidner, and Scholarios (1990); Statman (1992); and Zeidner and Johnson (1994).

These empirical comparisons have used the Project A database and show the improvement in MPP in standard deviation units, that is, as a proportion of the standard deviation of the MPP distribution. Each experimental condition was investigated with several synthetic samples (usually 20). The researchers used the means and standard deviations of the MPP values, calculated over the 20 samples, to form the basis of statistical tests of the significance of improvements in MPP resulting from the experimental conditions, usually compared to current assignment methods. Standard errors were typically very small, and nearly all differences were statistically significant.

Using the full regression weighted predictor battery, and a linear programming algorithm, to make optimal assignments to the nine "Batch A" MOS in the Project A database leads to an increase in MPP of about 0.15 SD when compared to current methods. Increasing the number of predictor tests, the number of job families, and decreasing the selection ratio, all improve MPP substantially. The test selection method, job clustering method, and overall selection and classification strategy have much smaller effects. These results represent a substantial potential improvement in MPP for "real" classification versus the current selection and assignment system. The actual improvement obtained by implementation of specific classification procedures will be less because of the damping influence of various constraints.

An alternative procedure, developed as part of Project A, also used Monte Carlo-based simulation procedures to estimate mean actual performance (MAP) rather than MPP. The derivation, evaluation, and use of this estimator is described later in this chapter.

Alternative Differential Job Assignment Procedures

The previous section reviewed methods for estimating the degree to which a particular classification goal (e.g., MPP) can be increased as a result of a new classification procedure, compared to a specified alternative. That is, the estimation methods portray the maximum potential gain that can be achieved, given certain parameters, if the prescribed procedure is used in an optimal fashion. However, the ability of the real-world decision-making procedures to realize the gain is another matter.

Current Army Allocation System

The Army currently uses a computerized reservation, monitoring, and person/job match (PJM) system labeled REQUEST (Recruiting Quota System). REQUEST operates to achieve three goals: (a) ensure a minimum level of aptitude (as assessed by ASVAB) in each MOS by applying minimum cut scores, (b) match the distribution of aptitude within jobs to a desired distribution, and (c) meet the Army's priorities for filling MOS/training seats.

Using functions related to these goals, REQUEST computes an MOS Priority Index (MPI) that reflects the degree of match between the applicant and the MOS and uses the MPI to produce a list of MOS in order of Army priority. The program first lists the five MOS that are highest in priority, and the classifier encourages the applicant to choose one of them. If the applicant is not interested in these jobs, the next five high priority jobs are shown and so on until the applicant chooses a job (Camara & Laurence, 1987; Schmitz, 1988).

The current system does not represent "true" classification in the sense that an entire set of job assignments is made as a batch such that the goal of classification (e.g., MPP) is maximized. The current system seeks to ensure that one or more limited goals for each job are met, even though the resulting assignments are suboptimal in terms of maximizing total gain. However, a new experimental system, the Enlisted Personnel Allocation System (EPAS), has been developed to incorporate a true classification component as part of the assignment algorithm. The EPAS prototype was developed over the course of a parallel (to Project A) project, usually referred to as Project B.

EPAS

The EPAS system is designed to (a) maximize expected job performance across MOS, (b) maximize expected service time, (c) provide job fill priority, and (d) maximize reenlistment potential. EPAS was designed to support Army guidance counselors and personnel planners (Konieczny, Brown, Hutton, & Stewart, 1990).

The following maximization problem provides a heuristic for understanding the view of the classification process taken by EPAS:
Maximize

$$Z = \sum_{i=1}^{n} \sum_{j=1}^{n} c_{ij} X_{ij} \qquad (1)$$

subject to

$$\sum_{i=1}^{n} X_{ij} = 1$$

$$\sum_{j=1}^{n} X_{ij} = 1 \tag{2}$$

where the variables, i and j index the applicants and jobs, respectively. The two constraints specify that each job is filled by a single applicant, and each applicant is assigned to a single job, respectively. The variable c_{ij} is a weight that represents the value of assigning applicant i to job j.

However, there are many factors that make the problem more complex than is indicated in the equation, including sequential processing of applicants, an applicant's choice of suboptimal assignments, complications caused by the Delayed Entry Program (DEP), and temporal changes in the characteristics of the applicant population. Consequently, the optimization approach taken by EPAS is considerably more complex than the simple formulation shown above.

For example, in "pure" classification the optimal allocation of individuals to jobs requires full batch processing, but in actual applications, applicants are processed sequentially. EPAS attempts to deal with this complication by grouping applicants into "supply groups" defined by their level of scores on the selection/classification test battery and by other identifiers, such as gender and educational level. For a given time frame the *forecasted* distribution of applicants over supply groups is defined, and network and linear programming procedures are used to establish the priority of each supply group for assignment to each MOS. For any given period, the actual recommended job assignments are a function of the existing constraints and the forecast of training seat availability.

Consequently, the analyses performed by EPAS are based on the training requirements and the availability of applicants. EPAS retrieves the class schedule information from the Army Training Requirements and Resource System (ATRRS), and provides this information, along with the number of training seats to be filled over the year, to the decision algorithm. It then forecasts the number and types of people who will be available to the Army in each supply group over the planning horizon (generally 12 months). The forecasts are based on recruiting missions, trends, bonuses, military compensation, number of recruiters assigned, characteristics of the youth population, unemployment rates, and civilian wages.

Based on the requirements and availability information, EPAS performs three kinds of analysis: (a) policy analysis, (b) simulation analysis, and (c) operational analysis. The first two of these analyses are designed to aid personnel planners, and the third primarily supports Army guidance counselors.

The policy analysis allocates supply group categories to MOS, including both direct enlistment and delayed entry. The allocation is based on a large-scale network optimization that sets a priority on MOS for each supply group. The analysis is used primarily for evaluating alternative recruiting policies, such as changing recruiting goals or delayed entry policies. The alternative maximizing functions that can be used to determine the optimal allocation include expected job performance, the utility of this performance to the Army, and the length of time that the person is expected to stay in the job. Other goals include minimizing DEP costs, DEP losses, training losses, and training recycles. Constraints include applicant availability, class size bounds, annual requirements, quality distribution goals, eligibility standards, DEP policies, gender restrictions, priority, and prerequisite courses.

The simulation analysis mode provides a more detailed planning capability than is possible with the policy analysis mode. The simulation analysis produces detailed output describing the flow of applicants through the classification process. The simulation analysis may be based on the same network optimization that is used for policy analysis, or it may be based on a linear programming optimization. The linear programming model provides a more accurate representation of the separate requirements for recruit and initial skill training, and consequently produces a more accurate analysis. The linear programming model requires much more computing time than for network formulations.

The operational analysis component provides counselors with a list of the MOS that are best suited to each applicant. The primary differences between the operational analysis and the policy analysis components are that the operational analysis allocates individual applicants to jobs, rather than supply groups, and performs sequential allocation of applicants. The operational module uses the lists of MOS provided by the policy analysis as the basis of its allocation procedure.

The ability of EPAS to "look ahead" derives from the interactions between the policy analysis over the planning horizon and the operational analysis. The policy analysis provides an optimal allocation over a 12-month period. This solution is one ingredient to the sequential classification procedure used by the operational analysis. Individual assignments of MOS to an individual are scored according to how close they are to the optimal solution. Highly ranked MOS are those that are in the optimal solution. MOS that are lower ranked would increase the cost (reduce the utility) of the overall solution. The MOS are ranked inversely according to this cost.

Even this cursory view of EPAS should convey the complexity of the issues with which a real-time job assignment procedure in a large organization must deal. Also, and perhaps most importantly, ignoring them does not make them go away.

PART 2: ESTIMATING CLASSIFICATION GAINS: DEVELOPMENT AND EVALUATION OF A NEW ANALYTIC METHOD

An assumption underlying much classification research is that mean predicted performance and mean actual performance are equal when (a) least-squares equations are used to develop the predicted performance scores on very large samples, (b) assignment is made on highest predicted scores, and (c) no quotas for jobs are used (Brogden, 1959). Because even these conditions rarely exist in actual practice, an alternate method for estimating classification efficiency is described in this chapter.

The remainder of this chapter is divided into three sections. The first section pertains to the statistical definition of two estimators of classification efficiency. One estimator (reMAP) is for estimating actual means of performance for a future group of applicants that would be assigned to the nine Batch A MOS jobs. The second (eMPP) is a refined estimator of the means of predicted performance for the same applicants. Both estimators purport to be indices of classification efficiency. The second section describes a set of empirical, Monte Carlo experiments designed to test the accuracy of the two estimators: eMPP and reMAP. Such a demonstration is necessary because the estimators are novel. The third section uses the developments described in the first two sections to estimate the potential classification efficiency under various conditions that could plausibly be obtained in situations represented by the Project A data base.

Development of eMPP and reMAP

Given the situation in which predicted performance scores for several jobs are available for applicants, one may elect to assign each applicant to the job where the highest predicted performance is observed. This simple assignment strategy was proposed by Brogden (1955). More complex strategies may involve the simultaneous assignment of individuals in a sample of applicants. For instance, optimizing techniques, such as linear programming, have been proposed to accomplish assignment under constraints such as incumbency quotas for individual jobs, differential job proficiency requirements for specific jobs, and minimum work-force standards (McCloy et al., 1992).

The purpose of this section is to clarify the issue of how group means of predicted performance relate to the actual criterion performance of the corresponding groups when an assignment strategy is employed.

Relevant Parameters of the Applicant Population

In the population of applicants, the vector of predicted performance, $\hat{Y}$, has a multivariate distribution. Its variance-covariance matrix, $\sum_{\hat{y}}$, is symmetric about the diagonal, that is,

$$\sum_{\hat{y}} = \begin{bmatrix} \sigma_{11} & \sigma_{12} & \cdot & \sigma_{1P} \\ \sigma_{21} & \sigma_{22} & \cdot & \sigma_P \\ \cdot & \cdot & \cdot & \cdot \\ \cdot & \cdot & \cdot & \cdot \\ \sigma_{P1} & \sigma_{P2} & \cdot & \sigma_{PP} \end{bmatrix} \qquad (3)$$

so that $\sigma_{ij} = \sigma_{ji}$, and the correlation between the ij-th pair of predictors is

$$r_{ij} = \sigma_{ij}[\sigma_{ii}\sigma_{jj}]^{-1/2}$$

The population means of $\hat{Y}$ are

$$E(\hat{Y}) = \begin{bmatrix} E(\hat{y}_1) \\ E(\hat{y}_2) \\ \cdot \\ \cdot \\ E(\hat{y}_P) \end{bmatrix} \qquad (4)$$

where p is the number of job assignments

The unobservable vector of actual performance, Y, also has a multivariate distribution. For purposes here, each value, y_j, in this actual performance vector is a standard score with the expectation of zero and variance of one.

Additionally, predicted performance, $\hat{Y}$, is linearly related to actual performance, Y. The term most commonly applied to characterize the magnitude of the relationships is "validity," which is the correlation between each predictor, $\hat{y}_i$, and each actual performance measure, y_i. Thus, there is a matrix, V, of validities so that

$$
V = \begin{bmatrix}
v_{11} & v_{12} & \cdot & v_{1P} \\
v_{21} & v_{22} & \cdot & v_{2P} \\
\cdot & \cdot & \cdot & \cdot \\
\cdot & \cdot & \cdot & \cdot \\
v_{P1} & v_{P2} & \cdot & v_{PP}
\end{bmatrix} \tag{5}
$$

where each row represents the validity of the i-th predictor for predicting the actual performance for the j-th job in the applicant population. The covariance of the i-th predictor with the j-th actual performance is $v_{ij}\sigma_{ii}^{1/2}$. The matrix of covariances, $\sum_{\hat{y}_y}$, is

$$
\sum\nolimits_{\hat{y}_y} = \text{Dg}\{\sum\nolimits_{\hat{y}}\}^{1/2} V \tag{6}
$$

where $\text{Dg}\{\sum_{\hat{y}}\}^{1/2}$ is a diagonal scaling matrix consisting of standard deviations on the diagonal and off-diagonal zeros.

Mean Values of Predicted Performance

Suppose that a sample of applicants has been assigned to the P number of jobs according to a chosen assignment strategy. There exists a matrix of means of the observed values of predicted performance scores for each job. For each job, there is a group of n_j individuals assigned so that

$$
m_{ij} = \sum_{k=1}^{n_j} \hat{Y}_{ijk}/n_j \tag{7}
$$

where $\hat{y}_{ijk}$ is the i-th predicted performance score of the k-th individual assigned to the j-th job. Thus, the observed values of mean predicted performance consist of a P by P matrix, $M_{\hat{y}}$, of means where the rows represent predictors and the columns represent jobs:

$$
M_{\hat{y}} = \begin{bmatrix}
m_{11} & m_{12} & \cdot & m_{1P} \\
m_{21} & m_{22} & \cdot & m_{2P} \\
\cdot & \cdot & \cdot & \cdot \\
\cdot & \cdot & \cdot & \cdot \\
m_{P1} & m_{P2} & \cdot & m_{PP}
\end{bmatrix} \tag{8}
$$

Brogden (1955) suggests that the mean of the diagonal elements of this matrix, MPP, indicates the classification efficiency realized by applying the assignment strategy based on the predicted performance scores of applicants:

$$\text{MPP} = \sum_{j=1}^{P} n_j m_{jj} \bigg/ \sum_{j=1}^{P} n_j \tag{9}$$

Classification Efficiency Defined in Terms of Actual Performance: Definition of the Re-estimate (reMAP)

With respect to mean actual performance, Brogden (1955) argued that MPP is a satisfactory approximation of the expected mean actual performance (MAP) in standardized units (Mean = 0, SD = 1). Using a limiting case argument, he contended that, as the sample sizes on which least-squares prediction equations are estimated become very large, the resulting prediction composites asymptotically approach the expected values of actual criterion performance. Brogden gave no additional consideration of actual performance.

This argument has been cited by Scholarios, Johnson, and Zeidner (1994) with the implication that MPP is approximately the same as MAP when samples used to develop the prediction equations range in size from about 125 to 600. It is not clear that MPP is an unbiased estimator of MAP when developmental samples are small.

A simple case in which an applicant is both randomly drawn and randomly (or arbitrarily) assigned to the j-th job demonstrates this issue. The expected actual performance in the j-th job of such an applicant is

$$E(y_j) = v_{jj} z_{\hat{y}_j} \tag{10}$$

where

$$Z_{\hat{y}_j} = [\hat{y}_j - E(\hat{y}_j)]/\sigma_{jj}^{1/2}$$

and y_j is the actual performance of the applicant for the j-th job, $\hat{y}_j$ is the corresponding observed predicted performance, which has the validity v_{jj} (from Equation 5), a population mean of $E(\hat{y}_j)$, and a standard deviation of $\sigma_{jj}^{1/2}$.

Equation 10 expresses the extent of regression that is to be expected by conditioning a prediction of actual performance on the observed value of predicted performance. However, it is true *only* for an applicant who is randomly assigned to the j-th job. When an assignment strategy is applied, the observed values of $\hat{y}_j$ are *not* random but, rather, are conditioned on the observed values of predicted performance for all P of the jobs. Thus, additional conditions are placed on the expected value, $E(y_j)$.

To illustrate the issue, consider a simple case of assignment based on Brogden's strategy of assigning each applicant to the job with the highest observed $\hat{y}_{ij}$. For this hypothetical case, there are two predictors for two corresponding jobs. The variance of each predictor is .75, and the covariance is .375. Thus, each predictor has a standard deviation of .866 and the correlation between them is .50. Each of the two variates has a mean of zero.

Because this simple case meets all of Brogden's assumptions, the expected mean predicted performance for each of the two jobs is the same and may be obtained using Brogden's allocation average (Brogden, 1955). The allocation average is $R(1 - r)^{1/2}$ A, such that $R = .866$, $r = .5$, and the tabled adjustment, A (referred to previously as $f(m)$), is .564. The allocation average is .345. The expected values of a randomly selected observation, $\hat{y}_1$ and $\hat{y}_2$, for the assigned applicants in each of the two jobs are as shown:

	Job	
Predictor	1	2
1	.345	−.345
2	−.345	.345

The expected mean of $\hat{y}_1$ for the applicants assigned to job 1 is .345. The corresponding expected mean of $\hat{y}_2$ for job 1 is less because of the conditions of the assignment strategy. In fact, in this simplified case, the expected mean of predicted performance for the predictor not targeted for each job is negative.

Unless the validity of $\hat{y}_2$ for predicting job 1 and the validity of $\hat{y}_1$ for predicting job 2 are both zero, there is a conflict. The conflict is that both $\hat{y}_1$ and $\hat{y}_2$ are valid predictors of job 1 (or job 2), and they make contradictory predictions for the same sample of applicants. That is, $\hat{y}_1$ predicts the mean performance to be $+.345$ standard deviation units and $\hat{y}_2$ predicts it to be $-.345$ standard deviation units.

Clearly, both predictions cannot be true. The apparently paradoxical situation arises because the assignment strategy introduces additional conditions on the observed predicted performance scores. Specifically, it selects extreme cases based on comparison of the observed values of predictors. In this example, it compares $\hat{y}_1$ and $\hat{y}_2$ for each applicant.

Because the paradoxical effect is introduced by conditional assignment, a linear equation reflecting the conditions may be defined, which accounts for the effects of the assignment of extreme scores (often denoted as regression effects) as follows:

$$y_{ij} = \beta'_j[\hat{Y}_i - E(\hat{Y})] + \epsilon_{ij} \tag{12}$$

where $\hat{Y}_i$ is the P-vector of predicted performance for the randomly chosen i-th applicant, and β_j is the P-vector of regression weights that minimize the expected square of the error, $_{ij}$. This least-squares solution is determined by solving for β_j in the normal equations,

$$\sum_{\hat{y}}\beta_j = \mathrm{Dg}\{\sum_{\hat{y}}\}^{1/2}V_j \tag{13}$$

where the variance-covariance matrix, $\sum_{\hat{y}}$, is defined in Equation 3, V_j is the j-th column vector of validities in Equation 5, and the matrix, $\mathrm{Dg}\{\sum_{\hat{y}}\}^{1/2}$, is the scaling matrix from Equation 6. Accordingly,

$$y_{ij} = \beta'_j[\hat{Y}_i - E(\hat{Y})] \tag{14}$$

defines y_{ij}, the expected value of the actual criterion performance (y_{ij}) under the conditions imposed by an assignment process.

The value y_{ij} is hereafter referred to as a *re-estimate* of actual performance (reMAP). The term, re-estimate, was chosen because the y_{ij} have already been defined as estimates of actual performance. The re-estimation is necessary because of the use of the conditional assignment strategy. The problem is analogous to the cross-validation issue.

The mean of the re-estimates, y_{ij}, for a sample of n_j applicants assigned to the j-th job would constitute a measure of classification efficiency with respect to that job, that is,

$$m_{y_j} = \sum_{i=1}^{n_j} y_{ij}/n_j \tag{15}$$

Furthermore, the weighted mean of the appropriate re-estimates across jobs estimates the overall classification efficiency of an assignment strategy in terms of actual criterion performance, that is,

$$\text{MAP} = \sum_{j=1}^{P} n_j \, m_{y_j} \bigg/ \sum_{j=1}^{P} n_j \tag{16}$$

Sample Re-Estimation of Mean Actual Performance

Unfortunately, the re-estimate, y_{ij}, is defined in terms of population parameters that are not ordinarily known. The potential for practical use depends on obtaining satisfactory estimates of the variance-covariance and validity matrices ($\sum_{\hat{y}}$ and V) defined in Equations 3 and 5, respectively. Furthermore, estimation of the unknown values of $E(y_i)$ is required.

It is beyond the scope of this chapter to summarize all issues regarding the estimation of the elements of these two matrices. Recall that they are parameters of the population from which the applicants have been drawn. Generally, the only statistics available are obtained from previous validation research, and, unfortunately, these statistics are frequently based on samples where covariances have been restricted in range and validity estimates are subject to "shrinkage." Details of how the estimates were obtained for the Monte Carlo studies are described in the next section of this chapter.

For now, suppose that satisfactory estimates

$$S_{\hat{y}} = \text{Est}(\textstyle\sum_{\hat{y}}) \tag{17}$$

and

$$V = \text{Est}(V) \tag{18}$$

are available. Then, estimates of the P × P matrix of regression coefficients, B, required for the re-estimates is

$$B = S_{\hat{y}}^{-1} \, \text{Dg}\{S_{\hat{y}}\}^{1/2} \, V \tag{19}$$

where the j-th column of elements, B_j, in B constitute estimates of β_j in Equation 12.

Thus, using sample data, the re-estimate of actual performance for the i-th applicant assigned to the j-th job is

$$\text{Est}(y_{ij}) = B_j'[\hat{Y}_i - G(\hat{Y})] \tag{20}$$

where $\hat{y}_i$ denotes the P-vector of predicted performance scores for the applicant and $G(\hat{Y})$ constitutes a vector of "guesses" of the values of $E(\hat{Y})$.

With respect to these expected "guessed" values for the $E(\hat{y}_i)$, one might estimate them from the applicant sample if the sample is large. Also, one might reasonably assume them to be zero if regression methods were used to develop the prediction composites.

A re-estimate of the classification efficiency for the j-th job can then be written as follows:

$$\text{Est}(m_{y_j})n_j = \sum_{i=1}^{n_j} \text{Est}(y_{ij}) \tag{21}$$

Additionally, a re-estimate of overall classification efficiency may be computed as

$$\text{Est(MAP)} = \sum_{j=1}^{P} n_j \, \text{Est}(m_{y_j}) \bigg/ \sum_{j=1}^{P} n_j \tag{22}$$

A Theoretical Expectation for Mean Predicted Performance (eMPP)

The re-estimates of expected actual performance for applicants assigned to jobs using an assignment strategy depend on the estimation of the elements of the matrix of means of predicted performance (Equation 8). To obtain these estimates, one may go through the process of developing the predictor variates for each job and collecting a sample of applicants on which to base the re-estimates.

However, it is of practical value to be able to forecast the results of assignment at a point in time before the applicant samples are actually obtained. This capability may be expected to provide useful information regarding the selection among assignment strategies or assist in the development of predictors.

Building on the work of Tippitt (1925) and Brogden (1951, 1959), this subsection develops the rationale of the statistical expectation for the matrix of means of predicted performance. The development continues with a proposed method of estimating the values based on statistics that are often available from samples used in predictor development.

For a given situation where the predictors, $\hat{Y}$, have been developed for a given set of P number of jobs, the three parameters that define the expectation of the matrix of means of predicted performance are as follows:

1. $E(\hat{Y}) =$ the vector of applicant population means (Equation 4).
2. $\sum_{\hat{y}} =$ the variance-covariance matrix (Equation 3).
3. $Q =$ a P-vector of quotas for the jobs.

Not previously mentioned is the vector Q, which consists of proportions. The element of Q, q_i, is the proportion of the applicant sample that is to be assigned to the i-th job. Thus, it is a value that is positive and less than or equal to 1.00. Also, the sum of the elements of Q must be less than or equal to 1.00.

The fact that these are the three relevant parameters becomes evident by examining a case where the exact statistical expectation can be defined. Consider again the simple case of assigning people to one or the other of two jobs in which there is a performance estimation equation for each job. Under the rule of Brogden's assignment strategy, the expected values of $\hat{y}_1$ and $\hat{y}_2$ for a randomly selected point are completely determined by the bivariate normal distribution with the specified variance-covariance.

The specific function for the expected value of the mean, m_{11}, of $\hat{y}_1$ for those assigned to job one would be

$$E(m_{11}) = E(\hat{y}_1) + \int_{-\infty}^{\infty} \int_{\hat{y}_2}^{\infty} \hat{y}_1 f\left(\hat{Y}, E(\hat{y}_1), \sum_{\hat{y}}\right) d\hat{y}_1 d\hat{y}_2 \qquad (23)$$

where

$$f\left(\hat{Y}, E(\hat{y}_1), \sum_{\hat{y}}\right) = (2\pi)^{-1} \left|\sum_{\hat{Y}}\right|^{-1/2}$$
$$\times \exp\{-1/2[(\hat{Y} - E(\hat{Y}))' \sum_{\hat{y}}^{-1}(\hat{Y} - E(\hat{Y}))]\},$$

which is the density function for the point defined by $\hat{y}_1$ and $\hat{y}_2$ in the bivariate normal distribution of $\hat{Y}$. The expected values of all four means, m_{ij}, may be defined by appropriate substitutions. Moreover, the form may be readily generalized to incorporate the Brogden assignment strategy for any number of jobs by adding an integral for each added job and augmenting the matrices with an added predictor for each job. Thus, for the Brogden assignment strategy, it is clear that the first two of the three parameters listed above completely determine the expectation of the means of predicted performance.

The third parameter of quotas, Q, does not affect the definition where the Brogden assignment strategy is applied because incumbency quotas are not invoked by the Brogden strategy.

The type of modification required for Equation 23 to incorporate quotas depends on whether the quota for each job applies as a proportion of the population of applicants or as a proportion of a particular sample of applicants. If the quota for job 1 is a proportion of the population of applicants, the lower limit of the inside integral would become a value, z, such that

$$q_1 = \int_{-\infty}^{\infty} \int_{z}^{\infty} f(\hat{Y}, E(\hat{y}_1), \textstyle\sum_{\hat{y}}) d\hat{y}_1 d\hat{y}_2 \tag{24}$$

In practice, the value of z may be a random variable. Job incumbency quotas ordinarily would be applied to a particular sample of applicants because any particular sample would be assigned to jobs with a fixed number of vacancies at the time the assignments are made.

It is beyond the scope of this chapter to exhaust the complexities of the variations that may arise in defining a function of the form of Equation 23 for varied general applications. The purpose of introducing the definition here is limited to providing the basis for contending that the three parameters that determine the expectation of $\hat{Y}$ are as listed above. Examination of the equations supports the contention.

For the purposes noted here, it is sufficient to state that a function exists that determines the expectation of any element, m_{ij}, in the matrix, $M_{\hat{y}}$, as follows:

$$E(m_{ij}) = F_s(i, j, P, Q, E(\hat{Y}), \textstyle\sum_{\hat{y}}), \tag{25}$$

which is the expected value for the mean of the j-th predictor in the group assigned to the i-th job among P number of jobs and where the predictors, $\hat{Y}$, have the expectation and covariance of $E(\hat{Y})$ and $\sum_{\hat{y}}$, respectively.

The subscript of F_s in Equation 25 denotes a function for a particular assignment strategy, that is, the s-th strategy. For instance, F_B may denote the Brogden strategy, or F_{LP} may denote the strategy that employs a linear programming algorithm to assign the applicants. Thus, the function F_s belongs to a family of functions dependent on (a) the specific assignment strategy that is applied, and (b) the multivariate distribution of $\hat{Y}$.

At this point, it is clear that the parameters that determine the expected result of applying an assignment strategy make it cumbersome, if not prohibitive, to attempt mathematical definition of the general range of forms that F_s may incorporate. Also, the function F_s depends on parameters that are ordinarily unknown in practice. Accordingly, an estimator based on sample data is proposed as

$$\text{Est}(m_{ij}) = F_s(i, j, P, Q, G_{\hat{y}}, S_{\hat{y}}) \tag{26}$$

where $S\hat{y}$ is defined (Equation 17) as the sample estimator of $\sum_{\hat{y}}$, and $G_{\hat{y}}$ is a vector of "guesses" of the values of $E(\hat{Y})$ in the population of applicants. As in Equation 20, the "guesses" are "reasonable" guesses if empirical estimates are not available.

The calculus of analytically evaluating a form such as Equation 23 as a general case is formidable and rewriting the form to fit more than a nominal range of situations and assignment strategies is prohibitive. Consequently, a numerical solution for the function F_s, which appears in Equations 25 and 26, is necessary. The approach proposed uses Monte Carlo methods and the implementing software can be run on personal computers with reasonable computational capabilities.

The required Monte Carlo procedure applies the selected assignment strategy to simulated, random samples from the known or assumed population of applicants. The needed statistics to be used as the estimates of MPP, such as those defined in Equation 7, are simply computed from the simulated samples in the same way as they would have been computed from a real sample.

The capability of obtaining random observations, $\hat{Y}$, from the simulated applicant population is the first requirement. One option may be to sample a very large, finite population of applicants that has been derived from an existing database of applicants. Conceivably, one might also contrive a large finite database that could be assumed to have the distribution properties of the future applicant population. For general purposes, it is often reasonable to assume that the distribution of $\hat{Y}$ in the population of applicants is multivariate normal. This provides a convenient source of pseudo-random observations in the form of a multivariate normal, pseudo-random number generator.

Accordingly, for present purposes, the distribution of $\hat{Y}$ is assumed to be multivariate normal with assumed expectation of either $E(\hat{Y})$, for Equation 25, or $G_{\hat{y}}$, for Equation 26. Also, the multivariate distribution has the variance-covariance of either $\sum_{\hat{y}}$, for Equation 25, or $S_{\hat{y}}$, for Equation 26.

Next, an algorithm for implementing the chosen assignment strategy is presumed. For practical application, this choice could be critical in that the precise method of assignment directly affects the numerical values of the resulting estimates.

Finally, the procedure is simply that of repeating the following steps enough times to obtain the desired accuracy of the numerical results:

1. Obtain a simulated sample size N from the assumed population of applicants.

2. Apply the assignment algorithm to the sample, imposing the operational quota constraints.
3. Compute the P × P matrix of sample means of predicted performance scores. The more times the process is repeated, the more accurate the resulting matrix of estimates of mean predicted performance will become. The following section describes the implementation of the method using linear programming assignment for each of 100 samples of approximately 500 applicants.

Monte Carlo Demonstration of Accuracy of eMPP and reMAP

A demonstration of the accuracy of the sample estimators of mean predicted performance (eMPP) and mean actual performance (reMAP) was carried out by Rosse, Whetzel, and Peterson (1993). The accuracy of both estimators based on sample data was considered satisfactory. However, because the conditions of the Project A validation studies vary somewhat from those of the previous evaluation, a further demonstration of the accuracy of eMPP and reMAP, under conditions specific to the Army, was conducted using Monte Carlo procedures that simulated:

1. Gathering predictor and criterion data.
2. Developing weights for predictor composites.
3. Computing eMPP and reMAP for groups that might be assigned using an assignment algorithm.
4. Sampling again for applicants from the population and assigning them to jobs using the chosen assignment algorithm.
5. Computing eMPP and reMAP for the assigned groups for comparison to the estimates.

Defining the Simulated Population

The sample statistics for the Longitudinal Validation first-tour sample (LVI) data were used to simulate a population of applicants, and the covariances were defined such that multivariate observations drawn from the population could be generated using a pseudo-random number generator. This simulated population, while not exactly the same as the population from which the Army actually draws applicants, was assumed to have covariance properties very similar to the actual population from which the LVI samples arose and from which Army recruits would be drawn in the future. The predictor variables ($n = 33$) and the criterion variable (Core Technical

Proficiency for each of the nine MOS included in the investigation) are described in previous chapters.

The simulation provides an opportunity to observe a separate criterion for each person for each MOS with the appropriate covariances with the predictor variables. Obviously, this kind of observation cannot be obtained in the "real world" because it would require the simultaneous assignment of each applicant to all nine MOS. However, the presence of an "actual" criterion score on all nine criteria for each simulated applicant provides the capability of comparing the proposed estimators to the simulated "actual" performance.

To construct a plausible covariance matrix with the required 42 variables (the 33 predictors and 9 criteria), a series of steps were performed. It was decided that the covariances should approximate those found in the 1980 Youth Population norming sample (Mitchell & Hanser, 1984), which contains only the nine ASVAB variables. The remainder of the variables were experimental measures from the Project A samples and were assumed to have been directly or indirectly restricted in range.

The first step then consisted of correcting the nine covariance matrices and the corresponding mean vectors of predictors for range restriction. The nine corrected matrices were then pooled to form a single matrix of covariances for predictors. The pooling was a weighted sum of the covariances with the between-groups variances (based on the corrected means) added into the final matrix. This provided covariances that were assumed to approximate the covariances that would be found in the 1980 Youth Population if the experimental variables had been included in that study. The resulting matrix of covariances became the assumed population covariance structure for purposes of the Monte Carlo investigations.

To include the criterion variables in the correction, each of the sample matrices of predictor covariances for the nine MOS was corrected for restriction of range using the assumed population described above. Then, the criterion variable for each group was appended to the matrix so that the covariances of predictor variables with the criterion were corrected for restriction of range. (All range restriction corrections were made using the Lawley method cited in Lord and Novick [1968].)

Each row of covariances of predictors with the criterion was appended to the population matrix to provide the needed covariances of predictor variables with all nine of the criterion variables. The covariances among the nine criterion variables were not included because they were not involved in any of the computations. The final matrix contained covariances between all 42 variables and this matrix was used in the Monte Carlo investigations to generate 42 scores (33 predictors and 9 criteria) for each simulated applicant (or recruit), using a pseudo-random number generator capable of sampling the multivariate normal population.

Simulated Validation Studies

The investigations were designed to simulate the approximate conditions of the actual Project A validation analyses. However, the validation studies were repeatable because they used simulated data. In all, the simulated validation studies were repeated 30 times for each particular investigation.

The simulated validation studies approximated the same conditions as the "real" study. Each sample consisted of the appropriate predictor variables and the appropriate criterion drawn from the simulated population. The samples were restricted by using cutoff scores (on the appropriate operational ASVAB Aptitude Area composite) supplied by the Army. To accomplish this, the ASVAB composite score for each MOS was computed for each simulated observation and, if it fell below the cutoff for the MOS corresponding to the simulated sample, the observation was discarded. Sampling continued until the number of observations for each MOS was equal to the actual developmental sample sizes in the LVI sample data.

The covariance matrices for each of the nine simulated samples were then corrected for restriction of range using only the ASVAB variables from the 1980 Youth Population, as in the actual Project A validation studies. Using the covariance matrix for each of the nine MOS, least-squares regression weights for forming predicted performance composites were obtained. The validity of each composite was estimated by adjusting the foldback multiple correlation for shrinkage, using the Rozeboom Formula 8 (1978). Additionally, the validity of each composite for predicting the criterion in each of the eight remaining MOS was computed. This was accomplished by applying the predictor weights in each of the simulated samples for all MOS except the one in which the weights were developed. Thus, these validity estimates consisted of the Pearson correlation between the predictor composite and the criterion. Finally, an estimate of the covariances of the predictor variables was obtained by pooling the nine simulated MOS covariance matrices.

At this point, the information needed to compute eMPP and reMAP was available; that is:

1. $S_{\hat{y}} = \mathrm{Est}(\sum_{\hat{y}}) =$ the matrix of estimates of covariances of predictor composites (see Equation 17), and
2. $V = \mathrm{Est}(V) =$ the estimate of the validities of each predictor composite for predicting each criterion (see Equation 18).

Numerical Evaluations
for eMPP and reMAP

The numerical evaluations for estimating mean predicted performance followed the approach described earlier. The incumbent quotas were assumed to be proportional to the Project A developmental sample sizes. For example, there were 3,083 observations distributed across the nine MOS in the LVI samples. Because 551 of them were in MOS 13B, the quota assumed for 13B was $551/3083 = .179$.

The numerical analysis used Monte Carlo evaluations of Equation 25 to obtain a 9 by 9 matrix of estimated means of predicted performance scores, one mean for each combination of predictor composite and criterion.

The assignment algorithm for this particular demonstration assumes that the future applicant samples would contain some fairly substantial number of applicants. The assignment would consist of finding the highest predicted performance among a group of applicants, assigning the corresponding applicant to the MOS for which the highest of the nine predicted performance scores was realized, and then removing the applicant from further consideration. The process is repeated for the applicants still remaining for consideration and continues until the incumbency quota for any one MOS is filled. At that point, the MOS that is filled to quota is removed from further consideration. The process is continued until all applicants are assigned. This assignment method was chosen because of its simplicity and speed of computation. It was considered a satisfactory approximation to the results that would be obtained using a linear programming algorithm, which would maximize overall MPP. Using the Monte Carlo method, the process was simulated 50 times.

For each of the nine MOS, each simulated applicant had nine values corresponding to predicted performance on each of the nine predictor composites. A 9 by 9 matrix of means was then computed by dividing the sum of predicted scores in each cell by the number of assignments for the cell. Each element of this 9 by 9 matrix constitutes an evaluation of the function defined in Equation 26 for this particular method of assignment. The diagonal elements constitute the estimate of mean predicted performance, eMPP, for each of the nine MOS. The weighted mean of the nine diagonal elements constitutes an overall estimate of mean predicted performance.

More importantly, the information for computing estimates of actual criterion performance (reMAP) is available at this point. Specifically, the reMAP is computed using Equation 20 for each of the nine MOS. An overall estimate of reMAP is also obtained by a weighted mean of the estimates for each of the nine MOS.

Simulated Actual Assignment of One Thousand Applicants

To demonstrate that the statistics eMPP and reMAP are accurate in forecasting the results that would be realized if the Army actually used the predictor composites as developed and assigned recruits based on the same assignment algorithm, it was necessary to continue the simulation process to include the gathering of simulated, "future" applicant data.

To accomplish this, after each simulated validation study was completed, a sample of 1,000 simulated applicants was drawn from the same population of applicants from which the developmental samples were drawn. However, unlike the "real world," criterion scores for all nine MOS were known for every applicant. Thus, when the MPP is computed for each simulated group of assigned applicants, it is also possible to compute the mean *actual* performance for each group.

The means of predicted performance can be compared to the means of the estimates, eMPP, and the means of actual performance can be compared to the means of the estimates, reMAP. If the two estimators, eMPP and reMAP, are accurate, they should be the same as the MPP and MAP obtained from the simulated group of "real" applicants (allowing for sampling error).

Results of Three Monte Carlo Investigations

Three Monte Carlo investigations were conducted that included all of the processes described above (i.e., simulating validation studies, obtaining eMPP and reMAP, and assigning 1,000 "future" applicants). All three studies used the same simulated population as the source of data for both developmental sample and applicant data. For each investigation, the complete process was repeated 30 times; the results reported here are based on the averages across the 30 repetitions.

The three investigations differed in the predictor variables used in predictor equations as follows:

1. Nine ASVAB subtests, for the first investigation.
2. Nine ASVAB subtests, the spatial composite, and eight computer-administered composites, for the second investigation.
3. Nine ASVAB subtests, eight ABLE composites, and seven AVOICE composites, for the third investigation.

Tables 16.1 through 16.6 present summaries of the results of each of the three Monte Carlo investigations. Tables 16.1, 16.3, and 16.5 contain

TABLE 16.1

Means of Developmental Sample Statistics for Monte Carlo
Investigation Using ASVAB Only

MOS Group	Sample Sizes[a]	Foldback Correlation	Adjusted Validity[b]	True Validity	Selection Ratio
11B	235	.741	.716	.739	.679
13B	551	.447	.416	.417	.750
19K	445	.487	.454	.452	.672
31C	172	.661	.611	.610	.498
63B	406	.623	.600	.596	.665
71L	251	.833	.819	.813	.601
88M	221	.554	.496	.513	.679
91A	535	.679	.666	.666	.600
95B	270	.751	.730	.740	.596

Note: Across 30 repetitions.
[a]Sample sizes are the same for each of the 30 repetitions.
[b]Rozeboom Formula 8 (1978).

TABLE 16.2

Means of Estimates of Mean Predicted and Mean Actual Performance
(eMPP and reMAP) Compared to Simulated Results of Assigning 1,000
"Real" Applicants: First Investigation

MOS Group	Developmental Samples			1,000 Applicants	
	Quota	eMPP	reMAP	MPP	MAP
11B	.077	.924	.829	.929	.847
13B	.179	−.172	−.226	−.167	−.217
19K	.145	−.116	−.180	−.130	−.200
31C	.056	.914	.747	.956	.768
63B	.131	.092	.034	.084	−.009
71L	.081	1.414	1.373	1.405	1.357
88M	.071	.459	.289	.463	.273
91A	.173	−.128	−.147	−.119	−.147
95B	.087	.847	.766	.833	.772
Mean		.284	.216	.286	.210

Note: Across 30 repetitions.

TABLE 16.3

Means of Developmental Sample Statistics for Monte Carlo Investigation Using
ASVAB, Spatial, and Computer Tests

MOS Group	Sample Sizes	Foldback Correlation	Adjusted Validity[a]	True Validity	Selection Ratio
11B	235	.802	.765	.771	.670
13B	551	.482	.424	.427	.753
19K	445	.517	.452	.453	.674
31C	172	.724	.641	.639	.498
63B	406	.664	.624	.623	.666
71L	251	.837	.809	.816	.604
88M	221	.608	.506	.527	.669
91A	535	.701	.675	.681	.594
95B	270	.794	.760	.773	.599

Note: Across 30 repetitions.
[a]Rozeboom Formula 8 (1978).

TABLE 16.4

Means of Estimates of Mean Predicted and Mean Actual Performance (eMPP and
reMAP) Compared to Simulated Results of Assigning 1,000 "Real" Applicants:
Second Investigation

MOS Group	Developmental Samples			1,000 Applicants	
	Quota	eMPP	reMAP	MPP	MAP
11B	.077	1.177	1.037	1.197	1.106
13B	.179	−.134	−.251	−.140	−.220
19K	.145	−.016	−.172	−.011	−.177
31C	.056	1.179	.940	1.168	.932
63B	.131	.136	−.001	.137	.025
71L	.081	1.315	1.227	1.308	1.232
88M	.071	.573	.272	.562	.291
91A	.173	−.060	−.134	−.068	−.136
95B	.087	.946	.811	.927	.862
Mean		.366	.228	.364	.248

Note: Across 30 repetitions.

TABLE 16.5

Means of Developmental Sample Statistics for Monte Carlo Investigation Using
ASVAB, ABLE, and AVOICE Tests

MOS Group	Sample Sizes	Foldback Correlation	Adjusted Validity[a]	True Validity	Selection Ratio
11B	235	.794	.738	.737	.675
13B	551	.510	.439	.441	.755
19K	445	.548	.468	.477	.673
31C	172	.747	.642	.653	.506
63B	406	.663	.608	.608	.669
71L	251	.857	.824	.827	.606
88M	221	.656	.537	.559	.679
91A	535	.699	.664	.675	.598
95B	270	.782	.732	.744	.602

Note: Across 30 repetitions.
[a]Rozeboom Formula 8 (1978).

TABLE 16.6

Means of Estimates of Mean Predicted and Mean Actual Performance (eMPP and
reMAP) Compared to Simulated Results of Assigning 1,000 "Real" Applicants:
Third Investigation

MOS Group	Developmental Samples			1,000 Applicants	
	Quota	eMPP	reMAP	MPP	MAP
11B	.077	1.076	.870	1.061	.862
13B	.179	−.039	−.162	−.036	−.155
19K	.145	.130	−.025	.134	−.018
31C	.056	1.251	.941	1.323	1.032
63B	.131	.256	.100	.249	.091
71L	.081	1.406	1.311	1.430	1.327
88M	.071	.871	.557	.848	−.602
91A	.173	−.114	−.182	−.098	−.163
95B	.087	.922	.775	.880	.764
Mean		.434	.281	.437	.294

Note: Across 30 repetitions.

summary information regarding the 30 simulated validation studies. This information includes:

- The sample sizes for each of the groups for each repetition.
- The foldback correlation (multiple correlation in the sample).
- The adjusted validity estimate based on Rozeboom's Formula 8 (1978).
- The "true" validity computed on the population.
- The selection ratio representing the proportion of simulated applicants accepted according to the AFQT cutoff scores.

Tables 16.2, 16.4, and 16.6 contain the average of the 30 estimates of mean predicted performance (eMPP) and estimated mean actual performance (reMAP) computed from developmental sample data.

The results of these three Monte Carlo investigations suggest that the estimators, eMPP and reMAP, for assessing classification efficiency are quite accurate. The critical comparisons are eMPP with MPP and reMAP with MAP. For the eMPP-MPP comparison, the discrepancies are .002, .002, and .003 across the three investigations. For the reMAP-MAP comparisons, the discrepancies are .006, .02, and .013.

Importantly, note that the individual MOS comparisons are similarly close, especially in the pattern across MOS, though the absolute values of the discrepancies are, of course, a bit larger. Finally, note that mean MPP and mean eMPP consistently overestimate mean MAP and mean reMAP by sizeable amounts. MPP overestimates MAP by .026, .116, and .134 in these three investigations and eMPP similarly overestimates reMAP.

Advantages and Disadvantages of Practical Application of eMPP and reMAP Estimators

Compared to the Brogden Allocation Average, the eMPP estimators offer the advantage of estimating MPP on the individual job level as well as the aggregated mean across all jobs among which assignments were made. Moreover, the eMPP estimators are not restricted to any simple assignment algorithm such as that outlined by Brogden, but can be applied for any assignment algorithm that can be computerized. Additionally, the patterns of variances and correlations of predictor composites need not conform to the assumptions of equality made by Brogden.

An obvious disadvantage is that the eMPP estimators cannot be calculated from a simple formula but require a Monte Carlo simulation procedure.

This is not a serious disadvantage now, as it was when Brogden developed the Allocation Average.

Both the Allocation Average and eMPP estimators are based on predicted performance. This is a major disadvantage because, as shown above, mean predicted performance is not a particularly good estimator of mean actual performance under conditions where assignment algorithms are likely to be applied. Thus, any estimate of the mean predicted performance based on validation statistics from finite samples is subject to being spuriously inflated by the conditions imposed by the assignment algorithm. An unbiased estimate of the gain in classification efficiency would require an adjustment analogous to cross-validation.

Accordingly, the reMAP estimators based on mean actual performance have been offered as the most useful estimator. As with eMPP estimators, the reMAP estimators may be applied at the level of individual jobs as well as for the aggregate of jobs. The metric of the estimators is the metric of actual performance and not the metric of predicted performance. The estimator is calculated from sample-based validation data, as is the Brogden Allocation Average.

Applications of Classification Efficiency Estimates in Project Samples

In the previous sections, the statistical concepts for estimating mean predicted performance (eMPP) and mean actual performance (reMAP) were developed, and the accuracy of the estimates was demonstrated. In this section, the estimators are applied to the LVI sample results to investigate the implications of certain issues important to decisions about classification strategies for the Army.

The specific issues addressed here are the effects of:

1. Least-squares weighting compared to synthetic weighting.
2. Various combinations of the experimental tests with the ASVAB.
3. Classification on individual MOS (in terms of reMAP).
4. The criterion (Overall Performance or Core Technical Proficiency) on classification efficiency.

The synthetic weighting systems resulted from the Army's Synthetic Validity Project (described in Chapter 15). In this project, job components that were common across a range of jobs were identified, and job incumbents rated the extent to which each component or task was an important and frequent part of their jobs. A group of psychologists judged the validity of predictor constructs included in Project A for these job components. Prediction equations can then be developed for any Army job by combining these judgments. The results of that research showed that the judgment-based approach produced validity coefficients very close to those from least-squares, sample-based methods. Thus, the important question, described in this chapter, is whether they are satisfactory for estimating classification efficiency in terms of predicted and actual performance.

The obvious advantage of the synthetic validation procedures is that they do not require the gathering of empirical criterion data but, rather, the application of relatively inexpensive experimental procedures in order to arrive at the weights. Accordingly, the generalization of the LVI results to additional MOS would be relatively easily accomplished if confidence in the effectiveness of the procedures exists.

The second issue involves combining experimental tests with the ASVAB for operational use in selecting and assigning Army recruits. Decisions would be required regarding which of the experimental tests to use and how to combine them for satisfactory classification of the recruits among MOS. This section presents results about the classification efficiency of various predictor combinations.

The third issue involves reviewing the classification efficiency results for individual MOS and determining the extent to which standard deviation units of predicted performance above zero (the classification efficiency of random assignment) in some jobs is offset by standard deviation of predicted performance units below zero in other jobs. It is important for the Army to know the extent to which critical Army jobs are predicted to have lower levels of job performance as a result of classification. This section presents classification efficiency results for individual jobs, as well as means across jobs.

The fourth issue involves the criterion used for the prediction of performance. Several criteria were identified during the analyses of first-tour job performance. These included Core Technical Proficiency, General Soldiering Proficiency, Effort and Leadership, Personal Discipline, and Physical Fitness and Military Bearing. In addition, a weighted combination of these five criteria, Overall Performance, was developed (Sadacca, Campbell, White, & DiFazio, 1989). This section compares the classification efficiency resulting from performance predictions of Core Technical Proficiency and Overall Performance.

Method

Weighting systems. The predictor scores used in these analyses were taken from the ASVAB, operationally administered when the soldiers were inducted, and from the paper-and-pencil and computerized tests administered in the Project A Experimental Battery. As indicated above, least-squares weights and synthetic weights were computed on the synthetic validity variable set, described below.

Least-Squares Weights. In all, 108 sets of least-squares (LS) weights were computed for the eMPP and reMAP estimations: nine MOS, six sets of predictor variables (shown below), and two criteria. Each of the sets of LS weights was computed using the common matrix of correlations among predictor variables and the appropriate vectors of correlations with the criterion variables. Each of the 108 sets of LS weights was used to define a predictor composite corresponding to the appropriate MOS and criterion.

The validity of each predictor composite for predicting its own criterion was obtained by computing the multiple correlation and adjusting it for "shrinkage" using the Rozeboom Formula 8 (1978). The validities of the predictor composite for predicting the criteria in other MOS were directly computed from the correlations of the predictors with the appropriate correlations with the criterion variables. These validity estimates did not require adjustment for "shrinkage." The standard deviations of the LS composites were determined by the multiple correlations. Specifically, the standard deviation of a composite of standardized regression weights (in the sample) is equal to the multiple correlation.

Synthetic Validity Weights. There also were 108 sets of weights based on the Army Synthetic Validity project methods. The validities of these weights for predicting all criteria were directly estimated using the correlations of predictor test variables and the correlations with criteria. None of these validities required adjustment for "shrinkage" because they were not estimated from the existing sample. Each set of weights based on the synthetic validation methodology was adjusted so that the standard deviation of the corresponding composite was equal to the correlation of the composite with the appropriate criterion. This was done so that the definition of the metric of the synthetically derived weights would be comparable to the metric of the least-squares weights.

Predictor variables. The components of each of the five variable sets included in the investigations are shown in Table 16.7. Note that,

TABLE 16.7

Predictor Variables Used in Classification Efficiency Analyses

Attribute Set	Components	Attribute Set	Components
ASVAB	• Verbal composite • Quantitative Composite • Speed/Accuracy (Computer) • MC, EI, AS subtests	ABLE	• Physical Condition scale • Work Orientation, Control scales • Cooperation, Stability scales • Energy scale

Spatial	• Reasoning
	• Assembling Objects, Map,
	  Maze, Orientation,
	  Object Rotation
			• Dependability composite
			• Dominance, Self-Esteem
			  scales

Computer	• Basic Speed, Basic
	  Accuracy
	• Perceptual Speed,
	  Perceptual Accuracy
	• Short-Term Memory
	• Target Shoot: Mean
	  Log Distance
	• One-Hand Tracking:
	  Mean Log Distance, Two-Hand
	  Tracking: Mean Log Distance
	• Cannon Shoot: Mean
	  Time Discrepancy
	• Mean median movement
	  time across 5 tests
		AVOICE	• Structural/Machines
			  composite
			• Rugged/Outdoors
			  composite
			• Protective Services
			  composite
			• Computers, Electronics,
			  Electronic Communications,
			  Drafting, Audiographics scales
			• Science scales
			• Leadership/Guidance scale
			• Aesthetics scale
			• Clerical/Admin.,
			  Warehousing/Shipping, Food
			  Service Prof., Food Service
			  Employee scales

Subsets of the variables from these covariance matrices were used for all analyses:
ASVAB only
ASVAB + spatial
ASVAB + computer-administered psychomotor
ASVAB + ABLE
ASVAB + AVOICE
ASVAB + all experimental predictors

for this investigation, the ASVAB component scores are slightly different that those traditionally seen. Four ASVAB factor scores were used, but computer-administered measures were used for perceptual speed and accuracy rather than the Numerical Operations and Coding Speed subtests. This was done because the synthetic validity methods used this approach, and we wished to make direct comparisons of weighting systems on the same set of variables (i.e., the 27 predictors in Table 16.7).

TABLE 16.8

Weights Used for Calculating Overall Performance Across Five Criteria[a]

MOS	Core Technical Proficiency	General Soldiering Proficiency	Effort and Leadership	Personal Discipline	Military Bearing
11B Infantryman	22.9	18.5	29.1	17.2	12.3
13B Cannon Crewmember	22.7	19.2	27.7	18.3	12.1
19K Armor Crewmember	29.4	21.1	20.5	17.9	11.0
31C Single Channel Radio Operator	29.0	20.3	22.0	17.3	11.4
63B Light Wheel Vehicle Mechanic	27.5	18.1	23.5	21.1	9.9
71L Administrative Specialist	24.1	19.9	22.7	21.0	12.3
88M Motor Transport Operator	26.1	22.8	21.8	15.4	14.0
91A Medical Specialist	26.9	16.6	23.1	22.5	11.0
95B Military Police	20.0	27.8	20.5	19.1	12.6

[a]From Sadacca, Campbell, White, and DiFazio (1989).

Criteria.   Core Technical Proficiency, defined in Chapter 11, consisted of hands-on and job knowledge measures of technical skill. Components were unit weighted; that is, they were combined by standardizing them within MOS and then adding them together.

Overall Performance was a weighted combination of the five criterion components: Core Technical Proficiency (CTP) as mentioned above, General Soldiering Proficiency (GSP), Effort and Leadership (ELS), Personal Discipline (PD) and Physical Fitness and Military Bearing (MB). The weights for the five criterion components, described by Sadacca et al. (1989), are shown in Table 16.8.

Sample.   The sample information required for computing eMPP and reMAP consisted of:

1. Estimated covariances of predictor tests in the population from which future recruits will be drawn.
2. Estimated validities of each of the predictor tests for predicting the criteria for all MOS among which assignments are to be made.

There were 32,075 soldiers in the Project A database for whom all experimental test scores were available. These data also include the nine ASVAB subtest scores. These data are presumed to have been restricted in range through selection, and thus are not representative of the population of applicants.

To obtain the estimated covariances of predictor tests in the population of applicants, the covariances based on the sample ($N = 32,075$) were corrected for range restriction (Lord & Novick, 1968) based on the nine ASVAB subtest scores found in the 1980 Youth Population.

To obtain validity estimates for the two criterion variables that are the subject of these analyses, the LVI data for which criterion information exists were used. Thus, for each of the nine MOS, there exists a matrix of covariances between predictor tests and between each test and each of the criteria.

The covariances in each of the nine matrices were also presumed to have been restricted in range by selection. At this point, the nine ASVAB subtest scores were not needed for the correction because the full matrix of corrected covariances based on the larger sample ($N = 32,075$) could be (and was) used as a basis for correcting the covariances of tests with criterion variables.

The result of these steps was a matrix of covariances for the predictor variables based on 32,075 observations presumed to be representative of the 1980 Youth Population. Also, for each MOS, there was a set of covariances between the predictor tests and the criteria. Then, all of the covariances were transformed to correlations so that the covariances were expressed in terms of standardized z-scores (mean $= 0$ and SD $= 1$).

Quota conditions. Two quota conditions were compared: (a) job assignments were made for all individuals, or (b) job assignments were made for the top 95% (5% were eliminated on the basis of the AFQT). Under both conditions, MOS assignments were made in proportion to actual accessions for fiscal year 1993.

For the first condition, 50 samples were generated with 501 applicants in each sample. There were no rejections, quotas for each MOS were proportional to FY93 accessions, and assignments were made by the linear programming strategy. In FY93, 24,258 individuals entered into the target MOS. Table 16.9 shows that of the total, 7,320 (30.2%) were assigned to MOS 11B, 1,826 (7.7%) were assigned to MOS 13B, and so on.

To simulate these quotas in the second condition, 50 sets of 527 applicants were generated. The lowest 5% were rejected, thus simulating the Army's actual rejection rate for FY93 on the initial AFQT screen. The remaining 501 applicants were assigned to MOS according to proportions entering those MOS in FY93. As shown in Table 16.9, of the 501 simulated applicants remaining after the 5% rejection, 151 were assigned to the 11B

TABLE 16.9

Proportion and Number of Soldiers Selected Into Nine Project A MOS in Fiscal
Year 1993 and in Simulations

	FY 93		Simulations	
MOS	Proportion Assigned	Number Assigned	Proportion Assigned	Number Assigned
11B Infantryman	30.2	7,320	30.1	151
13B Cannon Crewmember	7.7	1,826	7.6	38
19K Armor Crewmember	7.7	1,863	7.6	38
31C Single Channel Radio Operator	1.6	382	1.6	8
63B Light Wheel Vehicle Mechanic	12.5	3,046	12.6	63
71L Administrative Specialist	4.6	1,116	4.6	23
88M Motor Transport Operator	8.1	1,963	8.2	41
91A Medical Specialist	16.3	3,968	16.4	82
95B Military Police	11.4	2,774	11.4	57
Total	100.0	24,258	100.0	501

MOS (30.1%), 38 were assigned to the 13B MOS (7.6%), and so on. The
proportions shown are slightly different from those used in FY93 because
of rounding.

Results

Estimates of mean actual performance, reMAP, at the level
of individual jobs.   Tables 16.10 through 16.15 present detailed results for three of the six subsets of variables listed in Table 16.7. As can
be seen in these tables, the estimated classification efficiency gains are not
distributed equally for the individual MOS. Although the organization as a
whole benefits from increased aggregate performance, individual jobs may
not. Maximizing aggregate performance utility might present a different
picture. Also, policy makers could decide to impose a constraint on mean
performance losses on some MOS, which would of course result in a less
than maximum gain organization-wide.

It is important to note that these results are highly dependent on a very
specific set of conditions of assignment. In this case, the conditions approximated are those where a linear programming algorithm is to have

TABLE 16.10

Values of Two Classification Efficiency Indices for Assigning Army Applicants
Under Two Conditions of Assignment Strategy and Two Predictor Composite
Weighting Systems: Predictor Set = ASVAB Only and Criterion = Core
Technical Proficiency

| | | Assign All Applicants | | | | | Assign 95% of Applicants | | | |
| | | LS Weights | | Synth Weights | | | LS Weights | | Synth Weights | |
MOS	Quota	eMPP	reMAP	eMPP	reMAP	Quota	eMPP	reMAP	eMPP	reMAP
11B	.301	.651	.651	.433	.499	.287	.680	.680	.470	.524
13B	.076	−.579	−.579	−.538	−.680	.072	−.431	−.431	−.350	−.506
19K	.076	−.612	−.612	−.517	−.500	.072	−.468	−.468	−.405	−.383
31C	.016	−.027	−.133	−.087	−.206	.015	−.006	−.112	−.043	−.169
63B	.126	−.055	−.055	−.048	.048	.120	−.016	−.016	−.001	.095
71L	.046	.580	.532	.460	.389	.044	.630	.579	.484	.415
88M	.082	−.338	−.338	−.443	−.499	.078	−.278	−.278	−.371	−.431
91A	.164	−.063	−.063	−.083	−.216	.156	.000	.000	−.036	−.170
95B	.114	.745	.705	1.095	1.116	.108	.789	.748	1.147	1.169
All	1.000	.172	.163	.142	.132	.951	.231	.222	.200	.189

been applied to raw predicted performance scores with a specific, albeit "realistic," set of incumbency quotas. The results at the level of individual MOS could be dramatically altered by changing the distribution of incumbency quotas, altering the metric of the raw predicted performance scores, or using an altered assignment algorithm that included differential priority (utility) information, that is, directly valuing some MOS higher than others. It seems unlikely that the specific conditions that have been investigated here would be of interest for immediate operational application; they serve primarily to highlight the important point that the "mean" classification efficiency values, although very important, can disguise some deleterious effects at the level of the individual MOS.

An important issue is how well the results of the LVI data will generalize to other MOS not included in the study. In terms of classification efficiency, these results would indicate that adding groups to the assignment process beyond those already included in an investigation of classification efficiency could involve substantial risk. This is the case because the changes

TABLE 16.11

Values of Two Classification Efficiency Indices for Assigning Army Applicants
Under Two Conditions of Assignment Strategy and Two Predictor Composite
Weighting Systems: Predictor Set = ASVAB Only and Criterion =
Overall Performance

| | Assign All Applicants | | | | | Assign 95% of Applicants | | | | |
| | LS Weights | | Synth Weights | | | LS Weights | | Synth Weights | |
MOS	Quota	eMPP	reMAP	eMPP	reMAP	Quota	eMPP	reMAP	eMPP	reMAP
11B	.301	.682	.666	.679	.683	.287	.706	.690	.701	.705
13B	.076	−.048	−.048	−.064	.040	.072	−.007	−.007	−.048	.056
19K	.076	.119	.084	−.065	−.055	.072	.140	.101	−.046	−.035
31C	.016	−.127	−.127	−.034	.049	.015	−.099	−.099	−.021	.062
63B	.126	.094	.094	.040	.101	.120	.111	.111	.056	.119
71L	.046	.134	−.026	.018	−.154	.044	.162	−.002	.031	−.147
88M	.082	−.162	−.162	−.060	−.089	.078	−.117	−.117	−.047	−.080
91A	.164	.065	.065	−.063	−.154	.156	.084	.085	−.047	−.136
95B	.114	.084	.084	.084	.083	.108	.112	.112	.104	.098
All	1.000	.244	.219	.194	.188	.951	.260	.244	.213	.206

to the individual MOS in expected performance are largely unknown, and
could result in a substantial undesired reduction in important MOS.

Estimates of Mean Actual Performance, (reMAP), Averaged Across MOS

Table 16.16 shows the average estimates of reMAP, extracted from Tables 16.10 through 16.15, for easier reference. It also summarizes results
from the other three subsets of predictors. The table shows the means and
standard deviations of the indices across the six sets of predictor variables.

Before considering the five issues raised at the beginning of this section,
note first the general effect of classification over and above the effect of
selection. The values in the "All Assigned" part of Table 16.16 show the
effect of classification, because all applicants are assigned, and no one is
selected out. The values in the "95% Assigned" part of the table show
the combined effects of selecting out 5% of applicants and classifying the
remainder. A working estimate of the gain resulting from selection can be

TABLE 16.12

Values of Two Classification Efficiency Indices for Assigning Army Applicants
Under Two Conditions of Assignment Strategy and Two Predictor Composite
Weighting Systems: Predictor Set = ASVAB + ABLE and Criterion = Core
Technical Proficiency

MOS	Quota	Assign All Applicants				Quota	Assign 95% of Applicants			
		LS Weights		Synth Weights			LS Weights		Synth Weights	
		eMPP	reMAP	eMPP	reMAP		eMPP	reMAP	eMPP	reMAP
11B	.301	.610	.506	.619	.650	.287	.618	.511	.661	.691
13B	.076	−.340	−.463	−.515	−.676	.072	−.200	−.337	−.325	−.499
19K	.076	−.487	−.734	−.505	−.510	.072	−.322	−.596	−.402	−.406
31C	.016	.408	−.293	−.061	−.160	.015	.483	−.246	−.037	−.131
63B	.126	−.052	−.312	.015	.099	.120	.012	−.262	.068	.149
71L	.046	.547	.357	.575	.575	.044	.621	.427	.611	.603
88M	.082	−.107	−.572	−.391	−.475	.078	−.020	−.503	−.320	−.407
91A	.164	.041	−.079	−.049	−.198	.156	.068	−.053	.006	−.142
95B	.114	.718	.610	.553	.228	.108	.756	.650	.613	.289
All	1.000	.226	.044	.160	.097	.951	.280	.090	.225	.160

obtained by subtracting the appropriate values in the "All Assigned" part
from the "95% Assigned" part. (For example, .189 − .132 = .057 selection
gain for ASVAB only, Core Technical Performance.) We say "working
estimate" because the proportions assigned to each MOS differ across the
"All Assigned" and "95% Assigned" conditions, as described above (see
"Quota Conditions"), confounding such effects with selection effects.

Least-Squares and Synthetic Weights. In general, the weighting system made a small to very small difference, but not in a consistent direction. For the Core Technical Proficiency (CTP) criterion, least-
squares weights produced slightly higher reMAP values for the ASVAB
only, ASVAB plus Spatial, and ASVAB plus Psychomotor predictor sets,
but synthetic weights produced slightly higher values for ASVAB plus
ABLE and ASVAB plus AVOICE. The weighting systems showed virtually identical reMAP values when all predictors were used for CTP; while
the ASVAB plus AVOICE predictor showed the largest difference in favor
of the synthetic weights.

TABLE 16.13

Values of Two Classification Efficiency Indices for Assigning Army Applicants
Under Two Conditions of Assignment Strategy and Two Predictor Composite
Weighting Systems: Predictor Set = ASVAB + ABLE and Criterion =
Overall Performance

| | | Assign All Applicants | | | | | Assign 95% of Applicants | | | |
| | | LS Weights | | Synth Weights | | | LS Weights | | Synth Weights | |
MOS	Quota	eMPP	reMAP	eMPP	reMAP	Quota	eMPP	reMAP	eMPP	reMAP
11B	.301	.599	.544	.681	.671	.287	.637	.577	.697	.685
13B	.076	−.059	−.209	−.073	.012	.072	.024	−.174	−.053	.040
19K	.076	.043	−.160	−.077	−.102	.072	.093	−.125	−.055	−.083
31C	.016	.227	−.650	−.035	−.346	.015	.311	−.652	−.023	−.376
63B	.126	.230	.043	.041	−.089	.120	.256	.057	.054	−.071
71L	.046	.242	−.105	.014	−.193	.044	.298	−.059	.029	−.165
88M	.082	.437	.221	−.083	−.250	.078	.462	.243	−.065	−.227
91A	.164	.226	.093	−.046	−.101	.156	.256	.118	−.033	−.087
95B	.114	.327	.076	.171	.449	.108	.354	.116	.182	.456
All	1.000	.333	.168	.205	.184	.951	.372	.198	.220	.200

As shown in Table 16.16, averaged across all the predictor sets, the reMAP differences between the two systems are in the third decimal. However, the synthetic weights consistently show less variation in reMAP values across predictor sets (about 1/2 the standard deviation value of least-squares weights) no matter which criterion or quota system is in effect.

Predictor Combinations. These results show that the ASVAB-only predictor set produces nearly as much, if not more, gain than the ASVAB combined with other predictors. For CTP, the highest gain is produced by ASVAB plus Spatial using least-squares weights, but it is only .004 greater than ASVAB only. Most of the other least-squares combinations are noticeably smaller.

For Overall Performance, the ASVAB-only combination (least-squares weights) also shows the highest gain. However, the differences in reMAP values are much smaller across the predictor combinations, no doubt because of the importance of the other predictors for predicting this more comprehensive criterion. The highest synthetically weighted predictor

TABLE 16.14

Values of Two Classification Efficiency Indices for Assigning Army Applicants
Under Two Conditions of Assignment Strategy and Two Predictor Composite
Weighting Systems: Predictor Set = ASVAB + All Experimental Predictors and
Criterion = Core Technical Proficiency

| | | Assign All Applicants | | | | | Assign 95% Applicants | | | |
| | | LS Weights | | Synth Weights | | | LS Weights | | Synth Weights | |
MOS	Quota	eMPP	reMAP	eMPP	reMAP	Quota	eMPP	reMAP	eMPP	reMAP
11B	.301	.523	.313	.439	.389	.287	.561	.349	.467	.417
13B	.076	−.237	−.475	−.268	−.423	.072	−.066	−.330	−.180	−.333
19K	.076	.021	−.245	−.563	−.688	.072	.145	−.132	−.402	−.521
31C	.016	.898	.428	−.257	−.080	.015	.892	.417	−.193	.019
63B	.126	.159	−.167	.203	.206	.120	.217	−.107	.227	.228
71L	.046	.711	.441	.700	.745	.044	.810	.527	.733	.782
88M	.082	.211	−.347	−.104	−.300	.078	.317	−.275	−.046	−.238
91A	.164	.211	.029	.090	−.192	.156	.269	.084	.151	−.122
95B	.114	.808	.598	.717	.406	.108	.817	.606	.757	.464
All	1.000	.352	.090	.211	.082	.951	.417	.148	.262	.139

combination is about .02–.03 points less than the ASVAB only least-squares
weighted combination.

Interestingly, the ASVAB plus AVOICE combination produces the highest reMAP value for the synthetic weights, in *all* cases. It significantly outperforms the least-squares weights for ASVAB plus AVOICE in all four conditions, and outperforms all least-squares combinations except ASVAB only or ASVAB plus Spatial for CTP.

The Criterion. Table 16.16 shows that higher reMAP values are obtained using the Overall Performance criterion than using the CTP criterion. This holds true for all four quota/weighting system conditions when values are averaged across all predictor combinations. These differences were about .03 points (for 95% Assigned) to .07 points (All Assigned). It also holds true for all but two of the 24 separate comparisons across predictor combination/quota/weighting system conditions—those two being ASVAB plus Spatial and ASVAB plus AVOICE combinations in the "95% Assigned," least-squares conditions. These findings in favor

TABLE 16.15
Values of Two Classification Efficiency Indices for Assigning Army Applicants
Under Two Conditions of Assignment Strategy and Two Predictor Composite
Weighting Systems: Predictor Set = ASVAB + All Experimental Predictors and
Criterion = Overall Performance

| | Assign All Applicants | | | | | Assign 95% Applicants | | | | |
| | | LS Weights | | Synth Weights | | | LS Weights | | Synth Weights | |
MOS	Quota	eMPP	reMAP	eMPP	reMAP	Quota	eMPP	reMAP	eMPP	reMAP
11B	.301	.629	.487	.609	.588	.287	.656	.512	.633	.614
13B	.076	.083	−.328	−.048	−.077	.072	.179	−.315	−.033	.092
19K	.076	.382	.094	−.052	−.063	.072	.455	.141	−.036	−.036
31C	.016	.706	−.540	−.014	−.152	.015	.776	−.526	.000	−.135
63B	.126	.305	−.057	.062	−.035	.120	.350	−.019	.083	−.017
71L	.046	.577	−.122	.058	−.116	.044	.627	−.082	.068	−.108
88M	.082	.701	.300	−.064	−.261	.078	.752	.333	−.048	−.246
91A	.164	.349	.122	−.010	−.085	.156	.378	.153	.008	−.073
95B	.114	.613	.283	.167	.261	.108	.640	.306	.185	.277
All	1.000	.485	.184	.198	.161	.951	.527	.214	.218	.180

of Overall Performance are somewhat surprising. They may be due to the greater predictability of the more comprehensive criterion because of its higher reliability (but we note that the CTP criterion is highly reliable itself, see Chapter 12), its inclusion of all five major components of job performance, or the differential weighting across MOS of the five major components.

Classification Efficiency of Full Versus Reduced Prediction Equations

In Chapter 13, estimates of the population selection validity were computed for prediction equations using (a) all the Experimental Battery predictor composite scores plus the four ASVAB factor scores, and (b) two reduced equations that were limited to 10 or fewer predictors (including ASVAB). The two reduced equations were obtained via an expert judgment procedure that emphasized either maximizing selection validity or maximizing classification efficiency for the nine Batch A MOS when CTP was used as the maximizing function. These three equations were also compared in terms of their classification efficiency by using both eMPP and

TABLE 16.16

Values of Two Classification Indices Averaged Across Nine Army Jobs for Two
Criteria, Two Assignment Strategies, Two Weighting Systems, and Six
Predictor Composites

| | All Assigned | | | | 95% Assigned | | | |
| | LS Weights | | Synth Weights | | LS Weights | | Synth Weights | |
	eMPP	reMAP	eMPP	reMAP	eMPP	reMAP	eMPP	reMAP
				Core Technical Proficiency				
ASVAB only	.172	.163	.142	.132	.231	.222	.200	.189
ASVAB + spatial	.194	.167	.156	.099	.255	.226	.215	.155
ASVAB + psychomotor	.262	.120	.184	.093	.320	.176	.232	.139
ASVAB + ABLE	.226	.044	.160	.097	.280	.090	.225	.160
ASVAB + AVOICE	.266	.088	.172	.141	.331	.149	.230	.200
ASVAB + all preds	.352	.090	.211	.082	.417	.148	.263	.139
Avg across sets	.245	.112	.171	.107	.306	.169	.228	.164
SD across sets	.058	.044	.022	.021	.061	.047	.019	.023
				Overall Performance				
ASVAB only	.234	.219	.194	.188	.260	.244	.213	.206
ASVAB + spatial	.256	.188	.197	.187	.280	.209	.208	.201
ASVAB + psychomotor	.361	.177	.187	.150	.389	.197	.204	.168
ASVAB + ABLE	.333	.168	.205	.184	.372	.198	.220	.200
ASVAB + AVOICE	.346	.124	.205	.201	.374	.142	.220	.216
ASVAB + all preds	.485	.184	.198	.161	.527	.214	.218	.180
Avg across sets	.336	.177	.198	.179	.367	.201	.214	.195
SD across sets	.081	.028	.006	.017	.087	.031	.006	.016

Note: Values in standard deviation units.

reMAP to evaluate the effects of three sets of job assignments based on
linear programming.

Each set of job assignments made use of one of the three prediction
equations. Consequently, it is possible to ask whether the expert judgments produced a difference in the two sets of reduced equations in terms
of the estimates of classification efficiency yielded by each one. If the

TABLE 16.17
Values of Two Classification Indices Averaged Across Nine Army Jobs for the
Core Technical Proficiency Criterion and Three Types of Prediction Equations

| | Aggregate Classification Efficiency | | | |
| | eMPP | | reMAP | |
	All Assigned	95% Assigned[a]	All Assigned	95% Assigned[a]
Full Equation (All Predictors)	.325	.401	.081	.153
Reduced Equation: Selection	.248	.317	.113	.180
Reduced Equation: Classification	.278	.361	.136	.217

Note: Least-squares weighting system. Values in standard deviation units.
[a] Applicant pool reduced 4.9% by prior selection on AFQT.

expert judgments achieved the intended objective, then the reduced equations developed to maximize classification should yield higher estimates of
classification efficiency than the reduced equations developed to maximize
selection validity.

The results, averaged across MOS, are shown in Table 16.17. The estimation procedure again used linear programming to make job assignments
in proportion to FY93 accessions under the two conditions of (a) no prior
selection, and (b) elimination of 5% of the sample, using AFQT. As before,
each set of job assignments was repeated 50 times on simulated samples
of applicants.

The top row in Table 16.17 is analogous to the sixth row (ASVAB +
all predictors) in Table 16.16, columns 1 and 2, and 5 and 6 (least-squares
weights). The actual values in the two tables are slightly different because
Table 16.17 is based on an independent set of simulated samples and, for the
ASVAB, this table used the four factor scores instead of the nine subtest
scores that were used in the computations for Table 16.16. The values
in Table 16.16 are slightly higher, which may mean that using the four
ASVAB factor scores loses a small amount of classification information,
as compared to the full set of nine subtests.

A comparison of the full equation with the reduced equations (using
reMAP) shows that the reduced equations produce greater classification

efficiency than the full equation, presumably because they contain less "noise." The result is not in the same direction for eMPP because it does not correct for "shrinkage" at the job assignment stage. This shrinkage is greater for the longer equation. That is, eMPP is proportionally more inflated when more predictors are used.

Comparison of the classification gains produced by the two sets of expert-developed reduced equations shows a small advantage in favor of the equations that were in fact intended to emphasize classification. The classification equations produced a 15 to 20% greater gain than the selection equations.

These are tantalizing results, and they invite additional research as to how maximum potential classification efficiency can best be achieved, and of how such gains will be affected by variation in the critical constraints that are part of any operational system.

CONCLUDING COMMENTS

This chapter has used classification efficiency analyses to provide information relevant to a number of issues around the use of the ASVAB and Project A/Career Force experimental predictors. Each of these issues has been discussed above. Some more general conclusions are offered here.

First, these analyses highlight the intricacy of studying classification efficiency and the considerable amount of research remaining before we reach stable ground. The results presented in this chapter sound a cautionary note for the acceptance of mean predicted performance, as measured by Brogden's Allocation Average or by more elaborate simulations, as the appropriate index of classification efficiency. MPP is, after all, intended as an estimate of Mean Actual Performance (MAP). An alternative estimate of MAP, called reMAP, seems to more closely match the behavior of MAP in practical situations. We have striven to provide a comprehensive rationale and explanation of this estimate and welcome its scrutiny by other interested investigators.

Second, it seems clear that classification strategies can increase aggregate performance, certainly over random allocation of individuals, and perhaps in fairly realistic scenarios such as the "95% assigned" condition investigated here. We say "perhaps" because these investigations point out the relative fragility of any classification strategy. That is, modifying the mix of jobs that are the targets for classification, changing the proportions assigned to each job, or causing increases or decreases in the underlying validity of predictor composites for the jobs can produce rather dramatic shifts in the expected increase in level of productivity, *especially at the individual job level.* These two points seem to suggest the need for relatively specific modeling exercises aimed at particular instantiations of more general classification strategies when operational classification procedures are being considered.

Finally, a not unreasonably optimistic interpretation of these results suggests that a single multiple aptitude test battery such as ASVAB alone can provide useful classification efficiency. It also appears that judgmental methods, as operationalized in the Army's synthetic validation strategy and in the reduced equation analysis, can be used (a) to create predictor equations with relatively small losses in classification efficiency from that to be expected using relatively unobtainable least-squares equations, and (b) to select optimal sets of predictors that maximize classification efficiency with virtually no loss in selection validity.

17

Environmental Context Effects on Performance and the Prediction of Performance

Darlene M. Olson, Leonard A. White, Michael G. Rumsey, and Walter C. Borman

The Project A research program explored the relationships between the characteristics of individuals and their performance. For the most part, it did not take into account the effects of the situation or environment on performance, or on the predictor-performance relationship. Environmental differences may also contaminate measurement (Brogden & Taylor, 1950b) or restrict criterion variance (Steel & Mento, 1986). However, two related research efforts by ARI and contractor staff did examine the relationship of environmental characteristics to individual performance. This chapter summarizes their efforts.

Schneider proposed "the idea that environments and people are not separable and that the people in an environment make it what it is" (1987b, p. 440). He viewed the inseparability of people and environments as an explanation for homogeneity within an organization. Yet to the extent that an environment is defined in terms of individuals within that environment, this conceptualization would seem to imply a very fluid environment, which changes as people change. One person's environment is not another person's environment. Studies of supervisor-subordinate dyads (e.g., Graen, 1976) suggest that supervisors often act substantially differently toward different subordinates.

The idea that "people in an environment make it what it is" is a powerful explanatory tool, but it has its limits. There are other factors that impact upon the environment, including history, rules and regulations, and external expectations. These factors interact with and constrain the influence of factors defined by current organizational membership. They help ensure that the mission, goals, and functions of an established organization such as the U.S. Army will not change radically in a short period of time. They thus foster environmental stability.

This, then, is our view of the organizational environment. It has some degree of institutional stability and social homogeneity, yet it is unique for every individual. This uniqueness is a function of at least two factors: differences in perception and differences in social interactions. Each individual perceives the environment differently as a function of his or her own personality and cognitive processes. Further, each individual interacts uniquely with his or her own peers, supervisors, and subordinates. These interactions help define the working environment for that person.

The purposes of the research efforts described in this chapter were to (a) investigate dimensions of the overall work environment for U.S. Army enlisted jobs, (b) examine patterns of relationships between individual work environment factors and different kinds of performance measures, and (c) investigate potential moderating effects of work environment on the relationships between individual differences and job performance. Particular attention was focused on leadership as a major component of the work environment.

This chapter is presented in two parts. The first part focuses on leadership, as reported by subordinates, as an environmental property. It will examine whether relationships between individual differences and performance vary as perceived leader behaviors vary. The second part presents a more comprehensive view of the work environment. An instrument assessing a wide array of work environment variables was developed and administered in conjunction with the Project A predictors and performance measures. The development of this instrument and the relationships found between different components of the work environment and person and performance variables is summarized.

LEADER INFLUENCES ON RELATIONSHIPS BETWEEN INDIVIDUAL CHARACTERISTICS AND PERFORMANCE

The Leadership Environment

Longitudinal research indicates that the quality of leader-subordinate work relationships is predictive of job success (Wakabayaski & Graen, 1984). In addition, some investigators (e.g., Barnes, Potter, & Fiedler, 1983) have suggested that the prediction of job performance from general ability is moderated by type of leadership.

With the emergence of interactive leadership approaches (e.g., Graen, 1976; Jacobs, 1971) has come a recognition of the reciprocal contributions subordinates make to the leadership process. Although leaders may tend to have a characteristic style, they vary their behavior substantially in response to subordinates' actions and needs. Graen has shown that leaders form different kinds of working relationships with their subordinates, which can range from "in-group" relationships characterized by mutual support and trust to "out-group" interactions where both parties do only what is required by the formal employment contract.

Past research has shown that subordinates' performance is a powerful determinant of subsequent treatment by superiors (e.g., Greene, 1975). Generally, poor performers are more likely to have low quality relationships with their superiors. However, this phenomenon has been investigated primarily in the laboratory. There also is evidence that relatively stable personal dispositions enable some subordinates to form more positive relationships with superiors. Graen and his associates (Graen, Novak, & Sommerkamp, 1982) demonstrated that the strength of subordinates' need for growth influenced the formation of effective relationships with superiors.

The focus of this effort was on perceived leadership and its relationship to individual difference variables and job performance. The model examined in this research assumes that job performance is influenced by a new incumbent's capabilities measured prior to enlistment and by characteristics of the work environment. The specific purposes were to (a) examine relationships among dimensions of leader behavior and subordinate performance, and (b) explore possible moderating effects of leadership on the relation between general cognitive ability and job performance.

Categories of Leaders' Behavior

During the past 35 years, researchers have proposed many different taxonomies detailing the activities of leaders. Based on extensive research, Yukl and his colleagues (e.g., Yukl & Nemeroff, 1979; Yukl & Van Fleet, 1982) developed a comprehensive taxonomy of 12 leader behavior dimensions that are general enough to apply to different kinds of supervisors, yet specific enough to provide relatively homogeneous categories of leader behavior.

These 12 dimensions were used as the starting point for the present investigation. Critical incident workshops conducted with 80 NCOs in both combat and noncombat MOS generated a total of 474 examples of leader behaviors thought to influence soldier performance. These examples and a review of pertinent sources resulted in the addition of one new category, "Discipline/Punishment," to the Yukl taxonomy and the modification of other categories to more specifically address the Army environment. The expanded list of 13 categories was then reduced to 9 on the basis of a classification exercise conducted by two of the authors and a panel of 31 additional NCOs. These nine categories are shown in Table 17.1. A 60-item questionnaire, with at least 5 items in each category, was developed and administered as part of the Project A predictor field test to 696 first-tour soldiers in five MOS.

The Relationship of the Perceived Leadership to Individual Differences and Job Performance

The next step was to focus on the relationships between perceived leadership and individual difference variables and job performance in two samples.

Preliminary Field Sample Analyses

The 696 first-tour soldiers described above were administered the Supervisory Behavior Rating Scale (SBRS) consisting of the 60 items based on the nine categories of leader behavior identified above. Principal components factor analysis (with promax rotation) of the items resulted in four factors that were descriptive of leader behavior. The factors were Support/Inspiration, Structuring Work, Fairness/Discipline, and Participation. Scale

TABLE 17.1

Categories of Leader Behaviors

1. Planning
2. Monitoring
3. Informing
4. Leading by Example
5. Recognizing and Rewarding
6. Training and Developing
7. Permitting Participation
8. Supporting
9. Disciplining/Punishing and Use of Constructive Criticism

scores were formed by summing the responses to the items loading highest on the factor. In addition, a total leadership score was generated by summing the four scale scores.

Supervisors evaluated soldiers using the Army-wide and job-specific rating scales. Soldiers also completed the hands-on and job knowledge tests (see Chapter 8). The Armed Forces Qualification Test (AFQT) was used as a measure of general cognitive ability for each soldier.

Correlations between the summated total score of perceived leadership provided by each soldier and each of the performance measures revealed that the highest correlation was between the Quality of Perceived Leadership and Army-wide performance ratings ($r = .20$). Perceived leadership correlations with the other performance measures were as follows: job-specific ratings ($r = .12$), hands-on tests ($r = .09$), and job knowledge tests ($r = .01$). Within the set of Army-wide performance dimensions, strongest relationships were obtained between the SBRS dimension of Supportive and Participative Leadership and ratings of subordinates' Adherence to Regulations and Willingness to Provide Extra Effort.

Hierarchical regression analysis was used to estimate the incremental validity contributed by perceived leadership climate to the relationship between cognitive ability (i.e., AFQT score) and performance. The AFQT scores were entered first in the regression, followed by Leadership and the Ability by Leadership interaction. Results showed no statistically significant increase in R^2 because of inclusion of the Ability by Leadership interaction in the model.

Concurrent Validation Sample Analyses

Possible interactions between the Perceived Leadership measure and a more comprehensive set of variables were examined in the CVI sample by Hough, Gast, White, and McCloy (1986). On the basis of item analysis using the field test data, the Supervisory Behavior Rating Scale was revised and renamed the Supervisory Behavior Questionnaire, and was composed of the four factors (Support/Inspiration, Structuring Work, Fairness/Discipline, and Participation) described above. Scale scores were generated for each factor and an "Overall Quality of Perceived Leadership" score was obtained by summing the four scale scores.

From the Project A predictor battery, the following predictor scores were used: (a) the AFQT, (b) three spatial ability factors scores (Spatial Reasoning-Power, Spatial Reasoning-Speed, and Spatial Orientation), (c) three temperament factor scores and the physical condition scale from the Assessment of Background and Life Experiences (ABLE), (d) six interest factor scores from the Army Vocational Interest Career Examination (AVOICE), and (e) six desired work outcome scores from the Job Orientation Blank (JOB) (Peterson et al., 1990). Performance measures included the total hands-on and job knowledge test scores, overall composites of the Army-wide and MOS specific rating scales, and the three Army-Wide Rating factor scores (Technical Skill and Effort, Personal Discipline, Physical Fitness/Military Bearing). The sample, from the first-tour concurrent validation data collection, comprised 5,161 first-tour soldiers in the nine Batch A MOS.

Among the total set of Project A predictors examined, only the ABLE Dependability score ($r = .23$) had a correlation above .15 with the Total Quality of Perceived Leadership score. Of the four factor scores from the Supervisory Behavior Questionnaire, the Participation factor score yielded the highest correlations, also with the ABLE. The multiple correlation between the ABLE scales and Participation was .33, with the Achievement Orientation factor alone correlating .21 with Participation.

The relationships between Perceived leadership and performance were also examined. Leadership was most strongly related to supervisory ratings. For three of the four Leadership factors, the correlations with the overall composite Army-Wide rating score ranged from .18 to .23. No correlations above .09 were found between any of the Leadership factors and the total hands-on and job knowledge test scores.

Next, possible moderating effects of leadership on the relationships between predictor and performance measures were examined. The summated

TABLE 17.2
Moderating Effect of Perceived Leadership on Correlations between
Dependability and Rated Performance

Subordinates' Rated Performance	Correlations with Subordinates' Dependability Rated Leadership Quality	
	Low	High
Technical Skill and Effort	.21	.10
Integrity and Control	.29	.24
Appearance	.21	.10

Note: Differences in correlations of .08 or more are significant at $p \leq .05$.

Overall Quality of Leadership score was used to divide the sample into thirds, and correlations between predictor and performance variables for the upper and lower thirds were calculated. Only for the Dependability factor was any evidence of a moderating effect found, with significantly ($p < .05$) higher correlations between Dependability and two supervisory Army-wide ratings factor scores within the Low Perceived Quality of Leadership group than in the High group (see Table 17.2).

Conclusions from Leader Component Research

This research focused on how the leadership environment relates to individual difference predictors, performance criteria, and the link between the two. It used the Yukl model of leader behavior to develop a nine-dimension leadership taxonomy tailored to the Army environment, which can be parsimoniously represented in terms of four factors.

Using these factors, Hough et al. (1986) found that there was generally no relationship between subordinates' cognitive ability and their perceptions of leader climate. Nor was there any evidence that perceived leader climate moderated relationships between general cognitive aptitude (as measured by AFQT) and job performance.

These researchers did find a relationship between personality/temperament and perceptions of leadership climate. The more dependable the soldier, the higher he or she rated the overall Quality of Leadership, particularly when the soldier perceived the quality of leadership to be low. As Hough et al. noted (1986, p. 9), "it appears that a soldier's personal trait of "dependability" is less important to ratings of their effectiveness when they are in units with better leaders."

Dependability is composed of three scales: Nondelinquency, Traditional Values, and Conscientiousness. Low scores on this dimension are linked to indiscipline and attrition. It may be that effective leaders can, through support, structure, discipline, and participatory leadership, overcome shortcomings in subordinates' dependability.

The present research demonstrated in a field setting that perceived leadership is related to Army-wide ratings, which feed into "will do" performance factors. This finding can be interpreted as showing that perceived quality of leadership influences typical soldier performance or as showing that soldier performance influences perceived quality of leadership. Our interpretation is that, to some degree, both conclusions are correct. Leadership effects on performance may be understood in terms of exchange theory (Graen, 1976), which views the interaction between leader and subordinate as a reciprocal influence process that develops over time. Supervisors will evaluate subordinates more favorably if they are perceived as willing to work hard and support the mission. In return for their support, these soldiers are likely to receive more individualized attention, information, and other resources from their supervisors. This, in turn, serves to reinforce and sustain subordinate effort. The finding that the perceived quality of leadership can moderate the relationship between subordinates' dependability and their rated performance is also consistent with this view. Although this moderating influence was not sufficiently great to seriously challenge the use of personality predictors for selection, it does point to Dependability as a factor whose importance may increase as the effectiveness of one's leaders declines.

THE GENERAL ARMY WORK ENVIRONMENT

Much of the research on the work environment has focused on potentially inhibiting environmental effects. During the early 1980s, Peters and O'Connor initiated a program of research to study aspects of the work situation, or "constraints," that might act to interfere with the use of individual abilities and motivation in performing job activities (Peters & O'Connor, 1980). This interference would have the most severe impact on the performance of highly capable and well-motivated individuals who would also experience more dissatisfaction and frustration than their counterparts with lower levels of ability and motivation. Schneider (1987a, 1987b) broadened the focus of environmental effects research beyond constraints, exploring potentially enhancing effects as well.

For selection purposes, it is particularly important to examine the possible interactive effects of cognitive abilities, temperament, and work environment on job performance. Schneider (1978) and Peters and O'Connor (1980) proposed that environmental factors may moderate the relationships between ability and performance. In contrast, Schmidt and Hunter (1977) have contended that the prediction of performance from ability is stable across situations and over time for various jobs.

Much of the support for environmental moderator effects has come from laboratory research (O'Connor, Peters, & Segovis, 1980; Peters, Fisher, & O'Connor, 1982; Schneider, 1978). Results from field research (e.g., Watson, O'Connor, Eulberg, & Peters, 1983) have been less supportive.

The current effort built on earlier investigations of environmental variables to generate a set specifically suited to the Army. This environmental taxonomy then served as the basis for developing an instrument to assess the individual's perception of the Army work environment, the Army Work Environment Questionnaire (AWEQ). The AWEQ was then used to investigate questions relating to the relationship between the work environment and the extraordinarily broad range of individual characteristics and job performance variables developed in Project A.

Developing the AWEQ

The development of the AWEQ, which is described in Olson and Borman (1989), will be briefly summarized here. A critical incidents (Flanagan, 1954) approach was used, involving workshops with Army participants to generate incidents of effective and ineffective performance influenced by situational factors. Incidents were sorted by six psychologists into 14 environmental dimensions, which were defined to encompass situations enhancing or facilitating performance as well as those inhibiting or interfering with performance.

Following factor analysis, a 110-item AWEQ was reduced to a 53-item version, consisting of five factors. Conceptually, three of the factors are more directly linked to performance of job functions: General Situational Constraints, Training/Opportunity to Use Skills, and Job/Task Importance. The remaining two are more indicative of climate dimensions: Supervisor Support and Unit Cohesion/Peer Support.

TABLE 17.3
Correlations between Work Environment Constructs and Performance Measures

Work Environment Constructs	Performance Measures			
	Army-wide Ratings	*MOS-specific Ratings*	*Job Knowledge Tests*	*Hands-on Tests*
General Constraints	10	00	−07	−06
Supervisor Support	22	12	05	00
Training/Opportunity to Use Skills	07	12	06	23
Job/Task Importance	22	12	07	06
Unit Cohesion/Peer Support	12	09	09	06

Note: $N = 4,951$.

AWEQ Results

Correlations with Performance

The administration of the AWEQ to 5,080 first-tour Army enlisted soldiers in the Batch A MOS in CVI was used to assess the relationship between AWEQ factors and four summary performance measures. The four performance measures included an Army-wide measure of Overall Soldier Effectiveness and composite scores for the MOS-specific rating scales, hands-on measures, and job knowledge tests. As shown in Table 17.3, three correlations above .20 were observed: Supervisor Support with Army-wide performance ($r = .22$), Job/Task importance with Army-wide performance ($r = .22$), and Training/Opportunity to Use Skills with hands-on task proficiency ($r = .23$). None of the other work environment constructs correlated above .12 with these measures.

Regression Analyses

Moderated regression analysis was used to examine the relationships of individual difference measures, perceptions of the work environment, and their interactions to the same four summary measures of job performance among the same 5,080 soldiers. Jobs were divided into the four following categories: Combat, Clerical, Operations, and Skilled Technical.

Four regression models were explored for each of the four performance measures (Army-wide ratings, MOS-specific ratings, hands-on proficiency and job knowledge) within each job category. One model regressed each of the performance variables against AFQT and the three ABLE factor scores (Achievement, Dependability, and Adjustment) to determine the contribution of individual differences to job performance (Individual Differences Model). A second, Environmental Model, examined the contribution of the five work environment dimensions. A Full Model included both individual differences and environmental factors. A fourth model added interactions among the individual difference and environment predictors to the full model. All correlations are uncorrected.

The multiple correlations for the Full Model are shown in Table 17.4. The regression analyses showed that, while the Individual Differences Model generally yielded higher multiple correlations than did the Environmental Model, the Environmental Model was a more powerful predictor of

TABLE 17.4
Multiple Correlations for the MOS Cluster Regression Models

Predictor Set	Overall Effectiveness Rating	Personal Discipline Rating	Hands-on Score	Job Knowledge Score
Clerical Jobs				
Indiv Diff (ID)	.30	.26	.40	.57
Environment (E)	.26	.26	.24	.20
ID + E	.36	.35	.45	.57
Combat Jobs				
Indiv Diff (ID)	.33	.39	.24	.50
Environment (E)	.22	.24	.22	.17
ID + E	.35	.41	.33	.53
Operations Jobs				
Indiv Diff (ID)	.26	.30	.14	.40
Environment (E)	.20	.20	.32	.26
ID + E	.30	.33	.35	.47
Skilled Technical Jobs				
Indiv Diff (ID)	.33	.32	.20	.33
Environment (E)	.32	.30	.26	.17
ID + E	.41	.40	.33	.37

hands-on job proficiency for both the Operations and Skilled Technical job categories. The amount of variance accounted for generally increased by about 1% when interactions were added to the Full Model.

IMPLICATIONS OF ENVIRONMENTAL FINDINGS

The results of this research can be discussed in terms of three main topic areas: (a) the meaning of environmental variables, (b) the importance of environmental variables, and (c) the implications of these findings for the relationship between individual differences and job performance.

Meaning of Environmental Variables

The environmental variables examined here clearly represent perceptions of the environment. But are these perceptions accurate? One might suppose that, because all individuals in a given organizational unit experience essentially the same organizational environment, divergent perceptions regarding that environment would necessarily indicate that at least some of these perceptions must be inaccurate. However, as noted above, there is reason to think that not everyone is exposed to the same environment even within the same unit. Studies of supervisor-subordinate dyads (e.g., Graen, 1976) suggest that supervisors often act substantially differently toward different subordinates (e.g., providing different levels of personal and work-related support). Herein this means that low agreement within a unit on a work environment factor such as Supervisor Support may reflect real differences in these levels of support, not simply misperceptions on the part of some or all respondents. Thus, although we found here relatively low within-unit agreement for AWEQ items, the meaning of this finding is not entirely clear.

Although we have no empirical basis for determining the "real" accuracy of AWEQ scores, we can reason by analogy that, just as other types of judgments in a social context seem to provide a degraded but nonetheless meaningful representation of reality, much the same might be said of judgments about the environment. For example, performance judgments have been found to be influenced by a rater's cognitive ability, adjustment, self control, and likability (Borman, 1979b), but are nonetheless considered to contain a substantial true score component as well. Lord and Maher (1991) have suggested that social perception may be guided by "internal mental models or symbol systems of the world." Cultural and gender differences may also impact on whether or not different people perceive the "same" organizational world. However, a common organizational culture will "create fairly similar mental models for organizational members" (Lord & Maher, 1991).

Importance of Environmental Variables

The results described above strongly support the proposition that, to fully understand individual job performance, one must consider the environment in which such performance takes place as well as the ability and temperament of the performer. In Table 17.4, the model incorporating both individual difference and environmental components provided substantially better prediction of performance in general than a model containing only individual difference components.

Two different types of environmental variables were identified herein: (a) those more directly linked to performing job functions, and (b) those describing the worker's job climate. This dichotomy appears to be somewhat analogous to a distinction between the two proficiency first-tour job dimensions, which can be viewed as representing "can do" performance, and the remaining three more motivationally-oriented or "will do" performance dimensions.

Only the functionally oriented "Training/Opportunity to Use Skills" environmental factor had a substantial relationship with either of the two "can do" performance dimensions. The relationship between this factor and hands-on performance appears to have a straightforward explanation. Those who have trained more on their job tasks are likely to perform better when tested on a sample of these tasks.

The relationship between work environment and "will do" performance appears more complex. One of the strongest environmental predictors of Army-wide performance, Supervisor Support, was a social climate factor. The relationship between Support and rated performance was also observed in the leadership research reported in an earlier section of this chapter and, as noted there, fits well with the concept of leader-subordinate exchange. However, Job/Task Importance, identified here as a functional environmental factor, had a comparably strong relationship with rated Army-wide performance. One explanation for this finding is that those who view their jobs as important are likely to be motivated to perform well, are likely to translate this motivation into increased effort, and are thus likely to be perceived by raters as better performers.

The modest level of the correlations between General Constraints, identified as a single environmental factor in this research, and the summary performance measures suggests that a model focusing principally on constraints is too restrictive to capture the full complexity of the relationship between environmental variables and job performance. The environment can be facilitating as well as constraining. Where constraining it may be so in subtle ways, involving, for example, limited opportunities to use job skills or impoverished relationships with supervisors.

If the Army work environment is perceived as particularly facilitating or constraining, then there could be concern regarding the extent to which it may contaminate performance measurement or restrict performance variability. Although the results obtained here are not sufficiently dramatic to provide a basis for alarm, they do suggest some ways in which the environment and performance are intertwined. The supervisor-subordinate relationship does appear to impact upon the rating that the subordinate receives. Whereas this could be viewed as a contaminating factor, those elements of the relationship that seem to be pertinent also seem to be elements that contribute to effective subordinate performance. Thus, the contamination is perhaps less than a cursory examination of the results might suggest. Similarly, the fact that the subordinate's perception of job/task importance and that the subordinate's training and opportunity to use skills impact on evaluations of performance do not necessarily make the performance evaluations any less accurate. Rather, they shed light on the context in which performance takes place and provide clues as to how the environment might be manipulated to improve the performance of all job incumbents.

Implications for Person-Performance Relationships

Our findings suggest that differences among soldiers in ability and personality interact with their environmental perceptions to a limited extent in the prediction of various performance outcomes. When the work environment interactions are compared with those obtained in the analysis of leadership perceptions, few consistent patterns emerge. The finding that suggests the relationship between dependability and rated performance is moderated by leadership effectiveness remains the most prominent observed interaction.

From a selection standpoint, the most problematic outcome would be evidence that our individual difference predictors work effectively only in certain situations. Considerable effort has been expended in an attempt to identify those environmental factors likely to effect such an outcome. The environmental factors we identified were important predictors of performance and, in many cases, did interact significantly with our individual difference variables. However, the interactions were generally neither particularly large nor consistent. This failure, ironically, is good news, supporting the robustness of Project A individual difference measures and the current Army selection instrument across the range of conditions that occur naturally in an Army environment.

VI

Application of Findings: The Organizational Context of Implementation

18

ABLE Implementation Issues and Related Research

Leonard A. White, Mark C. Young, and Michael G. Rumsey

From the beginning of Project A, there was a certain degree of tension between short-term and long-term implementation objectives, and between the goal of broad, systematic change and more narrowly focused objectives. The Project A research strengthened the case for retaining cognitive tests while providing a strong foundation for the use of new temperament, spatial, and psychomotor tests in the selection and classification process. It also paved the way for a new promotion system based on more comprehensive predictive assessment leadership potential.

However, major changes to Army personnel systems do not happen quickly or easily. The centerpiece of the current selection system represents the culmination of a process that began in 1917 with the first Army cognitive test battery, the Army Alpha, and ended with the introduction of the ASVAB in 1976. A complex administrative structure has been built around this selection system, including testing stations, mechanisms for delivering examinees to the stations, mechanisms for providing feedback to examinees and to appropriate service personnel, and joint service committees that monitor the testing process and review proposed changes. Before any major system change can be implemented, the impact on all aspects of this structure must be considered, joint service concurrence obtained, and a formal scientific review committee must approve the proposed change. Moreover, a number of administrative steps must be taken to ensure that the test is properly normed, that it will be free of race and sex bias in an operational context, that multiple forms are developed, that the potential for test compromise is minimized, and that an operational system for effectively scoring the tests and providing feedback is implemented. Yet these steps are only the final ones in the implementation process. Before they can reasonably be initiated, the new testing procedure must be shown to represent an improvement over the existing one, and some reassurance is needed that the benefits shown in an experimental context can reasonably be presumed to generalize to an operational one.

This context is important for understanding the history of implementation of Project A products. It partially explains why the process of implementation tends to be slow, and why the proper time for judging the success of applying research products is not immediately after research completion, but rather many years beyond. Moreover, there is another reason why an evaluation at this stage would be premature. The finding that a particular measure has incremental validity beyond the current operational selection system does not immediately suggest the appropriate manner in which such a measure should be operationally used. The ABLE and the Project A spatial and psychomotor tests are cases in point. The ABLE has been found to add to the ASVAB in predicting the "will do" job performance components. However, there are coaching and faking issues that present more concern in some contexts than others. Spatial and psychomotor tests have been found to add to the ASVAB in predicting certain types of gunnery performance. However, there are additional sets of questions and issues associated with trying to determine how best to capitalize on the predictive validity of these instruments in a selection and classification context.

The complexities involved in making changes to the Army's personnel system also partially explain why it has been necessary to maintain a balance between systemic implementation and efforts of more limited scope, which often, although not necessarily, tend to require less lead time. Although it was always understood that the completion of the entire research program would take many years, there would also be a need to address short-term problems and to sustain sponsor interest in these projects while waiting for the final results.

Much of the energy devoted to implementation of products of this research has focused on the new predictors, particularly the psychomotor and spatial tests and ABLE. In fact, the history of research associated with

ABLE implementation is so extensive, and represents so well the different implementation issues confronted in this entire research effort, that we devote the remainder of this chapter to this topic. Chapter 19 then will address the implementation issues associated with several other Project A predictor measures.

ABLE IMPLEMENTATION

The Project A research showed that the personality constructs measured by ABLE were predictive of enlisted job performance and first-tour attrition (White, Nord, Mael, & Young, 1993) and that ABLE tapped qualities needed for successful performance that were not captured by currently used screening tools. These findings generated much enthusiasm for further evaluating ABLE's potential for use in the Army's personnel selection and classification decision system.

Early discussions with the Army leadership centered on the use of ABLE for applicant screening and on its value as an indicator of NCO and officer leadership potential. Later, there was interest in using ABLE for personnel classification and job assignment decisions and as a training needs diagnostic tool for new recruits.

The prospect of using ABLE for operational decisions raised questions pertaining to selection utility, fakability, and the logistics of test administration. At this juncture, it became clear that additional research beyond the scope of Project A was needed to address these issues. Although this research was conducted within a military context, we believe the issues addressed here have broader relevance and implications. This chapter highlights the most significant findings relating to theory and application in industrial and organizational psychology.

Soon after the Project A concurrent validation, it became clear that shorter ABLE forms would be needed in virtually any implementation scenario. The development and evaluation of shorter (114-item) forms was one of the earliest implementation activities and will be the subject of the next section of this chapter. As part of this early implementation research, the disparities between the criterion-related validity findings between the CVI and LVI analyses described previously in Chapter 10 were explored in more depth.

The promising nature of the early research prompted the development and evaluation of even shorter forms (70 items) of the ABLE, which were intended primarily for the prediction of first-tour attrition. This research included an evaluation of the instrument's cost-effectiveness and other operational concerns. The research on the 70-item ABLE is the subject of the second major substantive section of this chapter. Although the findings of this research were also very promising, the ABLE was still not considered ready for implementation because of concerns about the effects of coaching and faking. Accordingly, a great deal of research effort has been expended in the identification and managing of these effects. This research is the subject of the third section of this chapter. Finally, the chapter will discuss a number of efforts associated with implementing ABLE for postenlistment applications.

DEVELOPMENT AND VALIDATION OF A SHORTER FORM OF ABLE (ABLE-114)

Given the pressures to minimize testing time in preenlistment screening and elsewhere, an early implementation concern was that the full, 199-item ABLE required nearly one hour for some examinees to complete, which exceeded the time available for most, if not all, potential operational uses. Accordingly, there were two major efforts to create shorter forms and then validate them against measures of job performance. A 114-item form of ABLE was developed following scale construction procedures recommended by Jackson (1970). Items were dropped from the longer form based on low discriminant validity and/or a low contribution to internal consistency reliability (White & Young, 1994). The resulting scales on the 114-item form are closely aligned (all convergent validities, $r > .86$) with corresponding composites on the 199-item ABLE (see Hough, Eaton, Dunnette, Kamp, & McCloy, 1990, for a description).

Results from the LV sample showed that the new, shorter scales reliably measure the intended constructs, with a median internal consistency of $r = .81$. Correlations among measures of the six temperament constructs and Physical Condition ranged from .15 to .65 (mdn $r = .45$). This effort illustrated the feasibility of measuring the temperament constructs of interest to our Army sponsors within operational testing time constraints.

Relation to Five-Factor Model

In the last decade, the Five-Factor Model (FFM; Costa & McCrae, 1992) has emerged as a conceptual framework for personality research (Barrick & Mount, 1991; Costa & McCrae, 1995). Table 18.1 shows, for a sample of college students, how the ABLE-114 composites relate to the FFM.

TABLE 18.1

Relationships Among ABLE Factor Composites and NEO Big Five Constructs

ABLE Construct	NEO Construct				
	Neuroticism	Extraversion	Agreeableness	Conscientiousness	Openness
Achievement	−.21**	.24**	−.01	.75**	−.02
Dominance	−.37**	.44**	−.29**	.34**	.04
Dependability	−.12	−.04	.46**	.37**	−.22**
Adjustment	−.77**	.19**	−.06	.24**	−.09
Cooperativeness	−.38**	.29**	.58**	.20**	−.02
Internal Control	−.19*	.19*	.27**	.32**	.01
Physical Condition	−.22**	.32**	−.14*	.21**	−.05

Note: $N = 143–150$. $^*p < .05$. $^{**}p < .01$.

As displayed in Table 18.3, three ABLE constructs correspond closely to primary dimensions in the FFM; NEO-Conscientiousness is aligned with ABLE-Achievement, NEO-Neuroticism (reverse scored) converges with ABLE-Adjustment, and NEO-Agreeableness fits with ABLE-Cooperativeness. However, Dependability, Dominance, and Internal Control, all subsequently confirmed as important to military performance, have no clear counterparts among the primary five factors (see Hough, 1992 for a related discussion). Some relationships emerged between two of these three divergent constructs and facets of the FFM. Dependability was correlated with Deliberation, $r = .48$ ($p < .01$), which is a facet of Conscientiousness; and Straightforwardness, $r = .49$ ($p < .01$), which is a facet of Agreeableness. Persons scoring higher on these two facets are more planful, not impulsive, and tend to be open and honest about their intentions. Dominance had its highest correlation, $r = .66$ ($p < .01$), with Assertiveness, which is a facet of Extraversion.

Relation of ABLE-114 to Job Performance and Attrition

In Project A, the original content scales were used separately or in composites for estimating validity of temperament constructs against job performance criteria (J.P. Campbell & Zook, 1994; Hough et al., 1990). Here we discuss the criterion-related validity of the ABLE-114. We also examine why the predictive validities of these temperament measures were sometimes lower than the concurrent estimates of these same relationships.

First-Tour Performance

Table 18.2 displays correlations between ABLE-114 composites (screened for missing data and random responding) and the first-tour performance criteria for both the predictive (LVI) and concurrent (CVI) validation samples. The validity estimates shown in Table 18.2 are based on results from the nine Batch A MOS for which the full array of criterion measures were administered. The mean validity coefficients across these jobs were computed using unit weighting, as opposed to weighting by sample size. The correlations were not adjusted for restriction of range or criterion unreliability. Corrections for range restriction were not applied because most potential operational uses of ABLE under consideration focused on its selection utility over and above the existing employment screens.

As shown in Table 18.2, the ABLE-114 composites were significantly correlated with the first-tour performance criteria in both validation samples. Achievement, developed primarily to predict work effort, along with Dominance and Dependability, emerged as the best predictors of Job Effort. Although they were statistically significant, the predictive validity estimates of both Achievement and Dominance were disappointing in comparison to the CVI results, and raised some concern about their selection utility. We will return to these LVI/CVI differences in criterion-related validity later in this section.

A different pattern of temperament-performance relationships was obtained for the Personal Discipline criterion. Dependability, measured at entry to the Army, had the highest correlation with soldier's Personal Discipline over the first two years on the job ($r = .22$). Cooperativeness was also predictive of soldiers' level of Personal Discipline ($r = .11$).

Physical Condition, perhaps more of a biodata scale than a temperament measure, was the best predictor of soldiers' Physical Fitness and Military Bearing. Achievement was also significantly correlated with this criterion, perhaps because maintaining physical fitness is an important aspect of military performance and has a role in promotion decisions.

Second-Tour Performance

The focus for the second-tour pre-implementation analyses was a sample of 590 soldiers who had completed ABLE upon entering the Army and were retested about five years later during the second-tour criterion

TABLE 18.2

First-Tour Predictive and Concurrent Validity Estimates for Temperament Constructs (ABLE-114)

Construct	Core Technical Proficiency		General Soldiering Proficiency		Effort & Leadership		Personal Discipline		Physical Fitness & Military Bearing		Attrition (LV Only)
	LV[a]	CV[b]	LV	CV	LV	CV	LV	CV	LV	CV	1 yr/3 yr
Achievement	.03	.07	.02	.05	**.12**	**.28**	.07	.19	.20	.26	−.06/−.03
Dominance	.06	.07	.03	.08	.11	.22	.01	.05	.15	.22	−.05/−.01
Dependability	.06	.11	.10	.10	.14	.17	**.22**	**.30**	.14	.16	−.08/−.12
Adjustment	.07	.09	.06	.11	.06	.17	.02	.10	.14	.16	−.13/−.07
Cooperativeness	.02	.05	.02	.05	.11	.17	.11	.22	.10	.12	−.07/−.07
Internal Control	.01	.05	.02	.05	.06	.15	.05	.15	.11	.16	−.07/−.05
Physical Condition	−.06	−.05	−.04	−.02	.09	.13	.04	.00	**.31**	**.32**	−.09/−.07
Social Desirability	−.09	−.08	−.07	−.07	.02	.03	.06	.07	.08	.07	−.01/.01

Note: $p < .05$ for all mean correlations in bold.

[a]Predictive design using data from LVI (minimum $N = 3,254$ for performance measures, $N = 27,610$ for attrition).

[b]Concurrent design using data from CVI (minimum $N = 3,751$).

administration. Thus, unlike the first-tour measures, the concurrent and predictive validity estimates against the second-tour criteria are based on the same soldiers.

Table 18.3 displays these relationships for the second-tour performance constructs. Because of the small sample sizes in each job, the data were combined across the nine MOS (ignoring job) prior to computing these relationships. As in the first-tour analyses, the correlations were not corrected for range restriction or criterion unreliability.

Personality-performance relationships in the second-tour generally paralleled those obtained for the first-tour. Achievement and Dominance, assessed concurrently with performance, had the highest correlations with Job Effort and Leadership, but the predictive validity coefficients for these scales were much lower. In contrast, the concurrent relationships between Dependability and soldiers' Personal Discipline and Leadership generally held up in the predictive validation. The CV results were also an accurate indicator of the significant predictive relationship between soldiers' dispositional motivation to exercise and stay fit (i.e., Physical Condition) and soldiers' Fitness/Bearing in the second-tour.

Relation of ABLE-114 to Attrition

Attrition is costly to the Army because approximately one-third of new recruits' fail to complete their initial obligated tour of enlistment. Attrition reflects soldiers' success in adapting to military life and meeting minimum Army academic, physical, and disciplinary standards. New recruits entering the Army are required to adjust to multiple life stressors, including a change of residence, often being separated from family and friends, and a new job that is highly structured, physically demanding, and requires a full-time commitment.

In the ABLE research, several temperament dimensions emerged as predictors of first-term attrition, as displayed in Table 18.2. For these analyses, attrition was coded as 1 when a soldier was separated before completing his or her obligated 12 and 36 months of service, respectively, and as 0 otherwise. Early on, during the first year of enlistment, Physical Condition and Adjustment were among the best predictors of a soldier's likelihood of adapting to military life (or its opposite, attrition). These relationships can be understood in terms of the physically demanding nature of Army training and the stresses new recruits' face in transitioning from civilian to Army life. Dependability had a relatively lower correlation with early attrition, but emerged as the best predictor of attrition after three years.

TABLE 18.3

Second-Tour Predictive and Concurrent Validity Estimates for Temperament Constructs (ABLE-114)

Construct	Core Technical Proficiency		General Soldiering Proficiency		Effort		Leadership		Personal Discipline		Fitness & Bearing	
	LV	CV	LV	CV	LV	CV	LV	CV	LV	CV	LV	CV
Achievement	.01	.12**	.03	.16**	.06	.26**	.13**	.29**	.07	.18**	.14**	.22**
Dominance	.02	.07	.04	.18**	.10*	.26**	.15**	.30**	.01	.10*	.15**	.23**
Dependability	.01	.01	.06	.04	.10*	.16**	.16**	.18**	.20**	.20**	.05	.10*
Adjustment	.02	.09*	.06	.14**	.00	.16**	.07	.20**	.00	.03	.07	.15**
Cooperativeness	.00	.02	-.02	.02	.06	.08*	.09*	.07	.13**	.07	.09*	.05
Internal Control	-.03	.03	.03	.10*	.02	.12**	.11**	.19**	.07	.13**	.02	.12**
Physical Condition	-.02	-.01	-.02	.02	.05	.06	.05	.02	-.01	.00	.28**	.30**
Median Validity	.01	.03	.03	.10	.06	.16	.11	.19	.07	.10	.09	.15

Note: Both the predictive (LV) and concurrent (CV) validity estimates are based on the same soldiers ($N = 590$).

* $p < .05.$ ** $p < .01.$ Pairs of validity estimates (LV vs. CV) in boldface are significantly different from one another ($p < .05$).

These findings created much interest in using ABLE as an attrition-risk screen for Army applicants.

Effects of the Type of Validation Design on Criterion-Related Validity

In addition to attrition screening, there was also considerable interest in using ABLE as an indicator of leadership potential and for assessing soldiers' work motivation and their likelihood of staying out of trouble. However, one unexpected concern with using ABLE to predict these types of criteria was the disparity between the predictive and concurrent validities, particularly for the Achievement and Dominance scales, and to some extent Adjustment. These findings raised questions about the stability of these relationships and the utility of ABLE for predicting leadership and job performance in both the first and second tour. Accordingly, we investigated several possible reasons for these validation design effects to better understand their implications for potential operational uses of ABLE.

Our initial analyses focused on the second-tour data for which concurrent and predictive validities were estimated for the same sample, of soldiers. In this sample, differences in the quality of the performance criteria could not account these validation design effects because the same performance measures were used for both estimates. In addition, demographic differences between recruits and job incumbents or problems of sample attrition were largely ruled out as explanations.

Several reasons for this pattern of LVI/CVI validity coefficients were investigated, including greater socially desirable responding among new recruits (as opposed to job incumbents), the temporal instability of the ABLE scales, and the effects of Army job experience on responses to ABLE. Analyses indicated that the first two factors led to slightly lower predictive validities (relative to concurrent estimates), but could not account for much of the drop in the criterion-related validity of Achievement and Dominance in LVI (White & Moss, 1995).

The most important factor contributing to the validation design effects appeared to be the effects of Army job experience (or lack of it) in interaction with the item job content. The potential impact of Army job experiences is certainly not hard to understand because, for many new recruits, this is their first extended full-time job and first time living away from home. To explore this effect, three psychologists and one military officer familiar with Army occupations classified the 114 ABLE items into one of three job content categories reflecting the extent to which Army job experiences were likely to influence examinees' responses to that item (interclass $r = .76$). These raters were blind to the item-level criterion validities when making their judgments of job content.

Those items classified by the raters as high in job content generally pertained to expending job effort, working with others, or leadership roles, and had a face-valid relationship to Army job requirements. We hypothesized that the responses of incumbents' to items high in job content would primarily reflect their motivation and interpersonal behavior in the Army work context (as opposed to more generalized experiences such as high school); and as a result would show higher concurrent validities that would overestimate the predictive relationships. In contrast, items low in job content tapped behavioral tendencies and attitudes prior to enlistment or manifestations of these competencies outside Army life. For these items, the concurrent validities were expected to approximate the predictive relationships.

Table 18.4 presents the mean item-level validity coefficients by job content category for the second-tour performance criterion constructs. The results show that items high in job content had concurrent validities that were significantly above the predictive relationships (White & Moss, 1995), particularly for the Leadership and Effort criteria. In contrast, for the set of items (about 20%) classified as low in job content, the concurrent

TABLE 18.4

Mean Second-Tour Validity Estimates of ABLE Items By Job Content Category, Research Design, and Criterion Construct

Job Content Category	Number of Items	Effort		Leadership		Personal Discipline		Fitness & Bearing	
		LV	CV	LV	CV	LV	CV	LV	CV
Low	24	.047	.066	.058	.037	.053	.047	.094	.097
Moderate	63	.031	.095	.063	.123	.035	.058	.047	.083
High	27	.017	.114	.059	.128	.019	.073	.052	.099

Source: White & Moss (1995).

validation results provided relatively accurate estimates of the predictive values. A parallel analysis of the item-level validities by job content category against the first-tour performance criteria showed similar results (White, 1999).

Finally, the proportion of items classified as low (vs. high) in job content varied by temperament scale; and these scale content differences are correspondent with the observed pattern of CVI/LVI validity coefficients. Specifically, for Dependability and Physical Condition, the LVI and CVI validity estimates were comparable and most items on these scales were classified into the low job content category. Conversely, Achievement and Dominance, with a high proportion of items classified as moderate or high in job content, showed higher concurrent validities that did not generalize to the predictive context.

Because responses to ABLE are influenced by Army job experience, concurrent estimates of the predictive validities must be interpreted with caution. Note that the predictive relationships for Achievement (similar to NEO Conscientiousness) are consistent with the results of meta-analyses (Barrick & Mount, 1991). We interpreted the higher concurrent validities of Achievement and Dominance as reflecting the fact that these scales were primarily tapping soldiers' temperament as expressed in the Army environment as opposed to broader situations (e.g., summer employment or high school). Other researchers (Schmit, Ryan, Stierwalt, & Powell, 1995) also provided evidence that context-specific items have higher criterion-related validity. In terms of our implementation strategies, this argues for administering ABLE to job incumbents (or retesting if ABLE is given to Army applicants) in order to obtain these higher criterion-related validities for use in postenlistment decision making. Several such potential applications are discussed in a subsequent section of this chapter.

Summary

Temperament constructs, measured by the 114-item form developed for implementation, showed significant predictive and concurrent relationships with job performance in both the first-tour and second-tour. Importantly, the ABLE scales developed for operational testing have low correlations with ASVAB composites and with recruits' educational attainment, which are the primary tools used by the Army for applicant selection and classification decisions. Thus, in the context of the Army's applicant screening measures, most of ABLE's criterion-related validity would be incremental.

DEVELOPMENT AND EVALUATION
OF AN ATTRITION SCREEN

The significant personality-performance findings coincided with the Department of Defense's interest in developing screening tools to reduce the high attrition among first-term enlistees. Accordingly, two equated 70-item, 20-minute forms of ABLE (ABLE-70) were developed for this purpose (White et al., 1993). Scales for Achievement, Adjustment, and Dependability were included on ABLE-70. Higher predictive validities against attrition would have been obtained by including a measure of Physical Condition on ABLE-70, but the validated item pool for this construct was not large enough to support the immediate need for two alternate forms. The ABLE-70 also contained a Social Desirability scale to detect faking.

Evaluation of ABLE-70 as an Attrition Screening Tool

The sample used to investigate temperament-attrition relationships consisted of 38,362 soldiers in the LV sample with complete data on all variables. The records of 277 soldiers who died, or separated from the enlisted force to become officers, were excluded. In these models, attrition was coded as 1 when a soldier separated before 36 months of service and as 0 otherwise.

One issue was whether these ABLE-attrition relationships could be accounted for by other individual difference measures used in applicant screening, or by personnel policies related to attrition. Consequently, a multivariate model was used to isolate the incremental effects of individuals' temperament on attrition with other variables controlled. Table 18.5 presents the means and standard deviations of the independent variables and the expected direction of their relationship to attrition. CAT IIIB consists of those individuals scoring in the 31st to 49th percentiles on the Armed Forces Qualification Test (AFQT). CAT IV are those persons in the lowest AFQT score category eligible for enlistment. The MOS-AA (MOS Aptitude Area Score) is a specific composite of ASVAB subtests, which is used for classification into particular occupations. The GED is the group who has passed the General Equivalency Examination. HSDG designates high school diploma graduates. The DEP (Delayed Entry Program) is a U.S. Army program in which recruits are permitted to contract for a job and then delay enlistment until a training seat becomes available.

TABLE 18.5
Variables in the Attrition Models

Variable	M	SD	Description	Expected Effect on Attrition
ABLE-T	51.40	28.61	ABLE-T Percentile	−
ABLE-SocD	16.82	3.37	ABLE Social Desirability	?
Age	20.31	2.86	Age in Years	+
CAT IIIB	.28	—	Aptitude Category IIIB = 1; Else = 0	+
CAT IV	.10	—	Aptitude Category IV = 1; Else = 0	+
MOS-AA	108.96	11.77	MOS Aptitude Area Composite	−
Combat MOS	.52	—	Combat = 1; Noncombat = 0	+
DEP	3.85	3.19	Months in DEP	−
ETERM2	.13	—	2 Yr. Term = 1; 3–4 Yr. = 0	−
GED	.02	—	GED = 1; Else = 0	−
HSDG	.93	—	HSDG = 1; Else = 0	−
Female	.10	—	Female = 1; Male = 0	+
White	.72	—	White = 1; Nonwhite = 0	+
ATT36	.26	—	Attrition Within 3 Yrs = 1; Else = 0	NA

The ABLE-70 screening composite, referred to as ABLE-T, comprised three scales measuring Achievement, Dependability, and Adjustment. It was interpreted as measuring a broad construct of adaptability and sacrificed some of the interpretability of the individual content scales in exchange for greater reliability, for the simplicity of a single score, and for less elaborate equating of alternate forms. Correlations between ABLE-T and the other predictor variables in the model (e.g., AFQT, race, gender) were uniformly low.

Attrition Models

Two logistic regression attrition models were estimated: one including all variables, and one that excludes ABLE-related variables.[1] These models

---

[1]Logistic regression was used for these analyses because we wished to model the *probability* of an event (attrition) as a function of various individual characteristics (age, education, etc.). The logit specification is preferred to linear regression for this problem because (a) unlike linear regression, it will always generate predicted probabilities of attrition that range from 0-1, and (b) it will provide unbiased estimates of the standard errors of the coefficients.

TABLE 18.6

Logistic Regression Coefficients for 36-Month Attrition (N = 38,362)

Independent Variables	With ABLE	Without ABLE
Intercept	*.4758 (.4831)*	*.3995 (.4745)*
ABLE-T	**−.0480** (.0040)	—
ABLE-T^2/100	**.0748** (.0095)	—
ABLE-T^3/10,000	**−.0361** (.0063)	—
ABLE-SocD	*.0066 (.0041)*	—
Age	**.0974** (.0396)	*.0587 (.0393)*
Age^2	*−.0011 (.0008)*	*−.0004 (.0008)*
CAT IIIB	*.0253 (.0355)*	*.0395 (.0352)*
CAT IV	*−.0514 (.0525)*	*−.0257 (.0519)*
MOS-AA	**−.0139** (.0015)	**−.0155** (.0015)
Combat MOS	**.2438** (.0267)	**.2252** (.0265)
DEP	**−.1367** (.0158)	**−.1349** (.0157)
DEP^2	**.0078** (.0013)	**.0077** (.0013)
ETERM2	**−.9462** (.0484)	**−.9029** (.0481)
GED	**−.2771** (.0842)	**−.2350** (.0835)
HSDG	**−1.041** (.0511)	**−1.0382** (.0507)
Female	**.6935** (.0422)	**.6744** (.0420)
White	**.4227** (.0315)	**.5023** (.0310)
Attrition	.26	.26
Model χ^2	2434 (17df)	2137 (13df)

Note: Standard errors are shown in parentheses.

$p < .05$ for all coefficients except those in italics.

are presented in Table 18.6. The difference in chi-squares between the two models is 297 (4 *df*, $p < .001$), indicating that the addition of ABLE to the model provides a highly significant increase in explanatory power.

Figure 18.1 shows the relationship between ABLE-T and 36-month attrition. The overall model explained 53% of the variance in mean attrition rates when the sample was grouped on ABLE percentile scores (see White et al., 1993, for a detailed discussion of the accuracy of the model). In the logistic specification, the linear and higher order ABLE terms are clearly significant, indicating that the attrition effect of a small change in ABLE score is generally larger for low scores than for high scores. As can be seen in Figure 18.1, the effect of ABLE screening is most noticeable for scores below the 20th percentile, with almost no effect for scores above the 40th

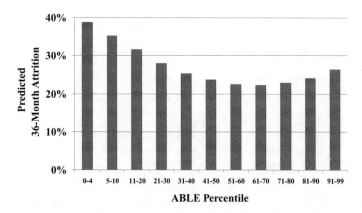

FIG. 18.1.   Relation of ABLE to predicted 36-month attrition.

percentile. The effect of the Social Desirability scale is nonsignificant, indicating that, at least in this specification, this measure is not predictive of attrition. In addition to ABLE, the effects of the remaining variables are generally consistent with the results of past research.

Examination of Other Operational Considerations

Legal, Sensitivity, and Fairness Assessment

As a serious candidate for implementation, the ABLE received a legal and sensitivity review by the Assistant General Counsel (Personnel and Health Policy). The General Counsel's review was favorable and found no legal or sensitivity objections to ABLE. It should also be noted that during preenlistment processing, applicants to all of the Services are asked questions about prior arrests, fines or convictions, and their use of drugs and alcohol. Compared with these examples, ABLE's items are not sensitive. An important test of an instrument's sensitivity is the respondents' reactions to the items that remain. Judging by the reactions of nearly 60,000 examinees in Project A, ABLE's items are not offensive and do not violate sensitivity norms.

In addition, research has consistently shown that race/ethnic and gender differences on ABLE are small. This applies to all versions of the ABLE (199-item full form, ABLE-114, and ABLE-70). Where differences are noted, women and minorities often had the higher scores (see Chapter 6 in this volume; White et al., 1993).

Is ABLE Screening Cost-Effective?

The findings relating to ABLE's criterion validity and lack of adverse impact were encouraging; however, many questions had yet to be answered regarding its operational utility. One particular issue relates to screening candidates in the prime applicant categories (i.e., high aptitude high school graduates), where recruiting is expensive and difficult. Applicants in these categories who are rejected by ABLE are not easily replaced, and this could prevent the Army from meeting its annual recruiting goals. Although there is no accepted single approach for estimating cost-benefit outcomes, recruiting costs have generally been excluded from such models, with one noted exception (Martin & Raju, 1992). However, recruiting costs within the Army are high, and because these costs escalate at an increasing rate for the most desirable recruit categories, they cannot be ignored (Schmitz & Nord, 1991).

Determining optimal cut scores. The Army's annual recruiting needs were broken into seven market segments known as *mission boxes.* Market segments are specified in terms of the desired aptitude (AFQT) scores, educational levels, and gender proportions. Because of variations in marginal recruiting costs for the different market segments, ABLE-70 screening could have positive utility for some markets, but not for others. Separately, for each of the seven different mission boxes used by the Army, the utility of ABLE was evaluated at all feasible cut scores. The utility of a given ABLE enlistment standard was modeled as a function of the anticipated reduction in training and recruiting costs resulting from the lower attrition of ABLE-screened applicants, adjusted downward for the costs of recruiting additional candidates to replace those screened out by ABLE, and for test administration costs. Thus, the key variables in the analysis were (a) the number of recruits needed to yield the target number of soldiers completing their initial term of enlistment (which depends on the attrition rate of selectees), and (b) the number of applicants required to find enough qualified recruits that depends upon the selection standard. The ABLE-T cut score yielding the highest selection utility to the Army was assumed to be the optimal enlistment standard for that labor market segment relative to the baseline case in which ABLE is not used in the selection process.

We used the logistic regression model described earlier to determine the expected reduction in attrition that would result from using every possible ABLE cutoff score. To estimate the cost of attracting and processing the applicants to replace those that would be rejected by ABLE at each

TABLE 18.7
Recruiting Market Characteristics

Market Segment	Description	Q^0	Q^*	η	MC
GMA	Grad, Male, I-IIIA (AFQT > 49)	22,000	48,000	.8	$16,758
GFA	Grad, Female, I-IIIA (AFQT > 49)	5,000	10,000	.8	$14,683
GMB	Grad, Male, IIIB (AFQT = 31–49)	10,500	15,000	1.2	$6,494
GFB	Grad, Female, IIIB (AFQT = 31–49)	1,700	2,000	1.2	$4,598
GM4	Grad, Male, IV (AFQT = 15–30)	20,000	5,000	∞	$3,270
HMA	GED, Male, I-IIIA (AFQT > 49)	4,700	5,000	1.2	$3,750
NMA	Nongrad, Male, I-IIIA (AFQT > 49)	4,700	5,000	1.2	$3,750

Note: Q^0 = number of recruits available at constant marginal cost
Q^* = total number of recruits needed
η = elasticity of marginal cost with respect to changes in Q^*
MC = marginal cost of Q.

cutoff score, we relied on estimates produced by Kearl and Nord (1990). Recruiting costs vary for each market segment depending upon the number of recruits needed, the available applicant population within each segment, the "taste for military service" within each segment, and external economic conditions (e.g., youth unemployment). Table 18.7 shows the marginal recruiting costs for each market segment. As can be seen in Table 18.7, high quality applicants were, at the time of the analysis, up to five times more expensive to replace than lower quality applicants ($16,758 vs. $3,270).

Training costs were estimated from the Army's Manpower Cost Model (AMCOS) at $14,130 per trainee. This included only those variable costs, including pay and allowances and travel, which are responsive to changes in class size and can be reduced if lower attrition rates lead to reduced training loads. For this analysis, we treated all training costs for a recruit who fails to complete his or her initial term of enlistment as wasted resources. Even when attrition occurs after training, the portion of training investment that is recouped through subsequent productive service may be relatively small. Our analysis of the LVI showed that the first-tour performance of attritees averaged .7 SD below the performance of soldiers who completed their initial term of enlistment.

The results of these analyses are perhaps best understood by examining the graphs shown in Figure 18.2. The dotted curve on each graph shows the

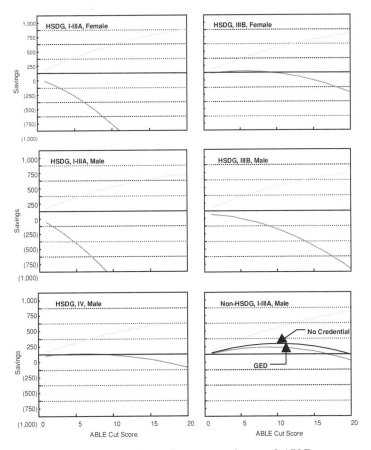

(Solid curve shows estimated net savings per accession at each ABLE score. Dotted curve show estimated "gross" savings — resulting from reduced accession requirements, not accounting for costs of attracting and processing additional applicants.)

FIG. 18.2.   Net and gross savings per accession as a function of ABLE cut score.

total savings at each ABLE cut score resulting from reductions in training and recruiting costs because of reduced attrition. The solid curve shows the *net* savings after the costs of testing and attracting additional applicants are accounted for. The optimal cut scores are the ones coinciding with the maximum point on each of the net savings curves. As can be seen in Figure 18.2, the highest utility is obtained by using ABLE to screen applicants who do not possess a traditional high school diploma. The savings for nongraduates results from the combined effect of a low baseline survival rate, the strong relationship between soldiers' temperament and attrition rates at the low end of the ABLE score range, and relatively low recruiting costs (e.g., many are walk-ins). The graphs also show that a slight savings can be achieved by using ABLE to screen high school diploma graduate applicants in the lower AFQT categories. This recommendation is driven primarily by the low (and constant) marginal recruiting costs for these groups.

Sensitivity analysis of recruiting cost assumptions.   There is always some uncertainty associated with estimating recruiting costs, and a key issue is the sensitivity of the "optimal" selection standards to variations in recruiting cost estimates. To investigate this issue, sensitivity analyses (e.g., Rich & Boudreau, 1987) were conducted to determine how variations in assumptions about recruiting costs would affect the estimated savings from "optimal" selection. Evaluating marginal cost yielded a function that would specify the marginal cost that would make any given cut score optimal. Comparing this value to the estimate of actual marginal cost, we can see how the optimal cutoff score would change if the baseline estimate was changed. Figure 18.3 shows the results of these calculations for each applicant market.

In Figure 18.3, the (estimated) optimal cost-effective cut score is at the intersection of the maximum recruiting cost function (solid curve) and the estimated actual recruiting cost function (dotted curve). Our recommendation of no ABLE screening for applicants in the prime recruiting market appears to be quite robust. According to the sensitivity analyses, marginal recruiting costs for higher quality recruits must be cut by more than half before any screening would be cost effective, or the criterion-related validity of the ABLE screening composite would have to be increased significantly. In contrast, relatively small changes in the recruiting cost estimates for nongraduates and high school graduates in the lower AFQT categories could produce substantial changes in the recommended cut score. These analyses were provided to decision makers to help them evaluate the robustness of our screening recommendations and to understand the sensitivity of the ABLE's selection utility to changes in the recruiting market conditions.

Performance Utility

Additional benefits of implementing ABLE selection standards are derived from improved job performance among selected applicants. Although there has been considerable research in the civilian sector to estimate the

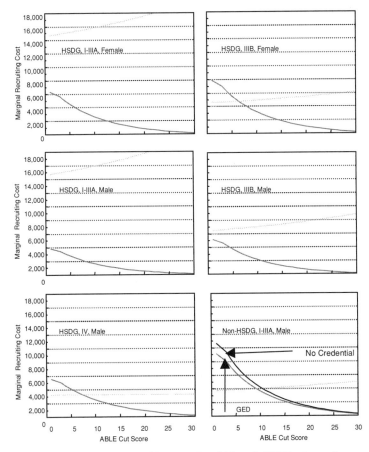

(Solid curve is maximum recruiting costs for which each ABLE cut score is
cost-effective. Dotted curve shows estimated actual recruiting cost at each cut
score.)

FIG. 18.3. Sensitivity of optimal cut score to recruiting cost estimates.

dollar value of changes in job performance, its relevance to the military context has been questioned. We argue that because a volunteer Army must
compete with civilian markets to attract manpower, the value to society
of the output produced by that manpower must be approximately equal
to its price. The discounted cost of first-tour performance at the time of
the analysis was estimated to be $56,580 over 39 months, which was the
average term of first enlistment (Kearl & Nord, 1990). This cost includes
basic military compensation and average training costs. To estimate the
dollar value of one standard deviation increase in performance, we used

the conservative rule that it is equal to 40% of salary (Hunter & Schmidt, 1982). When these job performance gains are considered, the benefits of ABLE screening in all recruiting markets would be higher.

Potential Use of ABLE for Classification

Our analysis shows that the added value of ABLE screening is greatest in market segments where recruiting costs are relatively low. In higher quality segments, which constitute over one half of Army accessions, ABLE's selection utility was substantially offset by added recruiting costs. For these markets, the implementation strategy could consider a shift from selection to potential uses of ABLE for improving personnel classification decisions. For newly enlisted recruits, classification decisions determine to which of over 200 enlisted occupations the individual will be assigned and trained. Improper or suboptimal person-job matches may result in poorer job performance, extensive retraining, higher attrition, and a lower likelihood of reenlistment.

An advantage of using ABLE for classification is that potential benefits from reduced attrition and improved performance can be achieved without incurring increases in recruiting costs. In addition, potential problems with applicant faking and coaching might be lessened if ABLE were used as a classification tool for improving the person-job match.

If significant differential prediction holds, performance gains would be obtained by using ABLE to place recruits into jobs or job families where they are most apt to perform well and complete their enlistment obligation. In addition, some Army jobs require as little as four weeks of training whereas others require nearly one year, with training costs for new hires being 15 to 20 times as much for the latter as for the former. Added reductions in training costs could result from using ABLE to identify recruits with lower attrition propensity for assignment to MOS where the training period is relatively long and expensive.

Summary

Our analysis established ABLE's utility in preenlistment selection and classification decisions. However, the Services decided not to implement ABLE-based selection procedures. This was largely due to concerns about its fakability and potential compromise. Some individuals believed that any large-scale operational screening using self-report measures, like ABLE, would lead to widespread faking and degradation of predictive validity over time. This belief was based in part on the U.S. Army's prior operational experience with a biodata instrument called the Military Applicant Profile (MAP). In comparison with its research phase, higher test scores and much lower validities were obtained during MAP's brief implementation period (Walker, 1985).

There was also concern that applicants might receive outside guidance (i.e., coaching) on how to score well on ABLE. Because little was known about the potential impact of faking and coaching, new research was required to guide ABLE implementation decisions. Our initial work focused primarily on ABLE's fakability and coachabililty and the use of the Social Desirability scale to detect such effects. We also began exploring strategies for managing possible effects of faking and coaching and their impact on criterion-related validity in likely future implementations. In the next section, we summarize our research findings relating to this controversy.

COACHING AND FAKING ISSUES

Documentation of Effects

Effects of Faking and Coaching on Construct Scores

In an early effort to address these issues, Hough and her associates (Hough et al., 1990; Chapter 6 in this volume) conducted a directed faking experiment in which new recruits were asked to complete the ABLE while imagining themselves as applicants for the Army. They were further told to respond to ABLE in a way that would maximize their chances of getting a high score on the test and being selected for the job. The results clearly establish that examinees could, when instructed to do so, exaggerate their self-reports to make themselves appear like more ideal job candidates. We subsequently replicated these findings and additionally found that external coaching, accompanied by a few practice items, led to even greater score inflation (about 1 SD) than individual attempts at faking (Young, White, & Oppler, 1991). Thus, these data indicate that coaching would be an even greater cause for concern than individual attempts at faking.

We believe that results from these faking and coaching experiments generally show the upper limits of fakability. However, substantial score inflation, presumably because of faking, has been observed among job applicants as well (e.g., Hough, 1998; Rosse, Stecher, Miller, & Levin, 1998; Walker, 1985). In these samples, the applicants typically scored between .30 and .60 SD higher on the personality measures than did job incumbents.

Effects of Socially Desirable Responding on Criterion-Related Validity

A critical question for personnel decision makers is how to interpret test profiles inflated by socially desirable responding and whether such socially desirable responding undermines the criterion-related validity of the self-report information. One model of the effects of faking on validity has examined socially desirable responding as a suppressor variable. The idea here is that faking, either deliberate or subconscious, leads to inflated scores and masks, or suppresses, the true predictive validity of the self-report assessment. This suppressor effect can be removed by statistically partialling social desirability variance from the predictor-criterion relationships. It is this adjusted temperament score that would provide valid information for personnel decisions. However, several investigators have found that partialling social desirability variance has small or negligible effects on temperament-performance relationships (Barrick & Mount, 1996; Ones, Viswesvaran, & Reiss, 1996). These results have led some to conclude that social desirability is not a response bias that affects criterion-related validity. However, this optimism seems premature as social desirability may operate in other ways to attenuate criterion validity.

Another model we investigated is that social desirability moderates the predictor-criterion relationships. As a moderator, social desirability interacts with the predictor measures so that the magnitude of the corresponding criterion-related validity coefficient varies by level of faking. The primary study investigating moderator effects of social desirability was reported by Hough et al. (1990). Using ABLE data from CVI, Hough found some evidence for lowered criterion-related validity with high levels of faking. However, her overall conclusion was that the temperament-performance relationships remained stable even when respondents were distorting their responses in an unusually positive direction. However, as discussed earlier in this chapter, findings from a concurrent validation may not always generalize to longitudinal studies, and it is these predictive validities that guide most of our implementation strategies.

Our analyses of moderator effects of social desirability in the LVI sample followed closely the procedures used by Hough et al. (1990) in their analysis of the CVI data. For these analyses, Social Desirability scale scores were used to classify subjects into one of three groups representing different

TABLE 18.8

Criterion-Related Validity Estimates of ABLE Scales as a Function of Social
Desirability Classification and Criterion (LV Sample)

Scale	Effort & Leadership			Personal Discipline			Physical Fitness & Military Bearing			24-Month Attrition		
	L	M	H	L	M	H	L	M	H	L	M	H
Achievement	.16	.14	.02	.09	.05	-.08	.19	.16	.14	-.06	-.02	.00
Dominance	.14	.17	.03	.03	.00	-.12	.16	.15	.15	-.05	-.02	.01
Dependability	.16	.11	.00	.22	.18	.05	.11	.08	-.01	-.14	-.08	-.02
Adjustment	.09	.09	.02	.03	-.01	-.03	.13	.12	.07	-.11	-.06	-.02
Cooperativeness	.11	.11	.02	.12	.10	-.07	.09	.06	.06	-.09	-.04	-.01
Internal Control	.04	.07	.02	.03	.07	.03	.07	.09	.06	-.06	-.03	-.02
Physical Cond	.11	.09	-.01	.05	-.02	-.12	.32	.28	.23	-.10	-.08	-.07
N	2,417	1,089	369	2,495	1,123	380	2,496	1,121	381	25,109	11,381	3,664

Note: L = Low; M = Moderate; H = High. Validities in boldface are significantly lower than Low social desirability validities at $p < .05$ (one-tailed).

levels of faking. Those classified as high fakers, about 10% of the sample, had mean Social Desirability scores comparable to those of coached examinees in our directed faking experiments.

As displayed in Table 18.8, results from LVI showed a much different pattern of findings than those reported by Hough et al. (1990). In LVI, high levels of response distortion in a positive direction attenuated the predictive validity of the self-report information. With high levels of faking, Dependability was no longer predictive of Personal Discipline ($r = .05$), and none of the temperament scales retained their validity as predictors of Job Effort. High and moderate levels of faking also undermined the validity of Dependability and Adjustment and predictors of attrition. Physical Condition was the only scale that maintained its criterion-related validity in the face of high levels of socially desirable responding.

As a follow-up to these findings, participants in the directed faking experiments were tracked to determine their attrition status 24 months later. Paralleling the results from the LVI sample, the highly inflated ABLE profiles resulting from external coaching were no longer valid predictors of attrition (Young, White, & Oppler, 1992). Individual attempts at faking, without coaching, led to moderate score inflation, and also reduced, but did not eliminate, the criterion-related validity of the temperament scales against attrition.

Summary

The findings from LVI, with its multiple performance criteria, closely paralleled those from the directed faking experiments. High levels of socially desirable responding, easily produced by coaching, severely curtailed the criterion-related validity of temperament measures. Less extreme levels of faking also attenuated validity, but with less consistent effects. Therefore, without effective strategies to control or manage faking, ABLE's utility could be compromised.

Managing the Effects of Faking and Coaching

These research findings led to the investigation of three approaches for managing faking and coaching effects: (a) warning statements, (b) the detection of faking, and (c) adjustment of scores for faking. In an operational context, some combination of these strategies might be used in a complementary fashion.

Warning Statements

Previous research with biodata inventories has shown that warning statements can effectively suppress faking. In some cases, respondents were warned of faking-detection scales (Doll, 1971; Schrader & Osburn, 1977). Other types of warnings have included the threat of response verification and consequences for detected faking (Trent, Atwater, & Abrahams, 1986). The question here was whether warnings and/or consequences for faking would be effective in suppressing attempts to elevate ABLE scores. Consistent with the biodata research, subjects who were warned of faking detection items had ABLE scores comparable to those responding honestly (Palmer, White, & Young, 1990). However, because of variations in the faking and warning instructions, the extent of this suppression differed across experiments.

Even if scale means with warnings are comparable to those in the honest condition, validities may be adversely affected. It is possible that the warned applicant changes from a fake good stance to some other, albeit still invalid, one. In a follow-up to Palmer et al. (1990), warnings reduced score inflation among examinees instructed to fake good, without degrading the criterion-related validity of temperament constructs against attrition. These preliminary results were encouraging. In line with these findings, the results of a recent meta-analysis of 15 studies concluded that warnings combined with consequences were effective in reducing applicant faking ($d = .27$; $n = 7,461$) on noncognitive selection measures (Dwight & Donovan, 1998). As a cautionary note, the effectiveness of warning statements may need to be investigated when more intense coaching or incentive for faking is provided. We also recognize that coaching may include inoculation against warnings, such as strategies to avoid detection, which may undermine their effectiveness.

Detection of Faking

Accurate detection of faking is important for managing and monitoring socially desirable responding in an operational environment. Applicants identified as having inflated their scores might be asked to retest, or the faking index could be used to adjust scores for socially desirable responding. When respondents attempt to raise their scores by faking, temperament construct scores are increasingly contaminated by social desirability variance.

The Social Desirability scale can be used to detect high levels of faking among first-time examinees (e.g., Hough et al., 1990; White et al., 1993; Young et al., 1992). It shows the largest increases of all ABLE scales when examinees are distorting their responses in a positive direction. Results from ARI research show that the Social Desirability scale correctly identifies about 67% of examinees successfully coached to look good, while erroneously classifying only 5% of those instructed to respond honestly. It is somewhat less effective in detecting moderate levels of faking as indicated by research on similar types of measures (Drasgow, Levine, & McLaughlin, 1991). Research on other approaches is ongoing, including the use of "appropriateness measurement" procedures, based on item response theory, to supplement traditional social desirability scales (Zickar & Drasgow, 1996).

Adjustment of Scores for Social Desirability

Effects on criterion-related validity.   For one approach, regression techniques were used to remove the variance from the temperament measures related to social desirability. Applying these corrections to the data from the deliberate faking experiments showed that score adjustments partially restored the criterion-related validity of the ABLE scales against attrition, having its greatest effect on the highly inflated scores of coached examinees. However, in other samples, partialling social desirability from the temperament scales showed less consistent effects for improving criterion-related validity. Thus, although there is some indication that adjusting scores for faking may, at times, restore predictive validity, no method has consistently worked well, and research is continuing.

Effects on selection decisions.   Because faking leads to score inflation, there was also a concern that deliberate faking would have a significant effect on the quality of applicants hired in a top-down selection system. Deliberate faking would enable applicants who might otherwise be rejected (on the basis of their noninflated scores) to be selected at any given enlistment standard on ABLE. This suggests a potential situation in which applicants with inflated scores might have a better chance of being selected than applicants who did not distort their responses, and who have a higher true score for predicted performance.

To investigate this issue, we conducted a series of simulated hiring decisions using data from the LVI. Our analysis showed that a disproportionate number of examinees flagged as faking (high scores on Social Desirability) had scores in the top percentiles on ABLE and were underrepresented in the lower range of the distribution below the 15th percentile. Thus, by distorting their self-reports, these individuals greatly enhanced their chances of passing any ABLE enlistment standard, assuming no adjustments for faking were made. Applying adjustments for faking resulted in different simulated hiring decisions than would have been made using the uncorrected scores, and greatly reduced the number of individuals with inflated scores who were ranked as highly qualified. Although, such corrections do not always improve criterion-related validity, we believe their use may be justified both as a deterrent to faking and to help decision makers compare job candidates' scores unconfounded by social desirability effects.

Some investigations have argued that social desirability may be indicative of individual differences in social competence, or measure valid trait variance in conscientiousness, or adjustment; and thereby be positively related to performance (Christiansen, Goffin, Johnston, & Rothstein, 1994; Ones et al., 1996). However, in our implementation research Social Desirability consistently showed low or nonsignificant correlations with both job performance criteria and attrition (as shown in Table 18.2). Where significant relationships have been observed, socially desirable responding has been associated with lower Technical Proficiency, higher turnover, and somewhat higher Personal Discipline and Physical Fitness. In summary, we found no consistent support for the notion that Social Desirability is predictive of performance or that individuals who distort their responses perform better on the job than those who do not.

Summary

In sum, several strategies show promise for managing the effects of faking and coaching on ABLE. Based on our current knowledge, no one approach appears to be satisfactory by itself. However, the combination of multiple strategies (i.e., warnings, detection of faking, and score adjustments) may be able to address these concerns.

Alternative Methods for Measuring Temperament Constructs

Even if effective controls for faking were implemented, ABLE's highly transparent and nonverifiable nature could make it a target for criticism. Accordingly, we are now using the lessons learned from Project A in exploring alternative methods for measuring ABLE temperament constructs. In one approach, we are using a forced-choice item format to reduce fakability and coachability. In another, we are investigating the use of rational biodata scales for measuring temperament constructs.

Assessment of Individual Motivation (AIM)

To address faking concerns with ABLE, a paper-and pencil measure of ABLE constructs called the Assessment of Individual Motivation (AIM) was developed by White and colleagues (White & Young, 1998). Each AIM item presents four behavioral statements, and examinees are asked to choose which statements are most and least descriptive of themselves. The strategy here is to minimize faking and coachability by balancing the self-statements within the tetrad in terms of social desirability. AIM's quasi-ipsative scoring constrains construct score values without creating the serious psychometric problems associated with purely ipsative measures (Hicks, 1970).

The development of AIM began in 1993, and the prototype instrument was completed in 1996. Between FY94 and FY96, trial versions of AIM were administered to over 5,000 new recruits. An early version of AIM showed substantial convergence with ABLE measures of the same constructs (median $r = .69$). In our deliberate faking experiments, AIM was much less fakable than ABLE, and coaching strategies that led to large score increases with ABLE ($+1SD$) were ineffective with AIM (White & Young, 1998; Young & White, 1998). Preliminary analyses also revealed that AIM is predictive of first-term attrition, showing the characteristic curvilinear relationship observed with ABLE.

In response to these encouraging findings, an AIM preimplementation research program was initiated in 1998 in which 22,000 Army recruits were tested on AIM. At the time of this writing, 9-month attrition data were available for 5,000 soldiers who were tested on AIM when they entered the Army. The relationship between AIM and attrition in this sample ($r = -.15$; $R = .17$) is highly similar to that observed for a sample of airmen ($n = 8,500$) who completed AIM under a parallel Air Force research program. Importantly, the AIM-attrition relationships seen in both samples are strikingly similar to the Army's past findings with ABLE (White & Young, 1998). In the Army sample, AIM had a higher criterion-related validity than both AFQT score and educational attainment against the attrition criterion. Preliminary findings from these recruit samples also indicated that AIM screening would not adversely impact females or minorities.

As a result of these findings, the Army has implemented AIM in a new pilot program for expanding the recruiting market for nonhigh school diploma graduates. Candidates for the program are being tested on AIM at Military Entrance Processing Stations (MEPS) nationwide. This new experimental program, called GED Plus was initiated in February 2000.

In other research, AIM has also been shown to be related to the duty performance and personal discipline among correctional officers working in military prisons ($R = .44$), and its utility as a training needs diagnostic in this environment is currently being evaluated. In addition, AIM was also predictive of success in explosive ordnance disposal (EOD) training at the U.S. Naval EOD School, which trains service members from all four services. Finally, the U.S. Coast Guard has initiated research to link AIM with measures of new recruit attrition and performance.

Biodata Measurement

A parallel research effort has been undertaken to develop biodata scales for measuring ABLE constructs. The biodata items refer to past behaviors and life events that most individuals would have been exposed to by adulthood, and that are indicative of the targeted constructs. These items are not limited to those that are objective or externally verifiable and are rationally keyed. Results showed that these rational biodata scales can approximate the temperament constructs they are intended to measure, have somewhat higher criterion-related validity, and are less fakable (Kilcullen, White, Mumford, & Mack, 1995; White & Kilcullen, 1992).

In a second approach, objective and verifiable biodata items were keyed to produce analogs to the five ABLE scales used in the research (Mael & White, 1994). The methodology used in keying these items is described in Mael and Schwartz (1991), and is referred to as "quasi-rational keying" in that it has elements of rational and empirical keying (Mael & Hirsch, 1993). In sum, biodata measures, configured through various rational and quasi-rational approaches, may provide another way of measuring temperament constructs while reducing susceptibility to faking.

POSTENLISTMENT APPLICATIONS

ABLE has also been evaluated for several postenlistment applications. Much of this research has been conducted with Special Forces (SF) and Army Rangers, including both officer and enlisted personnel. Special Forces are an elite branch of the U.S. Army. SF units are proficient in deep reconnaissance, counter terrorist measures, and direct action in all types of terrain. Rangers are effective small unit leaders. In several studies, temperament constructs, notably Adjustment, were predictive of successfully completing the Ranger qualification course and passing the Special Forces Assessment System, which is used to select candidates for Special Forces training (DeMatteo, White, Teplitzky, & Sachs, 1991). To minimize concerns about faking, recent research has used an in-service form of AIM in lieu of ABLE for measuring temperament constructs in this context (Kilcullen, Mael, Goodwin, & Zazanis, 1999).

There is also interest in using ABLE/AIM for assessing leadership potential among military personnel. Dominance, Achievement, Dependability, and Adjustment were all predictive of leadership criteria in the Project A research. These relationships were highest for soldiers who completed ABLE after serving 3 to 4 years in the Army. In research with Ranger units, Achievement, Dependability, and Adjustment (measured by AIM) were linked to advancement into leadership positions, with concurrent validities ranging from .19 to .49. In the Army's Expanding the Concept of Quality in Personnel (ECQUIP) project (Peterson et al., 1999), Achievement and Dominance were highly predictive of the leader effectiveness criteria among NCOs with criterion-related validities comparable to those in the second-tour validation (see Table 18.3). As a follow-up to this work, we are conducting additional studies of AIM's selection utility for making promotions to supervisory NCO positions in the Army.

In other research, ABLE was used by the Marine Corps as a decision-aid for designating job assignments following training. This implementation involved the placement of Marine Security Guards (MSG) who provided security services at U.S. diplomatic and consular facilities throughout the world. Most ABLE scales were significantly related to MSG success training and later performance in the field (Wiskoff, Parker, Zimmerman, & Sherman, 1989). As a result of this research, ABLE was used to aid embassy assignment decisions, with low scoring trainees assigned to less sensitive environments. These postenlistment applications of ABLE/AIM were judged successful and, notably, free from problems of response distortion. We are continuing to monitor their progress and to explore new implementation opportunities.

DISCUSSION

This chapter has described the results of the ABLE implementation research, a story that continues to unfold. Short ABLE forms were developed for use in preenlistment screening and for postenlistment selection and placement decisions. Temperament/personality constructs, reliably measured by these shorter forms, predict conceptually related criteria, with validities comparable to those reported in the literature (e.g., Barrick & Mount, 1991). Selection simulation studies using samples of new recruits also suggest that ABLE screening would not adversely impact women or minorities.

Soldiers' level of Adjustment and motivation to stay fit (i.e., Physical Condition) was mostly highly correlated with early attrition. In contrast, the validity of Dependability increased over time and showed the highest correlation with attrition after three years. These findings add to growing evidence that the time at which the criterion is assessed moderates the relationship between temperament and performance. In addition, the association between temperament and attrition is curvilinear and the product-moment correlation underestimates the true predictive relationship. A better model of this nonlinear function is obtained using polynomial regression.

The criterion validation results are interpreted as supporting the position of Hough and colleagues (e.g., Hough & Schneider, 1996) that, within the temperament domain, the best predictors are identified using a construct-oriented approach (as was used in developing ABLE). The Five Factor Framework (Costa & McCrae, 1992) has provided a useful starting point for the temperament taxonomy; however, additional refinements appear to be in order to make it more useful for identifying work-related competencies. Four ABLE constructs (Dependability, Dominance, Internal Control, and Physical Condition) predictive of job performance criteria are not represented by primary factors in the FFM. This indicates the need for more research at a bandwidth narrower than the Big Five and the need to investigate attributes outside the Big Five framework.

The utility analyses highlight the importance of considering recruiting costs when evaluating the utility of any selection measure. Sensitivity analyses are also recommended to determine how changes in key variables (e.g., recruiting costs) would affect utility estimates and the recommended cut score. ABLE had the highest utility for screening where recruiting costs are relatively low. For the higher quality labor market segments, implementation strategies shifted from preenlistment screening to ABLE's potential for improving classification decisions.

The results of our implementation research also confirmed concerns about the effects of faking on the criterion-related validity of self-report temperament scales. Other research (White & Kilcullen, 1998) found similar negative effects of faking on validity in four independent studies involving both military and civilian personnel. To manage possible effects of faking and coaching, we recommend using one or more of the following: (a) validity scales to detect socially desirable responding, (b) warning statements about the consequences of faking, and (c) score adjustments to correct inaccurate, inflated self-reports.

We are continuing to explore new temperament assessment approaches that are more resistant to deliberate faking and less coachable. There is some evidence that rational biodata scales measure temperament constructs with higher criterion-related validity and less susceptibility to socially desirable responding (Kilcullen et al., 1995; Kilcullen et al., in press). The development and experimental operational use of AIM (White & Young, 1998; Young & Rumsey, 1998), a new forced-choice approach for measuring temperament constructs, represents another promising step toward control of deliberate faking that will be monitored closely.

The ABLE implementation research also highlighted several problems with using concurrent designs to estimate the predictive validity of self-report measures of temperament. Our analyses indicated that higher concurrent validities resulted primarily from the effects of incumbents' Army job experience in interaction with the job content of the predictor test items (White & Moss, 1995). Other researchers (e.g., Schmidt & Ryan, 1993) have also raised cautions about generalizing results of concurrent studies to job applicants.

The differences in the concurrent and predictive validities of ABLE may be interpreted as suggesting that temperament dimensions differ in terms of their domain specificity. That is, true scores on some measure (e.g., Achievement) might legitimately vary as a function of the context, or frame-of-reference, within which the individual responds to the items. One could legitimately be classified as a high-achiever relative to one domain or occupation, but as an average achiever in another. One the other hand, attributes like Dependability may vary less as a function of context and these tendencies may generalize widely across situations. It follows that an individual could have more than one Achievement score depending on the context or frame-of-reference, but perhaps only one Dependability score.

A FINAL WORD

When ABLE was initially considered for operational use, there were many obstacles to its implementation. At that time, several important technical issues were unrecognized or poorly understood. Findings from the ABLE implementation research have added to the growing evidence and optimism that temperament measures can make an important contribution to personnel selection, assessment, and job assignment systems, albeit within a very real set of constraints.

19

Application of Findings: ASVAB, New Aptitude Tests, and Personnel Classification

Clinton B. Walker and Michael G. Rumsey

The remaining implementation issues relate to the major personnel functions of selecting applicants for entry-level jobs and then classifying them (i.e., matching selectees with appropriate specialties). In this chapter, we will describe both ongoing and projected work on those two functions.

Using the findings of Project A to evaluate the effectiveness of ASVAB in ongoing Army enlisted selection required no new implementations. These findings have important implications for the maintenance and renewal of the operational system. Concurrently with the initiatives to implement ABLE, ARI also moved psychomotor and spatial aptitude tests from Project A toward operational use.

Two other research programs in combination with Project A comprise a broad initiative to improve the Army's classification and assignment system. In one, Zeidner and Johnson (1994) developed procedures for generating more powerful ASVAB Aptitude Area Composites. Second, the Enlisted Personnel Allocation System (EPAS) project developed software for using the Aptitude Area Composite scores to make better person-job matches in a personnel system that has multiple priorities (Greenston, McWhite, Mower, Walker, Lightfoot, Diaz, & Rudnick, 1999).

IMPACT ON THE ARMED SERVICES VOCATIONAL APTITUDE BATTERY (ASVAB) PROGRAM

The applied impact of Project A starts with the ASVAB itself. Although ASVAB had been administered for Joint Service selection and classification since 1976, well before Project A, its validity had been shown against performance in only *entry-level training* programs. Without evidence that training success relates closely to *job success*, the meaning of training-oriented validations was unclear. Project A addressed this issue in the Army context while each of the other Services launched parallel efforts as part of a Joint Service collaboration (Wigdor & Green, 1991).

As noted in earlier chapters, we found that ASVAB performs its selection function very effectively; it strongly distinguishes those who can perform the job well from those who cannot, and it is an excellent predictor of the future job performance of applicants for enlistment. If Project A had shown ASVAB not to be an effective selection instrument, managers would have had difficulty defending its continued use. The findings have justified continuing to use ASVAB for selection and classification and for a number of related functions, such as keeping the Congress informed of the quality of the force and ensuring that each occupational grouping has sufficient high aptitude soldiers to get its job done. In both cases, ASVAB scores are the primary component of the definition of "quality in personnel."

Paradoxically, the success of Project A in demonstrating the validity of ASVAB worked to discourage implementing new selection tests. In the eyes of many, it would be hard for new tests to improve on that level of functioning.

NEW APTITUDE TESTS

In Project A, 16 new tests of aptitudes were developed and validated. Six of these were conventional (i.e., pencil-and-paper, multiple choice) tests of aptitudes for dealing with spatial information. Ten others required a computer and a special response device with joy sticks, buttons, and slides. The computerized tests, such as tracking a moving object and identifying an object quickly and accurately, involve precision in movement and timing.

In parallel with Project A's evaluation of predictors against measures of the totality of job performance, ARI research staff used other performance measures to evaluate different combinations of spatial and psychomotor tests as predictors of visually-guided gunnery performance in tank crewmen at the Armor Center (Smith & Graham, 1987) and anti-tank gunners at the Infantry Center (Grafton, Czarnolewski, & Smith, 1988). These small sample tryouts produced promising evidence for some of the new tests.

The Skills, Selection and Sustainment (S3) Program

By December 1987, ARI had briefed GEN Maxwell Thurman, Commander of the U.S. Army Training and Doctrine Command (TRADOC), on the results from both Project A and the small gunnery projects. GEN Thurman ordered Project A tests to be implemented the following February in entry-level training at the Army centers where operators of advanced weapon systems are trained. This implementation was to be part of a program known as Skills Selection and Sustainment, or S3. The Centers were to use the test scores to select incoming trainees for special new training and to track the examinees into gunners' duty positions in the force. Also, the Training Centers were directed to develop and disseminate training packages for sustaining gunnery skills after initial training. For three sites, ARI put together and installed a testing package that included Project A computers, four promising aptitude tests (two spatial and two computerized psychomotor ones), and scoring materials. At a fourth site, the user chose unique batteries of Project A tests for each of three MOS, which ARI installed.

The intended context of this implementation was that of a testbed—an opportunity to evaluate the effectiveness of these measures in an operational environment. However, in effect, it became a more substantial experimental implementation, but with limited resources. As new funding was not provided, the Training Centers had to pay for the testing out of already programmed resources. TRADOC Headquarters provided command support; although centers formally complied, their philosophical agreement was not a precondition for implementation. As a result, scores from the new tests were never incorporated into the systems for making personnel decisions.

Despite these limitations, the testbed advanced the process of achieving ultimate implementation in three ways. First, the practicality of such testing was shown by the success of personnel at the Training Centers in carrying out the testing themselves. Over 19 months, host site personnel administered the package to 18,000 incoming Infantry trainees and 7,500 incoming Armor trainees.

Second, the positive results from the small tryouts in 1987 in tank and anti-tank gunnery training were replicated and extended. For S3 trainees scoring well on the Project A tests, their anti-tank gunnery showed faster train up and higher levels of accuracy (Smith & Walker, 1988). Reanalysis of those data (Busciglio, Silva, & Walker, 1990) found that the short test battery produced a 100% gain in variance accounted for in firing accuracy over using ASVAB alone. In the Armor trainees (Graham, 1988), the new tests showed a .15 superiority in validity over the ASVAB General Technical composite. Trainees who had scored in the upper third of the Project A score distribution had a 16% higher hit rate and 10% faster engagement rate than those in the lower third. Further analysis of these data found a 50% gain in variance accounted for in a composite measure of speed and accuracy in gunnery over using ASVAB alone (Busciglio, Silva, & Walker, 1990). Only at the Air Defense Artillery Center, where the high cost of operating the anti-aircraft gunnery simulator limited us to a very small evaluation, did the estimated validities not support use of the Project A tests (Gast & Johnson, 1988). Those poor validities were ascribed to the use of two fire-and-forget (i.e., homing) weapon systems, which involved relatively little visually-guided tracking.

The third impact was the credibility of the results. Staff at the Infantry School analyzed and briefed the early results to the Commander of the Infantry Training Center. On seeing that they were positive, he approved continuation of the program and use of the test scores. In Europe in 1990, US Armor units that were preparing to compete in the Canadian Army Trophy, a NATO competition in tank gunnery, were briefed on ARI's gunnery data. The briefings persuaded them to ask to use the tests in their system for selecting crews for the competition.

Enhanced Computer Administered Testing (ECAT) Program

Because the funding needed to continue the S3 program was not on the horizon, while a higher impact opportunity for implementation was, ARI concurred when the end users at the Training Centers requested the program's termination in September 1989. Throughout 1989, ARI had been participating in a Joint Service panel to recommend a set of new tests for evaluation as possible subtests in a future computerized ASVAB (Bloxom,

1989). That DoD project was the Enhanced Computer Administered Testing Program (ECAT).

Test Selection for ECAT

For the ECAT panel to make the most informed decision about which Project A tests to include in any future test battery, it was necessary to have validation data on individual tests rather than on the spatial and psychomotor composites that had been used in Project A analyses. Busciglio (1991) reanalyzed the Project A CVI data using backward stepwise multiple regression analyses to examine the contribution of individual tests in predicting a selected set of first-tour performance measures for each MOS.

Criteria consisted of two types: comprehensive and specific. Comprehensive criteria (see Chapter 11) included the General Soldiering and Core Technical Proficiency composite scores, as well as separate Hands-On, Job Knowledge, and School Knowledge scores and total score on the Army's Skill Qualification Test (SQT). The SQT was a comprehensive paper-and-pencil test of MOS-specific technical knowledge that the Army used for periodically requalifying incumbents in their specialties. In all, 86 equations were computed for the comprehensive criteria (43 criteria × 2 orders of entry into the regression equation [ASVAB first vs. new tests first]). The more specific criteria included scores on a selected set of hands-on tasks. These criteria were identified on the basis of their judged conceptual relevance to one or more of the Project A spatial and psychomotor measures. For these criteria, a total of 56 equations were calculated.

These analyses served as a vehicle for identifying the most promising Project A spatial and psychomotor tests in terms of adding most often to ASVAB. In predicting comprehensive criteria, three spatial tests led the way: Assembling Objects (entered 48 times), Figural Reasoning (40), and Map (33). Only two ASVAB subtests, Auto/Shop (74 times) and Mathematics Knowledge (68), surpassed Assembling Objects on this basis. The leading computerized measure was the Target Identification Test percent correct score (32).

For predicting the specific criteria, the leading Project A measure was Decision Speed on the Target Identification Test (entered 18 times), followed by Assembling Objects (13) and Figural Reasoning (12). Here, the three leading tests were from the ASVAB: Mathematics Knowledge (28), Mechanical Comprehension (22), and Auto/Shop Information (20).

Additional information about specific spatial and psychomotor tests came from analyses conducted by Silva (1989) on TOW and tank gunnery performance using S3 data. Predictors included ASVAB, two spatial tests (Mazes and Orientation), and two psychomotor tests (One- and Two-hand Tracking). Again, a backward regression approach was followed. Two accuracy criteria were used for TOW gunnery: an overall score and a pass/fail measure. Two-hand Tracking and Mazes added significantly to ASVAB subtests in predicting the overall score. The criterion of pass/fail on the first qualifying trial was also significantly enhanced by Two-Hand Tracking.

For tank gunnery, the measure of performance was a speed/accuracy composite from the Unit Conduct of Fire Trainer (UCOFT) simulator (Smith & Graham, 1987) of a tank crew's tasks. The backward regression approach used to build TOW prediction models was also used for the UCOFT analysis. In addition to the ASVAB subtests, both Two-Hand Tracking and Mazes added validity to predicting the Speed/Accuracy score on the UCOFT. Although Orientation and Mazes had equal zero-order correlations with the Speed/Accuracy score, Mazes shared more variance with Speed/Accuracy once both the ASVAB subtests and Two-Hand Tracking were included. In summary, the usefulness of Two-Hand Tracking was strongly supported for both TOW and tank gunnery. Mazes also added predictive power.

Busciglio's (1991) and Silva's (1989) findings were cumulatively supportive of, in particular, two spatial tests—Assembling Objects and Figural Reasoning—and two perceptual/psychomotor tests—Target Identification and Two-hand Tracking. Another consideration favoring Assembling Objects and Figural Reasoning was that their differences in scores by gender in the large samples of Project A were quite small compared with such differences on the technical subtests of ASVAB. Valid tests that have modest or no group differences are generally preferred over those with large differences, all other things being equal, as they promote the goal of equal opportunity. Another consideration that favored the Project A spatial tests was that they could be administered on paper as well as on computer. In 1989, the switch from paper to computerized ASVAB was by no means certain and the ASVAB High School Testing Program was expected to continue using the paper medium indefinitely. Thus, this flexibility on the part of the spatial tests was a practical advantage. Earlier research on the prediction of TOW and tank gunnery (Czarnolewski, 1989; Grafton et al., 1988; Smith & Graham, 1987) provided support for several of the other Project A tests, including One-hand Tracking, and Orientation.

Based on a combination of such evidence and of theoretical promise, the Joint Service panel (Bloxom, 1989) selected nine tests for the ECAT battery, as shown in Table 19.1. Six of these were Army tests from Project A; three

TABLE 19.1

Tests Evaluated in the Enhanced Computer Administered Testing (ECAT) Program

Aptitudes/Tests	Source
Working Memory	
Integrating Details (using spatial information)	Navy
Mental Counters (using numerical information)	,,
Sequential Memory (using numerical information)	,,
Psychomotor	
One-hand Tracking	Project A
Two-hand Tracking	,,
Perceptual Speed and Accuracy	
Target Identification	,,
General Aptitude (Non-verbal/non quantitative)	
Figural Reasoning	,,
Spatial	
Assembling Objects	,,
Orientation	,,

Note: The assignment of tests to aptitudes here is not definitive; different authors assign all but the Tracking and Target ID tests somewhat differently. In Project A, Figural Reasoning was considered a spatial test.

were from the Navy. The Navy tests were chosen to provide measurement of working memory.

Execution of the ECAT Project

Details of the process and results of the ECAT project can be found in a special issue of *Military Psychology* (Wolfe, 1997). In ECAT, a sample of almost 12,000 new recruits in 17 Army, Navy, and Air Force schools took the battery in Table 19.1 just before starting basic training. The recruits' scores on ASVAB, which they had taken when applying for enlistment, were gathered from central personnel files. The criterion was success in training as measured by performance on primarily the hands-on tests that were a part of the regular program of instruction.

The Army initially contributed three MOS to the ECAT validation, selected for both being combat occupations and having good hands-on measures in their training programs: TOW Gunner (11H), Field Artillery Fire Support Specialist (13F), and Tank Crewman (19K). As the ECAT data collection got underway, the UCOFT high fidelity simulator of tank gunnery was withdrawn at the Armor Center because of cuts in training funds. The other available indicators of success in tank crew training turned out to be statistically unusable, so Tank Crewmen (19K) were not included in the analysis sample.

The power of the new tests to predict the examinees' success in training was exhaustively analyzed. Because the ECAT tests were expected to supplement ASVAB, or to replace only a very small number of the present ASVAB subtests, some of the analyses looked at the statistical properties of practical (in terms of testing time) subsets of the whole set [ASVAB plus ECAT] rather than at individual tests. In both the Navy (Held & Wolfe, 1997; Wolfe, 1997) and Army (Sager, Peterson, Oppler, Rosse, & Walker, 1997) analyses of the data, ASVAB was a very strong predictor of the trainees' performance, which replicated a major result of Project A on a different sample of examinees and on different performance measures.

Also as in Project A, some of the new tests added to the predictive power of ASVAB for some of the occupations, with the amount of the increment being statistically significant and valuable, but small. Moreover, some of the ECAT tests surpassed some of the ASVAB subtests for some of the occupations. In Army analyses to identify comprehensive test batteries that maximized absolute validity, the ECAT tests most frequently included were Two-hand Tracking, Target Identification (Decision Speed), and Figural Reasoning (Sager et al., 1997). In Navy analyses that examined the impact of adding each separate ECAT test to the existing ASVAB, the tests which most frequently made significant contributions were the two tracking tests, Assembling Objects and Figural Reasoning. In a second validation that used the ECAT predictors, Carey (1994) found Assembling Objects to provide the greatest increment over ASVAB for predicting hands-on performance in two Marine Corps mechanical MOS. Assembling Objects had also made the best showing of the new tests in Project A. The differences in findings across the three projects may be the result of differences in the occupations and performance measures that were examined.

As in the analyses of the Project A data (J.P. Campbell & Zook, 1996), the Army analyses of ECAT were designed to identify batteries that optimized the following three objectives: selecting the best performers, matching persons' aptitudes to job requirements most closely (i.e., classification), and minimizing differences between gender and racial groups. The optimal ECAT batteries for any one of those objectives tended to be different from the batteries that optimized another. One further step before implementation will be to make the tradeoffs among these objectives mindfully when choosing new subtests for ASVAB in the future. Such tradeoffs *cannot* be avoided by just continuing to use the present ASVAB; they are made by default when they are not made purposefully (Wise, 1994).

Coaching and Practice

As the accumulated evidence from Project A, ECAT, and other research began to build momentum for the implementation of one or more spatial tests, research into the possible contamination of test scores by practice and coaching took on a new urgency. In a review of research on such issues, Silva and Busciglio (1993) noted that practice effect sizes up to 1.60 SD and coaching effect sizes up to 1.26 had been found for spatial tests. Greater practice effects tended to be associated with (a) shorter periods between test administrations, (b) the use of latency measures rather than accuracy, and (c) the use of the same test form at both test administrations. Coaching effects tended to be greater to the extent that the coaching was directed to the specific content or form of the test items.

Busciglio and Palmer (1996) examined the effects of practice, nonspecific coaching (i.e., strategies for taking tests in general, such as not wasting time trying to answer difficult questions), and test-specific coaching on scores for three ECAT tests: Assembling Objects, Figural Reasoning, and Orientation. To evaluate specific coaching, the authors developed strategies for solving each test's type of item accurately and relatively quickly. The effect of practice was examined both separately and in combination with coaching.

In general, a number of coaching and practice effects were obtained, consistent with previous findings on spatial tests (Busciglio & Palmer, 1996). Across all combinations of coaching, practice, and tests administered, the greatest effect was for specific coaching on the Orientation test. Although Assembling Objects and Figural Reasoning showed lower coaching effects, they did show sizable practice effects. The authors suggested possible strategies to reduce these effects, including adding more practice items and making the items more dissimilar. This research did not compare the effects of coaching and practice on the new tests with those on ASVAB.

Implementation in ASVAB

Based on the whole fabric of evidence, practical considerations, and policy, the Department of Defense's Military Accession Policy Working Group recommended including Assembling Objects in the next data collection to renorm ASVAB on the American youth population. That data collection took place in 1997–98 and the results were undergoing evaluation in 1999. Meanwhile, the executive agent for ASVAB, the Defense Manpower Data Center, has taken the pool of Assembling Objects items that ARI developed (Busciglio, Palmer, King, & Walker, 1994), developed additional items, and prepared them all for administration by computer. This version of Assembling Objects is being administered as an experimental test along with operational CAT-ASVAB to gather data on its properties in computerized form (John Harris, DMDC-West, personal communication, June 1999). Owing to a concern for testing time, its potential role in future operational testing would probably be as a replacement for an existing ASVAB subtest, not as an addition to the present battery.

Spatial Tests and Land Navigation

In 1989, the Army's Special Forces School approached ARI for help in solving a problem: the high rate of attrition of students for failures in land navigation in both the initial two-week orientation course and the six-month qualification course. ARI, judging that land navigation requires spatial aptitude, responded by providing three of the six spatial tests from Project A: Map, Orientation, and Assembling Objects. In a series of validations (Busciglio & Teplitzky, 1994; Teplitzky, 1995), Assembling Objects again proved to be the best of the new tests. Since then, the Special Forces School has implemented Assembling Objects in the initial assessment process as a supplemental indicator for making decisions about marginal candidates.

CLASSIFICATION AND ASSIGNMENT

Improvements in job performance through changes in selection testing are expected to occur primarily by adding new selection tests. On the other hand, the existing ASVAB can be used to make substantial improvements in job performance through changing procedures for classification and assignment. An individual is now assigned to a particular MOS based on a number of considerations, one of which is the person's pattern of scores across the complete set of ASVAB tests. Assignment to any one group of MOS is based on examinees' scores on the unique ASVAB Aptitude Area Composite for that job set. Each such composite is the group of ASVAB subtests that has been found to give the most accurate prediction of individuals' performance in that job set. Project A produced data sets that make it possible to re-examine which groups of ASVAB subtests are best for assigning qualified applicants to each set of Army jobs. Early Project A analyses had already resulted in a change in the way ASVAB tests were used for classifying individuals into clerical jobs (Weltin & Popelka, 1983), and an MOS-wide analysis of archival data under Project A resulted in reassignment of a number of MOS to different ASVAB classification composites (McLaughlin, Rossmeissl, Wise, Brandt, & Wang, 1984).

Subsequent to the above activities, Johnson and Zeidner (1990, 1991; Zeidner & Johnson, 1994) used Project A data to develop a set of procedures under the rubric of Differential Assignment Theory for estimating the mean gain in predicted performance across all job assignments if a test battery were used to make classification decisions as well as selection decisions (see also Chapter 16). By simulating the assignment outcomes from using different combinations of tests, test weights, and job sets, they estimated the effects of alternative classification strategies in terms of gains in mean predicted performance (i.e., average level of incumbents' performance across the whole set of jobs being examined) on top of the gains over random assignment that are possible from the current ASVAB Aptitude Area Composites. Those gains ranged from 91% of mean predicted performance to 177%, depending on the number and nature of job families that are used. Research in this complex area has continued (Zeidner, Johnson, & Scholarios, 1997), and the use of new composites generated by this research to replace existing composites is now being considered.

Project A, with criterion data of unprecedented relevance and comprehensiveness, made it possible to estimate classification gains more precisely than ever before. Although it was necessary to supplement this data set with others that provided more complete job coverage, Zeidner and Johnson were able to use the Project A data to good effect in generating a new set of recommended composites.

Improving the ASVAB classification composites is but one step to a more optimal matching of persons' aptitudes with the demands of jobs; it is also possible to make better use of the existing composite scores. The present system asks only one question regarding a candidate's scores: do they meet the *minimal* requirements for a particular MOS? In the present assignment system, all candidates who satisfy that minimum are treated as though they are equally qualified for the job.

Another Army project that started concurrently with Project A—called Project B, or the Enlisted Personnel Allocation System (EPAS) (Konieczny, Brown, Hutton, & Stewart, 1990) sought to improve person-job matching by using linear programming methods. A prototype of EPAS was developed and evaluated that uses more of the information in examinees' Aptitude

Area Composite scores. It does this by offering available Army jobs to applicants based on their *highest* Aptitude Area Composite scores. In addition, the variety of jobs that might be offered to any applicant was expanded by lengthening the time horizon over which upcoming jobs are to be filled.

Developmental research found that EPAS would produce major improvements in applicants' future job performance (Greenston et al., 1999). By 1999, EPAS was moving toward operational use in the Army's system for processing applicants for enlistment.

DISCUSSION OF IMPLEMENTATION REALITIES

It has now been (as of 1999) about 14 years since ARI first began working with prospective users to promote implementation of early products from Project A, and from that time to the present day we have been involved in numerous implementations or potential implementations of Project A products. At the outset of the project, there was every reason to be optimistic about the prospects for implementing the research products. We recognized early on that high-level support from Army leadership would be needed throughout the project, so a General Officer Steering Committee was established to ensure that critical leaders supported actions taken at key stages. Not only have a number of these and other leaders expressed support for use of Project A products, they have actively pushed us in the direction of implementation.

In many respects, we are pleased with the outcomes of the work described in this book. They have profoundly influenced the way we look at our screening measures. They have given us confidence in a cognitive screening approach while simultaneously alerting us to the need for screening on characteristics of motivation and adjustment. Finally, they have shown the potential utility of psychomotor, spatial, and temperament measures while informing us of other issues that must be resolved in any use of such measures for making personnel decisions.

Yet the record of implementation of new predictor tests that we have described is mixed. We have a product, Assembling Objects, that is now being administered with the operational ASVAB, but not yet being used in selecting and assigning applicants. We have another, ABLE, which is not currently used operationally but has spawned a successor, AIM, which is being used for screening in an experimental program. Then we have psychomotor and spatial tests that were earlier administered in an operational context but whose scores have not been used for selecting and classifying examinees. Yet we have found that the process of trying to implement new measures, even with the strong scientific and military support enjoyed by Project A, has often been unexpectedly difficult and frustrating. We believe that the most vexing problems relate to the many stakeholders in the system and organizational inertia.

Some Obstacles

Stakeholders

The "user" for Army selection and classification tests is not one person, agency, or organizational unit; instead it is a large network that includes many different players. The stakeholders include (a) the agency responsible for administering entrance tests and managing applicant records and databases, (b) Army guidance counselors who try to persuade qualified applicants to accept an available Army job, (c) recruiters who must fill the available positions with new qualified volunteers, (d) the office that sets policy for and runs the Army personnel system, (e) the Army training establishment, and (f) the active forces, which employ the personnel that the selection, classification, and training systems have found qualified to enter the force. Moreover, for current and possible new ASVAB subtests, an elaborate system of policy and technical review at the joint service level is required. In addition, Congress, as a consumer of test scores, which are one of the indicators of the quality of the military forces, is also a major player in this arena.

These players make different uses of selection and classification tests; some use the test materials, some the scores of individuals, some the aggregated scores, and some the people whom the tests had a part in selecting. Implementing a new test tends to require the simultaneous and continuing approval of most of these players, but it may take the disapproval of only one of them to stop a test from being used operationally. Whenever key personnel change within any one node of this net, that change may require selling the new players from scratch on the merits of a test. Thus, odds alone make it harder to put a new test into operation than to postpone or otherwise block implementation.

Even when most of the players in the network of potential users recognize a costly personnel problem, that may not be sufficient to mobilize an effective solution. From 1973 to the mid-1990s, 30 to 40% of new recruits failed to complete their first enlistment successfully. That high turnover had high costs, both in the expense of recruiting and training replacements for the "attritions," and in the intangible negative impact on recruiting of returning large numbers of unhappy attritees to the civilian population. Finally, in the mid-1990s, the network started working together to produce and implement a set of system-wide remedies.

The case of attrition shows that it is not only the elusiveness of consensus among the users that makes it hard to implement new selection and classification procedures; it is also true that players may have legitimate, mission-related conflicts of interests with each other. Attrition could be reduced by improving selection, training, leadership, or any combination of those three. But each of the three remedies would have a cost, and the cost of each would be borne by a different player in the user network. Each player, in trying to hold costs down, would have a legitimate motive for trying to hand the action off to the other players. Similarly, a new selection or classification procedure that could benefit some players by improving the performance of trainees and soldiers might require changes in personnel files, databases, and regulations, these at some cost to operators in the personnel system.

In general, the organizational player/user that receives the benefit of an improvement in selection or classification is not the player/user that pays the bill for the improvement. Getting players/users to support a change in selection/classification is hard when the costs and benefits are not equally shared.

Organizational Inertia

The next circumstance working against implementation is that large, complex organizations resist change in general. In the Army, for one, a number of operational and political realities result in a powerful tilt toward preserving the ongoing system and resisting changes to that system. One persuasive reality is that the current selection and classification system is perceived to be working well. It is generating soldiers who are perceived to be of high quality based on their ASVAB scores and educational attainment, and the resulting Army is performing better than its foes. The second reality is that the operators and supporters of the current system form a natural constituency in favor of the status quo. This group is not unalterably opposed to change, but they need to be convinced. The third reality is that personnel selection and classification is a risk-averse process because its results are very public; it is the venue for dealing with issues in equality of employment opportunity; and it affects the lifeline of the personnel system,

Army recruiting. These specific realities reinforce the predictable tendency of any large organization to resist implementing new personnel tests.

Another reality is that, unless a new test or procedure has extraordinarily strong support or is part of a broader push toward organizational change, it will not be allowed to fundamentally impact upon other personnel systems but will need to be adaptable to these systems before it is implemented. For example, where the assignment of a tank crewman to the gunner's position is traditionally determined by the progression from Loader to Driver to Gunner to Tank Commander, a new test that measures aptitude for gunnery is not likely to be allowed to alter the assignment of duties. A pessimistic corollary to this principle is that, if researchers cannot anticipate personnel system changes that might occur during the development of new selection and classification systems, the selection and classification products may be dead on arrival.

Seeds of Success

The organizational obstacles that we have reviewed to this point are not peculiar to the Army except in the specific players involved; they are general facts of organizational life, and they are very powerful. Although the obstacles to implementing changes in Army selection and classification are formidable, however, they are occasionally surmountable. Assembling Objects and the AIM, scion of Project A's ABLE, are illustrative. The commonality in these cases is the perception at high management levels of an acute problem. Shortfalls in recruiting have now made first-tour attrition unacceptable. The press of that problem has lowered obstacles to trying out AIM in preenlistment screening. In fact, the use of AIM as a component of a program to expand the recruiting market has led to its embrace by key decision makers. In the case of Assembling Objects, it has the special merits of measuring an aspect of general aptitude that ASVAB does not (viz., spatial aptitude), of adding to ASVAB in predicting job performance, and, unlike most other measures of spatial aptitude, not showing large gender differences in scores at the expense of women. Thus, at a point in history when the military expects recruiting to be increasingly difficult, Assembling Objects offers a way to improve ASVAB without creating an obstacle to women's qualifying for enlistment based on their validly predicted job performance.

At moments of acute need such as these, tools and procedures that are available off-the-shelf will be favored over those that can be implemented three to four years downstream. If the research community is fortunate enough to have an instrument that has already gone through extensive development and testing, a process that, as in the hardware community, can easily take a generation, and if the instrument happens to fit the need, then this is the ideal environment for implementation. It is almost impossible to shape a research program to generate tools to be available exactly when the user community perceives they are needed. However, if the focus is on developing tools that can improve the current procedures, at least researchers will have some hope of ultimate implementation.

What can researchers do to promote implementation in such an environment? They can first ensure that the instruments they develop meet the standard legal, practical, ethical, policy-related, and scientific criteria. Most of the tests that were newly developed in Project A strongly meet those criteria. Second, researchers can persist by looking for alternative settings where implementation of a new product could help reduce a personnel problem. In general, smaller applications are easier to get approved and installed. Or a discontinued implementation could guide improvement of a new product and strengthen the case for its renewed implementation. Third, the researchers can prepare themselves ahead of time by identifying the relevant players in the user network, identifying those users' practical and political issues, overcoming any objections that users might make, and only then promoting implementation.

None of these steps will guarantee implementation of testing products. Ultimately, it is the users' place to determine whether or not to implement based on their assessment of the impact on the whole operational system. It is the researchers' obligation to ensure that this decision is made with the best information possible. In the end, the implementation scorecard will be based not on how many products were transferred to operational use, but on the net benefit to the organization from implemented products. We are confident that the products from Project A can score well on this criterion. Moreover, we hope these lessons learned will help make selection and classification researchers' future implementation efforts a little less like pushing a large rock up a rather steep hill.

VII

Epilogue

20

Implications for Future Personnel Research and Personnel Management

John P. Campbell

The series of projects that we have referred to as Project A spanned a considerable time period. They are in fact still continuing in the form of subsequent projects that deal with further implementation research, the development of new personnel assignment models, the development of new predictor and performance measures, and additional projects that attempt to extend Project A, both in terms of modeling additional properties of the personnel systems and in terms of anticipating the personnel system needs of the future. As the result of a broad range of technology advances, the increased diversity of its missions, the changing nature of potential threats, and changes in the labor force itself, the Army has in fact entered a very dynamic period (i.e. 2000–2020) in which it must develop and adapt more quickly and deal with almost continually changing requirements. The Army's situation is not unlike the issues faced by human resource management in the civilian labor force (Ilgen & Pulakos, 1999). The Project A data base, the models of performance and performance determinants that were developed, and the measurement and data collection procedures used are all playing critical roles in virtually all current and proposed research efforts that are attempting to deal with this more dynamic environment

(Ford, R. Campbell, J. Campbell, Knapp, & Walker, 2000). Consequently, even though this book comes 18 years after Project A first began, the work is still ongoing and the database itself is heavily used.

The work described in this book spanned the period from 1982–1995. There was an overall project plan and a detailed set of objectives for that period. Over the course of its formal life, Project A involved dozens of research personnel and support staff from four organizations, three advisor/oversight groups, a National Research Council panel, and contributions from literally hundreds of individuals in the Army itself.

What is still a bit difficult to believe is that the original project plan was carried out and completed in virtually the same form in which it was proposed, and that the original objectives were met. How was that possible?

First, Army management was extraordinarily supportive. The objectives were important to them. They understood the questions being asked, and they understood what it would take to answer them. In short, they were, and are, very knowledgeable about human resource management and the role that applied research plays in developing new information and new systems. Consequently, very large samples of job incumbents were provided when they were needed. None were permitted to duck their obligation to cooperate.

Second, one consequence of having multiple advisory/oversight groups was that the work of the project took on a very "public" nature. We all knew that we were quite visible and that dropping the ball would not be a good thing to do.

Third, as described in Chapter 3, the project design fundamentally depended on being ready to collect data on particular dates from two specific cohorts of Army accessions. These dates were cast in stone, literally years in advance. Consequently, everyone involved in measurement development and data collection planning knew that all procedures and instrumentation needed to be ready by a certain date or the entire project would fail. Similarly, those people logistically responsible for the samples knew that if the samples were not ready to participate by a certain date, then all of the R&D investment would be lost. This was a powerful set of forces.

Fourth, despite having to prepare what seemed like an endless number of briefings and having to worry constantly about deadlines, everyone found the work encompassed by Project A to be intrinsically interesting, challenging, and fun. Everyone had the opportunity to use all their skills, and then some. Everyone got the opportunity to learn new skills and to develop new ideas, and most people took advantage of the opportunity.

Finally, the research teams took on many of the characteristics of what we would now call the high performance work team. That is, everyone knew the overall project plan and how their contributions fit. They knew what would happen if they did not produce. It seems fair to say that all principal team members were committed to the goals of the project and were invested in its quality. Perhaps because of the nature of graduate training in applied psychology and the way the project participants were selected, there was considerable de facto cross-training. Everyone could judge when the specifications for a measure were good or bad, whether the results of a pilot test were indicative of more development, or when a statistical estimation procedure was a reasonable one. Everyone could do their own analysis and critically evaluate the analyses done by others. It was not the case that everyone worked on their own part and then passed it on to a principal investigator without knowing how it fit with the work of others or how it became part of the overall effort. Because of the high degree of cross-training, the management of the project simply had to be very participative. The participants would have rebelled against anything else. Not necessarily by design, the team members turned out to be individuals that did not shy away from participation. Neither did anyone seem to put their own personal agenda ahead of accomplishing project goals to the fullest extent possible.

Early on in the project, we tried to utilize a computerized project management tool in the spirit of (but not identical to) PERT. It did not work. Maintaining the software system and satisfying its data requirements took much effort and produced progress reports of limited construct validity. For a project of this size, and given the nature of the participants' training and experience, the model of the high performance team worked better. That is, everyone knew the goals and milestones quite well. Everyone accepted accountability for them, the level of information sharing was high, and there was an extremely high degree of participation on all planning and evaluation issues. This meant a lot of face-to-face interaction. Although we had a primitive form of e-mail, one wonders what the current emphasis on terse, distant electronic communication would have meant for this kind of participative, information-rich interaction. For example, we spent much discussion time trying to make sure that when two people used the same words they in fact were talking about the same thing, and that when they used different words they were in fact not talking about the same thing. The latter issue produced a lot of pseudo-disagreements that simply evaporated when the details were examined.

This is our best explanation for why this very ambitious project, which had a size, scope, and need for coordination that was new to personnel research, did not crash and burn or substantially depart from its original proposed plan. It illustrates some old truths, but perhaps it illustrates some new ones as well.

THE SUBSTANTIVE IMPLICATIONS

It is all well and good that the project did what it proposed to do on time, and that it was a rewarding experience for the participants. What is the legacy of its substantive outcomes? Are they of use only to the Army, which some might argue is a unique organization? Do they have implications for human resource management in general? For Industrial and Organizational Psychology practice? For applied psychological research? For basic research questions? We have tried to address these issues in the individual chapters, but what about the overall picture? As our last word in what is a rather long and detailed volume, we offer the following brief synopsis.

Job and Occupational Analysis

For purposes of developing measures of individual performance, Project A used multiple methods to describe the substantive content of a representative sample of jobs. Even though the Army has a rich database of task descriptions, and even though NCOs and officers were a fertile source of critical incidents, the strong conclusion must be that one method is not enough. There is probably no personnel research purpose that would not be better served by multiple methods. Both for developing performance measures and inferring critical performance determinants (i.e., KSAs), the enterprise needs to know (a) the content of the work that is required, (b) the criticality of different dimensions, (c) the level of difficulty or complexity at which individuals must perform, and (d) the conditions under which the individual should be able to operate. No one method can provide all of these.

The Importance of Taxonomic Theory

Although not everyone on the project may have started with a firm belief that taxonomic models of predictors and criteria are fundamental for selection and classification research, the necessity of thinking in terms of the latent structure soon became apparent to everyone. Even the diehards were pushed in this direction because, while Project A attempted to collect data on a representative sample of jobs, the specific MOS in the sample were not the primary interest. The goal was to generalize findings to the entire population of jobs encompassed by the enlisted selection and classification system. Consequently, both predictors and criteria had to reflect the latent structure that applies to all jobs in the population. From this perspective, *any* investigator who uses one or more predictor or criterion measures should be able to locate the variable(s) being measured in a known (or at least specifiable) taxonomic structure. Substantive research results should be organized around latent variables (e.g., need for achievement), not around methods (e.g., the interview).

To the extent that the latent structure for a particular domain becomes more completely known and agreed upon, the more interpretable and usable the accumulated research knowledge becomes. We think Project A clearly showed this and that subsequent research on predictors and criteria have been influenced accordingly. Project A was really the first personnel research effort to develop systematically a substantively defined structure for job performance (i.e., the first-tour five-factor performance model). We believe that it helped change the way the field thinks about the criterion problem and performance assessment. The real hope is that it will someday soon lead to a *generally agreed upon* substantive model, most likely hierarchical, that can be used as a universal framework to interpret research on performance assessment and prediction. To make this happen, every user of a criterion measure must specify the substantive component of performance (general or specific) that is the goal of measurement.

The project also offered taxonomic models for abilities and personality. It also made it painfully obvious that we lack any sort of taxonomic theory for "knowledge" and for "skill." The work of the Secretaries Commission on Achieving Necessary Skills (SCANS, 1992) and the development of the Occupational Information Network (O*NET; Peterson, Mumford, Borman, Jeanneret, & Fleishman, 1999) are steps toward this goal, but much more needs to be done.

Implications for Performance Measurement

Because the project design included large samples from two cohorts (i.e., the concurrent and longitudinal samples), and because the same latent variables were assessed with multiple measures in each cohort, it was possible to test alternative latent structure models using confirmatory techniques. Project A presented the first real opportunity to investigate the nature of performance in this way. In addition to the taxonomic notion that performance does indeed have a replicable latent structure, there are additional specific implications that we think are critical.

The Rating Method

Ratings as a method for the assessment of job performance have a generally bad press. There is, after all, much evidence for unreliability, halo, and leniency. The rating method represents a complex process in information processing and social cognition that is rampant with opportunities for biased and error-filled judgments (Morgeson & Campion, 1997). The conclusion from Project A must be that, in spite of all these considerations, ratings are a valuable measurement method *if* significant attention is paid to using them effectively. For Project A, this meant that (a) the dimensions to be rated were carefully developed and defined, and were very meaningful to the raters; (b) there were at least 20 to 30 minutes of rater training; (c) the ratings were made in a setting that ensured the raters would take sufficient time and give careful attention to the rating task; and (d) the goals of the rater were commensurate with the goals of the researchers. Although one might consider the above conditions as minimal, they probably go far beyond the conditions under which ratings have been used in most studies. Asking someone to perform such a complex judgment task without at least the above conditions being present is simply asking for an unsuccessful result.

The Project A rating measures yielded reasonable distributional properties, had reasonable single-rater reliabilities, and produced a factor structure that was highly replicable across samples. Again, a method should not be forever damned based on the negative results of very inexpert applications, even if the inappropriate applications are in the majority.

The Role of the Measurement Goal

A frequently asked question about performance measurement concerns which type of criterion measure is best. The implication is that there must be a near-ultimate criterion lurking someplace. For example, the National Research Council panel (Wigdor & Green, 1991) took the position that the hands-on job sample simulation was the preferred criterion measure, always. We hope we have at least dispelled the myth of the "ultimate criterion" once and for all. The intent was to also counter the argument that there is always one preferred measurement method.

By design, different measurement methods permit different sources of variation to operate. For example, the job sample simulation is a standardized "test" environment that controls for motivational differences as a source of variance. The intent is for all individuals to work at a maximum effort level. Individual differences in effort should not be a significant source of variation in performance. Using a measurement method that controls for, or does not control for, a specific source of individual differences is a choice to be made by the investigator or the practitioner. The choice depends on the potential sources of variation that the investigator or practitioner wants to capture, not on being more or less ultimate. The moral is that investigators must also include such specifications in their criterion measurement plan.

The General Factor versus Specific Factors

Because of the generally positive manifold in the intercorrelation matrix for any set of job performance measures, even when method variance and unreliability are controlled (Viswesvaran, Schmidt, & Ones, 1993), there will always be a general factor. However, the general factor is not there because there is only one general performance requirement. It arises most likely because individual differences in general mental ability and individual differences in the predisposition toward conscientious effort are determinants of performance on virtually all aspects of most jobs, even for performance requirements that entail very different content (e.g., electronic troubleshooting vs. rewarding subordinates appropriately). However, a general factor does not preclude the importance of specific factors for selection and classification.

The Project A results showed significant differential prediction across performance factors within jobs. However, differential prediction across jobs was limited largely to the "core technical factor." The other factors mean essentially the same thing in terms of substantive content, no matter what the job, at least for this population of jobs. There are some clear implications here. One is that attempts to evaluate classification efficiency should not focus on measures of overall performance. That may weight the criterion with substantial variance for which differential prediction would never be expected. Also, for selection purposes, using only an overall performance measure would preclude being able to explicitly weight the different components of performance or to impose "minimum standards" for some but not others.

Again, we believe that Project A has provided enough evidence and stimulated enough subsequent research on the substantive nature of performance that the naïve use of the term "overall performance" should become a thing of the past, or at least that the users of such language will feel a strong sense of shame and guilt.

Implications for the Study of Individual Differences

Project A devoted considerable time to identifying the taxonomy of predictor constructs that held the most promise for enhancing both selection and classification for the enlisted personnel system. The evaluations of selection validity and classification efficiency for the total test battery have been reported in some detail in previous chapters, but what are some of the broader implications?

The Role of Personality

In retrospect, the development and validation of the ABLE was one of the primary reasons for the recent resurgence of research on personality for selection purposes. In the early 1980s, the measurement of personality for selection purposes was still held in low regard. As noted in Chapter 6, the Project A literature review categorized previous validity estimates by type of criterion and by major personality dimensions, which presented a more encouraging picture. That is, when specific personality dimensions were used to predict performance dimensions to which they would be linked on a priori theoretical grounds, the validity estimates were much higher. This finding, together with the positive results from the concurrent validation, were a major impetus for the much larger role that personality measurement currently plays in personnel selection research.

The additional research reported in this volume reaffirms the value of personality measurement, but it also cautions about the reactivity to experience of some types of items and the use of concurrent designs. The implementation problems are also examined in some detail. The implementation research, which began under the Project A contract, is still ongoing. The use of personality data for decision making is an excellent example of how basic research, applied research, and implementation concerns all interact and cross-fertilize each other.

General Mental Ability versus Differential Prediction

The issue here is well-known and has been argued many times in many places. That is, for purposes of personnel decision making, is it possible to account for significant criterion variance with measures of specific abilities after the effects of a measure of the general factor have been controlled? The advocates of general mental ability (GMA) as the dominant explanation ask two principal empirical questions. First, will adding additional trait measures to the equation provide incremental validity for the selection decision? Second, will the inclusion of additional variables in the prediction equation yield significant amounts of differential prediction of performance across jobs?

Based on the results reported in this volume, as well as subsequent meta-analyses (e.g., Schmidt & Hunter, 1998), there is certainly no denying the dominant role of GMA in the prediction equation for virtually any job. However, the principal lessons from Project A are that the degree to which incremental validity and/or differential validity are possible is influenced significantly by the component of performance being predicted and the range of predictor variables that can be used.

Differential prediction across jobs should be greater to the extent that the performance measure is a "purer" (i.e., more construct-valid) measure of the substantive/technical content of the job or occupation. The Project A samples yielded differential prediction across jobs on the Core Technical Performance (CTP) factor but not on the other performance factors. However, even though the MOS from which data were collected were sampled from a population of jobs, the total population is still restricted to entry-level positions in a relatively narrow range of occupational specialties compared to all the jobs in the civilian labor force. It is also true that the CTP criterion score is probably still too much a function of declarative knowledge rather than the fully practical skills that would be exhibited in a "real" situation. All of which is to argue that the Project A estimates of differential validity are undoubtedly still underestimates of what would be true in a less constrained situation.

Classification gains, compared to selection, are greater if a wider variety of ability variables (e.g., perceptual and psychomotor) as well as dispositional and experience variables can be considered. It is also true that because the Army's selection and classification systems recruit people with no prior job experience or specific occupational training, predictive variables representing occupationally specific knowledge and skill could not be used. This is another constraint on the degree of differential prediction that is possible.

The project results also made clear that there is differential prediction across performance components within jobs. The field had not generally thought of differential prediction in this way before. The finding is critical because it highlights that GMA may not be enough for effective selection if one or more of the nontechnical performance factors are judged to be critical for achieving the organization's goals.

Estimating Classification Efficiency

The Project A study design and database also provided a rare opportunity to estimate classification gains under a variety of conditions, without having to assume the simplifying conditions required by the Brogden-type estimator. Zeidner and Johnson and their colleagues (e.g., Scholarios, Johnson, & Zeidner, 1994) carried out an extensive series of Monte Carlo simulation studies using the Project A database and showed that small but operationally significant classification gains could be realized using only a battery of ability tests. Our own analyses (Chapter 16) showed that somewhat larger estimated gains could be obtained if the entire Project A Experimental Battery, plus ASVAB, could be used. When generalized to an organization of this size, the estimated payoff, although still relatively small in terms of the average gain per selectee, is quite large in the aggregate.

Another important conclusion in this regard is that the statistical estimation of classification efficiency or classification gain is a complex matter. One major consideration is that it incorporates two types of "cross-validation." First, the selection-decision effects of the job-specific predictor weights must be cross-validated. Second, the classification decision effects of the assignment algorithm must also be evaluated for capitalization on chance. That is, classification is also a maximization procedure and some portion of the total estimated gain could be because of making differential job assignments based in part on chance fluctuations in an individual's predicted performance scores across jobs. Johnson and Zeidner (1990) handled this problem via simulated empirical cross-validation. In Chapter 16, we attempted to develop a more generalized unbiased estimator of the actual classification gain. We hope it is of some interest to other researchers.

Another major issue here is the comparison of estimates of maximum potential classification gain with the potential gain that can be realized with a specific operational system. As reviewed in Chapter 16, a number of parameters and constraints can influence the actual classification outcome. The Army now has a fully functional prototype of a "true classification" algorithm, the Enlisted Personnel Allocation System (EPAS), that can incorporate and evaluate the effects (using Project A data) of many factors (e.g., selection ratios, assignment priorities, assignment quotas, acceptance rates). This system has been used extensively to simulate classification outcomes under a variety of operational conditions (Greenston et al., 1999). In this instance, the Project A data have provided a very useful test bed for evaluating the effects of a variety of human resource management strategies.

Predicting Future Performance from Previous Performance

Because of its longitudinal design, Project A was able to estimate the consistency of individual performance across three career stages (training performance, entry-level performance, and supervisory performance) for a large sample of individuals. Further, it was possible to portray these results in terms of covariances among true scores. The high degree of convergent/divergent validity for the performance factors across career stages was further evidence that being able to specify the latent structure enhances our understanding of the nature and dynamics of the performance domain. One of the most significant aspects of this pattern was that leadership performance has a broader set of determinants than any other performance component. This makes a great deal of sense if we think of leadership/supervision as not "one thing" but as a number of distinguishable roles that perhaps have different determinants (e.g., the leader as technical trainer, performance model, goal facilitator, source of support and recognition, communicator of information, resolver of conflicts), which in turn has a number of implications for selection and training.

Beyond the Army

The original objectives set by the sponsor were met. Using well-developed measures and large representative samples, it was possible to estimate the validity of the current system and to estimate the degree of selection validity and classification efficiency that could be achieved from the current state-of-the-art, given substantial (but not unlimited) resources. The performance components were measured reliably and with considerable construct validity. The levels of predictive accuracy were high.

But what about the Army as a unique organization and the generalizability of any findings to the civilian sector? Certainly in some respects the Army is a unique organization. No civilian organization has a similar mission, and some of the components of individual performance have unique aspects. However, the bulk of the performance domain for the enlisted occupational structure has civilian counterparts. The current Army is a volunteer organization. It competes in the job market with other employers, and people can quit and seek other employment. The enlisted personnel corps is reasonably representative of the civilian labor force in similar jobs with similar levels of experience. It is our firm belief that the major implications of the project's methods and results are not constrained by the uniqueness of the Army as an organization and have broad applicability to understanding the world of work.

SOME LAST THOUGHTS

With the strong support of the Army, Project A achieved its stated objectives. However, as described in Chapters 18 and 19, there was no immediate wholesale implementation of the project's findings into the enlisted personnel and classification system. This was certainly not unexpected. For both good and not so good reasons, implementation must deal with a variety of system constraints, not all of which can be anticipated. It would be a mistake to try to design even very applied research projects such that implementation could virtually be guaranteed. It would lead to a very narrow focus. It is never possible to predict all the future constraints. More importantly perhaps, it is also not possible to anticipate all the ways in which the results will prove to be valuable. The Project A results *have* had an impact on the operational system (e.g., Zook, 1996), and the database is used almost continuously to answer specific questions from the management or ARI researchers. The findings have also provided the foundation for subsequent projects, and they constitute the test bed for the development of the next generation of personnel assignment procedures (Greenston et al., 1999).

The above realities argue again for the necessity of placing the measures and variables used in a particular study within a model of the relevant latent structure that is specified as well as possible. It facilitates the interpretation of results, the integration of findings across studies, the identification of future research needs, and the use of the findings for unanticipated applications. If Project A did nothing else, it subscribed to this idea and showed the value of modeling both the predictor and performance domains as well as possible. Subsequent investigators have used the database to test alternative structural models of the linkages among abilities, personality, job experience, job specific knowledge and skill, and the major components of performance (e.g., Borman, White, & Dorsey, 1995; Borman, White, Pulakos, & Oppler, 1991). These efforts also convincingly show that a clear focus on the latent structure will illuminate the gaps as well as the strengths in our research knowledge. For example, the lack of research attention devoted to the latent structure of "job-relevant knowledge" and "job-relevant skill" became painfully obvious. These deficiencies have also presented problems for the development of the Occupational Information

Network (O*NET), as well as the work of the National Skills Standards Board (NSSB) and the efforts of all those who are trying to deal with the skill requirements for the future labor force.

Continually trying to improve our models of relevant domains, as well as the interrelationship among them, is as critical for (good) practice as it is for (good) science. We began Project A with high respect for both our practice and our science. The respect for both and the appreciation for how they are so strongly interrelated were even greater at the end.

References

Abbe, C. N. (1968). *Statistical properties of allocation averages* (Research Memorandum 68-13). Washington, D.C.: U.S. Army Behavioral Science Research Laboratory.

Abrahams, N. M., Alf, E. F., Kieckhaefer, W. F., Pass, J. J., Cole, D. R., & Walton-Paxton, E. (1994). *Classification utility of test composites from the ASVAB, CAT-ASVAB, and ECAT batteries* (Contract N66001-90-D-9502, Delivery Order 7J16). San Diego: Navy Personnel Research and Development Center.

Abrahams, N. M., Neumann, I., & Rimland, B. (1973). *Preliminary validation of an interest inventory for selection of Navy recruiters* (Research Memorandum SRM 73-3). San Diego, CA: Navy Personnel and Training Research Laboratory.

Abrahams, N. M., Pass, J. J., Kusulas, J. W., Cole, D. R., & Kieckhaefer, W. F. (1993). *Incremental validity of experimental computerized tests for predicting training criteria in military technical schools* (Contract N66001-90-D-9502, Delivery Order 7J13). San Diego: Navy Personnel Research and Development Center.

Ackerman, P. L. (1987). Individual differences in skill learning: An integration of psychometric and information processing perspectives. *Psychological Bulletin, 102,* 3–27.

Ackerman, P. L. (1988). Determinants of individual differences during skill acquisition: Cognitive abilities and information processing. *Journal of Experimental Psychology: General, 117,* 288–318.

Ackerman, P. L. (1989). Within task intercorrelations of skilled performance: Implications for predicting individual differences? (A commentary on Henry & Hulin, 1987). *Journal of Applied Psychology, 97,* 360–364.

Ackerman, P. L. (1996). A theory of adult intellectual development: Process, personality, interests, and knowledge. *Intelligence, 22,* 227–257.

Allen, S. J., & Hubbard, R. (1986). Notes and commentary: Regression equations for the latent roots of random data correlation matrices with unities on the diagonal. *Multivariate Behavioral Research, 21*, 393–398.

Alley, W. E., Berberich, G. L., & Wilbourn, J. M. (1977). *Development of factor-referenced subscales for the Vocational Interest Career Examination* (AFHRL TR 76-88). Brooks AFB, TX: Personnel Research Division, Air Force Human Resources Laboratory.

Alley, W. E., & Matthews, M. D. (1982). The Vocational Interest Career Examination: A description of the instrument and possible applications. *The Journal of Psychology, 112*, 169–193.

Alley, W. E., Wilbourn, J. M., & Berberich, G. L. (1976). *Relationships between performance on the Vocational Interest Career Examination and reported job satisfaction* (AFHRL-TR-76-89). Lackland AFB, TX: Personnel Research Division, Air Force Human Resources Laboratory.

American Educational Research Association, American Psychological Association, & National Council on Measurement in Education (1985). *Standards for educational and psychological testing.* Washington, DC: American Psychological Association.

American Educational Research Association, American Psychological Association, & National Council on Measurement in Education (1999). *Standards for educational and psychological testing.* Washington, DC: American Psychological Association.

Anastasi, A. (1958). *Differential psychology: Individual and group differences in behavior* (3rd ed.). New York: MacMillan.

Anastasi, A. (1982). *Psychological testing* (5th ed.). New York: MacMillan.

Arvey, R. D., & Dewhirst, H. D. (1979). Relationship between diversity of interests, age, job satisfaction, and job performance. *Journal of Occupational Psychology, 52*, 17–23.

Asher, J. J., & Sciarrino, J. A. (1974). Realistic work sample tests: A review. *Personnel Psychology, 27*, 519–533.

Astin, A. W. (1964). Criterion-centered research. *Educational and Psychological Measurement, 24*, 807–822.

Austin, J. T., & Hanisch, K. A. (1990). Occupational attainment as a function of abilities and interests: A longitudinal analysis using project TALENT data. *Journal of Applied Psychology, 75*, 77–89.

Austin, J. T., Humphreys, L. G., & Hulin, C. L. (1989). A critical reanalysis of Barrett et al. *Personnel Psychology, 42*, 583–596.

Azen, S. P., Snibbe, H. M., & Montgomery, H. R. (1973). A longitudinal predictive study of success and performance of law enforcement officers. *Journal of Applied Psychology, 57*, 190–192.

Balma, M. J. (1959). The concept of synthetic validity. *Personnel Psychology, 12*, 395–396.

Barge, B. N., & Hough, L. M. (1988). Utility of biographical data for predicting job performance. In L. M. Hough (Ed.), *Utility of temperament, biodata, and interest assessment for predicting job performance: A review and integration of the literature* (ARI Research Note 88-02, pp. 91–130). Alexandria, VA: U.S. Army Research Institute for the Behavioral and Social Sciences.

Barnes, V., Potter, E. H., & Fiedler, F. E. (1983). Effects of interpersonal stress on prediction of academic performance. *Journal of Applied Psychology, 69*, 686–697.

Barrett, G. V., & Alexander, R. A. (1989). Rejoinder to Austin, Humphreys, and Hulin: Critical reanalysis of Barrett, Caldwell, and Alexander. *Personnel Psychology, 42*, 597–612.

Barrett, G. V., Caldwell, M. S., & Alexander, R. A. (1985). The concept of dynamic criteria: A critical reanalysis. *Personnel Psychology, 38*, 41–56.

Barrick, M. R., & Mount, M. K. (1991). The Big Five personality dimensions and job performance: A meta-analysis. *Personnel Psychology, 44*, 1–26.

Barrick, M. R., & Mount, M. K. (1996). Effects of impression management and self-deception on the predictive validity of personality constructs. *Journal of Applied Psychology, 81*, 261–272.

Bentz, V. J. (1968). The Sears experience in the investigation, description, and prediction of executive behavior. In J. A. Myers (Ed.), *Predicting managerial success.* Ann Arbor, MI: Foundation for Research on Human Behavior.

Bloxom, B. (1989, July). *Report of the Technical Advisory Selection Panel.* Unpublished memorandum to the Military Accession Policy Working Group. Monterey, CA: Defense Manpower Data Center.

Bordelon, V. P., & Kantor, J. E. (1986). *Utilization of psychomotor screening for USAF pilot candidates: Independent and integrated selection methodologies* (AFHRL-TR-86-4). Brooks Air Force Base, TX: U.S. Air Force Human Resources Laboratory.

Bordin, E. S., Nachman, B., & Segal, S. J. (1963). An articulated framework for vocational development. *Journal of Counseling Psychology, 10*, 107–116.

Borman, W. C. (1979a). Format and training effects on rating accuracy and rater errors. *Journal of Applied Psychology, 64*, 410–421.

Borman, W. C. (1979b). Individual difference correlates of accuracy in evaluating others' performance effectiveness. *Applied Psychological Measurement, 3*, 103–115.

Borman, W. C. (1991). Behavior, performance, and effectiveness. In M. D. Dunnette & L.M. Hough (Eds.), *Handbook of industrial and organizational psychology* (Vol. 2), pp. 571–621. Palo Alto, CA: Consulting Psychologists Press.

Borman, W. C., & Brush, D. H. (1993). Toward a taxonomy of managerial performance requirements. *Human Performance, 6*, 1–21.

Borman, W. C., & Motowidlo, S. J. (1997). Task performance and contextual performance: The meaning for personnel selection. *Human Performance, 10*, 99–110.

Borman, W. C., Motowidlo, S. J., Rose, S. R., & Hanser, L. M. (1987). *Development of a model of soldier effectiveness: Retranslation of materials and results* (ARI Research Note 87-29). Alexandria, VA: U.S. Army Research Institute for the Behavioral and Social Sciences. (ADA 181832)

Borman, W. C., White, L. A., & Dorsey, D. W. (1995). Effects of ratee task performance and interpersonal factors on supervisor and peer performance ratings. *Journal of Applied Psychology, 80*, 168–177.

Borman, W. C., White, L. A., Pulakos, E. D., & Oppler, S. H. (1991). Models of supervisory job performance ratings. *Journal of Applied Psychology, 76*, 863–872.

Bownas, D. A., & Heckman, R. W. (1976). *Job analysis of the entry-level firefighter position.* Minneapolis, MN: Personnel Decisions, Inc.

Bray, D. W., Campbell, R. J., & Grant, D. L. (1974). *Formative years in business.* New York: Wiley.

Brayfield, A. H. (1942). Review of the Kuder Preference Record. *Occupations, 21*, 267–269.

Brayfield, A. H. (1953). Clerical interest and clerical aptitude. *Personnel and Guidance Journal, 31*, 304–306.

Brennan, R. L. (1983). *Elements of generalization theory.* Iowa City, IA: ACT Publications.

Brogden, H. E. (1946a). An approach to the problem of differential prediction. *Psychometrika, 11*, 139–154.

Brogden, H. E. (1946b). On the interpretation of the correlation coefficient as a measure of predictive efficiency. *Journal of Educational Psychology, 37*, 65–76.

Brogden, H. E. (1951). Increased efficiency of selection resulting from replacement of a single predictor with several differential predictors. *Educational and Psychological Measurement, 11*, 173–196.

Brogden, H. E. (1954). A simple proof of a personnel classification theorem. *Psychometrika, 19*, 205–208.

Brogden, H. E. (1955). Least squares estimates and optimal classification. *Psychometrika, 20*, 249–252.

Brogden, H. E. (1959). Efficiency of classification as a function of the number of jobs, percent rejected, and the validity and intercorrelation of job performance estimates. *Educational and Psychological Measurement, 19*, 181–190.

Brogden, H. E., & Taylor, E. K. (1950a). The dollar criterion–applying the cost accounting concept to criterion construction. *Personnel Psychology, 3*, 133–154.

Brogden, H. E., & Taylor, E. K. (1950b). The theory and classification of criterion bias. *Educational and Psychological Measurement, 10*, 159–186.

Browne, M. W., & Cudeck, R. (1993). Alternative ways of assessing model fit. In K. A. Bollen & J. S. Long (Eds.), *Testing structural equation models* (pp. 136–162). Beverly Hills, CA: Sage.

Brush, D. H., & Owens, W. A. (1979). Implementation and evaluation of an assessment classification model for manpower utilization. *Personnel Psychology, 32*, 369–383.

Busciglio, H. H. (1991). *The usefulness of Project A spatial tests for predicting comprehensive performance measures* (ARI Research Note 91-17). Alexandria, VA: U.S. Army Research Institute for the Behavioral and Social Sciences. (AD A 232 069)

Busciglio, H. H., & Palmer, D. R. (1996). *An empirical assessment of coaching and practice effects on three Project A tests of spatial aptitude* (ARI Research Note 96-70). Alexandria, VA: U.S. Army Research Institute for the Behavioral and Social Sciences.

Busciglio, H. H., Palmer, D. R., King, I., & Walker, C. B. (1994). *Creation of new items and forms for Project A Assembling Objects test* (ARI Technical Report 1004). Alexandria, VA: U.S. Army Research Institute for the Behavioral and Social Sciences. (AD A282 727)

Busciglio, H. H., Silva, J., & Walker, C. B. (1990, June). *The potential of new Army tests to improve job performance.* Paper presented at the Army Science Conference, Durham, N.C.

Busciglio, H. H., & Teplitzky, M. T. (1994). *Predicting land navigation performance in the Special Forces qualification course* (ARI Technical Report 1015). Alexandria, VA: U.S. Army Research Institute for the Behavioral and Social Sciences. (AD A289 792)

Butler, F. J., Crinnion, J., & Martin, J. (1972). The Kuder Preference Record in adult vocational guidance. *Occupational Psychology, 46,* 99–104.

Camara, W. J., & Laurence, J. H. (1987). *Military classification of high aptitude recruits* (FR-PRD-87-21). Alexandria, VA: Human Resources Research Organization.

Campbell, C. H., Campbell, R. C., Rumsey, M. G., & Edwards, D. C. (1986). *Development and field test of task-based MOS-specific criterion measures* (ARI Technical Report 717). Alexandria, VA: U.S. Army Research Institute for the Behavioral and Social Sciences. (ADA 182645)

Campbell, C. H., Ford, P., Rumsey, M. G., Pulakos, E. D., Borman, W. C., Felker, D. B., de Vera, M. V., & Riegelhaupt, B. J. (1990). Development of multiple job performance measures in a representative sample of jobs. *Personnel Psychology, 43,* 277–300.

Campbell, D. P. (1965). The vocational interests of APA presidents. *American Psychologist, 20,* 636–644.

Campbell, D. P. (1971). *Handbook for the Strong Vocational Interest Blank.* Stanford, CA: Stanford University Press.

Campbell, D. P., & Hansen, J. C. (1981). *Manual for the SVIB-SCII.* Stanford, CA: Stanford University Press.

Campbell, J. P. (1986, August). *When the textbook goes operational.* Invited address at the annual meeting of the American Psychological Association, Washington, D.C.

Campbell, J. P. (Ed.) (1987). *Improving the selection, classification, and utilization of Army enlisted personnel—Annual report, 1985 fiscal year* (ARI Technical Report 746). Alexandria, VA: U.S. Army Research Institute for the Behavioral and Social Sciences.

Campbell, J. P. (1990). Modeling the performance prediction problem in industrial and organizational psychology. In M. D. Dunnette & L. M. Hough (Eds.), *Handbook of industrial and organizational psychology* (2nd ed., Vol. 1, pp. 687–732). Palo Alto: Consulting Psychologists Press.

Campbell, J. P., Gasser, M. B., & Oswald, F. L. (1996). The substantive nature of job performance variability. In K. R. Murphy (Ed.), *Individual differences and behavior in organizations* (pp. 258–299). San Francisco: Jossey-Bass.

Campbell, J. P., McCloy, R. A., Oppler, S. H., & Sager, C. E. (1993). A theory of performance. In N. Schmitt & W. C. Borman (Eds.), *Personnel selection in organizations* (pp. 35–70). San Francisco, CA: Jossey-Bass Publishers.

Campbell, J. P., McHenry, J. J., & Wise, L. L. (1990). Modeling job performance in a population of jobs. *Personnel Psychology, 43,* 313–333.

Campbell, J. P., & Oppler, S. (1990). Modeling of second-tour performance. In J. P. Campbell & L. M. Zook (Eds.), *Building and retaining the Career Force: New procedures for accessing and assigning Army enlisted personnel—Annual report, 1990 fiscal year* (ARI Technical Report 952, pp. 337–360). Alexandria, VA: U.S. Army Research Institute for the Behavioral and Social Sciences.

Campbell, J. P., & Zook, L. M. (Eds.) (1990). *Building and retaining the career force: New procedures for accessing and assigning Army enlisted personnel—Annual report, 1990 fiscal year* (ARI Research Note 952). Alexandria, VA: U.S. Army Research Institute for the Behavioral and Social Sciences. (ADA 252 675)

Campbell, J. P., & Zook, L. M. (Eds.) (1991). *Improving the selection, classification, and utilization of Army enlisted personnel: Final report on Project A* (ARI Technical Report 1597). Alexandria, VA: U.S. Army Research Institute for the Behavioral and Social Sciences. (ADA 242921)

Campbell, J. P., & Zook, L. M. (Eds.) (1994). *Building and retaining the career force: New procedures for accessing and assigning Army enlisted personnel—Annual report, 1992 fiscal year* (ARI Research Note 94-27). Alexandria, VA: U.S. Army Research Institute for the Behavioral and Social Sciences. (ADA 284129)

Campbell, J. P., & Zook, L. M. (Eds.). (1996). *Building and retaining the career force: New procedures for accessing and assigning Army enlisted personnel—Annual report, 1993 fiscal year* (ARI Research Note 96-73). Alexandria, VA: U.S. Army Research Institute for the Behavioral and Social Sciences. (ADA 309090)

Campbell, R. C. (1985). *Scorer training materials* (ARI Working Paper RS-WP-85). Alexandria VA: U.S. Army Research Institute for the Behavioral and Social Sciences.

Carey, N. B. (1994). Computer predictors of mechanical job performance: Marine Corps findings. *Military Psychology, 6*, 1–30.

Carretta, T. R. (1987a). *Basic Attributes Test (BAT) System: A preliminary evaluation* (AFHRL-TP-87-20). Brooks Air Force Base, TX: U.S. Air Force Human Resources Laboratory.

Carretta, T. R. (1987b). *Basic Attributes Test (BAT) System: Development of an automated test battery for pilot selection* (AFHRL-TR-87-9). Brooks Air Force Base, TX: U.S. Air Force Human Resources Laboratory.

Carretta, T. R. (1987c). *Field dependence–independence and its relationship to flight training performance* (AFHRL-TP-87-36). Brooks Air Force Base, TX: U.S. Air Force Human Resources Laboratory.

Carretta, T. R. (1990). *Cross-validation of experimental USAF pilot training performance models* (AFHRL-TR-89-68). Brooks Air Force Base, TX: Manpower and Personnel Division, U.S. Air Force Human Resources Laboratory.

Carretta, T. R. (1991). *Short-term test-retest reliability of an experimental version of the Basic Attributes Test battery* (AL-TP-1991-0001). Brooks Air Force Base, TX: Human Resources Directorate, Armstrong Laboratory.

Carretta, T. R. (1992). *Predicting pilot training performance: Does the criterion make a difference?* (AL-TP-1991-0055). Brooks Air Force Base, TX: Human Resources Directorate, Armstrong Laboratory.

Carroll, J. B. (1991a). No demonstration that *g* is not unitary, but there's more to the story: Comment on Kranzler and Jensen. *Intelligence, 15*, 423–436.

Carroll, J. B. (1991b). Still no demonstration that *g* is not unitary: Further comment on Kranzler and Jensen. *Intelligence, 15*, 449–453.

Carroll, J. B. (1993). *Human cognitive abilities*. New York: Cambridge University Press.

Cascio, W. F. (1991). *Applied psychology in personnel management* (4th ed.). Englewood Cliffs, NJ: Prentice Hall.

Cattell, R. B. (1971). *Abilities: Their structure, growth and action*. Boston: Houghton-Mifflin.

Cattell, R. B., Eber, H. W., & Tatsuoka, M. M. (1970). *Handbook for the Sixteen Personality Factor Questionnaire (16PF)*. Champaign, IL: Institute for Personality and Ability Testing.

Center for Human Resource Research (1991). *NLS Handbook, 1991*. Columbus, OH: Ohio State University.

Chia, W. J., Hoffman, R. G., Campbell, J. P., Szenas, P. L., & Crafts, J. L. (1989). Analysis of job components: The development and evaluation of alternative methods. In L. L. Wise, J. M. Arabian, W. J. Chia, & P. L. Szenas (Eds.), *Army synthetic validity project: Report of Phase I results* (ARI

Technical Report 845). Alexandria, VA: U.S. Army Research Institute for the Behavioral and Social Sciences.

Christiansen, N. D., Goffin, R. D., Johnston, N. G., & Rothstein, M. G. (1994). Correcting the 16PF for faking: Effects on criterion-related validity and individual hiring decisions. *Personnel Psychology, 47*, 847–860.

Claudy, J. G. (1978). Multiple regression and validity estimation in one sample. *Applied Psychological Measurement, 2*, 595–601.

Comrey, A. L. (1970). *EITS manual for the Comrey Personality Scales.* San Diego, CA: Educational and Industrial Testing Service.

Costa, P. T., Jr., & McCrae, R. R. (1992). *Revised NEO Personality Inventory (NEO-PI-R) and NEO Five-Factor Inventory (NEO-FFI) professional manual.* Odessa, FL: Psychological Assessment Resources.

Costa, P. T., Jr., & McCrae, R. R. (1995). Solid ground in the wetlands of personality: A reply to Block. *Psychological Bulletin, 117*, 216–220.

Crafts, J. L., Szenas, P. L., Chia, W. J., & Pulakos, E. D. (1988). *A review of models and procedures for synthetic validation for entry-level Army jobs* (ARI Research Note 88-107). Alexandria, VA: U.S. Army Research Institute for the Behavioral and Social Sciences.

Cronbach, L. J., & Gleser, G. C. (1965). *Psychological tests and personnel decisions* (2nd ed.). Urbana: University of Illinois Press.

Cudeck, R. (1989). Analysis of correlation matrices using covariance structure models. *Psychological Bulletin, 105*, 317–327.

Czarnolewski, M. Y. (1989). *Criterion development and Project A validities for the DX164 TOW2 simulator* (ARI Technical Report 863). Alexandria, VA: U.S. Army Research Institute for the Behavioral and Social Sciences.

Dahlstrom, W. G., Welsh, G. S., & Dahlstrom, L. E. (1972). *An MMPI handbook, Vol. I: Clinical interpretation.* Minneapolis: University of Minnesota Press.

Dahlstrom, W. G., Welsh, G. S., & Dahlstrom, L. E. (1975). *An MMPI handbook, Vol. II. Research applications.* Minneapolis: University of Minnesota Press.

Darley, J. G., & Hagenah, T. (1955). *Vocational interest measurement.* Minneapolis, MN: University of Minnesota Press.

Davis, R. H., Davis, R. A., Joyner, J. N., & deVera, M. V. (1987). *Development and field test of job-relevant knowledge tests for selected MOS* (ARI Technical Report 757). Alexandria, VA: U.S. Army Research Institute for the Behavioral and Social Sciences.

Dawis, R. V., & Lofquist, L. H. (1984). *A psychological theory of work adjustment: An individual-difference model and its applications.* Minneapolis: University of Minnesota.

DeMatteo, J. S., White, L. A., Teplitzky, M. L., & Sachs, S. A. (1991, October). *Relationship between temperament constructs and selection for Special Forces training.* Paper presented at the 33rd Annual Conference of the Military Testing Association, San Antonio, TX.

DiMichael, S. G., & Dabelstein, D. H. (1947). Work satisfaction and work efficiency of vocational rehabilitation counselors as related to measured interests (Abstract). *American Psychologist, 2*, 342–343.

Doll, R. E. (1971). Item susceptibility to attempted faking as related to item characteristic and adopted fake set. *The Journal of Psychology, 77*, 9–16.

Dolliver, R. H. (1969). Strong Vocational Interest Blank versus expressed vocational interests: A review. *Psychological Bulletin, 72*, 95–107.

Dolliver, R. H., Irvin, J. A., & Bigley, S. S. (1972). Twelve-year followup of the Strong Vocational Interest Blank. *Journal of Counseling Psychology, 19*, 212–217.

Drasgow, F., Levine, M. V., & McLaughlin, M. E. (1991). Appropriateness measurement for some multidimensional test batteries. *Applied Psychological Measurement, 15*, 171–191.

DuBois, P. H. (1964). A test-dominated society: China, 1115 B.C.–1950 A.D. In *Proceedings, ETS Invitational Conference on Testing.*

Dunnett, S., Koun, S., & Barber, P. (1981). Social desirability in the Eysenck Personality Inventory. *British Journal of Psychology, 72*, 19–26.

Dunnette, M. D. (1962). Personnel management. *Annual Review of Psychology, 13*, 285–314. Palo Alto, CA: Annual Reviews, Inc.

Dunnette, M. D. (1963). A note on the criterion. *Journal of Applied Psychology, 47*, 317–323.

Dunnette, M. D., & Hough, L. M. (1993, November). Personality factors in work performance. In *Does Applied Science Pay?* Symposium in honor of Professor Henk Thierry, University of Amsterdam, Amsterdam.

Dwight, S. A., & Donovan, J. J. (1998, April). *Does warning applicants not to fake actually reduce faking?* Paper presented at the 14th Annual Conference of the Society For Industrial and Organizational Psychology. St. Louis, MO.

Eaton, N. K., Goer, M. H., Harris, J. H., & Zook, L. M. (Eds.) (1984). *Improving the selection, classification, and utilization of Army enlisted personnel—Annual report, 1984 fiscal year* (ARI Technical Report 660). Alexandria, VA: U.S. Army Research Institute for the Behavioral and Social Sciences.

Edwards, A. L. (1959). *Edwards Personal Preference Schedule manual* (Rev. ed.). New York: Psychological Corporation.

Egbert, R. L., Meeland, T., Cline, V. B., Forgy, E. W., Spickler, M. W., & Brown, C. (1958). *Fighter I: A study of effective and ineffective combat performers* (HumRRO SR-13). Alexandria, VA: Human Resources Research Organization.

Eitelberg, M. J., Laurence, J. H., Waters, B. K., & Perelman, L. S. (1984). *Screening for service: Aptitude and education criteria for military entry.* Washington, DC: Office of the Assistant Secretary of Defense.

Ekstrom, R. B., French, J. W., & Harman, H. H. (1976). *Manual for Kit of Factor-Referenced Cognitive Tests.* Princeton, NJ: Educational Testing Service.

Ekstrom, R. B., French, J. W., & Harman, H. H. (1979). Cognitive factors: Their identification and replication. *Multivariate Behavioral Research Monographs, 79*, 1–84.

Equal Employment Opportunity Commission. (1978). Uniform guidelines on employee selection procedures. *Federal Register, 43*, 38290–38315.

Eysenck, H. J. (1939). Review of "primary mental abilities," by L. L. Thurstone. *British Journal of Psychology, 9*, 270–275.

Eysenck, H. J., & Eysenck, S. B. G. (1975). *Manual for the Eysenck Personality Questionnaire.* San Diego, CA: Educational and Industrial Testing Service.

Flanagan, J. C. (1948). *The Aviation Psychology Program in the Army Air Forces* (Report 1). AAF Aviation Psychology Program Research Reports, U.S. Government Printing Office.

Flanagan, J. C. (1954). The critical incident technique. *Psychological Bulletin, 51*, 327–358.

Flanagan, J. C. (1965). *Flanagan Industrial Test Manual.* Chicago: Science Research Associates.

Fleishman, E. A. (1967). Performance assessment based on an empirically derived task taxonomy. *Human Factors, 9*, 349–366.

Fleishman, E. A. (1973). Twenty years of consideration and structure. In E. A. Fleishman & J. G. Hunt (Eds.), *Current developments in the study of leadership.* Carbondale, IL: U. of Southern Illinois Press.

Fleishman, E. A., & Hempel, W. E. (1956). Factorial analysis of complex psychomotor performance and related skills. *Journal of Applied Psychology, 40*, 96–104.

Fleishman, E. A., & Mumford, M. D. (1988). Ability requirements scales. In S. Gael (Ed.), *Job analysis handbook for business, industry, and government* (Vol. 2, pp. 917–935). New York: Wiley.

Fleishman, E. A., & Quaintance, M. K. (1984). *Taxonomies of human performance: The description of human tasks.* Orlando: Academic Press.

Fleishman, E. A., Zaccaro, S. J., & Mumford, M. D. (1991). Individual differences and leadership: An overview. *Leadership Quarterly, 2*, 237–243.

Ford, L. A., Campbell, R. C., Campbell, J. P., Knapp, D. J., & Walker, C. B. (2000). *Soldier characteristics for the 21st century—Phase II Final Report* (ARI Technical Report 1102). Alexandria, VA: U.S. Army Research Institute for the Social and Behavioral Sciences. (ADA 38004)

Furnham, A., & Craig, S. (1987). Fakability and correlates of the perception and preference inventory. *Personality and Individual Differences, 8*, 459–470.

Gade, E. M., & Soliah, D. (1975). Vocational Preference Inventory high point codes versus expressed choices as predictors of college major and career entry. *Journal of Counseling Psychology, 22*, 117–121.

Gael, S. (1988) (Ed.) *The job analysis handbook for business, industry, and government.* New York: John Wiley & Sons.

Gast, I. F., Campbell, C. H., Steinberg, A. G., & McGarvey, D. A. (1987, August). *A task based approach for identifying junior NCO's key responsibilities.* Paper presented at the meeting of the American Psychological Association, New York.

Gast, I. F., & Johnson, D. M. (1988, November). *Evaluating psychomotor and spatial tests for selecting Air Defense gunners.* Paper presented at the annual meeting of the Military Testing Association, Arlington, VA.

Ghiselli, E. E. (1973). The validity of aptitude tests in personnel selection. *Personnel Psychology, 26*, 461–477.

Gibbons, F. X. (1983). Self-attention and self-report: The "veridicality" hypothesis. *Journal of Personality, 51*, 517–542.

Glaser, R., Lesgold, A., & Gott, S. (1991). Implications of cognitive psychology for measuring job performance. In A. K. Wigdor & B. F. Green (Eds.), *Performance assessment for the workplace.* (Vol. II). Washington, D.C.: National Academy Press.

Goldberg, L. R. (1981). Language and individual differences: The search for universals in personality lexicons. In L. Wheeler (Ed.), *Review of personality and social psychology* (Vol. 2, pp. 141–165). Beverly Hills, CA: Sage.

Gordon, L. V. (1978). *Gordon Personal Profile Inventory manual.* New York: Psychological Corporation.

Gottfredson, G. D., & Holland, J. L. (1975). Vocational choices of men and women: A comparison of predictors from the Self-Directed Search. *Journal of Counseling Psychology, 22*, 28–34.

Gough, H. G. (1975). *Manual for the California Psychological Inventory.* Palo Alto, CA: Consulting Psychologists Press.

Graen, G. B. (1976). Role-making processes within complex organizations. In M. D. Dunnette (Ed.), *Handbook of industrial and organizational psychology* (pp. 1201–1245). Chicago: Rand McNally.

Graen, G. B., Novak, M. A., & Sommerkamp, P. (1982). The effects of leader-member exchange and job design on productivity and satisfaction: Testing a dual attachment model. *Organizational Behavior and Human Performance, 30*, 109–131.

Grafton, F. C., Czarnolewski, M. Y., & Smith, E. P. (1988). *Relationship between Project A psychomotor and spatial tests and TOW gunnery performance* (SCTA Working Paper RS-WP-87-10). Alexandria, VA: U.S. Army Research Institute for the Behavioral and Social Sciences.

Graham, S. E. (1988, November). *Selecting soldiers for the Excellence in Armor Program.* Paper presented at the annual meeting of the Military Testing Association, Arlington, VA.

Greene, C. N. (1975). The reciprocal nature of influence between leader and subordinate. *Journal of Applied Psychology, 60*, 187–193.

Greenston, P., McWhite, P., Mower, D., Walker, S., Lightfoot, M., Diaz, T., & Rudnick, R. (1999). *Toward optimized classification in the U.S. Army: Development of the Enlisted Personnel Classification System.* Manuscript submitted for publication. Alexandria, VA: U.S. Army Research Institute for the Behavioral and Social Sciences.

Guilford, J. P. (1957). *A revised structure of intelligence* (Report No. 19). University of Southern California Psychological Laboratory.

Guilford, J. P. (1975). Factors and factors of personality. *Psychological Bulletin, 82*, 802–814.

Guilford, J. P., Zimmerman, W. S., & Guilford, P. P. (1976). *The Guilford-Zimmerman Temperament Survey handbook.* San Diego, CA: Educational and Industrial Testing Service.

Guion, R. M. (1965). *Personnel testing.* New York: McGraw Hill.

Guion, R. M. (1976). Recruiting, selection, and job placement. In M. D. Dunnette (Ed.), *Handbook of industrial and organizational psychology* (pp. 777–828). Chicago: Rand-McNally.

Guion, R. M., & Gottier, R. F. (1965). Validity of personality measures in personnel selection. *Personnel Psychology, 18,* 135–164.

Hahn, M. E., & Williams, C. T. (1945). The measured interests of Marine Corps women reservists. *Journal of Applied Psychology, 29,* 198–211.

Hansen, J. C. (1983). *Measurement of interests.* Unpublished manuscript, Minneapolis, MN: Personnel Decisions Research Institute.

Hanson, M. A. (1994). *Development and construct validation of a situational judgment test of super-visory effectiveness for first-line supervisors in the U.S. Army.* Unpublished doctoral dissertation, University of Minnesota.

Hanson, M. A., & Borman, W. C. (1992). *Development and construct validation of the Situational Judgment Test* (Institute Report #230). Minneapolis, MN: Personnel Decisions Research Institute.

Harmon, L. W., Hansen, J. C., Borgen, F. H., & Hammer, A. L. (1994). *Strong Interest Inventory: Applications and technical guide.* Stanford, CA: Stanford University Press.

Harvey, R. J. (1991). Job analysis. In M. D. Dunnette & L. M. Hough (Eds.), *The handbook of industrial and organizational psychology* (Vol. 2, pp. 72–163). Palo Alto: Consulting Psychologists Press.

Hedges, L. V. (1982). Fitting categorical models to effect sizes from a series of experiments. *Journal of Educational Statistics, 7,* 119–137.

Heist, P., & Yonge, G. (1968). *Manual for the Omnibus Personality Inventory, Form f.* New York: Psychological Corporation.

Held, J., & Wolfe, J. H. (1997). Validities of unit weighted composites of the ASVAB and the ECAT battery. *Military Psychology, 9,* 77–84.

Henry, R. A., & Hulin, C. L. (1987). Stability of skilled performance across time: Some generalizations and limitations on utilities. *Journal of Applied Psychology, 72,* 457–462.

Herzberg, F., & Russell, D. (1953). The effects of experience and change of job interest on the Kuder Preference Record. *Journal of Applied Psychology, 37,* 478–481.

Hicks, L. E. (1970). Some properties of ipsative, normative, and forced-choice normative measures. *Psychological Bulletin, 74,* 167–184.

Hinrichsen, J. J., Gryll, S. L., Bradley, L. A., & Katahn, M. (1975). Effects of impression management efforts on FIRO-B profiles. *Journal of Consulting and Clinical Psychology, 43,* 269.

Hogan, R. (1982). A socioanalytic theory of personality. In M. M. Page (Ed.), *1982 Nebraska Symposium on Motivation* (pp. 55–89). Lincoln, NE: University of Nebraska Press.

Holland, J. L. (1966). *The psychology of vocational choice.* Waltham, MA: Blaisdell.

Holland, J. L. (1973). *Making vocational choices: A theory of careers.* Englewood Cliffs, NJ: Prentice-Hall.

Holland, J. L., Magoon, T. M., & Spokane, A. R. (1981). Counseling psychology: Career interventions, research and theory. *Annual Review of Psychology, 32,* 279–305.

Horn, J. L. (1989). Cognitive diversity: A framework of learning. In P. L. Ackerman, R. J. Sternberg, & R. Glaser (Eds.), *Learning and individual differences* (pp. 61–116). New York: Freeman.

Horst, P. (1954). A technique for the development of a differential prediction battery. *Psychological Monographs: General and Applied, 68*(5, Whole No. 390).

Horst, P. (1955). A technique for the development of a multiple absolute prediction battery. *Psychological Monographs* (No. 390).

Horst, P. (1956). Multiple classification by the method of least squares. *Journal of Clinical Psychology, 12,* 3–16.

Horst, P., & MacEwan, C. (1957). Optimal test length for multiple prediction: The general case. *Psychometrika, 22,* 311–324.

Hough, L. M. (1992). The "Big-Five" personality variables—Construct confusion: Description versus prediction. *Human Performance, 5*, 139–155.

Hough, L. M. (1998). Effects of intentional distortion in personality measurement and evaluation of suggested palliatives. *Human Performance, 11*, 209–244.

Hough, L., Dunnette, M. D., Wing, H., Houston, J., & Peterson, N. G. (1984, August). *Covariance analyses of cognitive and non-cognitive measures of Army recruits: An initial sample of Preliminary Battery data.* Paper presented at the Annual Convention of the American Psychological Association, Toronto, Ontario, Canada.

Hough. L. M., Eaton, N. K., Dunnette, M. D., Kamp, J. D., & McCloy, R. A. (1990). Criterion-related validities of personality constructs and the effect of response distortion on those validities. *Journal of Applied Psychology, 75*, 581–595.

Hough, L. M., Gast, I. F., White, L. A., & McCloy, R. (1986, August). *The relation of leadership and individual differences to job performance.* Paper presented at the meeting of the American Psychological Association, Washington, D.C.

Hough. L. M., & Schneider, R. J. (1996). Personality traits, taxonomies, and applications in organizations. In K. R. Murphy (Ed.), *Individual differences in behavior in organizations.* San Francisco: Jossey-Bass.

Howard, A. (1995). *The changing nature of work.* San Francisco: Jossey Bass.

Hoyt, C. J. (1941). Test reliability obtained by analysis of variance. *Psychometrika, 6*, 153–160.

HRStrategies (1994). *Revised technical documentation for the General Aptitude Test Battery.* Unpublished manuscript, HRStrategies, Gross Pointe, MI.

Hulin, C. L., Henry, R. A., & Noon, S. L. (1990). Adding a dimension: Time as a factor in the generalizability of predictive relationships. *Psychological Bulletin, 107*, 328–340.

Humphreys, L. G. (1979). The construct of general intelligence. *Intelligence, 3*, 105–120.

Humphreys, L. G. (1986). Commentary. *Journal of Vocational Behavior, 29*, 421–437.

Humphreys, L. G. (1992). Ability testing commentary: What both critics and users of ability tests need to know. *Psychological Science, 3*, 271–274.

Humphreys, L. G., Lubinski, D., & Yao, G. (1993). Utility of predicting group membership and the role of spatial visualization in becoming an engineer, physical scientist or artist. *Journal of Applied Psychology, 78*, 250–261.

Humphreys, L. G., & Montanelli, R. G. (1975). An investigation of the parallel analysis criterion for determining the number of common factors. *Multivariate Behavioral Research, 10*, 193–206.

Hunter, J. E. (1980). *Test validation for 12,000 jobs: An application of synthetic validity and validity generalization to the General Aptitude Test Battery (GATB).* Washington, DC: U.S. Employment Service, U.S. Department of Labor.

Hunter, J. E. (1986). Cognitive ability, cognitive aptitudes, job knowledge, and job performance. *Journal of Vocational Behavior, 29*, 340–362.

Hunter, J. E., & Hunter, R. F. (1984). Validity and utility of alternative predictors of job performance. *Psychological Bulletin, 98*, 72–98.

Hunter, J. E., & Schmidt, F. L. (1982). Fitting people to jobs: The impact of personnel selection on national productivity. In E. A. Fleishman & M. D. Dunnette (Eds.), *Human performance and productivity. Vol. 1: Human capability assessment.* Hillsdale, NJ: Lawrence Erlbaum.

Hunter, J. E., & Schmidt, F. L. (1990). *Methods of meta-analysis: Correcting error and bias in research findings.* Newbury Park, CA: Sage.

Intano, G. P., & Howse, W. R. (1991). *Predicting performance in Army aviation primary flight training* (ARI Research Note 92-06). Alexandria, VA: U.S. Army Research Institute for the Behavioral and Social Sciences.

Intano, G. P., Howse, W. R., & Lofaro, R. J. (1991a). *Initial validation of the Army aviator classification process* (ARI Research Note 91-38). Alexandria, VA: U.S. Army Research Institute for the Behavioral and Social Sciences.

Intano, G. P., Howse, W. R., & Lofaro, R. J. (1991b). *The selection of an experimental test battery for aviation cognitive, psychomotor abilities and personal traits* (ARI Research Note 91-21). Alexandria, VA: U.S. Army Research Institute for the Behavioral and Social Sciences.

Jackson, D. N. (1967). *Personality Research Form manual.* Goshen, NY: Research Psychologists Press.

Jackson, D. N. (1970). A sequential system for personality scale development. In C. D. Spielberger (Ed.), *Current topics in clinical and community psychology.* New York, Academic.

Jackson, D. N. (1976). *Jackson Personality Inventory manual.* Goshen, NY: Research Psychologists Press.

Jacobs, T. O. (1971). *Leadership and exchange in formal organizations.* Alexandria, VA: Human Resources Research Organization.

Jensen, A. R. (1980). *Bias in mental testing.* New York: The Free Press.

Jensen, A. R. (1986). *g*: Artifact or reality? *Journal of Vocational Behavior, 29*, 301–331.

Jensen, A. R. (1992). Ability testing commentary: Vehicles of *g*. *Psychological Science, 3*, 275–278.

Johnson, C. D., & Zeidner, J. (1990). *Classification utility: Measuring and improving benefits in matching personnel to jobs* (IDA Paper P-2240). Alexandria, VA: Institute for Defense Analysis.

Johnson, C. D., & Zeidner, J. (1991). *The economic benefits of predicting job performance: Vol. 2. Classification efficiency.* New York: Praeger.

Johnson, C. D., Zeidner, J., & Scholarios, D. (1990). *Improving the classification efficiency of the Armed Services Vocational Aptitude Battery through the use of alternative test selection indices* (IDA Paper P-2427). Alexandria, VA: Institute for Defense Analysis.

Johnson, E.G., & Zwick, R. (1990). *Focusing the new design: The NAEP 1988 technical report.* Princeton, NJ: Educational Testing Service.

Jöreskog, K. G., & Sörbom, D. (1986). *LISREL VII: Analysis of linear structural relationships by maximum likelihood, instrumental variables, and least squares methods.* Morresville, Indiana: Scientific Software, Inc.

Jöreskog, K. G., & Sörbom, D. (1989). *LISREL VII: A guide to the program and applications* (2nd ed.). Chicago: SPSS Publications.

Kass, R. A., Mitchell, K. J., Grafton, F. C., & Wing, H. (1983). Factorial validity of the Armed Services Vocational Aptitude Battery (ASVAB), Forms 8, 9, and 10: 1981 Army applicant sample. *Educational and Psychological Measurement, 43*, 1077–1087.

Kearl, C. E., & Nord R. D. (1990). *How much soldier quality? Cost effective recruit selection policy for a smaller Army.* Paper presented at the Army Science Conference, Durham, NC.

Kettner, N. (1977). *Armed Services Vocational Aptitude Battery (ASVAB Form 5): Comparison with GATB and DAT tests* (Technical Research Report 77-1). Fort Sheridan, IL: Directorate of Testing, U.S. Military Enlistment Processing Command.

Kilcullen, R. N., Mael, F. A., Goodwin, G. F., & Zazanis, M. M. (1999). Predicting U.S. Army Special Forces field performance. *Human Performance in Extreme Environments, 4*, 53–63.

Kilcullen, R. N., White, L. A., Mumford, M. D., & Mack H. (1995). Assessing the construct validity of rational biodata scales. *Military Psychology, 7*, 17–28.

Knapp, D. J., & Campbell, J. P. (1993). *Building a joint-service classification research roadmap: Criterion-related issues* (AL/HR-TP-1993-0028). Armstrong Laboratory: Brooks Air Force Base, TX. (ADA 269735)

Knapp, D. J., Carter, G. W., McCloy, R. A., & DiFazio, A. S. (1996). The role of job satisfaction in performance, attrition, and reenlistment. In J. P. Campbell & L. M. Zook (Eds.), *Building and retaining the career force: New procedures for accessing and assigning Army enlisted personnel—Annual report, 1993 fiscal year* (ARI Research Report 96-73, pp. 215–244). Alexandria, VA: U.S. Army Research Institute for the Behavioral and Social Sciences.

Knapp, D. J., Russell, T. L., & Campbell, J. P. (1993). *Building a joint-service classification roadmap: Job analysis methodologies* (HumRRO Report IR-PRD-93-15). Alexandria, VA: Human Resources Research Organization. (ADA 293419)

Konieczny, F. B., Brown, G. N., Hutton, J., & Stewart, J. E. (1990). *Enlisted Personnel Allocation System: Final report* (ARI Technical Report 902). Alexandria, VA: U.S. Army Research Institute for the Behavioral and Social Science.

Kranzler, J. H., & Jensen, A. R. (1991a). The nature of psychometric *g*: Unitary process or a number of independent processes? *Intelligence, 15,* 397–442.

Kranzler, J. H., & Jensen, A. R. (1991b). Unitary *g*: Unquestioned postulate or empirical fact. *Intelligence, 15,* 437–448.

Kuder, G. F. (1977). *Activity interests and occupational choice.* Chicago: Science Research Associates.

Kuhn, T. S. (1970). *The structure of scientific revolutions.* Chicago: The University of Chicago Press.

Kyllonen, P. C., & Christal, R. E. (1988). *Cognitive modeling of learning abilities: A status report of LAMP* (AFHRL-TP-87-66). Brooks Air Force Base, TX: U.S. Air Force Human Resources Laboratory.

Kyllonen, P. C., & Christal, R. E. (1990). Reasoning is (little more than) working memory capacity. *Intelligence, 14,* 389–433.

Landy, F. J., & Farr, J. L. (1980). Performance ratings. *Psychological Bulletin, 87,* 72–107.

Lau, A. W., & Abrahams, N. M. (1971). *Reliability and predictive validity of the Navy Vocational Interest Inventory* (Research Report SRR 71-16). San Diego, CA: Navy Personnel and Training Research Laboratory.

Lawshe, C. (1952). Employee selection. *Personnel Psychology, 5,* 31–34.

Linn, R. L. (1968). Range restriction problems in the use of self selected groups for test validation. *Psychological Bulletin, 69,* 69–73.

Linn, R. L. (1986). Comments on the *g* factor in employment testing. *Journal of Vocational Behavior, 29,* 340–362.

Linn, R. L. (1988). *Educational measurement* (3rd ed.). New York: MacMillan.

Linn, M. C., & Petersen, A. C. (1985). Emergence and characterization of sex differences in spatial ability: A meta-analysis. *Child Development, 56,* 1479–1498.

Lord, F. M., & Novick, M. R. (1968). *Statistical theories of mental test scores.* Reading, MA: Addison-Wesley.

Lord, R. G., & Maher, K. J. (1991). Cognitive theory in industrial and organizational psychology. In M. D. Dunnette & L. M. Hough (Eds.), *Handbook of industrial and organizational psychology* (2nd ed. Vol. 2, pp. 1–62). Palo Alto, CA: Consulting Psychologists Press.

Lubinski, D., & Dawis, R. V. (1992). Attitudes, skills, and proficiencies. In M. D. Dunnette & L. M. Hough (Eds.), *Handbook of industrial and organizational psychology* (Vol. 3, pp. 1–59). Palo Alto, CA: Consulting Psychologists Press.

Maccoby, E. E., & Jacklin, C. N. (1974). *The psychology of sex differences.* Stanford, CA: Stanford University Press.

Mael, F. A., & Hirsch, A. C. (1993). Rainforest empiricism and quasi-rationality: Two approaches to objective biodata. *Personnel Psychology, 46,* 719–738.

Mael, F. A., & Schwartz, A. C. (1991). *Capturing temperament constructs with objective biodata* (ARI Technical Report 939). Alexandria, VA: U.S. Army Research Institute for the Behavioral and Social Sciences.

Mael, F. A., & White, L. A. (1994). Motivated to lead: Dispositional and biographical antecedents of performance. In H. O'Neil & M. Drillings (Eds.), *Motivation: Theory and research.* Hillsdale: Erlbaum.

Markus, H. (1983). Self-knowledge: A expanded view. *Journal of Personality, 51,* 543–565.

Martin, S. L., & Raju, N. S. (1992). Determining cutoff scores that optimize utility: A recognition of recruiting costs. *Journal of Applied Psychology, 77,* 15–23.

McArthur, C. (1954). Long-term validity of the Strong Interest Test in two subcultures. *Journal of Applied Psychology, 38,* 346–354.

McCloy, R. A., & DiFazio, A. S. (1996). Prediction of first-term military attrition using pre-enlistment predictors. In J. P. Campbell & L. M. Zook (Eds), *Building and retaining the career force: New procedures for accessing and assigning Army enlisted personnel—Annual report, 1993 fiscal year* (ARI Research Report 96-73, pp. 169–214). Alexandria, VA: U.S. Army Research Institute for the Behavioral and Social Sciences.

McCloy, R. A., Harris, D. A., Barnes, J. D., Hogan, P. F., Smith, D. A., Clifton, D., & Sola, M. (1992). *Accession quality, job performance, and cost: A cost-performance tradeoff model* (FR-PRD-92-11). Alexandria, VA: Human Resources Research Organization.

McCloy, R.A., & Oppler, S. (1990). End-of-training measures. In J. P. Campbell & L. M. Zook (Eds), *Building and retaining the career force: New procedures for accessing and assigning Army enlisted personnel—Annual report, 1990 fiscal year* (ARI Technical Report 952, pp. 201–246). Alexandria, VA: U.S. Army Research Institute for the Behavioral and Social Sciences.

McCormick, E. J., Jeanneret, P. R., & Mecham, R. C. (1972). A study of job characteristics and job dimensions as based on the Position Analysis Questionnaire (PAQ). *Journal of Applied Psychology, 56*, 347–368.

McGee, M. G. (1979). Human spatial abilities: Psychometric studies and environmental, genetic, hormonal, and neurological influences. *Psychological Bulletin, 86*, 889–918.

McHenry, J. J., Hough, L. M., Toquam, J. L., Hanson, M. A., & Ashworth, S. (1990). Project A validity results: The relationship between predictor and criterion domains. *Personnel Psychology, 43*, 335–354.

McHenry, J. J., & Rose, S. R. (1988). *Literature review: Validity and potential usefulness of psychomotor ability tests for personnel selection and classification* (ARI Research Note 88-13). Alexandria, VA: U.S. Army Research Institute for the Behavioral and Social Sciences.

McLaughlin, D. H., Rossmeissl, P. G., Wise, L. L., Brandt, D. A., & Wang, M. (1984). *Validation of current and alternative ASVAB area composites, based on training and SQT information on FY1981 and FY1982 enlisted accessions* (ARI Technical Report 651). Alexandria,VA: U.S. Army Research Institute for the Behavioral and Social Sciences.

McRae, G. G. (1959). *The relationship of job satisfaction and earlier measured interests.* Unpublished doctoral dissertation, University of Florida.

Messick, S. (1988). The once and future issues of validity: Assessing the meaning and consequences of measurement. In H. Wainer & H. Braun (Eds.), *Test validity.* Hillsdale, NJ: Erlbaum.

Meyer, E. C. (1980). *The hollow army* (White Paper). Washington, DC: Department of the Army.

Mischel, W. (1968). *Personality and assessment.* New York: Wiley.

Mitchell, J. (1988). Job analysis in the U. S. military. In S. Gael (Ed.), *The job analysis handbook for business, industry, and government.* New York: John Wiley & Sons.

Mitchell, K. J., & Hanser, L. M. (1984). *1980 youth population norms: Enlisted and occupational classification standards in the Army*, Unpublished manuscript. Alexandria, VA: U.S. Army Research Institute for the Behavioral and Social Sciences.

Mitchell, T. W., & Klimoski, R. J. (1986). Estimating the validity of cross-validity estimation. *Journal of Applied Psychology, 71*, 311–317.

Montanelli, R. G., & Humphreys, L. G. (1976). Latent roots of random data correlation matrices with squared multiple correlations on the diagonal: A Monte Carlo study. *Psychometrika, 41*, 341–347.

Morgeson, F. P., & Campion, M. A. (1997). Social and cognitive sources potential of inaccuracy in job analysis. *Journal of Applied Psychology, 82*, 627–655.

Morrison, R. F. (1977). A multivariate model for the occupational placement decision. *Journal of Applied Psychology, 62*, 271–277.

Mosier, C. I. (1951). Problems and design of cross-validation. *Educational and Psychological Measurement, 11*, 5–11.

Mulaik, S. A., James, L. R., Van Alstine, J., Bennett, N., Lind, S., & Stilwell, C. D. (1989). Evaluation of goodness-of-fit indices for structural equation models. *Psychological Bulletin, 105*, 430–445.

Münsterberg, H. (1913). *Psychology and industrial efficiency.* Boston: Houghton Mifflin.

Nathan, B. R., & Alexander, R. A. (1988). A comparison of criteria for test validation: A meta-analytic investigation. *Personnel Psychology, 41*, 517–536.

Neisser, U. (1996). Intelligence: Knowns and unknowns. *American Psychologist, 51*, 77–101.

Norman, W. T. (1963). Toward an adequate taxonomy of personality attributes: Replicated factor structure in peer nomination personality ratings. *Journal of Abnormal and Social Psychology, 66*, 574–583.

North, R. D., Jr. (1958). Tests for the accounting profession. *Educational and Psychological Measurement, 18*, 691–713.

Nunnally, J. C. (1967). *Psychometric theory.* New York: McGraw-Hill.

O'Connor, E. J., Peters, L. H., & Segovis, J. (1980, August). *Situational constraints, task-relevant abilities, and experienced frustration.* Paper presented at the annual meeting of the Academy of Management, Detroit.

Olson, D. M., & Borman, W. C. (1989). More evidence on relationships between the work environment and job performance. *Human Performance, 2*, 113–130.

Ones, D. S., Viswesvaran, C., & Reiss, A. D. (1996). Role of social desirability in personality testing for personnel selection: The red herring. *Journal of Applied Psychology, 81*, 660–679.

Oppler, S. H., Campbell, J. P., Pulakos, E. D., & Borman, W. C. (1992). Three approaches to the investigation of subgroup bias in performance measurement: Review, results, and conclusions [Monograph]. *Journal of Applied Psychology, 77*, 201–217.

Oppler, S. H., Childs, R. A., & Peterson, N. G. (1994). Development of the longitudinal validation sample first-tour performance model. In J. P. Campbell and L. M. Zook (Eds.), *Building and retaining the career force: New procedures for accessing and assigning Army enlisted personnel—Annual report, 1991 fiscal year* (ARI Research Note 94-10) (pp. 125–154). Alexandria, VA: U.S. Army Research Institute for the Behavioral and Social Sciences.

Oppler, S. H., Peterson, N. G., & Russell, T. (1994). Basic validation results for the LVI sample. In J. P. Campbell and L. M. Zook (Eds.), *Building and retaining the career force: New procedures for accessing and assigning Army enlisted personnel—Annual report, 1991 fiscal year* (ARI Research Note 94-10) (pp. 155–194). Alexandria, VA: U.S. Army Research Institute for the Behavioral and Social Sciences.

Organ, D. W. (1997). Organizational citizenship behavior: It's construct cleanup time. *Human Performance, 10*, 85–98.

Owens, W. A. (1975). *UGA Biographical Questionnaire.* Athens, GA: University of Georgia.

Owens, W. A. (1976). Background data. In M. D. Dunnette (Ed.), *Handbook of Industrial and Organizational Psychology.* Chicago: Rand McNally.

Owens, W. A. (1978). Moderators and subgroups. *Personnel Psychology 31*, 243–248.

Owens, W. A., & Schoenfeldt, L. F. (1979). Toward a classification of persons [Monograph]. *Journal of Applied Psychology, 64*, 569–607.

Palmer, D. R., White, L. A., & Young, M. C. (1990, November). *Response distortion on the Adaptability Screening Profile (ASP).* Paper presented at the Annual Conference of the Military Testing Association, San Antonio.

Pearlman, K. (Chr.) (1995, April). *Is the "job" dead? Implications of changing concepts of work for I/O Science and Practice.* Panel presentation at the 14th Annual Conference of the Society of Industrial and Organizational Psychology, Orlando, FL.

Peters, L. H., Fisher, C. D., & O'Connor, E. J. (1982). The moderating effect of situational control of performance variance on the relationship between individual differences and performance. *Personnel Psychology, 35*, 609–621.

Peters, L. H., & O'Connor, E. J. (1980). Situational and work outcomes: The influences of a frequently overlooked construct. *Academy of Management Review, 5*, 391–397.

Peterson, N. G. (Ed.) (1987). *Development and field test of the Trial Battery for Project A* (ARI Technical Report 739). Alexandria, VA: U.S. Army Research Institute for the Behavioral and Social Sciences.

Peterson, N. G. (1993). *Review of issues associated with speededness of GATB tests.* Washington, DC: American Institutes for Research.

Peterson, N. G., Anderson, L. E., Crafts, J. L., Smith, D. A., Motowidlo, S. J., Rosse, R. L., Waugh, G. W., McCloy, R., Reynolds, D. H., & Dela Rosa, M. R. (1999). *Expanding the Concept of Quality in Personnel: Final report* (Research Note 99-31). U.S. Army Research Institute for the Behavioral and Social Sciences.

Peterson, N. G., & Bownas, D. A. (1982). Skill, task structure, and performance acquisitions. In M. D. Dunnette & E. A. Fleishman (Eds.), *Human performance and productivity* (pp. 49–106). Hillsdale, N.J.: Erlbaum.

Peterson, N. G., Hough, L. M., Dunnette, M. D., Rosse, R. L., Houston, J. S., Toquam, J. L., & Wing, H. (1990). Project A: Specification of the predictor domain and development of new selection/classification tests. *Personnel Psychology, 43*, 247–276.

Peterson, N. G., & Houston, J. S. (1980). *The prediction of correctional officer job performance: Construct validation in an employment setting.* Minneapolis, MN: Personnel Decisions Research Institute.

Peterson, N. G., Houston, J. S., Bosshardt, M. J., & Dunnette, M. D. (1977). *A study of the correctional officer job at Marion Correctional Institution, Ohio: Development of selection procedures, training recommendations and an exit information program.* Minneapolis, MN: Personnel Decisions Research Institute.

Peterson, N. G., Houston, J. S., & Rosse, R. L. (1984). *The LOMA job effectiveness prediction system, Technical Report #4: Validity analyses.* Atlanta, GA: Life Office Management Association.

Peterson, N. G., Mumford, M. D., Borman, W. C., Jeanneret, P. R., & Fleishman, E. A. (1995). *Development of a Prototype Occupational Information Network (O*NET) (Vols. I & II).* Salt Lake City, UT: Utah Department of Employment Security.

Peterson, N. G., Mumford, M. D., Borman, W. C., Jeanneret, P. R., & Fleishman, E. A. (Eds.) (1999). *An occupational information system for the 21st century: The development of O*NET.* Washington, DC: American Psychological Association.

Peterson, N. G., Owens-Kurtz, C., Hoffman, R. G., Arabian, J. M., & Whetzel, D. L. (Eds.). (1990). *Army Synthetic Validation Project, Report of Phase II Results, Volume I* (ARI Technical Report 892). Alexandria, VA: U.S. Army Research Institute for the Behavioral and Social Sciences.

Peterson, N. G., Russell, T., Hallam, G., Hough, L., Owens-Kurtz, C., Gialluca, K., & Kerwin, K. (1992). Analysis of the experimental predictor battery: LV sample. In J. P. Campbell, & L. M. Zook (Eds.), *Building and retaining the career force: New procedures for accessing and assigning Army enlisted personnel–Annual report, 1990 fiscal year* (ARI Technical Report 952) (pp. 73–199). Alexandria, VA: U.S. Army Research Institute for the Behavioral and Social Sciences.

Prediger, D. J. (1982). Dimensions underlying Holland's hexagon: Missing link between interests and occupations? *Journal of Vocational Behavior, 21*, 259–287.

Primoff, E. S., & Fine, S. (1988). A history of job analysis. In S. Gael (Ed.), *The job analysis handbook for business, industry, and government.* New York: John Wiley & Sons.

Pulakos, E. D., & Borman, W. C. (Eds.) (1986). *Development and field test of Army-wide rating scales and the rater orientation and training program* (ARI Technical Report 716). Alexandria, VA: U.S. Army Research Institute for the Behavioral and Social Sciences. (ADA 182101)

Pulakos, E. D., White, L. A., Oppler, S. H., & Borman, W. C. (1989). An examination of race and sex effects on performance ratings. *Journal of Applied Psychology, 74*, 770–780.

Ree, M. J., & Earles, J. A. (1991a, August). *Estimating psychometric g: An application of the Wilk's theorem.* Paper presented at the annual meeting of the American Psychological Association, San Francisco, California.

Ree, M. J., & Earles, J. A. (1991b). Predicting training success: Not much more than *g. Personnel Psychology, 44*, 321–332.

Ree, M. J., Earles, J. A., & Teachout, M. S. (1992). *General cognitive ability predicts job performance* (AL-TP-1991-0057). Brooks AFB, TX: Human Resources Directorate, Armstrong Laboratory.

Ree, M. J., Mullins, C. J., Matthews, J. J., & Massey, R. H. (1982). *Armed Services Vocational Aptitude Battery: Item and factor analysis of Forms 8, 9, and 10* (AFHRL-TR-81-55). Brooks Air Force Base, TX: U.S. Air Force Human Resources Laboratory.

Rich, J. R., & Boudreau, J. W. (1987). The effects of variability and risk in selection utility analysis: An empirical comparison. *Personnel Psychology, 40*, 55–84.

Riegelhaupt, B. J., Harris, C. D., & Sadacca, R. (1987). *The development of administrative measures as indicators of soldier effectiveness* (ARI Technical Report 754). Alexandria, VA: U.S. Army Research Institute for the Behavioral and Social Sciences.

Roe, A., & Siegelman, M. (1964). *The origin of interests*. Washington, DC: American Personnel and Guidance Association.

Rosse, R. L., & Peterson, N. G. (1991). An investigation of the use of least squares validity estimators and correction formulas when population values are available for predictor intercorrelations. In L. L. Wise, N. G. Peterson, R. G. Hoffman, J. P. Campbell, & J. M. Arabian (Eds.), *Army Synthetic Validation Project, Report of Phase III Results, Volume I* (ARI Technical Report 922). Alexandria, VA: U.S. Army Research Institute for the Behavioral and Social Sciences.

Rosse, J. G., Stecher, M. D., Miller, J. L., & Levin R. A. (1998). The impact of response distortion on preemployment personality testing and employment decisions. *Journal of Applied Psychology, 83*, 634–644.

Rosse, R. L., Whetzel, D. L., & Peterson, N.G. (1993). *Assessment of the classification efficiency of selection/assignment systems*. Washington, DC: American Institutes for Research.

Rothstein, H. R. (1990). Interrater reliability of job performance ratings: Growth to asymptote level with increasing opportunity to observe. *Journal of Applied Psychology, 75*, 322–327.

Rotter, J. B. (1966). Generalized expectancies for internal versus external control of reinforcement. *Psychological Monographs, 80* (1, Whole No. 609).

Rounds, J. B., Jr. (1981). *The comparative and combined utility of need and interest data in the prediction of job satisfaction*. Unpublished doctoral dissertation, University of Minnesota.

Rozeboom, W. W. (1978). Estimation of cross-validated multiple correlation: A clarification. *Psychological Bulletin, 85*, 1348–1351.

Roznowski, M. A. (1987). *Elementary cognitive tasks as measures of intelligence*. Unpublished doctoral dissertation, University of Illinois at Urbana-Champaign.

Ruch, F. L., & Ruch, W. W. (1980). *Employee Aptitude Survey: Technical report*. Los Angeles: Psychological Services.

Rulon, P. J., Tiedeman, D. V., Tatsuoka, M. M., & Langmuir, C. R. (1967). *Multivariate statistics for personnel classification*. New York: Wiley.

Russell, T. L., Reynolds, D. H., & Campbell, J. P. (1994). *Building a joint-service classification research roadmap: Individual differences measurement* (AL/HR-TP-1994-0009). Brooks Air Force Base, TX: Armstrong Laboratory.

Sackett, P. R., Zedeck, S., & Fogli, L. (1988). Relations between measures of typical and maximum job performance. *Journal of Applied Psychology, 73*, 482–486.

Sadacca, R., Campbell, J. P., White, L. A., & DiFazio, A. S. (1989). *Weighting criterion components to develop composite measures of job performance* (ARI Technical Report 838). Alexandria, VA: U.S. Army Research Institute for the Behavioral and Social Sciences.

Sager, C. E., Peterson, N. G., Oppler, S. H., Rosse, R. L., & Walker, C. (1997). An examination of five indices of test battery performance: An analysis of the ECAT battery. *Military Psychology, 9*, 97–120.

Sands, W. A., Waters, B. K., & McBride, J. R. (Eds.) (1997). *Computerized adaptive testing: From inquiry to operation*. Washington, DC: American Psychological Association.

Schaeffer, R. H. (1953). Job satisfaction as related to need satisfaction in work. *Psychological Monographs, 67* (14, Whole No. 364).

Schletzer, V. M. (1966). SVIB as a predictor of job satisfaction. *Journal of Applied Psychology, 50*, 5–8.

Schmidt, F. L. (1988). Validity generalization and the future of criterion related validity. In H. Wainer & H. Braun (Eds.), *Test validity*. Hillsdale, NJ: Erlbaum.

Schmidt, F. L., & Hunter, J. E. (1977). Development of a general solution to the problem of validity generalization. *Journal of Applied Psychology, 62*, 529–540.

Schmidt, F. L., & Hunter, J. E. (1981). Employment testing: Old theories and new research findings. *American Psychologist, 36*, 1128–1137.

Schmidt, F. L., & Hunter, J. E. (1998). The validity and utility of selection methods in personnel psychology: Practical and theoretical implications of 85 years of research findings. *Psychological Bulletin, 124*, 262–274.

Schmidt, F. L., Hunter, J. E., Croll, P. R., & McKenzie, R. C. (1983). Estimation of employment test validities by expert judgment. *Journal of Applied Psychology, 68*, 590–601.

Schmidt, F. L., Ones, D. S., & Hunter, J. E. (1992). Personnel selection. *Annual Review of Psychology, 43*, 627–670.

Schmit, M. J., & Ryan, A. M. (1993). The Big Five in personnel selection: Factor structure in applicant and nonapplicant populations. *Journal of Applied Psychology, 78*, 966–974.

Schmit, M. J., Ryan, A. M., Stierwalt, S. L., & Powell, A. B. (1995). Frame-of-reference effects on personality scale scores and criterion-related validity. *Journal of Applied Psychology, 80*, 607–620.

Schmitt, N., Gooding, R. Z., Noe, R. A., & Kirsch, M. (1984). Meta-analyses of validity studies published between 1964 and 1982 and the investigation of study characteristics. *Personnel Psychology, 37*, 407–422.

Schmitz, E. J. (1988). Improving personnel performance through assignment policy. In B. F. Green, H. Wing, & A. K. Wigdor (Eds.), *Linking military enlistment standards to job performance: Report of a workshop*. Committee on the Performance of Military Personnel. National Research Council. Washington, DC: National Academy Press.

Schmitz, E. J., & Nord, R. (1991). The Army manpower procurement and allocation system. In J. Zeidner, & C. D. Johnson (Eds.), *The economic benefits of predicting job performance—Volume 3: Estimating the gains of alternative policies*. New York: Praeger.

Schneider, B. (1978). Person-situation selection: A review of some ability situation interaction research. *Personnel Psychology, 31*, 381–397.

Schneider, B. (1987a). E = f(P, B): The road to a radical approach to person-environment fit. *Journal of Vocational Behavior, 31*, 353–361.

Schneider, B. (1987b). The people make the place. *Personnel Psychology, 40*, 437–453.

Schoenfeldt, L. F. (1974). Utilization of manpower: Development and evaluation of an assessment-classification model for matching individuals with jobs. *Journal of Applied Psychology, 59*, 583–595.

Scholarios, T. M., Johnson, C. D., & Zeidner, J. (1994). Selecting predictors for maximizing the classification efficiency of a battery. *Journal of Applied Psychology, 79*, 412–424.

Schrader, A. D., & Osburn, H. G. (1977). Biodata faking: Effects of induced subtlety and position specificity. *Personnel Psychology, 30*, 395–404.

Schratz, M. K., & Ree, M. J. (1989). Enlisted selection and classification: Advances in testing. *Military personnel measurement: Testing, assignment, evaluation* (pp. 1–40). New York: Praeger.

Schwab, D. P. (1971). Issues in response distortion studies of personality inventories: A critique and replicated study. *Personnel Psychology, 24*, 637–647.

Sebring, P., Campbell, B., Glusberg, M., Spencer, B., & Singleton, M. (1987). *High school and beyond 1980 sophomore cohort third follow-up (1986) data file user's manual*. Washington, DC: Center for Education Statistics.

Secretary's Commission on Achieving Necessary Skills (SCANS). (1992). *Learning a living: A blueprint for high performance*. Washington, DC: U.S. Department of Labor.

Sevy, B. A. (1983). *Sex-related differences in spatial ability: The effects of practice*. Unpublished doctoral dissertation, University of Minnesota.

Silva, J. M. (1989). *Usefulness of spatial and psychomotor testing for predicting TOW and UCOFT gunnery performance* (ARI Working Paper WP-RS-89-21). Alexandria, VA: U.S. Army Research Institute for the Behavioral and Social Sciences.

Silva, J. M., & Busciglio, H. H. (1993, January). *Impact of practice and coaching*. Paper presented at the Military Accession Policy Working Group Meeting, San Diego.

Smith, E. P., & Graham, S. E. (1987). *Validation of psychomotor and perceptual predictors of Armor Officer M-1 gunnery performance* (Technical Report 766). Alexandria, VA: U.S. Army Research Institute for the Behavioral and Social Sciences.

Smith, E. P., & Walker, M. R. (1988, November). *Testing psychomotor and spatial abilities to improve selection of TOW gunners.* Paper presented at the annual meetings of the Military Testing Association, Arlington, VA.

Smith, P. C. (1976). The problem of criteria. In M.D. Dunnette (Ed.), *Handbook of industrial and organizational psychology* (pp. 745–775). Chicago: Rand McNally College Publishing Company.

Smith, P. C., & Kendall, L. M. (1963). Retranslation of expectations: An approach to the construction of unambiguous anchors for rating scales. *Journal of Applied Psychology, 47,* 149–155.

Society for Industrial and Organizational Psychology (1987). *Principles for the validation and use of personnel selection procedures* (3rd ed.). College Park, MD: Author.

Sorenson, R. C. (1965). *Optimal allocation of enlisted men—Full regression equations versus aptitude area scores* (Technical Research Note 163). Washington, DC: U.S. Army Personnel Research Office. (AD 625 224)

Spearman, C. (1927). *The abilities of man.* New York: MacMillan Co.

Spearman, C. (1939). Thurstone's work reworked. *Journal of Educational Psychology, 30,* 1–16.

Staff, AGO, Personnel Research Branch (1943a). Personnel research in the Army, I. Background and organization. *Psychological Bulletin, 40,* 129–135.

Staff, AGO, Personnel Research Branch (1943b). Personnel Research in the Army, II. The classification system and the place of testing. *Psychological Bulletin, 40,* 205–211.

Staff, AGO, Personnel Research Branch (1943c). Personnel research in the Army, III. Some factors affecting research in the Army. *Psychological Bulletin, 40,* 237–278.

Statman, M. A. (1992, August). *Developing optimal predictor equations for differential job assignment and vocational counseling.* Paper presented at the 100th Annual Convention of the American Psychological Association, Washington, DC.

Steel, R. P., & Mento, A. J. (1986). Impact of situational constraints on subjective and objective criteria of managerial job performance. *Organizational Behavior and Human Decision Processes, 37,* 254–265.

Steele, D. J., & Park, R. K. (1994). Final data editing and score imputation. In J. P. Campbell & L. M. Zook (Eds.), *Building and retaining the career force: New procedures for accessing and assigning Army enlisted personnel—Annual report, 1991 fiscal year* (ARI Research Note 94-10) (pp. 101–124). Alexandria, VA: U.S. Army Research Institute for the Behavioral and Social Sciences.

Sternberg, S. (1966). High speed scanning in human memory. *Science, 153,* 652–654.

Sternberg, S. (1969). The discovery of processing stages: Extensions of Donder's method. *Acta Psychologica, 30,* 276–315.

Stoker, P., Hunter, D. R., Kantor, J. E., Quebe, J. C., & Siem, F. M. (1987). *Flight screening program effects on attrition in undergraduate pilot training* (AFHRL-TP-86-59). Brooks Air Force Base, TX: U.S. Air Force Human Resources Laboratory.

Strong, E. K., Jr. (1931). *Vocational interest blank for men.* Stanford, CA: Stanford University Press.

Strong, E. K., Jr. (1943). *Vocational interests of men and women.* Stanford, CA: Stanford University Press.

Strong, E. K., Jr. (1955). *Vocational interests 18 years after college.* Minneapolis, MN: University of Minnesota Press.

Stuit, D. B. (1947). *Personnel research and test development in the Bureau of Naval Personnel.* Princeton University Press.

Tellegen, A. (1982). *Brief manual for the Differential Personality Questionnaire.* Unpublished manuscript, University of Minnesota.

Teplitzky, M. L. (1995, June). *Spatial abilities and land navigation performance.* Paper presented at the Army Science Conference, Orlando, FL.

Thorndike, R. L. (1949). *Personnel selection.* New York: Wiley.

Thorndike, R. L. (1986). The role of general ability in prediction. *Journal of Vocational Behavior, 29,* 332–339.

Thorndike, R. M., Weiss, D. J., & Dawis, R. V. (1968). Canonical correlation of vocational interests and vocational needs. *Journal of Counseling Psychology, 15,* 101–106.

Thornton, G. C., & Gierasch, P. F. (1980). Fakability of an empirically derived selection instrument. *Journal of Personality Assessment, 44*, 48–51.

Thurstone, L. L. (1938). *Primary mental abilities*. Chicago: University of Chicago Press.

Thurstone, L. L., & Thurstone, T. G. (1941). *The Primary Mental Abilities Tests*. Chicago: Science Research Associates.

Tilton, J. W. (1937). The measurement of overlapping. *Journal of Educational Psychology, 28*, 656–662.

Tippitt, L. H. (1925). On the extreme individuals and range of samples taken from a normal population. *Biometricka, 17*, 364–387.

Toquam, J. L., Corpe, V. A., & Dunnette, M. D. (1991). *Literature review: Cognitive abilities—theory, history, and validity* (ARI Research Note 91-28). Alexandria, VA: U.S. Army Research Institute for the Behavioral and Social Sciences.

Toquam, J. L., McHenry, J. J., Corpe, V. A., Rose, S. R., Lammlein, S. E., Kemery, E., Borman, W. C., Mendel, R. M., & Bosshardt, M. J. (1988). *Development and field test of behaviorally anchored rating scales for nine MOS* (ARI Technical Report 776). Alexandria, VA: U.S. Army Research Institute for the Behavioral and Social Sciences.

Trent, T. T., Atwater, D. C., & Abrahams, N. M. (1986, April). Biographical screening of military applicants: Experimental assessment of item response distortion. In G. E. Lee (Ed.), *Proceedings of the Tenth Annual Symposium of Psychology in the Department of Defense* (pp. 96–100). Colorado Springs, CO: U.S. Air Force Academy, Department of Behavioral Sciences and Leadership.

Trimble, J. T. (1965). *Ten-year longitudinal followup study of inventoried interests of selected high school students*. Unpublished doctoral dissertation, University of Missouri.

Tupes, E. C., & Christal, R. E. (1961, May). *Recurrent personality factors based on trait ratings* (ASD-TR-61-97). Lackland Air Force Base, TX: Aeronautical Systems Division, Personnel Laboratory.

Tyler, L. E. (1965). *The psychology of human differences* (3rd ed.). New York: Appleton-Century-Crofts.

Vernon, P. A. (1990). The use of biological measures to estimate behavioral intelligence. *Educational Psychologist, 25*, 293–304.

Vernon, P. E. (1950). *The structure of human abilities*. London: Methven.

Viswesvaran, C., Schmidt, F. L., & Ones, D. S. (1993, April). *Theoretical implications of a general factor in job performance criteria*. Paper presented at the 8th Annual Conference of the Society of Industrial and Organizational Psychology. San Francisco.

Wakabayashi, M., & Graen, G. B. (1984). The Japanese career progress study: A 7-year follow-up. *Journal of Applied Psychology, 69*, 603–614.

Walker, C. B. (1985, February). *The fakability of the Army's Military Applicant Profile (MAP)*. Paper presented at the Association of Human Resources Management and Organizational Behavior Proceedings, Denver, CO.

Wallace, S. R. (1965). Criteria for what? *American Psychologist, 20*, 411–417.

Walsh, W. B. (1979). Vocational behavior and career development; 1978: A review. *Journal of Vocational Behavior, 15*, 119–154.

Waters, B. K., Barnes, J. D., Foley, P., Steinhaus, S. D., & Brown, D. C. (1988). *Estimating the reading skills of military applicants: The development of an ASVAB to RGL conversion table* (Final Report No. 88-22). Alexandria, VA: Human Resources Research Organization.

Waters, L. K. (1965). A note on the "fakability" of forced-choice scales. *Personnel Psychology, 18*, 187–191.

Watson, T. W., O'Connor, E. J., Eulberg, J. R., & Peters, L. H. (1983, October). Measurement and assessment of situational constraints in Air Force work environments: A brief summary. *Proceedings of the 25th Annual Conference of the Military Testing Association, 25*, 662–627.

Welsh, J. R., Jr., Kucinkas, S. K., & Curran, L. T. (1990). *Armed Services Vocational Aptitude Battery (ASVAB): Integrative review of validity studies* (AFHRL-TR-90-22). Brooks Air Force Base, TX: U.S. Air Force Human Resources Laboratory.

Welsh, J. R., Jr., Watson, T. W., & Ree, M. J. (1990). *Armed Services Vocational Aptitude Battery (ASVAB): Predicting military criteria from general and specific abilities* (AFHRL-TR-90-63). Brooks Air Force Base, TX: U.S. Air Force Human Resources Laboratory.

Weltin, M. M. & Popelka, B. A. (1983). *Evaluation of the ASVAB 8/9/10 Clerical composite for predicting training performance* (ARI Technical Report 594). Alexandria, VA: U.S. Army Research Institute for the Behavioral and Social Sciences.

Wernimont, P. F., & Campbell, J. P. (1968). Signs, samples, and criteria. *Journal of Applied Psychology, 52,* 372–37.

White, L. A. (1994). Development of composite scores for the Assessment of Background and Life Experiences (ABLE) instrument. In J. P. Campbell and L. M. Zook (Eds.), *Building and retaining the career force: New procedures for accessing and assigning Army enlisted personnel*—Annual report, 1991 fiscal year (ARI Research Note 94-10) (pp. 25–32). Alexandria, VA: U.S. Army Research Institute for the Behavioral and Social Sciences.

White, L. A. (1999, June). *The temperament measurement component of Project A: Research findings and future directions.* Paper presented at the annual meeting of the American Psychological Society, Denver, CO.

White, L. A., & Kilcullen, R. N. (1992, August). The validity of rational biodata scales. In M. G. Rumsey (Chair) *Biodata advances: Bridging the rational and empirical perspectives.* Symposium presented at the annual meeting of the American Psychological Association, Washington, DC

White, L. A., & Kilcullen, R. N. (1998, April). *Effects of socially desirable responding on the criterion-related validity of temperament measures.* Paper presented at the 14th Annual Conference of the Society for Industrial and Organizational Psychology, St. Louis, MO.

White, L. A., & Moss, M. C. (1995, May). *Factors influencing concurrent validities of personality constructs.* Paper presented at the 10th annual meeting of the Society of Industrial and Organizational Psychology, Orlando, FL.

White, L. A., Nord, R. D., Mael, F. A., & Young, M. C. (1993). The Assessment of Background and Life Experiences (ABLE). In T. Trent & J. H. Laurence (Eds.), *Adaptability screening for the armed forces.* Washington, DC: Office of Assistant Secretary of Defense (Force Management and Personnel).

White, L. A., & Young, M. C. (1994). Development of composite scores for the Assessment of Background and Life Experiences (ABLE). In J. P. Campbell & L. M. Zook (Eds.), *Building and retaining the career force: New Procedures for accessing and assigning Army enlisted personnel—Annual report, 1991 fiscal year* (ARI Research Note 94-10). Alexandria, VA: U.S. Army Research Institute for the Behavioral and Social Sciences.

White, L. A., & Young, M. C. (1998, August). *Development and validation of the Assessment of Individual Motivation (AIM).* Paper presented at the annual meeting of the American Psychological Association, San Francisco, CA.

Wigdor, A. K., & Green, B. F., Jr. (1991). *Performance assessment for the workplace (Vols. I-II).* Washington, DC: National Academy Press.

Wilk, S. L., Desmarais, L. B., & Sackett, P. R. (1995). Gravitation to jobs commensurate with ability: Longitudinal and cross sectional tests. *Journal of Applied Psychology, 80,* 79–85.

Wilkinson, L. (1988). *SYSTAT: The system for statistics.* Evanston, IL: SYSTAT, Inc.

Wilson, G., Keil, C. T., Oppler, S. H., & Knapp, D. J. (1994). The LVII data file. In J. P. Campbell & L. M. Zook (Eds.) *Building and retaining the career force: New procedures for accessing and assigning Army enlisted personnel—Annual report, 1992 fiscal year* (ARI Research Note 94-27) (pp. 125–138). Alexandria, VA: U.S. Army Research Institute for the Behavioral and Social Sciences.

Wing, H., Peterson, N. G., & Hoffman, R. G. (1984, August). *Expert judgments of predictor-criterion validity relationships.* Paper presented at the annual meeting of the American Psychological Association, Toronto, Ontario, Canada.

Wise, L. L. (1986, March). *Criterion data preparation.* Presentation to the Project A Scientific Advisory Group, Minneapolis, MN.

Wise, L. L. (1994). Goals of the selection and classification decision. In Rumsey, M. G., Walker, C. B., & Harris, J. H. (Eds.), *Personnel selection and classification* (pp. 351–361). Hillsdale, N. J.: Erlbaum.

Wise, L. L., Arabian, J. M., Chia, W. J., & Szenas, P. L. (Eds.). (1989). *Army synthetic validation project: Report of Phase I results* (ARI Technical Report 845). Alexandria, VA: U.S. Army Research Institute for the Behavioral and Social Sciences.

Wise, L. L., & McDaniel, M. A. (1991, August). *Cognitive factors in the Armed Services Vocational Aptitude Battery and the General Aptitude Test Battery.* Paper presented at the meeting of the American Psychological Association, San Francisco, CA.

Wise, L. L., McHenry, J. J., & Campbell, J. P. (1990). Identifying optimal predictor composites and testing for generalizability across jobs and performance factors. *Personnel Psychology, 43,* 355–366.

Wise, L. L, McHenry, J. J., & Young, W.Y. (1986). *Project A Concurrent Validation: Treatment of missing data* (ARI Working Paper RS-WP-86-08). Alexandria, VA: U.S. Army Research Institute for the Behavioral and Social Sciences.

Wise, L. L., & McLaughlin, D. H. (1980). *Guidebook for the imputation of missing data.* Palo Alto, CA: American Institutes for Research.

Wise, L. L., McLaughlin, D. H., & Steel, L. J. (1977). *The Project TALENT data bank handbook.* Palo Alto, CA: American Institutes for Research.

Wise, L. L., Peterson, N. G., Hoffman, G., Campbell, J. P., & Arabian, J. M. (1991). *Army synthetic validity project: Report of Phase III results—Vol. I.* (ARI Technical Report 922). Alexandria, VA: U.S. Army Research Institute for the Social and Behavioral Sciences.

Wise, L. L., Wang, M., & Rossmeissl, P. G. (1983). *Development and validation of Army selection and classification measures, Project A: Longitudinal research database plan* (ARI Research Report 1356). Alexandria, VA: U.S. Army Research Institute for the Behavioral and Social Sciences.

Wiskoff, M. F., Parker, J. P., Zimmerman, R. A., & Sherman, F. (1989). *Predicting school and job performance of Marine Security Guards* (PERSEREC Technical Report 90-003). Monterey, CA: Defense Personnel Security Research and Education Center.

Wolfe, J. H. (Ed.) (1997). Special Issue: The Enhanced Computer Administered Test (ECAT) Project. *Military Psychology,* 9(1).

Worthington, E. L., & Dolliver, R. H. (1977). Validity studies of the Strong Vocational Interest Inventories. *Journal of Counseling Psychology, 24,* 208–216.

Young, M. C., & Rumsey, M. G. (1998, August). *Army pre-implementation research on the Assessment of Individual Motivation (AIM).* Paper presented at the annual meeting of the American Psychological Association, San Francisco, CA.

Young, M. C., & White, L. A. (1998, June). *Development of a measure to predict soldier attrition and motivation.* Paper presented at the 21st Army Science Conference, Norfolk, VA.

Young, M. C., White, L. A., & Oppler, S. H. (1991, October). *Coaching effects on the Assessment of Background and Life Experiences (ABLE).* Paper presented at the 33rd Annual Conference of the Military Testing Association, San Antonio, TX.

Young, M. C., White, L. A., & Oppler, S. H. (1992, October). *Effects of coaching on validity of a self-report temperament measure.* Paper presented at the 34th Annual Conference of the Military Testing Association, San Diego, CA.

Young, W. Y., Austin, K. C., McHenry, J. J., & Wise, L. L. (1986). *Concurrent validation codebook file: M3AMOZV2 (Batch Z MOS summary file version 2).* Washington, DC: American Institutes for Research.

Young, W. Y., Austin, K. C., McHenry, J. J., & Wise, L. L. (1987). *Concurrent validation codebook file: M3AMOSV3 (Batch A MOS summary file version 3).* Washington, DC: American Institutes for Research.

Young, W. Y., Houston, J. S., Harris, J. H., Hoffman, R. G., & Wise, L. L. (1990). Large-scale predictor validation in Project A: Data collection procedures and data base preparation. *Personnel Psychology, 43,* 301–311.

Young, W. Y., & Wise, L. L. (1986a). *Concurrent validation codebook file: M2AMOSV1 (Batch A MOS summary file)*. Washington, DC: American Institutes for Research.

Young, W. Y., & Wise, L. L. (1986b). *Concurrent validation codebook file: M3AMOZV1 (Batch Z MOS summary file)*. Washington, DC: American Institutes for Research.

Yukl, G. A., & Nemeroff, W. F. (1979). Identification and measurement of specific categories of leader behavior: A progress report. In J. G. Hunt & L. L. Larson (Eds.), *Crosscurrents in leadership*. Carbondale: Southern Illinois University Press.

Yukl, G. A., & Van Fleet, D. D. (1982). Cross-situational, multimethod research on military leader effectiveness. *Organizational Behavior and Human Performance, 30,* 87–108.

Zeidner, J., & Johnson, C. D. (1994). Is personnel classification a concept whose time has passed? In M. G. Rumsey, C. B. Walker, & J. B. Harris (Eds.), *Personnel selection and classification* (pp. 377–410). Hillsdale, N. J.: Erlbaum.

Zeidner, J., Johnson, C. D., & Scholarios, D. (1997). Evaluating military selection and classification systems in the multiple job context. *Military Psychology, 9,* 169–186.

Zickar, M. J., & Drasgow, F. (1996). Detecting faking on a personality instrument using appropriateness measurement. *Applied Psychological Measurement, 20,* 71–88.

Zook, L. M. (1995). *Research findings on soldier selection and their implications for Army Policy and Programs* (Final Report). ARI Contract MDA903-93-D-0032. Alexandria, VA: Human Resources Research Organization.

Zook, L. M. (1996). *Soldier selection: Past, present, and future* (ARI Special Report 28). Alexandria, VA: U.S. Army Research Institute for the Behavioral and Social Sciences. (ADA 321806)

Zytowski, D. G. (1976). Predictive validity of the Kuder Occupational Interest Survey: A 12- to 19-year followup. *Journal of Counseling Psychology, 3,* 221–233.

Author Index

Subject Index

621